BARBARA BRUCE COLE

California Central Coast Pioneer Families

Originally published in the *Santa Maria Valley Genealogical Society & Library Quarterly*, 1980-2003

Volume I

Genealogical Research by

Barbara Bruce Cole

Santa Maria, California
Janaway Publishing, Inc.
2009

California Central Coast Pioneer Families. Two Volumes

Copyright © 2009 by Santa Maria Valley Genealogical Society

ALL RIGHTS RESERVED. Written permission must be secured from the
Santa Maria Valley Genealogical Society or the publisher to use or reproduce any part of this book,
in any form or by any means, including electronic reproduction,
except for brief quotations in critical reviews or articles.

Published by
Janaway Publishing, Inc.
732 Kelsey Ct.
Santa Maria, California 93454
(805) 925-1038
www.JanawayPublishing.com

2009, 2018

ISBN: 978-1-59641-186-9 (Two-Volume Set)
ISBN: 978-1-59641-418-1 (Volume One)
ISBN: 978-1-59641-419-8 Volume Two)

Second Printing: September 2018

Cover photograph courtesy of the Santa Maria Valley Historical Society.

Made in the United States of America

Dedicated to Barbara Bruce Cole

Barbara Bruce Cole had a strong sense of Noblesse Oblige that she claimed was influenced by her own extensive research on her maternal Puritan heritage. We might attribute her organizational skills to her paternal Scandinavian heritage.

Early on, Barbara laid out her original intent:

> *This is a condensation of material gathered for a book tentatively entitled, Related Pioneer Families of the Central Coast -- families related in a round-about way to Laurentine S. Cole, 1828-1894, ... Several dozen families are being collected, most having settled earlier than Coles; there is much intermarriage, and scattering, to the north as far as Santa Cruz and south to Santa Maria.*

Barbara's grasp of detail on individuals and their myriad connections was evidence of her incredible memory. The flavor of her person is easily seen in the gentle humor so often written into her commentary. All of this in addition to participating in a full family life and her church duties.

We hope to do justice to her intent.

Introduction

This substantial body of research reflects Barbara Cole's vision, ability, and dedication to the genealogy of the early settlers of our Santa Maria Valley and adjacent areas of San Luis Obispo County of California's central coast. Later groups that migrated to the area were not researched; the exception being a person who married into the subject families.

Since 1977, the Santa Maria Valley Genealogical Society's research *Quarterly* published extensive findings by Barbara Bruce Cole. From 1992, Barbara was most often Ye Editor herself, at which point she rarely claimed authorship of the well-documented research. She also oversaw the publishing of data such as local newspaper abstracts, mortuary indexes, and cemetery listings. Most often compiled by Society members at her urging, Barbara always gave excellent guidance and generous credit.

An inherent value of gathering all of this under one cover is reflected in the national interest by several of the foremost genealogy archives and libraries subscribing to SMVGS's *Quarterly* until discontinued upon her death in 2004. Unfortunately, those using her findings did not always attribute credit where due. SMVGS hopes to correct such oversight by publishing her compiled work under copyright.

Barbara Cole often stated that one of the principal functions of genealogical societies is to make available the earliest records of the area. With the permission of her beloved family, the SMVGS attempts to continue with Barbara's intent.

Thanks To The SMVGS

On pages 118 to 120, my late wife, Barbara, tells how she and I got interested in genealogy and family history. But since she wrote that text in 1986 (quoted in dedication), it does not explain how or why she did so much later research into the histories of other families who lived in the central coast area of California in the late 19th and early 20th centuries.

Briefly stated, it was just a matter of her having found such research to be such an enjoyable challenge, such a great puzzle to solve, that she just couldn't quit until ill health forced her to do so. Once she had figured out the Coles and the other families with which the Coles came to California from Wisconsin in 1874, there was always another challenge ahead. What did these people do, where did they go, and whom did their children marry here in California? It became a classic case of one thing leading to another.

In the late 1980's and early '90's, Barbara and I used to visit the California State Library in Sacramento two or three times a year, and we would stay there for a week. Barbara would sit there all day, poring through Census records, birth and death indexes, and searching through microfilmed newspapers for obituaries, making new discoveries all along the way. We had a lot of fun doing that.

How pleased she would be, how gratified she would feel, if she knew that her work was held in such esteem by the current members of the Santa Maria Valley Genealogical Society that they have seen fit to compile her work into this remarkable volume. She cannot thank you for publishing this book, but I can, and I do. Thank you all so very much!

David L. Cole

Table of Contents

VOLUME I

List of Photos	8
Abbreviations	9
Abbott	11
Abeloe	14
Abernethy	21
Adam	26
Baker	37
Bartron	46
Battles	54
Bloomer	58
Blosser	59
Bonilla-Lukeman	68
Bowers-Parnell	70
Bradley	74
Brewster-Russell	75
Brown	78
Bunce	95
Chaffin	101
Christensen	108
Clements	112
Clemons	117
Cole	120
Colver-Stevens	132
Davis	140
Davisson	172
DeNise	174
Doane	177
Dodge	182
Drum-Drumm	184
Earl	200
Edmands	212
Elvidge	219
Fine	222
Fleck	224
Forrester	227
Foster	245
Fox	254
Ganoung	257
Garrett	260
Gates	262
Gragg	264
Gray	266
Haas-Whitney	272
Harriman	276
Hecox	281
Hobbs	285
Hopper	299

VOLUME II

Jenkins	311
Jensen	312
Jessee	322
Logan	326
Lownes	335
McBane	336
McCartney	339
McNeil	341
McPhaul	351
Miller	354
Moore	364
More	368
Morrison	375
Nicholson	382
Nielsen	395
Nixon	397
Norris	402
Orand	412
Parnell	415
Phillips	416
Prell	422
Rosenblum	423
Runels	433
Russell	442
Scott	445
Snow	462
Speed	463
Stephens	466
Stokes	478
Stowell	483
Sturgeon	503
Swain	514
Tilley	517
Toy	518
Travers	523
Turek	526
Twitchell	530
Waite	569
Wheat	572
Wise	584
Young	586
Zabriskie	591
Zerfing	596
References	598
Index	599

List of Photographs
Located at end of Volume I

G.W. Battles

G.M. Doane, Sr.

Gragg Family: Carrie, Judge James A., Mamie, Mrs Mary Elizabeth Payne Gragg, Irwin, Lovell

Adam Family: Ronald McDonald Adam, Esther Bradley Adam, Alexander Adam, William Adam

Nora Davis and Verda Davis

Edna Clare Blosser, Alida Christina Blosser, Mary Anna Blosser, Nellie Blosser

George Mason Doane

Mrs Duncan Earl

George Elvidge and Sarah Elvidge (Mrs George Chaffin)

Miss Margaret More

Earl Gates, Curtis Tunnell Sr. and ?

Anna Albrecht Miller, wife of Isaac Miller, Sr.

Issac Miller, uncle of Joel Miller

Joel Miller, nephew of Isaac Miller

Edith Hamann Miller, wife of Isaac Jr.

Nellie Bradley

Paul Bradley

Louisa Bradley

Charles Bradley

Blanche Morrison

Nellie and Seth Waite

Abbreviations

@:	at (usually age)	EV:	Evergreen Cemetery, Lompoc
a:	acres	F:	Father
abt:	about	f:	farmer
acc:	accident	F&AM:	Free & Accepted Masons
AF:	Ancestral File, Church of Jesus Christ of Latter Day Saints	FHC:	Family History Center at the Church of Jesus Christ of Latter Day Saints
AFB:	Air Force Base	FOE:	Fraternal Order of Eagles
AG:	Arroyo Grande, SLO County, CA	GAR:	Grand Army of the Republic
AGUHS:	Arroyo Grande Union High School	gch:	grandchildren
		gdtr:	granddaughter
AG cem:	Arroyo Grande Cemetery	genl:	general
Anc File:	Ancestral File	GER:	Germany
Atas:	Atascadero, CA	ggch:	great grandchildren
atndt	attendant	gnc:	grand niece
b.:	born	gnph:	grand nephew
BofA:	Bank of America	GR:	Great Register of Voters
ben:	benefits	groc:	grocery
Benj:	Benjamin	gson:	grandson
bio:	biography	Guad:	Guadalupe, California
b/l:	brother-in-law	h:	house
bkpr:	bookkeeper	hskpr:	housekeeper
blksm:	blacksmith	IGI:	International Genealogical Index, LDS
bo:	boarder	imm:	immigrated
br:	brown	INDEX:	*The Salinas City Index 1873-1882.* Newspaper Abstracts, Monterey County Genealogical Society, no date
bro:	brother		
Bwy:	Broadway		
bur:	buried	inf:	infant or informant
c:	circa	IOGT	Independent Order of Good Templars
CA:	California	IOOF cem:	Independent Order of Odd Fellows Cemetery, SLO County
Carp:	Carpenteria		
CDI:	California Death Index	JP:	Justice of the Peace
cem:	cemetery	JPL:	Jet Propulsion Laboratory
cen:	census	K of P:	Knights of Pythias
ch:	children	LA:	Los Angeles, California
ch or CH:	church	lab:	laborer
CHI:	Chicago	LaG	La Graciosa, California
ck	creek	LAI:	Los Alamos, California
clk:	clerk	LDS:	Church of Jesus Christ of Latter Day Saints
clnrs:	cleaners		
co or Co:	County	LO:	Los Olivos, California
Congl min:	Congregational Minister	M::	Mother
Cor de Ped:	Corral de Piedra	m:	married
d.:	died	mcht:	merchant
dau:	daughter	ME:	Methodist Episcopal Church
Dir:	directory	McK:	*McKenney's Coast Counties Directory* 1884-5
Dist:	District		
div:	divorced	mdse:	merchandise
dk, drk:	dark	Mech:	Methodist Church
d/l:	daughter-in-law	MEN:	Mendocino
drvr:	driver	MB/C:	Morro Bay/Cayugas
DTel:	*San Luis Obispo Daily Telegram*	MG:	Minister of the Gospel
Ed.:	Editor	M/H:	Morrison & Haydon, *History of San Luis Obispo County & Environs* 1917
emp:	employed or employer		
eng:	engineer	min:	minister

M/M: Mr & Mrs
mntnc: maintenance
MTrib or MT: *San Luis Obispo Morning Tribune*
mv: moved
n/a: not available
na, nat: naturalization or naturalized
nat/f: naturalization of father
nc: niece
n.d.:   no date
NDGW: Native Daughters of the Golden West
neph: nephew
n/n: nieces and nephews
Note: comments by Barbara Cole
nr: near
NP   Notary Public
NS: Nova Scotia
NSGW: Native Sons of the Golden West
NYG&B: New York Genealogical & Biographical Society
obit: obituary
OES: Order of Eastern Star
OM: Old Mission Cemetery, SLO
ONT: Ontiveros, *San Ramon Chapel Pioneers* 1990
PCRR: Pacific Coast Railroad
pct: precinct
PG,Pc: Pine Grove Cemetery, Orcutt-SM
phbk: phone book
PM   Postmaster
pntr: painter
POB: post office box
POR: Portugal
POSM: Post Office Santa Maria, California
PR: Paso Robles, California
Prot Epis: Protestant Episcopal Church
PV: *From Acorns to Oaks, A Potter Valley History-1855 to 1985*, Shelton
r, res: residence/resided
Rbt: Robert
recs: records
Re&In: Real Estate & Insurance
reg: registered
ret: retired
Rev: Reverend
Review: Yearbook of Santa Maria Union High School
rr: railroad
RR: rural route
rt: right
s: single
SB: Santa Barbara
sch: school

SCT: Scotland
SCz: Santa Cruz
s/d, s/dau: step daughter
SF: San Francisco, California
Sisk: Siskiyou County, California
s/l: son-in-law
SLO: San Luis Obispo, California
SLOCGS: San Luis Obispo County Genealogical Society
SM: Santa Maria, California
SMJC: Santa Maria Junior College
SMUHS: Santa Maria Union High School
SMv: Santa Maria valley
SMVGS&L: Santa Maria Valley Genealogical Society and Library
SMVRR: Santa Maria Valley Railroad
SON: Sonoma, California
SPRR   Southern Pacific Railroad
s/s, s/son: step son
SS: Social Security
Ssben: Social Security benefits
SSDI: Social Security Death Index
STAN: Stanislaus
stu: student
svt: servant
SYV: Santa Ynez Valley
tp: township
(*T*):   *Santa Maria Times*
Temp cem: Templeton Cemetery, San Luis Obispo County, CA
tmstr: teamster
trctr: tractor
TRIB: *San Luis Obispo Tribune*
trkdrvr: truck driver
T-T: *San Luis Obispo Telegram-Tribune*,
T/W: *History of Santa Barbara & Ventura Counties*, Thompson & West, 1883
UCal: University of California Berkeley
UO: Union Oil Company
v: valley
Valley: *This Is Our Valley,* Carlson 1959 (SM Valley Historical Society)
Vols   Volunteers
VR or Voter reg: California Voters Registration
wf: wife
whsmn: warehouseman
whsle   wholesale
wid: widow or widower
WIN: Winneshiek
Wit. or wit: witness(es)
Wm: William
WOW: Woodmen of the World
y: year

ABBOTT
PIONEERS OF THE CALIFORNIA CENTRAL COAST

Alvin B Abbott b. CAN 26 Aug 1826 (IGI: 26 Aug 1825, of Hatley, Quebec)
 d. Guadalupe 22 Apr 1893 @68; Guad cem
  obit Apr 29: Masonic funeral
 F: CT; M: MA

1878. Abiel Boynton Abbott d. Salinas City 29 July 1878 @70; bro of Carlisle, John, Alvin
 -*The Salinas City Index* (b. 28 Nov 1808 Quebec, Stanhead, CAN – IGI)
1880 cen: Arroyo Grande pct
1883. Patron T/W; res AG f b. CAN; to CA 1850; to county 1878, 40a AG
1884. AG News. Mr A B Abbott, res of AG 6y, formerly of Salinas, sick; going to Phoenix
 Old Pioneer. To be absent 3m. Dau/law Mrs D E Abbott will accompany him.   (*Times*) Oct 11
1890 GR: 65 CAN f Guad; American parents. reg Sep 10
 "Many States Were Represented by Arroyo Grande's Pioneers…A B Abbott, a native of
 Canada, owned a large farm which was later known as the L Routzahn home."   –Madge 229
 Abbott mentioned again twice as an early AG valley pioneer.
  m.
Louisa C Tripp b. PA 8 July 1834
 d. Guad 9 Sep 1894; Guad cem
 F: CT;   M: NY
1894. Guadalupe Notes. Mrs Abbott, mother of Mrs John Hart, was buried Tuesday (-Sep 11)
 -Sep 15

1. Don Elwin Abbott b. 1856 (1852 cem)
 1928 in Los Angeles d. Los Angeles 7 Feb 1932 @76; Guad cem
  obit Tue Feb 9 p.5; 2 sons, dau, 1gch. former res of
  Salinas and AG; 30 yrs in LA. Service conducted by
  Nojoqui tribe of Red Men of SM; he organized the
  McKittrick lodge of Red Men

 m.
 Martha Ann Edgar b.
  d. (Fresno co 2-1-22 @62)?

 a. dau b. Salinas City 21 May 1878 - *Salinas Valley*
 b. Clyde Abbott *Index;* in San Francisco 1932
 c. Frank Elwin Abbott b. 21 Sep 1890
  1932 in Bakersfield d. Los Angeles co 28 Mar 1942
 d. Mattie May Abbott b. Lompoc 4 Mar 1885—SB co recs
  May Emory in San Francisco 1932

2. Jennie E Abbott b. CA c1858
 1880 cen: SM pct, no hus d. (San Francisco 19 Mar 1939 @81)?
 1928 in Los Angeles
 1934 in Los Angeles
 1936 phbk: Jennie A Graves r2120 W 11th Los Angeles
  m. at res of Alvin Abbott nr Salinas City 11 Feb 1875 by Rev W H Wilson
   - *Salinas Valley Index*

 Hugh Graves b. Salinas valley c1854
 1882 GR: 28 CA saloonkpr d. Oakland Mar 1890 @37 –*Times* Mar 15
  SM reg Aug 16 obit in T from *Salinas Journal*; hip abscess; tried
 1883-4 McKenney Dir: Paraiso and Tassajara and other hot springs, then to
  liquors SM Oakland hospital; wife, 2 sons, sis Mrs A J Gillette,

    1884 lost property in SM fire   SLO; bro Thomas, Gonzales; uncle Wm, Napa;
    1886 GR: as 1882, crossed out   dispatch received by Capt Al. Graves
    1887. Local Brevities. Mr   F: George Graves
        Thomas Graves, of Gonzales,   (Annilethi J Gillette d. Stanislaus co 7-21-1933 @86
        passed through town last   spouse AJ)?
    Sunday, on his way home from Cayucos with 237 head of calves.
                                                    –*San Miguel Messenger* June 24
   a.   Benjamin Hugh Graves   b. CA 15 Aug 1876
                           d. Marin co CA 27 June 1952
   b.   Frederick C Graves   b. CA 7 July 1878
        "Fred"   d. Los Angeles co 5 Feb 1958
3.   Mary Eudora Abbott   b. Sonoma co 25 June 1861; m. @20 of AG
                           d. Guadalupe 9 June 1934 @72; Guad cem
                           obit June 9 p.4; father to CA 1852 (!)
                           hus son 3 sis bro; 3ch dec, 2 bro deceased
    m. Arroyo Grande 13 Oct 1881 by H Holdridge ME ch, A447; wit: Hugh Graves, SM;
        Jennie E Graves, SM; bride "formerly of Salinas City."   –*Salinas Valley Index* Oct 20
Frederick Wilber Abernethy 1857-1939; see Abernethy chart
4.   Caroline M Abbott   b. (Sonoma co) 17 Sep 1864; m.1 @17 of AG;
    1880 cen: w/parents   m.2 @26 of Guad
    1928, 1934 in LA "Lee"   d. Los Angeles co 22 May 1944
        m.1 AG 20 Oct 1881 by Rev H H Dobbins, A448;
           wit: John Abbott, AG; Wm Findley, AG
Frank Barker   b. Portugal c1850?; m. @30 of AG
    1890 GR: 38 POR f AG   d. Guad 12 Nov 1890 @45 (*Times*); AG cem
    na Aug 1871 Marin co US Ct; reg July 18 1888
4.   m.2 at home of bride's parents Guad 26 Aug 1891 by Rev A M Prewitt (*Times*)
   Oliver Perry Lee   b. IN c1862; m. @29 of AG; parents IN
    "Perry"   d. Los Angeles co 4-5-1933 @70 spouse CM
    1890 GR: 26 IN f Cor de Ped reg July 18 1888
    1892 GR: 31 5'10 dk complexion grey eyes blk hair f IN res AG Pct AG #2 PO AG;
        reg Sep 2
    1895. Perry Lee farm on Branch Mill Ditch –Madge
    1906 Dir: O P Lee lab rMain; Mrs (Santa Maria)
5.   Lulu Abbott   b. 13 Aug 1868; m. @18 of Guad
    1928, 1934 in LA   d. Los Angeles 2 Feb 1948
    1936 phbk: Mrs Lulu Hart r1229 W 23d Los Angeles
        m. at res of Frank Barker AG 16 May 1887 by F S Woodcock MG, C62
           wit: A B Abbott, Guad; John Hart, Guad (*Times*)
   John Hart jr   b. ENG Sep ? 1867; m. @20 of Guad; consent of parents
    1890 GR: 23 ENG painter   d. (Los Angeles co 13 Jan 1939 @70 spouse C)?
    Guad; by na of F;   F: John Hart 1838-1905; Guad cem
    reg Sep 10
    1890. G B Hopper has a fine two seater spring wagon for sale—of his own manufacture. It
        was brought up from Hart & Son's shop at Guad, the other day where it had received the
        required number of coats of paint and varnish.   –Nov 15
    1893. John Hart jr & J Abbott, Guadalupe stables
    1897. Guad Notes. Mr Keeney is adding to his stock and John Hart jr is painting him a
        sign   –Nov 20
    1900 cen: tp #9 Guadalupe
    1906 Dir: John sign painter Main st r same; Mrs (Santa Maria)

1909 Dir: Hart John Painter r305 E Main; Mrs Lulu
1914 Dir: No
1932. death of Harriet Hart Jessee Los Angeles. survived by bro John, LA; nc Mrs G L Watson, Mrs Coralee Maggord, neph Clarence J Hart, all LA   —Oct 4
Father John Hart to Guad 1880.

   a. Clarence John Hart   b. (Guad) 28 Aug 1887
       1906 Dir: painter Main st   d. Los Angeles 15 Feb 1940
       1909 Dir: painter 305 E Main
       1932 in LA
       1936 phbk: Clarence J r3353 Garden av LA

   b. Johnnie Hart   b. Guad 23 June 1889 (*Times*)
       d. Guad 17 Oct 1889 @3mos 21 or 24 day; Guad cem

   c. John Hart jr   b.
       d. 17 Jan 1892; Guad cem

   d. Hazel L Hart   b. Guad 12 July 1890 (*Times*)
       1906 Dir: Miss stu Main st   d. Los Angeles co 14 May 1970 surname Watson
       1909 Dir: Miss sls ldy 305 E Main
       1932 in LA
       m.
       G L Watson   b.

   e. Coralee Hart   b. SM 17 May 1902 (*Times*)
       1932 in LA   d.
       m.
       Maggord (Maggard)?

6. Alvin Carlyle Abbott   b. CA 2 Apr 1874
    1900 GR: 26 AG #2 PO AG   d. Fresno co 5 Oct 1947 @73
    1928 Fresno
    1934 Academy (Fresno co)

7. Elmer Irwin Abbott   b. Salinas City CA 3 Mar 1876   –*Salinas Valley Index*
    "Irwin"   d. Los Angeles 17 Oct 1928 @52; Guad cem
    1888. Honor roll, Guad   obit Thu Oct 18; to LA 10 yrs ago; 4 sis 2 bro
      sch –*Valley*
    Sp-Am war CoE 6 CAL INF

ABELOE
DANISH PIONEERS OF THE CENTRAL COAST

Michael Abeloe   b. Aabenraa DK 12 July 1816
  (Æble = apple ø + island)   d. DK 3 April 1878
                                           F: Hans Peter Abeloe
  m. DK 1 Nov 1850   M: Anna Dorthea Morgensen
Johnne Petersen
  Children, all born Aabenraa
1. Hans Peter   b. 16 Feb 1852
2. Peter Andreas   b. 11 April 1853
    imm. 1872   d. San Luis Obispo 29 May 1930 IOOF cem
   1892 GR: 39 5'7½ fair complexion blue eyes blond hair farmer;
     r Laguna; precinct Los Osos; PO SLO, nat 7 Apr 1879 SLO Co. Ct
   in Nipomo 1882, Laguna 1888; to Templeton c1905, to SLO by 1916
  m. San Luis Obispo 7 Nov 1881 by C L Woods, A451
    wit: A Lauritzen, C H Jasperson, SLO
  Ingeborg Beck   b. nr Aabenraa DK 7 Nov 1861
                                 d. Laguna dist, SLO Co 30 Sep 1896 IOOF cem
                                 F: d in DK
                                 M: Margaret Marie 1835-1894 IOOF cem SLO
                                         m.2 Peter M. Petersen 1830-1913 IOOF cem
  a. Mary 1882-1907 IOOF cem, m. Peter Peterson Yager jr 1878-1935 IOOF cem; 2 ch
                                         or Andrew Yager 1877-1949 IOOF cem
  b. Johanna 1883-1940 SM cem, m. Lawrence H Jensen 1877-1931 SM cem; 5 ch
                                     See Jens Peder Jensen chart
  c. Michael 1886-1909 Temp cem single
  d. Emma 1889-1970 Temp cem, m. Harry Ernest Marquart 1885-1971 Temp cem; 3 ch
  e. Petra 1893-1977, m. Nelson Glass Voshall 1888-1974; 1 ch
  f. Margerette 1896-1968 IOOF Cem, m.1 Chris Antone Yager 1881-1955 IOOF cem; 2 ch
                                       m.2 Frank Ignatius McGerry 1895-
3. Michael jr 1857-1946; see his chart
4. Jacob Jacobsen; w Maren   b. 18 Sep 1859
5. Anne Marie   b. 22 Oct 1861; imm. c1882
                         d. Lompoc 4 Mar 1935 EV cem
  m. St. Stephen's ch, San Luis Obispo 24 Feb 1886 by A W Summers
    wit: Eva Miles, Oso Flaco; A W Summers
  Lars Jenzen Kolding   b. Copenhagen DK 14 Nov 1849
   "Jens"   d. Lompoc 27 Mar 1929 EV cem
   1892 GR 43 5'4½ fair blu brown scar on thumb rt hand DK; r pct, PO Nipomo
    nat 14 Aug 1890 SLO Sup Ct.; lived in Nipomo, Port Harford, Foxen Cnyn, Garey, Santa
    Rita Cnyn La Purisima Cnyn. See ONT 250-1
  a. Mary 1886-1970 EV cem   m.1 Fred Neal Olinger 1880-1918 EV cem; 7 ch
                                         m.2 Chas Alfred Dittman 1880-1961 EV cem; no issue
  b. Mikael 1888-1959 EV cem   m. 1915 Winifrey Genevieve Pine 1896-1964 EV cem; 3 ch
                                         (Winefred Geneva Pine – ONT)
  c. Jens 1890-1917 single
  d. Johanna 1891-1972   m. 1915 Wm T Odenbaugh 1889-1944; 1 ch
  e. Lars 1893-1979   m. 1916 Rachael Estelle Streeter 1893-1989; 4 ch
  f. Wensen "Vincent" 1894-1966   m.1917 Neva Estelle Robison 1901-1993; 3 ch
  g. Trine 1896-1967 EV cem   m. 1917 Rufus Henry Martin 1890-1943 EV cem; 4 ch

  h. Hans 1899-1945 EV cem   m.1 Grace Eudora Moore 1901- ; 1 ch
              m.2 1933 Ruth May Robison 1913- ; 1 ch
  i. Anna 1899-1990   m. 1923 Geo Mehlschau 1897-1985; 2 ch
  j. Otto Andrew 1902-1964 EV cem m. 1922 Helen Durfee White 1902-1975
   EV cem; 2 ch
 6. Catherine Marie   b. 26 Oct 1863
  "Kate"   d. Lompoc 19 Sep 1926; EV cem
   m. San Luis Obispo co 2 Oct 1883
  Otto Thevador Martin Westermeyer   b. Eltena GER 17 Mar 1846
   nat SLO 3 Mar 1879   d. Lompoc 25 May 1916 EV cem
   No issue   F: Christopher Westermeyer
 7. Marie Dorthea   b. 21 Nov 1865
   1910 cen: imm. 1885, 11 births,   d. Nipomo 13 Aug 1947 @81/8/22; SM cem
    11 living
   m.1 San Luis Obispo co 25 Mar 1886;
    wit: Otto Westermeyer SLO; Andrew Lauritzen SLO
  Soren Paulsen   b. Jutland DK 4 Feb 1854
   1892 GR: 38 6'3 lt blu lt mole left   d. Nipomo 21 Dec 1900 @46; SM cem
    cheek, farmer DK; r pct PO Nipomo; nat 19 Oct 1887 SLO Sup Ct. wit: Lawrence
    Damm, Peter Lauritzen
  a. Mary 1886-1928 EV cem   m. Edward Wineman jr 1880-1964 EV cem; no issue
  b. Hanna 1888-1964 SM cem   m. Harry Taylor Cheadle 1884-1975 SM cem; 4 ch
  c. Lillie Cecelia 1889-1978, Temp cem m. Ted Edmond Johnson 1886-1977 Temp cem; 5 ch
  d. Paul S 1891-1940 SM cem   m. Juanita Dana 1890-1975 SM cem; 5 ch
  e. Margaret 1892-1979 SM cem; single
  f. Anna 1894-1975   m. Jas Christian Nelson 1892-1968; 5 ch
  g. Yancy 1897-1976   m. Jennie "June" Cooper 1883-1966; no issue
  h. Samuel 1899-1970   m. Nina Mary Wright 1902-1965; 1 ch
(7)   m.2 Nipomo 4 Oct 1902 by S M Dana JP, F391
    wit: Lauritz Larsen Holt, Nipomo; John Theodore Jensen, Nipomo
  James (Jens) Hans Jensen   b. Aabenraa DK 8 Aug 1872
   1910 cen: Nipomo SM Rd   d. Nipomo 24 Feb 1944 @71/6/16; SM cem
   imm. 1886; nat 7 Mar 1894 SLO;   F: Jen Hans Jensen; to Watsonville 1890's
   wit: Lauritz Larsen Holt, Thomas Jensen   M: Anna Catherine Weid (White)
  i. Francis 1903-1995 m. Margaret Detlefsen 1906-1996; 3 ch
  j. Ernest James or John 1904-1979 SM cem; m. Eva Clara Dutra 1912-1986 SM cem; 3 ch
  k. Dorothy Elizabeth 1909-1986 SM cem; single
 8. Jes Christian   b. 28 Oct 1867
 9. Johnanne Marie m. Hans Clausen   b. 12 Sep 1870

Note: The Abeloe family is well documented in *The Family History of Anna Maria (Abeloe) Kolding*, by Neva Better Kolding Dittman. Laura Abeloe and others contributed to the work, with photos; see it at the Lompoc Historical Society.

Michael Abeloe, Jr   b. Aabenraa DK 8 June 1857; m. of Nipomo
 1900 cen: Nipomo (imm. 1881)   d. at home 8 June 1946, 89th birthday, SM cem
 1904: to Lakeview   obit Mon June 10 p.1, 9 gch, in CA 6y, here 37 y
 1910 cen: Orcutt-Los Alamos Rd; imm. 1885
 1892 GR: 35 5'5 fair complexion blue eyes light hair farmer b. Ger. r Nipomo. nat Oct 13

   1887 SLO Sup Ct (wit: Otto Westermeyer, SLO (sister Kate's husband): Peter Lauritzen)
    m. Nipomo 23 Aug 1894 by Tillford Dagger JP, D451
     wit: Hans Mehlschau, Mary Mehlschau, Nipomo
  Laura Jensen   b. Loite DK 3 May 1872, see Jensen chart
   1900 cen: 4 births, 4 living   m. of Nipomo
   1910 cen: 8 births 6 living   d. at home 19 Apr 1936 @64/11/16; SM cem
   1936: 5 children living   obit Mon Apr 20 p.2 6 gch, 29y Los Alamos
   imm. 1891 (1900 cen), 1890 (1910 cen) or @17 (obit)
  1. Minnie Helene   b. Nipomo 11 Aug 1895; m. of Orby
                 d. Orby 4 Jan 1919 @23/4/27; SM cem
    m. Santa Maria 20 June 1917 byL J Morris JP
     wit: Hannah Leonore Abeloe, George M. Lawton, Orby
   Glenn Everitt Baker   b. Hollister CA 7 July 1893; m. of Orby
    to SMv 1908, Union Oil, hiway   d. Santa Maria 29 Nov 1972 @79/4/22; SM cem
    mtrcycle officer; Chief of Police etc. F: George Buchanan Baker
    1940-1 Dir: truck driver   M: Lucinda Imogene Smith
    SB Co Rd Dist 5 h 615 W Mill   m.2 1920 Emma Belle Emerson 1902-1987
    1955-6 Dir: truck dispatcher   Issue: Emma Belle (Van Nelson) b. 1921,
    h 615 W Mill   Roland Lewis b. 1922
   a. Glenn Robert   b. Careaga ranch 30 Oct 1918
    SMUHS 1937; single   d. USS Caldwell nr Borneo 11 May 1945
    reared by g'parents   @26/6/11; reinterred SM cem 1948
  2. James Peter   b. Nipomo 9 Apr 1897; m. of Harriston
   1940-1 Dir: f Los Alamos   d. Orcutt 4 June 1971 @74/2/25; SM cem
   1955-6 Dir: rancher h 330 Park, Orcutt
    m. at home of bride Santa Maria 17 March 1926;
     wit: Hannah Abeloe, Carl Abeloe, Harriston
   Edith Edwards   b. Santa Barbara 2 Aug 1906; m. of SM
                 d. Orcutt 30 Aug 1986 @ 80; SM cem
                 F: William Spencer Edwards 1879-1963
                 M: Ada Ryan 1884-1963
                  1930 Dir: Edwards W S & Son nursery 221 N Smith
                  1940-1 Dir: same
   a. James Edward   b. Santa Maria 8 Dec 1929
    1955-6 Dir: rancher r 330 Park, Orcutt. single
   b. Kenneth William   b. Santa Maria 13 Oct 1938
    m. (div)
    Margaret Rose Clark   b. Louisville KY 27 Sep 1949
  3. Carl Arthur   b. Nipomo 10 June 1898
   1940-1 Dir: Los Alamos   d. Los Alamos 30 Jan 1982 @83/7/20; SM cem
   1955-6 Dir: Same
   1982 pall bearers: nephews Lawrence, James, Herman, Donald, Kenneth Abeloe;
    great-nephew Michael Abeloe
    m. Howard ranch nr Los Alamos 3 Nov 1935 by Rev W F S Nelson;
     wit: Fred Dudley Howard, Laura Abeloe
   Elinor Howard   b. San Francisco 26 April 1909
                 d. Los Alamos 5 July 1953 @45/2/11; SM cem
                 F: Fred Dudley Howard 1858-1937
                 M: Phoebe Chart Laws 1868-1935
   1935 wedding guests: Wm and Maude Ferguson; Emil and Anna Pfiitzner with Dorothy and
    Claus; Les and Faith Battelle with Jean, Michael and Laura Abeloe, James and Edith

Abeloe and Jimmie, Phoebe Howard and son Fred Laws Howard; Herman and Mary Abeloe with Herman and Donald; Lawrence and Ada Abeloe with Buddy and Nadine; Hazel I Ewald, Marjorie Hearn, Mrs Georgia L. Beal, Bill and Hannah Shefty, Glenn Robert Baker, Marion Helmquist

1953 pall bearers: Henry Confaglia, Dale Douglas, Walter Barca, Alvin Robbins, Johnny Bastanchury, Tony Serpa

  a. Carl Clifford   b. Howard/Abeloe ranch 6 Aug 1936
      m. Charlene Joyce LaFontaine   b. SM 2 Jan 1941
  b. Laura Christine; single   b. Howard/Abeloe ranch 12 Mar 1938
  c. Marion Fred "Butch"; single   b. Howard/Abeloe ranch 12 Apr 1939
4. (Jo) Hanna Leonora   b. Nipomo 8 July 1899
    in Richmond 1936   living in Santa Maria 1997
      m. at home of bride 15 Feb 1929 by Rev W F S Nelson
         wit: Edith (Edwards) Abeloe, James Peter Abeloe, ring bearer: Glenn Robert Baker;
           flower girl: Emma Belle Baker (divorced)
William Lester Shefty   b. Colby KS 15 Feb 1900
   ranch worker Goleta   d. Las Vegas NV 6 Dec 1966
   shipyards Richmond   F: B J Shefty
   Celite, Lompoc, etc.   m.2 1950 Amelia Louise (Haug) McAdams

1929 Nipomo Notes. Miss Hannah Abeloe Weds William Shefty At Pretty Ceremony. Those present at the wedding were Mssrs and Mesdames M Abeloe, James Abeloe, Glenn Robert Baker of Harriston, Hans Mehlschau, J H Jensen, Laurence Jensen, George Mehlschau and son; P Jensen, Miland Jensen, Mrs M Jensen, Mrs Albert Jensen, Mrs Ed Wineman, Misses Margaret Paulson, Mattie Mehlschau, Dorothy Jensen, Ida and Johanna Jensen; Hans Mehlschau and Ernest Jensen, all of Nipomo; Mrs Chris Yager and family, and P A Abeloe of San Luis Obispo; Mr and Mrs L Kolding of Lompoc; Mrs James Jensen and daughter; Mrs Tom Jensen; Tillie, Margaret and Thomas Jensen; Mr and Mrs Glenn Baker and children; Mrs W S Edwards and Albert Edwards of Santa Maria; and Mrs M E Wood and Miss Rhoda Wood of Los Angeles. The Nipomo Pythian Sisters honored her last week, when she was the recipient of a lovely gift from the organization of which she is a member.   - clipping

  a. Lorraine Lila (adopted)   b. Salinas 14 Mar 1940
      m. c1961
    Richard Steve Pico   b. Los Alamos 26 Dec 1929
5. Herman Walter   b. Nipomo 12 Aug 1900
   auto mechanic   d. Santa Maria 21 Oct 1992 @92 SM cem
   1940-1 Dir: shop frmn Frank L Roemer h 829 W Cypress
   1955-6 Dir: emp Roemer & Rubel h 2210 N Bwy
      m. Minerva Club, Santa Maria 13 Jan 1930. Matrons of Honor: Mrs Cecelia (Bello)
        Freitas, Santa Maria; Mrs Hannah (Abeloe) Shefty, Goleta. Best man: Joseph Freitas
        Ushers: Manuel Brass, Carl Abeloe, Arthur Pinheiro
Mary Gloria Bello   b. Garey 27 July 1911
   1955-6 Dir: receptionist; living Santa Maria 1977
   Dr Harold T Case r 2210 N Bwy   F: Manuel Deus Bello 1883-1966
                                         M: Maria Gloria Faria 1887-1982
  a. Herman Walter jr   b. Santa Maria 10 Oct 1930
     1955-6 Dir: USN r 2210 N Bwy
       m. 1 (div)
     Helen Ruth Starnes   b. Belmont NC 4 May 1936
       m.2
     Young Soon Park   b. Ondong Korea 20 Apr 1957

   b. Donald Leland   b. Santa Maria 24 Dec 1932
     1955-6 Dir: US Navy r 2210 N Bwy
       m.
   Marilyn Louise Michl   b. Olney IL 10 Dec 1935
6. Lawrence Henry   b. Nipomo 1 Jan 1902
   1940-1 Dir: slsmn Hanson Equipt;   d. Santa Maria 5 Nov 1984 @82/10/4; SM cem
     r Star rt; also mech, Orcutt Star rt (Ada)
   1955-6 Dir: slsmn h 116 E Alvin
     m. Rickard ranch, Los Alamos 28 Apr 1925 by Rev R F Nelson
       wit: Carl Arthur Abeloe, Henry Monighetti
   Ada Erda Monighetti   b. Monte Carasso (Caruso?) Switz 8 May 1906
                                            d. Santa Maria 12 Oct 1994
                                            F: Henry Monighetti 1884-1951
                                            M: Maria Monighetti 1882-1964
  1951. Barbecue…Mr & Mrs Carl Abeloe…for nephew Jimmie at Camp Roberts. Mr &
    & Mrs James Abeloe, son Kenneth, Orcutt, Beverly Eggler and Ronnie Wyse, Mr &
    Mrs Lawrence Abeloe went to Santa Barbara to visit her sister Mrs Dona
    McDevitt and daughter Kathy.   – date lost
    a. Lawrence Lambert "Buddy"   b. Careaga ranch 28 Apr 1926
      1955-6 Dir: trctr opr Box 111 Los Alamos   d. Orcutt 5 Dec 1991
        m.
    Carley Jeanne Cassidy   b. Salinas 8 Aug 1925
    b. Nadine Mildred   b. Careaga ranch 7 Feb 1930
                                         d. same 11 Mar 1945 @15/1/4
                                           SM cem; tractor accid.
7. Laura Christine   b. Nipomo 12 Jan 1903
                                   d. Lakeview district 30 Oct 1906 @3/9/18
                                   SM cem
8. Robert Kenney   b. before or after move to Lakeview?
                                   20 Oct 1904
                                 d. Lakeview district 7 Jan 1905 @2 mos 12 d
                                 SM cem

Notes on the Abeloe Family by Laura Abeloe
Michael and Laura

    Mike was a seaman in Denmark but became a farmer in California. Laura and Mike lived and farmed in Nipomo (location unknown) until 1904 when they moved to the Lakeview district, southwest of Santa Maria. In 1909 they moved to the large Careaga ranch, seven miles west of Los Alamos. In 1919 they moved into the former "Harris" schoolhouse located on the ranch. Laura served as a Trustee on the Careaga-Orby school district for several years. She also worked at the school as a custodian, sometimes with the help of her daughter Hannah. Some of the children remember her bringing cookies and lemonade to the school. Laura and Mike raised their grandson, Glenn Robert Baker, after his mother died in 1919. Laura was taking care of her mother, in 1929, when Mette died at the age of 86.

James and Edith

    James and Edith lived and farmed on the Careaga ranch in the Los Alamos valley for 23 years. Their first home was on the south side of the ranch, 6½ miles west of Los Alamos, until 1929. It later became the home of the Walter Barca family. In 1929, they moved to the north side of the Careaga ranch, 7 miles west of Los Alamos, next door to Mike and Laura Abeloe, and they lived there for 20 years. In 1949 the family moved to Park Street, in Orcutt. James was a farmer, first with his father, "Mike Abeloe and Sons" and later in partnership with his brother Carl, as

"Abeloe Brothers Farming". He served on the Orcutt Elementary School District for twelve years and was a charter member of the Los Alamos Valley Men's Club. He also belonged to the Woodman of the World and the Neighbors of Woodcraft. Edith worked for Joey's Food Market in Orcutt, approximately 20 years. She was a member of the Justamere Club in Los Alamos, serving as President for several years. Edith was also a member of the Santa Maria and Orcutt Senior Citizens.

Carl and Elinor

Carl and his brother, James were in partnership as "Abeloe Brothers Farming". They had continued their father's farming operation which was previously known as "Mike Abeloe and Sons Farming". The family leased farmland from a wide area throughout Santa Barbara County. Carl was a charter member of the Los Alamos Men's Club, a member of the Los Alamos Senior Citizens and had been a Trustee of the Los Alamos Elementary School Board. Carl and Elinor were active in the Los Alamos Grange and the Los Alamos Community Church, where Carl was a Trustee. Elinor was a pianist and loved cooking and gardening. She belonged to the sewing circle of the Community Church and was skilled in needlework. In 1995, some families in Los Alamos still have her work displayed in their homes.

Hanna and Bill Shefty

Bill comes from a large family of 14 brothers and sisters. He was living on a ranch north of Goleta when they were married. He worked in the farming and construction trades in several places including the Doty ranch north of Goleta, the shipyards in Richmond, and the Celite Corporation in Lompoc, where they bought a home on "F" Street. They also lived in Salinas and San Francisco. Bill was working in the state of Washington when they divorced.

Hanna later lived in Monterey for many years, then in San Jose. She moved to Los Alamos in 1993 and to Santa Maria in 1994. She has worked as a sales clerk, a babysitter, a Western Union Messenger during World War II, and as a housekeeper. She also worked on large cruise ships traveling to foreign ports by tending children. She is a seasoned traveler, touring many foreign countries, and was an avid cross-country hiker in her younger days. She was still walking up to a mile or so at the age of 95.

Lawrence and Ada

At the time of their marriage, the Monighetti family was living on the Rickard ranch about two miles west of Los Alamos and the Abeloes were living on the Careaga ranch about seven miles west of Los Alamos.

Lawrence first farmed with his father and brothers, then he worked in Santa Maria for International Harvester Company as a salesman for 25 years. He later worked at Valley Farm Company for 5 years before he retired.

Lawrence and Ada's first home was 7¼ miles west of Los Alamos. The house was located just west of the bridge that crosses San Antonio Creek. The Everitt Brickey family later lived there, in the 1950's. Their 2nd home was 6¾ miles west of Los Alamos, located near the foothills. In 1945, they moved to Santa Maria. Ada worked briefly as a sales clerk for Griset Hardware on E Main St, then at Holser and Bailey's Department Store for 5 years. Her last job was at Haslam's Department Store where she worked for many years before she retired.

Lawrence and Ada were avid gardeners. They belonged to Santa Maria Valley Beautiful and received many awards for the landscaping of their home on E Alvin St. Lawrence was a member of the Santa Maria Historical Society.

Notes on the Careaga-Harris Ranch
It is situated west of Los Alamos and south of Orcutt

1842 - A Mexican land grant of 48,000 acres, called Rancho Los Alamos, is issued to Jose Antonio Carrillo.

1873 - 18,000 acres of the land grant is purchased in partnership by Juan Careaga, Ramon Careaga, and Daniel Harris.

1883 - The three partners subdivide the 18,000 acres into 3 approximately equal parcels, about 6000 acres each.

1909 - Laura and Mike settle on the 6000 acre parcel belonging to Ramon Careaga. They lived and farmed here for the rest of their lives. They moved only once, in 1919, from the south side of the road to the north side of the road. But the Post Office that serviced the Careaga ranch was restless. It moved many times: from La Graciosa, to Los Alamos, to Careaga, to Orby, to Harriston, and finally to Orcutt.

The Six Different Post Offices of the Careaga Ranch

1872/1877	La Graciosa, Cal	Stage Coach stop-11 miles northwest of the new village of Los Alamos
1877/1905	Los Alamos, Cal	Various locations within the township of Los Alamos
1905/1909	Careaga, Cal	5 miles west of Los Alamos - at the Pacific Coast Railway Station
1909/1924	Orby, Cal	9¼ miles west of Los Alamos (Lompoc-Harris Rd) Union Oil Company Steam Plant
1924/1934	Harriston, Cal	9 miles west of Los Alamos (junction of Lompoc-Harris Rd and Hwy 135)
1934/today	Orcutt, Cal	Township of Orcutt, 12 miles northwest of Los Alamos

If you were to ask anyone along the old Los Alamos Ranch Route where they lived…most likely they would simply say "in Los Alamos".

Vol. XXIX, No. 1, Spring 1997, p. 13

Corrections and Additions [Page numbers refer to those in Quarterly]

p.10. Father Kills Son on Ranch at Los Alamos. 78-Year-Old Fred D Howard Held in Jail Here for Death of Son. Reported Killing to His Daughter. Calmly Related How They Argued over Greasing a Car and He Shot. Fred D Howard shot his son Fred L, 31 on the Howard ranch 1½ miles north of Los Alamos…The elder Howard went to the home of his daughter Mrs Abeloe on an adjoining ranch and said "I've shot Fred." Fred was survived by his sister, Mrs Carl Abeloe; 2 half-sisters, Mrs L E Battele, Los Angeles, and Mrs Charles Tumbleson, Pacific Grove.
-Mon Nov 1 1936 p.1

p.11 William Morrison, Crash Victim, Killed Instantly. Ex-Mail Carrier, Scout Leader, is Traffic Fatility. Lawrence H Abeloe, 38, resident of the Barca ranch near Harris Station, an employee of Hanson Equipment Co, driving a loaded panel truck, crashed into Morrison's pick-up at the intersection of Betteravia lateral and Lower Orcutt Road at 5:30 pm. William Newton Morrison was born in Arkansas, had been in Santa Maria valley 11 years. Survived by widow Josie, son Wm Porter Morrison; daughters Mrs Annie Scharer, Pasadena and Mrs Winnie Rosenbrock, San Dimas; 2 brothers, Richard Morrison, Ontario, and David Morrison; two sisters Mrs Lula Caldwell, Oklahoma City, and Mrs Emma Pruitt, Chickasha, OK; 3 gch, as well as 7 half-brothers and sisters. – Fri Nov 15 1940

Vol. XXIX, No. 4, Winter 1997, p.18

ABERNETHY
PIONEERS OF THE CALIFORNIA CENTRAL COAST

Robert Abernethy   b. IRE c1815; parents SCT
   1880 cen: Guad blksmith   d. 29 Dec 1896; Guad cem
   1883 T/W; R Sr blacksmith Guadalupe
       R Jr hdwr, tinsmith Guadalupe
   no voter registrations found   *Santa Maria Times* not available for 1896
   m.
Caroline P(hebe) Travers   b. CAN 6 July 1822
   1900 cen: w/Anna Guad   d. Spokane WA 28 June 1912 @90; Guad cem
     9 births 5 living   obit July 6: from CAN to Racine WI; to CA 1875
         to Spokane c1908 to live w/son; 9 births 4 living
         4 dec: 3 sons 1 dau; 1 bro Will lvg, 1 Rbt dec
         F: Boyle Travers d. 1890s?
         M: Hannah Laraway 1799-1895

1.   James Abernethy   b. 27 Nov 1844
         d. 5 June 1878; Guad cem

2.   Anna P Abernethy   b. (Racine) WI May 1848
     1900 cen: Guad no hus   d. Spokane WA 24 Dec 1912 @69; Guad cem;
       6 births 3 living m/32 yr   "Hannah Anna"
         obit Jan 11 1913: *Week's News of Guadalupe*: went
       m. 1868   to Spokane w/mother; 2 little dau 1 son, bros, rels
   Charles Cornelius Goodfellow   b. NY c1849
     1890 GR: 49 NY bldr   d.
     Guad reg Sep 30
     1894. Mrs Carrie Goodfellow of Guad was in town Wed & paid the *Santa Maria Times* a
     call.   –Sep 15
     a.   Carrie Goodfellow   b.
         1888. Honor roll, Guad sch –*Valley*
     b.   child   b. SB co 12 Mar 1880 –Co Birth records
         (Edward Albert Goodfellow)   b. 26 Mar 1880
         d. Alameda co 11 Mar 1952)?
     c.   Brownie L Goodfellow   b. CA Dec 1883
     d.   Carl A Goodfellow   b. CA Apr 1886

3.   Robert Abernethy   b. (CAN) c1848
     1879 GR: 31 GB (?) tinsmth   d.
     na Sep 1869 Sac City Co Ct
     1880 cen: Guad tinsmith b. CAN
     1888. office Sprague st, between Post and Mill, Spokane Falls, WA Terr –ad
     1912 in Spokane
       m. c1874
   Mary R   b. WI c1852
         d.
         F: NY;   M: CT
     a.   Leila/Lulu A Abernethy   b. c1875
     b.   Elma? R (son) Abernethy   b. c1878
     c.   Flossie Abernethy   b.
         1912 in Spokane to gm's funeral, single

4.   Harriet J Abernethy   b. (WI)? May 1849
     "Hattie"   d. (Los Alamos) May 1885; LAl cem

       m. Santa Barbara 25 Nov 1882
William Gewe   b. Stemshorn, Honover GER 8 Mar 1850
  bio Phillips II 254   d. (Los Alamos) 17 July 1931; LAI cem
  imm 1868; to CA 1875;   F: Henry Gewe
  to Guad 1876 w/Hart   M: Mary Overman
 Bros m.2 1886 Cassie Downing
 1882 Blaksm shop Los Alamos; retired 1911
1879 GR: 28 GER blksm Guad na Aug 20 1877 SLO Co Ct
1880 cen: @29 Guad w/Thos Hart; horse shoer
1883-4 McKenny Dir: Whitcher & Gewe blksm LAI
1890 GR: 39 GER blksm Los Alamos na 1877 SLO Co Ct
1906 Dir: Bell st Los Alamos genl blksm; Mrs, Henry R clk, Hattie Miss
1922-23 Dir: farmer Los Alamos; Mrs Cassie hskpr; Gewe Henry R postmaster,
  insurance notary public office post office; Wm A machinist
  Robbins Ernest A (Hattie M) constable; Alvin stu PO Box G Los Alamos
a.   Henry Robert Gewe   b. (Los Alamos) 9 Mar 1884
                                 d. at home 14 Oct 1980 @96
    m.1   notice Oct 14
  Mabelle Alexander   b. 18 Dec 1892
                                 d. 18 Jan 1919; LAI cem
                                 no obit found

  = Robert A Gewe
    1959, 1979 in Glendale
      m.2
  Mabell Wilson   b. Tecumseh NE 4 Oct 1882
   1940-1 Dir: Henry R   d. 14 Mar 1959 @76; LAI cem
    (Mabell A) postmaster   obit Mon Mar 16 p.2: 40y Los Alamos
    Robert A stu   son 8gch s/son
   1955-6 Dir: Henry R   M: Garner
    (Mabell A) ins Los Alamos   m.1 Adams
  = her son Harold Adams
    1955-6 Dir: Harold (Priscilla) emp Coca-Cola h700 E Main
          Priscilla emp Schneider News Agency r700 E Main
    1972 Dir: Adams Priscilla Y Mrs clk Smith Trans r1600 E Clark space 165
    1976 Dir: Adams Priscilla clk Smith Trans h1380 W Main space 38
    1982 Dir: no Priscilla
b.   Hattie Mae Gewe   b. Los Alamos 19 May 1885; m. of Los Alamos
                                   d. (Los Alamos) 18 Dec 1979 @94
                                      obit Thu Dec 20 p.11; son bro 2gch neph
                                        nc Dr Catherine Robbins, Pasadena
        m. at home of Wm Gewe by Rev Chapman of SM 7 Jan 1907 (*Times*)
  Ernest Alva Robbins   b. (CA) 16 Dec 1883; m. of Los Alamos
   1906 Dir: Los Alamos. Robbins   d. 9 Oct 1956; LAI cem
    John W f 1 m E LO rd; Mrs;   obit Thu Oct 11 p.5; long illness
    Martin H f; Ernest f   M: Baber
   1940-1 Dir: Ernest A
    (Hattie) constable Los Alamos
  = Alvin W Robbins   b. 27 Aug 1909
    m.   d. Los Alamos May 1987
  Marguerite Tognazzi   b. *see ONT*
    or Margaret   d.

  1940-1 Dir: Alvin W (Mgt) ser sta; F: Victor Tognazzi 1861-1940
   Robbins & Howard ser sta Los M: Jennie Locarnini 1869-1932; LAI
   Alamos (station built by Gewe 1923)   cem
  1955-6 Dir: Robbins Alvin Shell Serv 1906 Dir: Victor f:Mrs: 6m W of Los
   Los Alamos h918 E Cypress SM,   Alamos
   Alvin W Shell Ser Sta Los Alamos, 1932. Survivors: hsband Victor, 3
   Marguerite at home Los Alamos   sons: Frank, Dante (d.1958 @63),
 + Alvin W Robbins jr 1936-1968;   Chas Tognazzi, LAI; 3 dau: Olga
  Los Alamos cem   Tognazzi, Mrs Margaret Robbins,
  = Billy Robbins 1979 in Nipomo   LAI; Mrs Alma Howard, Fullerton.
  = Susan Robbins 1979 in Nipomo 4 bro: John and Pete (d.1945 @68)
    Locarnini, Orcutt; Joe Locarnini, AZ;
    Chas Locarnini, Modesto; sis Marie
    Locarnini, Switzerland. 1gch. former
 by 2nd wife res Cayucos –Mon Feb 19 1932
 c. William Andrew Gewe b. (Los Alamos) 17 Dec 1895
  USN WWI d. Contra Costa co 24 May 1941 @46; LAI cem
   obit Mon May 26 p.1
   car struck by train nr Byron Springs
   sch bus driver. Left Los Alamos "short time
   ago to live on ranch nr Byron Spr w/aunt."

5. Caroline P Abernethy b. 11 Nov 1851
 "Carrie" d. Guadalupe 29 Mar 1885 @c33 (*Times*); Guad cem
  m.
 George R Walls b. NY (1846)
  1884 GR: 38 NY Miner** d. San Jose 7 Dec 1922 @76; Guad cem; Civil War
  Guad reg Aug 3 notice Dec 9; no survivors listed
 a. Fred Walls
  1888. Honor roll, Guad sch –V
  **Miner: Jose Rubalcava, Rancho de Guadalupe Historical Society, has researched
   the Abernethy gold mine, said to be about two miles north of Casmalia. The owner,
   Samuel Nash, also proprietor of the Gilt Edge Creamery in Guadalupe, founded in
   1893, sold the mine to one of the Buells about 1896. Unfortunately a severe storm
   flooded the mine, which collapsed, thus ending the enterprise.
6. (Isabella Abernethy 1851-1878; Guad cem; is this a daughter or dau-in-law?)
7. Elmer Abernethy b. 1850s
   d. young
8. William A Abernethy b.
  1890. Wm Abernethy of d.
   Stockton to Guad to visit parents and friends. –Jan 11
  1912 in Spokane
9. Henry Abernethy b. CAN 1855
  1879 GR: 23 CAN tinsmth d. (Alameda co 7 Oct 1918 @63) spouse E
  Guad na Aug 7 1879 SLO Co Ct reg June…
  1912 in San Leandro
  m.
 Eliza d. (Alameda co 21 May 1937 @79) spouse H
10. Frederick Wilber Abernethy b. CAN April 1857; m. @24 of Guad C/E IR NY
  to Guad 1876 (1874 -*Valley* d. (Guad) 3 Nov 1939 @82; Guad cem
  1879 GR: 21 CAN tnsmth Guad obit Sat Nov 4 p.3; Agent SP Milling co
  na June 18 1869 SLO Co Ct son gson no other close relatives

1882 GR: 25 CAN tnsmth Guad…reg Aug 15 1882; 1886: same
1883-4 McKenny Dir: F W Abernethy stoves & tinware Guadalupe
1890. F W Abernethy returned from Spokane a few days ago and was in this town for a few days. He gave a glowing account of the prosperity of his future home and left here for that city, with his family on last Wednesday morning. We hope Fred will realize his most sanguine expectations and that he will be most eminently successful in his new vocation. –Apr 26
1896 returned to Guad;   1900 cen: Guad 4 births 3 living
1906 Dir: engineer, Guad; Mrs
1910 cen: Powell st (=Cook st) Santa Maria; 4 births 2 living; foreman lumber mill
1922-3 Dir: agt SP Milling co rGuad
1925 Dir: Guad, Fred (Mary) mgr SP warehouse
1928 Dir: Fred (Mary) mgr SP warehouse Guad
    m. Arroyo Grande 13 Oct 1881 by H Holdridge ME ch, A447
      wit: Hugh Graves SM; Jennie E Graves, SM

Mary Eudora Abbott   b. Sonoma co 25 June 1861; m. @20 of AG
  "May"   d. Guad 9 June 1934 @72; Guad cem
                               see Abbott chart
                             F: Alvin B Abbott 1827-1893
                             M: Louisa C Tripp 1834-1894

a.   Roy Frederick Abernethy   b. (Guad) Apr 1882
   1900 cen: Guad   d. (Guad) 14 Nov 1918 @36; influenza; Guad
    poultry dealer   cem; notice Fri Nov 14 p.3
   1906 Dir: R F eng Guad
   1910 cen: w/parents single
      m. San Luis Obispo 28 Dec 1910 by M Ternes, I131
        wit: Edward Wise, Guad; Lottie Wise, Guad
   Edith C Wise   b. 12 Sep 1886; m. @24 of Guad
    Confirmed St Pat's ch   d. 20 Dec 1961 @75; Guad cem
     AG 7 Oct 1901; sponsor   obit; 60y Guad; 40y tchr; retired 1957
     Lottie Wise   6gch 3ggch
    1906 Dir: Miss stu Guad   F: Edward Hale Wise 1837-1916
    1920 cen: tp #9 Guad hskpr   M: Margaret   1859-1918
     Own Income widow;   see Wise chart
     Raymond 7; bro Edw Wise 27 bkpr gen mdse store
    1922-3 Dir: Edith C hskpr Guad
    1925 Dir: Mrs Edith schtchr Guad
    1928 Dir: Mrs Edith schtchr; Raymond stu Guad
    1940-1 Dir: tchr rGuadalupe st Guad
    1955-9 Dir: tchr Box 163 Guad
    1961. pall bearers: Raymond Lopez, Kermit McKenzie, Thomas P Weldon,
      Fred Gracia, Leo Acquistapace, Albert Cicero
  = Raymond F Abernethy   b. Guad 10 July 1912
    1913. Guadalupe Happenings. The d. SM 12 Jan 1986 @73; Guad cem
     little son of M/M Roy Abernethy   obit Tue Jan 14 p.19; 20y w/Smith
     is reported to be very ill. –Jan 4   Transportation; ret 1975 H & R
    1931 SMUHS; 1935 San Jose State Block; 5 yr partner with Glenn
    1940-1 Dir: emp Golden St Ltd   Porter & Assoc; wid, 3 sons 5 dau;
     r114 Guadalupe st Guad   14gch 5ggch 24 foster ch
    1955-6 Dir: laundromat, constable h4605 2d Guad
    1976 Dir: dock foreman Smith Trans h685 Guadalupe st Guad

    1976 Dir: Porter Glen & Tina mgr H & R Block h4922 Cherry Orcutt
    1982 Dir: Porter Glenn E & Tina P H & R Block h4922 Cherry Orcutt
    1986. pall bearers: Raymond Lopez jr, Michael & Jimmie Lopez, Damon Zaragoza, Tim & Chad Hedrick
     m.
    Bettie J Pritchett   b. Shawnee OK 15 Aug 1928
             d. Guad 23 Feb 1998 @69; obit Wed Feb 25 A7; 47y Guad, formerly Olivehurst. 30 foster ch 3 sons 1 dau named; bro 2 sis; 1 bro 2 sis deceased
             F: Charles Daniel Pritchett 1891-1988
             M: Oma Serena Menser 1895-1969
    1956. Officers' Wives Install Staff. Branch USDB Officers' Wives Club…Mrs Raymond Abernethy, outgoing president…photo
    1969. pall bearers: Charles Pritchett, Larry Pritchett, Danny Abernethy, Anthony Abernethy, Stephen Shaffer, Bill Hedrick
    1988. pall bearers: Danny Abernethy, Anthony Abernethy, Steven Mackey, Jeff Shaffer, Tim Hedrick, Chad Hedrick
    1998. pall bearers: Raymond Lopez jr, Michael Lopez, Jimmie Lopez, Damon Zaragoza, Tim Hedrick, Chad Hedrick
     Survivors bro & sis: Buck Pritchett, Guadalupe; Jeannie Hedrick, Guadalupe; Anna Shaffer, Salinas; deceased: Faye Mabray, Ada Mae Callaway, Fred Pritchett.
   + Joann Abernethy (Raymond Lopez) in Guad 1986
    1982 Dir: Raymond & Joan emp Hy Manomi & Sons h930 Olivera Guad (H Y Minami)
   + Serena Abernethy (Frazier) in Guad 1986
   + Rayma Abernethy (Rbt Brayton) in Guad 1986, 1998
    1976 Dir: Rayma Abernethy wtrs Far Western r685 Guadalupe st
    1982 Dir: Brayton Rbt & Rayma h665 Guadalupe st
   + Raedine Abernethy (Werthman) SB 1986
   + Barbara Abernethy (Waren) SB 1986
   + Raymond Abernethy jr in Guad 1986, 1998
    1998. arrested @38 for violation of parole etc –May 23 A2
   + Anthony Abernethy in SM 1986, Nipomo 1998
    1976 Dir: emp Columbia Records r685 Guadalupe st
    1982 Dir: Anthony & Angelina elec tech VAFB h4417 Elm Guad
   + Danny Abernethy in Guad 1986, 1998
     m. 1974 Barbara Jean Ruiz b. 1950 –ONT 112
    1982 Dir: Jas D & Barbara J emp Getty Oil h1155 Guadalupe st
 b. Fred Clive Abernethy   b. Guad 2 Dec 1885 (*Times*)
   1910 cen: w/parents single d. (Guad) 22 July 1973 @87; Guad cem
   1922-3 Dir: gas eng Guad   obit Mon July 23 p.2; r685 Guad st
   1940-1 Dir: emp SP Milling   neph Ray; gnc, gneph
   rGuad st   Single
   1955-6 Dir: lab h685 Guad st
 c. Alda May Abernethy   b. Guad 25 June 1888 (*Times*)
               d. Guad 30 July 1888 @1 mo 4 day (*Times*); Guad cem
 d. Edna Marguerite Abernethy b. (Spokane) WA Feb 1892
               d. (Guad) 10 Oct 1909 @17/6; Guad cem

Other Abernethy, Guad cem: Ella May b. 9 Apr 1943; d. 12 Apr 1943

ADAM
SANTA MARIA VALLEY PIONEERS

The Adam family arrived in the Santa Maria Valley in the fall of 1869, at which time there were already several families braving the wind and sand. Of the earliest families, the descendants are, for the most part, not many, having moved away or dwindled away; however, the Adam clan is still well represented in the valley, so that it may well be said that they take the prize for long residence, certainly more so than other pioneer families chronicled in these pages in recent years. It can hardly be doubted that the more than 9000 acres of city and country property distributed from the estate of William Laird Adam has enabled his descendants to maintain, and that comfortably, their residence in this, their ancestral place. We note the continuity of address in city directories, even as we see, also the building of more modern dwellings in the fashionable part of town.

The Adam family is well represented in county histories as well as in historical articles in the newspapers over the years. We do not here attempt to recapitulate their lives, except in bits and pieces shown on the chart. The pall bearers are listed because most are relatives; others are the movers and shakers of the community.

The Memoirs of William Laird Adam, California Pioneer 1836-1903, prepared for printing by Donald M. Prentice from the original manuscript, can be found in the Genealogy Section of the Santa Maria Public Library. Adam was literate and detail conscious, which makes for interesting and educational reading. Unfortunately, "he did not have enough time to complete the Memoirs beyond arrival of the wagon train at San Bernardino". That lack is somewhat filled by the above-mentioned biographies.

Mr Prentice gathered as much family information on the descendants as was possible for him; he has names only-no dates or places, so this compilation complements his work.

This outline precedes Chapter 1 of the Memoirs:

1836 to 1850	What I remember of Scotland
1850	Voyage Liverpool to New Orleans thence up the Mississippi river to Saint Louis Mo.
1850-1857	Winter in Saint Louis thence up the Missouri to Council Bluffs thence to Salt Lake
51,52,53	Life in Salt Lake to City
53	Journey Salt Lake to Cedar City
53,54	Life in Cedar City
54	Journey Cedar City to San Bernardino
55	Life in San Bernardino and Journey to Sta. Barbara
56	Journey to San Joaquin then to San Jose Mission
56,57,58	Life in San Jose
58,59	Up the Frazer River moved to Pajaro
Nov 60	Married to Elizabeth Connor
61,62,63,64	Farmers Life in Pajaro Life there Moved to Salinas Life there
69	Moved to Santa Maria Life there

Mr Prentice lists the siblings of Wm. Laird Adam, and had wished to include information on them as well, but was unable to gather the necessary material. A note on Alexander, the youngest of William's brothers, stated that he was living in Monterey County in 1903 and "has had much trouble in the latter part of his life." Thanks to some facts in the Lompoc Historical Society's collection, further investigation was stimulated so as to add a bit about Alexander, who accompanied Wm. here.

William Laird Adam   b. Old Swallow Haugh, Old Moukland,
  1860: SCz co Pajaro tp   Lanarkshire, Scotland 7 Aug 1836
  1869: to Santa Maria   christened Bothwell 21 Aug 1836
  1870: SMv dairyman   d. San Francisco 14 Dec 1903 @67/4/7; SM cem
  1875: Agricola school org'd,   obit Dec 18
    W L Adam sec.   F: William Thom Adam 1796-____; contractor
  1880: SM storekpr, farmer   M: Isabelle Laird d. Scotland c1844
  1880: taxpayers on $500 or more: W.L. Adam $16,905. -T/W 231
  1883-4 McKenney Dir: W.L. Adam genl merch Santa Maria
  1888 GR: 51 Sct ranchero SM; naturalized Dec 5 1887 SB Sup Ct
  1890 GR: 54 Sct farmer; nat as above
  1893: W L Adam is very sick with la grippe, but improving... -Dec 2
  1900: Santa Maria landowner
    also deputy post master, director/president bank of Santa Maria;
    president/secretary Santa Maria Union High School, etc. etc.
    m. San Jose Nov 1860
Elizabeth (O)Connor   b. Frampton Quebec 1838
     d. at home nr SM 21 May 1898 @60/2/15;SM cem
      obit May 28; also Card of Thanks
     F: James Connor (b. IRE) of Santa Clara Valley
     M: b. England
11 births, 10 living 1898; 8 living 1927; 5 left, all SM 1939; 4, 1940; 3, 1944

1. William Connor   b. nr Watsonville 16 Sep 1861
  1880: w/parents, clerk   d.1035 W Main st 16 Dec 1944 @83/3/0; SM cem
  1890 GR: 28 CA mcht SM #1   house built 1904; obit Mon Dec 18 p.1
  1900: SM   Santa Clara U. bio 1909 Dir; O'Neill 465
  1906 Dir: rancher 3 m NW; Mrs; Irma Miss; Phyllis Miss
  1909 Dir: stock dealer, rancher W Main; Mrs Ada; Miss I A; Miss P E; E C
  1922 DIR: rancher Garey dist; rW Main, Fairlawn dist; Mrs Ada V
  1944 Pall bearers: Fred O. Sherrill, Wm Porter, John Gray, W P Adam, Dewey Werling,
    Jas Adam
        m. at bride's home Guadalupe 10 Jan 1888 (*Times*)
  Ada Vere Kelley   b. San Francisco 28 Feb 1865
     d. 6 Oct 1943 @78/7/8; SM cem
      obit Thu Oct 7 p.1; bro W F Kelley, SB
     F: Joseph Kelley
     M: Catherine Langais (1841-1897 OM cem SLO)?
    4 births, 4 living 1910
    a. Irma A   b. SM 4 Nov 1888 (*Times*)
      1922 Dir: Irma C Adam   d. 26 Jan 1983 @94/2/22; SM cem
        steno SMG&P Co rFairlawn dist
        m.
      George Pratt
    b. Phyllis Elizabeth   b. SM 18 May 1891; SSDI
         d. (SB) Apr 1975; lived in King City
        m.
      Frank Marshall
    c. Elmo Charles   b. SM 17 Nov 1893 (*Times*)

    1922 Dir: rancher Suey   d. San Francisco 18 Mar 1943 @48; SM cem
       dist (1920: single)   obit Fri Mar 19 p.1; 20 yrs in SF
    m. (wife not named in obit)
    1943 Pall bearers; Donald Prentice, Thomas Adam, Wm Porter, John Adam,
      Kenneth Adam, W P Adam
  d. Leonard Henry   b. 15 Apr 1895 (Co birth rec)
    1922 Dir: Leonard (Mrs   d. 13 July 1976 @81/2/28; SM cem
      Winnie) rancher Garey rd   obit Wed July 14 p.2. WWI
    1947-48 Dir: farmer & pres SMv Water Conservation Dist. rGarey
    m.
    Winifred Gertrude Smith   b. Norwalk CA 8 Jan 1898
      to SMv 1919   d. at home 6 Oct 1989 @ 91; SM cem
          obit Mon Oct 9 p.12
          sis Catherine Lee Werling, SLO
          bro Ralph Edward Smith, Balboa Island
    =John Kelley (living in Fort Bragg 1989); "Jackie" only gch 1944
2. Mary Conner   b. Watsonville 4 Mar 1863
   Confirmed Guadalupe   d. 13 Jan 1939 @75/10/9; SM cem
    8 July 1877 @14; sponsor   obit Sat Jan 14 p.2; bio O'Neill 160
    Mary Emerick   educated Convent of Sacred Heart, SLO
  1922 Dir: Mary C Adam hskpr r519 S Bwy (Porters' house)
    Single
  1939: Eight Nephews to Bear Body to Grave…Wm, Leonard, John, Thos, James Adam,
    Wm Porter, all of SM; Kenneth & Roderick Sheehy, Watsonville
3. Isabella/Belle   b.Watsonville 1864; m. @31 (!) of Santa Maria
   Confirmed Guadalupe   d. at home 201 Jefferson st Watsonville noon
    8 July 1877 @13; sponsor   Fri 17 Jul 1931. Obit Sat July 18 p.5
    Theresa Fleck   Valley cem Watsonville
   m.1 at home of bride's parents nr Santa Maria 27 April 1898 by Rev Lynch, B16
    wit: Joseph Sheehy,Watsonville; Mary Adam, SM (moved to Watsonville thereafter)
  Patrick R (Henry?) Sheehy   b. CA 1865; m. @33 of Watsonville
           d.
    m.2 by 1928 J P Mann   (not mentioned in Belle's obit)
  a. Kenneth (Byra Wood)   (living in NYC 1931; in Watsonville 1939)
    =Robert Patrick
    =Terrence Wm
  b. Roderick/Wm R   (living in Watsonville 1931)
  c. Gladys (Martinelli)   d. before 1931
    =Charles
    =Patricia
    =Barbara
  d. Isabel single in 1931
4. James Eugene   b. (Watsonville) Oct 1865
   Confirmed Guadalupe   d. Santa Barbara 9 Aug 1910 @44/7/23; SM cem
    8 July 1877 @11; sponsor   bio Phillips II 191
    Wm Adams (sic) jr
  1888 GR: 23 CA farmer SM
  1888 Polk Gazetteer: Adam & Blosser (Jas Adam, Garrett Blosser) Meat Mkt SM
  1890 GR: 24 CA rancher SM #2
  1900: SM 4 births, 4 living

1910: S Bwy 7 births, 6 living
1906 Dir: rancher 1½ m SW; Mrs
1909 Dir: rancher, stock dealer 1½ m SW; Mrs; W P stu; Miss B M stu
    m. at the bride's home Los Berros by Rev Lynch 25 Apr 1892 (*Times*)
      moved to Pismo Beach, operated the Pismo Hotel until 1897;
    came back to west Stowell rd.

Mary Aloysius Donovan	b. Watsonville May 1870 (cen) or
1920: Co rd SMv	Castroville 25 May 1869 (obit)
1922 Dir: Mrs Mary hskpr	d. at home of dau Mrs Shipsey Pismo Beach
SW city limits	25 Sep 1957 @88/4/0; SM cem
1938, 1950 ph/bk: Mrs J E	obit Thu Sep 26 p.8. 6 yrs in Pismo
W Stowell rd	sis Miss Agnes Donovan, Mrs Catherine
	Williams (hus Cramer J Williams)
	F: Patrick Donovan 1840-1906; to AGv 1881
	M: Jane McCart(h)y 1842-1920

  1957 Pall bearers, all grandsons: John Adam jr, Richard Adam, Wm Adam, Jim Adam,
    Kenneth Ford, Gerald Shipsey

Note: Some of the property on West Stowell Road was developed into a housing tract called Adam Park. William Laird Adam Elementary school and Adam Park (a real park) are located a few blocks east and south, off Stowell Road.

a. William Patrick/Pat	b. Pismo 14 Feb 1893 (*Times*)
1922 Dir: W P (Pauline)	d. at home 935 W Stowell Rd 1 Jan 1972
rancher r400 E Main	@78/10/17; SM cem. obit Mon Jan 3 p.2
1939,1950 ph/bk: W Stowell	
m.	
Pauline Nevada Martin	b. Martin dist SMv 2 Mar 1898 (*Times*)
1922 Dir: Pauline sten	d. 18 Nov 1985 @87/6/16; SM cem
B of SM r400 E Main	F: Robert Franklin Martin 1865-1929
	M: Harriet Louise Newlove 1870-1921

  1972 Pall Bearers, all nephews: John F Adam jr, Richard E Adam, Gerald W Shipsey,
    James E Shipsey, Patrick Williams, Thomas Williams
    =Patricia Ann (Gerald Patrick Mahoney) 1950 ph/bk: Nance Rd SM
    =James Eldon 1925-1989 (Vivian Mildred Tonascia)
      1951-2 Dir: Jas (Vivian) farmer 602 E Church; Vivian dental nurse Dr W L Smith
    =Wm Patrick jr (Georgina Griset)
    =Jane Marie (Louis Donald Drenon)

b. Elizabeth Mary/Bessie	b. Pismo 29 Oct 1894 (*Times*)
1916: Local items.	d. (SLO) 30 Mar 1961; OM cem SLO
Bessie Adams (sic) spent week end with relatives at Los Berros. -Jan 15	
m.	
William T Shipsey	b. (SLO) 7 Sep 1892
	d. (SLO) 30 Mar 1948; OM cem SLO
	F: Wm Shipsey 1851-1922; OM cem SLO
	bio Davis Encyc 1915 p.359, photo
	mayor SLO 1898-1902
	M: Annie Barry 1863-1950; OM cem SLO

    =Kathleen Elizabeth (Lyons) div
    =Gerald Wm (Dorothy Nadine McDougal)
    =James Edward (Bruna Louise Frances Coni)

   c. Dorothy M   b. Pismo 2 Sep 1896
                                                             d. 11 Dec 1976 @80/3/9; SM cem
                                                                    obit Mon Dec 13 p.3. 18 gch, 7ggch
         m. Santa Maria 17 Aug 1921
      Albert E Ford   b. Gas City IN 8 July 1894
        Paso Robles HS   d. 4 July 1982 @87/11/26; SM cem
        to SM 1917   bio *Who's Who SM*
     1930 Dir: r111 W Morrison   F. John Ford;   M: Grace
     1940-1 Dir: attdnt Gilmore Ser Sta, h111 W Morrison
     1947-8 Dir: emp Camp Cooke h111 W Morrison
        Dorothy Secy Vanaas & Taylor (20 years, per obit)
    =Kenneth Earl 1922-1971; SM cem (Leona 1921-1981)
       1940-1 Dir: stu r111 W Morrison
       1947-8: Kenneth (Leona) USCCA* h624 W Fesler
           *USC College of Aeronautics, Hancock Field
    =Miriam F (F David Schnebly) (in Portola Valley 1976)
    =John Robert (in Glendale 1976)
   d. John Francis   b. SM 8 Feb 1898 (Co birth rec)
      1920: w/mother   d. 10 Sep 1973 @75/7/2; SM cem
      1922 Dir: farmer SW city limits
      1938 ph/bk: Lower Orcutt Rd
      1950 ph/bk: 316 Mariposa Way
        m.
     Hester Florence Myers   b. 14 Jan 1898; m. of Berkeley
                                             d. 23 May 1989 @91; SM cem

     =John Francis Jr
     =Richard Edward
   e. Kenneth A   b. 16 Mar 1901
      1920: w/mother   d. 8 July 1968 @67/3/23; SM cem
      1940-1 Dir: h729 E Cypress
      1951-2 Dir: rancher 725 E Cypress
        m. 22 June 1932
     Mary Adele Johnston   b. 2 July 1911
                                              d. 17 Nov 1967 @56/4/6; SM cem
                                              F: Wm Fletcher Johnston 1876-1951
                                              M: Anita M Castro 1880-1969
                                                     see ONT 193; *Valley* 25; M/H 944(Castro)
     =Mary Ann (Edwin John Fumia 1924-1974)
     =Kathryn Elizabeth (George Shiffrar) see ONT 278-80
     =Janet Rose (Norman Conrad Kalland)
   f. twins   b. 7 Dec 1904 (*Times*)
     infant   d. @1 mo 16 da; bur 23 Jan 1905 SM cem
     Janet Bernice   d. 11 Oct 1976 @71/10/3; SM cem; obit Thu
       1940-1Dir: secy SM Conservation Water   12 Oct p.12
         Dist; rEl Paseo Cts
       1976 Pall Bearers, all nephews: John Adam, Willard Adam, Wm P Adam jr,
          Gerald Shipsey, John Ford, Gerald Mahoney
       m.   Joseph Francis Rowan   b. 14 Nov 1901
       No issue   d. 5 Oct 1988 @86; SM cem
       1940-1Dir: Rowan & Green Mens Wear 106 W Main; hEl Paseo Cts

5. Charles Augustus   b. (Watsonville) Dec 1867
   Confirmed Guadalupe   d. at home of sister Mary Adam 401 W Main
   1 Apr 1886 @18; sponsor   21 Aug 1923 @55/8/1; SM cem.
   James Mahoney   obit Wed Aug 22 p.1; lived w/Porters
   1890 GR: 22 CA f SM #2
   1900 GR: 33 Huasna;   1900 cen: Huasna, stock raiser, next to Porters
   1902 GR: 34 Huasna
   1906 Dir: rancher 2mW (no wife)
   1909 Dir: stockraiser r S Bwy Cor Cook St (no wife, just sisters)
     m. 1897
   Mary J Porter   b. CA Nov 1875
    1900: no issue   d.
                                     F: Arza Porter 1838-
                                     M: Rosa Sparks 1851-1915

6. Thomas Bernard   b. Santa Maria Aug 1870
   Confirmed Guadalupe   d. 12 Oct 1940 @70/1/22; SM cem
   1 Apr 1886 @16; sponsor   obit Sat Oct 12 p.1; Mon Oct 14 p.2
   Basil Fox   r222 E Main; bio Phillips II 142
   1906 Dir: banker rBroadway; Mrs (22 years w/Valley Savings Bank)
   1909 Dir: banker 719 S Broadway; Mrs
   1920: 103 E Cook
   1922 Dir: Ths B (Grace) prop Calif Mkt rCook and Broadway (w/S R Obarr)
   1939 ph/bk: T B Adam meats 114 E Main
   1940-1 Dir: 222 E Main (house built by J B Arellanes)
   1940: The oil industry on the floor of the valley began with Adam's discovery of oil
       five years ago.
   1940 Pall bearers, all nephews: Leonald Adam, Wm P Adam, John F Adam,
      Kenneth Adam, James Adam, Wm A Porter, Byron Thornburg, Lasalle
      Thornburg. Honorary pall bearers: W L Hopkins, Will Johnson, Isaac Miller,
      Henry Tilley, Benjamin Granas, Joe Davis, Wm MacDonald, Jesse Chambers,
      Walter Smith, Leo P Scaroni
     m. Oakland 18 May 1905
   Grace Thornburgh   b. Santa Maria 24 Aug 1885
   San Jose St Col   d. 17 Mar 1967 @81/6/23; SM cem
                                     obit Sat Mar 18 p.2; r222 E Main
                                   F: Jesse Hunt Thornburgh 1840-1913
                                   M: Caroline B Fee 1849-1929
                                      See M/H 346 for Thornburgh; *SM Vidette*
                                      16 Dec 1927 for Fee, to SM 1874
   1967 Pall Bearers, all nephews: James E Adam, James R Adam, Wm A Porter,
      Robert Sheehy, Donald N Prentice, Byron H Thornburgh
     a. Elizabeth Caroline   b. 11 July 1906 (*Times*)
        1922 Dir: stu HS r101 E Cook   d. 25 Nov 1958 @52/4/14; SM cem
        m.
        Frederick Orlo Sherrill   b. 1903
          1939 ph/bk: 525 S Bwy   d. 5 May 1952 @48/4/15; SM cem
           1947-8 Dir: h222 E Main; 1950 ph/bk: same
        =Frederick O jr 1935-1996 (Karen Laughter)
        =Elizabeth Ann (Robert Lee Newark)
     b. Thomas B II   b. 27 Jan 1913
        1940-1 Dir: farmer 222 E Main   d. 21 Aug 1980 @67/6/24; SM cem

    1950 ph/bk: same   obit Sat Aug 23 p.9 (no wife or ch)
    1951-2 Dir: Thos B jr (Lucile) farmer 222 E Main
      Adam Berry Farm, T B Adam, P.O. Box
    1980 Pall bearers: Donald H Taylor, Keith Lapp, Donald Prentice,
      W A Porter, James Battles, Robert W Bond, Ed Phipps
7. Anastasia/Nessie   b. Santa Maria 26 Dec 1871; m. @27 of SM
 Confirmed Guadalupe   d. 23 Feb 1954 @82/1/27; SM cem
 1 Apr 1886 @13; sponsor   obit Tue Feb 23 p.1. r 519 S Broadway
  Elizabeth Adam
  m. nr Santa Maria 25 Oct 1899 by Rev M Lynch, F202
   wit: Arza Porter, Santa Barbara; Kate Adam, Santa Maria
 Isaac James Porter   b. Santa Barbara 24 Mar 1871; m. @28 of Huasna
  1900: Huasna (SLO co)   d. @65/0/19; bur 26 Feb 1937 SM cem
  1902 GR: 30 Huasna   F: Arza Porter 1838-
  1909 Dir: cattleman r 403   M: Rosa Sparks 1851-1915
   S Bwy; Mrs Nessie   See M/H 55 for Isaac J Sparks
  1910: W Cypress 3 births 3 living   bio Phillips I 356; Valley 64
  1918: built 519 S Broadway
  1922 Dir: Isaac (Anna S) ret r 519 S Bwy; Rose, stu; Elizabeth, stu
   a. Elizabeth Ann   b. nr SM 25 Aug 1900 (*Times*)
    Mills College   d. 19 Aug 1991 @90; SM cem
    Supt County Hospital SM   obit Wed Aug 21 B7 1 gch
   m. 1936
    Donald Marion Prentice   b. Pana IL 15 Nov 1905
     to SM 1925 grad CIT   d.
    Supt Casmite Co in   bio *Who's Who SM*
     Casmalia, 1930   F: John A Prentice; M: Dicey B
   1947-8 Dir: oilman h1106 S Bwy; 1951-2 Dir: Oil Opr, r same
   =Mary Katherine (Thomas Rhodes Wolf) div. she in SB 1991
   =John Anthony (Sharon Harris) div. he in SM 1991
  b. Rosa Anastasia   b. 1902
    Single   living in Santa Maria 1992
  c. William Arza/Bunny   b. SM 19 Oct 1908 (*Times*)
   cattle rancher Huasna   d. 6 Feb 1993, injured in auto accident
             @84; SM cem. obit Tue Feb 9 A5 7gch
   m. 1937
    Josephine Poncetta   b. 22 Dec 1910, SSDI
              d. (San Jose) April 1983
              F: Joseph Poncetta 1883-1957
   1957 Pall bearers: Bunny Porter, Chas Cossa, Herman Goodman,
    George Guntle, Eddie and Frank Capitani
   =Anastasia (Richard Emslie) div. she in SB 1993
   =Isaac Joseph (Christine Gamble) in SB 1993
   =Rosemary (Joseph Eugene Doud jr) in SM 1993
   =Charles Robert (Gerilyn Bartel) in SB 1993
8. Margaret/Maggie   b. 1873
              bur Thornburgh cem 1877 @4; reinterred
               SM cem 1884
9. Kenneth   b. Santa Maria Jan 1874/5 (cen)
 Confirmed St Pat's Ch AG   d. Oakland 1 Feb 1899 @23/11/24; SM cem
 3 June 1894 @19; Sponsor __ Donovan   endocarditis

10. Katherine A   b. Santa Maria Nov 1876
    1909 Dir: w/Charles A,   d. Los Angeles 20 Dec 1928 @52; SM cem
       S Bwy cor Cook   obit Fri Dec 21 p.1; Sat Dec 22 p.5
    1910: w/Porters   funeral from Porters' residence
        m. Santa Maria 3 Dec 1912 (bio) or 9 Nov 1912 (Co record)
    Joseph Adam Rembusch   b. Batesville IN 27 July 1869; m. @44
       Professor of Music   d. 29 Oct 1961 @92/3/2; SM cem
       to SM 1907   bio M/H 841
       SM Band; resigned 1914   F: Peter Rembusch b. FR d. 1898 @80
       No issue   M: Frances Snyder d. 1883
11. Carlyle Alexander   b. Santa Maria 5 Mar 1881
    Confirmed St Pat's Ch AG   d. watching the Elks' Parade on Porters'
       3 June 1894 @14; sponsor   porch 31 May 1952 @81; bur San Jose
       Patrick Donovan   obit June 2 p.3
        m.
    May Laffie   died in San Jose?
  1910 living on West Main; in San Jose 1923,1924; returned to Santa Maria 1935
    to manage Carl Adam ranch on Guadalupe road
        a. Francis Laird (predeceased father?)
        b. Constance M (Francis Silliman) (living in Watsonville 1952)
        c. Bernice G (predeceased father?)
        d. James Richard (Katherine Caulfield) (living in Santa Maria 1952)
12. Anna Elizabeth   b. on ranch 1 mi W of Santa Maria
                                               2 Jan 1886 (*Times*)
    1909 Dir: w/Charles A,   m. @23
       S Bwy cor Cook   d. at home cor Blosser and Donovan rds 9 Nov
                                               1959 @73/20/8; SM cem
                                               obit Mon Nov 9 p.1 8 gch
        m. 26 Oct 1909 –*SLO Tribune* Oct 29
    Charles Leo Preisker   b. Visalia 15 Aug 1885; m. @24
       to SM 1894   d. 6 May 1966 @80/8/21; SM cem
                                               bio *Who's Who SM Valley* XVIII 191ff,
                                               "Mister Politics"
                                               F: Thomas Jefferson Preisker
                                               M: Louise Arizona Strube 1843-1931
  1906 Dir: Preisker Thos City Attorney office Main st, r same; Mrs Leo student;
    Nora Miss student
  1909 Dir: Preisker & Preisker, Attorneys-at-Law, Office on Broadway, adjoining new
    Post Office
    Preisker Thos Attorney r W Main & Thornburg sts; Mrs Louise
    C L Attorney, r same; Miss Nora, student, r same
  1922 Dir: Preisker Chas L (Anna E) Atty, Preisker, Preisker & Goble
    B of SM bldg; r401 W Main
    Thos Atty Preisker, Preisker & Goble, rLong Beach
  1931 Mrs Thomas Preisker   b. Tucson AZ, d. Inglewood CA @88, to Inglewood 1917
    Survived by dau Nora Preisker, son CL; sisters May Montgomery, Los Angeles,
    Mrs Carrie M Squier, Los Angeles, Mrs Anna Lutnesky, Santa Maria. 3 gch
        a. Miriam Louise   b. 11 May 1912
           m.
           Arthur G. Ainscough 1940-1 Dir: Ainscough Tractor co h109 W Pershing

```
        =Peter Thomas              1947-8 Dir: slsm Farm Equipt Co h1011 S Bwy
          (Roselyne Gentry)        1950 ph/bk: 1017 S Bwy
    b. Patricia Ann                              b. 17 Mar 1919
        m.
      James D McLanahan      1947-8 Dir: S Blosser rd; 1950 ph/bk: same
        =Sharon
        =Ann (Jaques Prevost)  div. (Wm Benge)
        =Susan
        =Charles Leo
        =Julia
    c. Katherine Mildred                         b. 2 Oct 1921
        m.
      Mark Durley  (living in Claremont 1959)
        =Laird
        =Odette
```

1916. Locals. The sidewalk in front of the Adams' estate on Main street has been completed this week and makes a big improvement. John Leyva had the contract and he did a very good job. A walk will also be laid from the corner to the alley of the M E Church property.

Mr and Mrs C L Preisker and little daughter and Mr and Mrs Warren McNeil returned on Friday from an enjoyable trip in Mr Priesker's new Chalmers machine to San Francisco and San Joaquin valley points. Mr Preisker combined business with pleasure on the trip and studied road conditions as he went along.   - Aug 19

William Thom Adam's Second Family

"...father married a young woman, much younger than several of his married daughters-who resented the intrusion."   -*Memoirs* p.10

1860: Santa Cruz co Pajaro tp PO Watsonville: Wm 64, Margaret 38 b. SCT
    John 7 b. Utah, James b. CA 1855, Agnes b. CA 1855
1900: Monterey Co San Antonio tp
  (#2 Alexander Adam and son Wm A)
  #6 John T Adam b. UT Nov 1853 m/22yrs
      Mahala J b. CA Apr 1869 parents MO 4 births 3 living
      John R b. CA Nov 1853, Ruby P b. CA Nov 1890; Ths H Meritt neph b. 1887
  #7 Wm Z Adam b. CA June 1879 m/0 yrs, Rosetta b. CA Oct 1877
New Pleito cemetery, in CCCGS *Bulletin* (now SLOCGS) 4 #10 p.174 (Oct 1971)
    Adam Donald R 1904-1916 (d. Monterey co 24 Aug 1916 @11)*
        Rosetta A 1876-1928 (d. SLO co 18 Jan 1928 @51)*
    Wm Z 1869-1964 (26 June 1879-Aug 1964; SSDI)
    Alexander 1838-1928
    James R no dates (d. Monterey co 5 Jan 1920 @64)*
*California Grand Death List
Wm Zembruz Adam m. 25 Dec 1899 Rosetta Doty, lived in Bryson
                                    -Hardenbrook Genealogy, Lompoc Historical Society

ALEXANDER ADAM

Alexander Adam   b. Scotland; chr 30 June 1839 Bothwell,
  1860: Watsonville w/father   Lanarkshire; d. 1928; New Pleito cem
  1870: SMv next to Wm L   F: William Thom Adam

```
    1880: Santa Maria                      M: Isabel Laird d. Scotland c1844
    1888 GR: 48 SCT of SM; by nat of father; 1890 GR: Same
    1900: Monterey co San Antonio tp divorced
          m. Guadalupe 11 Feb 1878 by John Dunbar JP, B262
Esther Spencer                             b. London ENG; m. @16 of Santa Maria; imm.1872
    1900: Lompoc m/2                       d. (buried Forest Lawn, Los Angeles)
    1 birth; 1 living (!)                  F: _____ Spencer; died England
                                           M: Elizabeth 1816-1914; m.2 1870 Paul Bradley
1. William Alexander                       b. Santa Maria valley Feb 1878 (?)
    1900: w/father                         d.
2. Ronald MacDonald                        b. Santa Maria valley 8 Sep 1884 (Times)
                                           d. Lompoc 5 Apr 1953; Sta Barbara mausoleum
       m. Lompoc 10 Nov 1905                  obit Lompoc Historical Society
    Malinda Jane Hardenbrook               b. MT 17 Apr 1884
                                           d.
                                           F: Charles Kelley Hardenbrook 1847-1924
                                           M: Jennie Walker 1859-1894
                                               see Hardenbrook Genealogy, Lompoc Hist Soc
       a. Kathryn L    m. 1931 William Watkins Conner
       b. John Donald  m. 1933 Rozan Mildred McDougal
       c. Kenneth Laird                    b. 10 Oct 1916
            BA USC 1939                    d. 27 July 1966; Evergreen cem Lompoc
                                               see Who's Who in the West 1963-4
            m.  19 Oct 1941                    publisher Lompoc Record
            Harriet Ailene Hall            b. 1919
            =Rennie Laird; =Margaret Malinda; =Mary Adrienne; = Jeffery Wm
1891 Honor Roll, Agricola School, SMv: Carl, Ronald, William Adam…        -This is Our Valley
```

Note: Esther Adam m.2 Ramona Hotel 29 Apr 1898 by Rev J M Hilbish (*Times*)
    John S Graham   b. CA Dec 1865
                                           F: Benjamin F Graham 1815-1903
                                           M: Safrano: see Drumm chart
    J S Graham, "formerly of Lompoc," was reported ill in Los Angeles in 1908. –Lompoc *Record*
He was living in Lompoc when his brother, J Will Graham, MD, died there in 1914. One of the
Graham sisters married a man named James Adams.

Vol. XXVIII, No. 1, Spring 1996, p. 18

Corrections and Additions   [Page numbers refer to those in Quarterly]

p.11   1. b. Phyllis Elizabeth Adam m. @24 of Santa Maria
            m. St Stephens Epis Ch SLO 9 Aug 1916 by C H L Chandler. Wit: W C Adam,
               Leonard Adam, E. Marshall, Mrs W C Adam, Miss Gertrude Marshall, Irma Adam
               Benton Franklin Marshall   -SLOCGS *Bulletin* 28:2 Summer 1995 p.48

p. 14   5. Charles A Adam of Huasna
            m. Arroyo Grande 4 Nov 1896 by M. Lynch, B105; Wit: Kenneth Adam, SM;
               Mary Trussell, Santa Barbara; Mary Jane Porter of Huasna

Vol. XXVIII, No. 2, Summer 1996, p.14

p. 17   William Zimry (NOT Zembruz) Adam b. CA m. @20 of Bryson
           consent of father given for Wm
       m. 24 Dec 1899 by D G Wright, F72
          wit: Mrs O Sayler, Lockwood; Julia A Ward, Pleyto
    Rosetta Grace Doty b. IA m. @23 of Bryson

Note: A trip to the Bryson area with the San Antonio valley Historical Society in May was valuable in acquainting us participants with members of the Adam clan who still reside in that vicinity. Alexander Adam's son William Alexander was known as "Fancy Bill" and his nephew, William Zimry, was called "Buckskin Bill". Buckskin's daughter, Velma Adam Dayton, for many years was the social correspondent from the Valley to the *King City Rustler*.

p. 18   2. Ronald Adam. He did not go north with his father and brother; rather, was listed in Lompoc on the 1900 census, a 15-year-old typesetter, thus beginning his life-long newspaper career.

Vol. XXVIII, No. 2, Summer 1996, p.14

William Laird Adam family

p.12.   Patrick H Sheehy = Henry P Sheehy died in Watsonville. Attending the funeral: Mrs Jas Adam, Wm Adam, Thos Adam, Mrs Mary Adam, Mrs J A Rembusch, brothers and sisters of the widow.   –Local Paragraphs Sat Oct 18 1913
        Dewey Werling (27 Dec 1898-1 Mar 1989, SS benefits to Templeton) was a pall bearer for Wm Connor Adam, and, apparently, brother-in-law of Winifred Smith Adam. There is a display on the Werling family in the Paso Robles Area Pioneer Museum.
p.13.   Vivian M Adam died 11-19-1975, SB co.
p.15.   Silver Anniversary Catholic Daughters of America Court 1079…Mrs Don Prentice, Miss Rosa Porter, Mrs Joe Rowan, Mrs Isaac Porter (in wheelchair), Mrs Mary Adam, Miss Agnes Donovan et als, photo by Stonehart.   –Sat Feb 14 1953 p.4
p.17.   Miriam Louise Preisker Ainscough died in Santa Barbara 13 Nov 1996. Grad. U C Berkeley 1934, m. 1935. Survivors: husband, son Peter T of Paris, France; 2 grandchildren; sisters Patricia McLahan (sic), SM; Katherine Durley, Napa co.   –Fri Nov 15 1996 A-3

Alexander Adam family

p.18.   In the case of Esther Adam vs Alexander Adam, Sup Ct SLO granted custody of the younger child Ronald to Mrs Adam.   –50 Years Ago, Feb 28, 1946
        The marriage of Esther Adam of Santa Maria and John S Graham of Lompoc is recorded in SLO co, E293.
        William Alexander Adam died in SLO co 4-24-1973. The *Paso Robles Daily Press* ran an article on the 94th birthday of Bill Adam, Nov 15 1971. There is also an interview in the *King City Rustler*, 1959, exact date not at hand.

Vol. XXIX, No. 4, Winter 1997, p.20

BAKER
FROM MENDOCINO COUNTY TO SANTA MARIA VALLEY
PIONEERS OF THE CALIFORNIA CENTRAL COAST

Henry Womack Baker   b. St Joseph MO 13 Oct 1818; "1st white child"
       d. at home of dau Mrs Hopper Santa Maria 8 Sep 1909
         @90/10/26; SM cem
         obit Sep 11; funeral from res of Geo Hopper
         12 ch; 8 (4 sons 4 dau) surviving

   left home @18; to Mexico; Mexican War; to CA 1850; in IA 1853-57; to CA 1857, Sonoma co
     1860 Napa co; to Potter Valley 1867; to Morro 1883; SM 1884
                 -From *Acorns to Oaks, A History of Potter Valley 1855-1985,* Shelton
   also obit of Mrs Baker Apr 29 1899

1860 cen: Napa hotelkpr

1867. bought and built up Baker Springs; sold in 1879 to N P Compton; full page ad in
   Paulson's Hand-book and Directory of Napa, Lake, Sonoma and Mendocino Cos, 1874:
   Baker Springs H W Baker, Prop'r. Situated 28 Miles North of Ukiah, Men Co. Cal…
   A Fine Bath-House…The Best Natural Soda Water…Mr Baker bestows the best of care
   upon visitors…no more delightful spot for a few weeks' holiday…   -*PV* 46, 100

1870 cen: Mendocino co Calpella tp PO Ukiah

1880 cen: same JP

1888-1898 JP Santa Maria

1890 Golden Wedding anniversary (*Times*) date lost

1890 GR: 71 MO f SM #1 reg Aug 4

1906 Dir: H W ret SM

1908. 90th Birthday Tuesday last, family dinner: Major P, Henry, Mart, Mrs Geo Hopper, Mrs
   Waltrip, Mrs Young from Mendocino co, Mrs G W Curryer. Baker to CA 1850s; about
   20y SM   –Oct 17

1909 Dir: H W r709 S Lincoln
     m. Buchanan co MO 1840

Elizabeth Wilkerson   b. nr Boonesboro KY 14 Dec 1823
       d. Santa Maria 23 Apr 1899 @75/4/9; SM cem; inf
         J E Hamilton; obit Apr 29, May 6; 12 ch, 9 (5 dau
         4 sons) living; 39gch 18ggch. 2 ch dy

1.   Sarah Baker   b. no data
2.   Eliza Jane Baker   b. MO Feb 1842
     1900 cen: Little Lake tp   d. (before 1905?)
     widow 9 births 8 living
        m. (1858?)
     Presley F Muir   b. KY c1818
     1880 cen: Mendocino co   d. (before 1898)
       Little Lake pct
     1889. Mrs E J Muir of Willits, mother of Mrs J E Hamilton, eldest child of Grandpa
       Baker is in town for a short visit. (death of mother)   –May 6
     (his son?) Jeremiah Francis Muir   d. Mendocino co 1898 @c50
     (his son?) John J Muir   d. Mendocino co 21 May 1909 @58
     a.   Henry Baker Muir   b. CA 8 Oct 1859
        1880 cen: w/parents   d. Alameda co 14 Mar 1942
         clerking in store   obit on Rootsweb; 1 of 10 ch; much

1900 cen: Ukiah capitalist   business detail
3 births 1 living; Susan Brown*, sister Apr 1834 wid 3/2 IN KY 2 in household
1891. Irvine & Muir incorporated by Henry B Muir and C A Irvine, Grange Bldg, Main st Centerville (Potter Valley); moved to Willits, set up several stores. 1930 fire; Muir wanted out, but bought 150 shares in the new Potter Valley store.
                                 -*PV* 25, 45, 80; photo 155

*Susan J Brown d. MEN co 1917 @83

	m. 1886	
	Emma Caroline Hargrave	b. CA 22 Jan 1859; parents KY
		d. Alameda co 13 Jan 1947; M: Wood
	= Ora Muir	b. CA Mar 1890
b.	James L Muir	b. CA c1863
	m.	
	Flora Weeks	b. (OH Mar 1869; parents OH steno divorced)
	1900 cen: Ukiah daughter w/	d.
	Martin Weeks 1837-; tchr	F: Martin L Weeks 1837-1909
	= Gladys Muir	b. CA 12 Dec 1891
		d. Alameda co 14 Jan 1982; surname Tuttle
c.	Margaret Elizabeth Muir	b. CA 5 Dec 1865
		d. Sacramento co 21 Feb 1951 @85
	m. c1883	
	John Edward Hamilton	b. NY May 1853; parents IRE
	1890 GR: 37 NY tchr	d.
	Guad reg Oct 6	

1890. An Invitation On Behalf of the Trustees and the pupils of the Guadalupe school and in my own name, I hereby extend a cordial invitation to the public to be present at the flag raising ceremony, on Thanksgiving Day, Thursday, Nov 27, 1890 at 1:30 PM. J E Hamilton, teacher. Guadalupe, Cal, Nov 19, 1890.
1890. Mrs J E Hamilton left Monday to visit friends & relatives in Mendocino co.
                                 -Feb 15

1890. Our Busy People. Jerry Muir the popular landlord of the Arroyo Grande Hotel took a run over in the early part of the week.   –Mar 29
1890 GR: Muir J F 43 MO Hotelkeeper AG reg April 7 1890
1892 GR: Muir Jeremiah Francis 46 5'9½ dk blu dk f MO AG AG #1 AG reg Aug 22 (he must be a half-brother)
1898. Mrs J E Hamilton received a sad intelligence Tuesday night that her brother J F Muir of Mendocino county was dead, age about 50. So far no particulars have been received.   –Sep 10 (nothing else found)
1900 cen: SM school principal 4 births 2 living
1900. Geo Hopper and wife, Mrs J E Hamilton and Mrs May Baker drove to Los Alamos Friday morning to attend the funeral of B P Whitney, a relative of theirs.
                                 -Feb 3 (see last page)
1900. Jack Hamilton and family returned to their Santa Maria home Friday night. Their trip did them a world of good and Jack is in the best of trim for his school duties.   –Aug 4
1900. J D Rogers, brother of our wealthy oil man, Bud Rogers, was married to Mrs Jerry Muir at Ukiah July 2, 1900. M/M Rogers are well known here and have many friends who extend to them their heartiest congratulations.   –Aug 4

1902. Professor J E Hamilton who was in Santa Barbara and Los Angeles for the past two weeks connected with the Board of Education, returned home Tuesday.
    -June 4

Earthquake damage…J E Hamilton, Principal Grammar school…   -Dec 13, 20

1905. Mrs Davis and Miss Lulu Hamilton, nieces of J E Hamilton, are visiting here.
    See 6a. Geo T Hopper   -Apr 8

1906 Dir: Hamilton J E Principal Grammar Sch r cor Main & Vine
    Mrs M E; Miss Ethel stu

1909 Dir: Hamilton Mrs J E Boarding House r310 E Main; Miss Ethel stu

	= Edward Muir Hamilton	b. 1887
		d. 13 Jan 1893 @5/5/17; SM cem; only son of J E Hamilton (*Times*)
	= Ethel Hamilton	b. SM 29 Dec 1893 (*Times*)
	= Charles E Hamilton	b. SM 30/31 Dec 1895 (*Times*)
		d. El Dorado co 17 July 1967
	= (infant)	(bur 3 Jan 1902)?
d.	Austin J Muir	b. CA Nov 1867
	1880 cen: w/parents	d.
	1900 cen: Little Lake tp stock raiser; 5 births 5 living	
	m.1888	
	Laura A Bigelow	b. WI 8 July 1866 F: WI; M: NY
	1880 cen: Little Lake	d. Fortuna CA 28 May 1962 @95
	w/parents	F: Horace Bigelow 1823-
		M: Jane Flintcraft 1846-
	= Raymond Muir	b. CA 21 Nov 1888/9
		d. Santa Clara co 11 Feb 1946
	= Guy Muir	b. CA Apr 1891
	= Leta M Muir	b. CA Aug 1893
	= Hattie Jane Muir	b. CA 6 May 1896
		d. Napa co 7 May 1958; surname Jacobs
	= Bessie A Muir	b. CA Apr 1899
e.	Emma Alice Muir	b. CA c1870 (cen) 22 Dec 1867 (CDI)
		d. Sonoma co 10 May 1957; surname Rupe
f.	William Martin Muir	b. CA 13 Nov 1872
	1900 cen: w/mother; no wife	d. Mendocino co 11 Mar 1950
	m. (1900)	
	Kate	d. Mendocino co 11 Mar 1931 @55; surname Muir; spouse W M
	1900 cen: Katherine Muir b. CA July 1875 F: OH; M: MI, m/0 0 births 0 living daughter w/Rebecca McCullough Dec 1836 wid 11/11 MI OH2 nurse Little Lake tp	
g.	Iva E Muir	b. CA c1876
h.	Della M Muir	b. CA July 1878
	1900 cen: w/mother	
i.	Lewis E Muir	b. CA 26 Aug 1882/3
	1900 cen: w/mother	d. San Francisco 14 Mar 1948
3.	Mary E Baker	b. (Buchanan co) MO 1844
	1899 Mendocino co	d. Alameda co 25 Aug 1917 @70 (?)
	1909 Berkeley	
	m.	

Nathaniel Waltrip b. (MO c1837)
  d. Mendocino co 23 May 1905 @68

 a. James B Waltrip b. CA Mar 1867; parents MO
   1900 cen: Ukiah bartender d. Alameda co 26 Apr 1929 @62; spouse A
   m. 1895
   Ettie b. CA Jan 1871; F: IRE; M: MO
   = Lewis (?) Waltrip b. CA July 1887
 b. Louis E Waltrip b. CA 12 Jan 1876
   d. San Bernardino co 28 Oct 1945; M: Baker

4. Margaret F Baker b. MO c1848
  1888. Maggie Taylor of d. Santa Maria 5 Nov 1896 @48/5/17; SM cem
   Mendocino co is visiting her parents M/M Baker –Mar 10
  1899. Mrs M F Taylor died over two years ago… -May 6
  m.
  James Taylor b. MO? c1837 (cen); F: KY; M: IN
   1880 cen: Mendocino co d. Mendocino co 6 Nov 1920 @90 (?)
   Little Lake pct
  a. Minnie F Taylor b. CA 14 Sep 1866
    d. Santa Clara co 11 Feb 1947 @80; surname
    Matlock
  b. William H Taylor b. CA c1869
    (Wm H d. SF 9-14-1920 @51; spouse F)?
  c. Oscar E Taylor b. CA c1871
  d. Albert (Ross) Taylor b. CA c1876 (cen); (15 July 1875
    d. SLO co 12 Oct 1956)?

5. Martha E Baker b. MO 1852
  1899 in Phoenix d. (before 1936)
  1909 in AZ
  m.
  J W Davenport d. (John W (M) @70 d. Los Angeles co 10-16-1922)?

6. Lucinda Emeline Baker b. St Joseph MO 23 Dec 1853
  1899 in SM d. at home of M L Hopper 517 E Cypress SM 5 May
  1936 in SM: 517 E Cypress 1939 @85/4/12; SM cem; obit Sat May 6 p.1
   m. *Potter Valley* 30 March 1869
  George Leigh Hopper b. San Jose 2 Mar 1848
   1870 cen: Mendocino co d. at home 709 S Lincoln SM 28 Jan 1931 @82/10/26;
    Calpella tp SM cem; obit Jan 29 p.1
   1880 cen: same no ch F: John Hopper 1821-1889
   1884 GR: 36 CA f SM M: Jane Leigh 1814-1898
    reg Aug 1 see Hopper chart; *PV* p. 132-4, 250
   1890 GR: 42 lab Ballard reg Aug 4
   1890. M/M H W Baker returned a few days since from a visit among relatives at Ballard.
    -Nov 22

   1892 GR: lab 47 5'5 light complexion blu eyes brown hair CA SM #2
   1900 cen: SM 4 births 2 living
   1901. Geo Hopper and family moved to Guadalupe to reside. –Dec 7
   1906 Dir: sexton rPine st SM; Mrs
   1909 Dir: Hopper Geo L Carpenter 709 S Lincoln; Mrs L E
   1910 cen: SM
   1910-11 Dir: ret 709 S Lincoln

1920 cen: 709 S Lincoln
1922-3 Dir: not listed
1925 Dir: Geo L (Lucinda) caretaker S M park r709 S Lincoln
1928 Dir: Geo (Lucinda) ret r709 S Lincoln

a. George T Hopper — b. (Potter Valley) March 1881
    1906 Dir: clk rPine st
    d. Santa Rosa 30 Jan 1954; SSDI @72
    1910 cen: Oakland
    obit (*Times*) Jan 30 p.8; bro of L M "Harper"
    1920 cen: 5237 James, Oakland
    of Broadway Bootery; one son
    1931 in Boise ID
    1936 in Denver
    1939 in Vallejo
      m. Thanksgiving Day 1905 Oakland (*Times*)
    Lulu Hamilton — b. (Mendocino co) CA 1885; m. of "northern California"
    d. 23 Dec 1967; SS# same as Geo
  = Victor (?) Hopper — b. c1910
  (Richard H Hopper b. 1 Jun 1909 d. Santa Clara co 30 Oct 1962; M: Hamilton)

b. Gertie Bell Hopper — inf ch of Geo Hopper d. SM 19 July 1883 (*Times*); SM cem

c. Martin Luther Hopper — b. SM 30 Aug 1885
    "Lute"
    d. Santa Rosa 4 Apr 1962 at home 1118 Morgan st @77; obit (*Times*) Apr 5 p.2; bro late Geo T; cousins Ray Baker, SM; Harry Hopper, Potter Valley; Elmer Hopper, Ukiah.

bio *Who's Who SM*: 22 yrs traveling salesman (sic); Bwy Bootery from 1922
bio Phillips I 371 (rife with inaccuracies)
1905. Orcutt News. Luther Hopper formerly in employ of Haslam & Co has accepted
    a position as bookkeeper with Forbes & Son.   –Dec 9
1906 Dir: r Pine st
    Forbes & Son General Merchandise, Orcutt
    Forbes J F merchant, Forbes & son; Mrs
     Aubrey merchant, Forbes & Son; Stella Miss
1920 cen: w/parents
1921. Luther Hopper departed yesterday to make his last trip for Nettleton Shoe Co
    of Syracuse NY. He will complete his route and return to Santa Maria the latter
    part of May to open a new shoe establishment in Santa Maria.   –Apr 20
1922-3 Dir: Hopper Mrs Inez bkpr Broadway Bootery r709 S Lincoln
    Hopper M L (Inez) Manager Broadway Bootery r709 S Lincoln
    Broadway Bootery M L Hopper Mgr 105 S Bwy (see adv)
    Broadway Bootery Inc. Laird-Schober, Utz and Dunn for Ladies
    Nettleton Florsheim for Men. Hollands Boys Shoes—Edwards
     Childrens Shoes. America's Foremost Line of High Grade Footwear
1925 Dir: Hopper M Luther prop Broadway Bootery r709 S Lincoln
    Mrs Inez bkpr Broadway Bootery r709 S Lincoln
1928 Dir: Hopper Luther M (Inez) prop Broadway Bootery r709 S Lincoln
1930 Bus Dir: Hopper Luther 709 S Lincoln
    Broadway Bootery 105 S Bwy
1938 phbk: Hopper M Luther Broadway Bootery 105 S Bwy; r517 E Cypress
1940-1 Dir: Hopper Inez owner of Broadway Bootery h123C E Cypress,
    Elmo Apts
1947-8 Dir: nobody

        m. Portland OR 29 Aug 1912
    Inez Clovinger   b. St Helens OR 1896?
    No issue   F: John Clovinger
                                    M: Mary McNulty

7.   Henry Ross Baker   b. IA 30 Oct 1854; m. @30
    1890 GR: 35 IA f SM #1   d. Santa Clara co 6 Feb 1943
    1896. Rice House, SM hotel, Henry R Baker, new proprietor.   –Jan 4
    1898-9 Asphaltea PO money order receipts: H R Baker   –ONT
    1899 in SM
    1900 cen: Sisquoc lab asphalt mine
    1901. Henry Baker and family leave this week for San Jose by private conveyance where
       they go to make their home.
    1909 in San Jose
    1936 in Sunnyside (?)
    1939 in Sunnyvale
        m. at the home of M/M Alvin Cox, Santa Maria 25 Dec 1889 by J W Bain.
           Wedding Bells…bride wore brown silk trimmed in fancy brocade…dinner
           at home of groom's parents, M/M/ H W Baker. list of gifts…   -Dec 28
    Malinda Jane Hood   b. MO 23 May 1862; m. @27
    Leanna/Linna/Linnie   d. Santa Clara co 15 Oct 1944 @82
   a.   Mary Baker   b. SM 7 Nov 1890 (*Times*)
      Sisquoc sch 1898/9
      3rd grade –ONT
      1909 Dir: w/M P Baker
      1910 cen: @18 nc w/Dudley D Stowe, W Chappel (sic), SM
   b.   Ruth E Baker   b. SM 28 Mar 1893 (*Times*)
      Sisquoc sch 1898/9   d. San Mateo co 25 Dec 1982; surname
      1st grade –ONT   Syverson
   c.   Henry Arthur Baker   b. SM 4 May 1895 (*Times*)
                             d. 15 Nov 1895 @6m 11d; whooping cough (*T*)
   d.   Edna Baker   b. SM 11 Feb 1898 (*Times*)
   e.   Elsie Baker   b. nr SM 5 Oct 1900 (*Times*)

8.   Martin Van Baker   b. IA 25 Jan 1857
    1892. M V Baker and wife,   d. Willits 28 Apr 1939 @82/3/3; SM cem
      son and dau/law of Judge   obit Sat Apr 29 p.4; rancher Willits; wid, son, bro
      Baker and wife of this place   2 sis. Parents to CA a few mos after his birth; to OR
      started on Thursday for   1878; to SM 1905 for 1 yr
      their home in eastern Oregon. –date lost
    1899 in Burns OR
    1909 in NV
    1936 in Willits
        m. Oregon
    Alice Thornburg   b. KS 22 Jan 1869 M: Ong
                                    d. 27 Feb 1955 @86/1/5; SM cem;
                                      inf Roy (sic) C & Marie R Baker
                                      obit Mon Feb 28 p.8; 16y SM formerly Willits;
                                      50y CA son gson
   a.   Raymond Carl Baker   b. Silver Creek OR 5 June 1887
      1922-3 Dir: Roy C (Marie)   d. SM 10 Dec 1971 @84/6/5; SM cem
      teller Bank of SM   obit Mon Dec 13 1971 p.2. Cattle rancher
      r314 E Cypress   SM area since 1940. Past Master Willits

    1925 Dir: Ray C (Marie)   Lodge #365 F&AM, etc; rSuey Creek rd;
      bank clk r314 E Cypress   wife, son
    1928 Dir: R C (Marie R) bank teller r314 E Cypress; Mrs R tchr r same
    1940-1 Dir: same
    1947-8 Dir: Ray C meter rdr PG&E PO Box 906; Marie R tchr Box 906
    1955-6 Dir: Mrs Marie tchr Alvin Av sch POB 906
    1971. Pall bearers: Paul Hodel, Ted Verbryke, M G Holman, Angelo Novo, John
       Crowder, Curtis Gunderson. Honorary: Marion Rice, Fred Leissman, Bob Evje,
       George Radke, Palmer Lindberg, Ed Julius, Oscar Olson, Alden Lewis, Wm
       Ward, Thomas Hyland
          m.
    Marie H Redwine   b. Covelo Mendocino co 20 Apr 1895
      Grad San Jose State   d. Santa Maria 30 May 1991 @96; SM cem
      1900 cen: Round Valley tp   inf Rbt M Baker son
        MEN co   obit Sun June 1 A7; res rural SM; son, d/l,
      1913: taught in Willits; married,   1 nc 1 neph
        thence to SM   F: George Robert Redwine 1864-1956
      1920. 42y elementary   M: Amy Belle O'Farrell 1869-1950
        teacher; retired 1961
    1936 Pioneer Picnic: Mrs Ray Baker accompanied a duet
    1943 Pioneer Picnic: Mrs Ray Baker presented a program of songs by children of the
       pioneers
    1944 Pioneer Picnic Maria (sic) Baker presented songs, dances, and instrumental
       numbers.   –*The Story of the Pioneer Picnics,* Tesene, 2002
    1956. California Pioneer Judge Dies Here. George Robert Redwine @91.
      b. Georgetown, Placer co 1864; to Mendocino co @7 mos. JP 40 yrs Covelo,
      retired 1948. Also deputy sheriff, constable, State Fish & Game Commissioner.
      Lived with daughters Mrs Marie Baker and Mrs Mildred Andrews (1898-1961)
      in Santa Maria. Three gch: Robert M Baker, Sacramento; Colleen M Buckaloo,
      Santa Maria; Marvin R Andrews, SLO; 2ggch. SM cem.   –Mon Jan 23
    1972 Dir: R M Baker r1095 McCoy La; Robt M (Eileen) sec mgr Convention Hall
       r1095 McCoy La #64
    1976 Dir: Robt M Baker & Eileen sec treas County Fair Grounds; r same

9.   Robert G/T Baker   b. CA c1859   d. young
10. Emma A Baker   b. CA Apr 1862
      1880 cen: married, w/parents   d. Napa co 17 Sep 1936 @74
      1899 in Mendocino co
      1909 in Westport (Fort Bragg)
         m. c1880
    Thomas L Young   b. MO/IA June 1854 F: IA; M: IN
      1900 cen: Long Valley tp   d. Mendocino co 18 Mar 1922 @67
        MEN co teacher 8 births 7 living
    a.   Kate E Young   b. CA Jan 1881
    b.   Roy Orsen Young   b. CA 19 Nov 1882
                                          d. Alameda co 19 May 1957 @74
    c.   May A Young   b. CA Dec 1884
    d.   Guy U Young   b. CA Jan 1889
    e.   Ruth E Young   b. CA Aug 1892
    f.   Dora E (cen) Young
        (Dora G Young   b. CA 21 Nov 1895
                                        d. Santa Clara co 5 Oct 1950 @54; M: Baker)

    g.   Myrtle Young   b. CA Nov 1898

11. Major Ransom P Baker   b. Petaluma 1 Oct 1863 (cem) 5 Oct 1862 (obit, *Who's*
    "Mage"   *Who*) m. @28
    Bio *Who's Who SM*: to   d. at home 123 W Chapel 2 Dec 1936 @72/1/1; SM
      SM 1883 @22 (sic)   cem; obit Wed Dec 2 (photo) 2 bro 2 sis
      1930: 2 bro 4 sis   director Gas Co, Security-Natl Bank; pres C of C etc
    Bio O'Neill 125 (photo)
    1890 GR: 24 (sic) CA f SM #1 reg Aug 4
    1899. Major Baker has been wearing his hat unusually low for some days past. He
      succeeds pretty well in hiding the scar but the story couldn't be suppressed. A false
      step threw him against a sharp corner at his house Monday night and it required several
      stitches to close the wound he received. Maj got off light, for his hurt need only have
      been a little deeper to have caused his death.   –May 6
    1900 cen: SM no births
    1900. Mage Baker returned Tuesday from his northern trip. Geo Hopper returned from
      the city Thursday evening.   –Sep 15
    1906 Dir: M P Baker Mcht Herron & Baker r Chapel st; Nellie Mrs
        Herron & Baker General Merchants Bwy
        Herron James W Mcht r Pine; Mrs (Irma Trott)
    1909 Dir: Baker M P grocer 123 W Chapel; Mrs N D (sic); Miss Mary E (Henry's dau?)
    1910 cen: SM w/L W Blosser no births 123 W Chapel retail mcht groc
    1910. Advertising plate, 7",   "Compliments of Herron & Baker Co.
      lilies of the valley   Santa Maria, Cal 1910"
    1914 Dir: Major P (Nell B) pres & mgr Herron & Baker h123 W Chapel
    1922-3 Dir: M P (Nellie) farmer r123 W Chapel
    1925 Dir: M P (Nellie) ret r same
    1931 pres Pioneer Assn
    1936. estate of Major Baker …   –Dec 9
        m. Santa Maria 16 Feb 1893 by George Weaver
    Nelle Blosser   b. Santa Maria valley 24 Oct 1869 "1st white child";
      1947-8 Dir: Nellie B   m. @23
        wid M P homkr   d. Santa Maria 17 Apr 1949 @79
        h123 W Chapel   obit Mon Apr 18 p.1
          F: Lorenzo Waugh Blosser 1844-1920
          M: Anna Van Valkenburgh 1846-1926

12. Dora Adelaide Baker   b. Potter Valley 2 May 1867; m.1 @19 of SM
    1880 cen: w/parents   d. SON 23 Apr 1962 @94/11/12; bur May 18; SM cem
    1899 SF Curryer
    1908 still Curryer
    1936 in SF surname Griffith
    1939 in SM surname Griffith
        m. at home of bride 24 Nov 1886 (*Times*) by F S Thomas, min, C352
          wit: Geo G (sic) Smith, Geo Curryer
    George Willard Curryer   b. OH 1859; m. @27 of SM
      c1881 to SM   d. at home Nipomo 22 Mar 1932 @72
      1884 GR: 24 OH clk SM   obit Wed Mar 23 p.1; pioneer, 15y Nipomo, 53y SM
        reg May 19   area; Curryer st named after him, wife, son 1 dau
      1890 GR: 31 OH truckman   F: Daniel Curryer 1813-1889
        SM #2 reg Aug 4   M: Rachel J 1826-1889

1885. Important Land Sale. Messrs Daniel Curryer, Geo C Smith and Geo W Curryer purchased of Mr Conner 80 acres south of Main st west of town to the railroad to make town lots; $4,130.   –Dec 26 (Smith & Curryer's Addition to the Town of Santa Maria)

- a. Carl W Curryer b. SM 28 June 1889 (*Times*)
  1932 in Piedmont d. Bend OR Apr 1987
- b. Gladis Curryer b. SM 12 June 1893
  d. San Francisco 2 Mar 1894 @c8mos (*Times*); SM cem

George m.2
May Amanda   b. Mt Sterling IL 1853
d. Nipomo 28 Dec 1933 @80/9/22; SM cem
obit Fri Dec 29 p.6; to CA Sep 1897
2 dau 1gdau; 14y Nipomo

her daus: Olive M Scott 1932 in SF, 1933 in Nipomo; Bertha K Satnam 1932, 1933 in Barstow gdau: Blanche E Premo (?) Porterville

Two of Judge Baker's sisters, "Jane (Sabra)", husband Newton Porter Rogers, and Martha Ann, widow of Henry Long, settled in Potter Valley the same year Baker did; Martha's second husband was B P Whitney. Whitneys came south, as did a nephew, Newton J Rogers.   –See *PV*

Benjamin Piper Whitney was born in Maine in 1834 and died in Los Alamos in 1900. A blacksmith, he registered to vote in Los Alamos in 1888 and 1890. In 1894 his steam engine exploded and blew several men around; the event was chronicled in the *Santa Maria Times* and repeated in the Harriman chart in an article about other Maine natives, the Harrimans. Martha was listed in the 1906 Directory on Centennial street in Los Alamos, where she died in 1908. The children shown on the 1880 census of Calpella tp, Mendocino co, were Stillman E Whitney (1865-1919), Emma Whitney @11, John Whitney @7, and Charlie @7. No trace of them has been noticed in these parts.

The Rogerses, Newton P and Sarah J (who died in Mendocino co in 1929 @95) were enumerated in Willitsville, Mendocino co, in 1880; they had six children, of whom one, at least, came to Santa Maria. Newton Jasper Rogers registered to vote in Santa Maria in 1888 and 1890; he was listed in the 1906 Directory at the corner of Main and Miller, with Mrs A F, occupation butcher in each case. He died in San Joaquin co in 1934.

Other Potter Valley settlers came south for a time but returned to Mendocino or left for elsewhere after a few years. Thomas Edward Long registered to vote in Santa Rita in 1884; he was 23, born in MO, and likely a son of Martha's. His grandsons left their mark on California by founding Longs Drug Stores.   –*PV* p.137

Thomas Edward Long's wife was Agnes Carner, and a couple of her Carner cousins lived around here for a time also. There was a large Carner clan in Potter Valley.

BARTRON
SANTA MARIA VALLEY PIONEERS

Patrick Henry Bartron
    b. Barton, Tioga co NY 19 Apr 1842
    d. at home N Curryer st Santa Maria 1 Feb 1920 @78
      obit Feb 2 p.1; wid, 4 dau 3 sons
    F: Hanyon
    M: Joanna Louisa Bartron
    GF: James Bartron, who reared Henry

bio Guinn 1253: moved early in life to Potter co PA, educated and apprenticed as well-borer. Enlisted in Co K 149 PA Inf in Civil War; returned to PA, working in lumber 4 years. To WI 1871, married, returned to PA, grist/saw mill. To CA 1878, near Hanford; 1881 to Santa Barbara co. GAR.

1880 cen: Tulare co Mussel Slough tp
1884 GR: 38 US f SM reg May 19
1887 Local Dots. Mr Bartron, residing a short distance north of town intends planting out
    1200 walnut trees this coming winter.   -Sep 17
1888 During the past few months Mr H Bartron, poultry dealer living one mile north of town,
    has made the following shipments of poultry and eggs: 8220 dozen eggs, 104 dozen
    chickens, 368 turkeys. This makes a pretty good showing as Mr B. only devotes his
    spare time to running his poultry wagon outside his farm work.   -Jan 7
1889 H Bartron & Co have opened up in the building formerly occupied by Jeweler Jones on
    Main street near the post office where they propose to do a general commission business;
    thus handling all kinds of farm produce. The attention of farmers is called to the
    advertisement of this new firm, elsewhere in today's issue. (no ad found)   -Apr 27
1890 GR: 46 NY f SM #1 reg Aug 9
1891 Mr Bartron says there is no change in the poultry market, though he is still in the
    business.   -June 20
1893 H Bartron the old stand-by poultry man of this valley made a business call on Saturday
    last and he is now paying $4 to $4.50 per dozen for hens, 14 cents per pound for turkeys.
    Eggs are 15 cents per dozen. Who says poultry don't pay.   -Apr 29
    H Bartron will Deliver Dressed Turkeys! Dressed Chickens! Dressed Ducks! Etc.
    Tuesdays & Saturdays. Right At Your House.   -Dec 30
1894 Mr Hemmingway has bought the John Barry building and lease on the Braun lots on
    Main street and H Bartron will open a meat market therein.   -Jan 20
    H Bartron will open a new meat market in the building recently vacated by Shrite the
    painter-just west of Braun's blacksmith shop.   -Jan 20
    H Bartron has opened a new meat market on Main street next door to Braun's
    blacksmith shop. He will run a meat delivery wagon taking all kinds of farm produce in
    exchange for meats or for cash. Wait for his wagon.   -Jan 27
    E Morrison sold the Bartron meat market two very fine beeves during the week. -Mar 10
1896 Mr Bartron is in the well boring business with G W Hemmingway.   -Jan 11
1900 cen: Santa Maria well digger 7 births 7 living
1906 Dir: P H Bartron f 1½ mi N; Mrs; Ethel Miss
1910 cen: N Pacific st Santa Maria water well borer
1914 Dir: Barton (sic) Henry (Elsie) (sic) lab h302 N Pacific
1920 cen: 311 N Curryer Santa Maria
    m. Pine Valley, Clark co WI 14 Feb 1871

Alsie Anna Dodge   b. Mendon, St Joseph co MI 21 Mar 1849
  1922-3 Dir: Mrs Alsie hskpr   d. Santa Maria 1 Mar 1925 @75; SM cem
    r510 N Curryer   obit Mon Mar 2 p.5; 4 dau 3 sons 16 gch

1922. Alsie Bartrum (sic) sur-   Card of Thanks…M/M J H Mahurin, M/M John Grant,
    viving sister of Rinaldo Dodge   M/M Bert Bartron, M/M James Bartron, M/M R E
    See last page   Bartron, Mrs Anna McCann, Mrs Kitty Gaxiola.
   -Wed Mar 4

    1925 Dir: Mrs Alsia (sic) hskpr   F: John Ellison Dodge d. 1850
       r300 N Curryer   M: Anna Wadsworth Hutchins 1810-1886; SM cem
                                         m.2 Jonathan Clough

1. Louise Ellison Bartron   b. Clearfield co PA 19 July 1873 (Koons)
   to SM 1881   16 July 1877 (death cert.) 1878 (1900 cen)
   1920 in Los Alamos   d. Bellflower 4 Dec 1941; res Orcutt
   1925 in Santa Maria   obit Fri Dec 5 p.2, Sat Dec 6 p.4; 4ch, 3 sis 2 bro
   1934 in Orcutt
   1941 survived by sisters Mrs Chas Seddwick (sic), Oakland; Mrs Ann Wilkerson, Morro
      Bay; Mrs Ray Anderson, Arroyo Grande; brothers R E Bartron, Paso Robles;
      Gilbert (sic) Bartron, Long Beach; children Henry E Mahurin, Santa Maria; Mrs
      Pearl Noris (sic), Orcutt; Alsia Mahurin, Orcutt; Mrs Irene McCrackett, Bellflower.
      Note: Mrs Anderson is a niece.
        m.   1903
  John Henry Mahurin   b. Kern co 22 Sep 1877
    bio O'Neill 348   d. Santa Barbara hospital 2 Feb 1939 @61; auto acc nr
                                       Chico Dec 2
    1906 Dir: J H f 2mi N   obit Thu Feb 2 p.1; wife, son 3 dau 4 gch 4 bro 2 sis
    1908 to Maricopa   SM Police 1922-24; Chief 1925-27
    1917 Dep Sheriff Inyo co   F: Wm Mahurin[6] (1846-1908) Thomas[5] John[4] Samuel[3]
                                        Stephen[2] Ebenezer[1]
    1917 to Los Alamos   M: Cyrena Caroline Cox 1855-1917
    1923 Samuel Mahurin is visiting his brother night officer John Mahurin…lives in southern
        part of the state.   -Dec 28
    1925 Dir: J H (Louisa) city ofr r1137 W 2d; Miss Pearl C stu
    1928 Dir: J H (Louisa) lab r1137 W 2d;   1930 Dir: J H r 3½ mi S on Hwy
    1931 Amos Mahurin returned to his home in Bakersfield following visit here with relatives.
                                                                                                                                                 -Nov 4
    1935 Orcutt Notes. The John Mahurin family, living on Twyford's place east of town, are
        moving to Big Grove Auto Camp.   -Nov 15 (sold it Mar 1937)
    1938-9 Dir: John H (Louise E) S on Hwy 101
    1939 survived by brothers Thomas M Mahurin (1883-1960), Turlock; Samuel Mahurin
        (1885-1962), Sawtelle; Charles Edward Mahurin (1891-1969), Norwalk; Amos M
        Mahurin (1894-1945), Buellton; sisters Mrs Martha (Olive) LaBorde (1880-1958),
        Santa Maria (Pierre LaBorde 1862-1935); Mrs Rosanell Kirner (1889-1957), Santa
        Maria (Thomas R Kirner 1882-1945); deceased: Mary C Black 1873-1918 (John P
        Black 1862-1933); William C Mahurin 1874-1935]
    1940-1 Dir: John H (Louise E) Box 248 RR #1 (=2½ mi S Hwy 101 -obit)
  a. Henry Ellison Mahurin   b. (SM) 15 Oct 1903 (*Times*) SSDI
    1939 in SM   d. Fresno w/dau Mrs Gordon Bauer 26 Mar 1972
    1940 K of P; @ 37 trk   @68 obit Mon Mar 27 p.2; wid son dau; rSB
      drvr, suspended   20 y
    1945-6 Dir: Henry E (Mae K) emp SM Ice & Cold Stg h621 S Oakley
        Mae K slsldy Mary Doll r621 S Oakley
    1947-8 Dir: Henry E (Mae K) app engr Ice Puller SM Ice & Cold Stg h808 W Cook
    1970 in Santa Barbara
      m. Burbank Fri July 5 1929 by Wm Malloy (?) JP; to live in Sisquoc   –*Times* Thu July 9

    Mae Katheryn Scribner   b. MA 22 Sep 1908; SSDI
                                                                 d. Santa Barbara 15 Jan 1996 @87
                                                                 M: Nison
= Florence Louise Mahurin   b. 2 Feb 1931
    m. Gordon Wayne Bauer   b. IA 10 June 1926; SSDI
                                                          d. SLO 23 May 1974 @47
        1974. Dusting Copter Crashed near Morro. Aerial Control Helicopter Spraying,
           Dusting & Seeding Co. Crashed on Fairview Ranch 4 mi E of Morro Bay;
           widow, 3 ch.   -*SLO Telegram-Tribune* Thu May 23 p.1
= Leonard Eugene Mahurin   b. 29 Nov 1933; SSDI; d. 13 May 1997
       m. Santa Barbara co 6 May 1961 Ellen Louise Schulze
b. Irene Alice Mahurin   b. Santa Maria 10 Feb 1906 (*Times*)
                                                        d. Lake Isabella 17 Sep 1970 @64/7/7; SM cem
                                                            on vacation. Obit Sat Sep 19 p.4; 2 gch 2 ggch
                                                            r1008 W Cypress
          m.1 San Luis Obispo co 24 Nov 1924, N395
    Curtis Henry Volk   b. Oconto Falls WI 20 Feb 1903
       1922-3 Dir: Volk Edw   d. San Luis Obispo Tue Mar 4 1953; SM cem
         millman Doane's   obit Wed Mar 5 p.3; chemist Union Sugar;
              rFairlawn dist   rNipomo Mesa
                                                             F: Edwin Bunn Volk 1877-1954; SM cem
       1925 Dir: Curtis H   M: Cora Moss 1877-1954; SM cem
         (Irene) mech Union Sugar r1113 W 2nd SM
       1938-9 Dir: Nipomo. C H Volk mech hlpr U sugar; E B Volk carp Puritan Ice; Merrill
          Dean Volk emp U sugar; Ralph Perry Volk mach hlpr U Sugar
       1940-41 Dir: same
       1947-8 Dir: Curtis H chem Nipomo
       1953. father in Nipomo; bro Ralph P Volk, Grover city; Merrill D Volk, Nipomo
= Caroline Henriette Volk   b. Santa Barbara 9 Dec 1925
       1953 in SM   d. 31 Oct 1967 @41/10/22; surname
                                                              Hunnicutt SM cem; inf Maurice
                                                              Hunnicutt, obit Wed Nov 1 p.2, Fri Nov 3
           Carol Henriette (Volk) Rimell m. SLO co 16 Feb 1947; 11-89   p.1; lgch
Leland Rudolph Teixeira
       1947-8 Dir: Teixeira Carol R clk Jr S Lndy & Clnr 210 Rice Ranch Rd Orcutt
          Leiland (sic) trk drvr Jordano Bros no address Orcutt
       1955 Manuel Teixeira 601 W Fesler, died from auto accident Dec 18 @60. widow
          Irene; 7 sons: Clarence & Raymond, Morro Bay; Arthur, Melvin, Leland, SM;
          Gerald, US Marines, 29 Palms; Manuel jr, Lompoc; daus: Mrs Dorothy Novo &
          Mrs Lorraine Bettancourt, Morro Bay; Mrs Shirley Konasky & Barbara Ann
          Teixeira, Santa Maria. Siblings: Mrs Mary Ramalho, Santa Maria; Mrs Mamie
          Gerard & Mrs Rose Marie Machado, San Jose; Joe Teixeira & Mrs Emily
          Cardoza, Oakland; Mrs Lorraine Smith, Long Beach.   –Wed Dec 28
       1955-6 Dir: Teixeira Leland (Carol) trk drvr Jordano Bros h1019 W Church
       1962 Dir: Leland R (Carol H) mgr Jordanos Inc h1019 W Church
          same through 1969 (with Carol!)
       1965 Dir: Carol Teixeira h723 S Curryer #13
       1970 Dir: Leland R (Ivalea) liq slsmn Jordanos h1019 W Church; same 1972
   + Daniel Lee Teixeira b. 22 July 1948; in Bass Lake 1979
       1972 Dir: Danny rt slsmn Pepsi Cola h135 Pabst Ln
   + Vickie Ann Teixeira (Bello) b. 19 Sep 1949; in SM 1979

      1972 Dir: Bello Gary J (Vickie A) slsmn Coca Cola Bottlg h1632 N Miller
b. Irene Alice Volk m.2 SLO co 31 Dec 1929, R385
  Eugene William Randall   b. Switzerland 1 Jan 1897
  "Happy"   d. Santa Maria 22 Jan 1952 @54
  1938-9 Dir: E W (Helen) welder   obit Wed Jan 23 p.3; emp Union Sugar
    r327 W Cook
  1952 Survived by 8 cousins: Ted, Wm, Kenneth Bianchi, Santa Maria; Leo Bianchi,
       Petaluma; John Bianchi, Santa Barbara; Woodrow Bianchi, Betteravia; Mrs Leo
       Bunds, Mountain View
b. Irene Alice Randall m.3 at home of bride's parents 11 July 1934
  by L J Morris JP, 307-239
  Andrew Jack Jensen   b. OR 27 May 1905
    1934 Miss Irene Alice Randall, dau   d. 3 July 1979 @74/1/6; SM cem; no obit found
      of M/M Dan (sic)   F: Hans Peter Jensen 1867-1942; SM cem
      Mahurin, Andrew J Jensen, son of   M: Catherine Marie Christiansen 1867-1936;
      M/M Hans Jensen, both of Orcutt   SM cem
    Attended by her sis Mrs Pearl Jennings, Orcutt. Blue ensemble with white flowers.
    Guest Mrs Anna McKinnon and children; to live on Jensen ranch.
    Note: Mrs McKinnon is groom's sister.   -Sat July 14
    1938-9 Dir: Andrew emp. Ths B Adam r528 S Bwy;   1942 U S Army
b. Mrs Irene McCrackett in Bellflower 1941
b. Irene Alice Jensen m. (again) SB co 20 Sep 1944: 616-428
  Andrew Jack Jensen
    1947-8 Dir: Andr J dairymn whsmn SM Ice & Cold Stg; rVets Tlr Ct #32
    1955-6 Dir: Andrew(Irene) h1008 W Cypress
c. Pearl Caroline Mahurin   b. Santa Maria 14 June 1908
                                                d. at home Orcutt 2 Sep 1978 @70/2/28; SM cem
                                                obit Tue Sep 5 p.8; hus, son
  m.1 at home of bride's parents south of Santa Maria 10 Sep 1929 by L J Morris
    JP. Maid of honor Mrs Irene Volk; best man Henry Mahurin. To live in Van Nuys.
    Barbecue, old time dancing; music by Thos B Rice and Louis Sibilio. Guests:
    M/M L J Morris, M/M Fred Schaeffer, M/M H E Mahurin, M/M C B Sedgwick,
    M/M J C Maynard, M/M John N Grant; M/M T Phillips, M/M E E Henderson
    M/M A Mahurin, Misses Thelma Lyon, Ida Perry, Alsie Mahurin, Caroline Volk,
    Mary Haddon; Mrs Clara Dodge, Mrs T C Chaddick; Messrs Ralph Grant, T B Rice,
    Fred Orp, H E Orp, J B Orp, Emmett Dodge, Bert Lee, Earl W Crane.
                                                                                             -Wed Sep 11 p.5
  Earl Jackson Jennings   b.   m. of Van Nuys
                                                d. 1935; bur Hartwell OK
    1928 Dir: Earl Jennings mech RFD Santa Maria
    1938-9 Dir: Pearl Jennings wtrs Beacon Coffee Shop
  = Earl John Jennings   b. 13 Jan 1931
    (Bobbie)
        m.2 1938
  Dresden D Norris   b. Orcutt 2 Dec 1902
    1938-9 Dir: Dresden D carp   d. Santa Maria 31 July 1981 @78; SM cem
      r110 Norris St Orcutt   F: Robert Brent Norris 1854-1919
    1940-1 Dir: Dresden same;   M: Anna Bertha Pfiitzner 1871-1960
      Mrs Pearl C hswf   See Norris chart
    1955-6 Dir: Dresden (Pearl) bldg contr   m.1 1924 Luella May Moody
      h855 Union Orcutt

    d. Alsie Cyrena Mahurin   b. 10 Mar 1920; SSDI
        1941 in Orcutt, single   d. Deschutes co OR 22 Sep 1996
        m. after 1941
    R O Barnes
2. Myra D Bartron   b. Hanford 21 Oct 1879; m. @19 of SM
    to SM @2   d. Santa Maria 1 Feb 1934 @53/5/11; SM cem,
    1920 in Annette   obit Feb 2; r303 N Curryer; hus dau 2 sons 2gch
    1925 in San Miguel   3 sis 3 bro
       m. Santa Maria 2 Nov 1899 by S S Sampson, F234
         wit: S D Munger, SM; W L Adam, SM   -*Times* Nov 4
  John Nish Grant   b. CA 1 Jan 1875
    1900 cen: SM, also bro Rbt   d. Santa Barbara 15 Apr 1954 @79/3/14; SM cem
    1906 Dir: f 1 1/2 mi NW; Mrs;   obit Mon Aug 19; son 3 bro sis 3 gch 3ggch
      also R B (bro)   F: J W Grant pio Santa Maria & Bitterwater valleys
    1910 cen: SM Co Rd 3 births   M: Margaret Nish
      3 living; also bro Rbt
    1940-1 Dir: John N f r303 N Curryer;   1945-6 Dir: John L (sic) h303 N Curyer
    1947-8 Dir: same;   1953 in Santa Barbara
    1954 surviving brothers: Robert Bruce Grant (1872-1955) (Christine Sulan 1884-1951)
        Pozo; Fred Grant, Morro Bay; Adam L Grant (1881-1966), Cholame; sis Mrs
        Viva A Anderson (1880-1966), Cholame; (another bro Archie Grant 1890-1940)
   a. Margaret Alsie Grant   b. (SM) 10 Sep 1900
       1934 in Creston   d. San Luis Obispo 6 June 1953 @52; Santa
                                               Margarita cem, res Santa Margarita
       m.
    Samuel Cullen   b. CA 24 Dec 1896; SSDI
      1900 cen: Santa Margarita   d. Santa Margarita 7 Dec 1974 @77; Santa
        tp, LasPilitas-Huer-Huero   Margarita cem, obit *T-T* Mon June 8 p.22;
      1953 in Santa Margarita   hus, 2 sons, dau; father, bro, 2gch
                                            F: John Cullen 1846-1918; Santa Margarita cem
                                            M: Harriet E Austin 1856-1924; Santa Marg. cem
    =Myra Jane Cullen   b. Santa Margarita 9 Aug 1927
                                  d. Santa Maria 3 Apr 1999 @71
        1949 Atascadero HS grad   obit: 5 ch 2 bro 12gch 6ggch
        1953 Myra J Weed in San Francisco
      + Frank Eugene Weed in Lewisville TX 1999
          m. (2)
      Eugene Stanley Marino   b. 24 June 1926; d. SB 14 May 1989 @62
         1982 Dir: Eug S & Myra J security guard h1715b N Pine SM
       + John Paul Marino in Santa Maria 1999
       + Myra Gene Yates in Ft Smith AR 1999
       + Robert Denton Marino in Santa Maria 1999
       + Antonio Stanley Marino in Santa Maria 1999
    = Samuel James Cullen
       1953 in USAF TX
       1999 on Cullen ranch, Creston
    = Daniel Archie Cullen
       1953 in Santa Margarita; 1999 in Buellton
    = (Edward J Cullen 12 Oct 1923-30 May 1928 Santa Margarita cem)?
  b. Ralph Owen Grant   b. (SM) 1904
     1934 in SM   d. SB co 29 July 1934 @29/9/2; SM cem;
                                      no obit found

   c. Basil F Grant   b. (SM) 29 Sep 1909; SSDI
       1934 in SM   d. Riverside co 3 Sep 1984
       1938-9 Dir: Bazil (sic) lab h303 N Curryer
       1940-1 Dir: Bazil (sic) Grant lab h303 N Curryer
       1945-6 Dir: Bazil F(Jean) emp Sinton & Brown h 501E Mill, Laura Grant super A T Co
           r501 E Mill (Assoc Tel Co)
       1953, 1954 in Los Angeles
3. Adelbert H Bartron   b. Santa Maria 23 Nov 1883
    "Bertie"   d. Los Angeles co 18 Oct 1955 @71
    1934 in Long Beach
    married; no issue; step-son call Bartron
4. Anna Isabelle Bartron   b. Santa Maria 23 July 1886; m.1 @19 of SM; m.2 of SM
                                          d. Alameda co 30 Dec 1950 @64
      m.1 San Luis Obispo 31 Jan 1906 by E P Unangst, Sup Ct Judge, G269
   John C Aubert   b. CA or CAN/Fr; m. @26 of SM (1910 cen:@27!)
      1906 Dir: Aubrey (sic) J C   d.
         drvr SM Lndry; r same   parents French-Canadian
      1910 cen: next to Bartron carpenter
    a. Leslie P Aubert   b. (SM) 15 Sep 1906
      m.2 Los Angeles 19 Feb 1916, dau of M/M Bartron of SM   -*Times* Feb 26
   Charles Welborn
      1920 Mrs Wilbourne (sic) in Long Beach;   1925 Anna I McCann in San Fernando
      1934 Alma (sic) Wilkerson in Long Beach; 1941 Mrs Anna Wilkerson in Morro Bay
      1950 Ana (sic) Bartron Cortez
5. Ethelyn Kathryn Bartron   b. Santa Maria 14 Nov 1888 (*T*); m.1 @18 of SM
    Ethel/Kitty   d. San Leandro 3 Nov 1965 @76/11/19; SM cem
       m.1 San Luis Obispo 24 Sep 1906 by C P Kaetzel JP, G374
          wit: Jas Cooper, SLO; Hollis Green, SLO
   Clyde Elmer Knotts   b. Elwood IN Feb 1883
      1910 cen: w/Bartron   d. San Luis Obispo 13 Apr 1929 @46; AG cem; rNipomo
        house painter 1 birth   obit Mon Apr 15; son 3 sis 5 bro
      1914 Dir: Clyde printer (sic)   F: Emery Knotts 1842-1912
        r205 E Cook; also bro   M: Lenora A Fry 1849-(before 1900)
        Warren, mach
      1916-17 VR: 5'10½ in Nipomo
      1929 Nipomo Notes. Clyde Knotts survived by son Ulvin, Lompoc; 3 sisters: Minnie
          Adams (1871-1951), Taft (Hubert Adams); Lola Kimball (1885-1960), Garden
          Grove; Lillie Kessler (1868-1956) San Diego; 6 brothers: Burnett (1870-1944);
          Ray (1887-1930); Ulvin (1880-1930); Ralph (1890-1952); Warren (1892-1945); all
          Nipomo; Leslie (1879-1951), Pismo Beach; nieces/nephews.
          (deceased: Herman Edward 1873-1914)
   a. Ulvin V Knotts/Jack V Knotts   b. 22 May 1907; mother Bartron
      1910 cen: w/ Bartron   d. Pittsburg CA 15 Feb 1997 @89
      1920 cen: w/Bartron
5. Kittie E Knotts m.2 SLO co 24 Feb 1915, J326
   James David Gaxiola   b. (SLO) 12 Nov 1889
      1914 Dir: J D Gaxiola   d. Monterey co 22 Dec 1943 @54
        RFD2 Box 15 SLO   F: (Vincent) David Gaxiola
      1920 Dir: w/Bartron   M: Louisa E (Avegeno?) (1876-1901, Old Mission cem,
      1925 Mrs Kitty Gaxiola in San Fernando   SLO)
      m.3 by 1929

Charles B Sedgwick	b. Stockton? Santa Maria? 11 Mar 1888; SSDI
1934 Mrs Charles in	d. San Leandro 24 June 1974 @86/3/13; bur SM cem 1980
Oakland	F: George E Sedgwick 1860-1931
	M: Mary M Blower
	m.1 1909 Katherine/Katie C Peterson
6. James Martin Bartron	b. nr Santa Maria 15 July 1891 (*T*); m. @21 of SM
1910 cen: w/parents	d. nr Bakersfield 1 May 1941; SM cem
1914 Dir: Jas (Carrie) drvr	obit Fri May 1 p.1; dropped dead; wf, 2 dau
h503 W Mill	Shell Oil Co
1920 cen: 505 W Mill SM	

   1922-3 Dir: James (Carrie) oil wkr 301 N Curryer; J M rPacific & Mill
   1925 in Venezuela;   1934 in Ventura
    m. San Luis Obispo 2 Jan 1912 by Wm Mallagh I356
      wit: Mrs Kittie Knotts, SM; Otto D Sinsheimer, SLO

Caroline Emma DeBoux	b. CA 31 Jan 1893
"Carrie E"	d. Arroyo Grande 21 Oct 1969 @76; AG cem
	obit Thu Oct 23 p.2; 23y 277 E Cherry, AG, formerly
	SM, 7 gch 12 ggch
	F: John Marie DeBoux 1843-1912
	M: Manuela Lenora Linares 1850-1918
	m.2 Elford C McMaster
a. Irene Matilda Bartron	b. (Santa Maria) 7 Mar 1913
	d. San Luis Obispo 16 Dec 1991 @78

    m. SLO co 24 June 1933, S450
  Raymond William Anderson

b. Dorothea E Bartron (Mooney)	b. (SM) 1919
1969 in Oxnard	d.

Carrie McMaster in Arroyo Grande 1947, 1964
   1918 Manuela DeBoux survived by 2 sons 6 dau: Mra Sarah Loustalot, Santa Maria;
     Mrs Helen (Clara) Martinez (1890-1964), Santa Maria (Joaquin Louis Martinez
     1885-1954); Carrie Bartron, Santa Maria; Mrs Josie (Josephine) Martinez (1879-
     1948), Watsonville; Mrs Lulu (Lenora Mary) Gularte (1898-1986),
     Watsonville; Mrs Annie Lugo, Paso Robles (Joe B Lugo); Peter DeBoux (1883-1933),
     Los Alamos; Frank DeBoux (1887-1960), Army Training, American Lake;
     (deceased: Mattie I DeBoux 1891-1913)
   1947 Stanley Leonard Martinez, son of Joaquin L & Helen, died as a result of an auto
     accident 14 Nov 1947, @31. Sister Mrs Margaret Schurtz (1911-1989), San Luis
     Obispo; 3 aunts Mrs Carrie McMaster, Arroyo Grande; Mrs J P Martinez,
     Watsonville; Mrs W L Lovier, Morro Bay; uncle Fred DeBoux.
   1964 Helen Martinez survived by daughter Margaret Schurtz, 2 sisters Mrs Carrie
     McMaster, Arroyo Grande; Mrs Anita Lovier (1886-1973), Morro Bay; (William
     Henry Lovier 1878-1943)

7. Roy Ernest Bartron	b. Santa Maria 7 July 1894; m.1 @20
1925 in Albany OR	d. Richmond CA 25 Oct 1942 @49/9/15; SM cem
1935 in Paso Robles	obit Wed Oct 28 p.1 Former Resident Dies in North
electrician	wife, 3 dau 2 sons; in Richmond 7 mos, shipyard
1941 in Paso Robles	

    m.1 Santa Maria 13 Aug 1913 by L G Morris JP. Alsie Bartron and Melissa Bonilla,
     mothers, consenting. Divorced 15 Apr 1921 SLO co L 251

Ynez Melissa Bonilla	b. Gilroy 21 Jan 1900; m. @15 of SM
	d. New Woodstock NY visiting dau Mrs Doreen Allen

                           21 July 1975 @75/6/0; SM cem; obit Wed July 23,
                             r324 W Chapel, 68y SM, son 2 dau 5 sis 10gch 8ggch
                   F: Walter R Bonilla 1870-1943
                   M: Melissa J McAfee 1877-1926
                        m.2 William Oswald Lukeman 1896-1970
    a. Rosalyn E Bartron   b. Santa Maria 3 April 1915   d:
      1942 Mrs Rosalyn Stepner moved recently from Santa Maria to National City
      1943 M/M Harry Stepner and children Lois and Alan of Los Angeles visiting here
          with parents, M/M Lukeman, when word received of W R Bonilla's death.   -July 30
      1975 Mrs Rosalyn Thayer in Santa Barbara
      1995 in Santa Maria
7.   m.2 Albany OR 23 July 1922
    Cassandra Gertrude Brock   b. 31 July 1895; SSDI
    "Cassie"   d. (Indio) Dec 1974
      1938 phbk: R E Bartron   F:
        1511 Oak st Paso Robles   M:
      1942 in Santa Maria
    b. Romaine Edythe Bartron   b. CA 21 Jan 1920; SSDI
        1942 in SLO   d. Orange co CA Sep 1987
            m. San Luis Obispo co 11 July 1937, V225
      Eric Konrad Luttropp   b. MA 25 Feb 1916
                                          d. San Benito co 22 Oct 1996 @80
                                          M: Silvia (Silva?)
      = Laurence Lane Luttropp   b. SLO co 10 Mar 1940
      = Richard Konrad Luttropp   b. SLO co 10 Sep 1944
      = Sandra Ruth Luttropp   b. SLO co 18 Jan 1946
    c. Roy Patrick Bartron   b. OR 7 Sep 1922; SSDI
        1942 USN   d. Sacramento 26 Mar 1996
    d. James Bartron   b. OR 4 Oct 1924
        1942 in SLO   d.
    e. Beverly Bernita Bartron   b. Paso Robles 26 June 1929
        1942 in SLO
            m.1 San Luis Obispo co 22 Dec 1948, 13-103
      John Ambrose Halcomb
          m.2
      Earl Koons

Member Bee Koons has done much research on this family; additions, corrections, questions may be directed to her: 1591 Larson Lane, Fallbrook CA 92028-4390.

Vol. XXXIII, No. 2, Summer 2001, pp.11,12

Corrections and Additions   [Page numbers refer to those in Quarterly]

p.4   Patrick Henry Bartron was born in Athens, Bradford county, Pennsylvania on 19 April 1846. –Information supplied by Beverly Koons, 1591 Larson Lane, Fallbrook CA 92028-4390

Vol. XXXIV, No. 1, Spring 2002, p.19

p.8   Sam Cullen's mother was Harriet Elizabeth Callaway, not Austin; dau. of William Dudley Callaway (1833-1881) and Rachel Jane See (1837-1925), -from Family Tree Maker

Vol. XXXV, No.1, Spring 2003, p.11

BATTLES
SANTA MARIA VALLEY PIONEERS

The Battles family was one of the very first to settle in the Santa Maria Valley, coming here from the Sacramento area with the Holloways and Hiram Sibley, among others, in 1868. Grant, the youngest Battles child, was 5, and his reminiscences of the early days were highly regarded in the Pioneer Association, of which he, and his son Jim after him, were prominent members. Jim's daughter-in-law, Janice, submitted an article on the Battles family, which was printed in this publication in 1974. Many of the earliest families are no longer represented in the valley, but Battleses are, not only in the flesh, but in Battles Road and one of the newer elementary schools, George Washington Battles School, on – Battles Road!

Following is an article by U. G. Battles taken from the Golden Anniversary Edition of the *Santa Maria Times,* Monday, May 9, 1932:

Valley Beautiful, But Wild, Pioneers Found

As pioneers, with all the hopes and sacrifices the word denotes, more than a dozen settlers came into this valley in 1868 and 1869 when the country was overrun with longhorn cattle, wild mustangs, tall lush grass and high clover.

With all hopes they came, for the valley was fertile, the climate salubrious. It was a good place to live as may be noted from a list of the old timers, who with their families, came, saw, and stayed. That there were sacrifices to be made, hardships to be faced was taken as a matter of fact for what community, newly-created, does not face such conditions, particularly since the awards, fully realized were great?

These reflections, recalling a period beginning nearly 63 years ago were voiced by Ulysses Grant Battles at his home just south of town where he has lived since coming with his parents, brother and sisters to Santa Maria. No other resident, he believes, has been here as long as he has.

Over many hard trails the pioneers came and on their way they passed many a future Eldorado. Occasionally they stopped but then pushed onward until they came to this valley to remain, to fulfill their hopes and ambitions.

Here From Illinois

Battles was born in Ipava, Ill., April 16, 1863, and two years later, in a covered wagon, part of a train carrying 400 persons, his parents set out for the promised land. His father, George Washington Battles, had been in the mining country of California in '51 and '52 and was anxious to return. They stopped one winter along the way and, arriving in California, tried living in several towns but found the climate did not agree with them.

Finally, in the forepart of November, 1868, they arrived at Suey Canyon, a swing station on the stage line, and camped there a few weeks while a cabin was constructed near the present site of their home.

Although only five years old, Battles declared he had a vivid picture in his mind of the valley at the time.

Wild Looking Place

"The valley was a wild looking place but beautiful to behold", he said. "There were flocks of elk, deer, bands of mustangs, and longhorn cattle, undisturbed by the advance of man. There were no settlers' cabins and only about three adobes, one at Guadalupe, Los Alamos and Suey Canyon.

"My father and brother, Rollin, secured lumber at Mallagh's Landing on the other side of Pismo Beach to build the cabin. There was no port but vessels would anchor offshore and lighten their cargoes in or out. To do our shipping we had to go all the way to San Luis Obispo.

"In 1869 more settlers began coming in and settling the land which was unsurveyed. Each settler picked his acreage and though no other formality, usually attendant upon the taking of land, was observed at the time, his rights were respected. In 1869 a government engineer surveyed the land with the assistance of my father and brother.

"I remember when W. L. Adams (sic) started his first store here just two miles northwest of the present Santa Maria business district.

Changed Stage Line

"When the town first started it was called Central City, but this was later changed to Santa Maria, at the suggestion of John Crosby, who was instrumental in getting the stage line to come through here instead of Guadalupe.

"Later, because there was a Central City, Col., which made it hard for post office employees to determine the state on account of the little difference between the abbreviations, Cal. and Col., the town's name was changed back to Santa Maria.

"In 1869 father circulated a petition for a school house, which was built entirely by settlers. The money was raised here. In the following year help was secured from Santa Barbara. I was among the first students.

Great Fire Started

"A great fire occurred not long after we came here. It started this side of Guadalupe and the blaze crackled over a hundred feet high, it seemed, swept on to Santa Maria and past as far as Los Alamos. Most of the settlers had cleared around from improvements which prevented the fire from doing any damage to their property. It was a great sight, that fire, with the deer, mustangs and cattle fleeing before it.

"I believe my father's cabin was the second settler's structure in Santa Maria Valley. The first, in my opinion, was built by John B. Prell.

"An early phenomenon occurred in the valley with the appearance of myriads of red spiders. Where they came from, we often wondered. Open places would appear as patches of red. Wagon ruts were clearly outlined by two red streaks.

Grasshopper Plague

"We also had a grasshopper plague for about two years. The grasshoppers were so thick they would sometimes gather in huge clusters, like bees. They would get on wagon wheels in huge lob-lolly masses. On the sides of buildings they would hop, clinging to the walls or to each other. The buildings would thus present a curious appearance. They hopped everywhere into everything. Wells had to be sealed over, otherwise these hoppers would fill them up with their huge numbers. But they finally died out or hopped away."

Battles was married November 8, 1899, to Miss Ella F. Hourahane of Ireland. Two children were born to this union, Mary Theodosia, now Mrs Carroll, and James George, both of Santa Maria.

```
George Washington Battles           b. Hanover NY 15 June 1816
   To PA 1824                       d. Santa Maria 3 Jan 1905 @88/6/9; SM cem
   1850: Elk Ck, Erie co PA            obit Jan 7
   1860 Ipava IL: JP                F: Asa Battles 1786-1848
   1865: to CA from Lewis IA        M: Elizabeth Brown
   1868 to SM Valley    1879 GR: 63 NY f SM    1890 GR: 74 NY f SM #1
   Patron T/W           bio Guinn p.879, photo
      m. 9 Oct 1839
Freelove Crouch Bartlet             b. Reed's Borough VT 16 Sep 1816
                                    d. IL 17 Nov 1855
```

1. Olive Eb. Elk Ck PA 19 July 1841; d. Oct 1871
2. Frances Mb. Elk Ck PA 30 Nov 1842; d. 19 Feb 1843
3. George W jrb. Dundee Kane co IL 5 Dec 1844; d. 15 Jan 1845
4. Rollin Eugeneb. Elk Ck PA 27 Aug 1848; m. @37 of SM
1879 GR: 30 PA f Sisquocd. Berkeley CA 28 June 1907 @58/10/1
1890 GR: 42 PA SM #1obit July 6 p.1
bio Storke p.393
to Berkeley 1904. SMUHS *Review*, 1905, noted departure of the Battles boys
"the last of last semester."
m. San Luis Obispo 28 Oct 1884 by Henry H Hall, Garden St ME ch, A631
wit: John B Miner, Guad; Ida M Battles, Guad
Mary Elizabeth Minerb. IA/Salem OR 12 Feb 1861; m. @23 of Guad
1910: Berkeleyd. 1 Dec 1926
F: Hudson A Miner(1850: Winnebago co WI)
M: Electa(1880: Guadalupe)
a.Eugene (Rollin)b. nr SM 27 Apr 1887 (*Times*)
1920: 927 N Curtis, Alhambrad. (Pasadena CA 19 Apr 1967, SSDI)
T Gertrudeb. CA 1891
= Robert Eugeneb. 1913?
b.Myron Horaceb. SM valley 22 May 1889 (*Times*)
d. Santa Clara co 24 Sep 1937 @48
1920: Patient, Agnews State Hospital for the Insane
c.George Hudsonb. nr SM 18 Feb 1903 (*Times*)
d. Berkeley 6 Dec 1918 @15
5. Alice Lucinab. Elk Ck PA 5 Sep 1849
d. Long Beach CA 30 Nov 1933 @84; Guad cem
m. Guadalupe 15 Nov 1871
William McPhaul1828-1893; see McPhaul chart
6. Rosa Alsinab. Dunham tp McHenry co IL 16 Sep 1852
d. 9 Feb 1853
7. Cora Augustab. Dunham tp McHenry co IL 17 June 1854
d. 13 Mar 1855
(GW Battles) m.2 Fulton co IL 22 Aug 1856
Matilda Ione Franceb. Pleasant tp Fulton co IL 20 Aug 1833
d. 1 Apr 1861
8. Ida Mayb. Ipava IL 17 Aug 1858
d. Santa Maria 11 Aug 1897 @38/11/25; heart failure/
childbirth; SM cem; obit Aug 14
m. at home of Mr and Mrs G W Battles 25 Dec 1895 by Rev J M Smith
wit: Rollin Battles, Henry Grisingher
Samuel J Dorlandb. Heller CAN (13) Aug 1841; m. @53
Carpenterd. in his room at Orrs', SM, 10 Dec 1906 @65/3/26
SM cem. Imm. 1860 obit (*Times*)
F: NYM: IR
a.Ida M (Stotera)b. SM Wed 11 Aug 1897 (*Times*)
living in Long Beach 1933
living with Alice McPhaul, SMUHS Class of 1918
SMUHS Alumni Notes 1921: bkpr Santa Barbara
9. Carrieb. Ipava IL 31 Dec 1860
d. 29 March 1862
(GW Battles) m.3 Fulton co IL 25 Sep 1862

Rachel Edna Kinsey	b. Freeport OH 5 Feb 1836
	d. at res of U G Battles Santa Maria 22 Dec 1911 @72
	SM cem; obit Dec 23 p.1
	F: OH M: DE

10.   Ulysses <u>Grant</u>   b. Ipava IL 16 Apr 1863; m. @37 of SM
     1884 GR: 21 IL f SM   d. Santa Maria 31 Oct 1935 @72; SM cem obit (*Times*)
     1890 GR: 27 IL f SM #1
        m. San Luis Obispo 8 Nov 1899 by Rev Fr Lynch, F47.
          wit: Cramer Williams, Los Berros; Kate Williams, Los Berros

Ella Frances Hourihan   b. Skibbereen, Co Cork IR 14 Mar 1869
  bio O'Neill p.176   d. Santa Maria 26 July 1950 @81/4/14 SM cem obit (*T*)
                           F: John Hourihan
                           M: Mary Donovan

    a. James George   b. Santa Maria 5 May 1905 (*Times*)
       Pres. Pioneer Assn 1955   d. SM 24 Jul 1990 @85; r Rosemary Rd
                                    SM cem obit Thu July 26
        m. 26 Jan 1936
        Thelma Louisa Chamberlain   b. Santa Barbara 24 Jan 1906
          tchr Foxen Schl 1954-5 (Ont) F: Glenn Chamberlain
          last tchr Pleasant Valley sch SM M: Edith Doty
      = James G jr   b. 1937 (Wanette King)
      = Glenn Edward   b. 1938 (Janice Rae Barca)
      = Myron Grant b. 1939 (Carol Rotheimer; div) lvg Pawnee City NE
      = Barbara Jean b. 1941 (John Jordan) lvg San Jose 1990
   b. Mary Theodosia   b. Santa Maria 22 Apr 1908 (*Times*)
        m.1   living Santa Ynez 1994
        Kenneth Carroll
          m.2 Los Angeles 18 June 1937
        James Gerred Ruckle   b. Forest Grove OR 28 May 1905
                                    d. 22 Feb 1983; Oak Hill cem Ballard
      = Sharon Ann   b. 1938 (Carl E Tobin)
      = Sheila Lynn   b. 1940 (Robert Holmes Boehringer)
      = Kathleen Gayle b. 1948 (Marvin Larry Brown)

Special thanks to Janice Battles for much information, including the eleven children of G W Battles. Ye Ed. must have lost one; so much for protestations of accuracy.

Vol. XXVI, No. 2, Summer 1994, pp. 9, 10

Corrections and Additions   [Page numbers refer to those in Quarterly]

p.8.   Rollin Battles' widow Mary Miner m.2 before 1918 S A Davis

p.9.   Ida Dorland grad SMUHS 1918; at Heald's Business College, per 1920 *Review*
         Battle-Dorland marriage – lengthy write-up Dec 28 1895

p.10.   Kenneth Charles Carroll died 1 Sep 1977. His father was Charles N Carroll 1859-1944, survived by wife Jean, children Lila Breen, Catherine Billington, Joseph M, Wm J and Kenneth C Carroll.   –Jan 3 1944 p.3

Vol. XXX, No. 1, Spring 1998, pp.8, 9

BLOOMER
San Luis Obispo County   Santa Cruz County

Fell from wagon.   Wheels of Header Wagon Passed Over Body With Fatal Results

A fatal accident occurred on a ranch some two miles from Templeton yesterday, shortly after the noon hour, in which William Bloomer received injuries from which he died last night at 10 o'clock. The unfortunate man was working on a header wagon, from which he was accidentally thrown by a sudden jerk.

Before he could get out of the way, and before the horses could be stopped, the wheels passed over the body leaving him helpless and unconscious. He was taken to his home where he died last night at 10 o'clock.

Dr Nichols held an inquest this afternoon and the postmortem examination showed that the base of the skull had been crushed, the left shoulder had been dislocated and the arm broken, the body was bruised and other injuries had been suffered.

The deceased was a native of Ireland, 48 years old, and married.
-*San Luis Obispo Breeze* Wed July 24 1901 p.1

William Bloomer   b. IR Dec 1852
                           d. Templeton 23 July 1901 (2B #1217)
   1892 GR: 40 5'8 fair blue brown f IR Templeton. nat/f. Reg Sep 17
   m. 1880 (1900 cen; San Luis Obispo co, Salinas tp)

Elizabeth   b. Scotland May 1861?
  1910: 364 Pacific, Santa Cruz, rooming hs, wid.
  1920: w/son, Santa Cruz

1. Sarah I (Melford L Doane) See Doane chart

2. William Robert   b. CA May 1886
                           d. Santa Cruz 1-19-1950 (EB)
    1910: w/mother
    1920: 12 Wood, Santa Cruz
  a. June Marie   b. c1917

3. Grace E   b. CA Mar 1890
   1910: w/mother
   1920: San Francisco

4. Jessie M   b. CA Nov 1893
   1910: w/mother; steno

BLOSSER
PIONEERS OF THE CALIFORNIA CENTRAL COAST

Jacob Blosser b. PA 1807   1880 cen: 70
  1850 to CA: Stockton d. Lake Valley MEN co 22 Mar 1890 @82
  1880 cen: Little Lake pct
  1890. Intelligence was received this week by S M and L W Blosser that their father, who lived
    in Little Lake Valley, Mendocino county, was taken suddenly ill on Friday of last week, and
    died on Saturday afternoon. He had reached the advanced age of 82.   –Mar 29
      m.
Martha W   b. VA/PA 1805   1880 cen: 72
  8 sons. see #6   d.
1. Nicholas J Blosser   b. PA Jan 1834
    1880 cen: Willitsville,   d. MEN co 1 Apr 1919 @85
      blacksmith
    1900 cen: Willitsville, 2 births 2 living, mill wright
      m. 1867
    Elizabeth G   b. NY Dec 1833; parents GER
        d. MEN co 12 Oct 1917 @84 spouse NJ
    a. Frederick Clayton Blosser 1870-1940
        1880, 1900 cen: w/parents
2. Thomas G Blosser   b. PA Aug 1836
    1880 cen: w/parents   d. 21 Nov 1920 @84 spouse MJ
    1900 cen: Little Lake 0/0
      m. 1894
    Mary J   b. CA Dec 1864; F: KY; M: MO
3. Samuel Martin Blosser   b. VA 1839
    1850 to CA; patron T/W   d. at home Fresno 26 Sep 1926 @87/7/5; SM cem
    1879 to SB co   obit Tue Sep 28 p.5; SMv 40y; to San Jose 1919,
      prop SM Hotel; 40a POSM   thence Fresno. 2 dau son, 2 bro 1 bro dec =L W
    1880 cen: SM
    1881. trustee Central Sch Dist; SM Band
    1882 GR: 43 VA hotelkpr SM
    1890 GR: 51 VA livryman SM #2
    1906 Dir: Blosser Samuel, Prop. Exchange Hotel, Main st, r same
        S. Mrs r Exchange Hotel
        Mattie Miss r Exchange Hotel
    1909 Dir: Blosser S M Carpenter South Lincoln st
        Mrs S M res same; Miss M R Missionary res same
      Blosser Mrs S M Second Hand Furniture Store 211 E Main
    1910 cen: S Bwy(?) m/42 7 births 3 living
    1914 Dir: Blosser S M (Harriett E) bldg contr h208 W Jones; Miss Mattie r same
      m. Willits July 1866
    Harriet E Whitcomb   b. IN 1851; parents NY
    1888 Polk Gazetteer: d. at home Fresno 1 Oct 1928 @76/7/13; SM cem
      Harriet, propr Farmers' Home   possible brothers 1880 census Little Lake: all b. IN,
    1890. Mrs S M Blosser,   parents NY; Orin Whitcomb @38; Charlie Whitcomb
      prop Crosby's Dining   @48; Henry Whitcomb @44; married, with families;
      Palace. –Jan 11   Elkanah Whitcomb @26; obit Wed Oct 3 p.3; son
    1894. Rice House (Blosser   2 dau sis (sic) Mattie Blosser, all Fresno; 2 gs 3 gd
      & Son)   all Fresno. nc: Mrs M P Baker,

1896. Sam Blosser's family   Mrs C V Gardner, Mrs Elmer Rice, SM
    in charge of Pismo   1880-1908 Exchange Hotel SM
    Hotel. –Jan 4

1900. Mrs Sam Blosser has opened a bakery in the room used formerly by Miss Ella Hourihan for dressmaking parlors. Clean, sweet bread and rich pies and cakes will always be found there, fresh and at right prices.   –Feb 24

1902. Exchange Hotel. Mrs Etta Young and sister Miss Mattie Blosser visiting parents at Exchange Hotel.   –Dec

1909. For sale entire stock of M/M S M Blosser's Exchange Hotel in vacant building just east of John Long's blacksmith shop, opposite Pioneer stables.   –Mar 17
(fire closed hotel)

   a.   Almeda E Blosser   b. CA 1868
                                         d. 4 Mar 1890 @21/7/22; SM cem; la Grippe (*T*)

   b.   Daniel M Blosser   b. CA Dec 1869; m. @24 of SM
      1900. If you are going to put   d. Fresno 3 Sep 1935 spouse M
        up a tank it would pay you to see Dan Blosser. He will put you up an adjustable roundhoop tank, all set up and ready for use, at the very lowest price.   –Feb 24
      1906 Dir: D M draughtsman, r cor Pine and Lemon sts; Mrs
      1909 Dir: no
      1926, 1928 Fresno
      1935. Society Notes. Santa Marians Go to Blosser Funeral - M/M C V Gardner, Mrs Major Baker, Mrs Helen Walker, Mrs Thomas Adam and Mrs Fred Sherrill attended the funeral service of the late Daniel Blosser, in Fresno yesterday…heart attack…born Willits 64 years ago…lived in Santa Maria valley many years. Surviving children: Mrs E W TeWinkle, Bakersfield; Mrs Hastings Pilcher, Oakland; Mrs C D Bartlett, Yuba City; Fred C Blosser, Fresno.   –Fri Sep 6 p.3
         m. Santa Maria 15 Aug 1894 by Rev Joseph Hemphill,
            wit: M P Baker, Adelia Hemphill (*Times*)
      Maude G Thornburgh   b. IA Feb 1874; m. @21 of SM
       1913 in Fresno   d. Fresno co 17 Oct 1930 spouse D
                                    F: Jesse Hunt Thornburg(h) 1839/40-1913
                                    M: Caroline B Fee 1849-1929
       = Almeda Jae Blosser   b. SM 4 Dec 1895 (*Times*)
                                      d. Kern co 22 Aug 1982; surname Stickler
       = Carrie V Blosser   b. SM 30 June 1897 (*Times*)
       = Fred Claire Blosser   b. 4 Oct 1902
                                     d. Fresno co 13 Nov 1955
       = dau   b. SM 15 Feb 1906 (*Times*)

   c.   Rosetta Modesta Blosser   b. Willits 17 Nov 1871; m. of SM
       "Etta"   d. Pasadena (15) Jan 1947 @75/1/28; SM cem
       1926 in Stockton   obit Thu Jan 16 p.8; 12y Pasadena
       1928 in Fresno
          m. SLO 2 July 1898 by Louis Lamy JP, E313
             wit: Chas Pedraita, Miss Theresa Pedraita
      Wilmot Lewis Young   b. Horsehead NY 1864; m.2 of SM
       1890 GR: 26 NY carp   d. SM 28 Nov 1918 @54/9/17; SM cem
         Lompoc   obit Fri Nov 29 p.3; 25y SM; Eagles
       1906 Dir: W L Young   F: Lewis Wiggins Young 1835-1919
         prop The Jesse Moore   M: Sarah Elizabeth Langdon d. c1900
         rChurch st; Mrs   see Young chart

        1909 Dir: W L Young, Knotts & Young, r205 W Cypress; Mrs E
        1910 cen: 205 W Cypress, emp retail liquor
        1918. Card of Thanks for son and brother: L W Young, Louise V Whitney,
           F C Young, A H Young

	= Floyd W Young	b. Orcutt 15 Feb 1907 (*Times*)
	1947, 1963 in Pasadena	d. San Francisco 8 May 1985;
	2 ch: Bonnie Young Woodruff	spouse R C
	in Westminster 1963; Don Young in Upland 1963	
d.	Martha R Blosser	b. Willits 11 Jan 1875
	"Mattie"	d. Pasadena 8 Jan 1963 @87/11/27; SM cem
	Single	obit Mon Jan 21 p.2; neph, gnc gnph
	1926, 1928 Fresno; 1947 Pasadena	
e.	George Elmo Blosser	b. SM 8 Dec 1888 (*Times*)
		d. 31 Oct 1889 @0/10/23/ (*Times*); SM cem
f.	Hazel Knight Blosser	b. 1893
		d. 5 Oct 1894 @0/17/12 (*T*); SM cem; "cholic"

4.   William A Blosser   b. VA July 1841
       1880 cen: Little Lake pct   d. MEN co 23 Nov 1922 @80 spouse R
       1900 cen: Little Lake tp 5 births 4 living
         m. 1874
       Roxana A Whitcomb   b. IA Feb 1854; parents IN
                                            d. MEN co 24 Jan 1927 @71 spouse W A

a.	Valmour A Blosser	b. 25 Dec 1875
	not on 1900 cen w/parents	d. Santa Clara co 27 Sep 1960
b.	Harry G Blosser	b. CA 19 May 1877
	1900 cen: w/parents	d. Santa Clara co 6 Aug 1961
c.	Bertha A Blosser	b. CA Apr 1882
d.	Elsie R Blosser	b. CA May 1889

5.   Lorenzo Waugh Blosser   b. (W)VA May 1845 (cen) 1844 (obit)
       1851 to Stockton   d. at home of dau Mrs Gardner SM 2 May 1920 @75;
       1869 to SM   SM cem
       1870 cen: SMv blacksmith   obit Mon May 3 p.3; 5ch Staunch Methodist
       1882 GR: 37? VA blksm SM
       1888 Polk Gazetteer: Lierly & Blosser (Wilson S Lierly, Lorenzo W Blosser) livery SM
       1890 GR: 46 VA f SM #2
       1900 cen: SM 6 births 6 living
       1901. A pleasant surprise party was tendered Mrs L W Blosser last Monday night by the
          Ladies Aid Society of the ME Church. The occasion was Mrs Blosser's 54th birthday
          and she was well remembered by the members of the family and the church with which
          she has been actively identified for many years. Mrs Blosser was the recipient of some
          very handsome presents. During the evening an excellent lunch was served accompanied
          by general merriment and a good time.   –Nov 2
       1906 Dir: Blosser L W ret r Broadway; Mrs; Edna Miss stu
       1909 Dir: Blosser L W Rancher, West Chapel; Mrs A; Mrs (sic) E C res same
       1910 cen: W Chappel (sic) 6/6
       1914 Dir: Lorenzo W (Anna) h109 W Mill
       1919. 55th Wedding Anniversary on Mother's Day, May 12, at home of daughter Mrs
          Elmer Rice; Four generations attended: Mrs Lierly, her daughter Irene Ellis,
          granddaughter Eleanor Ellis. Present: Mrs Garrett Blosser, Mrs Willis (sic) Lierly,
          Mrs Irene Ellis and Eleanor of Taft; M/M M P Baker, Dr/M E E Blosser and children
          Elbert and Teddy of Santa Barbara; M/M C V Gardner and children, Hilda and Anna

Luise (sic); M/M Elmer Rice. Judge Crow of Santa Barbara sent congratulations.

-Wed May 14

    m. Stockton 12 May 1864

Anna Van Valkenburg   b. Chatham NY Oct 1846
 1851 to Stockton   d. at home of dau Mrs Rice, Garey rd SM 19 July 1926
 1917. Surviving nc of Chas   @79; SM cem; obit July 19 p.5; 4 dau 1 son;
 Sedgwick (1829-1917)   sis Mrs Ida (sic) Hamm, Chatham NY
 1921. Mrs M P Baker, Mrs   F: Garrett Van Valkenburg
 L W Blosser and Mrs   M:
 E C Rice left for St Augustine Florida to visit Mrs Blosser's sister Mrs Ada Hann (sic).

-25 Years Ago, Feb 16 1946

 1922-3 Dir: Mrs Anna hskpr r rural
 1925 Dir: Mrs Anna ret SM RFD

a. Garrett Lorenzo Blosser   b. Stockton 23 May 1865; m. of SM
  1886 GR: 21 CA lab SM   d. 27 Jan 1918 @52/10/4; SM cem
  1890 GR: 25 CA livrymn SM #2   obit Feb 2; 4 sis bro; dep sheriff 18y
  1898. ad Hart House Livery Stable, Blosser & Brown, Props. Horses Boarded by the
   Day, Week or Month. Buggies, Carriages, Horses and Picnic Turnouts. Horses
   Carefully Groomed. Next to Hart House. Santa Maria Cal   –Sep 10
  1898. Garrett Blosser. Regular Republican nominee for Constable of 7th Judicial
   District. Election Tue Nov 8 1898.   –Sep 10
  1898 constable
  1900 cen: SM livery 2 births 2 living
  1905. Marshall, tax & license collector
   Horn Bardin, Tom Steele and Garrett Blosser owned horses raced at the Santa
   Maria track; partners Steele, Bardin and Blosser had interests in livery stables in
   Arroyo Grande, Pismo Beach and Santa Maria.   –Madge
  1906 Dir: Bardin H H liveryman rMain st; Mrs
   Blosser G L City Marshal, Blosser & Blosser, livrymn, Main st; rChurch; Mrs
   E E Dr liveryman, Blosser & Blosser, r cor McClelland & Chapel; Mrs
  1909 Dir: Bardin H H Livery Stable r E Main; Mrs Jennie
    Blosser G L Livery r309 W Church; Mrs M A; Miss Mabel stu; E G stu
  1910 cen: W Church 2/2 own income
  1914 Dir: Bardin Henry H (Jennie) city marshal and mgr S M Livery & Feed co
    h419 E Main; Henry R stu; Ramona
    Blosser Garrett L (Mary) constable 126 W Main and pres S M Livery &
    Feed co h309 W Church; Mabel stu
  1916. H H Bardin, pound master
  Note: Thomas J Steele d. 1911 @56, AG cem
   Bardins came to SM from Salinas 1905, apparently returned there. Their son Ralph
   Henry Bardin (1893-1968) was a long-time dentist in SM.
   See Madge for Steele & Bardin families

    m. SLO 17 July 1893 by J W Van Cleve VDM, D302
     wit: John Kabel, SM; John H Conway (?), Sisquoc (*Times*)

Mary Antoinette McClaine   b. CA 13 Sep 1865; m. of SM
 1886. Confirmed St Isidore Ch   d. 9 May 1958 @92/7/26; SM cem
 Guad @20 1 Apr sponsor   obit May not available
 Mary Stockdale   F: José McClaine/McLane
 1922-3 Dir: Mrs Mary A hskpr   M: Georgia Maria Gregoria Fuentes
  r319 W Church; Mabel L tchr; Ernest surveyors helper
 1925 Dir: Mrs Mary hskpr r319 W Church; Ernest, clk

      1940-1 Dir: Mary hmkr h321 W Church; Ernest clk Harpers Café r321 W Church
= Mabel M/L Blosser   b. SM 1 Dec 1895 (*Times*)
   1903. Park fund benefit program: d. Kern co 13 Oct 1965 @69
     37ch, incl Mabel –V
   1949, 1950, 1952 in Lebec
       m. Smailes
= Ernest Garrett Blosser   b. 26 July 1899
   1920 cen: w/mother   d. @52/6/5; bur Feb 5 1952; SM cem;
   1947-8 Dir: Ernest bartender   inf Mrs Mabel Smailes
     Harper's Café   obit Fri Feb 3; lifelong res SM.
     r321 W Church;   Mother, sis Mabel Smailes, Lebec;
     Mary hmkr h321 W Church   Dr E E Blosser, Exeter
     Harper's Cocktail Lounge Harry Harper 111 W Main
   Single

b.   Mary Anna Blosser   b. 18 Apr 1867; m. @18 of SM
     "May"   d. Taft 21 Sep 1931 @64; SM cem; obit Sep 21
     1882. Surprise birthday party   3 sons 2 dau 3 sis SM; bro Exeter; gch
       @14 for Girlie Blosser.   –Apr 22
        m. Cosmopolitan Hotel SLO 11 May 1885 by John W Hinds MG, B49
          wit: C W Marriott, SM; S K Martin, SM; left for Tulare and parts
          north . . .   –May 16 (*Times*)
   Wilson St Clair Lierly   b. IL 1858; m. @26 of SM
     1880 cen: 21 IL svt w/Millard   d. Taft 18 May 1933; SM cem
       Blodgett family, SM   F: (Wilson Lierly 1809-1894)
     1881. SM Band   M: (Sarah Zimmerman 1809-   ) see *PV* 259
     1882 GR: 23 IL stable kpr SM
     1883-4 McKenney Dir: Lierly W livery stable SM
     1890 GR: 32 IL livery SM
     1890. Lierly to San Francisco with fine racing horses . . .   –Jan 11
       Mrs Lierly, mother of our townsman W S Lierly, departed for her home in
       Mendocino on Tue.   –Feb 15
     1898. Rube Hart and W S Lierly deserve praise for their acts in caring for the trees
       at the park.   –Sep 10
     1900. W S Lierly and Johnny Adams are home again from the county seat. Neither of
       them have aught to say against the sheriff or jailor, so we guess their stay was
       pleasant.   –Feb 24
     1912. ad. Taft Harness Shop—Midway Stables. Lierly & Son, Prop.
       South Taft Block 1072   –*Taft Driller* 11 Dec 1912
     1932. (from an article by Arthur M Keene, Editor of the *Daily Midway Driller*, Taft)
       Former Santa Maria Liveryman Does Fine Business Now in Taft . . . still rents
       horses and mules for use in handling grading construction . . . has a string of heavy
       trucks . . . Lierly & Son . . . (Wray) his business proves that Taft is not a one horse
       town.   –(*Times*) Fri Jan 22 4 paragraphs
     1932. Lively Factor In Two Communities Closely Related. Santa Maria and Taft
       Beneficiaries of W S Lierly . . . spent half a century in Santa Maria and the oil city
       of Taft . . . to Santa Maria from Mendocino county in 1882 and opened the
       Champion livery stables . . . 27 years . . . dealer in horses and . . . all matters
       connected with the livery business . . . one of six who put $1500 in trust for the
       Methodist church of Santa Maria . . . The original church . . . built mostly from
       lumber salvaged from a wrecked shop . . . to Taft in 1909 . . . livery and teaming
       . . . Later . . . trucking . . . He still owns two horses, so it cannot be said of Taft that

it is a one-horse town . . . "Father of Taft's Schools," . . . first school held in a tent until a building could be erected . . . In Lierly's days here, Santa Maria boasted some of the best buggy and harness horses in the State, and a good race track, too . . . Champion Stables . . . located at the southwest corner of Broadway and Chapel street . . . five children, all married . . . all born in Santa Maria.

–*Valley Vidette* Fri June 10

= Elwin G Lierry
   1932 in LA
b. SM 13 May 1886 (*T*) 12 May CDI
d. Los Angeles co 6 Aug 1945

= Lorenzo William Lierly
   1932, 1949, 1950 in AG
b. SM 28 Aug 1888 (*T*); m. @25 of Taft
d. (AG) 24 July 1965; AG cem; inf Grace Lierly, 343 S Halcyon rd AG; poultry farm

   m.1 SLO 14 July 1913 by C W F Nelson MG, J4
     wit: Mrs P J Saulsbury, Paso Robles; Mrs L W Blosser, SM
   Edna May Saulsbury
b. nr SM 7 Dec 1888 (*Times*); m. @25 of Paso Robles
d. (AG) 31 July 1937 @48; AG cem
F: David E Saulsbury 1862-1925
M: Permelia Jane Beckett 1869-1936

   + Vida June Lierly (McLaurin)
   + Lois Lorraine Lierly (Nelson)
   + Harold Claire Lierly
   m.2
   Grace Ethel Theobald
b. IL 29 July 1897 M: Mead
d. Fresno 3 Dec 1995; AG cem

= Wray Lucas Lierly
   1932 in Taft
   1949 in Riverside
   1950 in Long Beach
b. 20 Aug 1891 CDI 27 Aug (*Times*)
d. Los Angeles co 25 Aug 1956

= Irene Lierly
b. nr SM 21 Oct 1893 (*T*) 20 Oct CDI
d. Los Angeles co 29 Mar 1969

   m.1 C E Ellis; 1932 in Culver City
   m.2 Coulter; 1949, 1950 in El Monte

= Nellie Lierly
   1932, 1949, 1950 in Taft
   m. C W Williams
b. SM 7 Sep 1895 (*Times*)
d. Kern co 1 Sep 1954

c.   Nelle Blosser
b. SMv 24 Oct 1869
d. SM 17 Apr 1949
obit Mon Apr 18 p.1. 6 Blossers, 2 left: Dr E E Blosser, Exeter; Edna C (Elmer) Rice, SM. Deceased: Alida (Chas Gardner), Garrett L Blosser –wife Mary living; Mary A Lierly d. Taft. n/n: Mabel Smailes, Lebec; Ernest Blosser, SM; L W Lierly, AG; W L Lierly, Riverside; Irene Coulter, El Monte; Nellie Williams, Taft; Theodore and Elbert Blosser, Exeter; Mrs Hilda Taylor, Mrs Anna Gill, SM

   m. 1893
   Major Ransom P Baker
b. Petaluma 1 Oct 1863
d. at home SM 2 Dec 1936 @72
F: Henry Womack Baker 1818-1909

                                  M: Elizabeth Wilkerson 1823-1899
      No issue   see Baker chart

d.   Elbert Eldridge Blosser   b. 24 July 1875
     1909 Dir: dentist   d. Exeter CA 29 July 1958 @83; Exeter cem
       419 S Bwy; Mrs   obit Tue Aug 5 p.10; to Taft 1920
     1910 cen: S Bwy 0/0   dentist Exeter 1922-1945; 2 sons 2 nc, Hilda
     1914 Dir: Elbert E Blosser   and Anna; b/l Elmer C Rice
       (Ora) Bagby & Blosser dentists h417 S Bwy
       Bagby & Blosser (H G Bagby, E E Blosser) dentists IOOF Bldg
         124 W Main
     1949, 1952 in Exeter
       m. at home of bride's parents SM 15 June 1904 by Rev Clague (*Times*)
    Ora Phena Trott   b. CA 27 Aug 1879
                                      d. Exeter 17 Nov 1955; obit Tue Nov 22 p.5
                                      severe injuries auto acc 5 wks ago
                                      F: George Joseph Trott 1853-1919
                                      M: Mary E Oakley 1858-1925
     = Elbert George Blosser   b. 1 Dec 1912
       1918. Albert (sic), son of   d. Los Angeles co 31 Mar 1981
         Dr E Blosser, SB, has flu. –Nov 23
       1949, 1950 in Exeter
       1958 in Inglewood
     = Theodore L Blosser   b. 2 Nov 1916 (*Times*)
       1949, 1950 in Exeter
       1958 in Pahrump WA

e.   Alida Christine Blosser   b. 29 Jan 1882
      "Allie"   d. (17) Feb 1938 @56/0/19; SM cem
     1900 cen: w/parents   obit Fri Feb 18 p.1
        m. SM 16 Apr 1902 by Rev S S Sampson (*Times*)
    Charles Virgil Gardner   b. NY 8 Feb 1881
     1894 to SM—   d. 16 Aug 1947 @66/6/8; SM cem
     1906 Dir: Chas V clk   F: Wright Gardner 18__-1913
       rBwy; Mrs   M: Helen Virgil 1834-1924
       Wright, druggist, rMcClelland st; Mrs H; Louise W same
     1909 Dir: C V, Druggist rSBwy; Mrs
          Wright, Druggist r403 S McClelland, Mrs H; Miss Louise Stu
          Gardner-Wheaton Co Druggists & Jewelers 106 W Main st
     1914 Dir: Chas V(Alida) v-pres Gardner-Wheaton Co h415 S Bwy
         Louise W bkkpr r419 S Bwy
         Gardner-Wheaton Co, Wright Gardner pres, C V Gardner v-pres
           druggists, jewelers and opticians 106 W Main
         Wright (Helen L) pres Gardner-Wheaton Co h419 S Bwy
     1922-3 Dir: Gardner-Wheaton Drug Co (The Rexall Store) C V Gardner mgr
          114 S Bwy
          Charles V (Alida) mgr Gardner-Wheaton Drug Co r415 S Bwy
     1925 Dir: C V (Alida) prop Gardner's Drug Store r415 S Bwy
         Hilda stu r415 S Bwy
     1928 Dir: Gardner-Wheaton Drug Co C V Gardner prop, 124 S Bwy
          C V (Alida) mcht r415 S Bwy; Hilda stu; Anna stu
     1940-1 Dir: C V Mgr Gardner-Wheaton Drug Co r201 E Mill

      Gardner-Wheaton Drug Co C V Gardner mgr 119 S Bwy
  = Hilda Frances Gardner   b. 26 Oct 1907 (*Times*)
                d. 10 Oct 1992 @84; Gordon G Gill
      m.   neph inf; SM cem
  Albert Jackson Taylor   b. 19 May 1906
   "Al"   d. 16 Mar 1989 @82; SM cem
   1940-1 Dir: Albert (Hilda)   F:
    emp Gardner-Wheaton   M: Ruiz
    Co 415 S Bwy
  = Anna Louise Gardner   b. 19 Sep 1913
                d. 2 June 1986 @72; SM cem
      m.
  Albert Grove Gill   b. 8 Aug 1910
   "Bert"   d. MEN co 21 Oct 1983 @73/2/13;
   1928 Dir: Gill Bert stu r219 S Bwy   SM cem
    Grayson Hotel   F: Albert Grove Gill 18 -1949 @65
   1940-1 Dir: Albert G ("Bert")   M: Moore
    (Anna L) Mgr Grayson Hotel; r same
  + Gordon Garner (sic) Gill   b. SM 20 May 1932; grad UC 1955
     m. SM 27 Dec 1955
   Anne Elizabeth Dorsey   b. SM 8 June 1933
   4 ch   F: Harry Custer Dorsey 1878-1961
                M: Ethel-May Palmer 1902-1991
                see *Reaching for High C,* Ethel-May
                (Palmer) (Dorsey) Conrad, 1984

 f. Edna Clare Blosser   b. SM 22 Apr 1886
   1907. Grad st Normal Sch   d. 15 Feb 1950 @63/9/10; SM Cem; inf Wm H
    San Diego –June 14   Rice; obit Feb 3; hus bro 17 n/n; in SM:
   1910 cen: w/parents   Patricia Boyd, M/M Wm C Rice; M/M Owen
   1914 Dir: Edna Blosser   S Rice, Mrs Bert Gill, Mrs Al Taylor, Ernest
    r109 W Mill   Blosser; taught grade sch SM 9y
     m. 4 Aug 1915
   Elmer Charles Rice   b. nr SM 18 Jan 1881
    bio Phillips II 182   d. 14 Oct 1975 @94/8/26; SM cem
    dairy farm   F: William Hickman Rice 1856-1951
   1906 Dir: Elmer C f   M: Florence Lee Coiner 1861-1945
    3½ m SE rfd; also W H f, Mrs; Owen T, Marion B stu, Gertrude A Miss stu,
    Wm T stu
   1909 Dir: Rice W H Pres Valley Saving Bank, r401 W Cypress (house built by
    Thomas Sands Brown 1825-1905 in 1904; see Brown chart)
    also Mrs F L, W T, G A, E C
   1914 Dir: w/parents farmer
   1925 Dir: Elmer C (Edna) f rGarey rd
    same for years
   No issue
6. (twin) John Adam Blosser   b. IA 6 Sep 1849
   1880 cen: w/parents   d. at home of brother L W Blosser 11 June 1915 @65
   1900 cen: Little Lake tp   obit June 12 p.1; to CA 1850. res Willits, wife, son,
   2 births 2 living   dau. 1 of 8 brothers. burial Willits
    m. 1888

	Ora E Morgan	b. CA May 1864; parents F: CT; M: PA
	1880 cen: Little Lake	d. MEN co 17 July 1931 @66 spouse J A
	w/parents	F: John A Morgan 1825-before 1900
		M: Unis/Annice? L 1823- living 1900
	a. Henry R Blosser	b. CA June 1889
	1915. teaching HS, Santa Rosa	
	b. Minnie H Blosser	b. CA Nov 1891
	1915. Teacher, Ukiah	
7.	(twin) Jacob Tobias Blosser	b. IA 6 Sep 1849
	1880 cen: w/parents	d. MEN co 10 June 1930 @80 spouse V
	1900 cen: Little Lake tp 2/2	
	1926 Tobias in Ft Bragg	
	m. 1888	
	Vernina (?) A	b. CA Dec 1867; parents MO
	a. Jesse D Blosser	b. CA Aug 1889
	b. May P Blosser	b. CA Feb 1894
8.	Daniel J Blosser	b. CA Feb 1853
	1880 cen: w/parents	d. MEN co 2 April 1931 @78
	1900 cen: bro w/Wm A, Single	
	1926 in Willits	

BONILLA–LUKEMAN
SANTA MARIA VALLEY PIONEERS

1914 Dir: Bonilla Walter R barber 119 E Main rE Main 1 mi E of city

1943 Walter Bonilla died at home Watsonville. 9 dau, 1 son Raymond, Oakland; daughters Mrs W O Lukeman, Santa Maria; Mrs Guy Ruperto, Santa Maria, Mrs Juanita Souza (Nita Christine 1895-1962), Santa Maria (Joseph C Souza 1894-1967); Mrs Thelma Vaughn, Santa Maria; Mrs Leona Philbrick, Santa Maria; Mrs Jeanne Romero, Santa Barbara; Mrs Elaine Martin, Richmond; Mrs Eva Vasconcellos, Watsonville; Miss Lucille Bonilla, Watsonville. –Fri July 30 p.1
   1940-1 Dir: Philbrick Geo L (Leona M) f E Main
        Ruperto Guy T (Norine) mgr Rex Café h600 N Ben Wiley
        Souza Jos C (Nita) emp Gas Co h112 N Thornburg
        1912: Joanita Christine Bonilla 17, Santa Maria
          m. Santa Maria 31 Dec 1912
        John Francis McGlashan 21, Gilroy

1962 Nita Christine Souza b. Capitola CA 20 May 1895; d. Santa Maria. Great-Granddaughter of (Jose) Mariano Bonilla (1807-1878), first judge of San Luis Obispo Co appointed by Fremont. r702 N McClelland with aunt Mrs Maude Goodale. 3 dau Mrs Lorraine Duncan, Shell Beach; Mrs Betty Schlinder, Princeville, IL; Mrs Bonnie Bouton, Monica, IL; 8 sis: Mrs Eva Madigan (1911-1998), Emerson, NJ; Norine Ruperto, Santa Maria; Mrs Thelma Canfield (1903-1983), Santa Maria; Mrs Ynez Lukeman, Santa Maria; Mrs Jeanne Romero Santa Barbara; Mrs Lucille Zahlke, Vallejo; Mrs Leona (Maude) Adams (1898-1980), Sacramento; Mrs Elaine (Edwina) Anzalone (1913-1981), San Francisco. -Thu Apr 12 p.2

1955-6 Dir: Goodale Mrs S W hmkr h702 N McClelland st

1970 William Oswald Lukeman b. Franklin, IL 1 Nov 1896; d. Santa Maria. r324 W Chapel. To Santa Maria 1917; electrician. widow Ynez; son W A, Santa Maria; 2 dau: Mrs Rosalyn Thayer, Santa Barbara; Mrs Doreen Allen (1922-1986), Cazenovia, NY; bro Claude Wood, Los Angeles. 10gch, 5ggch, n/n. –Mar 5 p.2
      m. San Luis Obispo 31 May 1921, L588 Ynez M Bartron
   1922-3 Dir: Lukeman Brothers "Willard Service" (W O & S F Lukeman) 114 W Chapel
        Lukeman Brothers Lompoc Santa Barbara Generator and Motor Repairs
        "Rewinding a Specialty" 114 W Chapel Santa Maria
        Willard Thread-Rubber Insulation
        Lukeman S F (Bessie D) prop Willard Service Station Lukeman Brothers
          r416 E Church
        Lukeman W C (Ynez) prop Willard Service Station, Lukeman Brothers
          r8 W Sola, Santa Barbara
   1925 Dir: Lukeman W O (Ynez) prop Willard Serv Sta r320 W Chapel
   1928 Dir: same r324 W Chapel
   1940-1 Dir: Lukeman W O (Ynez) oilwkr h 324 W Chapel
   1947-8 Dir: Lukeman W A farm lab r 324 W Chapel
        W O (Ynez) elec Elect Serv Co h324 W Chapel
   1955-6 Dir: Lukeman W A 1635 Canfield Ln Rt2 W O (Ynez) electn h324 W Chapel
        Wm A (Eleanor) drvr FitzGerald Bros h805 Las Flores

1975 Ynez survived by son Wm A, Santa Maria; 2 dau: Rosalyn Thayer, Santa Barbara; Doreen Allen, Cazenovia, NY; 5 sis: Mrs Doreen (sic) Anzalone, Santa Maria; Mrs Eva Madigan, Santa Maria; Mrs Jeanne Romero, Santa Barbara; Mrs Leona Adams, Sacramento; Mrs Thelma Canfield, Santa Maria. –Wed July 23 p.2

1972 Dir: Canfield Roy C (Thelma) A mntncmn S M Parks h411 W Sunset Madigan Eva L checker AFCO r411 W Sunset Anzalone Elaine emp Haanpaa rest home r508 N Mary Dr

1983 Thelma Angeline Canfield b. San Francisco 17 Jun 1903; d. at home. Pioneer Bonilla family. 2 sis: Georgine Romero, Santa Barbara; Eva Madigan, Santa Maria; n/n. Husband Roy C "Bud" Canfield d. 1977 -Thu May 31 p.8

1995 William Allen Lukeman b. Santa Maria 10 Oct 1923; pioneer Bonilla family. Truck driver FitzGerald Trucking. Wife Eleanor M. Lukeman, Santa Maria; Son William "Bill" H Lukeman, Santa Maria; daus Luanne M Reich, Phoenix; Joan R Houser, Henderson IA; sisters Rosalyn Thayer, Santa Maria; Doreen Allen, Woodstock, NY. 8 gch 1 ggch. Predeceased by parents Bill & Ynez Lukeman, daughter Karen E Dutra who died in 1979 @30. -Thu Dec 28 A7

1972 Dir: Dutra Gordon J (Karen) slsmn Bello's Sporting Goods h1011 W Cypress

BOWERS and PARNELL
SANTA MARIA BUSINESSMEN

Frank Bowers was well known in the Santa Maria Valley during his forty-year residence, almost thirty spent as the Ford Dealer. He came in 1905 as a superintendent for the Union Sugar Co., having entered that line of work in New York, his natal state, and gone on to greater responsibility in Colorado before being transferred to Betteravia (which name derives from the Spanish for sugar beet).[1] He retired from the factory in 1916, going into partnership with Harry Parnell, a fellow Union Sugar employee and mechanic, at the Santa Maria Garage.

The Santa Maria Garage, Wm. Donnelly and Harry Allott, proprietors, originally at 219 North Broadway, moved into the new Hart building, northeast corner of Broadway and Church Street, in 1909, having secured the Ford agency for Santa Maria. In the early days of the burgeoning automobile industry, almost anyone – garages, hardware stores, merchants, mechanics – could represent the various marquees, taking orders and making deliveries. By 1915 Ford was a leader, and that year handed out $50 rebates as promised because of having reached a sales goal. (T Oct. 9, 1915) Donnelly was motivated for unknown reasons to sell his business the next year to Bowers & Parnell; they took over on May 15, 1916. The 1917 Fords were received in September and business was good enough to impel Bowers & Parnell to construct a new building for their company across Church Street on the southeast corner of Broadway, contractors, Marriott & Edwards.

(*Times* Sep 22, 1917)

In 1918 Parnell sold his interest to Bowers' son-in-law, W. W. Stokes, also an alumnus of Union Sugar, and bought Sutherland's grocery, but by 1922 was selling cars again across Broadway from the old stand at the Crescent Garage, home of The Studebaker Motor Car. He was doing well enough to build a new house in 1927, at 1107 South Broadway, and changed business again; this time he joined Michael N. Firfires in managing the U.S. Grill, a relatively "nice" restaurant, which had been on east Main Street but was moved around the block to North Broadway. It would appear that Parnell's son-in-law, Henry Tilley, took over the Studebaker agency, having worked, up to that time, like his predecessors, at Union Sugar. Tilley and his partner, James P. Jensen, moved the business to 226 West Main Street, where both Champion Motors, the Studebaker agency, and The Automotive Garage, for repairs and Auto Club work, were located. Both Tilley and Jensen lived on Palm Court Drive, a new neighborhood in close proximity to Parnell's dwelling.

(1930 *A-Z Directory*)

Parnell dropped out of the restaurant business to work for Santa Barbara County for a few years until his death in 1936. Tilley followed suit, working in the 5th Road District and later in the County Clerk's office, from which he retired to Pismo Beach, where he lived 8 years.

The *Santa Maria Times* reported a "crash" at the corner of Airport and Orange Streets at 11 A.M., July 29, 1941, involving Tilley and Owen T. Rice; Henry was still suffering from the concussion when his brother William died in Los Angeles, August 4.

The 25th anniversary of Bowers & Stokes was advertised with a large spread in the *Santa Maria Times*, July 31, 1941, p.3, featuring photographs of the principals. Bowers died in 1945 and Stokes continued the business – see Stokes story. Mrs Bowers was active socially and in Catholic organizations; her biography is found in O'Neill. In that article Donnelly, above, is called Doyle, confusion generated, no doubt, from the fact that W. T. Doyle and Edmund Ontiveros operated The California Garage on North Broadway, most likely in the building vacated by Donnelly and Allott; in 1916 they were selling Buicks. North Broadway – Buicks; South Broadway – Fords; one hopes that was O'Neill's only inaccuracy.

BOWERS - BREEN

Conrad Bowers　　　　　　　　　　　b. and d. New York
Mary Brophy　　　　　　　　　　　　b. Ireland, d. New York
　　　　　8 children, 7 named, M/H p.935
1. Mary Ellen　　　　　　　　　　　b. (Rome) NY 1859
　　1922 Dir: N Lincoln　　　　　　d. at home of dau Mrs Doane Santa Maria 23 Feb 1932
　　　(Tunnell tract)　　　　　　　　　@72/7/27; SM cem
　　　　m.　　　　　　　　　　　　　obit Wed Feb 24 p.1; in SM 16y
　　Frank Eugene Breen　　　　　　b. NY 1858
　　　carpenter r 1005 S Broadway　d. Santa Maria 15 Nov 1921 @61; SM cem
　　　　　　　　　　　　　　　　　　　obit Wed Nov 16 p.2; heart attack, at work on
　　　　　　　　　　　　　　　　　　　Rubel bldg; in SM 5y
　　　　　　　　　　　　　　　　　F: James Breen
　　　　　　　　　　　　　　　　　M: Hannah Nightengale b. Rome NY 1839
　　　　　　　　　　　　　　　　　　　d. at res of Mrs Mary Breen 215 S Pine 28 May 1927
　　　　　　　　　　　　　　　　　　　@87; SM cem; obit Tue May 31
　　　　　　　　　　　　　　　　　　F: David Nightengale　M: Sarah
　　a.　Bertha Mary　　　　　　　　b. (Rome) NY 22 July 1884
　　　　1927: Sisquoc　　　　　　　　d. SM 8 May 1963; SM cem; r 306A E Cypress
　　　　　m. (2d wife)　　　　　　　　obit Thu May 9 p.16; in SM 50y
　　　　Frank B. Drumm　　　　　　b. Guadalupe 5 Feb 1886
　　　　(Benj Franklin)　　　　　　　d. Bakersfield 4 Jan 1980 @93; SM cem
　　　　1922 Dir: foreman　　　　　F: James Howard Drumm 1850-1916
　　　　Brookshire Oil Co　　　　　M: Mary C Stubblefield 1864-1894
　　　　　m.1 Clara Edith Rogers 1886-1912
　　　　= Mary Jane　b. SM 1921; d. SM; bur SM cem 2 June 1928 @6/9 r Sisquoc
　　b.　Anna Mae　　　　　　　　　b. Rome NY 9 May 1887
　　　　1920: w/parents　　　　　　d. Santa Maria 28 June 1975 @ 88/1/19; SM
　　　　　m. Santa Maria 4 April 1921　　　　　　　　　　　　　　　　　　cem
　　　　Dick V Doane 1891-1977; see Doane chart
　　c.　William Francis　　　　　　b. Rome NY 18 Dec 1889
　　　　to Betteravia 1912　　　　　d. SM 6 Jan 1960 @70/0/18; SM cem
　　　　1920: Betteravia Asst mach　　obit Fri Jan 8 p.2
　　　　1927, 1937: Sisquoc　　1940 Dir: Rice Ranch Oil Co, r Rice Ranch lease
　　　　　m. St Peter's Cath ch Rome NY 26 April 1911
　　　　Winifred Mary ____　　　　b. NY 2 Jan 1892
　　　　　　　　　　　　　　　　　　　d. at home Rice Rch Lease 30 Jan 1961
　　　　　　　　　　　　　　　　　　　@69/0/28; SM cem; obit Tue Jan 31 p.2
　　　　= William Junior　　　　　b. 10 Feb 1913; d. 17 Nov 1973 @60/9/7; SM cem
　　　　　Lorraine　　　　　　　　　Blochman sch; photo Ont p.323; obit Mon Nov 19 p.2
　　　　　　　　　　　　r 1133 George Ln Orcutt; plant opr Laguna Sanitation Dist
　　　　　+ Robert (in Oceano 1973)
　　　　　+ Virginia (Morrow) (WAC Okinawa 1973)
　　　　= Peggy (Miller) Blochman sch; Ont p.324 (in Nipomo 1960 '73)
　　d.　Francis J　　　　　　　　　b. (NY) 26 Mar 1899
　　　　Lila M　　　　　　　　　　　d. Fresno Aug 1988
　　　　1922 Dir: asst sub sta insp MCPS Corp r 406 W Chapel
　　　　1926 Dir: substa opr r 406 W Chapel; San Joaquin Power* Monthly mag June 1925
　　　　northern SB co issue: group photo Midland Counties Public Service Corp (FJBreen)

        still in Santa Maria 1932   *main offc Fresno
        Issue unknown

2. Agnes B   b. Rome NY 15 June 1881
   1932, 1945: Orcutt   d. 13 Feb 1957; SM cem; r 400 Clark, Orcutt
   m.   obit Thu Feb 14 p.3; in SM valley 46y
   Frank J Conaty   d. (San Joaquin co 12-8-1975: SSDI)
     1940 Dir: pipe fitr hlpr Rice Ranch Oil Co; r Orcutt
   a. Marie (Turner) (in Madera 1957)

3. Sarah (Sullivan) (in New York 1932; Brooklyn NY 1945)

4. Francis Joseph   b. Camden NY 3 Oct 1864
   1910: supt sugr fcty   d. Santa Maria 3 Jan 1945 @80; SM cem
   bio M/H p. 935   obit Thu Jan 4 p.1; 30y SM
    bio Phillips p.404; Bowers & Stokes Ford Agency
      m. Rome NY 10 June 1885
   Katherine Hellen Baulig   b. Lewis co NY 5 Dec 1866
    bio O'Neill p. 88   d. Santa Maria 8 Dec 1943 @77/0/3; SM cem
    r 900 S Broadway   F: Anthony Baulig b. GER; d. Rome NY @84
        M: Theresa Steiert b. GER; d. Rome NY @84
      7 births, 5 living 1910

   a. Genevieve   b. Rome NY 6 Feb 1886
      m. San Luis Obispo 7 May 1905   d. SM 3 Oct 1974 @88
    Oscar Mason Doane 1886-1960; see Doane chart

   b. Lauretta Catherine   b. NY 5 Feb 1887; m. @25 of Betteravia
      m. Santa Maria 15 March 1913   d. SM 2 Feb 1962; obit Sat Feb 3 p.1
    Walter William Stokes 1880-1967; see Stokes chart

   c. Francis   b. 4 Feb 1890; d. 24 Apr 1897
   d. Albertina   b. 12 Feb 1893; d. July 1893 @5mos
   e. Winifred Martha   b. Binghamton NY 22 Aug 1900
        d. SM 25 July 1990; obit Thu July 26
      1922 Dir: bkpr SM garage r 900 S Broadway
       m. Santa Maria 14 Aug 1926
     Henry August La Franchi   b. Guadalupe 25 Sep 1900
        d. at home 120 Palm Ct Dr 20 Jul 1985 @84
        obit Mon July 22 p.15
        F: Victor La Franchi 1875-1939
      1922 Dir: stu JC   M: Josephine   1876-
      1940 Dir: slsmn Bowers & Stokes; grad USC
    = Elaine B   b. 5 Sep 1927 (in Santa Barbara 1990)
    Donald W(aldo) Grisingher (in Santa Maria 1951)
      USN WWII   F: Frank Waldo Grisingher 1887-1962
        M: Helen Hourihan
   + Mary Katharine (Da Rin) (in Tustin 1985)
   + Donna (Brown)   (in Palos Verdes 1985)
   + David   (in Sunset Beach 1985)
   + Patricia (Weatherly) (in Santa Barbara 1985)

   f. Leona Katherine   b. (Boulder) CO 4 Jan 1904; bap Windsor CO
        d. SM 10 Jan 1977 @72; SM cem
      m.   obit Wed Jan 12 p.5; SB St Tchrs Col
     Jesse M Jordan   b. (3 June 1901; SSDI)
        d. (San Diego March 1968)
      1940 Dir: 218 S Elizabeth st; PG&E

```
               1955 Dir: 601 E Cypress, whrsmn PG&E
         = Leona Ann (Dille)    (in Santa Ynez 1977)
         = William              (in Sacramento 1977)
      g. Clifton F                     b. Santa Maria 12 Dec 1905
                                       d. 12 Feb 1978 @72/2/0; SM cem
            1922 Dir: stu 900 S Bdwy        obit Tue Feb 14 p.11
            1940 Dir: 145 Palm Ct Dr  teller BofA  1945: in Los Angeles
            1951 Dir: bartendr Ranchero Café   1955 Dir: stock clk r 320 W Hermosa
         Martha B
            1951, 1955 Dir: stno BofA
         = Frank J    1951 Dir: stu;   (in Escondido 1978)
         = Dan C      (in Santa Maria 1978)
5. Louis       (in New Jersey 1932; died before 1945)
6. Conrad      (in New York 1932; in Brooklyn NY 1945)
7. John        (in New York 1932; in Brooklyn NY 1945)
8. unknown
```

Vol. XXVI, No. 1, Spring 1994, pp.13, 14

Corrections and Additions   [Page numbers refer to those in Quarterly]

p.14.   MARRIAGE: Clifton Bowers married Martha Bardrick of Los Angeles in Los Angeles Wednesday. She grad Arroyo Grande HS. Chas Brown, son of Mr & Mrs John Brown of Santa Maria, a college mate, was best man.   –Fri June 8 1928
See Brown chart

   Mr & Mrs Matt Hammond, married in September, are back from Redding; he has joined Hammond Bros.   –Feb 7 1919

BRADLEY
SANTA MARIA VALLEY PIONEERS

Paul Bradley   b. Derbyshire England 1822 (bio); imm. 1846
   bio Storke 419   d. at home nr Garey 16 July 1890 @70/1/4
   1879 GR: 60 Eng f SM   SM cem obit July 19
      nat Aug 25 1867 Monterey Cal Dist Ct
   1870 cen: Santa Maria tp @47
   1880 cen: Sisquoc @59
   1882 GR: 60 Eng f SM nat as above
   1889: trustee Suey sch (ONT)
      m. in England
Elizabeth Spencer Mrs   b. England 1828 (cen); imm. 1872
   1900 cen: tp8 wd   d. at home of dau Mrs Seth Waite 23 Feb 1914
   1910 cen: w/Seth Waite   @98 (!). obit Sat Feb 28
      10 births 7 living
   1914 pall bearers: W A Haslam, Geo Trott, R Hart, J K Triplett, Thomas Boyd, A McNeil
1. (only) Nellie 1873-1938   See Waite chart.

     Paul Bradley came to the United States in 1846, residing in New York until 1850, when he came to California "around the Horn". After some moving about he settled in Monterey County, where he was naturalized in 1867; the next year he came to the Santa Maria Valley, starting with 480 acres, and ultimately acquiring over 4000 acres. In 1870 he visited England, and came back with a wife. In 1888 he built an "elegant two-story residence"—location not specified by Storke.
     His nephew, Charles Bradley, came at the behest of his uncle with his growing family, and was an influential personage in the valley during his long life. The Bradley Hotel, a landmark in Santa Maria and famous up and down the coast in its heyday, was built in 1888 by Reuben Hart. Bradley bought it in 1906, at which time it lost its original name, The Hart House. Built by George Doane, pioneer contractor, it was in use almost to the end of its 9th decade. It was demolished to make way for the Town Center Mall. See Doane chart
     Not much is known about Mrs Spencer. It appears that two of her nine Spencer children came with her to California: Esther, born in 1862, died before 1930, who married, first, Alexander Adam in 1878, and, second, John S Graham in 1898, and Elizabeth B, born in 1865, according to the 1880 census, but about whom nothing else has come to light. An older daughter, Stella (1860-1930), emigrated in 1889 with her husband, Joseph Elvidge, and four children; see Elvidge chart. In 1910, 7 of Mrs Spencer-Bradley's ten children were said to be living; in 1930, besides the youngest, Nellie Waite, there were two daughters and a son in England. Her own obituary lists only the three daughters living in California. The age given, 98, seems to be an exaggeration, as it is unlikely that a woman born in 1816 would be able to give birth in 1874. A recheck of the age given on the 1900 and 1910 censuses should be made.

SANTA MARIA. The Town of To-Day…in course of construction is The Hart Hotel which is modern built and with the furniture will cost $30,000…pioneers remaining…Charley Bradley and many others…   –*SLO Tribune* Fri May 18 1888

BREWSTER CONNECTIONS OF ISABELLA M. RUSSELL
of
CAMBRIA, SAN LUIS OBISPO AND SANTA MARIA

This article has been prepared from sources available locally, as well as Federal Census Records, and presented for what value it may have historically as well as genealogically.

CALLED TO REST
Mrs Chas Russell Passes Away Suddenly

Mrs Isabella Brewster Russell, beloved wife of Chas J Russell, passed away last Sunday evening…The funeral took place from the family residence on Wednesday noon, where a short service was held by Rev H T Murray of the Presbyterian church, after which the remains were taken to San Luis Obispo for interment…she was 57 years 7 months and 2 days of age, a lineal descendent of Elder Wm Brewster who emigrated to America with the Pilgrims in the Mayflower…she was born in Bristol, Wayne county, Ohio, September 8, 1846, and crossed the plains by team for California with her parents in 1862. She was married to Chas J Russell in Virginia City, Nevada, February 5, 1865. Mr and Mrs Russell moved to San Luis Obispo in 1869, and thence to Santa Maria, which latter place has been their home for the last eight years. Mrs Russell leaves a widower and seven children, three brothers and two sisters…Children are Mrs F A Dorn (Cora) of San Luis Obispo, Mrs A J Barclay (Harriet) of Reno, Nevada, Morris A Russell of Tonka, Nevada, and Frank H, Hazel, Ailene, and Earl of Santa Maria.

-Santa Maria Times April 15, 1904

U S Census, Wayne County, Ohio, Baughman Township, 2 Sept 1850
```
26   26   Calvin Brewster        63    Farmer    born   CT
          Harriet                36              PA
          Nancy                  10              OH
          John C                  8              OH
          Laura                   6              OH
          Isabel McCom___?        4              OH
          Silas R              3/12              OH
          Abram Daily            11              OH
```

U S Census, San Luis Obispo county, California, Santa Rosa Township, PO Cambria, 15 June 1870
```
          Russell, Chas J   32   Dairyman   $750   $1000    Born VT
          Ida (Isabel) M    24                              OH
          Clara (Cora) B     2                              NV
```
Note: These are not the only wrong names on this census.

San Luis Obispo County Great Register of Voters
2116   Brewster, John Calvin, age 32, born Ohio, occupation photographer, P O San Luis Obispo. Registered Aug 18, 1873
3698   Brewster, Silas Ralf, 26, Ohio, saddle maker, Cambria. June 29, 1877

U S Census San Luis Obispo County, California, North Higuera St 9 June 1880
```
114  119  Russell, Charles J   42   lumber merchant   VT   VT   VT
          Isabella M               wife               OH?  PA
          Cora B          12       dau                NV
          Hattie           9       dau                CA
          Morris A         3       son                CA
          Brewster, Ralph S 29 brother-in-law, harness maker  OH?  PA
          Plus three servants and five employees who are saddlers and harness makers
```

History of San Luis Obispo Co., Patron, Thompson & West, 1883
C J Russell, saddlery, in San Luis Obispo born VT, came to CA 1861, came to SLO 1869

C J Russell, (Brewster & Russell), Monterey St San Luis Obispo, in *Coast County Directory*… McKinney, 1884-5. Santa Cruz, San Diego, Ventura, Monterey, San Benito, Santa Barbara, San Luis Obispo and Los Angeles Counties.

S R Brewster and Madera Redmond married 17 Dec 1884 by D S Gregory, San Luis Obispo
-Book B page 6 San Luis Obispo Marriages

U S Census Santa Barbara County CA 7th township (Santa Maria) 1900
102	105	Russell	Charles J		Nov 1837,	age 62, m, 35 yr,		VT NH VT	no occ
			Isabelle M	wife	Sep 1846	53 9 births, 7 living		OH RI PA	
			Morris	son	Oct 1876	23, single, at school			dry goods clerk
			Hazel	dau	Nov 1884	15, single, at school		CA	
			Ailene	dau	Jan 1887	13, single, at school		CA	
			Earle	son	Jun 1888	12, single, at school		CA	

Cambria Cemetery: Sadie, daughter of C J and I M Russell, born Nov 8, 1873; died Dec 29, 1874

JOHN CALVIN BREWSTER

The pioneer photographer of Ventura, J C Brewster was of the eighth generation of the descendents of Elder William Brewster, of Mayflower fame. He was born Dec 3, 1841 in Wayne county, Ohio; the family moved to Iowa when he was eight, and he taught school there and in Missouri before he was 21. He began to learn the art of photography in 1860 in Warsaw, Illinois. He made the five-month trip to California in 1862 with his family, and lived in Sacramento for a time, where his father erected the Russ House, a famous hotel of that early period. He taught school for a while as well as continuing his photographic art, operating a gallery there, as well as in other places in the west where he traveled: Virginia City, Carson City, Idaho and in Salt Lake City with his brother-in-law until 1871. Going back to California, he worked in Visalia, then San Francisco where his mother resided, then spent some time in San Luis Obispo until locating in Ventura in 1874. He was among the first to adopt the Dry-Plate method, and his gallery was "splendidly equipped, and (was) filled with samples of his work which reflect great credit upon his skill."

He was married in Ventura in 1875 to Mrs Mary Oberia Hadley Sinclair, widow of J S Sinclair. He built a "nice two-story residence on Santa Clara Street." His son, Calvin Day, died in infancy, and daughter, Pansy Augusta, born August 15, 1880, married Dana L Teague August 14, 1909 and lived in Santa Paula. Teagues' three children were Mary, born December 8, 1913; Sarah, born April 23, 1917; and Robert Dana, born June 23, 1919.

BREWSTER GENERATIONS:
8. John C, Isabella M, Silas 5, et als
7. Calvin, b 1787, Canterbury, Windham co CT
   m 1837 Harriet Cramer b 1813 Strausburg, Lancaster co, PA
6. Jedediah, m May 19, 1773, Prudence Robinson, Canterbury
   Children: Elizabeth, Silas, Anson, Florina, Sarah, Calvin, Jedediah.
   Prudence d Jan 1789; he m Asenath Hapgood, moved to Berne, Albany co, NY.
5. Peleg, b 1717
4. Jonathan, went to Windham co CT 1729
3. Wrestling

2. Love
1. Sir William Brewster

      J. C. Brewster was a school trustee, Prohibition Republican, Elder in the Presbyterian Church, Treasurer of the YMCA, Honorary Member of the WCTU, and Treasurer and Depositary of the American Bible Society at Ventura.

Sources
A Memorial and Biographical History of the Counties of Santa Barbara, San Luis Obispo, and Ventura, California, Illustrated, by Mrs Ida Addis Storke, 1891
History of Ventura County, by Sheridan, 1926

OTHER BREWSTERS OF SAN LUIS OBISPO COUNTY

William Garland Brewster, 25, born Kentucky, rancher, registered July 7, 1879
Residence Santa Margarita

Garland W. Brewster and Mary A. J. Moody were married 26 Aug. 1880 by H. W. Featherston, Estrella   -Book 1, Page 390, SLO Marriages

G W Brewster, Patron of Thompson and West's *SLO County History*: 1883 b Kentucky, residence Estrella Ranch, business is farming, came to California in 1877, to San Luis Obispo County in 1878. PO San Miguel.

Garland Wm Brewster registered to vote Aug 16, 1892. b. Kentucky, age 38, 5'4" tall, dark complexion, grey eyes, dark hair, no scars, farmer, residence, Precinct and Post Office: Estrella

Stephen Guy Brewster, age 55, b. Missouri, carpenter, registered to vote Aug 25, 1875, Cambria.

Historic Houses of San Luis Obispo County C W Brewster's, 18th and Vine, Paso Robles. Built 1890.

For Charles J Russell, see Russell chart.

THOMAS SANDS BROWN   THOMAS ARCHER BROWN
1825-1905   SANTA MARIA VALLEY PIONEERS   1839-1924

Two Irish-born Tom Browns: 1825-1905   1839-1924
both married Irish girls but recently arrived;
both had sons named Robert who avoided marriage until over 40
both named sons John Archer and these same-name boys were cousins!

       The explanation is that the Tom Browns were brothers-in-law, although which wife is the sister is not clear.

       The article on the Brown surname, in the SMVGS & L *Quarterly*, Vol. IX, #2, pp. 228-232, states that Brown was a common Scottish name; that Brown was one of the choices, along with Black and White, offered to the Irish when the British conquerors ordered them to give up their ethnic surnames; add to that the fact that many Scots settled in Northern Ireland in the 17th century so that immigrants whose origin geographically is Ireland are Scots, ethnically, the conclusion may be reached that the Tom Browns were Scots-Irish, corroborated by their Protestant affiliation.

       Thomas Sands Brown was the older; he was born in 1825 according to records at the end of his life, although census and voters registrations around 1880 suggest two years earlier. He came to the United States in 1847, found his way to California in 1852, and was naturalized in the District Court of San Francisco (or Alameda county, depending upon which voters registration is correct) in 1853. He married in 1864, Rachel Brown, not long off the boat. They had four children when they made the move to Santa Maria valley. Both Toms are listed as Patron of Thompson & West's *History of Santa Barbara & Ventura Counties*, 1883, but only Thomas Sands is credited with land ownership. His son Benjamin died on the ranch on which he had been born, described in 1944 as being near the corner of Point Sal and Betteravia roads, that portion of Point Sal Road now being designated, appropriately, Brown Rd. Thomas S and Rachel Brown were charter members of the Santa Maria Presbyterian Church, and were said to be dutiful members, though it was undoubtedly a sometimes difficult seven or eight miles into town.

       Four births took place on the ranch; the last birth was twins, one of whom, Thomas S jr, lived only six months. T S Brown is on the Guadalupe cemetery list; this may be the infant, who is also memorialized on the seven-foot Brown obelisk in the Santa Maria cemetery with his parents and single brother, Ben. The markers for William J, his wives and two of his daughters are nearby.

       William lived near La Graciosa after his marriage in 1891, dairying. La Graciosa Items, Nov 7, 1897, reported that T S Brown and family were now residents of Washington district, leaving, presumably, one or the other son on the Guadalupe ranch. News from Guadalupe, July 12, 1902, stated that T S Brown of La Graciosa, has come to town to see about the sale of a house and two lots near First Street to Peter Ferrari. Mr Brown died at his residence on Cypress Street, Santa Maria, in 1905, and his wife, though much younger, declined rapidly thereafter and died in 1907.

       Besides the death in 1905, there were three Brown weddings: the double wedding of William to Eunice Day of Lompoc, and Mary to Nathaniel Irvine made the front page of the *Santa Maria Times*. Irvine, a brother-in-law, was associated with Irvine, Stratton & Co., wholesale grocers, San Francisco, with his brother, Alexander, (husband of Sarah J Brown), later called Irvine Bros. The bridesmaids, the Misses Brown and Boyd, were "Two pretty cousins from San Francisco". Four days later John's wedding took place in San Luis Obispo at the home of the Henry Mallorys, cousins of the bride, Maud Bidamon.

       William's first wedding had taken place in Vacaville in 1891 where his prospective father-in-law, the Rev Dr Beard, former minister of the Presbyterian church in Santa Maria, and moved, so Will hied himself thence to take Alphoretta Beard to wife, and brought her back to this valley, where they lived in the La Graciosa-Washington school district, which is roughly the area of Oak Knolls. Alphoretta died of a lung hemorrhage on a shopping trip in Santa Maria; her obituary sketch, unlike many which are sentimental fluff, contains valuable facts: birthdate in Missouri; family's move to Nevada in 1881; arrival in Santa Maria in 1887. She was the second daughter of the Reverend Doctor, although her sister is not mentioned as a survivor. (Jeannie Beard died in Estrella (SLO co), according to the *Santa Maria Times* 01 Sep 1894).

After William's second marriage in 1905 he took the family north, living for several years in Marin county, where his older daughter died of Bright's Disease. They were back in Santa Maria by 1910, living in the Fairlawn district, which was "way out of town" west of the railroad track, now Depot Street. In 1930, when *Who's Who in Santa Maria*, was compiled, he was proprietor of a second-hand store at 114 West Cypress, and living across the street, although when he died he was at 526 South Broadway. His widow died at 517 East Main Street, address also of her daughter, Edna Cunningham. That house was demolished in the early 1970's to make room for a bank. Mrs Cunningham moved to 523 East Orange St. This property was later purchased from her estate by David and Barbara Cole for their newly-wed son, whose family is still in residence.

Robert's late marriage was to an Irish-born woman with grown children, and they lived on his ranch between Santa Maria and Orcutt. At the age of sixty he fell down a well after which his health deteriorated to the point of nervous breakdown two years later, in which state of mind he "placed the barrel of a 12-gauge shotgun in his mouth and pulled the trigger". His wife outlived him by five years.

John Archer was born in 1882 and died in 1963; his cousin, John Archer was born in 1875 and died in 1894, so there is no confusion about who is meant in later records. John also is listed in *Who's Who in Santa Maria*; though he was a rancher, he started married life as a grocery clerk, and later was sales manager for Rubel Buick Co. In February 1910 his family "moved into their elegant new home on Cypress St. which was recently completed by Contractor Frank Mallory. Mr Brown's fine residence is quite an addition to the town's pretty homes." Upon retiring he moved to San Jose, where he died.

Joseph Samuel, the surviving twin, was said to have ranched near Point Sal all of his life, although the 1910 census lists him in the Fairlawn tract, working for the Pacific Coast Lumber Co., near the PCR depot; later directories list him on the ranch. His wife, Rausa Chaffin Brown, like Alphoretta, was accorded a valuable obituary. Her family came to Santa Maria valley in 1898, a date reiterated in the obituaries of her parents, William J W Chaffin and Nancy Chaffin. Mr Chaffin, a rancher, "went out into the potato patch near the house, and putting the barrel of a .22 rifle in his mouth, blew out his brains". This was in 1919, 11 years before Robert Brown's suicide. Mrs Chaffin died at 619 West Cook St in 1937.

Sarah and Mary, wives of the Irvine brothers, lived out their lives in the Bay area, although frequent visitors to their girlhood home. Annie and her husband, W J Phelps, started their marital housekeeping "on the Dutard ranch 4 miles south of Santa Maria" in 1895; this is roughly what is now the Tanglewood tract. Their son and heir was born in the Lakeview district, which may be described as east of Tanglewood; in 1906 their post office address was Casmalia, which is farther from the Tanglewood area than the center of Santa Maria is, so it may be assumed that they moved. Their later location was Isleton, on the Sacramento Delta.

Thomas Sands Brown's line was carried on by at least a dozen grandchildren; Thomas Archer had none at all.

THOMAS ARCHER BROWN

Thomas Archer Brown   b. Ireland 21 June 1839; imm. 1863; to CA 1863 to
                             Santa Barbara co 1873
                             d. nr Garey 24 Feb 1924 age 84 years; SM cem

	m. (Alameda) CA 23 Aug 1867	
Elizabeth Brown		b. Ireland 23 Oct 1839; imm 1867
		d. nr Garey 18 Aug 1925 age 85 yrs; SM cem

6 births, 3 living, 8th township (Santa Barbara) CA 1900

1. Robert James — b. (Alameda) CA 09 Jul 1868
   d. nr Garey 10 Mar 1910 age 41/8/1; SM cem

   m. aft 1900
   Ella Bell — b. Ireland Jun 1867/70; imm 1892/3; to SB co 1897
   d. Santa Maria 21 Feb 1935 age 63; SM cem

   No Issue

2. — b. & d. bef 1880?

3. Mary Elizabeth — b. Guadalupe Ranch 12 Jun 1873
   single — d. nr Garey 12 May 1894 age 20/11/01; SM cem

4. John Archer Brown — b. Guadalupe Ranch 25 Jun 1875
   single — d. nr Garey 12 Oct 1894 age 19/03/17; SM cem

5. Leslie Brown — b. Guadalupe Ranch 6 Jul 1877
   single — d. Santa Maria 29 Aug 1951 age 74; SM cem

6. Gordon Agnew Brown — b. Guadalupe Ranch 6 Aug 1877
   single — d. nr Garey 17 May 1934 age 51 yrs; SM cem

This family was enumerated on the 1880 census not far from the T S Brown family; they moved to Bradley Canyon before 1900. That census shows Ellen Bell, niece, in the household; apparently it is she who married Robert. At the time, Leslie was enumerated with his cousin, William on the west side of the valley.

The T A Browns celebrated their fiftieth wedding anniversary at a party in the home of their nephew, Joseph Brown, in 1917. The *Santa Maria Times* reported these guests; Leslie and Gordon Brown, Mrs Ella Brown, Benjamin Brown, Mr & Mrs Robt Brown, Mr & Mrs Wm J Brown with daus Elsie Brown, Edna & Alice Day.

Ref: The Thomas A Brown Bible Rec printed SMVGS&L *Quarterly,* Vol XI #1

SCRAPBOOK OF THOMAS ARCHER BROWN

1910   Robert J Brown Died Suddenly Of Heart Failure   Died at his home near Garey on Thursday, Robert James Brown, aged 41 years, 8 months and 1 day.

His death was due to heart failure and the news of his demise came as a shock to his many friends in this community. He was the eldest son of Mr and Mrs T A Brown and besides his parents he leaves a wife and two brothers to mourn his sudden death.

The deceased was a native of California and was a member of the Santa Maria Lodge No 90, Knights of Pythias, which order will conduct the burial service.

The funeral services will be held at the Presbyterian church in this city at two o'clock this afternoon and the remains will be laid to rest in the Santa Maria cemetery.

Santa Maria Lodge No 90, Knights of Pythias, will attend the funeral of their Brother Knight in a body and all members of the lodge are requested to meet at Castle Hall at 1:30 sharp

–*Santa Maria Times* Mar 12 p.1

T A Brown left for Los Angeles and other southern parts Monday and will be gone several days.   –*Santa Maria Times* Apr 10

Notice To Presbyterians

There will be a meeting of the members of the Presbyterian church next Friday evening at 7:30 for the purpose of calling a pastor if the way be clear, to transact other related business.

Vol. XXII, No. 1-4, 1990, pp.13, 14

It is earnestly hoped that every member of the congregation may be present.

By order of the Session   W H Rice   L W Young   T A Brown

1917   A Nice Party   Mr and Mrs T A Brown of Garey were given a dinner party at the home of Mr and Mrs Joseph Brown, Thursday evening, August 23 in honor of their fiftieth anniversary.

The house was tastefully and appropriately decorated yellow and gold being the prevailing tones.

The guests present were: Mr and Mrs Robert Brown, Mr and Mrs W J Brown, Mrs Ella Brown, the Misses Elsie Brown, Edna and Alice Day, and the Messrs Leslie and Gordon Brown, also Benj F Brown.   –Ibid Sat Sep 1 p.1

1919   Mr and Mrs T A Brown and son Leslie leave tomorrow for a week's visit in Los Angeles
–*Santa Maria Times* Nov 13

1924   Death Calls Pioneer Citizen Of S M Valley   Thomas Archer Brown, 84, a native of Ireland and resident of the Santa Maria valley for the past 51 years, passed away this morning at his home near Garey.

Mr Brown came to California 61 years ago. He lived at Alameda for a time before moving to this community. He was well known throughout this section. In 1867 he was married to Miss Eliza Brown.

The following relatives survive: the widow and two sons, Leslie and Gordon

Funeral services will be held Wednesday afternoon at 2 o'clock at the Albert A Dudley funeral home with the Rev W F Nelson in charge. Interment will be in the Santa Maria cemetery.
–*SM Daily Times* Mon Feb 25 p.1

1925   Death Calls Pioneer Citizen Of S M Valley   Mrs Eliza Brown, 85, a native of Ireland and a pioneer resident of California, passed away at her home near Garey Monday following a brief illness. Mrs Brown came to this state 60 years ago and had been a resident of the Santa Maria Valley for the past 27 (probably 52) years, where she was well known. Two sons, Leslie and Gordon Brown, both residents of the Garey community survive.

Funeral services will be held Thursday afternoon at 2 o'clock at the Albert A Dudley Funeral Home. The Rev Irving T Raab, pastor of the Presbyterian church of Santa Maria, will conduct the services. Interment will be in the Santa Maria cemetery.   –Ibid Aug 19 p.1

1934   Obituary Of Gordon Agnew Brown   Gordon Agnew Brown, 51, passed away at his ranch near Garey yesterday morning, May 17, 1934. The deceased was a native of Santa Maria Valley. He was born at Guadalupe, August 6, 1882, and lived in this valley during his entire lifetime. He has been a member of Lodge No 90, Knights of Pythias for over 30 years, and also a member of the Pioneers' Association.

Surviving relatives are one brother, Leslie Brown and several cousins.

Funeral services will be held at the Dudley Mortuary chapel Monday morning, May 21, 1934 at 10 o'clock with Rev S J Kennedy officiating. Lodge No 90, Knights of Pythias service will be conducted at the graveside.

Pallbearers will be C C Thompson, E W Boyd, J S Calderon, George McKinnon, A F Black and Arthur Haslam. (Dudley Mortuary Service)   -Ibid Fri May 18 p.6

1935   Obituary Of Mrs Ella Brown   Mrs Ella Brown, aged 63 passed away in a local hospital this morning after a period of failing health the past two years. She was a native of Ireland, having come to the United States 43 years ago. After living several years in Chicago, she moved to
Santa Maria Valley 38 years ago. She was the widow of the late Robert James Brown. Surviving relatives are in Ireland, except a brother-in-law, Leslie Brown of Garey.

Funeral services will be conducted Saturday afternoon at 2 o'clock in the chapel of Dudley Mortuary, Rev S J Kennedy officiating. Interment will be in the Santa Maria cemetery. (Dudley Mortuary Service) –Ibid Thu Feb 21 p.2

1942 Paragraphs of the Past. 25 years ago. Mr and Mrs Thomas A Brown of Garey were honored at a dinner party in the home of Mr and Mrs Joseph Brown. The T A Browns celebrated their 50th wedding anniversary. –Ibid Sep 4

1951 Funeral Services Tomorrow For 74 Year Old Native   Garey, Aug 30. Leslie Brown, 74-year-old retired farmer of this community, died yesterday in a Santa Maria hospital after a long illness. He was born July 6, 1887, near Betteravia and had lived in and near Garey most of his life.

Funeral services will be conducted at 2 PM in the chapel of the First Presbyterian church and members of the Knights of Pythias conducting the services. Interment will be in the Santa Maria cemetery.

Mr Brown was the son of the valley pioneer, Thomas A Brown, who came to this area from Ireland during Santa Maria's earliest days. He had been a member of the Knights of Pythias, Santa Maria Lodge No 90, for 48 years.

Survivors include four cousins: Joe S Brown of Betteravia, John Brown of San Jose, Mrs N Irvine of Lafayette and Mrs W F Phelps of Isleton. –Santa Maria Times Aug 30

(*Ed note*: Photo of Leslie Brown in *San Ramon Chapel Pioneers* by Ontiveros pg 339.)

THOMAS SANDS BROWN

Thomas Sands Brown
    b. Ireland Nov 1825; imm. 1847; to CA 1850
       naturalized SF or Alameda Dist Ct 1853
       to SB co 1873; 300 a Guadalupe Rancho
    d. Santa Maria 30 Apr 1905 age 79/5/18; SM cem

  m. Alameda co, CA 1864
Rachel Brown
    b. Ireland July 1844; imm
    d. Santa Maria 13 May 1907 age 62/10/09 SM cem

  9 births, 8 living Santa Maria Twp 1900
1. William James
    b. Alameda co 20 Sep 1865
    d. Santa Maria 30 Sep 1950 age 85; SM cem
    m.1) Vacaville, CA 10 Jun 1891/bride's fa, Rev J D Beard
       at his home assisted/Rev Donald Ross; to live near Santa Maria (*Santa Maria Times*)
  Alphoretta Beard
    b. MO 9 Aug 1871 (census/obit) or 16 Aug (tombstone)
    d. Santa Maria 3 Mar 1902 age 30/6/22; SM cem
    a. Gertrude S
       b. nr La Graciosa 24 Mar 1893 (SM Times)
       d. Marshall (Marin co) 4 Oct 1908
         age 15/6/14; SM cem
    b. Elsie Rachel
       b. Washington Dist (5 mi s SM) 15 Mar 1896
       d. Lompoc 22 Oct 1976; Evergreen cem
       m. Arthur Hapgood
         b. Clay Center KS 4 Oct 1882
         d. Lompoc 5 Mar 1974; Evergreen cem
       = James
       = Robert
    m.2) at home of Mrs T S Brown 10 Oct 1905/Rev W H Chapman double wedding
       with sister Mary.

       Eunice May (Brown) Day   b. Clay Center, KS 5 Jan 1880
                                             d. Santa Maria 26 Nov 1963 age 83
                                             F: b. Wales
                                           M: b. IA
                                           Her children: Edna L (Day) Cunningham 1898-1977
                                                  Alice Georgia (Day) Toy 1903 (see Toy chart)
      c.   Catherine Lucille   b. Santa Maria 2 Dec 1910
                                           d. Santa Maria 12 Feb 1944 age 44; SM cem
            m. Kenneth E France   b. 23 Jun 1906
                                           d. 29 Apr 1957; SM cem
    = Gary
    = Kenneth
    = Edwin
2.   Sarah Jane   b. Alameda co 6 Oct 1866; m. age 22
                                           d. Berkeley CA 3 Sep 1942 age 75; SM cem
      m. at bride's home in Guadalupe, 22 May 1889/Rev J D Beard
         to live in San Francisco (*Santa Maria Times*)
      Alexander Irvine   b. Ireland Nov 1857; m. age 31 of SF
                                         d. bef 1940
      (Children of Sarah Jane)
      a.   Violet Maybelle   b. San Francisco 1902 (census)
      b.   Dorothy A (Pettit)   b. San Francisco 1905 (census)
        = Kenneth
3.   Robert Henry   b. Alameda co, CA Dec 1867
                                         d. suicide on ranch, Coast Hywy n of Orcutt 13 Jul 1930
                                             SM cem
      m. San Luis Obispo 18 Jan 1909/Rev H H Hillard, H344;
        wit: Belle Williamson, (SLO); Sadie Robinson, SLO
      Joanna (Hutchison) Elliott   b. Ireland c1866
                                            d. Santa Maria 25 Apr 1935 age 80; SM cem
                                            Her ch: William H Reid
      No Issue   Marian (Robt Gray)
4.   Annie Elizabeth   b. Alameda co Jun 1869
                                       d. Santa Maria 28 Apr 1959 age 89; Lodi cem
      m. age 26 Santa Maria 13 Feb 1895/Joseph Hemphill
        wit: Robt Brown; Minnie Smith.
      William Joshua Phelps   b. IL Aug 1867; m. age 26
                                         d. SB co 24 May 1957
      a.   William Joshua, jr   b. Lake View 9 Jan 1896 (*Santa Maria Times*)
      b.   Ellen A   b. Mar 1897 (census)
      c.   Margaret   b. 11 Jun 1905 (*Santa Maria Times*)
5.   Benjamin Franklin   b. Guadalupe Ranch 28 Aug 1876
      Single   d. Guadalupe Ranch 10 Nov 1944 age 68; SM cem
6.   Mary Ellen   b. Guadalupe Ranch Aug 1880
                                       d. San Leandro, CA 27 Sep 1952 age 72
      m. at home of Mrs T S Brown 10 Oct 1905 (double ceremony/bro)
      Nathaniel Irvine   b. Ireland 1863
                                         d. Alameda co, CA 14 Aug 1959
      a.   Helen (Carlson)   b. Oakland, CA 1907 (census)
      b.   Doris (Parshall)   b. Oakland, CA 1909 ?
      c.   Frances (Reynolds)   b. after 1910

	d. Bernice (Muncy)	b. after 1910
7.	John Archer	b. Guadalupe Ranch 12/17 May 1882
		d. San Jose, CA 21 May 1961 age 81
		Madronia Cem, Saratoga, CA

m. at res of Mr/Mrs Henry Mallory, San Luis Obispo 14 Oct 1905/Rev Harry Hillard, G213
    wit: Robt H Brown, Santa Maria; Birdie Anderson, San Luis Obispo

Maude Ellis Bidamon	b. San Luis Obispo, CA 1883
	d. (Alameda co 11 May 1964)
	F: Benjamin Franklin Bidamon (1857-1942)
	M: Almira A Froom (1874-1893)
a. Charles Thomas	b. Santa Maria 29 Sep 1906
	d. Saratoga, CA
8. Thomas Sands, jr	b. Guadalupe Ranch 1 Nov 1884
(Twin)	d. Guadalupe Ranch? 4 May 1885 age 6 mo. 3 days; SM cem
9. Joseph Samuel	b. Guadalupe Ranch 1 Nov 1884
	d. Santa Maria 31 Mar 1963 age 78; SM cem

m. age 22 SLO 3 Apr 1907/Rev Harry Hillard G480
    wit: Geo Chaffin, SM; Ellen (Humphreys) Hillard, SLO

Rausa Chaffin	b. Lyra, Scoito co OH 14 Jul 1887; m. age 19
	d. Santa Maria 15 Oct 1945; SM cem
	F: Wm John Worth Chaffin (1846-1919)
	M: Nancy (1855-1937)

a. Viola K (Barnold Kinseth)
b. Gertrude (Carl Long) (___Weaver)
c. Muriel (Norris Bramlett)

THOMAS SANDS BROWN SCRAPBOOK

1892   T S Brown left for a visit in Oakland, where he had resided 20 years before.
    -Paragraphs of the Past, *Santa Maria Times*, Tue Sep 8 1942

1893   MARRIED: Martha Brown, niece of Mrs T S Brown of Santa Maria, Sep __1893 at the residence of bride's cousin, Mrs A Irvine, in San Francisco, to P A Leggett, by Rev Mr Duncan.
    –*Santa Maria Times*, Oct 21

1895   T. S. Brown brought in a crop of bronze turkeys to the depot for shipment on Wednesday morning. Ibid Jan 12
    A S J Phelps, former townsman, in real estate business in Los Angeles…   -Jan 26
    Robert Brown, son of T S Brown has returned home from a few weeks' to relatives in Frisco. Robert said that he was glad to get back to Santa Maria Valley and would not agree to make Frisco his home for all the city.   –Feb 2

Guadalupe Items:
    The vacant houses have all been taken and there is a demand for more. H H Johnson and T S Brown will erect several buildings in order to supply the present demand.   –Feb 9
    T S Brown came in a few days ago to inquire about a good cook. Any good cook out of employment will find it to her advantage to see him.   –Feb 9
    W H Phelps and bride have gone to housekeeping at their home on the Dutard* ranch 4 miles south of Santa Maria. Mr Phelps was *Santa Maria Times* caller Tuesday.   –Feb 23

A pleasant dinner party was given at the home of Mr and Mrs T A Brown on Thursday in honor of W J Phelps and bride. There were quite a number of relatives and friends present on that occasion and all report an enjoyable pastime and lots of good things to eat. –Feb 23
1897   La Graciosa Items: T S Brown and family are now residents of Washington district.
–Nov 6

Ed. Note: * Dutard Ranch – Warning notice of Executors of Estate of H Dutard. All persons forbidden to hunt, camp or trespass in any manner upon either the Jesus Maria or Casmalia Ranches. Any person or persons violating this warning will be prosecuted to the fullest extent of the law. P A Kise, Manager.   –*Santa Maria Times* Fri March 15 1903 p.3
1890   H Dutard, owner of the Jesus Maria ranch, was in town looking over other ranch properties with the idea of buying it if he finds the price and place to his liking.
–*Santa Maria Times*, Apr 22, 1940 "50 Years Ago"

1901   Married: At residence of brother W J Phelps, Sunday April 7, 1901. Henry L Nelson, Bakersfield, and Miss Ellen Phelps, in Santa Maria by M S Whiteside.   –*Santa Maria Times* Apr 13

1902   Death of Mrs Wm Brown   On Monday afternoon last, a gloom of sorrow was cast over our community when the sad news of the death of Mrs William J Brown was announced. Mrs Brown came to town in the morning and apparently enjoying her usual health, but was overcome by a hemorrhage of the lungs and expired at a few minutes past 12 o'clock.

The subject of this sketch was the second daughter of Rev Dr Beard, and was born in Missouri August 9, 1871. In 1881 the family moved to Nevada, and the following year came to Vacaville, this State, where they resided for five years. In 1887 the family moved to Santa Maria. One June 10, 1891 she was married to William J Brown, one of our highly respected young men. She was united with the Presbyterian Church when quite young, and had ever led a Christian life, was a dutiful and affectionate daughter, a true wife and a loving mother. Her untimely demise is mourned by a lonely father and mother, a kind husband and two daughters. A large circle of friends sympathize with the bereaved relatives in this dark hour of their misfortune…

Mrs Brown was aged 30 years, 6 months and 22 days. The funeral took place from the Presbyterian church on Wednesday at 11 o'clock, the service being conducted by Rev W S Whiteside and remains being laid to rest in the Santa Maria Cemetery.

Card of Thanks . . . Wm J Brown   *Santa Maria Times* March 8

Guadalupe   T S Brown of La Graciosa was in town on Business Wednesday. It is reported that he has sold his property consisting of a house and two lots, near First St., to Peter Ferrari.
-Ibid July 12   *Ed. Note*: Peter Ferrari married Miss Masdonati Orsolina of San Luis Obispo 3 Feb 1905, to live at Guadalupe.

1904   Notice to Builders   Bids will be received up to Friday April 29 for the construction of a residence Building. Plans and specifications can be seen at my house. T S Brown   –April 15

1905   T S Brown Passes Away   Thomas S Brown, one of the Valleys prominent and early settlers, breathed his last Sunday April 30th, after an illness of several months.

Mr Brown was 79 years, 5 months and 18 days of age, and the father of a large and fine family. He was a substantial member of the Presbyterian Church, and with his passing away it may be truly said that the community lost a true and noble man.

The funeral took place Tuesday from the family residence and was largely attended. A devoted wife, 5 sons and 3 daughters survive him.

Card of Thanks   We hereby extend our heartfelt thanks to the many kind friends who rendered us assistance during illness and burial of our late beloved husband and father. Mrs T S Brown and Family
–Ibid Sat May 6

1905   Marriage Of Popular Couple   At the residence of Mr and Mrs Henry Mallory in San Luis Obispo the marriage of Miss Maud Bidamon of that city and Mr John A Brown of Santa Maria was solemnized, only relatives and intimate friends being in attendance. Miss Bidamon was a former resident of Santa Maria and returning as the bride of a well-known and prominent young man she becomes the recipient of many hearty congratulations, which naturally are shared by her good-natured but rather timid husband.
–*Santa Maria Times* Oct 21

1905   Pretty Home Wedding   At high noon last Wednesday, at the home of Mrs T S Brown, Mr W J Brown was married to Mrs Eunice Day and Mr Nathaniel Irvine at the same time wedded Miss Mary Brown. Preceded by Messrs Robert and John Brown with Misses Boyd and Brown and groomsmen and bridesmaids, these young people formed a semi-circle under artistic floral decorations. Mrs Chapman played Mendelsohn's wedding march and Rev Mr Chapman used the beautiful and impressive Presbyterian marriage service. Only the immediate relatives were present.

After partaking of a splendid wedding feast the happy couples left in a shower of rice and well wishes for Santa Barbara, Los Angeles, and other points in southern California. They will stop at Santa Maria as they return to their homes near Berkeley.

The bridesmaids were two pretty cousins from San Francisco.

Mr Will Brown is well known to the people of Santa Maria Valley as a man of sterling qualities, and we have reason to believe that he has won in Mrs Day, of Lompoc, a woman worthy of the high compliment he has paid her.

Mr Irvine, a member of the large and popular wholesale grocery firm of Irvine…Stanton & Co…of San Francisco, has chosen for his wife Miss Mary Brown, who was born and brought up in this valley. She is universally admired for her quiet and modest disposition and for her earnest Christian charity.

May the Heavenly Fathers' richest blessing rest upon them in their new and happy relations.
–Ibid Oct. 14, p.1

1907   OLD SETTLER PASSES   Mrs Rachel Brown, Among Earliest Arrivals in This Valley, Passes Away after Lengthy Illness.   After an illness of almost two years, Mrs Rachel Brown passed peacefully away on Monday last surrounded by her loved ones. Mrs Brown was 61 years, 10 months and 9 days of age and had been a resident here since the first settlers arrived.

The deceased was the mother of a large and fine family, most of whom are now married and have families of their own. Adhering to the faith of her fathers, she united with the Presbyterian church in early life and loved to attend its services when health permitted. She was one of the charter members of the Presbyterian church here and as such was ever faithful in her devotion.

Her illness dates back to the death of her husband two years ago, since then she has been gradually getting worse. About two weeks ago it became evident that the end was nearing and she calmly resigned herself to await the Divine Call.

Services were held at the family residence on Thursday by Rev Chapman in the presence of the entire family and a large concourse of sorrowing friends. Many beautiful floral pieces were in evidence as she was tenderly laid by the side of her devoted husband in our Silent City.

The members of the family remaining are Wm J of Marin County; Robt H, Benj F, Joseph, John A, Mrs W J Phelps, Mrs Sarah Irvine and Mrs May Irvine, the latter residing in Berkeley.
–Ibid May 18 p.1

1908   Santa Maria (Special to The *Telegram*)   Santa Maria Sep 27.—W H Rice, who recently sold one of his large ranches to an oil company for a very comfortable fortune, has purchased the fine residence on Cypress street erected by the late T S Brown. It is a large one-story, modern structure, and is admirably adapted to the wants of Mr Rice's family.
–*Slo Daily Telegram* Tue Sep 29 p.3

Ed. Note: A photo and biography of William H Rice, 401 W Cypress, can be seen in the 1909 Santa Maria Directory. In 1908 he "purchased the fine Brown residence on Cypress and Thornburg Streets, where they now live." "Mr Rice is a man of large affairs, probably having heavier property, holdings than any other in the valley; among these are the home property, the Dutard ranch, large tracts on the Suey and in Pleasant valley and the Rice Ranch; he disposed of his ranch in Cat Canyon to the Old Mission Oil Company—the purchase price representing a snug little fortune." ...currently President of the Savings Bank. pp.167-8

1908   Notice   In the Matter of the Creating of a Reclamation District in the County of Santa Barbara, State of California. To the Honorable the Board of Supervisors of the County of Santa Barbara . . . The undersigned, your petitioners respectfully show:

I

That your petitioners propose to form a district for the reclamation of lands subject to flood and overflow and which are susceptible of reclamation, your petitioners desiring to reclaim the same, the following being a description of the lands composing and embraced within said proposed reclamation district, to wit: {among others}

      Brown, Robt H   Brown, John A
      Brown, Benj F   Irvine, May Brown
      Brown, Wm Jas   Irvine, Sarah J
      Brown, Joseph S   Phelps, Annie F

These heirs of T S Brown had, each, 1/8 interest in some part of the Guadalupe Rancho, plus other designated land.   -*Santa Maria Times* April 24

1910   Personals.   L L Peugh and family have moved into the residence recently vacated by John Brown. This brings Mr Peugh much closer to his office.
    John Brown and family have moved into their elegant new home on Cypress street which was recently completed by contractor Frank Mallory. Mr Browns' fine residence is quite an addition to the towns' pretty homes.   –*Santa Maria Times* Feb 26
Ed Note: Peugh was manager of the Home Telephone Co.

(1910) Born: A daughter to the wife of Wm Brown. (25 years Ago in Santa Maria valley.
-*Santa Maria Times* Tue Dec 10, 1935)

1919   Lt and Mrs W W Hedges, of New York are here with Mrs Hedges' sister Mrs Sam Gray. Lt Hedges is on a months' leave from his ship the USS Plattsburg. They came down from Shandon Monday where they were the guests of Mr and Mrs Robert Gray. The latter returned with them to spend Welcome Home Day in Santa Maria.   –*Santa Maria Times* Tue Nov 11 p.3

Local briefs: Mr and Mrs Robert Gray of Shandon, returned home today after several day's visit with relatives in Santa Maria. Lt and Mrs Hedges, of New York, who have been visiting Mrs Samuel Gray, a sister of Mrs Hedges, leave today for San Francisco accompanied by Mrs Robert Brown.
–*Santa Maria Times* Nov 14

1924   Local News.   Mrs Carl Toy is visiting her mother in this city for a few days. Mr and Mrs Toy formerly lived near Orcutt, but are now making their home in Ventura.   –Jan 4 p.5

1924   Local News.   Arrivals from San Pedro Monday for a couple of Days' visit with Mr and Mrs Sam Gray and Mr and Mrs Rbt H Brown are Lt and Mrs W W Hedges. Mrs Hedges is a niece of Mrs Brown.
   Mr and Mrs Robert Gray left Monday for their ranch near Shandon, after spending the weekend with relatives. Mrs Gray came down to see her brother, Dr W H Reid of Chicago, who has been visiting his mother, Mrs R H Brown.
   Dr Wm H Reid and Mortimer Flynn of Chicago departed Sunday for Los Angeles and San Diego, after a weekend visit with the formers mother, Mrs Rbt H Brown, on the highway near Orcutt. Having left Chicago in a blizzard last week, they are enchanted with California climate and plan to purchase a home in the southern part of the state.   –Mon Feb 11

1925   Mrs Carl Toy of Taft is a visitor at the home of her mother, Mrs W J Brown, of this city. Mrs Toy plans to be here for the week.   –April 1

1930   Valley Farmer Kills Himself   Robert H Brown Takes Own Life Sunday Afternoon
   Suffering from a severe nervous breakdown, Robert Henry Brown, 62-year-old valley rancher, committed suicide at his home on the Coast highway north of Orcutt yesterday afternoon. Brown placed the barrel of a 12-gauge shotgun in his mouth and pulled the trigger.
   The rancher was discovered by his wife, Joanna Brown, a stepdaughter, Mrs Robert Gray, who were in an adjoining room at the time of the tragedy.
   According to the widow, Brown has not been well for several years. His decline in health was rapid following a fall into a well on his ranch some time ago.   –Ibid July 14 p.1

Ed. Note: Biography of Robert H Brown, p. 2242, *A History of California under Extended History of Its Southern Coast Counties*, Gwinn, 1907

1930   Obituary   Robert Henry Brown
   Robert Henry Brown, 62, native of Alameda County, died yesterday afternoon, July 13, at his home on the Orcutt road.
   He had made his home in Santa Maria valley since 1873.
   Surviving relatives are, the widow, Mrs Joanna Brown, step-daughter, Mrs Marian Gray of Shandon; a step-son, William H Reid of Chicago, and the following sisters and brothers: Mrs Sarah Irvine of Berkeley; Mrs Mary Irvine of Berkeley; Mrs Annie Phelps of Isleton; Wm J, John A, Benjamin F, and Joseph S Brown, all of Santa Maria.
   The body is at the Dudley-Bradford Funeral home, and interment will be in the Santa Maria cemetery. No definite announcement as to the time of funeral has yet been made.   –Ibid p.5
   O b i t u a r y   Funeral services for Robert Henry Brown, who passed away at his ranch near Orcutt Sunday, will be held Wednesday afternoon at 2:30 o'clock at the Dudley and Bradford Funeral Chapel.
   Services will be conducted by the Christian Scientists, Stanley Breneiser in charge.
   Interment will be in the IOOF cemetery.   –Ibid Jul 15 p.3

1935   Obituaries   Joanna Hutchison Brown   Funeral services for Mrs Joanna Hutchison Brown, 80, who passed away Thursday, April 25, 1935, will be conducted in the chapel of the Dudley mortuary at 2 pm Sunday afternoon, April 28, 1935, by Stanley G Breneiser, Christian Science reader. Interment will be in Santa Maria cemetery.

The deceased, a widow of the late Robert H Brown, was a native of Ireland and had lived in this valley for 29 years. She is survived by a son and a daughter, William H Reid of Chicago, and Mrs Marian Gray of Shandon, Calif, a nephew, Alex Fee, Oakland, and a niece, Mrs W W Hedges of San Pedro. She was a member of the Christian Science church for the past 24 years.

–Ibid Thu Apr 25 p.4

1942   Pioneer Valley Woman With Four Brothers Living in Santa Maria Passes at 75

The four brothers of Mrs Sarah J Irvine, 75, former pioneer resident of the valley, received word today of her death yesterday in Berkeley. The brothers, John A Brown, William J Brown, Benjamin F Brown and Joseph S Brown, will attend funeral services tomorrow afternoon in the northern city.

The late Mrs Irvine came to the Santa Maria Valley with her parents, Mr and Mrs P S Brown, in the seventies, from Alameda county, where she was born Oct 8, 1866. Her marriage to the late Alexander Irvine, of the grocery firm of Irvine Bros., San Francisco, took place on May 22, 1889, and although she lived the remainder of her life in the bay area, Mrs Irvine was a frequent visitor to Santa Maria.

In addition to the brothers in Santa Maria, (the) deceased is survived by two daughters, Violet Maybelle Irvine and Mrs Dorothy Pettit, and a grandson, Kenneth Pettit, all of Berkeley. A sister, Mrs N Irvine, also lives in Berkeley, and another sister, Mrs W J Phelps, is a resident of Isleton.   –Ibid Fri Sep 4 p.1

1944   Dies On Ranch Where Born   B F Brown Lived Same Place 68 Years

Benjamin Franklin Brown died Friday at noon on his ranch near the junction of the Point Sal and Betteravia roads within 200 feet of where he was born 68 years ago, on August 28, 1876. Cause of death was a heart attack.

Brown was the son of Mr and Mrs Thomas S Brown, pioneers, who bought the property in 1872, and where he had lived since birth. He never married.

Brothers surviving are John A, Joseph S and William J all of Santa Maria. Two sisters surviving are Mrs N Irvine, Berkeley, and Mrs W J Phelps, Isleton. There are also several nieces and nephews.

Brown was a member of long standing of the Knights of Pythias, who will participate in rites in Santa Maria Cemetery, following services tomorrow at 2 pm in the chapel of Dudley Mortuary by the Rev Banes Anderson.   -Ibid Mon Nov 13 p.1
(See Biog. in *History of Santa Barbara County*, Phillips, 1927, p.348)

1945   Mrs Rausa Brown Dies After Illness   Mrs Rausa Brown died last evening in the family home on Point Sal Road, seven miles west of Santa Maria, after a four month illness. Born July 14, 1887, in Lyra, Ohio, she came to Santa Maria Valley in 1898, with her parents, William J and Nancy Chaffin, and had lived here ever since.

Mrs Brown was the wife of Joseph S Brown; mother of Mrs Barnold Kinseth, Ventura; Mrs Carl Long, Santa Maria; Mrs Norris Bramlett, Los Angeles; and the sister of Gladys Davis of Bakersfield; Shad Chaffin, Visalia; Thomas and George Chaffin of Orcutt; Willard Chaffin, San Jose; Merritt Chaffin of Taft, and Horace Chaffin of Santa Maria.

There are also five surviving grandchildren.

Funeral services will be held on 11 o'clock Thursday morning in the chapel of Dudley Mortuary, with interment in Santa Maria Cemetery. The Rev Frank Prewitt will officiate.

–Ibid Tue Oct 16 p.6

1950   Death Takes Valley Pioneer   Funeral services for William James Brown, 85, will be held at 2 pm Wednesday in the chapel of Dudley Mortuary. The Rev Phil W Barrett will officiate. Interment will follow in Santa Maria cemetery.

Deceased died Saturday afternoon at his home 526 south Broadway, after a long illness. Born September 20, 1865, in Alameda county, he had just celebrated his 85th birthday anniversary two weeks ago.

Brown came to Santa Maria in 1873. A merchant and prominent member of the Presbyterian church since 1887, Brown retired 8 years ago.

Deceased was the husband of Mrs Eunice Brown, Santa Maria, and the father of Mrs F E France and Mrs Edna Cunningham, Santa Maria; Mrs A R Hapgood, Lompoc, and Mrs C S Toy, Coalinga.

He was the grandfather of James and Robert Hapgood, Gary and Kenneth France, William Toy and Mrs Wm Jackson, and the great grandfather of Peggy and Bobby Hapgood.

He was the brother of Joseph S Brown, Santa Maria; John A Brown, San Jose; Mrs W J Phelps, Isleton, and Mrs N Irvine, Lafayette. —Mon Oct 2, p.1

1952   Mrs Mary Irvine, S.M. Native, Services Held   San Leandro—Funeral services were held at 3 pm today for Mrs Mary Ellen Irvine, 72, a native of Santa Maria. She died Saturday.

The services were conducted at Mountain View Mausoleum in Oakland, Estudillo Chapel of San Leandro was in charge of arrangements.

Mrs Irvine is survived by her husband, Nathaniel Irvine; four daughters, Mrs Helen Carlson of Lafayette, Mrs Doris Parshall of San Francisco, Mrs Frances Reynolds of Hayward and Mrs Bernice Muncy of Santa Barbara; two brothers, Joseph Brown of Santa Maria and John Brown of San Jose; a sister, Mrs Annie Phelps of Isleton, and ten grandchildren.

—Ibid Tue Sep 30 p.8

1955   Obituaries   Catherine L France   Mrs Catherine Lucile France, 44, a native of Santa Maria who was born here Dec. 2, 1910, died Saturday in a local hospital after a brief illness.

She is survived by her husband, Kenneth France of Santa Maria; sons: Gary, Edwin and Kenneth, Santa Maria; her mother, Mrs W J Brown, Santa Maria; sisters: Mrs Edna Cunningham, Santa Maria, Mrs Carl S Toy, Bakersfield, and Mrs Elsie R Hapgood, Lompoc.

Services will be in the Latter Day Saints church, Miller at Cook, at 1 pm, Wednesday, with Bishop David R Bickmore officiating; interment, Santa Maria cemetery. The Magner Funeral Home is in charge of arrangements. —Ibid Feb 14 p.8

1956   Obituaries   Charles Brown   Charles Thomas Brown, 50, died last night at his home in Saratoga, Calif.

Born in Santa Maria, Sept. 1906, he was a graduate of the Santa Maria schools. He was the son of Mr and Mrs John A Brown and grandson of valley pioneer, T A* Brown. He leaves his widow, Mary Jane Brown; son, Thomas; daughter Charlane, of Saratoga.   –*SM Times* Tue Mar 6 p.3
*T S Brown

Ed. Note: Graduating class of 1924½ : Class Pres (3), Class V-Pres (4); May Queen Contest officer (3); Masquerade Committee (2,3); Student Body Treas. (3)

1959   Obituaries   Annie E Phelps   Annie Elizabeth Phelps, 89, daughter of early pioneers of the Santa Maria Valley, died Thursday after a lingering illness which confined her to her bed for the past 10 years.

Born in Alameda County, she came to the Santa Maria Valley in the early 1870's with her parents, Thomas and Rachel Brown. Her father purchased the land known as the Brown Ranch located in the lower end of the valley.

Mrs Phelps was one of a family of nine children. Only two survive, Joseph S Brown, of Santa Maria and John A Brown, of San Jose. Also surviving is one son, William Joshuah Phelps II; two grandchildren and seven great grandchildren.

Interment was in Lodi. -*Santa Maria Times* May 2 p.2

1963   Joseph S Brown   Joseph Samuel Brown, 78, lifelong resident of the Santa Maria Valley, died Sunday in a local hospital. He resided at 509-A E. El Camino. His parents came to Santa Maria in 1873 and helped to organize the First Presbyterian Church here.

Born November 1, 1884 in Santa Maria Mr Brown farmed in the Point Sal area until his retirement in 1945. He was a member of the Grace Baptist Church.

Survivors include three daughters, Mrs Viola K Kinseth, Ventura, and Mrs Gertrude L Weaver and Mrs Muriel Bramlett, both of Whittier. Also one brother, John A Brown of San Jose, 7 grandchildren and 2 great-grandchildren.

Funeral services will be held at 11 am Thursday in the Chapel of the Dudley Mortuary with the Rev William Larson officiating.

Friends may call at the Dudley Mortuary from 7 to 9 pm Wednesday and if they so desire they make make (sic) memorials to the Grace Baptist Church.

Interment will be in the Santa Maria Cemetery. –Ibid Mon Apr 1

1963   Obituaries   John A Brown   Funeral services for John Archer Brown, 81, who died Tuesday in San Jose, will be held at 10 am Friday at the Oak Hill Mortuary, 300 Curtner, San Jose.

Born May 17, 1882, in the Santa Maria Valley, Mr Brown was a former sales manager at the Rubel Buick Sales. He left Santa Maria 15 years ago to make his home in the north. He leaves his wife, Maude E Brown of San Jose and two grandchildren. His son, the late Charles T Brown, preceded him in death.

Interment will be held in the Madronia cemetery in Saratoga. –Ibid Wed May 22 p.14

1963   Obituaries   Eunice Brown   Funeral arrangements are pending at the Dudley Mortuary for Mrs Eunice May Brown, 83, who died this morning in a local hospital.

Born Jan 5, 1880, in Clay City, Kansas, Mrs Brown resided at 517 E Main St.

–Ibid Nov 26 p.8

Eunice M Brown

Funeral services will be held at 2 pm Friday in the chapel of the Dudley Mortuary for Mrs Eunice Brown, who died Monday evening in a local hospital at the age of 83.

Mrs Brown, who was born Jan 5, 1880, in Clay Center, Kansas, was a member of the First Presbyterian Church and a 40-year resident of Santa Maria.

She is survived by three daughters, Mrs Edna Cunningham of Santa Maria, Mrs Alice Toy of Arroyo Grande, and Mrs Elsie Hapgood of Lompoc; a brother, Arthur Brown of Lompoc, five grandchildren and 9 great grandchildren.

Rev Jay Dee Conrad will officiate at the services.

Friends my call at Dudley Mortuary from 7-9 pm Thursday. –Ibid Nov 27 p.2

Addendum: 1905   Probate of Will.   The will of the late T S Brown of Santa Maria who died last April, was admitted to probate in the superior court on Monday last. The estate consists chiefly of real estate in town and in the vicinity of Guadalupe and is estimated about $60,000.

–Ibid June 17

Corrections and Additions   [Page numbers refer to those in Quarterly]

p.13   Thomas Archer Brown was naturalized in the San Luis Obispo Superior Court June 4, 1889; registered to vote in Santa Barbara County September 1, 1890, residence Sisquoc. His first-born, Robert James, 22, registered the same day.

The 1892 Voter Registration lists physical description, among other things:

Thomas A Brown, age 53, 5'8½", light complexion, blue eyes, brown hair, born Ireland, residence Sisquoc, Post Office Garey; reg. Sep 8.

Robert J Brown, age 24, 5'9½", light complexion, blue eyes, brown hair, born CA. res: Sisquoc. Reg. Sep 6.

Ye Editor was misled by the obituary of Eunice Brown, page 30, which averred that a surviving relative was her brother, Arthur Brown of Lompoc, when, in fact, her brother was Arthur *Hapgood,* well-known educator in Lompoc, who was also Eunice's son-in-law by virtue of his marriage to Eunice's, Elsie Brown. Myra Manfrina of the Lompoc Historical Society has favored us with Hapgood family data, with which we present this emendation of the Thomas Sands Brown chart.

p.17
1. William James
    1892: @26 5'11, light complexion, blue eyes, brown hair, b. CA, res. Guadalupe, P.O.
        Santa Maria, Reg. 17
    b. Elsie Rachel . . .
            m. Betteravia, CA 18 Nov 1917
        Arthur Richard Hapgood . . .   F: James Derry Hapgood 1857-
                                              M: Emma McLaughlin 1858-1946
                                                  (m.2 Emory Crist 1836-1915)

        = Arthur James b. 1919
        = Richard Warren 1922-1939
        = Robert Derry b. 1928
1. Wm Jas. m.2
        Eunice May Hapgood Day . . .   F: James Derry Hapgood
                                              M: Emma McLaughlin
                                              First husband: George Warren Day
                                              Her children: Edna . . .
                                                      Alice Georgia 1903-1969
p.18
4. Annie Elizabeth . . .
    Wm Joshua Phelps
        1890: @22 b. Illinois Farmer, Res. Maple, Reg. Sep 1, SB co.
        F: probably Augustus S J Phelps 1847-1925
7.   a.   Charles Thomas d. Saratoga 5 March 1956 (date inadvertently omitted)

Thomas Archer Brown Scrapbook Additions

1885   A Surprise Party. A surprise party was given to Mr and Mrs T A Brown of Guadalupe on Wednesday evening last, many of their friends took part. After some three hours dancing, a good supper was served, and at half past one in the morning all went home full of joy. Following is a list of those present: Ladies—Mrs T A Brown, Mrs T S Brown, Mrs J W Speed, Mrs W P Kemp, Mrs P Moore, Mrs M Fitzpatrick, Mrs M W Blodgett. Misses—M Brown, Annie Brown, Jennie Mead, Katy Fox, A Fox, May Kemp, Katy McBane, Miss Casenini. Gentlemen—T A Brown, T S Brown,

J W Speed*, Pat Moore, Luis Valenzuela, B Fox, Thos Fox, A Fox, J Briscow, Allen Mead, Chas Mead, W C Donnely, J Donnelly (sic), A McKelvey, H Bonetti, Wm Brown, Willie Kemp, M Fitzpatrick, R Brown, John McBane, M W Blodgett. –*Santa Maria Times* Sep 26

*Article on J W Speed is in Speed chart.

1888   T A Brown went to the county seat on business in the interests of the Presbyterian church. – Ibid Wed May 23

1908   Personals. Mrs T A Brown, who had the misfortune to break her leg several weeks ago, is reported to be getting along nicely. –Ibid Dec 26

Thomas Sands Brown Scrapbook Additions

1885   Guadalupe Items . . . T S Brown's many friends gave him a very enjoyable birthday surprise on Thursday evening of last week. –*Santa Maria Times* Nov 21

1888   Mr T S Brown, wife and two children will leave on Friday next for a six months visit in Ireland. They will go from here to San Francisco and on May 4th take the picnic excursion train which will reach Salt Lake City on the Sunday morning following, where the train will lay over during the day, giving the excursionists a chance to see the city and attend the various churches. It has been 41 years since Mr B left his native isle and 24 since his wife visited her people in that far away land. Mr Brown has a brother and sister and other relation (sic) to visit while Mrs Brown's father and mother are both living. The *Santa Maria Times* wishes them a pleasant trip and safe return –Ibid Sat April 21

1891   T S Brown's new residence on the Foster place south of town is almost completed. It is a fine building. –Ibid Sep 26

1894   Guadalupe Items . . . T S Brown and his mule were in town Tuesday. –Ibid June 2

Vol. XXIII, No. 1-4, 1991, p.13

Thomas Archer Brown family

p. 14   Thomas Archer Brown Scrapbook 1887. T A Brown insolvent debtor … - Oct 10

p.17   Mr & Mrs W J Brown announced the coming marriage of Elsie Brown to Arthur R Hapgood in Betteravia, Sunday Nov 18 1917. (*Times*)

      W J Brown's second wife, Eunice May Hapgood Day, had married George Warren Day at Stuart (between Los Alamos and Lompoc) 12 May 1897. Their elder daughter, Edna, graduated from SMUHS in 1919 and went to Heald's Business College, per 1920 *Review*. The 1922-3 Directory lists her in Betteravia, steno, where also was O F Cunningham, electrician. In 1927 Mr & Mrs O F Cunningham of Prescott, AZ, visited her parents, Mr & Mrs W J Brown. – Thu Mar 3. Mrs Cunningham was City Treasurer for some years, and is pictured as such in The *Times* Sep 29 1956. A divorcee, she lived with her mother at 517 E Main after the death of the step-father. Her grandmother, Mrs Emma Crist, 87, died in 1947, having, also, resided at that address, and Mrs Brown was there at her death in 1963. When the 500 block of East Main St was redeveloped, Mrs Cunningham moved to 523 E Orange St; Ye Ed's son purchased the property from her estate and is still in residence.

Vol. XXX, No. 3, Fall 1998, p. 20

p.18.　　Robert H Brown's wife, Joanna, often received visits from her daughter, Marion, wife of Robert Gray (1882-1977) prominent Shandon rancher, son of Samuel Gray (1860-1942) and Jennie McKeen (1860-1948), who lived at Oso Flaco in the 1890's, moving to the Graciosa area in 1897. – Oct 30. Gray owned 2 ranches in Santa Barbara County and nearly 3000 acres near Shandon. (See bio Samuel Gray M/H 278). Gray street in Orcutt is a reminder of Gray's Addition to the Town of Orcutt. In 1907 Robert J Gray and Wilbur T Smith were doing business as Pacific Realty & Stock Co in Santa Maria. – June 22. In 1918 Gray sold his Rancho del Rio in Cuyama and moved to Shandon to operate his father's large ranch. During that time Marion was the Shandon correspondent to the *San Luis Obispo Daily Telegram*. They left Shandon in 1952, living in Oroville until 1970, returning to Santa Maria.

p.18.　　The father of William J Phelps was Augustus S J Phelps (1847-1925). He was in real estate and moved from this area to Los Angeles in 1894. – Dec 15. The 1890 GR shows both father and son in Maple (near Lompoc).
　　　　Charles Thomas Brown died in Saratoga CA 5 March 1956

p.19.　　The daughters of Joseph S Brown and Rausa Chaffin were Viola K born 29 Mar 1912 (*Times*), Gertrude, born 17 Nov 1913 (- 25 Yrs Ago, Thu 17 Nov 1938); and Muriel, born c1918. In 1940, former residents Mr & Mrs Bernold Kinseth (Viola Brown) of Ventura visited her parents Mr & Mrs J S Brown in Betteravia.　　　　　　　　　　　　　　　　　　　　　　　　-Oct 17

p.20.　　1887. Going-away party for The Rev Dr Beard, father-in-law of W J Brown.　　– Nov 5
　　　　Thomas Sands Brown Scrapbook. 1897. La Graciosa Items. Mrs W J Brown has returned to her home here, after a pleasant visit with her parents in Arroyo Grande.　　　　– Aug 7
　　　　W J Brown and his father will exchange ranches, Billy going to the old home place in Laguna district and his father will move onto the farm in Washington district.　　– Oct 9 1897
　　　　La Graciosa. W J Brown ex-proprietor of the Washington dairy has disposed of his farm here to his father and will move to the homestead ranch at Laguna. T S Brown will occupy the farm in Washington district.　　　　　　　　　　　　　　　　　　　　　　– Oct 30 1897

p.26.　　1941. James Hapgood and Louise Sutter were married in San Jose; she daughter of Mr & Mrs George Sutter, he son of Mrs A R Hapgood of Lompoc. Mrs Edna Cunningham is aunt. Shirley Cunningham presented bouquets to guests at the door. List of Guests…　　- June 7 1941

p.27.　　1946. Lompoc Resident Dies in Local Hospital. Mrs Emma Crist, 87, had been with daughter Mrs W J Brown, 517 E Main st. Three grandchildren: Mrs Edna Cunningham, Mrs Catherine France, Santa Maria; Mrs Alice Toy, Bakersfield; son Arthur R Hapgood, Lompoc.
　　　　　　　　　　　　　　　　　　　　　　　　　　　　　　　　　　　– Fri Jan 4

BUNCE
PIONEERS OF THE CALIFORNIA CENTRAL COAST

Isaac Hopkins Bunce   b. Auburn NY 24 Dec 1831
   bio Storke 353: to CA 1851   d. at home nr San Luis Hot Sulphur Springs
   around the Horn. To SCruz,   9 Jan 1911 @79. obit SLO DT Mon Jan 9 p.1
   millwright, house carp.   former supervisor; under sheriff during
   to SLOco 1858. Co Sup   term of Mike Castro. To CA by Panama,
   1860,1870,1880 cen: SLO tp   built 1st sawmill Santa Cruz
   1892 GR: 60 5'8½ fair complexion hazel eyes grey hair 3d finger lh cut
       carp NY rAvila; precinct Beach; PO Root
   1900 cen: Arroyo Grande pct/Beach   1900 GR: 68 Beach pct PO Sycamore Spgs
   1910 cen: See Canyon
       Boland (sic) & Bunce, carpenters, contractors—Storke
       (Guillermo Borland m. Josefa Avila; Wm E. Borland, carpenter,
         d. Avila 18 Oct 1892 @64. –SLO Mortuary records)
   m. San Luis Obispo 22 Aug 1862 by Francisco Mora, A43
(Isabel) Juana Avila   b. Monterey CA Nov 1839 m. @21
   1900: 11 births 9 living   d. at home of son Henry 429 E Main St SM
     (9 per Storke)   20 June 1928 @88; SM cem
   1910: 11births 8 living   obit Wed June 20 p.1; to SM 1911
   1922 Dir: Isabelle J Mrs   bro Juan Avila; 18gch, 5ggch
     hskpr r722 E Main   F: Miguel Antonio Nicolas Avila 1798-1874
   1926 Dir: Mrs I H hskpr   M: Maria Encarnacion Inocenta Pico 1810-
     r722 E Main   See *Sp-Mex Fams* I 59 Avila: II 207 Pico
   1928: 3 dau 3 sons
1. Elizabeth   b. (Avila) 1863
   to SM 1909 (obit)   d. Santa Maria 19 Nov 1934 @70/4/3; SM cem
   in Fresno 1906, 1924, 1928, 1911   obit Tue Nov 20 p.4
   1934. In and Out of the City. Mr and Mrs Fred Ilenstine and small son from Santa Barbara
       spent weekend in SM. Mrs Minnie Brown and dau Juanita of Vallejo, former
          residents, visiting relatives…   -Tue Oct 30
   1934 pall bearers: A J Mesquit, Edward M James, C E Felmlee, Fred Ilenstine,
       Judge L J Morris, John U Brass.
     m. San Luis Obispo 2 April 1889 (Obit)
   Lewis Edgar Norman   b.
     prop women's apparel   d. at home 723 W Main St SM 17 May 1935 @60/9/15
     store (Fresno?)   SM cem. obit Sat May 18 p.4
                                       F: George W Norman (in SM 1935)
                                       sis Mrs Loretta Grube (Fresno 1935)
     a. Camille (Clinton D Rowley) in San Francisco 1934, 1935
       =Robert Norman Rowley
2. Lydia Ann   b. (Avila) 14 May 1867
   to SM 1900   d. Santa Barbara 22 Apr 1963 @95/11/8; SM cem
   m. 1890   obit Tue Apr. 23 p.8. 7gch 11 ggch
   Benjamin Spaulding Smyth   b. Pimlico England 31 Oct 1857
     1906 Dir: timekpr ½ mi E   d. at home 720 E Main St SM @93/5/28;
       Lydia Mrs   bur 1 May 1951 SM cem. obit Mon Apr 30 p.1
       Stella Miss stu   to US on a visit 1885; remained 6 mos
     1909 Dir: lab 618 E Main   Lompoc, to SLO, to SB, to SM 1891; 1st
       Lydia Mrs   service sta cor Bwy/Stowell; 7gch 2ggch

Stella Miss saleslady; Ethel Miss stu
1910 cen: 618 E Main 5 births 5 living
1930 Dir: Mrs r618 E Main
1938-9 Dir: Smythe J ret h720 E Main
1955-6 Dir: Smyth Benj (Lydia A) ret h720 E Main

a. Stella G b. 13 Jan 1891; SSDI
   1910 cen: tel ofc single d. 10 Oct 1981 (Santa Barbara)
   1922. Mrs Fred Ilestine (sic) of Abbott's Style Shop on 2-wk vacation, spent at home...
   1922 Dir: Ilenstine Mrs Fred clk Abbott's -July 6
     Abbott's Style Shop, Noel Abbott prop 107 N Bwy
   1926 Dir: Ilenstine Mrs Stella prop Estell's Novelty Shop r700 E Main
     lg ad: Estell's Specialty Shop. Millinery & Women's Ready-to-Wear. Bradley Hotel
        Bldg next to PO Mrs Stella Illenstine (sic), Prop
   1928 Dir: Estell's Specialty Shop 105 S Bwy
   m.
Fred W Ilenstine b. (SM) 13 Nov 1884 (*Times*); SSDI
   1922 Dir: chf clk Hotel d. 16 Feb 1968 (Santa Barbara)
     Bradley; r616 E Chapel F: Charles B Ilenstine 1832-1929
   1926 Dir: clk Hotel Bradley 1884: Chas Ilenstine contracted to
     r700 E Main; 1928: same remove bodies from Thornburgh cem
   1932 phbk: 210 Palo Colorado to new SM cem. - (*Times*) Mar 1, Mar 15
     Santa Barbara voter Santa Ynez 1890
   1951 phbk: 2925 Paseo del Refugio Santa Barbara
   1973 phbk: 616 San Ricardo Dr Santa Barbara
=son born before 1934

b. Ethel Juanita b. 19 Apr 1894
                                                            d. 9 Oct 1966 @72/5/20; SM cem
   m. obit Mon Oct 10 p.8. 5gch 2nc 1 nph
Edward Marion James b. Casmalia 11 July 1890; SSDI
   1938-9 Dir: bkpr SP d. 10 Dec 1968 @78/4/30; SM cem
     Milling Co h713 E Church obit Thu Dec 12 p.2
   1940-1 Dir: same F: Charles Edward James 1862-1934; SM cem
   1955-6 Dir: mgr SPM Co M: Margaret Jane 1861-1938; SM cem
     asphalt plant h713E Ch bro J G James, Huntington Beach
                                     sis Gertrude Milam Santa Barbara
   1968 pall bearers: Edw Goodchild, Henry Abels, Jake Will, Wm Zvolaneck, Wm Barnes,
     Chas Felmelee (sic)
=Edw M jr b. 14 July 1920; SSDI; d. 2 July 1994 (Ventura)
   1940-1 Dir: clk Felmlee Groc r713 E Church
   1955-6 Dir: Edw jr (Darlene) emp Rosemary Farm h323 Linda Dr SM
=Margaret L (E L Brenneman) (in Santa Maria 1966)
   1940-1 Dir: miss clk Haslam's r713 E Church
   (James Lee Brenneman 1919-1994 SM cem)
   (Linda Patricia Brenneman) d. 1958 @4; inf. Edw M James; SM cem

c. Sydney William b. 1901 (26 May 1901; SSDI)
   in Beverly Hills 1951 d. (Jan 1986 San Jose)?
   in Las Vegas 1963, 1966

d. Dorothy I b. 19 March 1903
                                                  d. 22 April 1986 @83; SM cem
   m. obit Thu Apr 24 p.26; 5gch

Charles E Felmlee · b. 14 Feb 1899
long-time trustee SMUHS · d. at home 28 March 1986 @87; SM cem; obit Sun Mar 30 p. 21; 5gch; at home 313 Las Flores Way SM; 3 markets, retired 1959

    1926 Dir: Houghton EG mgr Houghton's Groceteria E Main
      Groc & Fruits: Houghton E J   E Main
    1928 Dir: Houghton…120 E Main
      Fields & Felmlee Quality Cash Groc Thornburg & Lemon
    1930 Dir: Groceries - Houghton's No.4 120 E Main Quality Cash Grocery Every Thing A Good Grocery Store Should Have 603 S Thornburg at Lemon
    1933 phbk: Felmlee…714 E Main
    1938-9 Dir: Felmlee CE Houghton's Mkt (120 E Main) r714 E Main
    1940-1 Dir: Felmlee Groc 120 E Main; h714 E Main
      Houghton HG (Pearl) Bakery & Mkt 122 E Main; r514 E Cook
    1951 Felmlee and Gallison Buy Bert's Mkt…301 S Broadway
    …Felmlee, owner of the Market Spot, 120 E Main will own and operate the grocery and produce depts.…Roy Gallison, co-owner of Gallison's Cash Market, 211 S Broadway…meat dept…both…have been in the grocery business in Santa Maria for about 25 years and are well known… —Wed Oct 10 p.1 (Bert's Market, 1st "supermarket" in SM) See Rosenblum chart.
    1955-6 Dir: Felmlee…groc 301 S Broadway; h313 Las Flores Way
    1986: Felmlee survived by sisters Edna Reed, San Mateo and
    Helen Sawyer Morrill, Kansas.
=twins buried 25 Nov 1932 SM cem
=Mary (Naten) living in Santa Maria 1986
    (1932: Auto Demolished But Men Are Not Severely Injured…O M Paul, 34, 301 E Mill, F L Naten, 38, Orcutt…struck by heavily loaded vegetable truck on the coast highway…
=twins Joan Toomire, Fallbrook; Jane Koberg, Palo Alto (1986)   -Sat Mar 21)

  e. Margaret A · b. 1909
    m.1 Norman Edwards · living in San Mateo 1951
    m.2 Walter Straub · living in San Mateo 1963, 1986

3. Charles Alfred · b. (Sycamore Springs) 4 April 1870
  1892 GR: 22 5'6 fr br blk, scar 1h base · m.1 of Sycamore Springs; m.2 @39 of SM
    of thumb, lab CA Avila Beach · d. Santa Maria 16 Dec 1941 @71/8/12; SM cem
    Port Harford · spouse initials on death list PB; obit Wed
  1900 cen: w/Alfred, single · Dec 17 p.1 "Resident Here 40 Years Passes"
  1906 Dir: teamster SM · 2gch in Oakland, no wife
  1909 Dir: teamster rooms W Main St
  1910 cen: W Main St, roomer
  1922 Dir: driver C E Marriott r509 W Main (Santa Maria Transfer Co)
  1926 Dir: expressman r 209 S Vine;   1940-1 Dir: transfer emp h209 S Vine
    m.1 San Luis Obispo 2 Oct 1898, E339 by Wm Mallagh JP, no wit
Frances Calloway · b. (SLO) 1878; m. of SLO; d.
    F: Wm D Calloway 1833-___; IOOF cem SLO
    M: Rachel Jane   1837-1925; IOOF cem SLO
    1860, 1880 cen: SLO tp

  a. Floyd   living in Santa Maria 1941
    m.2 Santa Barbara 22 Dec 1913 (Co Marriage rec)
  Ava <u>Pearl</u> Wimmer Mrs · b. CA 1882; m.(2) @31 of Santa Maria
  1910 cen: E Cypress @27 m/1 9y CA3 dressmaker 2 births 2 living
    (Her daus: Maud b. c1903, Helen b. c1907, w/gpar Rbt & Nora Wimmer Betteravia 1910cen)?

4. Henry Jones   b. Sycamore Springs Nov 1871
    1900 cen: w/parents   d. Santa Maria 16 June 1945 @74
    1900 GR: 28 Beach pct PO SLO   SM cem. inf. HH Hinman. obit Sat June 16 p.21
         50 yrs section boss PCRR; ret 1942
    1906 Dir: RR foreman rMain St Los Alamos
    1910 cen: section foreman Los Alamos
    1911: Arroyo Grande
    1920 cen: 224 S Vine SM
    1922 Dir: road master PCRR r224 W Cypress;   1926: same
    1928 Dir: 429 E Main St SM
    1940-1 Dir: foreman PCRR h 400 E Orange SM
        m. 1904
  Mary de Jesus Ontiveros   b. Tepesquet 24 Dec 1878
    (Mary Jessie) or   d. Santa Barbara 26 Jan 1938 @57/1/2; SM cem
    "Amelia"—see ONT 79   obit Wed Jan 26 p.6; r400 E Orange
        F: Jose Florentino Ontiveros 1840-1911
        M: Tomasa Arellanes 1849-1928
    her dau Maclovia   b. 1896   d.____ survived Henry
    1920 cen: w/ Bunce, step-dau
    1938-9 Dir: Silva Mrs L A ret h400 E Orange
    Jessie I hskpr 400 E Orange
    Marjorie M hskpr 400 E Orange
    m.
    Louis Silva   b. CA 1894; parents POR
    1920 cen: w/Bunce
    1940-1 Dir: Silva Louis A trctr drvr Rosemary Gen Del
    =Jessie (Hinman)
    =Marjorie (Lapp)
    1940-1 Dir: Lapp Earl(Marjorie) trk drvr NBC co h S Miller
5. Alfred Lyman   b. Sycamore Springs Apr 1873; m @21
         d. Santa Maria 29 Mar 1924 @48/11/2; SM cem
         obit Mon Mar 31 p.1; 28y SMv
         musician Santa Maria Band
         Santa Maria Transfer Co
  1901: Al Bunce encountered a few of Santa Maria's frisky youth one moonlit night of this
    week, dressed in women's apparel and carrying on a general flirtation with all who
    could be interested. Bunce read the riot act and then dismissed the boys.   —Oct 26
    1906 Dir: tmstr rMain St; Mrs
    1909 Dir: wks for transfer co. r104 E Church St; Mrs L C
    1910 cen: 104 W? Church St wagon driver transfer co
    1920 cen: 315 E Main; 5 children at home;   1922 Dir: Al (Lucy) r704 W Main
        m. Guadalupe 5 Aug 1894 by M Lynch (*Times*)
  Lucia Concepcion Arellanes   b. CA May 1874
    1900: 2 births 2 living   d. (San Jose) 3-26-1954; living SJose 1925
    1910: 6 births 5 living   F: Juan Batista Arellanes 1838-1925
    1926 Dir: Lucy hskpr r429 E Main   M: Francisca Sanchez 1848-1926
    a. son W   b. Santa Maria 13 Sep 1895 (*Times*)
         d. Santa Maria 18 Sep 1895 (*Times*)
    b. Consuelo de Jesus (Collins)   b. SM 15 Aug 1896; SSDI
         d. (San Jose) 24 Sep 1984
    c. Garnita Lucille (Gates)   b. Santa Maria 13 Aug 1899 (*Times*)
         d. (before 1970) in Los Angeles 1924

    d. Isaac A   b. SM 3 Nov 1900; SSDI; m. @21 of SM
        1922 Dir: mus 704 W Main, Mrs   d. San Jose 20 Dec 1970 @68
                                                                         obit Mon Dec 21 p.2; 12 gch
             m.1 San Luis Obispo 20 Oct 1921 by H B Sellers, ME ch, M120
                 wit: Lucille Manahan, SLO; Albert Clark, SM
       Mildred Boosinger   b. CA m. @18 of San Luis Obispo
       = Antonio   d. 5 July 1922 @10 min; SM cem
          m.2
       Lucille A   b. (13 June 1906; SSDI)
                                                 d. (San Jose 1 Jan 1986) living SJ 1970
          =Dave; =Don; =James all in San Jose 1970
    e. Frances R (Soria)   b. 6 July 1904; SSDI
        1922 Dir: stu 704 W Main   d. San Jose 17 June 1986; living SJ 1970
    f. James W   b. 26 July 1905 (*Times*)
        1922 Dir: stu 704 W Main   d. (before 1970)
        1926 Dir: lab 429 E Main
6. Martha M   b. (Sycamore Springs) c1877; m. of SLO
                                               d. (Los Angeles co 9-17-1925 @50 WL)
         m. San Luis Obispo 30 Sep 1897 by V Aguilera, E220
              wit: C Bunce, SLO; Lizie (sic) Bunce, SLO
    William L Austin   b. ____ m. of Gilroy
        1906, 1911: Point Concepcion   (possibly b. Nov 1876, son of W H Austin of SLO
        1924: San Pedro   and Lompoc. See Storke 607)
7. John   b. (Sycamore Springs) 1878
        1902 GR: 26 (?) SLO #2   d. San Luis Obispo 2 June 1906 @ 25 (?)
           Single   obit *SLO MT* June 3. PCRR. died of injuries suf-
                                             fered years earlier while switching cars in rr yard
8. Minnie (Brown)   b. (Sycamore Springs) Jan 1880
                                               (in SM 1928, Vallejo 1941, 1963)
        1911: still single   d. (Solano Co 4-22-1965)?
        a. Juanita
9. Clarisa   b. 1880 (cen) no other data
10. Isaac William   b. (Sycamore Springs) Oct 1882
        1906: Port Harford   d. (Solano Co 12-26-1940) living in Vallejo
        1911: Coalinga   1924, 1928

Note: Lucia Concepcion Arellanes was confirmed at St Isidore's Church, Guadalupe 1 Apr 1886 @ 12; sponsor: Francisca Vidal

    Miguel Avila was the grantee of the San Miguelito Rancho of 22,125.89 acres. At his death in 1874 there remained 9909 acres, as shown on the county assessment rolls, owners Mrs Inocencia Avila, F Avila, Raphaela De la Guerra, J A Abila (sic), Joseph Borland, Refugio Castro, Santana Avila, Mrs Juana Bunce, Juan Abila (sic) and Adelina Jones. By 1870 Isaac Bunce owned 20 acres of that grant, "near the oil wells" the drilling of which led to the discovery of the hot sulphur water which became the focus of the resort known variously as Sycamore Springs, San Luis Hot Sulphur Springs, and, currently, Sycamore Mineral Springs Resort.

    A 32-page booklet advertising San Luis Hot Sulphur Springs, A M Smith, Prop., dating from about 1907, has many photographs of the facilities and surrounding terrain, explains the activities available, and has four pages of testimonials of cures effected by the water, as well as a list of several hundred people who had come from all over this country and also some foreign lands.

In December 1912 the San Luis Obispo County Automobile Club sponsored a "run" to the San Luis Hot Sulphur Springs. "About thirty machines filled to capacity" bore members and guests the dusty seven miles for a picnic. *SLO Daily Telegraph* Dec 11, 14, 16, 1912

Vol. XXVIII, No. 2, Summer 1996, p.11

Corrections and Additions   [Page numbers refer to those in Quarterly]

p.8.   Fred Ilenstine resigned as night clerk at Bradley Hotel to go to San Francisco for lucrative position.   –Oct 14 1916

p.11.   Minnie Bunce m. @25 of SLO. m. SLO 19 June 1911 by Mathew Ternes, Catholic, I231; wit: Lou E Norman, SM; Mrs Lizzie E Norman, SM.
William J Brown, b. CA m. @29 of SLO

Vol. XXIX, No. 4, Winter 1997, p.19

p.9   Frances Callaway, sister of Harriet Elizabeth Callaway, died in San Luis Obispo county CA 28 July 1934. Her second husband was John Faber.

CHAFFIN
SANTA MARIA VALLEY PIONEERS

The History of Robert Chaffin and His Descendants and of the Other Chaffins in America, Wm L Chaffin, 1912, (hereinafter (gen)in this article)

1. Robert Chaffin   b. c1695; inventory 15 Feb 1745
    m. Concord MA 15 Apr 1719 by Justice Minot
    Abigail Davis 22 Jan 1699-1752?   F: Samuel Davis; M: Abigail Reed
2. Francis Chaffin   b. Littleton MA 25 Jan 1730
                                             d. Valley Forge 28 Jan 1778
    m. 20 Apr 1756
    Rebecca Cummings of Littleton MA
3. Reuben Chaffin   b. Acton MA 14 Jul 1766
                                             d. Scioto co OH 1808
    m.1 Bolton MA 15 Dec 1788
    Eunice Walcott 24 Feb 1766-1799.   F: Jesse Walcott, Rev W; M: Rebecca
4. Shadrach Chaffin   b. Lisbon NH 8 Mar 1797
                                            d. Scioto co OH 13 Jun 1884 @87/3/5
    m.1   13 May 1819
    Sarah Salladay 1800-1840   F: Philip Salladay; M: Sarah C Flick
    m.2   3 Oct 1840
    Juliana Reynolds Hayward   d. 4 Apr 1890   F: Joshua Reynolds
    widow of Moses Hayward

Fifth Generation

David Sal(l)aday Chaffin   b. Scioto co OH 30 Nov 1828 (gen) or
    1855: to Iowa   10 Oct 1829 (obit) or Oct 1829 (cen)
    1860 cen: Benton co IA Eden tp   d. at home 500 S Bwy SM 7 Mar 1912 @83/4/8
        PO Unity; 1880 cen: same   SM cem. obit Sat Mar 16
    1892: to Santa Maria   F: Shadrach Chaffin; M: Sarah Sal(l)aday
    1900 cen: Santa Maria, capitalist, (died a very wealthy man—gen)
    1906: Treas, Director, Meridian Oil Co
    1906 Dir: farmer ¾ mi W
    1909 Dir: rancher r W Main; Mrs Emma; 1909-10 SBcoDir: farmer 920 W Main
    1910 cen: 500 S Bwy
    1912: survivors, sister Mrs Mary Lowe, Anamosa IA; ½ sis Mrs I J Emory, So Webster OH;
        ½ bro WJW Chaffin, SM. 2ch by 1st wf: Geo W, Ontario; Joseph L, SM;
        2ch by 2nd wf: Mrs F C Waterbury, Des Moines; Mrs C U Armstrong, SM
    1908: For Rent—160 acres, Chaffin place east of Pine Grove Sch, 6 mi south of Santa Maria
        Inquire of C U Armstrong.   -Oct 31
    1893: Mr Chaffin has built a new granary and made other improvements on his place near
        the school house.   -Nov 18 (?)
           m.1 Webster co OH 25 Nov 1853
Maria Thompson   b. OH 17 Sep 1833
                                         d. nr Vinton IA 21 Apr 1863

1. George W   b. Scioto co OH 17 Dec 1854
    1882: to South Dakota   d. Los Angeles 1-21-1921 @66
    1900 cen: Hand co SD.   1901: to SM   1905: to Ontario, Orange ranch (gen)
    1910 cen: Ontario, Orange grove. Living in Ontario 1912
    1920 cen: 1031 Grandview, Los Angeles
        m. 15 Aug 1880

  Mary Lawyer Fisk   b. MI 7 Feb 1852
    1900 cen: 7 births 5 living   d. Los Angeles 11-5-1920 @68
                  F: Peter Deton Lawyer; M: Lydia Laraway
    her dau Fay Fisk   b. IA June 1877
     1900 cen: w/Chaffins
    a. Rafe Chester Chaffin   b. SD 16 Aug (gen) Sep (cen) 1882
     spouse initial M C   d. Los Angeles 3-23-1958
     Los Angeles Extended Area phbk June 1936: Chaffin Rafe C MD   1137 S Westlake av,
      r 938 S Kingsley Dr photo facing p. 208 Chaffin gen; physician
    b. Jessie Alma Chaffin   b. SD 12 Sep 1886
      1920 cen: w/parents, S   photo facing p.210 Chaffin gen
    c. Adelbert Lawyer Chaffin   b. SD 29 July 1891; SSDI
      UCal (gen)   d. (Butte co) 9-9-1964
      1910 cen: w/parents; census enumerator
      spouse initial M
    d. Maria Chaffin   b. (SD) 4 Jan 1894; d. 6 May 1894
    e. George Chaffin   b. SD 4 Dec 1896 (gen)   1895 (cen)
      Chaffee HS (gen)   d. (Geo W 1966; Geo E 1960)?
                   living in Wilmington 1942
  2. Joseph Lewis   b. (Benton co) IA 12 Feb 1856
   1897: to CA, carpenter,   d. Santa Maria 20 Oct 1942 @86
     real estate holder   obit Wed Oct 21 p.1; Oct 22 p. 4; in CA 45 y
   1906 Dir: carp SM;   1909 Dir: Joe carp r W Mill
   1910 cen: not found. Was he in IA? 'to CA after death of wife' (obit)
   1912: living in SM;   1920 cen: wd 123 W Mill
   1920: Joe Chaffin Has Narrow Escape in Auto Wreck. -Jan 18 p.1
   1922 Dir: carp W Main, Fairlawn dist;   1926 Dir: same;   1930 Dir: 729 W Main
   1940-1 Dir: 123 W Mill carp
      m. 1882
   Stella Offenbach   d. Cherokee IA May 1911; long illness (gen)
    No issue
  3. Cornelia   b. 11 Oct 1858   d. 7 Jan 1859
  4. Susan   b. 12 Dec 1860   d. 18 Sept 1861
     m.2 Vinton or Cedar Rapids IA 7 Aug 1864 (gen vs obit)
   Emma Malinda Stewart   b. OH 13 Mar 1840
    1900 cen: 4 births 2 living   d. Long Beach CA 11 July 1924 @83/4/9; SM cem
    to Santa Barbara 1912 (gen)   obit Mon July 14 p.1. 25 yrs SM
      or 1915 (obit)   F: James C Stewart;   M: Harriet P Mason
   to Long Beach 1921
   1910: Personals: Mr & Mrs J H Stewart of Minneapolis visiting the Armstrong & Chaffin
     families; Mr Stewart is bro-in-law of Mr Chaffin.   -Mar 5
   1919: Local Briefs: Mrs JM Cook & sis, Mrs Emma Chaffin of Santa Barbara are home from
     extensive visiting in the east. Mrs Chaffin is guest of her dau Mrs CU Armstrong   -Nov 12
    Note: Harriet A Stewart (Mrs James M Cook)'s dau Viola L Cook of Des Moines
   married in 1910 Owen T Rice, son of pioneer John H Rice 1832-1896 and Mary Ann Long
   1836-1936.
   1924: survivors: daus Mrs Armstrong, Mrs Waterbury; bros J Hudson Stewart, Retail WA;
     Samuel S Stewart, Rockwell City IA.
  5. Kate Florence   b. IA 25 Aug 1865
                  d. 31 Jan 1884

6. Coral Patience b. IA 19 May 1867 (gen) 1868 (cen)
   social & civic leader,   photo facing p. 166 Chaffin gen
   Des Moines
      m. 12 July 1892
   Frank Calvin Waterbury b. IL Apr 1867 (cen)
     1900 cen: 1333 27th Des Moines d.
     1920 cen: 608 Country Club F: Dr Stephen Waterbury
       Blvd Des Moines M: Lydia E Overman
     bro Eugene W Waterbury MI May 1873 w/in 1900
   a. Carl Chaffin Waterbury b. IA 22 Feb 1894
   b. Chloris Patience Waterbury b. IA 24 Aug 1897
     1920cen: w/parents, S

7. Shadrach, MD b. IA 8 Feb 1869; photo facing p. 168
   Ann Arbor Med Sch (gen) d. Heath Ranch, Cuyama 13 July 1897 @28/5/11
      SM cem. obit July 17. consumption

8. Mary E b. 16 May 1875
   living in Long Beach 1924 d. (Long Beach) CA 2-22-1943
     m. Santa Maria 2 Dec 1896 by Geo T Weaver, pastor
      wit: Samuel Glade, Mrs John McMillan
   Charles Union Armstrong b. IL Feb 1864; m. @32
     1900 cen: next to D S Chaffin d. (Long Beach) CA 5-22-1956
     1906 Dir: atty-at-law F: Louis Armstrong
       W Main St; Mrs M: Mary Allen
    1909 Dir: atty-at-law r503 W Main, office 113 W Main; Mrs
    1909-10 SB co Dir: atty-at-law & notary public 113 W Main; h 503 W Main
    1910 cen: next to or w/D S Chaffin
    1920 cen: 500 S Bwy   1922 Dir: same
    1922 Dir: Armstrong & Schaeffer (CU&W) attys Bank of Santa Maria bldg
   a. Charles Armstrong b. & d. 15 May 1901
   b. David Leon Armstrong b. Los Angeles 28 Jan 1905
     reared, ed'd SM d. Nipomo 8 Sep 1985; SM cem
     18 yrs Nipomo obit Tue Sep 10 p.16. 2 gch
     supervisor in shipbuilding industry
     wf Mary L living in Nipomo 198_
    =Frank Armstrong living in Sacramento 1985
   c. Emma Lorita Armstrong (Norman) b. 26 May 1910
     living in Mazatlan Mexico 1985

Fifth Generation
William John Worth Chaffin b. Scioto co OH 29 Dec 1846
   1880 cen: Scioto co OH d. Santa Maria 8 June 1919 @72/5/9; SM cem
     Union tp obit June 9 p.1 suicide
   arrived SM 29 Oct 1899 F: Shadrach Chaffin
     M: Juliana Reynolds
   1900 cen: SM. 1901: purchased 83 acre ranch 4 mi S from D S Chaffin
   1906 Dir: farmer 4½ mi S; Mrs
   1909-10 SB co Dir: rancher 4 mi S. 1910 cen: Orcutt
     m. 31 Dec 1871
Nancy Call b. IN 11 Feb 1855
   1900, 1910: 11 births 11 living d. 619 W Cook SM 30 Aug 1937 @82/6/19; SM cem

1922 Dir: Mrs hskpr 619 W Cook   obit Aug 31 p.1. 22gch 12 ggch
1926 Dir: same; moved to town   F: Thomas Call
    from farm in 1919   M: Susan

1. Emma L   b. OH 31 Oct 1872
    d. Contra Costa co 4-1-1918 @61
    m. 12 Apr 1893
  Louis T Raybourn   F: Thomas Raybourn; M: Mary
  a. Jennis Raybourn   b. 26 Dec 1893
  b. William Worth Raybourn   b. 21 Dec 1895
  c. John Q Raybourn   b. 22 Nov 1898; SSDI
    d. Visalia Sep 1978
  d. Blanche B Raybourn   b. 24 May 1903
  e. Mattie May   b. 22 Mar 1906
  f. Shadrach C   b. 10 Dec 1908; SSDI
    d. July 1990 no zip code given

2. Julia   b. OH 9 Oct 1874
  1900 cen: w/parents, S   d. Fresno 4-12-1932 @57
    m. 25 Mar 1903
  Thomas S Raybourn   b. OH 6 Mar 1864
    1910 cen: Tulare co CA   d. Fresno 9-21-1937 @73
    1920 cen: Thornton av   F: Thomas Raybourn; M: Mary
    Fresno   sis Martha Raybourn KY 50 w/ in 1910
  a. Earl Shelton Raybourn   b. 15 May 1905 CA
  b. Lewis Wm Raybourn   b. CA 29 June 1906; SSDI
    d. Fresno Aug 1986
  c. Russell T Raybourn   b. CA 24 June 1911; SSDI
    d. (Dallas) June 1977

3. Shadrach   b. Scioto co OH 17 June 1876
  1912 (gen): Santa Barbara   d. Tulare co 12-16-1962
    street railroad
  1920 cen: Visalia. living in Visalia 1937, 1940, 1947, 1953
    m. 12 May 1909
  Ada (Leane) Beckett   b. Tulare co CA 1 Mar 1884
    d.
    F: Eugene Beckett; M: Ella
  a. Clarence Wm   b. Santa Barbara 3 Oct 1910 (gen)
    (not on 1920 census)
  b. Edwin   b. c1911
  c. Bernice   b. c1913
  d. Ella   b. 1920

4. Thomas   b. Lyra OH 29 Dec 1877 (obit) or 1878 (cen)
  1900 cen: w/parents   d. Santa Maria 9 Aug 1964 @86/7/10; SM cem
  1922 Dir: lab r Oakley av   obit Aug 10. res 530 N Mary Dr
  1926 Dir: lab Orcutt. 1940-1 Dir: lab Orcutt, 1955-6 Dir: h 4515 S Blosser, Single

5. George W   b. Lyra OH 15 Jan 1881
  to SM @19   d. Santa Barbara 21 June 1953 @72/5/6; SM cem
  1902: homestead 160 acres   obit Mon June 22 p.8. r 825 Pinal, Orcutt
    Cuyama valley
  1909-10 SB co Dir: rancher 3 mi S. 1910 cen: Orcutt. 1920 cen: Orcutt
  1926 Dir: Geo (Sarah) farmer; Miss Lila stu, Orcutt. 1930 Dir: lower Orcutt rd
    m. Santa Maria 25 March 1908

Sarah Elizabeth Elvidge 1881-1966: see Elvidge chart
- a. Leila Vivian (Hudson)   b. (Santa Maria) 29 Dec 1908 (*Times*)
  - 1927: Pres Girls League SMUHS; living in Oakdale 1953
  - =Shirley (Keene)   b. 15 Nov 1934; SSDI; living in Sharp Park 1953
  -      d. 20 Apr 1993 (Sharp Park)
- b. William George Chaffin   b. 1913; living in Auberry 1953,
  - SMJC, Navy   Big Creek 1966, Atascadero 1986
  - 1938-9 Dir: oil wkr r 830 Pinal, Orcutt. 1940-1 Dir: same
  - wf Ruby A   b. CA 25 June 1915; SSDI
  - 1938-9 Dir: mail carrier   d. Templeton 25 May 1986 @70; SM cem
  -    & news agency, Orcutt   obit May 27. res Atascadero. 2gch
  - left SM in 1940; in Big Creek   sister Doris Forrester, Orcutt
  - 1941-1975
  - =Linda (Gilbert Wilkes)   b. 10 May 1949 (*Times*)
  - living in Atascadero 1986, 1996

6. Willard L   b. OH 1 April 1883
   - 1910 cen: San Jose   d. San Jose 10-4-1952
   - 1920 cen: 66 Devine St San Jose. 1920 Dir: same clk Am Rwy Exp Co
   - 1922 Dir: h 482 N 5th, San Jose, 1926 Dir: same. 1929 Dir: h 45 Polhemus, San Jose
   - living in San Jose 1937, 1940, 1947
   -      m. 7 June 1906
   - Ethylin Adelaide Tobey   b. MN 18 Nov 1884; SSDI
   -      d. San Jose 9-21-1972? (fiche splotched)
   -      F: Almon Roscoe Tobey, d. San Jose 9-13-1924 @79
   -      M: Irona? Octavia
   - (Martha A Cline CA c1906 in this household 1920)

7. Charles Elmer   b. OH 29 Sep 1885; SSDI
   - 1909-10 SB co Dir: clk   d. Santa Barbara (obit) reg. Ventura co (CDL)
   -    h Lincoln cor Boone   20 Apr 1940 @54/6/11; SM cem. r 216 W Cypress
   - 1909 Dir: clk r 609 W Cypress,   obit Mon Apr 22 p.6. grocer
   -    Mrs A
   - 1910 cen: SM. 1920 cen: Barrett St, SM. 1922 Dir: clk Parnell Groc
   - 1926 Dir: clk r 924 W Barrett; 1937: Sauer's Wholesale Groc, SLO
   - 1940-1 Dir: C E r 216 W Cypress; Mrs h924 W Barrett
   -      m. 19 March 1909
   - Anna Bertha Wichman   b. (Waupaca co) WI 10 July 1885
   -    returned to SM from SLO   d. Santa Maria 8 June 1971 @85/10/28; SM cem
   -    1940, 1942 phbk: 924 W Barrett   obit Thu June 10 p.2. r 410B W Main
   -    1945-6 Dir: 924 W Barrett   F: William Wichman (1880 cen: Waupaca co WI)
   -    1955-6 Dir: 924 W Cook   M: Augusta Weeg 1862-1923; m.2 Entemann
   - a. Charles Frederick Chaffin   d. 13 Jan 1916 @ 1 mo 5 days (*Times*); SM cem
   - b. infant   buried 13 May 1918 @0/0; SM cem
   - c. foster dau Cecilia B Miller   b. CA 1909; living in SLO 1940
   - =Donald C Miller living in Los Altos 1971

8. Rausa   b. Lyra OH 14 July 1887; m. @19
   -      d. at home W of SM 15 Oct 1945
   -      obit Tue Oct 16 p. 6. 5gch
   -      m. San Luis Obispo 3 Apr 1907 by Rev Harry Hillard, G480
   -      wit: Geo Chaffin, SM; Ellen Humphreys Hillard, SLO
   - Joseph Samuel Brown   b. Guadalupe ranch 1 Nov 1884; m. @22
   -      d. Santa Maria 31 Mar 1963 @78; 7gch 2ggch

|||F: Thomas Sands Brown 1825-1905|
|||M: Rachel Brown   1844-1907|

    a. Viola A (Barnold Kinseth)   b. (SM) 29 Mar 1912 (*Times*)
                                                               living in Ventura 1945, 1963
    b. Gertrude Brown   m.1 Carl Long, living in SM 1945
                                          m.2 Weaver,   living in Whittier 1963
        1942 phbk: Carl R Long 517 E El Camino;   1945 phbk: same
    c. Muriel (Norris Bramlett)   b. c1918
        living in Los Angeles 1945, in Whittier 1963

9.   Horace Hazard (Hayard?)   b.   OH 30 March 1891; d. disappeared; no further data
    1910 cen: w/J S Brown, slsmn lumber yard
    1920 cen: 611 W Cook; 1922 Dir: foreman Union Oil co Plant, r 611 W Cook
    1926 Dir: bkpr Shell Oil co same; 1930 Dir: same
    1938-9 Dir: Chaffins Variety Store 317 Guadalupe St, Guad; h 611 W Cook
    1940-1 Dir: same; 1945-6 Dir: Varieties, Guad, r 715 N Miller
    1942 phbk: 715 N Miller; 1955-6 Dir: as 1945
        m. at home of bride's parents, Cypress St, Sat Sep 30 1916
            by J Walter Jordan DD (*Times*) (divorced)
    Ruth Margaret Young   b. Wilsonville NE May 1896
      1955-6 Dir: emp Miller St   living in Santa Maria 1996
      School r 715 N Miller   F: Floyd Clarendon Young 1872-1959
      to Santa Maria 1908   M: Mary Bell Anderson 1876-1947
    a. Mary Jean (Langley)   b. c1924; living in Connecticut 1996
        1932: Local Lass in Piano Contest. …student of only 18 mos, Mary Jean Chaffin won
            Wednesday's competition in the preliminaries…in Exposition Auditorium in San
            Francisco for the privilege of entering the Twelfth Annual Music Week Contest
            sponsored by the Civic assn of that city. The program…selected by San Francisco
            Music Teachers Assn under direction of Henrick Gjerdrum…here in a concert
            before the Harmony Club the past winter. Mary Jean Chaffin, little 8-year-old piano
            genius, will play the pages and pages of (two pieces) entirely from memory. The
            little pianist and her instructor Mrs Muriel Fisk…mother Mrs W H (sic) Chaffin and
            dau Georgianna left…this morn   –Mon Apr 18 p.3
    b. Georgina F (Utley)
        1940-1 Dir: stu r 611 W Cook
        1945-6 Dir: opr Dalessi Beauty Shop r 715 N Miller
        1955-6 Dir: Utley Willard B (Georgina) 495 Dal Porto Ln

10. Merritt Preston   b. OH 3 Aug 1893 (gen)   1892 (cen)
      w/Standard Oil   d. Taft CA 28 Apr 1947 @53/8/24; SM cem
      6 yrs in Taft (obit)   obit Mon Apr 28 p.1; heart attack; 3gch
      living in Taft 1928, 1937, 1940
      m.
    Cora Hazel Wylie   b. Santa Maria 12 Dec 1896
                                             d. at home Taft 5 Feb 1943 @45/1/23; SM cem
                                             obit Fri Feb 5 p.1; 2gch
                                           F: Richard Columbus Wylie 1867-1945
                                           M: Joanna S Leonard 1865-1935
    a. Preston living in Taft 1943. 1947: National Supply Store, Taft
        1928: Mr & Mrs M P Chaffin and son Preston from Taft visiting her sister Mr & Mrs
            Hugh Toy.   -Oct
        1933: R C Wylie family gathering Fourth of July…Mr & Mrs H D Toy Jr, Mr & Mrs
            Clifford Wylie of Santa Maria…Mr & Mrs M P Chaffin & Preston arrived yesterday;

   Mr & Mrs E G Keffer of Modesto and Mr & Mrs A H Dutton and Ruth of San Diego
    expected today…   –Sat July 1 p.2
    1943: survivors, Alice Toy and Clifford Wylie, Santa Maria; Eva Dutlow (sic), San
     Diego; Dorothy Keffer, Modesto; Leland Wylie, Alaska *Note:* See Toy chart
11. Gladys M   b. OH 28 March 1896
  1920 cen: w/Willard, S   d.
   m.1 Grisson, living in San Francisco 1937
    m.2 Davis, living in Los Angeles 1940, in Bakersfield 1947
     (1938 phbk: Davis Gladys M Mrs h 1035 S Figueroa, Los Angeles)?
    m.3 Tobey, living in San Jose 1953, 1964
  William W Tobey   b. SSDI d. San Jose 8-3-1963
  1954 Dir: Tobey Wm W (Gladys M) cabtmkr EA MacLean & Son h 1280 Hester Ave
  1966 Dir: Tobey Gladys M (wd Wm W) ret h1280 Hester Ave San Jose

Vol. XXVIII, No. 3, Fall 1996, p. 20

Corrections and Additions   [Page numbers refer to those in Quarterly]

p.18. Leila V Hudson's husband was Dorwin Hudson; they came for Thanksgiving from Los Angeles in 1928.

Vol. XXIX, No. 4, Winter 1997, p.19

p.19. Merritt P Chaffin and Cora H Wylie married October 9, 1915, Pres Ch by Rev Jordan.
                           -*Times* Oct 9

Vol. XXXI, No. 3, Fall 1999, p.6

CHRISTENSEN
EMIGRATION 1854 STYLE (DENMARK TO SALT LAKE CITY)

Below you will find the parts of the life story of Mads Fredrick Theobald Christensen that applied to his emigration in Dec. 1853 with the same group that our family was in. Here we are at last able to get a first-hand account of the long journey of nearly ten months duration that brought Bendt, his wife Margrethe, and their children, George, Christine, Hans Enoch, and Andrew B. to Utah.

Each new day of the trek brought new problems the majority perplexing, some sorrowful, a few inspiring — for every experience on the way was new and entirely different from the familiar farm life in green Hosterkob. Judging from the silent information that has been passed down to us concerning the emigration, most of the adventures must have been painful to our Nielsens. Records attest that sickness and death ravaged the Scandinavian company, and our family did not entirely escape tragedy when cholera struck after the immigrants reached the mouth of the mighty Mississippi. That part will be told later, but for now, lets look over the shoulder of Mads as he relives the eventful crossing, recording it just for us, it seems, in the hand of an experienced school teacher in Utah.

"Everything was now being arranged for the going to Utah. It was summer (1853) and the emigration did not start until Christmas time, ... The time for our departure for the great journey arrived. My benefactor, Jorgan Nielsen, a son of Bent Nielsen, of Hosterjob, near Copenhagen, furnished me with new clothing, enough to have lasted several years."

"On Dec. 22, 1853, 301 peoples boarded the steamer 'Slesvig', which left Copenhagen late in the afternoon. We sailed across the Baltic that night and arrived in Kiel Harbor next morning. The vessel was not large, but the billows on the sea were, and so we got rocked considerably and many were seasick…"

(Mads then tells that he was worried about his new clothes, and so he stood and waited to see the baggage unloaded off the steamer. His trunk, painted red with white lettering, so it would be easy to spot, was missing. He never saw it and George's generous gifts again.)

"...We went by train to Gluckstadon, the west coast of Glesvig. We crossed the North Sea by steamer and arrived safely at Hull, after a somewhat rough voyage, accompanied by much sea-sickness, which did not affect me, however. I was as fresh as the sailors and often in their way."

"...We were detained several days in Liverpool presumably on account of getting the ship in readiness for so long a voyage. The ship had to be supplied with provisions and fresh water, enough to last perhaps four or five months, in case of accidents or unfavorable weather causing delay... After several days we went aboard the Jesse Munn and started to float down the channel and out on the Atlantic, steering much to the south of west in order to get to a warmer zone where the vessel could take advantage of the trade winds."

"....We received our rations of food once a week. This was a regular allowance of uncooked food, such as peas, rice, salt, beef, sugar, coffee, and also fresh water once a day. The beef was salt beef. There was a kitchen range midship where an Irish cook held sway, abusing nearly every person who needed something cooked. Outside stood our cooking utensils in a long row from early morning until late evening, waiting their turn to get on the stove where they would get half cooked and then be taken away by us. Another cook in the adjoining kitchen prepared the meals for the crew, who also were rationed."

"...The two cooks could not agree and because of this they had a fight with the permission of the captain. It was held for the public in regular sailor style, which I had the nerve to witness. Entirely stripped to the waist, they went at each other with heavy blows to begin with, keeping it up for perhaps an hour, by which time they both were so jaded that the blows could not have hurt much."

"....For many days the weather was warm and the wind a dead calm, so the vessel scarcely moved. We could then play and dance on the deck just so we kept out of the way of the sailors who had their duties to perform. Again, we had wind storms, causing uneasiness for our safety."

"After some seven weeks of sailing, we passed the island of Cuba at some distance. At first its mountainous outlines against the sky appeared as outlines of clouds, but gradually they became more plain and distinct. I judge we did not get nearer than four miles, passed Florida and after several days, entered the muddy waters flowing out of the great Mississippi River, many miles out to sea. The changes of water could be seen long before we entered them."

"Soon a pilot vessel came out and lay alongside while the pilot boarded the ship and took charge of it. The next day we were in the Mississippi River and cast anchor off New Orleans. After inspection by the health officers, we were permitted to go ashore and view part of the city. Here we saw the slave market where slaves, male and female, were offered for sale. They stood in rows outside the dealers' place of business, where he would cry them off to passersby, much like other merchandise while the slaves were dressed so as to appear to the best advantage."

"After a delay of two or three days we were transferred to a large steamer with tremendous large side wheels as propellers. These steamers were floating palaces in appearance, painted white and handled mostly by crews of Negroes.

Owing to unusual low water in the Mississippi the passage was slow and tedious, which, in connection with the change of climate and differences in the mode of living, caused cholera of a very malignant type to break out among the emigrants, resulting in an unusual number of deaths."
"....We were on the steamer about ten days and landed in St. Louis."

"After arriving in St. Louis, March 11th, houses were rented for the temporary occupation of the emigrants who tarried there about a month until the next company of Scandinavian emigrants, under the direction of Hans Peter Olsen (Piercy) arrived. During the stay in St. Louis sickness continued among the immigrants and many more died of the cholera."

(*Note*: It was here in St. Louis that Margrethe Nielsen succumbed to Cholera, a specific date is not known but it was between March 11th and June 15th. Also a burial place is not known as the old Mormon cemetery has been erased and no records of it seem to exist.)

"....We bought our food at the grocery store where the price of nearly everything was five cents a pound. It was calculated that we should be there about six weeks so a number of the men took jobs on a railroad then being constructed in Illinois about forty miles from St. Louis. Another boy and myself went along to earn a few dollars. When we had worked there about three weeks we received word that the company had left St. Louis and gone to Kansas City, then a trading post. We quit work and asked for our pay... We boarded a steamer that was to take us to Kansas."

"....The company arriving in Kansas was provided with tents with which they formed a camp in the woods a mile or two from the city and there we waited while oxen, wagons and supplies were bought and prepared for the journey across the plains. While encamped here in the woods it rained considerably. One morning after a rainy night, we found everything in the way of fuel so wet we could hardly get a fire started..." (Mads here tells that he cut a deep gash in his leg while attempting to shave a wet log down to the dry part.)

This is about all the reference Mads made of the trip. We're very grateful for his account, though it does leave some things to be desired. For additional details, we need to look again into Andrew Jensen's, *The History of the Scandinavian Mission*, pages 87-90.

"After the arrival of the ' Jesse Munn' company from St. Louis," Jensen states, "the two companies were amalgamated and organized for the journey across the Plains, May 9th. Hans Peter Olsen was chosen leader of the amalgamated company and Christian J. Larsen as chaplain, while Bent Nielsen was chosen wagon master, Jens Hansen camp captain and Peter P. Thomsen captain of the guard. The company, which consisted of sixty-nine wagons, was divided into six smaller companes (sic) with ten to twelve wagons and a captain in each company. To each wagon were attached four oxen and two cows. There were also in the company a number of reserve oxen. From ten to twelve persons were assigned to each wagon. Elders Carl Capson, Anders Andersen, Peter Beckstrom, Jens Jorgensen, Anders W. Winberg, and Valentine Valentinsen were appointed captains of the six divisions. Oxen, wagons, tents and other traveling equipment, which the emigrants bought in St. Louis and Kansas City or vicinity, cost more than had been expected, on account of which a number of the emigrants ran short of means and were unable to furnish a full outfit."

"The more well-to-do, however, among whom we might mention Bro. Bent Nielsen from Sjaelland and Peter P. Thomsen from Falster, contributed freely of their means, so that none were left in the States through lack of money. Toward the close of May, another camping place was chosen about eight miles west of Kansas City, from which place the emigrants commenced their long journey over the Plains on Thursday, June 15, 1854."

"After camping in the woods for three weeks everything was in readiness and we started with six oxen hitched to each wagon. The prairie was soft and miry because of the rainy weather. For many miles there was not a trail or road and the oxen were not trained to pull wagons and knew nothing about 'gee' and 'haw' and less about our Danish talk. We had to tie long ropes to the heads of the lead oxen of each team to prevent them from taking their own course. Occasionally some ox would start to bellow and cause a stampede or panic of fear, and away they would run despite our holding tight to their ropes."

(*Note*: The quote above is taken from Mads narrative, now we return to Andrew Jensen's account.)

"This company of emigrants traveled over a new but shorter road than previous companies had done. After traveling about twenty miles from Kansas City, a halt was called because nearly all the teams were too heavily loaded, owing to the fact that the emigrants had taken too much baggage along, contrary to the instructions or counsel given. At the suggestion of Brother Olsen some of the brethren went to Leavenworth City, about thirty miles from the camping place, to consult Apostle Orson Pratt, who, in his capacity of emigration agent, had located temporarily in said city. Elder Pratt advanced the company sufficient money to buy fifty oxen, after which the journey was continued. A few days journey west of Fort Kerney the company, on the 5th of August, met Apostle Erastus Snow and other Elders from the Valley who had been called on missions to the States. Elder Snow held a meeting with the Scandinavian Saints and addressed them in their own language, which caused great rejoicing in the camp."

"Of all the emigrant companies, who this year crossed the Plains, the Scandinavians suffered the most with sickness (cholera), and during their temporary sojourn at the camping place near Westport, as well as on the steamboats, fatalities were more numerous. Scores fell as the victims of the dreadful disease and many of the Saints were compelled to bury their relatives and friends without coffins on the desolate plains. So great was the mortality among them that of the 680 souls who had left Copenhagen the previous winter only about 500 reached their destination. The others succumbed to the sickness and hardships of the journey. The survivors reached Salt Lake City, Oct. 5, 1854."

So ends Andrew Jensen's account of the 1854 emigration from Scandinavia which brought our family to Utah.

Extracted and condensed from the *Bendt Nielsen Family History*, who is my wife's Great Great Grandfather on her Maternal side, Wilfred W. Kesner

Notes on Emigration 1854 Style

Consulting Johnson's Family Atlas, 1861 edition, one finds Schleswig and Holstein on the map of Prussia, Norway, Sweden and Denmark. Keil is on the east coast of Holstein; from there a railroad is shown leading south to Hamburg, with a branch going west to Gluckstadt on the mouth of the river Elbe, which empties into the North Sea. This trip to Salt Lake City is much like that described in the Memoire of William Laird Adam, (see Adam chart). Originating in Scotland, the Adams, too, sailed from Liverpool, and cholera was a danger to their party four years earlier than the Danes'. Although the Adam clan stayed in Salt Lake City three years, they had moved on by the time our Danish contingent arrived.

The American Mormons sent missionaries early on to European countries, and made far more converts in Denmark than in either Norway or Sweden; in fact, Copenhagen, by 1850, was a center of emigration activity, as moving to Salt Lake City was implied by conversion. About 17,000 Danes made the trip, making them the second largest nationality in Utah in the early days. – See *Swedish Exodus*, by Lars Ljungmark, Swedish Pioneer Historical Press, 1979, p. 34.

CLEMENTS
CALIFORNIA PIONEERS

James Ely Clements						b. MA June 1811
								d. Santa Maria Fri 29 Mar 1901 @89/9/27; SM cem
								    funeral from Chas Sedgwick's
  1860 cen: San Joaquin co
    Douglas tp, PO Stockton;
  nephew John Holden 18 MO deaf/dumb in the household
  1880 cen: Stanislaus st, Stockton; parents MA
  1886. Mrs Kline of Mendocino, daughter of Mr Clemons (sic) and sister of Mrs Chas
    Sedgwick is visiting.						—Oct 9
  1890 GR: J E Clements 79 MA f SM #2; reg Sep 1
  1892 GR: James Ely Clements 81 5' 9½" fair complexion blue eyes grey hair miner MA
    res Huasna, pct Huasna, PO Santa Maria; reg Oct 18
  1897. "Grandpa" Clements managed to get down town a while Thursday and shake hands with
    old friends. He will celebrate his 86th birthday anniversary next week.		—May 29
  1900 cen: w/Chas Sedgwick
       m. (MA)
Aurelia C							b. Chester MA 1807
  to CA 1856							d. Santa Maria 20 Aug 1884 @77/0/16; SM cem;
								    inf Chas Sedgwick; obit Aug 23?

Known children
1. Charles Clements					b. MA c1838
      1860 cen: w/parents
2. Mary Ann Clements					b. Springfield MA Nov 1842
      1914 Dir: Mrs Mary A				d. at home Cypress st 29 June 1915 @72/6/29; SM cem
      r203 W Cypress					obit July 3 p.1: 33y SM; aged husband, son 2 dau
								Card of Thanks…Chas Sedgwick, Mrs Frank Smith,
								M/M John Watson –July 3
        m. Stockton CA 10 June 1858
    Charles Sedgwick					b. Columbia co NY Feb 1829; F: ENG; M: MA/NY
      bio Storke 490; to CA				d. at home of dau Mrs John Watson 30 May 1917
      via Horn 1849; river				 @87/3/21 SM cem; obit June 2 p.1; dau 2 sons;
      express Stockton-SF				 sis Mrs Thomas E Ketcham, Stockton; nc Mrs L W
      to SM Sep 1881; meat mkt			 Blosser (nee Anna VanValkenburg b. Chatham NY)
    1882. 6 ch, 3 buried Stockton (?)
      butcher, rancher
    Sedgwick and 2 ch had 160a each near Chimney Flat cyn north of Suey ranch
      -attribution lost
    1860 cen: San Joaquin co, Douglas tp, PO Stockton; Foreman's ranch
    1870 cen: 3d ward Stockton, butcher, son 2 dau
    1882 GR: 52 NY butcher SM; reg Sep 30
    1883. Santa Maria fire: Sedgwick House (meat mkt) 16x48 burned down
    1883-4 McKenney Dir: Chas Sedgwick meat mkt Santa Maria
             George E Sedgwick hotel Santa Maria
    1885. ads *Santa Maria Times* Dec
    1886. Mr Chas Sedgwick was called to Stockton on Saturday last by the intelligence of
      his father's death…@91.						—Sep 11
    1887. Personal Mention. Mr Charles Sedgwick left Wednesday morning to visit son
      George in Amador co.						—Nov 5

1888 Polk Dir: Chas Sedgwick meat mkt Santa Maria
1890 GR: 56 NY butcher SM #2; reg Aug 18
1891. 1st Annual Fair 37th Agricultural District Santa Maria: ad. Charles Sedgwick
   Wholesale & Retail Dealer in Fresh Meat of All Kinds…
1892 GR: 62 5'10 light complexion blue eyes white hair butcher NY res Huasna pct,
   Huasna PO, Santa Maria; reg Sep 21
1900 cen: Santa Maria butcher
1906 Dir: butcher rCypress st; Mrs Mary
      Orcutt: Sedgwick Charles, butcher; Mrs
            Thomas, butcher
            Charles B, butcher
      Sedgwick & Son, meat market
1909 Dir: Chas Sr stockman r203 W Cypress; Mrs M A; Chas Jr butcher
1910 cen: W Cypress st, own income; 6 births 3 living (?)

a.   George Edgar Sedgwick   b. (Stockton) Apr 1860
    1882 GR: 22 CA blksm   d. Santa Barbara co 12 July 1931 @60/2/14
    SM; reg Aug 17   spouse M; SM cem, out-of-town mortuary
    1884. witness to marriage of Ebenezer Hopkins and Sarah Stephenson, Santa
      Maria 13 June; C122
    1887. Mrs S E Crow returned from Stockton accompanied by her brother George
      Sedgwick who came on a short visit.   –Dec 24
    1890 GR: Geo E 30 CA butcher Huasna; reg Sep 15
    1892 GR: Geo E 32 5'10 fair brown dark f CA Huasna Huasna SM; reg Sep 10
    1898. Mrs Geo Sedgwick has a large music class at Guadalupe. Her pupils are to be
      congratulated at having so capable a teacher.   –Sep 24
    1900 cen: Santa Maria engineer (?); 5 births 5 living
      m.
  Mary Minnie Blower   b. NY Nov 1862?; parents ENG
            d.

= Mary J Sedgwick   b. CA Mar 1886
= Charles B Sedgwick   b. CA 11 Mar 1888
    1906 Dir: butcher Orcutt   d. San Leandro 24 June 1974 @86/3/13;
    1906 Dir: C B meat cutter   SM cem
      r223 W Fesler; Mrs Katie
    1910 cen: tp #10 (Orcutt) county rd, butcher shop
    1920 cen: 625 Chapala st Santa Barbara meat cutter
    1922-3 Dir: Chas R (sic) Los Olivos
    1924. Mrs Chas Sedgwick of Los Olivos…
    1926. Charley Sedgwick, Los Olivos…
        m.1 Mascarel Hotel, Santa Barbara 5 Apr 1909 by Rev Moore, (*Times*)
  Katherine C Peterson   b. CA? DK? 1888; parents DK
    "Katie"
  + Eldon Sedgwick   b. (Aug 1910)
              d. Oakland 4 Sep 1914
                @4/0/23; SM Cem; inf A Peterson;
                ill svl yrs; obit Sep 5;
                son of former residents
        m.2 (by 1929)
  Ethelyn Kathryn Bartron   b. Santa Maria 14 Nov 1888
    Mrs Chas Sedgwick   d. San Leandro 3 Nov 1965 @76/11/19
    in Oakland 1934, 1941   m.1 Knotts; m.2 Gaxiola; see Bartron chart

            F: Patrick Henry Bartron 1842-1920
            M: Alsie Anna Dodge 1849-1925
  = George Clair Sedgwick   b. SM 4 Feb 1891 (*Times*)
            d. Los Angeles co 26 Feb 1965
             @74/0/22; SM cem; inf Iowa
             Sedgwick

  = Darrell J Sedgwick   b. SM 12/13 Sep 1893 (*Times*)
            d. Santa Clara co 12 Dec 1961 @68

  = Ardis A Sedgwick   b. SM 7 June 1899 (*Times*)
            d. Folsom 24 Oct 1994 @95;
             surname Wancke

b. Ruth Sedgwick   b. (Stockton) c1864
  m.   (Ruth D Smith d. Los Angeles co 25 Apr 1915 @51)?
  Frank Smith (Franklin D Smith d. Los Angeles co 29 Jan 1935 @75
             spouse R)?

c. Alida Kate Sedgwick   b. Stockton 17 Apr 1866; m.1 @18 of SM;
  1886. Mrs S E Crow returned on m.2 of SM
   Sat last from an extended trip d. Bakersfield 14 Mar 1967 @100/10/27;
   to Stockton and various points SM cem; obit Wed Mar 15 p.4; 7y Arvin;
   in the San Joaquin valley.   gch include Mrs Marian FritzGerald (sic),
        -Sep 11   Bakersfield; John Watson, Yreka; d/l Mrs
             Minnie Hall, Bakersfield
  1890. New millinery goods at Mrs K A Crow's millinery parlors. A fine winter
   stock from which to select.   –Nov 22
  1891. Mrs K A Crow, milliner…   (*Times*)
   m.1 at the home of Chas Sedgwick 24 Nov 1884 by Rev Chas Leach ME, C163;
    wit: Mrs Anna Blosser; Mrs D S Leach
  Samuel Eugene Crow   b. Ashland IL 18 July 1860; m.1 @24 of SM
   1880 cen: SM w/parents   d. at home Santa Barbara 23 April 1941 @80
    student   obit Thu Apr 24 p.7; photo. 1876 to San
   1882 GR: 22 IL f SM   Diego; to SM 1891 (sic); 26y Supreme Ct;
             ret 1932. Organizer of SM Pioneer Assn
            F: Jerome Elmore Crow 1818-
            M: Eliza J 1824
            m.2 1906 Augusta Z Kabel 1870-1963
  bio Phillips II 203: to Brownville NE 1861; to Silver City NM 1875, then AZ, to CA
   1876; from Tehachapi to SM 1878. law school 1880. JP in SM to 1889, thence SB;
   judge of Supreme Ct 1906-
  1884. S E Crow admitted to practice before Supreme Courts of Santa Barbara and
   San Luis Obispo counties…   –article Aug 16
  1890 GR: 30 IL lawyer Santa Barbara #5
  1930. President Santa Maria Pioneer Assn; photo. –Pioneer Assn, Tesene, 2002
  1938 phbk: S E Crow atty Howard Canfield Bldg; r431 E Victoria SB
  = Carl Crow   b.
   1895. Carl Crow, attending school in Santa Barbara, is visiting his mother, Mrs
    Watson and grandparents M/M Sedgwick.   –Aug 24
   1941. survived father, living in San Francisco
  + Sterling Crow; had a daughter also surviving S E Crow, 1941
  + twins Stanley and Douglas Crow
  = Lois Crow   b. SM 22 Feb 1887 (*Times*)

		d. 9 Feb 1889 @1/11/17; SM cem; only dau of S E Crow gdau of Chas Sedgwick (*Times*)

c.   m.2 at the Ramona Hotel San Luis Obispo 13 Dec 1892
        by Rev Will A Knighten (*Times*)

John Nathaniel Watson   b. Rockford IL (20 Aug) 1862; m. of SM;
   1900 cen: wife and son   parents SCT
     w/Sedgwicks; 3 births 2 living   d. at home 205 W Cypress 22 Dec 1928
                                  @66/4/2; SM cem; obit Dec 22 p.5; former
                                  sealer of Wts & Msrs; wid, son, 2 gch,
                                  4 sis, 1 bro
   1909 Dir: John N mach 203 W Cypress; Mrs K A; Duncan S stu
   1910 cen: W Cypress; erector oil supply co
   1914 Dir: John N (Alida K) mach Fairbanks Morse & Co, 203 W Cypress
             Watson Ann E cash SM Gas & Power Co, 203 W Cypress
             Duncan mach Fairbanks & Morse Co, 203 W Cypress
   1922-3 Dir: John N (Alida K) sealer of wts & measures SB Co; r205 W Cypress
   1925 Dir: John N (Kate) sealer of wts & measures 203 W Cypress
   1928 Dir: J N (K Alida) sealer of wts & measures 205 W Cypress
   1928. pall bearers: F H Gates, Elmer Rice, M P Baker, Wm MacDonald,
     F C Twitchell, W L Smith

= Duncan Sedgwick Watson   b. SM 12 Aug 1894 (*Times*)
   1928 in Ventura   d. Los Angeles co 19 Jan 1950
                            @55/5/7; SM cem 2 ch
   1931. In and Out of the City. M/M Duncan Watson and family here from
     Ventura yesterday to visit relatives. –July 13. *Note:* the oil industry fizzled
     in Ventura in the early '30's, and many in that work moved to Long Beach.

d.   Thomas Clements Sedgwick   b. (Stockton) 27 Apr 1873; m. of SM
     1887. in school SM –*Valley*   d. SM 27 Apr 1952 @79; SM cem;
     1906 Dir: Thomas C butcher   obit Mon Apr 28 p.8; r8y w/Watson
       rCypress   213 S Lincoln
     1947-8 Dir: Watson Mrs John N hmkr h213 S Lincoln
       m. San Luis Obispo 28 Sep 1893, D333; consent of parents for Thomas,
         minor

Nelle Anna Tunnell   b. SMv 10 Mar 1872; m. of SM;
                         consent of parents
                  d. San Francisco 28 Jan 1948 @75/10/18;
                  SM Cem obit Wed Jan 28 p.8; 50y SF;
                  husband died in traffic accident; son d.
                  1918. she last of 10 ch. nc Mrs Ida Hawkins
                  to SF for funeral
                  F: Martin Luther Tunnell 1824-1903
                  M: Salina Haskins 1829-1903
                    see ONT, M/H

= Neil W? Sedgwick   b. SM 2 Jan 1896 (*Times*)
   1904. Neil Sedgwick   d. San Francisco 15 Dec 1918
     of SF visiting relatives   –July 1   age 22/11/13; SM cem
                                         obit Dec 21 p.2; nephew of Tom,
                                         Henry, and Geo Tunnell and Mrs
                                         John Watson. orchestra leader at
                                         Tait-Zincande (sic) Café, SF

        Nelle m.2
          Charles C Shattuck   b. CA 19 Jan 1880
                                            d. San Francisco 25 June 1943 @63/5/6;
                                               SM Cem "traffic accident"
                                        M: Sweat
        1917 phbk: Shattuck C C Sr r739 Haight av San Francisco
                            C C Jr r1273 27th av San Francisco
                    Tait-Zinkand Café 168 O'Farrell San Francisco
                    Zinkand Edw r434 10th av San Francisco
3.   Kate Clements   b. NY c1847
     1886. Mrs Kline of   d. (Katherine Klien d. Alameda co 27 May 1922 @77)?
        Mendocino…
    (1890 GR: Mendocino Co. Klein Peter Richard 40 GER Calpella; reg 20 Mar 1888)
                    (Peter Richard Klein d. @58 Santa Clara co 6-26-1906)
    There are discrepancies in the data, but it is presented as found.

CLEMONS
PIONEERS OF THE CALIFORNIA CENTRAL COAST

George Byron Clemons   b. OH 1841; d. Arroyo Grande 1917
   1870 cen: Mendocino co Anderson tp
   1880 cen: SE part of Monterey co   1890 GR: San Miguel
   1900 cen: Arroyo Grande;   1910 cen: Arroyo Grande 15 births 13 living
      m. (Mendocino co) 1865
Arminda Ellender Nunn   b. IL 1853; d. Shandon 1925
1.   Mary Ann Clemons   b. (Mendocino co) 1868; d. Ukiah 1962
      m. SLO co 1888; 7 children
    Daniel Hugh Lawson   b. nr Healdsburg 1862; d. Hayward 1943
2.   Aurora Jackson Clemons   b. Mendocino co 1870; d. Paso Robles 1952
3.   Lewis J Clemons   b. (Mendocino co) 1871; d. Saratoga 1964
      m. SLO 1895; 3 sons   Lena L Matthis
                                    b. (Watsonville?) 1876; d. Saratoga 1973
    a.   Lloyd Marvin Clemons   b. 1898-1964
       chiropractor Santa Maria 1929-; original organizer Elks' Rodeo 1944
         m.2 1931 Gertrude B McIntosh 1898-1973; Pres Pioneer Assn 1962
4.   Wesley James Clemons   b. Mendocino co 1873; d. San Jose 1954
      m. Paso Robles 1901; 5 children
    Minerva Gruwell   b. CA 1882; d. (San Miguel) 1911
5.   Homer Byron Clemons   b. CA 1875; d. Orange co 1938
      m.
Belle Berry (AF), spouse initial on death list L F
6.   Mattie Lucette Clemons   b. (San Miguel) 1877; d. (Gonzales) 1960
      m. San Miguel 1901; 5 children
    Otto Worth Tucker   b. KS c1872; d. Shandon 1925
7.   Margie Ellender Clemons   b. (San Miguel) c1879; d. (Arroyo Grande) 1899
8.   Henry Pomeroy Clemons   b. SLO co 1881; d. Paso Robles 1966
      m. Paso Robles 1905; 2 children
    Mabel Clare Correll   b. Selma 1885; d. Atascadero 1980
9.   Maggie B Clemons   b. (San Miguel) 1881; d. (San Miguel) 1887
10. Lottie Lula Clemons   b. (San Miguel) 1886; d. Santa Maria 1961
      m.1 San Luis Obispo 1907; 1 son
    Frederick Wolfe   b. NY c1875
      m.2; 1 dau
    John Edward Jullien   b. (Gilroy) 1893; d. (Santa Maria) 1976
     40 years Union Station Orcutt
11. Everett L Clemons   b. (San Miguel) 1888
                               d. (Huntington Beach) 1970
12. Susie Vera Clemons   b. (San Miguel) 1891; d. Cathey's Valley 1975
      m. Arroyo Grande 1920; 5 children
    Everett Ambrose Hopper   b. Adelaida 1881; d. Paso Robles 1964
    see M/H for Hopper clan
13. Stewart Nunn Clemons   b. San Miguel 1892; d. Santa Barbara 1956
   to Orcutt 1917; see *Old Town Orcutt,* Nelson, 1987
       m. San Miguel 1912; 3 sons
    Mary Adelaide Giraud   b. San Miguel 1894; d. Santa Maria 1979

14. George Colton Clemons b. (San Miguel?) 1893; d. Laguna Beach 1984
    wife unknown; dau Evelyn d. Garden Grove 1927 @9
15. Stanford B Clemons b. (San Miguel?) 1895; d. Lodi 1982; spouse G

Martin G Clemons b. NY Oct 1845
  1892 GR: 48 5'10 light complexion d. at home Goleta 17 Jan 1916 @71;
  brown eyes brown hair NY obit *SB Morning Press* Jan 18 p.3; 16y Goleta;
  rLaGraciosa PO Santa Maria; also lived in Lompoc; 50y CA; son & dau at home
  reg Sep 20
  1900 cen: tp #7 (Santa Maria) F: NY; M: SCT m/32 3 births 3 living
  1910 cen: tp #3 (Goleta) wid F: CAN/FR; M: NY
    The family story was that Clemons was from Quebec, French, a "wetback" who swam the
    St Lawrence River; he changed his name from St Clement to Clemons. –ONT 266
    This story probably belongs one generation back.
        m. c1868
Josephine M Scull b. OH Dec 1845
  d. (before 1905)
  F: Abel C Scull 1812-1899
  1877 GR: Skull Abil C 63 NJ f Santa Barbara; reg Mar 26 1875
  1879 GR: Scull Abel C 65 NY f Goleta (reg date not legible)
  1882 GR: Scull Abel C 68 NJ f Goleta; reg Aug 17
  1890 GR: 76 NJ f La Patera; reg Sept 13
  1899 d. Goleta 7 Feb @86/11; Goleta Cem. obit *Santa Maria Times* Feb 18; father of Mrs
    Clemons of Martin district
  Patron T/W: to CA 1849; to County 1863; 225a Goleta
      m.(2) @62 MEch SB 24 Jan 1869 Saran J Sherwood m. @29 (sic); d. 1920
        1900 cen: tp #3; b. FL Nov 1837; wid; 1 birth
          Carrie B Scull b. Nov 1869
          Carrie Scull d. Santa Clara co 10 May 1931 @50
  1900. Southside Squibs. The Clemons family are expected home from the San Marcus (sic)
    springs in a few days. –Sep 1
  1901. Southside Squibs. The Clemons family is still with us . . . decided not to move to Goleta
    property until some time in the future. –Jan 5
  Southside Squibs. Mrs Clemons has been sick for several days at the home of her daughter,
    Mrs Geo Nicholson. –Feb 16
1. Edward O Clemons b. CA 5 Nov 1868
     1900 cen: tp #7 single d. Santa Cruz co 22 Feb 1955
     1915, 1916 in Goleta
2. Aurilla Mae Clemons b. CA 31 Aug 1872; m. of San Miguel
     d. at home of brother Edward Clemons, Goleta,
       30 Dec 1914 @42/4; SM cem, obit Jan 2 1915 p.1
       m. San Luis Obispo 24 Sep 1894 by Rev Geo Willett, D461
         wit: Jas A Ford, SLO; Eva Clemons, San Miguel
   George Woodard Nicholson b. Ossian IA 15 Aug 1867; m. of San Miguel
     1906 Dir: Garey farmer d. Santa Maria 20 Nov 1949 @82/3/5; SM cem
     1909. trustee SMUHS obit Mon Nov 21 p.1; in valley 60y; co-mgr
       Suey ranch
     1914 Dir: RR #1; Geo, m.(2) 1918 Rosina Fischl Beutel 1880-1956; 2 ch
       Gladys, May, Philip F: Howell Powell Nicholson 1831-1921
       M: Caroline Woodard 1828-1920
       See Nicholson chart

    a.   Gladys Lenore Nicholson   b. Martin district 15 Nov 1895 (*Times*)
        SMUHS 1913   d. Santa Maria 9 Aug 1972 @76; SM cem;
        LA Normal; teacher   r829 E Central obit Thu Aug 10, p.2; 4 sons
                                                          5 dau ½ bro ½ sis 19 gch 2ggch;
                                                          see ONT, pp. 268-271 for names
        m.(1)
      Howard G Arbuckle 1898-1924; obit Feb 26, p.5; bur SB; American Legion
        m.(2)
      Leslie Andrew Peterson 1892-1948
    b.   Paul Woodard Nicholson   b. near Garey 9 Dec 1900 (*Times*)
                                                       d. (Garey) 4 June 1905; SM cem
        1901. Southside Squibs. At this writing the infant child of Geo Nicholson is very
          sick. It (sic) recovery is thought to be doubtful.   –Feb 16
    c.   Philip Livingston Nicholson   b. (Garey) 8 or 18 Dec 1905
                                                       d. 28 Dec 1914 at home of uncle Clemons,
                                                          Goleta, SM cem; obit 1 Jan 1915; diabetes,
                                                          pneumonia
3.   Eva/Evangeline Adelaide Clemons   b. CA Oct 1870
      1900 cen: w/father   d.
      1910 cen: w/father
      1916 w/father, single

COLE
A GENEALOGICAL ADVENTURE

This summer's trip to Illinois and adjacent ancestral dwelling places enabled us to make a cohesive story out of information gathered over the last decade, and gave us the grand satisfaction of having solved some mysterious family relationships.

Our latent interest in family history was stimulated during the bicentennial by a series of articles on local history by Doris Olsen of the *Santa Maria Times*. My husband's father, Linden S. Cole, born in Santa Barbara in 1894, reminded us that his grandparents had come from Iowa, as he thought, to California about the centennial year, and settled in the Cambria-San Simeon area; we decided that it would be simple enough to investigate their part in the local history of the next county, and set about doing so. Well, of course it wasn't simple, but it has been entertaining and highly instructive.

L.S. Cole, the only child of his parents' union, which union dissolved when he was 15, had few family stories from early childhood, and no contact with his father's family in adulthood to reinforce their retention. Our investigations, however, awakened memories long dormant, and led us, with his help, to a second cousin in Los Angeles who proved to have custody of the Cole Family Bible. We would still be at the starting gate without that Bible, and we wouldn't have found it without having jogged the patriarch's memory. It is fortuitous that we began when we did, for it proved to be the last year of his life, and as others can ruefully attest, once the old folks take their memories to the grave, there's no retrieval.

The Cole Family Bible, purchased soon after the marriage of Laurentine Sweet Cole and his first wife Catherine Jane Morris, Jo Daviess County, Illinois, 1853, is unusual in having not only names and dates, but also, concerning the children, place names, down to county and township. Three deaths, however, do not have such information, and therefore we have puzzled for ten years over this: a child was born in Clayton County, Iowa, in 1858; was the family still there when Catherine died in 1860? If so, how did Laurentine get to know Widow Laura Williams, 60 or more miles away in Bellevue, well enough to marry her 9 weeks later?

Soon after we undertook our family search, we joined the Santa Maria Valley Genealogical Society and Library, and were advised of the value of census records. Skeptical at first, we soon became addicts. Indexes were hard to come by at that time, so we would order a film and read through the whole thing. The first one we tried was the 1860 census of Jackson county, Iowa, the year and place of L.S. Cole's second marriage. He was not enumerated; we did find his prospective bride and family, a Cole family from South Carolina, and a single Cole girl, born in Illinois, in a McKinley family. Could be his sister, I thought, and made a note of the family which I have carried these ten years. It has been my habit to make note of any names which seem for any reason likely to be related, and it has stood me in good stead, as will be seen. Checking the Jo Daviess county, Illinois census for 1850, we hoped to find L.S. living with his parents; rather, he was living in an unrelated household, as were several other Cole children in that county. Later, I found another Cole 'orphan' in Jackson county, Iowa, duly recorded with the others in my notes.

According to the death notice in a Paso Robles (California) newspaper, L.S. Cole who died in 1894, a week before his grandson, Linden S. Cole was born, was a native of Springfield, Illinois. Investigation soon proved that there were no Cole families on the 1830 index for Sangamon county, Illinois, who had a son born March 1, 1828, as the Cole Family Bible records. There were both Cole and Sweet families in Morgan county, which is not far from Springfield, and, furthermore, one of those Sweet families had a son named Lorentine, seven years older than Laurentine Sweet Cole. Surely there must be a connection! We worked on that for years, until we exhausted the possibilities. Then I went back to my list of Cole orphans and their host families in Jo Daviess county; there was but one in which the mother was old enough to be Laurentine's mother - - Louisa Brown. Furthermore, the last child born to Laurentine was named Louisa, a name not used by the Morgan county Coles, so that was a plus factor. I sent to Jo Daviess County for a marriage for Stephen and Louisa Brown, early 1840s, but the response was negative.

In the meantime we had success tracing the lineage of the second Mrs Cole, Laura Culver, widow of Riley Williams. She it was whom my father-in-law remembered as Grandma Cole living in San Fernando Valley (California) and for whom he, as a small boy, gathered dried oranges from the packing shed to burn in the stove, but whose given name he had never heard. With much help from correspondence as well as travel we had traced her and her four siblings, Daniel, Oliver, Carlisle, and Lucy Culver, from Plattsburgh, New York to Huron, Erie county Ohio, thence, to Jackson County, Iowa, where three of them stayed. Lucy married Samuel Johnston in Ohio in 1847 and Abraham Hawks in Bellevue, 1865, and then dropped from sight, so, in an attempt to find her, I sought her children. Her oldest child, Martha, married John N. Brown in 1868, and even though Brown is a common name, his consistent use of his middle initial helped. The most valuable help came from names and places taken from photographs supplied by Culver relatives in Jackson county, enabling us to locate these people on the recently available 1900 and 1910 censuses. Knowing that many Iowa counties have enthusiastic genealogical societies, I wrote to the chapter in Cass county where the Browns and Johnstons had lived. Before I heard from them that they would include my query in a newspaper column, I received letters from three ladies, one a nonagenarian, who had known them. Another one, whose first husband, killed in WWII, was a grandson of Brown's, had access to her mother-in-law's scrapbook, and kindly sent me several obituaries.

It is the obituary of John N. Brown that brought all this together. His parents' names were not given, but when I looked on an Illinois map for Hanover, his birthplace, and found it to be in Jo Daviess county, it dawned on me that he was the baby John with Stephen and Louisa Brown and a Cole orphan in 1850. Due to faulty memory and poor record-keeping, I forgot that I'd tried for a marriage for them, so sent again, and this time the clerk came through with a marriage for a peculiar name, Scobin (it probably is Scobie) S. Brown and widow Louisa Cole. Getting braver, I sent for the marriage of another couple whose household included a Cole orphan, and that wife was a Cole.

The Brown obituary said that the family had moved to Putnam county, Missouri, when John was very young, and then to Bellevue, Jackson County, Iowa after the Civil War. To the 1860 census: disappointment. Another clue was that John was survived by his brother James, the last of fourteen children. I essayed to make a family of fourteen children by taking my six Cole 'orphans', adding the three youngest Brown Children, two older Brown children as found on the 1850 census, and throwing in a handful of the oldest Brown children already gone by 1850 - - it was possible. Also theoretical.

It all came together when we made our pilgrimage to Putnam county, Missouri, in July 1986. Our hopes were not strong, having found not even one land record for S.S. Brown in Jo Daviess county, Illinois, but as we happened to have some ancestors in another branch of the family to look for there, it made it worth our while to go. We did find land records for Stephen and Louisa Brown, so, hopes up, my husband (David) went to the probate office, and, lo and behold, a probate record for Louisa Brown, dated October (1859) - - no wonder the 1860 census didn't include them!

- - with a list of heirs, the first of whom was Laurentine S. Cole, and the rest were all my Cole orphans, every one. All of them had been living with one sibling or another, except for the one who lived for a time with Abraham Hawks, presumably the same Hawks who married Lucy Johnston later.

It would appear, then, that since L.S. Cole had three sisters, two of whom were married in Bellevue in 1860, it was natural for him, at the death of his (first) wife, wherever it occurred, to take his three little girls to his family who had already demonstrated loving care for one another.

To wind up this story, we needed a father for the Cole 'orphans.' We went to Springfield where the Illinois State Archives has a fine collection of materials. Looking for a young family in the vicinity of Springfield gave us several choices from the index. My feminine intuition concluded that Caroline Cole McKinley, the oldest Cole girl, married about the same time her mother remarried, which was not long after the death of her father. Caroline had probably named her first son Tom to memorialize her father. There was, indeed, a Thomas Cole on the Macon County census for 1830, but we needed a marriage about 1827, at which time Macon County had not yet been formed. We tried Fayette; no. Shelby; and there, among the first dozen marriages was Thomas Cole and Louisa Hawks.

A number of threads thus come together in these Jackson county, Iowa marriages:
    Louisa's son L S Cole married Laura Culver Williams in 1860
    Louisa's granddaughter Lovina McKinley married Carlisle Culver in 1864
    Louisa's baby brother? Abraham Hawks married Lucy Culver Johnston in 1865
    Louisa's son John Brown married Lucy Culver Johnston's daughter,
        Martha Johnston, in the house of Edward McKinley, whose wife was
        Louisa's daughter Sarah, in 1868

Those of you whose ancestors were monogamous, sedentary, or otherwise normal can't know the frustration on the one hand and the satisfaction on the other of those of us who really have to work to find our roots.

LOUISA HAWKS BROWN

Louisa Brown, widow, died October 1859, Unionville, MO
    Heirs: Laurentine S Cole, Joseph Cole, Flecta Luda of IL
                Caroline McKinley and Ellen Cole of Iowa
                Denyma A Hood, John Brown, Sarah Brown, James D Brown of MO
                - Sworn by Charles Hood, Administrator of the estate, 22 Oct 1859
                See also Putnam co, MO Mortality Schedule of 1860

Louisa Hawks married Thomas Cole 19 Dec 1827 Shelby co, IL
    ?Dau of George Hawks, died May 1855 Macon co, IL? No list of heirs
        included in Probate File No 271, Box 11
    Census: Macon co, IL 1830, 140
    Thomas Cole and Louisa her X mark Cole his wife mortgaged two 40 acre parcels
        T16N R1E Macon co, 15 Dec 1836, paid off by 19 Dec 1840; one parcel
        patented May 8, 1835, the other bought from James and Margaret Miller
        24 Nov 1836

1. Laurentine Sweet Cole   b. 1 March 1828 (near) Springfield, IL
                                                d. 5 August 1894 San Marcos, San Luis Obispo co CA

      m. 1. Catherine Jane Morris 3 Feb 1853 Rush Creek, Jo Daviess, IL
      m. 2. Laura Ann (Culver) Williams, widow of Riley Williams,
         16 Sept 1860 Bellevue, Jackson co, IA
    Census: 1850 Jo Daviess co, w/Esther Gable family, 1860? 1870 Hale,
       Trempealau co, WI to CA 1875; 1880 Junction City, OR

2. Caroline Cole b. c1829 IL. Married James McKinley c1844
   Census: 1860 Jackson co, IA, Bellevue

3. Mary Electa Adeline Cole b. c1832 IL
   m. Herginius Ludi 28 March 1850 Jo Daviess co, IL
   Census: 1850 Jo Daviess co, 1860 Jackson co, IA

4. Joseph Cole b. c1836 IL
   Census: 1850 Jo Daviess co, w/ Stephen Brown family

5. Denima/Denime/Denyma Ann Cole b. c1839 IL
   m. Charles Hood April 1, 1859 Putnam co, MO. Record says 'S A Cole'
   Census: 1850 Jackson co, IA w/ Abraham Hawks family; 1860 Putnam co, MO

6. Nancy Ellen b. c1841 IL
   Census: 1850 Jo Daviess co, w/ Herginius Ludi family; 1860 Bellevue, IA
     w/James McKinley family

Louisa Cole, widow, m. Scobie Stephen Brown 29 Sep 1844 Jo Daviess co, IL
    Census: 1850 Mill Creek, Jo Daviess co, IL. No land records
    Stephen S. Brown and Louisa her X Mark Brown his wife sold 120 acres
    Putnam co, MO; T65N R19W March 18, 1858, patented by Stephen S. Brown 13 June
     1857. Louisa Brown bought Lot 1 Blk 15, Unionville MO 26 March 1858
    sold 24 Sep 1883 by Mary E Bowman, formerly Brown, and William Bowman
    her husband, of Adams co, IL. Notarized in Mt Sterling IL

7. John Norriss Brown b. 10 March 1848 Hanover, Jo Daviess co, IL
   d. 9 Dec 1927 Griswold, Cass co, IA. Buried Griswold Cemetery
   m. Martha Ann Johnston March 10, 1868 Bellevue IA.
   Census: 1850 Jo Daviess co; 1860, 1870? c1875 MN; 1880 Harlan co, NE
   1900, 1910 Griswold IA

8. Sarah L. Brown b. c1849 Jo Daviess co, IL
   m. as second wife Edward McKinley 25 Feb 1864 Bellevue IA
   Census: 1850 Jo Daviess co, 1860 Putnam co, MO w/ Chas Hood family
   1870, 1880 Bellevue IA

9, James David Brown b. 1852 IL. Never married
   d. Nov/Dec 1929 Griswold IA. Buried Griswold Cemetery
   Said to be last of 14 children

COLE
SANTA MARIA MERCHANT OF THE EIGHTIES

As the end of the 1980s approaches, the original center of Santa Maria, Broadway and Main, that intersection formed by the corners of the section land of Messrs Cook, Fesler, Miller, and Thornburgh, is in the final throes of change. One hundred years ago the '80s saw the beginnings of change as in a windswept, sandy valley, a town took shape. Wooden structures sprang up, wooden structures burned down; reason and prosperity brought bricks to Santa Maria, and by 1890 substantial civilization was apparent. Charley Cole, though neither a founder nor a long-time resident, had a share in the growth during that decade, and looking at this place through his experiences, gives a glimpse of the era and its life. He came to town shortly after the *Santa Maria Times* began publication, and much of this history comes from its pages.

"Central City is growing like a mushroom...the village contains 2 hotels, 1 feed stable and camping-yard, 1 livery stable, 3 general merchants, 1 hardware store, 2 blacksmith shops, 2 meat markets, 1 barber, 2 paint shops, 1 restaurant, 2 saloons, 2 other general merchants, 2 drug stores, 1 undertaker, 1 variety store, 2 harness shops, a tin shop, 1 milliner, 2 boot and shoe shops, 1 clergyman, 2 lawyers, 1 dentist, 3 doctors and 1 J.P."
-Thompson and West, *History of Santa Barbara and Ventura Counties*, 1883, p. 319

It was to this that Charley Cole, 28, brought his bride, Jennie. He had learned the art of saddle and harness making at his father's elbow in Cambria, and had worked for a time in San Francisco for his brother-in-law, Frank Dalton of Dalton & Gray, commission merchants; Jennie was a highly regarded milliner in Cambria before her marriage. Which profession brought them to Santa Maria is anybody's guess. The first notice of their arrival is this ad in the *Santa Maria Times* of April 1883:

New Millinery Store!
I will open with a new stock of the latest novelties in the millinery and fancy goods about the first of May, and I respectfully invite the ladies to call and see the new styles. I have had many years experience in the millinery business and will endeavor to give satisfaction. Mrs C M Cole in the building formerly occupied by Newman & Son.

If the 1 millinery mentioned in Thompson and West was Mesdames Vincent and Graham, they soon had not only Mrs Cole but later that year Mrs S.M. Blosser competing with a candy and millinery store. On September 8, 1883, Jennie advertised her "Fall and Winter opening of millinery and fancy goods" and later that month her ads for her "large stock of Fall and Winter millinery goods" were regularly printed, through October 13. No ads in the issue of October 20; just the notice of the birth of a daughter to Mr & Mrs C M Cole. Impending maternity hadn't dampened her business zeal! There were no more Cole ads until December 8 when it was advertised that "Mr Chas Cole will open up about the 1st of January a new store next to Sherman's Bazaar. He will keep a general assortment of fancy goods, groceries, and all kinds of fruit." "Fresh fruit by every steamer," he later proclaimed, the source being Dalton & Gray, San Francisco, no doubt.

After but four months of business, Charley's store burned down in May, 1884 along with the rest of the north side of the first block on East Main St. He moved his stock into the building occupied by Mrs Cole's millinery establishment, and continued his business. Here, as elsewhere at the outbreak of fire, the custom was to remove as much of the contents of a building as possible, then knock down the walls, an easy task with these simple wooden boxes that passed for stores. As the *Times* commented "many of the buildings were but tinder boxes with cloth and paper linings." The next month Charlie moved his grocery and fruit business to the building next to B F Bell's.

"The room is being specially fitted up for him." New cloth-and-paper lining, don't you suppose?

As the Fourth of July approached, his one-liners were:
Protecnics At Cole's
P-H-I-Z ! Boom! At Charley Cole's

And these brief stories-

Charley Cole has rigged up a place to display his fireworks in front of his establishment and placed the toy pistols thereon; he surreptitiously loaded each with blank cartridges. In a few moments an innocent individual stopped and snapped one, and it was several moments before they could convince him that the top of his head wasn't blown off.

On the Fourth itself, "Charley Cole was awarded the privilege of keeping a refreshment stand at the park and he will be found there today with a full assortment of fruits, nuts, candies, etc."

The pictures of Santa Maria after the fire of 1884 show T A Jones' brick building, just a few months old, standing against the sky on the west side of Broadway. In 1885 M Fleisher, who had lost much in the fire, built a brick building, and "the commercial tourists, who have ample opportunity of judging, are nick-naming Santa Maria the 'biggest little city' on the coast." When, in September of 1887, Reuben Hart sold his blacksmith business and started the building of a "First Class Brick Hotel", its progress was duly noted in papers up and down the coast, as this "Big Little City" continued to improve.

Charley Cole improved with it. In 1884 he named his business "The Bonanza" and ran larger, more attractive ads in the paper. He bought a cider press; once he got in 100 lbs. of jerked venison that sold like hot cakes; he received a fine stock of Raymond and Squires' Ladies' and Gents' gloves; he stocked cigars, candies, toys…varieties. His one-liners mirror the style of the day: "We shall meet, but we shall miss her; there will be one vacant chair"…until she returns with a pound of those rich candies to be had at Cole's Bonanza.

The popular air with ladies when they visit Coles's Bonanza is "Sweet Buy And Buy"—The fresh candies look so tempting, you know.

Kole'S For Kandies
Kole Klaims The Kromo For Krismas Kards
Our Advertisers *Santa Maria Times* October 8, 1887

The ambitious proprietor of The Bonanza, Chas M Cole, commenced business in the Fall of 1883, by opening a small fruit store. At that time he had but a few dollars in his pocket with which to buy fruit. However, by perseverance he soon became able to lay in a small stock of candies, and today Charlie carries a stock of confections and variety goods to the amount of several thousand dollars and has also found it necessary to employ a clerk in order to wait on his customers with dispatch.

The previous month this story appeared: "One of our prominent citizens went into Cole's store the other day to make a purchase of some fruit. He asked, 'Is Mr Cole in?' 'Yes' replied the clerk in attendance, who was Mr Cole himself, excepting the hair on his upper lip, which had skipped, leaving Charley in disguise."

By 1888 Charley was Santa Maria agent for the *San Luis Obispo Tribune*, so his business received attention in that journal. "C M Cole at Santa Maria has a display of Xmas goods that would be a credit to a much larger town, and if the little folks are not made happy on Christmas morning, it will not be because Charley did not have the proper articles on call."

Aside from business, the Coles' name appeared in the papers mainly when their Cambria relatives came to visit, or when they went north for visits or lodge meetings. In 1885 Charles was one of the floor managers for the Thanksgiving Ball given by the Santa Maria Brass Band; in December Mr and Mrs Cole were among the 60 guests at the Whoofa-Whoofa Banquet given in Fleisher's Building. In June 1886 "Messrs Cole, Moore, and others had a way up time…sailing on Laguna Lake a few miles below town."

Prosperity continued: In August 1887 a second daughter joined the Cole family; in October "The store of Chas Cole is soon to be raised and a new covering added." In May 1888 Jennie had surgery by Drs. Lucas and Bagby; they amputated her "left limb" at the knee, as it had been paralyzed since her childhood and was useless—no wonder she hadn't attended the local balls and holiday dances. Charley's sister came from Cambria to help out with the children, the older not yet four, and the baby. Nothing was noticed in the papers about the disposition of the millinery business.

Charley augmented his business by becoming agent for Wheeler and Wilson sewing machines in 1889, and in May that year, the *Nipomo News* announced that "Cole, the fruit man of Santa Maria, will make two trips per week with fresh fruit and vegetables to Nipomo." His ads reminded that he would take county produce in exchange for goods. In June the San Luis Obispo County Board of Supervisors rejected his request to peddle without a license. Whether that inhibited his business or not, he decided in February 1890 to remove north, and left Santa Maria the end of March. In August the *Santa Maria Graphic* said, "C M Cole, a whilom (former) resident of Santa Maria had been heard from. He is in Washington, and the word comes that recently he accidentally chopped off one of his fingers. Charley ought to know better."

Charles M Cole, Santa Maria merchant of the eighties—why he left is a question as mysterious as why he came. After his departure the valley suffered a slump, to rise again with the discovery of oil; it has been up and down a number of times in the ensuing century. The new brick buildings, the pride of the town one hundred years ago, are gone; will the present efforts last as long?

George Mix Cole
        b. 20 Nov 1826, Shaftsbury, VT
        d. 5 May 1897, San Francisco, CA, at the home of his daughter, Jennie Dalton
        F: Micajah M. Cole[7] Peleg[6] Parker[5] Ebenezar[4] Benjamin[3] Hugh[2] James[1] of Plymouth, M
        M: Clarissa Martin, dau. of Ebenezer
        Saddler and harnessmaker in Cambria, CA, 1869-
  m. 1. 23 September 1850, Susquehanna, PA?
Sarah M. Easterbrooks/Estabrooks, etc. b. c1829 VT, d. c1856 WI
  No other information available
1. Jennie F.   b. 1 July 1851, Beaver Dam, WI
         d. 24 Aug 1934, Berkeley, CA
   m. 20 Jan 1870 San Luis Obispo, CA by A H Burton
  Franklin Dalton 1845-1921

  a. William H   b. Oct. 23, 1870
       m. 1897 Ella A Small
  b. Benton Charles   b. Feb. 7, 1872, d. May 29, 1922
                 Survived by sons Raymond & Harold
  c. May B   b. Sep. 8, 1873, d. Nov. 25, 1949
       m. William A Hargear
  d. Clyde Frank   b. March 5, 1876
  e. Herbert L   b. Aug. 2, 1877
  f. Ethel C   b. June 9, 1880, d. April 8, 1968
       m. Alexander J Barclay
  g. Russell C   b. June/July 10, 1888
       m. Catherine ____
2. Charles Mix   b. May 6, 1855, Beaver Dam, WI
               d. May 30, 1941, Solano County, CA
   m.1 February 22, 1882, Cambria, CA by Wilber F Wenk
  Jennie Bright 1857-1904
  a. Sadie Elizabeth   b. Oct. 17, 1883, Santa Maria, CA
                 d. May 4, 1950, Vallejo, CA
      m. Fred W. Mosier No issue
  b. Myrtle E   b. Aug. 8, 1887, Santa Maria, CA
                 d. Aug. 16, 1905, Stockton, CA
2.   m. 2. January 1, 1857, Beaver Dam ? Dodge co, WI
  Sophia Estabrooks   b. c1818 VT; widow of Hiram K Russell of
                 Saxton's River Village, VT
               d. c1898 CA
3. Clarissa /Clara/Claire M   b. Sep 21, 1861 Beaver Dam ? WI
   Single

Note: A Claire M Cole died 21 July 1946, Contra Costa County, CA. I haven't ascertained who it is.

Sources:
U.S. Census Susquehanna Co, PA, 1850; Dodge co, WI, 1860; San Luis Obispo co, CA, 1870,
   1880; San Francisco 1880, 1900
Cole, *The Descendants of James Cole of Plymouth 1633,* 1908
Vermont Vital Records
1850 Census Bennington co
Wisconsin Marriage Index
California Grand Death List
City Directories
Obituaries
County Histories

1. David Leigh Cole   b. Santa Barbara, CA June 13, 1931
   m. Santa Barbara, CA Feb 1, 1953

2. Linden Shirley Cole   b. Santa Barbara, CA   Aug 11, 1894
   m. Santa Barbara, CA Sep 24, 1919   d. Santa Maria, CA Nov 18, 1977

3. Mabelle Pearl Smith   b. Rocky Ford, CO Jan 18, 1898   d. Santa Barbara, CA Feb 17, 1956

4. Laurentine Exiva Cole   b. Bellevue, IA July 4, 1861   divorced Jan 18, 1911, King co WA
   d. Los Angeles CA June 10, 1932

5. Anna Mary Silliman   b. New Waterford, OH   May 3, 1856
   d. Santa Barbara, CA Jan. 10, 1916

6. Benjamin Breckinridge Smith   b. Cynthiana, KY   Nov 23, 1867
   m. Rocky Ford, CO July 2, 1896   d. Agnew CA July 3, 1949

7. Cora Pearl Knapp   b. Iowa July 16, 1875   d. Salinas, CA Mar 4, 1944

8. Laurentine Sweet Cole   b. Springfield, IL Mar 1, 1828
   m. Bellevue, IA Sep 16, 1860   d. San Miguel, CA Aug. 5, 1894

9. Laura Ann Culver   b. Plattsburgh, NY   Apr 29, 1829
   d. San Fernando, CA Feb 26, 1913

10. John Silliman   b. Lancaster co, PA   Jan 28, 1813   m. Pittsburgh, PA 1842
    d. Blairstown, IA   Aug 19, 1879

11. Nancy S Stevenson   b. Chambersburg, PA Mar 26, 1821
    d. Cleveland, OH May 29, 1900

12. Jonathan S Smith   b. Cynthiana, KY   Feb 23, 1827   m. Lincoln co KY   Nov 23, 1848
    d. Cynthiana, KY July 1896

13. Elizabeth Ann Lair   b. Lincoln co, KY   Aug 23, 1829   d. Cynthiana, KY   Mar 1897

14. David William Knapp   b. IA. 1845?   m. McDonough co, IL Dec 31, 1867
    divorced before 1880

15. Sarah Ellen Nicholes   b. Mc Donough co, IL   June 26, 1849
    d. Santa Barbara, CA Mar 13, 1919

18. Oliver Culver   b. Castleton? VT 1787?   d. OH? Feb 7, 1835

19. Abigail_____   b. NY/CAN? 1807?   m. about 1820, Plattsburgh, NY?

20. Samuel Silliman   b. Northampton co PA 1776   m. Lancaster co PA 1811?
    d. New Waterford, OH May 24, 1859

21. Elizabeth_____ b. 1792? d. Allegheny City, PA Aug 18, 1856

22. William Stevenson b. Dromore, County Donegal, Ireland 1788
    m. Chambersburg, PA 1820? buried Allegheny City, PA July 26, 1849

23. Elizabeth Snider Morton b. Chambersburg, PA July 21, 1800
    d. Allegheny City, PA Aug 5, 1871

24. Michael Smith b. VA Sep 29, 1789 m. Cynthiana, KY? July 4, 1816
    d. Cynthiana, KY June 3, 1853

25. Mary Howe b. KY Feb 24, 1795 d. Cynthiana, KY Sep 22, 1858.

26. John Pope Lair b. Lincoln co KY Sep 28, 1789 m. Jan 11, 1823?
    d. Lincoln co, KY July 5, 1833

27. Elizabeth Buchanan

28. David W Knapp b. d. Before 1845

29. Laura Jan Perkins b. VT Feb 15, 1823 d. Little Sauk, MN Apr. 4, 1892

30. George W Nicholes b. OH 1816?

36. Francis Culver b. CT July 2, 1758 m. Castleton, VT Mar 7, 1782
    d. Plattsburgh, NY May 1822

37. Mary Stevens b. CT.? Nov 14, 1763 d. Plattsburgh, NY June 9, 1827

40. John Silliman b. PA May 21, 1751

44. John Stevenson b. Ireland

46. George Morton

47. Catherine Faber

48. Michael Smith b. Washington co, MD 1752 d. Cynthiana, KY Nov 24, 1842

50. Christopher Howe b. VA

51. Elizabeth Harmon b. VA

52. Andrew Lair b. Philadelphia, PA bap Feb 18, 1750 m. about 1772
    d. Lincoln co KY 1826

53. Frances Hubbard b. VA 1752 d. Lincoln co KY 1792

54. Edward Y Buchanan

55. Ann Elizabeth Foster

58. William Perkins   Vermont/Michigan?

59. Clarice _____   Vermont/Michigan?

74. Rufus? Stevens

75. Lydia _____   b. CT 1741   d. Plattsburgh, NY Mar 23, 1817

80. Thomas Silliman   b. Ireland 1713   d. Northampton co? PA 1810

104. Matthias Lehrer   b. Rhineland 1714   d. Rockingham co VA 1787

105. Catherina Margaretha Moyer   b. Rhineland? 1720?   d. VA 1799

106. James Hubbard   b. VA.

107. Elizabeth Speers

160. Thomas Silliman   b. Ireland   d. PA 1762

161. Agnes _____   b. Ireland   d. PA 1778

LAURENTINE S. COLE BIBLE

Contributed by: David L Cole of Santa Maria, California

The Cole Bible is in possession of Mrs George Lombard, (of) CA, great-great granddaughter of L S Cole. Family Bible published in 1853.

MARRIAGES

February 3, 1853 Laurentine S Cole and Catherine J (Morris) were married by Mr Ritchie, Rushcreek, Jo Daviess Co., Illinois.

September 16, 1860 L S Cole and Laura Ann (Williams) were married by Mr McNulty, Bellevue, Jackson co, Iowa.

March 27, 1880 Edward F Nixon and Laura F Cole were married by Rev B F Baxton, Junction City, Oregon.

BIRTHS

Laurentine S Cole was born March 1, 1828

Catherine J (Morris) Cole was born March 3, 1832

Juliana R Cole was born Tuesday, December 13, 1853, Appleriver, Jo Daviess co, Illinois

Emma J Cole was born Thursday, April 24, 1856, Volga Township, Clayton, co, Iowa

Margaret E Cole was born May 9, 1858, Elk Township, Clayton, co, Iowa

Laurentine Exiva Cole was born July 4, 1861, Jackson co, Iowa

Laura Phidelia Cole was born April 10, 1865, Jackson co, Iowa

Louisa Cole was born June 25, 1868, Trempealeau co, Wisconsin

Roseyella Nixon was born January 11, 1881, Salinas City, California

Laurentine Nixon was born August 27, 1885, Soquel, Santa Cruz co, California

Roy Niel Hicklin was born April 2, 1888, Paso Robles, California

DEATHS

Catherine J Cole died July 7, 1860

Julyann Cole died January 29, 1865

Riley Williams died May 27, 1857

COLVER and STEVENS
of Beekmantown, New York

Francis Colver and Mary Stevens are the New England ancestors in the paternal lineage of Society member David L Cole. Their Ahnentafels are here presented, with several modest additions since 1986, and the line of descendants culminating in current Santa Maria residents.

1. Julia/Juliette Colver 1783-1867; m. Issac Delong
2. Daniel Colver 1785-1812; m.1 1806 Annie Winters, d. 1810; m.2 Martha Winters
3. Oliver Colver see below
4. Eunice Colver 1789-1864; m. Jacob Delong
5. Polly Colver 1792-1796
6. Francis Colver 1794-1866/8; m. 1815 cousin Olive Fisher 1791-1875
7. Polly Colver 1798-1798
8. William Colver 1800-1842; m. 1821 Rachel T   1798-1862
9. Luke S Colver 1802-1802

I. Oliver Colver b. Castleton VT c1787; d. Huron co OH 7 Feb 1835
        m. Beekmantown NY 24 Dec 1815
Abigail Gale b. CAN c1800; d. Jackson co IA 1871; m. 2 Conrad Huffman c1812-1871+
1. Daniel Culver 1820-1902; m. Evans NY 1848 Martha A Johnston 1827-1884
2. Oliver Culver 1823-1894; m. Erie co OH 1846 Ann Rebecca Shepard 1826-1905
3. Edward Carlisle Culver 1825-1886; m. Bellevue IA 1864 Lovina Martha McKinley 1849-
4. Laura Ann Culver see below
5. Lucy E Culver 1832-1866; m.1 Erie co OH 1847 Samuel W Johnston 1825-1863
        m.2 Jackson co IA 1865 Abraham Hawks

II. Laura Ann Culver b. CAN 29 Apr 1829; d. near San Fernando CA 26 Feb 1913
        m.1 OH c1844 Riley Williams c1821-1857
1. Lucy Awilda Williams 1844-1923; m. WI 1860 Exavia Francis Bresette 1837-1924
2. (Sarah) Josephine Williams 1849-1922; m.1 WI 1866 John Fellows Harriman 1837-1917[1]
        m.2 (Phoenix?) c1891 Edward Farley 1848-1918
3. Abigail A Williams 1853-1915; m. WI 1870 William Henry Bright 1846-1922
4. Riley Williams 1856-1943; m. Salinas CA 1882 Mary S Lynn 1862-1947
    m.2 Bellevue IA 16 Sep 1860 Laurentine Sweet Cole 1828-1894[2,3]
5. Laurentine Exiva Cole see below
6. Laura Phidelia Cole 1865-1940; m.1 Lane co OR 1880 Edward Frank Nixon c1848-[4]
        m.2 Fernando CA 1904 Charles W Paine 1860-1944
7. Louisa Cole 1868-1954; m.1 Santa Cruz 1882 John Roy Hicklin 1855-1916
        m.2 (Los Angeles) c1907 John Hart Vedder 1864-1937

III. Laurentine Exiva Cole b. Bellevue IA 4 July 1861; d. Los Angeles 10 June 1932
    m.1 Santa Cruz 1882 Josephine Hicklin c1866-c1890; son Eugene Sterling Cole
                                                          1886-1962
    m.2 Anna Mary Silliman Dunlap 1856-1916; son Linden Shirley Cole
    m.3 Seattle 1911 Sarah J Davis

IV. Linden Shirley Cole b. Santa Barbara 12 Aug 1894; d. Santa Maria 18 Nov 1977
        m.1 Santa Barbara 24 Sep 1919 Mabelle Pearl Smith 1898-1956; son David
        m.2 Las Vegas 1956 Ella Ann Hedge Hilliard Carpenter Crouch 1891-1976

V. David Leigh Cole b. Santa Barbara 13 June 1931
        m. Santa Barbara 1 Feb 1953 Barbara Bruce 1931-
1. Richard Linden Cole see below
2. Elaine Cole Schnepple b. Santa Barbara 1959; m. Santa Maria 1982; divorced
3. Kathleen Cole Wilson b. Santa Maria 1962; m. Santa Maria 1985; divorced

VI. Richard Linden Cole b. Santa Barbara 3 Nov 1954
   m. Santa Maria 4 Nov 1978 Catherine Marie Banta 1953-
  1. Caroline Mabelle Cole b. Santa Maria 1982
  2. Claudia Marjorie Cole b. Santa Maria 1985
  3. Cecily Margaret Cole b. Santa Maria 1986

---

[1] J F Harriman's father Jesse, see Harriman chart
[2] L S Cole, see Cole chart
[3] L S Cole's mother Louisa Hawks, see Cole chart
[4] E F Nixon, see Nixon chart

FRANCIS COLVER

August 1986   Accuracy *Not* Guaranteed

1. Francis Colver m. 7 Mar 1782, Castleton, VT
    b. 2 Jul 1758 Litchfield   Mary Stevens
    d. 9 May 1822 Beekmantown, NY

Revolutionary War Soldier
Capt. Thomas Sawyer's Co. of Provincial Troops, 1 May-30 Nov 1778
Capt. Parmelle Allen's Co. of Rangers, 1 Aug-17 Nov 1779
Detachment of men raised as a levy from Col. Thomas Lee's regt. of militia for the defense of the
    frontiers of the state of Vermont
Oct. 1781: Ten days at Castleton

Estate of Asher Colver, 13 August 1781
Francis, eldest son, appointed guardian of Joel, second son, age 14
Araunah Woodward and wife Charlotte, eldest daughter, appointed guardian of John, third son,
    age 11 years, 10 months
Azariel Blanchard and wife Eunice, widow of Asher, appointed guardian of Olive, second
    daughter, age 7 years, 6 months

Mill at Castleton
Francis operated sawmill, gristmill, and forge with his father's partners George Foote and Zadok
Remington and step-father Azariel Blanchard; eventually bought out the other heirs, later sold all
Castleton property and moved to Plattsburgh, New York, about 1795.

Petition to Governor and Council October 15, 1794
Francis Culver, Zadok Remington and others praying to be secured against further prosecutions at
law by Josiah Brush of Castleton by reason of the petitioners mill dam in said Castleton overflowing
his land and that commissioner might be appointed to assess the damages done by the overflowing
of said dam. *Note:* Another such complaint was lodged in Franklin Co., VT; may have been the
result of a rare hurricane a la 1938.

Plattsburgh
Francis Colver chosen officer for District 12 at Plattsburgh Town Meeting 3 April 1798
Culver Hill, 3 miles north of Plattsburgh: monument commemorating the battle with the British
Sept. 2, 1814, across the road not far from the stone house completed by Francis about 1815.
House later owned by Francis Jr., his daughters; became adjunct to the county poor house near the
end of the 19th century, then abandoned. Purchased, restored and occupied by the William Crosby
Family, c1970.

  2. Asher Colver m. 18 Sep 1755 Litchfield CT   3. Eunice Beach
     b. 19 Mar 1734 Litchfield CT   b. 27 Jun 1735 Wallingford CT
     d. 8 Dec 1776, Castleton VT   d. 12 June 1796

Vol. XXXII, No. 1, Spring 2000, pp.5,6

100 acre mill lot established by Col. Amos Bird, 1772, on outlet of Lake Bombasine, now Bomaseen; purchased 9 April 1773 by Asher Colver from Jabez Swift

    m.2 Azariel Blanchard, 25 Mar 1778

4. Daniel Colver m. 12 Feb 1723/4, Litchfield CT
    b. 19 Dec 1698 Lebanon CT
    d. 9 Apr 1734 Litchfield CT
    Original proprietor Litchfield lot 41, 15 acres
    Deed 6 Feb 1722

5. Deborah Goodrich
    b. 8 Jan 1706/7 Wethersfield CT
    d. 17 Sep 1755 Sharon CT
    m.2 Benjamin Boardman

6. Samuel Beach m. 23 Mar 1732; 2nd wife
    b. 29 Dec 1696, Wallingford CT
    d. 20 Jul 1765, Goshen? CT

7. Hannah Benham
    b. Dec 1708 Wallingford CT
    d. unknown
    m.2 Noah Wadhams

8. Edward Colver m. 15 Jan 1681/2 Norwich CT
    b. c1654, New London CT
    d. 7 Apr 1732 Litchfield CT
    Original proprietor Lebanon, Litchfield
    Lieutenant King Philip's War

9. Sarah Backus
    b. 14 Jun 1663, Norwich CT
    d. unknown

10. William Goodrich, Jr. m. 14 May 1706 Wethersfield CT
    b. 12 Jul 1686 Wethersfield   CT
    d. unknown

11. Margaret Orvis
    bap. 7 Apr 1687 Farmington CT
    d. unknown

12. John Beach m. 1 Dec 1678 Wallingford CT
    b. 19 Oct 1655 Milford CT
    d. Apr 1709 Wallingford CT
    Planter, 1675 Wallingford CT

13. Mary Royce
    b. c1658, Wallingford CT
    m.2 John Atwater 1718
    Wallingford CT

14. Joseph Benham m. 18 Dec 1706 Wallingford CT
    b. 5 Dec 1685 Wallingford CT
    d. 18 Apr 1754 Wallingford CT

15. Hope Cook
    b. 27 Sep 1686 Wallingford CT
    d. 30 Jan 1731 Wallingford CT

16. Edward Colver   m. 19 Sep 1638, Dedham MA
    b. c1610 Middlesex/Suffolk?, England
    d. 1685 Mystic CT
    Massachusetts Bay Colony 1635; Founder of Dedham
    to Connecticut 1653; Pequot War; Millwright/Wheelwright

17. Anne Ellis

18. William Backus m. by 1660, New Haven CT
    b. 1635?   d. 1721, Norwich CT
    Deputy, Norwich, to CT General Assembly

19. Sarah Charles
    bap Oct. 1640, New Haven CT
    d. 1663?

20. William Goodrich m. 22 Nov 1680, Wethersfield CT
    b. 8 Feb 1659/60, Wethersfield CT
    d. 27 Dec 1737, Wethersfield CT
    Train band, Wethersfield; Lieutenant

21. Grace Riley
    b. c1661
    d. 23 Oct 1712 age 51

22. *Probably* Samuel Orvis m. c1680 Farmington, CT
    b. May 1653, Farmington, CT?   d. unknown

23. Deborah

24. Thomas Beach m. c1654; of New Haven CT
    b. c1626   d. 1662 Milford CT?
    Moved to Milford CT c1626

25. Sarah Platt
    d. 15 May 1670
    m.2 Miles Merwin c1665

26. Jonathan Royce m. c1656, Norwich CT
    d. 1690

27. Mary Spinning/Spinage
    d. c1658

28. Joseph Benham m. 17 Aug 1682, Wallingford CT
    b. 25 May 1659, New Haven CT
    d. 1702 Wallingford CT

29. Hannah Merriman
    b. 15 May 1651, New Haven CT
    widow of John Ives

30. Samuel Cook m. 2 May 1667, New Haven CT
    b. 30 Sep 1641, Salem MA
    d. Mar 1702/3, Wallingford? CT
32. John Colver Middlesex, England
34. John Ellis
36. William Backus Walloon ancestry
    b. Norwich, England
    d. May 1664, Norwich CT
    Lived in Saybrook CT. To Norwich CT 1660
38. John Charles m. c1633 Charlestown MA?
    of New Haven and Branford CT
    d. 1673
40. William Goodrich m. 4 Oct 1648 Hartford CT
    bap. 13 Feb 1621/2, Bury-St.-Edmonds,
        Suffolk, England
    d. before 14 Nov 1676, Wethersfield CT
    Pequot War. Deputy, Wethersfield Connecticut Legislature
42. John Riley m. c1645, Wethersfield? CT
    d. 1679
44. George Orvis m. 1652
    d. 27 Apr 1664, Farmington CT
    In Farmington by 1658

31. Hope Parker
    b. 26 Apr 1650 New Haven CT
    d. 1686-1690, Wallingford CT
33. Christine
35. unknown
37. unknown

39. Sarah? Moss?

41. Sarah Marvin
    bap 27 Dec 1631 Great Bentley,
        Essex, England
    d. before 16 Jan 1701/2 Stratford
        CT   m.2 Wm. Curtis
43. Grace? Buck?
    b. 1624   d. 1703
45. Elizabeth Welbourne/
        Weyburn?
    d. 1694
    widow of David Carpenter
    m.3 Richard Bronson

46.
48. John Beach
50 Richard Platt m. c1633, England
    Christened 28 Sep 1603 Bovington, Hertz, England
    d. 1684/5, of New Haven and Milford CT
52. Robert Royce m. 4 Jun 1634, Martock,
        Somerset, England
    d. 1676
    Deputy, New London Connecticut Legislature
54. Humphrey Spinning m. 1640
    d. 1656. Of New Haven, Milford CT
56. Joseph Benham m. 15 Jan 1656/7, Boston, MA
    d. 1703. Of New Haven; early settler, Wallingford CT

58. Nathaniel Merriman m. c1647 New Haven CT
    b. c1614, London? England
    d.13 Feb 1693/4, Wallingford CT
    Pequot War; Sgt. New Haven Artillery Co
    New Haven Train Band 1664 Ensign.
60. Henry Cook m. 29? Jun 1629 Salem MA
    b. c1615? d. 25 Dec 1661, Salem MA
62. Edward Parker m. c1646 New Haven CT
    d. 1662

47.
49.
51. Mary Wood
    b. 1605
    d. unknown

53. Mary Sims
    b. Longsutton, Somerset, Eng
    d. 1696 Wallingford CT

55. unknown

57. Winifred King
    d. Staten Island?
    Accused of witchcraft 1697
    Wallingford CT; left town

59. Joan/Jane
    b. c1628
    d. 8 Dec 1709 Wallingford, 82nd yr

61. Judith Birdsall
    d. 1689
63. Elizabeth? Woods?
    d. 28 Jul 1677 New Haven CT
    widow of John Potter
    m.3 Robert Rose 1664?

82. Matthew Marvin   m. c1622, England   83. Elizabeth? Gregory
    1600-1680, to New England 1635   d. before 1647
    Original proprietor Hartford CT
    Early settler Norwalk CT

112. John Benham m. c1634,   113. 1st wife unknown
    Dorchester MA?
    d. 1661

For account of Winifred Benham, accused of witchcraft, see Jacobus, *Families of Ancient New Haven*, pp. 956-58.

References

Beach additions from *Lineage Book of the National Society of Daughters of Founders and Patriots of America, SSVIII 1948*
Bicentennial Ancestor Index, National Society Daughters of American Colonists
Blanchard Bible Record, Detroit Society for Genealogical Research, Vol. 12, No. 3, Page 70, Courtesy Marshall Blanchard, Wilton CT
Boston Marriages, Births, Etc., 1630-1699
Davis, *Early Families of Wallingford, Connecticut,* 1870
Giorgi, *Colver-Culver Genealogy,* 1985, and earlier versions
Hibbard, *History of the Town of Goshen, Connecticut, with Genealogies and Biographies,* 1897
Jacobus, *Families of Ancient New Haven,* 1981
Jacobus and Waterman, *Hale House and Related Families, Mainly of the Connecticut River Valley,* 1978
New York: *Clinton County Records;* Addie L. Shields, Clinton County Historian; Culver Family Bible
Orvis, *Outlines of the Orvis Family,* Sep 1913
Porter, *Plattsburgh 1785-1815-1902,* 1964
Records of Governor and Council, Montpelier, 1875
Shields, *Beekmantown, A Landmark in a Passageway,* 1976
S.U.N.Y., *The Centenary of the Battle of Plattsburgh,* 1914
Torrey, *New England Marriages Prior to 1700,* 1985
Vermont: *Castleton Town Records, Rutland Probate Records*
Vermont Soldiers in the Revolution
Woodruff, *A Genealogical Register of the Residents in Litchfield...1720-1800,* 1900
See also chart of Lucille M Donaldson 2460 Del Sur Dr, Albuquerque 87105-6016, in *American Genealogy Magazine,* Vol. 10, 2-3 Mar-Apr, May-June 1995 for Beach et al.

Compiler's Note

I would advance the same apologies and arguments that anyone having attempted to do this sort of work is well acquainted with. This effort is certainly not presented as definitive, but it is indeed presented as the final product of this collator on this subject.

Santa Maria, California
August 16, 1986
(signed) Barbara Bruce Cole
Mrs David L Cole

MARY STEVENS

August 1986   Accuracy *Not* Guaranteed

1. Mary Stevens m. 7 Mar 1782 Castleton VT   Francis Colver
    b. 14 Nov 1764 Killingworth CT
    d. 9 June 1824 Plattsburgh/Beekmantown, NY
2. Luke Stevens m. 19 Mar 1762 Killingworth CT 3. Lydia Chittenden
    b. 4 Aug 1736 Killingworth CT   b. 21 Jul 1740 Killingworth CT
    d. 5 Feb 1813 Castleton VT   d. 23 Mar 1817 Plattsburgh NY
    Note: "Malignant Fever", or typhoid pneumonia,
    killed 63, mostly adults, in Castleton in 1813;
    Stevens' son William died 7 Feb 1813
4. Timothy Stevens m. 3 Nov 1720 Killingworth CT   5. Mary Tooley
    No date available   b. 4 Jun 1700 Killingworth CT
6. Nathaniel Chittenden m. 6 Jan 1724/5   7. Lucy Nettleton
       Killingworth, CT   b. 1699 Killingworth CT
    b. 6 Jun 1701 Killingworth CT   d. Jul 1762 Killingworth CT
    d. Aug 1762 Guilford?
8. Timothy Stevens m. c1696 Killingly CT   9. Unknown
    b. 1664 Guilford CT
    d. 21 Feb 1711/12 Killingworth CT
10. *Possibly* Christopher/Cristanda Tooley m. c1683   11. Elizabeth?
       Killingworth CT
    d. 28 Jan 1717/18 (death date his or his son's?)
12. Nathaniel Chittenden m. 1690 Killingworth CT   13. Elizabeth Stevens, sister of No. 8
    b. 19 Aug 1669 Guilford CT   b. 14 July 1668 Killingworth CT
    Death date unknown   d. 15 Nov 1738
14. John Nettleton m. 21 Jan 1691/2 Killingworth CT   15. Sarah Woodmansie
    b. 1670 Killingworth CT   b. 16 Mar 1672 New London CT
    d. 1715   d. 1723 (Killingworth CT)
16. Thomas Stevens m. 1650 Milford CT   17. Mary Fletcher
    b. c1628 Gloucester England   b. 1634?
    d. 18 Nov 1685 Killingworth CT
    Corp. New Haven Troop 1654 from Guilford CT
    A founder of Killingworth CT Legislature 1671-1683
20. *Possibly* Edmond Tooley lived in New Haven 1644
    d. 19 Apr 1685
24. Nathaniel Chittenden m. c1668 Guilford CT   25. Sarah
    1643-1691 Guilford
26. Thomas Stevens No. 16   27. Mary Fletcher No. 17
28. John Nettleton m. 29 May 1670 Killingworth CT   29. Martha Hull
    c1648-1691 born Warwickshire   b. 10 Jun 1650 Windsor CT
30. Gabriel Woodmansee m. c1669 New London CT   31. Sarah
    d. 1685   m.2 Ricks/Rex
    Minister New London 1668
    (Woodmancy-se-see-sie-sey Wodmancy)
32. John Stevens/Stephens m. in England   33. Mary
    b. Gloucester England   b. probably of Kent
    d. 1 Sep 1670 Guilford CT   d. 1640's England
    Early settler Guilford. See Stephens Genealogy for story

34. John Fletcher m. c1634 Wethersfield CT
    1602-18 Apr 1662 Milford CT
    Deputy Milford, to New Haven Legislature

35. Mary Ward
    b. 1607?
    m.2 John Clark of Saybrook/Milford
    d. 22 Jan 1678/9 Framington CT

48. William Chittenden m. in England
    bap March 1594/5 Marsden Essex
    d. 1 Feb 1660/1 Guildford CT. Settled New Haven 1639. Lieut. New Haven Artillery 1653
    Deputy Guilford, New Haven Legislature

49. Joanna Sheaffe
    b. c1614
    m.2 Abraham Cruttenden
    bur. 16 Aug 1668

56. Samuel Nettleton m. c1636
    b.1605-10 Warwickshire England
    d.1655-58? Fairfield CT?
    Settled Milford 1639. Original proprietor Branford CT 1644

57. Maria
    b. in England
    d. 29 Oct 1658 Branford CT

58. Josiah Hull m. 20 Mar 1641 Windsor CT
    b. 1612-1620?
    d. 16 Nov 1675; death recorded in Windsor and Killingworth CT

59. Elizabeth Loomis
    d. after 1665

60. *Possibly* Robert Woodmancy of Boston MA
    See Rhode Island Genealogical Register April 1981, p.349

64. Edward Stephens Knight, d. c1670

65. Anne Crewe

70. Richard Ward

71. Joyce

96. Robert Chittenden of Cranbrook Kent England

98. Rev Edmund Sheaffe m. 30 May 1586 England
    bap 17 Mar 1559?

99. Elizabeth Taylor

116. George Hull 1590?-1659

118. Joseph Loomis m. 30 Jun 1614 Shalford Essex England
    b. c1588 Essex
    d. 25 Nov 1658 Windsor CT

119. Mary White
    b. 24 Aug 1590 Shalford
    d. 23 Aug 1652 Windsor CT

128. Thomas Stephens of Lypiatt Park and Little Sodbury Gloucester England. Barrister at Law, Attorney-General, Official at Court of James I.
    d. 26 Apr 1613 bur at Stroud Church Gloucestershire where stands a memorial mural of a praying figure…

129. Elizabeth Stone

130. Thomas Crewe, Knight of Northamptonshire

236. John Loomis
    b. 29 Jan 1562 Thaxted or Braintree Essex England
    12 Jun 1619 Braintree

237. Agnes Longwood/Lingwood

238. Robert White 1552-1617

239. Bridget Allgar

256. Edward Stephens, Lord Eastington and Chavenage

258. John Stone

472. John Loomis/Lummys
    bur 4 Dec 1567 Thaxted Essex England

473. Krysten Pasfield/ Bashfield/ Jackson

476. Robert White

477. Alice

478. William Allgar

479. Margaret

References

Abbott, *Families of Early Milford, Connecticut* 1979
Barbour, *Connecticut Vital Records*
Castleton, *Vermont Vital Records*

Vol. XXXII, No. 1, Spring 2000, pp.9, 10

Culver Family Bible, courtesy Addie L. Shields
Holmes, *Directory of the Ancestral Heads of New England Families 1620-1700*
Jacobus, *Genealogies of Connecticut Families: Stevens*
Nettleton Family Records, complied by W.O. Nettleton, Guilford, 1934
Stevens, *Stevens Genealogy: Some Descendants of the Fitz Stephen Family in England and New England,* 1904
Sumner, *Ancestry and Descendants of Amaziah Hall and Betsey Baldwin,* 1954 for Chittenden
Torrey, *New England Marriages Prior to 1700*
Talcott, *Families of Early Guilford, Connecticut* 1984
Virkus, *Compendium of American Genealogy*

for Hull, see *Dorset Pilgrims,* 1993

DAVIS
SANTA MARIA VALLEY PIONEERS

William W Davis   b. NY
     d. disappeared c1824
     m. Freeport NY 20 Oct 1820; divorced Seneca co OH 1 Aug 1828
Betsey Spencer   b.
     d.
     F: Moses Spencer 1780-1861
     M: Esther Albee

See *Pioneers Of The Bluestem Prarie*, Riley co Gen Soc, Manhattan KS 1976

1. Moses Spencer Davis   b. Freeport NY 6 Sep 1821
     d. Santa Maria 23 Mar 1895
     m. Lake co IN 24 Aug 1850
     Polly Jane Edgerton   b. Erie co PA 7 May 1830
     d. Santa Maria 22 Feb 1912
     F: Horace Edgerton
     M: Betsey Taylor

2. Mary Davis   b. 1824
     d.
     m.
     Amos Edgerton   b.
     d.
     F: Horace Edgerton
     M: Betsey Taylor

Betsey Spencer Davis m.2 Seneca co OH (Aug) 1828
Frederick Montgomery Davis   b. MA
     d.
     m.1 Martha   d. 30 Sep 1825; 5 ch

3. Harvey Augustus Davis   b. Seneca co OH 11 Feb 1831
     d. SLO co 1 June 1906 @74; AG cem
     m. Lake co IN 21 Sep 1857
     Amy Lucy Mann   b. Lake co IN 15 Sep 1841
     d. SLO co 15 June 1914 @74; AG cem
     F: Lyman Mann
     M: Almira N Taylor

4. Franklin William Davis   b. 1833
     d. Pottawatomie co KS
     m. into Obediah Taylor family of Lake co IN

5. George Berry Davis   b. 1837
     d. Pottawatomie co KS
     m. into Obediah Taylor family of Lake co IN

6. Frederick Montgomery Davis   b. Elkhart co IN 23 Dec 1839
     d. Manzana 19 May 1897 @59/4/25; bur Manzana
     m. (Pottawatomie co KS) c1870
     Sarah Ellen Forrester   b. (W) VA 1853/4
     d.
     F: George W Forrester
     M: Casandra Pin(n)ick 1817-1895

1916 City Happenings. Mr & Mrs F W Davis from St George KS are visiting Mr & Mrs
A H Davis and family.   –Aug 19

Moses Spencer Davis   b. Freeport NY 6 Sep 1821
   Co K 55 regt ILL Vol Inf   d. Santa Maria 23 Mar 1895 @73/6; SM cem
   photo in uniform SMV His Soc   obit Mar 30. 1 son 2 dau here, 2 dau in the east,
   1870 cen: Pottawatomie co KS   2 dead
     See *Pioneers of the Bluestem Prairie*, Riley co KS Gen Soc 1976, p.183
   to CA to stay 1888
   1890 GR: 68 NY SM #2
   1892 GR: 70 5'3 lt haz gry; NY; Sisquoc, PO SM
   1895: Moses S Davis Passes Away after a Short Illness…ME Ch…GAR vet. To CA 1852,
      mining. On way home to IN by sea was on the Yankee Blade wrecked off Point Concepcion
      1855; he and a brother, now in Santa Barbara, remained on the wreck until a coast steamer
      took them off and landed them in San Diego. Came here a second time 6 years ago… obit.
       m. Lake co IN 24 Aug 1850
Poly Jane Edgerton   b. Erie co PA 15 May 1830
   1900 cen: SM 7 births 5 living   d. Santa Maria 22 Feb 1912 @81/9/14; SM cem
   1906 Dir: Mrs M S rCypress st   obit Feb 24 p.1
   1909 Dir: Mrs M S W Fesler st
   1910 cen: W Fesler wid 7 births 5 living
   1898: Will Tunnell and family came down from their Sisquoc home Sunday, Mrs Davis
      returned with them Monday for a short visit. –June 4 Mrs M S Davis who went out to
      Manzana a couple of weeks ago to visit her daughter, Mrs Will Tunnell, was taken very ill
      and was brought home on a bed. Her many friends will be pained to hear of her sickness.
                                                                                       -June 18

1.   Ida Adell Davis   b. Lake co IN 2 July 1851
      in KS 1912, 1914   d. Los Angeles 2 June 1934 @82
       m. KS 11 Dec 1870
      John Collins jr   F: John Collins, early settler Pottawatomie co
                                                  M: Jane S
      Issue unknown
2.   Alvis Hilon Davis   b. Crown Point IN 5 Mar 1858
      to SM 1887   d. at home 924 S Bwy SM 5 Feb 1937 @78/11; SM cem
     1890 GR: 32 blksm; IN; Sisquoc   obit Sat Feb 6 p.1; 10gch
     1890: Garey Notes. Al. Davis to move to Cuyama.   –Oct 4
     1892 GR: 34 5'8½ lt gry aub blksm; IN; Sisquoc
     1892: Garey Brieflets. Mr A H Davis has succeeded to the ownership of the shop
       originally owned by Mr Woon. Mr Davis and family are of the first residents of
       Garey…they lived in Cuyama…   -Dec 24 See ONT. See Woon chart.
     1895: Long Valley Items. A H Davis of Garey is preparing to move his saw-mill to the
       Manzana.   –March 30
         Long Valley Items, May 8. Wm Miller hauled a load of machinery for the new saw
         mill to the Manzana last week for Davis & Co.   –May 11
         for Miller, see Forrester chart.
     1896 GR: 38 5'8½ lt gry aub blksm; IN; Sisquoc
     1897: The *San Luis Obispo Tribune* says that O W Maulsby has been appointed a delegate to
         the "Pine *F*ood Convention," and that he is a good man to send. If Mr M hankers after
         that kind of a diet, Messrs A H Davis & Co, of Manzana, can furnish it nearer home
         of the purest quality of pine lumber.   –Apr 17
         (a play on the typographical error, no doubt)

1900 cen: tp 8 Sisquoc blksm
1905: Alvis Davis has bought an acre of land on Bwy from Mr Speed and will begin the erection of a residence very shortly. —Jan 14
(SB co Bk 97 p.233 recorded Feb 11, 1905)

Note: Speed's 40 acres: NW4 SW4 S14 T10N R34W=between Bwy & Miller, Jones south to lot line north of Camino Colegio. SB co Bk 56 p.618 recorded 6 Jan 1898. Speed's Addition to the town of Santa Maria drawn and recorded 1908. See Speed chart.

1906 Dir: A H Davis lumber dlr r Bwy; Mrs; Ida Miss stu
1906: A H Davis, Mgr Pacific Valley Lumber Co's mills in Monterey co, vacation with family here. —July 14
1909 Dir: A H Davis mech r S Bwy; Mrs M; Miss Ida, Stanford; Chester A sch tchr; J D stu.
1910 cen: S Bwy machinist retail hdwr
1913: A H Davis suing Jacob Hanson for $400 due on auto. —Oct 11
1914 Dir: carp 924 S Bwy (Maggie)
1920 cen: 924 S Bwy
1922-3 Dir: 924 S Bwy: Alvis H, Dorian, Frank A, John D, L C
Davis Construction: F A, L C, A H Davis

1959: House Built in '04 (sic) Moves Off Broadway…another of the old Santa Maria landmark homes is being moved…opposite Santa Maria High School…built in 1904 by Alvis Davis…residence many years. The frame house of redwood and pine, some of it cut from early homesteads in the Manzana…to be moved to Nipomo Mesa…Sold by J D Davis to Craig F Smith & Assoc of SF…Virtually "out in the country" it was then located in the corner of a 40 acre field planted to fruit trees and vegetables. There were no streets in the area other than Broadway. The only other house nearby was that of John Speed, where the Saladin building is now…In the 1920's or thereabouts, the 40 acres, or a portion of it, was divided and sold for homesites, the first one selling for as low as $300 on South McClelland…Santa Maria High School was a frame building when the Davis family moved in…All in the family are graduates…and Mrs Ida Davis Devine, retired, now living in Berkeley, taught…for many years.
– Aug 1 1959 p.3 *Women's News*, Emma Brians Davis, Ed.

m. Wamego KS 30 June 1887; left for CA in Sep. Parents came next year

Margaret Jane Schatz   b. Wabaunsee KS 7 Dec 1860
  1900 cen: 6 births 6 living   d. Santa Maria (23) Jan 1948 @87/1/16; SM cem
  1910 cen: 6 births 6 living   obit Sat Jan 24 p.1 10gch 5ggch
   tchr 5y Wamego KS   F: George Stephan Schatz, early settler KS
1914 SLO Dir (incl SM): Schatz   M: Mary
  Ella, printer *SM Vidette* r924 S Bwy; Schatz Emma M r same
1933: John Stephen Schatz d. at sister's house 924 S Bwy 11 Oct @81. b. IL, in SM 6y.
  2 sis: Mrs Davis, SM; Miss Ella Schatz, KS; bro Geo S Schatz, OK. —Thu Oct 12 p.4
1948: sister-in-law Mrs Effie Schatz, Tonkawa OK

   a. Ida E Davis   b. (Garey) 16 Sep 1888
     tchr 30y SMUHS   d. Alameda 20 Aug 1971 @82/11/14; SM cem
     Editor *Review* 1905   obit Sat Aug 21 p.4; 4gch
     grad SMHS 1906; "promising student at Stanford"
     1910 cen: tchr
     1915 *Review*: tchr College City
     1918: Mrs Ida Hall with her children are here for the holidays with her parents,
        M/M A H Davis, S Bwy. —Dec 22
     1919: Ida Hall, vice principal Galt High Sch visiting family. —Jan 18
      M/M Hall visiting her parents… -July 18
      Mrs V Hall, Galt, teacher -Alumni Notes, 1919 *Review*

1925 *Review*: Mrs Hall AB Stanford, MA UCal; instructor Spanish
1925: Ida Davis Hall left for TX to visit relatives, then to summer school at U of
 Mexico. —10 Yrs Ago, July 23 1935
1927 *Review*: photo. Started teaching at SMUHS 1920
1932: Ida Davis Hall tchr French, German, Spanish, Italian SMJC
1940-1 Dir: Ida Davis Hall tchr HS&JC 112 W Camino Colegio
1947-8 Dir: same
1950 Dir: P B Devine 112 W Camino Colegio
   m.1
Volney Hall
   1934: Mrs Sarah Hall, Hillsberg, CA, died; grandmother of Enid and Fred Hall.
                                                              -Mon Nov 26
   Sarah A Hall 76 d. Sonoma co 15 Nov 1934 spouse initial L (CA Death List)
= Enid Hall b. SM 24 Dec 1916; d. Belmont 26 Sep 1980 @63/9/12; SM cem;
   obit Mon Sep 29 p. 15. Bro Fred, SF; uncles Audel & Dorian Davis, SM.
   1920 cen: gdau w/A H Davis; at Mt St Mary's, Los Angeles 1937; living in Alameda
   1971
      m. Joseph M. Carroll. Living in Wilmington 1979
         F: Chas N Carroll 1859-1944; see Battles chart
= Frederick V Hall b. Rio Vista 21 Feb 1918; d. SF 5 Dec 1997 @79
     obits Dec 10, Dec 12, Dec 16. Grad SMHS @15; (1934 CSF Seal Bearers, Enid &
     Fred Hall). Valedictorian. BS petroleum eng w/honors @19 UCal; 1st in class
     Army Air Corps Photo & Mapping Sch; P-38 pilot WWII…performance eng
     Pan American Airways, later Standard Oil of CA 25y; patented smog control
     device used on all cars sold in US at UC Berkeley 1937
     m. 1942 Barbara Spedick 4ch 6gch
a. Ida   m.2

Patrick Bernard Devine	b. 1874; to CA @19
pastel artist	d. SM (12) Jan 1954 @79/10/12; SM cem
Hopkins Art Inst (Now SF Art	obit Wed Jan 13 p.3, Thu Jan 14 p.6
Inst); Art Appraiser U S Customs	sis: Mary Fewer, SF; Mrs D J Sullivan
retired 1942	Waterbury CT

   1954: Pall bearers: Chester, Audell, Dorian, Chester Davis jr; Joseph Carroll, Fred
     Hall
   his first marriage: SF 1910 (*Times*)
   Lena Edith Thornburgh 1883-1976 obit Sat July 17 p.2, 60y Oakland; 1gs 1ggs
     F: Larkin Thornburgh 1862-1896
     M: Quintilla F Whaley 1861-1929
   = Roderick E Devine (1912-1992)? in Oakland 1954, 1976
   = Kathlyn/Kathryn Devine (1911-1996)? In Prescott AZ 1954, 1976
      m. Homer Keeton (1910-1987)?

b. Chester Alvis Davis   b. Garey 11 Apr 1890
   SMUHS 1907   d. SM 25 July 1977 @87/3/14; SM cem; obit
   1910 cen: tp5 pumper   Wed July 17 (sic) 6gch 3ggch r 3960 Orcutt
   1920 cen: w/parents   Rd
   1922-3 Dir: line walker, Orcutt dist; Mrs Nora E hskpr
   1925 Dir: C A (Ethel) oil worker r Orcutt
   1928 Dir: C A (Ethel) gas plant foreman Union Oil Co, r Orcutt
   1936: Lic to wed: Helen Brown of Los Olivos, dau of D O Brown, Los Olivos, niece
     of M/M Chester A Davis of Orcutt, and Edwin D Hammonds of Orcutt; to
     marry May 31.   –*Times* May 15 (18?)

    1940-1 Dir: const frmn Union Oil, Orcutt Rd (Ethel); later dir same
    m. 1920?
    Nora Ethel Barnes   b. Ballard 27 Aug 1897; SSDI
                                           d. Visalia 28 Dec 1983 @86/4/1; SM cem
                                           obit Thu Dec 29 p.16; 6gch 4ggch
                                         F: James A Barnes 1851-1910
                                         M: Amanda E 1863-
= Chester Alvis Davis jr (1920-1991 King City)?
    1955-6 Dir: Chester A (Louann) oil fld contr h216 Palm Ct Dr SM
    1961 Dir: (Louann H) mgr SP Milling hsame Freddi, stu, rsame
    in San Jose 1977, Groveland 1983
= Shirley M Davis in Visalia 1983; 4 children, Visalia 1967
    m. Phillip Edwin Berry 1924-1967. F: Chas Edwin Berry 1888-1949
    1955-6 Dir: P E (Shirley M) f 546 E Evergreen SM
c.   John Dorian Davis   b. SM 30 Jan 1892 (*Times*)
    SMUHS 1910   d. SM 11 Aug 1981 @89/6/11; SM cem
    1913: bkpr (*Review*)   obit Thu Aug 13; r921 S McClelland
    1914 Dir: clk P C Coal Co r924 S Bwy
    1917: took exam for Army.   –*Santa Maria Vidette* June 12
    1920 cen: w/parents
    1922-3 Dir: bkpr Davis Constr, 925 S Bwy
    1928 Dir: cement contractor r same
    1940-1 Dir: cement wkr; 1955-6 Dir: Davis Bros 924C S Bwy
    1976 Dir: J Dorian & Emma B ret 921 S McClelland
    m. Carmel Sat June 29 1957 by Joseph M Ewing, Pres Ch; attended by her sister,
    Mrs Harvey J Brackett of San Mateo and his brother Clifford Davis of Atascadero.
    Also Mrs Bernice Holt, Los Alamos; M/M James Brians & son Richard, Santa
    Maria; Richard M. Brians & daus Sandra, Phyllis, son Richard Grady, Modesto;
    Mrs Clifford Davis, Harvey Brackett, M/M Lawrence Vestal, Del Rio; Carl
    Hockett, Westminster; M/M Chester A Davis, M/M Chester Davis jr, M/M Phil E
    Berry, M/M F Audel Davis & Audel jr, all of Santa Maria. To live at 921 S
    McClelland.   –Mon July 1
    Emma Ramm Brians   b. 5 March 1893
      to SM 1928 w/1st hus   d. 17 June 1991 @98; SM cem
      1928: Mrs Frank Brians   arrangements pending June 18 A6; no obit
         entertained mothers of Episcopal Sunday School.   –Wed June 20
      1938 phbk: Emma Brians 223 E Church
      1940-1 Dir: Brians Emma Mrs *SB News-Press* rptr SM Valley h223 E Church
                 James clk Karl's Shoe Store r223 E Church
                 Richard "Dick" stu r223 E Church
      1947-8 Dir: Brians Emma rptr *SM Times* h116 S Curryer (started in Jan 1948)
                 James F (Audry) emp City of SM h621 S Oakley Apt 615
                 Audry scy Jack H Glines r same
      1957: Emma Brians to Marry Dorian Davis…photo. 25y newspaper work: 15y
         w/"out-of-town" paper, then news ed of the weekly *Courier* which was
         purchased by The *Sm Times*. 9½ y Women's Page ed; to retire upon marriage.
         (apparently she did not retire)   –Fri June 28
      Her first marriage: Inglewood 1917; div early 1930's
         Frank L Brians 1897-1970; see *Who's Who in SM*; obit June 9; WWI Army;
         WWII Navy; 4gch 3ggch; F: Morgan M Brians 1847-1928; M: Rosa Hostler
         1871-

                    = Richard M Brians 1919-1981; in Modesto 1957, 1970 3 ch
                    = James F Brians 1922-1992; Audrey G, 1 son, in Livermore 1970
                       SMUHS 1941
            Frank L Brians m.2 Lela G/K _____ 1901-1972; div 1946 (*Times*)
               1930. deputy game warden.   –Mar 10
               1936. Guadalupe News. Frank Brians' parents in Palmdale.   –July
               1938-9 Dir: Brians Frank (Lela) SB co Ag Dept 304 Guad st Guad
               1940-1 Dir: F L (Lelia) SM Co Ag Com h421 S Bwy
                    Lela Dress Shop 421 S Bwy
               1947-8 Dir: F L (Lela) h423b S Bwy
Note: Ye Ed. has much data on the Brians clan who came to SLO co in the 1860's from Sonoma co.
      d.   Frank Audel Davis   b. Garey 1 Aug 1894
            SMUHS 1914, Asst Ed *Review*   d. SM 25 June 1982 @87/10/24; SM cem
            also student body president   obit Mon June 28 p.8
            1914: home from Pomona for the holidays   -Dec
            Pomona College; also Stanford; WWI
            1920 cen: w/parents
            1922-3 Dir: Davis Constr r924 S Bwy; 1928 Dir: cement contr r same
            1938 Dir: Davis Bros Constr(L C, F A) cement contr 223 E Camino Colegio
            1940-1 Dir: same 1947-8 Dir: same 1955-6 Dir: Same
            1961 Dir: 1020 E McNeil; 1976 Dir: same
                m. (22) July 1932
            Vera Lucile Glines   b. Pine Grove 6 Sep 1896
            1922-3 Dir: Vera L Glines   d. SM 15 May 1983 @86/8/9; SM cem
            tchr SMUHS r603 S Bwy   F: John Thomas Glines 1875-1949
            same: Cassius H & Eva M Glines   M: Dora Beatrice Holloway 1873-1947
            (grandfather & aunt)   see Glines chart
            1925 Dir: Miss Vera L tchr r500 S Bwy; same: John T (Dora) county roadmaster
            1927 *Review*: faculty SMUHS hist/Eng, photo. Grad UC Berkeley 1919
               MA Pol Sci Columbia U 1925
            1928 Dir: Vera L tchr r223 E Camino Colegio; same: John T (Dora)
            = Audel Glines Davis b. 11 Feb 1934; m. Lynn Showers; 4 ch in Berkeley 1982
      e.   Eugene (G) Davis   b. Sep 1896 (cen) (Eugene L 21 Sep 1896;
                                                    SSDI)
            Editor in Chief *Review* 1915   d. (before Nov 1976) (d. 12 Jan 1976 Seal
            1920 cen: w/parents   Beach Spouse initial F)?
            1920: Local Briefs. Eugene Davis, well known SM lad, sailed today for Ipoli,
               Federated Malay States, where he is going with a contingent of engineers from
               Stanford U.   –Sat July 10
            1923: Eugene Davis of Hermosa Beach visiting parents.   –Dec 24
            1936: Former Resident Visiting in SM. M/M Eugene Davis & ch spent weekend
               w/parents M/M A H Davis, 924 S Bwy, returned to Long Beach. He was in Class of
               1915 SMUHS, now chief engineer of production dept in oil co in Los Angeles
               district. Family Barbecue: M/M A H Davis, M/M Eugene Davis & fam, M/M C A
               Davis & fam, M/M John Glines, M/M Leslie Holland & fam of Atascadero, Mrs Ida
               Davis Hall & fam and J D Davis.   –Mon May 18 p.3
            1937 in Long Beach; 1948 in Palos Verdes
            = Margaret Davis
            = Millicent Davis
            = Elenor Davis

  f. Lawrence Clifford Davis b. SMv 12 Nov 1899
    "Coon" d. Atascadero 12 Nov 1976 @77; SM cem
    Editor *Review* 1918 obit Sat Nov 13 p.11; 25y Atascadero
    stu body pres SMUHS 1920 *Atascadero News* Nov 18 A4; 4gch 5ggch
    sports SMUHS, Stanford 3 bros; Atascadero Plumbing Supply
    1920 cen: w/parents chf bldg insp SLO co 10y
    1922: Camozzi's Saloon in American Leg, Harvey R Cole Post 109
     Cambria is the last remnant (Atas); WWI. WWII
    of "the cowboy bar" in the east village. In 1922 Adriano Camozzi bought out the
    previous owner and hired Cliff Davis of Santa Maria to demolish the old wooden
    building, and construct a two story stucco hotel/card parlor/pool hall/barbershop
    complex. Davis charged $15,000, completing the job within a year. (during which
    time he met his bride to be, no doubt) He also built the Lyons house on Bridge st
    in 1922; after building several other homes in Cambria he became a county
    building inspector. He was grandfather of Sandy Sherer, a long time checker at
    Soto's market. –Cambria Historical Society, *Stroll Down Memory Lane*, 1997
    1922-3 Dir: oil wkr Bell Lease
    1925 Dir: carp r924 S Bwy
    1938 Dir: 921 S McClelland
    1940-1 Dir: Davis Bros Constr (L C & F A) concrete constr 921 S McClelland
      L C "Cliff" (Winifred) Davis Bros Constr 921 S McClelland
    1948 in Ventura
     m.1 1923; to live in San Luis Obispo –T Sep 4
      1932: Lawrence Clifford Davis vs Gladys Davis 17 Mar; SLO co R310
    Gladys Geraldine Shaug b. Pacific Valley (Monterey co) 12 Nov 1905
     cook Hearst Castle 18y d. Cambria 2 Sep 1982; Cambria cem; obit *SLO*
       Telegram-Tribune Fri Sep 8 A7; the
       Cambrian Sep 9 15gch 10ggch
      F: Charles Lawson Shaug 1874-1956
      M: Frances Marion Plaskett 1875-1966
    = Lawrence Clifford Davis jr in Ojai 1973, 1975, 1976, 1982
    = Faye Marion Davis 1924-1980 in Lompoc 1973, 1975
     m. (Lawrence) Williams (1922-1974)?
    Gladys m.2 28 May 1932, SLO S163
    Nicholas Yost 1906-1956 Cambria cem
    = Wayne Yost, in San Simeon 1982
    = Barbara Russo, in Glens Falls NY 1982
    = Sharon Veith, in Cambria 1982
  f. Cliff m.2 SM 13 May 1936 by L J Morris JP; attended by M/M R R Murphy.
    Newlyweds Visit in AZ on Trip. M/M Clifford Davis…to Hoover Dam and Kingman
    to visit her relatives…to live on West Church st –Fri May 15 1936 p.3
    Winnifred Peck Kuykendall b. San Angelo TX 28 Feb 1900
     OES Kingman AZ d. SM 12 Feb 1973 @72/11/14; SM cem
      inf: Margaret Jane Davis
      obit Tue Feb 13 p.2; also *Atascadero News*
      Thu Feb 15 A5; r9095 Lake View Dr; 7gch
      5 ggch
    1973: sisters Marie Braem, Santa Ana; Marjorie Marker/VanMarter, Kingman AZ;
     bro Nick Peck, Truth or Consequences NM
    = her son Roy W Kuykendall b. Kingman 2 Mar 1918; d. SM 19 Aug 1975
     obit Aug 20 p.2, Aug 21 p.2 wid Marjorie L, SM; dau Mrs Pamela V Reid, SM;

    step-bro Larry Davis jr, Ojai; step-sis Mrs Faye Williams, Lompoc, 2gch. To SM
    from Atascadero 1958; building inspector. WWII
    1940-1 Dir: Roy W Kuykendall atndt Craig Rich Ser Sta r921 S McClelland
  f. Cliff m.3
    Georgia Baldwin Mrs
    her sons: Harold Baldwin, in Richmond 1976; Ronald Baldwin, in SLO 1976

3. Mary Jane Davis   b. Lake co IN 2 Nov 1860
           d. young

4. May Lydia Davis   b. Lake co IN 11 Aug 1865
           d. (Westmoreland) KS 6 Dec 1960
  in KS 1912, 1914; Pasadena CA 1937; Westmoreland KS 1947-9
  m. (Westmoreland) KS 31 July 1883
  John Henry Whearty   b. Janesville WI 9 Mar 1856
           d. (Westmoreland) KS 28 Feb 1928
           F: John Whearty 1827-1907
           M: Ellen Hagerty 1833-1913
           See *Pioneers of the Bluestem Prairie* op cit #481,594
  children all born Westmoreland
  a. Nellie Mabel Whearty (Bertie Elwood Hough) in KS 1949
  b. Maude Beryl Whearty (Chas Isaac Hough) in KS 1949
  c. Roy Eugene Whearty   b. 27 Apr 1887
   to SM 1936   d. at home SM @62/5/6; bur 5 Oct 1949
   WWI   SM cem; obit Tue Oct 4 p.3. 1gch
   1940-1 Dir: Roy E (Viola) carp 306 W Tunnell; Bernice stu
   1955-6 Dir: Viola wid Roy cook Miller St sch h831 E Cook
   pall bearers members of the carpenters union.
   Viola M Frances Snodgrass   b. Wamego KS 13 Oct 1895
   cafeteria supt 20y retired 1961   d. 5 July 1988 @92; SM cem
               obit Wed July 6 p.16 5 gch
               F: Oliver Snodgrass
   = Bernice Whearty (Shelburn) in Modesto 1949, Palos Verdes peninsula 1988
    SMUHS 1940
   = Marjorie Whearty (Plumm) in Sunnyvale 1949, Sacramento 1988
   = Dorothy Whearty (Shubert) in Bakersfield 1949, single; in SB 1988
  d. Lelia Faye Whearty, single, in KS 1949
  e. Fannie Ella Whearty (Wm Franklin Grutzmacher) in KS 1949
  f. John Moses Whearty, single, in KS 1949
  g. Ruth Ida Whearty (Alfred Henry Maupin) in Pasadena 1949
  h. Lloyd Edward Whearty (Violet Frances Morford) in KS 1949

5. Lily Bell Davis   b. IN/KS? 25 Feb 1868
           d. (Pottawatomie co) KS 30 Aug 1870

6. Fannie Eleanor Davis   b. Pottawatomie co KS 22 Dec 1869; m. @20
  1940 phbk: Mrs W H   d. Santa Maria 2 Nov 1947 @77/10/10; SM cem
   118 W Tunnell   obit Mon Nov 3 1947 p.1; 62y SM 4gch 1ggch 1 sis
  1947-8 Dir: hmkr h109 W Fesler
   m. Santa Maria 9 June 1891 by J B Bain: wit: Nellie Blosser, M A Baker. -*Times* June 16
  William H Tunnell   b. Ukiah CA 5 Feb 1861; m. @29
   to SMv 1864   d. 8 Sep 1932 @71/7/3; SM cem
   bio Philips I 328   obit Sep 8 p.1
   1890 GR: 29 f; CA; Sisquoc   F: Martin Luther Tunnell 1829-1903
   1900 cen: tp8 (Sisquoc)   M: Salina Haskins 1829-1903

1906 Dir: f cor Bwy/Fesler; Mrs   See ONT 163; M/H 427; see Hopper chart
1909 Dir: Wm H rancher rFesler;
   Mrs F E; R W stu; Miss N M stu
1920 cen: SM
1922-3 Dir: Wm H (Fannie E) farmer r109 W Fesler
1925 Dir: Wm H (Fannie) ret same   1928 Dir: same   1930 Dir, 1938 phbk: same

   a. Roy William Tunnell   b. (Sisquoc) Sep 1891
     WWI   d. SM 20 Sep 1955 @64/0/18; SM cem
    1920 cen: w/parents   obit Wed Sep 21 p.1
    1922-3 Dir: f w/parents
    1925 Dir: Roy carp r507 N Lincoln; Mrs Ann bkpr, same
    1928 Dir: Roy (Ann) farmer r north SM
    1930 Dir: Roy W r north of SM; Ann M r507 N Lincoln
    1940 phbk: Roy W ranch n of SM; also 1943
    1947-8 Dir: Roy W (Nan S) ret f h118 W Tunnel; 1955-6 Dir: same
    1947-8 Dir: Tunnell Ranch c1000-1100 blk N Bwy RR1
    1955: Mrs R L Jeffrey of Burlington WA came to funeral
      m. (ONT says he married Gladys Tunnell) (Are Ann and Nan/Fannie 2 women?)
    Ann/Nan/Fannie Scoles   b. Atchison co MO 30 Sep 1895
    1976 Dir: Nan S (wid Roy)   d. SM 11 Oct 1978 @83; bur Burlington WA
    1961 Dir: same   death recorded as Nan and Fannie
    ret h118 W Tunnell   SS benefits to Mt Vernon WA
    came to SM 1944 (obit)   obit Thu Oct 12 p.6; bro Stanley S Scoles,
                                        Burlington WA; sis Mrs Blanche Jeffrey,
       = William Roy Tunnell   Mt Vernon WA; nieces/neph
         SMUHS 1948
       Said to be a resident of SM in 1955, but coming to funeral from Santa
         Monica; not mentioned in 1978 obit

   b. Nellie May Tunnell   b. (Sisquoc) 24 Oct 1893
     in SLO in 1915   d. SLO 30 July 1974 @80/9/6; SM cem; obit
     in SLO 1932, 1955, 1970   *SLO Telegram-Tribune* Wed July 31 p.2; 4gch
     m. (1915)
     Chester Lee Martin   b. SM 24 June 1891
     in SLO 1919, 1921   d. SLO 6 Dec 1970 @79/5/12; SM cem; obit
     SMUHS Oakland Poly   *SLO Telegram-Tribune* Dec 8 p.10
     ret 1957 from Fred H Johnson   F: Robert Franklin Martin 1865-1929
     Implement Co SLO   M: Henrietta Louise Newlove 1870-1921
    1970: Martin survived by bros Eugene, SLO; Dr Arthur, Whittier; sisters Mrs
      Pauline Adam, SM; Mrs Elsie Stoddard, Martinez; Mrs Viola Jessee, Stinson
      Beach, see Adam chart; Viola married Arthur Jessee, son of John V Jessee,
      see Jessee chart
    = Adela P Martin (Phillips) in Palo Alto 1970, 1974; dau Linda
    = Robert W Martin in SLO 1970, 1974

Note: R F "Frank" Martin purchased 2 acres on Broadway from J W Speed to erect an elegant residence…opposite Mr Blochman's ideal home…will add greatly to that already very attractive residential section. –June 9 1906. Martin had the entire 800 block as Davis had the entire 900 block. The Martin house became the Santa Maria Club; like the Davis house, it was in the corner of the property the rest of which was devoted to orchard and gardens.

   c. Veda Lillian Tunnell   b. (Sisquoc) 20 July 1900
     1920 cen: w/parents   d. Long Beach 23 Sep 1983 @83; SM cem
     1940-1 Dir: Dalessi Veda Beauty   obit Sun Sep 25 p.13; 3gch 7ggch

        Shop 624 S Bwy; r109 W Fesler
        1943 phbk: Dalessi Beauty Salon 624 S Bwy
        1947-8 Dir: Beauty opr h124 W Tunnell; 1955-6 Dir: 124A W Tunnell
        1973 Dir: same; 1947-8 Dir: Frances Beauty Salon 624 S Bwy (Frances Bianchi)
          in SM 1974
          m.

Alexander A Dalessi	b. (Los Berros) 6 Aug 1900
see Phillips II 185	d. Long Beach 22 March 1973
1925 Dir: A A (Veda) auto slsmn	F: Alexander Anselmo Dalessi 1858-1900
r124 W Tunnell	M: Adela Frances Rojas 1861-1911
1928 Dir: Alex (Veda) same	1930 Dir: A A Dalessi 118 W Tunnell

      = William T Dalessi in Huntington Beach 1974
7.   Rosa Evelyn Davis   b. Pottawatomie co KS 18 Jan 1872
      in Alaska 1912   d. Alaska June 1914
       m.
    Landy Marston

DAVIS
PIONEERS OF THE CALIFORNIA CENTRAL COAST

Harvey Augustus Davis	b. Seneca co OH 11 Feb 1831
Capt IN Inf (cem)	d. Arroyo Grande 1 June 1906 @74; AG cem
1890 GR: 59 lab; OH; Lompoc	consumption; funeral pd for by E C Davis
1900 cen:	

1906: Local & Business Items. Mr Davis of Arroyo Grande, brother-in-law of Mrs Polly Davis, died at that place last Sunday. Wm Tunnell and family of this place attended the funeral.   –June 9

    m. Lake co IN 21 Sep 1857. See *Pioneers of the Bluestem Prairie* p.184

Amy Lucy Mann	b. Lake co IN 15 Sep 1841
1910 cen: w/Edward	d. at home of son 1143 Murray av SLO 15 June 1914
4 births 3 living	@74 from effects of a fall last year; AG cem
1914: 2 sons 1 dau	obit *SLO Daily Telegraph* Tue June 16 p.7
1. Calvin Lewis Davis	former res Los Berros
1890 GR: 32 lab; IN; Lompoc	b. Lake co IN 31 Oct 1858
1900 cen: tp8 (Sisquoc)	d. Santa Barbara 8 Feb 1926 @67; AG cem
1902 GR: 43 Los Berros, PO Berros	
1910 cen: Nipomo & Los Berros rd	
1912 Dir: Los Berros	
1914: Los Berros	
1916-7 VR: 5'11; IN	
1920 cen: Nipomo pct	

      m. Pottawatomie co KS 23 June 1885

Rebecca Jane Edwards	b. IN 21 Feb 1868; F: IN; M: IN/OH
(Jennie)	d. at home SLO 29 Dec 1940 @72; AG cem
1910 cen: 10 births 7 living	notice *T-T* Mon Dec 30 p.4; obit *AG Herald-*
1916-7 VR: Mrs Jennie 5'3; IN	*Recorder* Fri Jan 3 1941 p.2; 15gch 2ggch
1940: 3 dau 5 sons	bro John Edwards, SLO; sis Mrs Olive Edwards,
	Chicago; Mrs Howard Edwards, Mitchell NE
a. Alvis A Davis	b. Pottawatomie co KS 8 July 1886
1910 cen: w/parents	d. Caldwell ID Feb 1969; SSDI
1912 Dir: Berros farmer	

      1916-7 VR: 5'10½; KS
      1920 cen: Nipomo pct
      in Caldwell ID 1940, 1947
      m.
    Hazel M   b. WI 19 Dec 1897; F: WI; M: Ger
                                              d. Caldwell ID Dec 1978; SSDI
  b. Charles F Davis   b. Pottawatomie co KS Jan 1888
    (Frank)   d. (Chas F (GS) SBco 3-6-1963)?
    1910 cen: w/parents
    1912 Dir: Berros lab
    in Santa Barbara 1940
    1939 phbk: Chas F Davis 970 Garcia rd SB; same 1940 phbk
  c. Glen Gilbert Davis   b. Santa Barbara 5 Dec 1892
    1910 cen: w/parents   d. SLO 5 Jan 1947 @54; IOOF cem; obit
    Los Berros to 1925;   *SLO Telegram-Tribune* Jan 6 p.7; 3 sons 3 dau
    Yoakum tract SLO 15y   4 bro 2 sis
    1931-house moving w/York, Davis & Bakke; in SLO 1940
      m.
    Myrtle
  = Earl Delano Davis in SLO 1947
  = George G Davis jr in SLO 1947
  = Walter C Davis in Detroit 1947
  = Elizabeth Glen Davis in SLO 1947
  = Caroline Rebecca Davis in SLO 1947
  = Mrs Doris Nicholson in Bellflower 1947
  d. Amy Ellen Davis   b. CA Sep 1896; m.1 @17 of Berros
    "Old Man Wheat", the patriarch of the Manzana settlement, claimed to have divine
      healing powers; one day he revived Amy, the 2-year-old daughter of Calvin Davis,
      when she was apparently dying in convulsions. All the women's help had failed, but
      he tossed her around, pounded and shook her and really snatched her from the jaws of
      death.   –ONT 354
    1910 cen: w/parents   d.
      m.1 Santa Maria 25 Sep 1912, Calvin L Davis consenting
    Antony C Correy   b.   m. @25 of SLO
      m.2
    Floyd Forsythe   b.
    in Santa Barbara 1940, 1947
    1940 phbk: Floyd Forsythe 609 W Cota SB
  e. Raymond G Davis   b. CA Jan 1898
    1920 cen: w/parents
    1940 in Burlingame; in SLO 1947
  f. Ralph E Davis   b. CA 1902
    1920 cen: w/parents   d. (3 Dec 1902-17 Feb 1991; SSDI)?
    in Oakland 1940; SLO 1947
  g. Lillian I Davis   b. CA 1906
    1920 cen: w/parents   d. (25 Oct 1905 – 8 June 1988 SLO; SSDI)?
      m.
    (L C) Ball, in SLO 1940, 1947
  h. Ruby Davis   b. CA c1912
    1920 cen: w/parents   d. before 1947
    in SM 1940

      m.
        Carl L Westfall   b. (15 Feb 1912; SSDI
          1940-1 Dir: Carl L (Ruby) oilwkr   d. Douglas co OR June 1985)?
          Pac Western Oil Corp h318 Mary dr
          1947-8 Dir: CL emp Five C Ref Box 1777 Orcutt; also L C Westfall, same employer

Note: Linder C Westfall, b. IN 1913 d. 1961; 35 yrs in SMv. Bro. Carl in Myrtle Creek (Douglas co) OR   –T Sep 16 1961 p.2

2.   Alice A Davis   b. IN 1861
                                          d. Santa Barbara before 1910
     m. (Pottawatomie co KS) 12 Mar 1878
   John Hand

3.   Lucy J Davis   b. IA 1865
     in SB 1909, 1914   d. Santa Barbara 26 Feb 1933 @68
      m.
   J (James) Y Wilson   b.
                                        d. (Santa Barbara 3-22-1937 @80)?
     1913. Arroyo Grande: Mrs Lucy Wilkeson (sic) from Santa Barbara visiting brother
       C L Davis and Mr & Mrs Davis. –Sep 27

4.   Edward Clinton Davis   b. Madison co IA 24 Sep 1870
     1902 GR: 31 Los Berros,   d. San Luis Obispo 25 Feb 1950 @79; IOOF cem; obit
       PO Berros   *SLO Telegram-Tribune* Mon Feb 27 p.10; r1127
     1910 cen: Nipomo & Berros rd   Upham st; 25gch 23ggch
     1912 Dir: Berros lab; also Edw C driver h1418 Carmel SLO (?)
     1914: 1143 Murray rd SLO
     1920 cen: 2305 Broad st SLO
     1920-1 VR: 5'10; IA; SLO #5
       m. c1900
   Mary Frances   b. Chicago 25 Dec 1885; parents IL
   (Mollie)   d. San Luis Obispo 30 May 1967 @84; IOOF cem; obit
     to KS farm; to Berros 1901   *SLO Telegram-Tribune* Thu June 1 p.16; 6 sons 8 dau
     to SLO 1911
     1910 cen: 5 births 5 living
     1967: 6 sons 8 dau
     a.   Dorothy D Davis   b. 7 Mar 1901; SSDI
        in SB 1950, 1967   d. 5 June 1991 no place given
        m.
      Charles Bausher   b. 14 Jan 1893; SSDI
        1940 phbk: painting contr   d. Santa Barbara Nov 1971
        620 E Alamar SB
        1967 phbk: 2204 Edgewater Way SB
      = Two sons, according to David L Cole, a SB native: one was "feeble minded", stood
        on the front lawn and stared at people; the other drove his father's truck into the
        mountains above SB shortly before school started, about 1946, and rolled it (and
        himself) off a cliff.
     b.   Gladys Erma Davis   b. c1903; in SB 1950, SLO 1967
          m. SLO co 16 March 1923; M489
       Fred Wm Cook
          1940 phbk: Fred W Cook r218 E Alamar SB
     c.   Daisy I Davis (Stoddard)   b. c1905; in Los Angeles 1950. Blythe 1967
     d.   Clinton C Davis   b. c1907; in New York 1950, 1967

e.	Pearl W Davis (Cox)	b. 27 Mar 1909 (*Times*); in Monterey 1950; Seaside 1967
f.	Rex Davis	b. c1912; in SLO 1950, 1967
g.	Zada Davis (Lewis) in SLO 1950, 1967	b. 9 Oct 1915; SSDI d. Monterey Dec 1986
i.	Richard Davis	b. c1918; in SLO 1950, Fresno 1967
j.	Arthur Davis	b. c1920; in Bakersfield 1950, 1967
k.	Frances Davis (Mitts) in Monterey 1950; Seaside 1967	b. 8 Jan 1922; SSDI d. Seaside 15 Feb 1996
l.	William Davis	b. in SLO 1950, Reno 1967
m.	Theodore Davis	b. in USN at sea 1950, El Monte 1967
n.	Sally Davis (Pierce)	b. in Spreckels 1950, Salinas 1967
o.	Ann(e) Davis (Spencer)	b. in SLO 1950, Los Gatos 1967

DAVIS
PIONEERS OF THE MANZANA

Frederick Montgomery Davis   b. Elkhart co IN 23 Dec 1839
  1870 cen: Pottawatomie co KS   d. Manzana 19 May 1897 @59/4/25
    PO Louisville lab single   bur Manzana, "impracticable to remove the body to
    w/Joshua Gann fam   the valley at this time." obit May 29
  1880 cen: Elko co NV Star Valley
  1890 GR: 50 f IN Sisquoc to KS 1869; 7y. to NV 1876 to Manzana 1886
    m. (Pottawatomie co) KS c1870
Sarah Ellen Forrester   b. (W) VA 1853/4
                                         d.

1.   Alonzo Edwin Davis   b. KS Aug 1871 (cen); 24 Aug 1872 (cem); m. of Garey
      1892 GR: 21 5'7 lt gry blk;   d. Sisquoc 26 Mar 1933 @61/7/21; SM cem
        scar on back of lh; KS; SM #2   obit Mon Mar 27 p.2. 4 sons 2 dau. 46y Sisquoc
      1896 GR: f 24 5'7½ dk gry blk
        scar lh; KS; Sisquoc
      1900 cen: tp8 w/David Spaulding
      1906 Dir: Garey, stockraiser; Mrs
      1910 cen: Manzana cyn, SB Forest Preserve; 2 births 2 living
      1920 cen: w/Arthur
        m. at home of bride's parents, Mr & Mrs B G Plaskett 4 May 1905 by Judge
           Whitelock (*Times*)
      Lucy Elizabeth Plaskett   b. Pacific Valley, Monterey co 22 Mar 1886
                                               m. of Pacific Valley
                                               d. Santa Maria 11 Mar 1975 @88/11/19; SM cem
                                               obit Wed Mar 12 p.2. r718 N East av
                                               14 gch 12 ggch. 70y SMv
                                               F: Byron G Plaskett 1845-1911
                                               M: Corrine Martha Bennett 1852-1931
      1947-8 Dir: Adrian (Marg L) Box 157 (Foxen Rd Dist)
           A L (Lucy E) Box 158; Lucy E Box 158
      1955-6 Dir: Rt 1 Box 157: Adrian L; Alfred E emp SP Milling; Alonza V;
           Jean Mrs; Leo L (Lillian) lab; Lucy E Mrs
      1975 pall bearers: Fred, Dennis, Edward, Brian Davis; Harold Barr; Rege Brannagan.
        Honorary: Chester, Dorian, Audell, Clifford, Eugene Davis; Jake Hill (Will?)

- a. Alonzo Virgil Davis   b. Sisquoc 15 Sep 1906 (*Times*)
     - 1951 Dir: RR 1 Box 158   d. SM 24 Jan 1994 @87; SM cem
         - obit Tue Jan 25 A-4. 4gch
         - welder Coast Rock, farmer, Sisquoc Grange
     - m.   Int U Operating Engs #12
     - Irene <u>Eunice</u> Martin   b.
     - 1960, 1971: Sisquoc   d. (living 1994)
         - F: Robert Sidney Martin 1877-1960
         - M: Jessie Irene Murphy 1889-1971
     - = Edward V Davis (in SM 1994)
     - = Carolyn Irene Davis (Harold Barr) (in SM 1994)
         - 1976 Dir: parts mgr VW Lompoc
- b. Alfred Eugene Davis   b. Sisquoc 9 Apr 1909
     - 1933: in Ojai   d. SM 29 Nov 1979 @70/7/20; SM cem
     - 1951 Dir: Plant Opr SP Milling   obit Fri Nov 30 p.18; 9 gch
     - Co Box 158   4 sons 2 dau 3 bro 1 sis 22y Coast Rock
     - 1976 Dir: ret 718 N East av
     - 1979 pall bearers: Steve Will, Jay Will, Rob Downy, Geo Hamill, Harold Barr, Lonnie Mohler. Honorary: Jake Will, Ron Corsby, Bill Williams, Cliff Cameron, Robert Allison, Les Lundgren, Leon Wickenden, Raymond Goodchild
         - m.
     - Jean L Aldrich   b.
     - = Alfred E Davis Jr (Jennifer B)   survived husband
         - 1976 Dir: plant opr Coast Rock Prod h2034 Lockwood Ln
     - = Dennis Davis (in Atascadero 1979)
     - = Ronald Davis (in SM 1979) 1976 Dir: Ronald H r718 N East av
     - = Clifford Davis (in SM 1979)
     - = Janet Davis (Bernard R Brannagan)
         - 1976 Dir: batchman Coast Rock Prod; Rt 1 Box 158a; Janet acct N Ray Guymon
     - = Joni Davis (in SM 1979)
- c. Adrian Leland Davis   b. 23 Jan 1912
     - 1951 Dir: Rt 1 Box 157   d. 6 Sep 1987 @75; SM cem
         - obit Tue Sep 8 p.17. SP Milling
     - m. 1939   2 bro 1 sis neph/nc
     - Margaret Louella Parker   b. 12 Nov 1913 (cem stone)
     - (Peggy)   d. 3 Jan 1991; SSDI
     - = No issue
- d. Atwell Alden Davis   b. 7 Nov 1917
     - d. 13 Oct 1921 @3/11/6; SM cem
- e. Sarah Ellen Davis   b. 19 Oct 1920
     - d. 30 Nov 1936 @16/1/1; SM cem
- f. Leo L Davis   b.
     - m.
     - Lillian
         - 1951 Dir: emp Airport Kitchen; RR1 Box 158
         - 1994: in Sisquoc
- g. Effie C Davis (Tucker)   b. (single 1933)
     - 1977 Dir: Tucker James H (Effie C) slsmn Calif Pools h324 E Grant
     - 1978 Dir: Tucker Effie C Mrs h324 E Grant
2. Arthur Curtis Davis   b. KS 16 May 1874
   - 1896 GR: 22 5'7 f lt blu br   d. 11 Apr 1937 @62/11/25; SM Cem "Uncle"

KS; Sisquoc
1906 Dir: Sisquoc stockraiser
1910 cen: Garey rd; also David C
   Spalding 72 S IL CT NC hired
1920 cen: Sisquoc
   Single

obit Mon Apr 12 p.1: "Sisquoc Farmer Drops Dead at Plow in Field" 51y Sisquoc

Note: Dave Spalding is said to have been an uncle of the Alvis Davis family. –The Good Years, Contreras, Sunday June 21, 1998 C-3. He died in Santa Maria Nov 1916 @80/8/24; buried SM Cem Nov 14, obit Nov 18. He lived 30 years on his ranch above Sisquoc, never married; only local survivor Pete Spalding, well known carpenter, a nephew. Other relatives in Payette ID. Pete died in 1928 @61; born in IL, he had been in Santa Maria 24 years, leaving his widow, Anna Mary, who died in 1943, and son, Earl W, who died in 1952. He had two brothers, Jesse, Mulhall OK, and John, in KS. Upon checking *Pioneers of the Bluestem Prairie* for Spalding/Spaulding, it was found that Mary Jane Whearty (1860-1940) was married to Lott W. Spaulding, and died in Payette ID. Mary Jane's brother John H Whearty, was the husband of May Lydia Davis, Alvis H Davis' sister. Dave Spalding could be Lott's brother, making him brother-in-law to Alvis' sister – not quite uncle, but some sort of shirt-tail relative.

Note: Jake L Will d. 1993; his widow, Evelyn Fenton Will, 92, died October 17 1998. The two sons, Jay and Steve Will, operate Coast Rock, a family business.

Who is This? NOTICE – To the ladies of Santa Maria and vicinity: I have taken over the management of the Beauty Parlor in the Hotel Bradley Barber Shop and would be pleased to have you call. I am direct from Kansas City and am up in all the latest in beauty culture. MRS F. H Davis   –Fri Sep 25 1925 p.5

1928 Dir: Davis Mrs Fayette, prop. Peacock Vanity Box, r109 W Fesler

DAVIS
PIONEERS OF THE CALIFORNIA CENTRAL COAST

Sylvester C Davis   b. Kingston NH 8 Oct 1833
  1850 cen: Kingston NH w/Sarah   d. Pacific st San Luis Obispo 30 July 1915 @81
    Fellows 70 MA; nr Hannah Davis   obit *MT* Sun Aug 1 p.1; Tue Aug 3; IOOF cem SLO
    39 NH; to CA 1859
  1860 cen: Marin co Bolinas, married; w/Daniel Olds 75 MA & wf;   to SLO co 1875
  1880 cen: San Simeon
  1882: District Clerk, Excelsior sch dist, Morro (T/W)
  1892 GR: 58 5'6 fr blu br f; NH; res Morro, pct Morro, PO Morro
  1900 cen: res Chorro, PO SLO;   1902 GR: 68; Chorro pct, PO SLO
  1912 Dir: h1060 Islay st SLO
  1915: pall bearers Chas St Clair, Wm Sandercock, Chas M Martin, F L Smith, G W Newton,
    W W Smithers. Survived by widow and 3 sons; had ranch beyond C H Johnson place.
    m. c1860
Mary C   b. ME/NH 1838-40 (cem: 1838-1920)
            d. at home of son 977 Pismo San Luis Obispo
               27 Feb 1921 @81; IOOF cem SLO
               obit/notice Feb 28 p.4; DT Mon Feb 28 p.5; 2 sons

1. Clarence Leroy Davis   b. Napa CA 17 May 1862; m. of Morro
    1892 GR: 30 5'8 fr gry br;   d. SLO 27 Feb 1955 @92/9/10; SM cem; obit *SLO*
      scar left wrist; f CA   *Telegram-Tribune* Mon Feb 28 p.2, Tue Mar 1 p.2

Morro, same, same to SLO in youth; harness shops in Morro & Cambria, then Guadalupe & Santa Maria 1898. to SLO 1944. 2ggch

1900: C L Davis has a lot of the best gloves made, which he is selling for $1 a pair. -*Santa Maria Graphic* Jan 5

1900 cen: Santa Maria 2 births 2 living

1900: Mrs Clarence Davis accompanied her sister, Mrs Arthur Davis, to her home at Morro this week. –Nov 3 Mrs S C Davis of San Luis, mother of Clarence Davis arrived Thursday on a few days visit. Mrs Clarence Davis returned Thursday after a weeks visit with Morro and San Luis friends. Dashiell and Black are having the rooms fitted up that were recently vacated by Davis' harness shop and will remove their cigar store into the same this week. –Nov 10

1904: M/M Davis, parents of harness dealer, Clarence Davis, here this week. Our Business Men and Pioneers of the Area. G M Doane Jr has a neatly appointed office in the new Wineman bldg with C L Davis the harness maker, who also shows a line of buggies and traps. He carries a large stock of farm implements of the well known Osborne make… (For Doane see chart) -Dec 16

1906 Dir: C L Davis harnessmkr Main st, rChapel; Mrs

1906: IDES. SLO, SM & AG Councils meet in SM. C L Davis on barbecue committee.
-*SLO Morning Tribune* June 3

1907: C L Davis oldest harness shop in Santa Maria. –June 14

C L Davis' Home Entered By Burglars…some time Monday afternoon during the circus…house ransacked…The intruders obtained a gold watch, a valuable heirloom belonging to Mrs Davis, which was made by her uncle 70 years ago in Switzerland. A number of minor articles were also taken…little value to the burglars…dear to their owners. No clue of the robbers could be obtained. –Nov 23

Note: the Beaty circus was in town

C L Davis, the pioneer harnessmaker, has engaged a first-class harnessmaker from Sacramento and his fine establishment is running as smooth as ever. Clarence has a fine equipped shop and is prepared to do any kind of work at the shortest possible notice. His stock is complete and purchasers can get anything they need from bridle ring to buggy robe.

M/M S C Davis of SLO visiting son Clarence. –Dec 28

1908: Davis Buys United Harness Co's Store . . . –Sep 26

1909: as 1906; r 401 W Chapel, Mrs Emma; Ralph; 1910: W Chapel, harness

1913: C L Davis shoe repair machine kept busy morning to night . . . does good work in short time. –Jan 18

1914 SLO Dir (has SM): harnsmkr 118 W Main; h401 W chapel

1922-3 Dir: Shoemkr 118 W Main; r401 W Chapel 1925 Dir: Same

1928 Dir: clerk res same

1930 Dir: w/Wm MacDonald, machinery 122 W Main

1930 Dir: Wm MacDonald Machinery and Supplies. Byron Jackson Pumps – Fairbanks Morse Gas Engines – Motors Pipe and Fittings. 122 W Main St

1936: Honored on Birth Anniversary. Clarence Davis of SM, guest of honor at Routzahn Park, AG, @76 (sic). To SLO @10; harness shop in SM many years before the coming of the automobile. –Tue May 19 p.3

Note: It is interesting to see how Davis accommodated to the rise of the automobile which caused phasing out of his business; it is a good example to people whose work is becoming obsolete.

1940-1 Dir: emp Wm MacDonald; MacDonald Wm (Belle) Pumps & Equipt 122 W Main h603 S Bwy (Wm MacDonald's wife was Belle Glines, aunt of Vera Glines Davis [Mrs F A])

1940: C L Davis 50th Anniversary . . . dau (Ray Benny) Ventura, gson Jimmie Stokes, Ventura; nephews A K Davis, Walla Walla, and wife; Dr Leslie Davis, Alameda; Chester Davis, San Diego. Mrs Davis' sister Rose Davis, SLO – husband was C L's brother. Married Episcopal Church, SLO Oct 2 1890. –Fri Oct 4

1955: dau Mrs Benning, Ventura; gsons Carl James Stokes, Sunland; Bennie Benning, Berkeley

    m. San Luis Obispo 2 Oct 1890 by R W Summers, Prot. Epis, B472
        wit: Mr/Mrs J H Orcutt, SLO

Emma Staudt
- b. PA Feb 1869 (cen) 8 Feb 1870 (obit); m. of Santa Paula (sic)
- d. Woodland 27 Dec 1962 @92/10/19; SM cem obit Sat Dec 29 p.2. 2 gch, lived a year w/dau
- F: G Frederick Staudt 1833-1909
  - 1892 GR: Frederick Standt (sic) 56 5'6 fr blu lt, painter Ger. Morro, same, same; Nat. 5 Aug 1886 McLennan TX Dist Ct
- M: Ger/Switz

  a. Ralph R Davis — auto mechanic
- b. nr SLO 11 Nov 1891 (MT)
- d. Los Angeles 1918 @26/7/8; SM cem obit June 22; appendicitis

  b. Ina Marie Davis
    in Ventura 1955; in Woodland 1962
- b. SM 18 Mar 1900 (*Times*)
- d.

    m.1 c1920 (married, living in Taft –*Review* 1921)

Carl Stokes
- b. Guadalupe 12 July 1899
- d. (Ventura) 17 Apr 1959; spouse initial V
- F: Wm C Stokes 1846-1925
- M: Matilda Virginia Fisher 1856-1937
- see Stokes chart.

1921: M/M C L Davis to Taft for Christmas w/dau Mrs Carl Stokes. –Dec 23
1923: M/M C L Davis to Taft to visit M/M Carl Stokes. –Dec 24

    = Carl James (Jimmy) Stokes

  b. Ina m.2
    A F (Ray) Benning
    = Bennie Benning

2. Arthur D Davis
    1900 cen: Morro
    1900 GR: Morro; 1902 GR: same
    1910 cen: Morro tp, Chorro pct f; 3 births 3 living
    1912 Dir: RFD #1 SLO
    1919 in SLO
    1920 cen: Santa Rosa st SLO
- b. CA Mar 1866; m. of Morro
- d. SLO co 21 Sep 1925 @63

    m. Cayucos 7 Apr 1895 by Earl O Lockard, Pres, D541
        wit: Geo W Gillespie, Cayocos; C Amelia Gillespie, Cayucos

Note: Ye Ed. has much data on Gillespie and related families of Cambria.

Rosa Staudt
    1902: Mrs Arthur Davis of Morro visiting sis Mrs Clarence Davis –Apr 12
    1920-1 VR: 5'4½; TX; SLO #8
- b. Waco, McLennan co TX 9 Feb 1878; m. of Cayucos
- d. at home SLO 13 Apr 1955 @77; SM cem; obit *SLO Telegram-Tribune* Thu Apr 14 p.2. 55y SLO. 3 sons sis Mrs C L Davis SLO; nc Mrs A F Benning, Ventura
- F: G Frederick Staudt 1833-1909

    a.   Leslie S Davis (Dr) — b. CA 17 Jan 1896
       1920 cen: w/parents — d. Hayward Aug 1971; SSDI
       1940 in Alameda
       1955 in Hayward
    b.   Alden K Davis — b. 1903 (6 Nov 1902)
       1920 cen: w/parents — d. (Laguna Beach Feb 1971; SSDI)?
       1924: Alden Davis of USC visiting mother, Rose. – *SLO Daily Telegram* Apr 15
       1937: 1219 Osos st SLO; grad UC Berkeley Elec Rsch Rods Corpn LA.
                                                     –See SLOCGS *Bulletin* 22:2 p57
       1940 in Walla Walla
       1955 in North Hollywood
    c.   Chester A Davis — b. 1908
       1920 cen: w/parents
       1940, 1955 in San Diego

3.   Charles Frederick Davis — b. SLO 29 Mar 1878 (Trib); m.1 @26 of SLO
    (Fred) — d. 1060 Islay St SLO 25 June 1919 @41; IOOF cem
   1902 GR: 42 (24) Chorro pct,   obit DT Thu June 26, bros Clarence, SM; Arthur, SLO
   PO SLO
   1910 cen: 753 Marsh st no occ
   1912 Dir: lab r1060 Islay st SLO
   1919: M/M C L Davis went to SLO today to attend the funeral of Mr Davis' brother who
      died there Wed.   –Fri June 27 p.5
     m.1 San Luis Obispo 31 Oct 1903 by Geo Willett, F537; wit: Frederick P Johnson,
       SLO; S C Davis, SLO. Maggie F Davis vs Chas F Davis Apr 25 1910 dismissed
       Chas F Davis vs Maggie F Davis June 13 1912 SLO co J206
   Maggie F Norton — b. ME, m. @29 of SLO; 2d mar (cen) parents ME
     1910 cen: Maggie M @34 — d.
     prop Lodging house 753 Marsh st SLO
     1920-1 VR: Maggie N Mrs 5'4; ME; SLO #6
3.   Chas. m.2 SLO co 26 April 1914, J147
   Laura May Carrow
     1920-1 VR: 5'5; CA; SLO #8
     survived husband
    a.   Freddie Davis

DAVIS
PIONEERS OF THE CALIFORNIA CENTRAL COAST

Jacob W Davis — b. IN 1830 (1880 cen: 40) parents NJ
  1880 cen: Barton co KS Bend tp — d. 10 May 1895 (probably burial date); AG cem
  1892 GR: 61 6'3 fr gry lt, middle   "Capt IN Inf"
    finger lh crooked, f, IN, Nipomo; same same
  m.
America Baker — b. IN (1880 cen: 37; 1900 cen: Nov 1844) parents IN
  1900 cen: Nipomo, wid   cem: 1838-1903
    5 births 4 living — d. 1310 Chorro st SLO 11 Mar 1904 @62; IOOF cem
  1904 . . . Her sons are powerful young   obit *MT* Sat Mar 12, apoplexy
    men of splendid character and physique who idolized their mother and are broken in great
    sorrow at her unexpected death. Mrs Davis was herself a person 6'2 in height and weighed
    273 pounds. She had never before been seriously ill.   –*SLO Morning Tribune*

1. William Davis   b. IN 1858
    1880 cen: listed first of children; not mentioned in Mrs Davis' obit; she claimed 5 not 6 births. He could have been a child of a previous marriage of Jacob's.
2. Charles S Davis   b. IN Jan 1869
    1900 cen: Nipomo   d.
    1900 GR: 31 SLO #4
    1902 GR: 32 SLO #2
    1904 Dir: 1310 Chorro SLO
      m. 1891
  Zeruia   b. IL Feb 1869; parents VA
    1900 cen: 3 births 2 living   d.
    1900: Mrs Chas Davis of Nipomo was calling on SM friends last Wed.   –Sep 1
    a.   b.
    b.   Hazel   b. CA May 1896
    c.   Hulda   b. CA Dec 1898
3. Amos W Davis   b. IN (1880 cen: 10; 1900 cen: Dec 1872)
    1898 GR: 26 6'2 lt br br; IN;   cem: 1879-1925
      Nipomo   d. 19 July 1925 @45 (sic); IOOF cem
    1900 cen: w/mother
    1900 GR: 28 Nipomo
    1902 GR: 30 SLO #2
    1904 Dir: lab 1310 Chorro SLO; also fireman rr
    1912 Dir: fireman SP Co h2017 Chorro SLO
    1920-1 VR: 6'3; IN; SLO #7
    1920 cen: 179 Islay st locomotive eng rr
    1925: Local Engineer Killed in Wreck…   -*SLO Tribune* Mon July 20 p.1
      Davis Funeral Is Held Today…Engineer Met Death in Train Wreck…at Sudden…
      Southern Pacific…in SLO 25y…wife Myrtle, son Clyde, 2 bro, Harry & Weed
      of SLO…   -*SLO Tribune* Wed July 22
      Engineer Killed in Train Wreck. C M (sic) Davis of SLO, engineer on a Southern Pacific freight train, was killed early yesterday morning when his engine collided with a south bound special passenger train loaded with U S soldiers at Sudden.
      The locomotive of the freight train was tipped over by a collision which occurred when the passenger train pulled into the station yard at Sudden. The freight train was on a side track but too close to the main line to allow the passenger to pass, according to the reports. The tender and baggage car on the passenger train were derailed but the crew and train-load of soldiers escaped injury.
      Davis, the only victim of the accident, died at Guadalupe early Sunday morning while he was being rushed to a hospital at San Luis Obispo.
      All south bound mail and passenger service over the Southern Pacific was halted for several hours while the track was being cleared at the scene of the wreck.
                                                                              –July 20 p.1
Note: Sudden (Sudden ranch) is south of Lompoc.
      m.
    Myrtle Wray   b. Jackson TN 1880
      1912 Dir: Myrtle tchr   d. at home 879 Islay st SLO 21 Jan 1953 @72; IOOF cem
        Nipomo st sch SLO   SLO; obit *SLO Telegram-Tribune* Fri Jan 23 p.6;
                                                    Wed Jan 21 p.9 OES; in SLO 46y
    1920-1 VR: Myrtle Wray Davis 5'8 TN SLO #7
    1953 pall bearers: Harold Bishop, Bernard Pennington, Fred Sholes, Elmer Grove, Alfred Bittick, Karl Sween

Note: Harold L Bishop (1880-1957) was an engineer for the SP; he married Daisy Phillips, daughter of General Marion Phillips (1855-1943) whose family chart is in SLOCGS *Bulletin* 23:4 pp. 93-99.

    a. Clyde W Davis   b. c1914
        in SLO 1950, 1953

4. Parlee Davis   b. IN (1880 cen: 5)
                    d. Bakersfield 18 May 1900 @23; AG cem
                       obit May 26
    m. Newsom's Springs SLO co 7 Apr 1895 by J L Eddy JP, D531
       wit: Charles Davis, Newsom's Springs; D F Newsom, Newsom's Springs
   John Thomas Scott   b. CA Oct 1872; m. of SM
     (Tom)   d. Santa Maria 11 Aug 1916 @44/9/15; SM cem
    1900 cen: Kern co tp 6   obit Aug 12
     wd teamster   F: John Cowhick Scott 1839-1901
                            M: Ella Elizabeth Cook 1848-1901
                              see Scott chart
    a. child   b. & d. 18 May 1896
    b. Ella P Scott   b. Santa Maria 6 Dec 1897 (*Times*)
       1900 cen: listed w/father, also w/J C Scott, SM
       1901: Tom Scott's little daughter had her arm broken this week a few miles south of town at the Foster place, but under Dr Paulding's careful attention she is doing nicely.   –Mar 2

5. Zenith Weed Davis   b. (Barton co) KS Mar 1880 or Preston IN (obit)
    1900 cen: Nipomo farm lab   m. @25 of SLO
     w/Alfred E Stonier   d. San Luis Obispo 20 Mar 1945 @65; IOOF cem SLO
    1902 GR: 22 SLO #2, also   obit *SLO Telegram-Tribune* Wed Mar 21 p.8; 53y CA
     22 Nipomo   to SLO 1902 nephews/nieces in KS
    1904 Dir: lab 1310 Chorro SLO
    m. San Luis Obispo 25 Sep 1905 by R M Dart, G195
       wit: Amos Davis, SLO; Ruah Davis, SLO
   Mattie M Riffe   b. OR; m. @18 of SLO; no further mention
    1892 GR: Riffe John W 58 5'5 lt gry br f; KY; Santa Margarita, same, same
       Riffe John 65 5'7½ lt blu gr f; MO; Templeton, same, same

Note: No Preston IN located in old gazetteers; Preston KS is in Pratt co, straight south of Barton co. (The obit writer was confused, no doubt.)

6. Harry S Davis   b. (Barton co) KS Mar 1883 (cen) 1884 (cem)
    1904 Dir: fireman 1310 Chorro   d. visiting Atascadero 12 Jan 1950 @65; IOOF cem; SLO
     SLO   obit *SLO Telegram-Tribune* Fri Jan 13 p.3
    1920-1 VR: 6'5½; KS; SLO #8   locomotive engineer SP 1900-1946
     apparently single

Note: Both Zenith and Harry's survivors were Myrtle and Clyde only. Thanks to the SLOCGS *Bulletin* for having published directories, voter registrations, cemetery readings, and mortuary records.

DAVIS
PIONEERS OF THE CALIFORNIA CENTRAL COAST

George Davis   b. New York City 9 May 1815 (M/H)
   bio M/H 349; see Storke 570   6 May 1816 (Storke)
    Black Hawk War; to Pacific   d. San Miguel 28 Jan 1891 @75/8/20

    Coast 1838 w/Hastings or   obit Palo Robles LEADER 1 Feb 1891
    Hudson Bay Co   wife, 4 sons, 4 dau
  to OR 1842, to CA 1843   F: Charles Davis b. Eng/Ire
  to OR 1847, to CA 1849   M: Sct/Ire
  hotel 4y Galt; 1854-60 Santa Cruz, thence San Antonio ck, Monterey co; sold ranch to RG Flint
  1870 to San Miguel. Sheep raiser. 13 births, 8 grew to maturity
  1880 cen: SLO co Salinas tp
      m. Sutter's Fort by Capt Sutter 17 July 1843; wit: General John Bidwell
Elecia Sumner   b. MS 25 Feb 1830; to AR as a child
                                      d. nr San Miguel 20 Feb 1913 @83
                                        obit DT Sat Feb 22 p.4
                                    F: Owen Sumner b. KY; to CA 1842
                                    M: Lucy Preston b. KY
  1880. San Miguel News –On Fri eve Jan 31st, a farewell party at Jeffereys (sic) Hotel for
    Mr J N Turner. Floor committee: Misses Mary Mahoney, May Davis, Ella Proctor, Annie
    Simmons, Annie Davis…Present: M/M D Speyer, M/M W N Jeffreys, M/M J Wilkerson,
    M/M Davis, M/M Peters, Mrs Simmons, Mrs J B Mahoney, Mrs J C Wade, Misses Mary
    Mahoney, Ella Proctor, Annie Simmons, May & Alice Davis, Annie Davis, Messrs E
    Schwarz, A Sittenfield, W T Shield, J B Davis, R Still, B Davis, D Mahoney, J Kelcher, J S
    Carter, Ed Proctor, J N Turner, J Gladhill, W R Huey. Mr Turner left for a new home in
    Cambria.   –*SLO Tribune* Feb 7
  1900 cen: w/Joseph; 13 births 8 living
  1910 cen: same
1.   David Davis   b. OR 1847
      1880 cen: w/parents   d. SLO 5 Oct 1929 @81; r San Miguel
      1892 GR: 44 5'7½ fr br dk 3d   obit DT Mon Oct 7 p.2. San Miguel cem, 2 bro 2 sis
        knuckle rh knocked in; f CA;   funeral from residence of Charles Davis, San Miguel
        San Miguel, same, same
      Single. Raised stock Indian Valley (Monterey co)
      1902 GR: 54 San Miguel;   1912 Dir: David farmer San Miguel
      1920-1 VR: 5'9 San Miguel
2.   Eliza Davis   b. OR June 1849
      1910 cen: Monterey co   d. Indian Valley, Monterey co 11 Nov 1912 @63
        Bradley tp
      wid 10 births 5 living
        m. San Luis Obispo co 19 Aug 1868 by B F Music, A96
      Newton Azbill (Azbell)   b. MO Jan 1844; parents KY
        1900 cen: Bradley tp;   d. before 1910
        10 births 7 living
        a.   John Azbill   b. CA Nov 1870
            1900 cen: next to parents   d. Sawtelle 6 Sep 1938 @67/7/13; Templeton
              m.1 1896   cem; obit DT Tue Sep 8 p.5; Sp-Am war vet
                                              1 son 1 dau
          Eva M   b. CA July 1877; m.2 @26 of Estrella
                                    d.
          Eva m.2 in Estrella 22 Sep 1903 by Albert Ore, ME Ch Estrella, F525
            wit: Mrs E McCord, Mrs Albert Ore, Estrella
          Alfred Mills   b. NJ m. @33 of Estrella
            1892 GR: 22 5'6 dk br blk f; NJ;   F: (Jed Mills 1844-1920) ? spouse initial A M
              Estrella, Estrella, San Miguel   1892 GR: 48 5'8½ dk br gry f; NJ; Estrella,

        1898: Member Estrella ME Ch   Estrella, San Miguel
        July 28   M: (Ann M d. 1929 @77) ? spouse initial J
- a. m.2
  Susie   d. 21 Feb 1941 @69/0/18; Templeton cem
  in Santa Margarita 1938
  = (John Edward Azbell m. SLO co 20 Sep 1926, 0 499
      Marjorie Adelaide Araujo)
- b. Jasper Azbill   b. CA 1872
  1910 cen: w/mother   d.
- c. Claude T Azbill   b. CA Mar 1883
  1900 cen: w/parents   d.
  1910 cen: Bradley tp
  m. 1910
  Emma M   b. CA 1880; F: IR; M: Eng
         d. (Emma F Azbill d. SLO co 1 Oct 1914 @34)
- d. Marguerite R Azbill   b. CA Feb 1884; m. @27 of Indian Valley
  (Maggie)   d.
     m. San Luis Obispo 25 May 1911 by C H L Chandler, St Stephen's Ch SLO, I220
        wit: Alfred Williamson, SLO; M W Chandler, SLO
  John T Lewis   b. CA m. @31 of Berkeley
- e. George B/M Azbill   b. CA Mar 1886
  (George B Azbill d. Monterey co 22 July 1926 @40; spouse initial WS)
- f. Theodore Azbill   b. Jan 1889
  1900 cen: w/parents   d. (before 1910?)

Note: SM cem: Raymond C Azbill 12-1-1914 – 6-1-1993 @78; Sandy Bettiga, dau, inf. He born Carlock IL; to Compton 1943; sis Edna McKinney, Riverton IL; bros Don, Rancho Marietta, Robert, Clinton, IL. Avanelle Louise Azbill 7-14-21 – 6-28-92; Raymond C, hus

3. Joseph Benjamin Davis   b. Sacramento 15 March 1852
   stock raiser, Davis Bros   d. SLO co 12 Apr 1924 @72
   1880 cen: w/parents
   1892 GR: 41 5'8½ fr blu br stock raiser; CA; San Miguel, same, same
   1900 cen: Monterey co Bradley tp
   1909 Leased Corriente Rancho
   1910 cen: San Miguel
   1912 Dir: Joseph B farmer San Miguel
   Single
4. Buchanan Davis   b. nr Santa Cruz 1857
   1880 cen: w/parents   d. SLO co 8 May 1933 @75
   1892 GR: 34 5'9¾ dk gry dk; CA; San Miguel, same, same
   1900 cen: San Miguel svt w/Chas Metzler
   1910 cen: w/Joseph
   1912 Dir: Buchanan farmer San Miguel
   1920-1 VR: 5'10; CA; San Miguel
   Single
5. Mary/May Davis   b. (Santa Cruz) 1859
   1880 cen: w/parents   d. (Monterey co 1-15-43 spouse initials BS)?
   1910 cen: San Miguel rd, San Miguel, wid 2 births 2 living, both at home, single
   1913 in San Miguel
   in Parkfield 1929, 1932, 1933

m. SLO co 17 Dec 1882, A527
Robert B Still b. MO
  1884 Coast Counties Dir: d. (before 1892?)
    Robert B Still, Estrella, stock raiser
  a. Percy B Still b. CA 16 Oct 1883 (SLO co birth rec)
  b. Silvey? Alvey? D Still (dau) b. CA c1886

6. Anna Davis b. San Antonio ck, Jan 1862; m. of San Miguel
  1880 cen: w/parents d. SLO 24 Feb 1933 @71; IOOF cem
  1900 cen: 1 birth 1 living obit DT Feb 25 p.1
  in SLO 1913, 1929, 1932

    m. San Miguel 16 Dec 1891 by Rev A L Mitchell, St John's Missionary Prot Epis Ch,
      D107; wit: B Davis, Alecia (sic) Davis, San Miguel

Robert George Flint b. London, ONT, 27 Feb 1862; imm. 1884
  1892 GR: 30 5'10½ dk blu dk, m. of San Miguel
    blind left eye, lab; IRE; San d. SLO 10 Oct 1933 @71; IOOF cem
    Miguel, same, same; obit Wed Oct 11 p.3 Thu Oct 12 p.4
    nat 12 May 1886 SLO Sup Ct
  1900 GR: 38 San Miguel F: Pirney Flint
  1900 cen: San Miguel f
  1902 GR: 40 San Miguel
  1910 cen: R st San Miguel

  a. Anna Ethel Flint b. San Miguel Dec 1894
    in SLO 1938 d. 1941; IOOF cem SLO
    1920-1 VR: Miss A Ethel Flint 5'8; San Miguel
      Howard L Hoy 6'1; IA; San Miguel
    = Florence Elizabeth Hoy in SLO 1938

"Nacimiento Ranch…ranch house built about 1870 by George Flint…about five miles west of San Miguel…two sons and two daughters…Charlotte was the oldest…quite an historian…tales…spiced with wit and humor…Bob Flint married Annie Davis, whose mother was reportedly the first white child born at Sutter's Fort…The Davis family lived for years 'out on the San Antone,' and later in San Miguel…Bob was a great horse fancier…took great pride in his stock…first to have a phonograph…Pete Flint was a bachelor…accomplished chef…worked many years at the mill. Bob's daughter Fannie…very popular…married and moved to Oroville." –*San Miguel At the Turn of the Century*, Stanley, 1976 pp.38-40 *Note:* Anna's mother was the first to be <u>married</u> at Sutter's fort, having come from Arkansas. An early birth was Celesta Ann Twitchell, born in a covered wagon at the gate of Sutter's Fort in 1849. –See Twitchell chart.

Peter Flint 1870-1943 and Charlotte H Flint 1861-1929 are buried in the IOOF cem SLO. The 1910 census shows them on R st, San Miguel, he an engineer in the flouring mill.

Robert Flint's death occasioned two historical obituaries, and correct the assumption in the San Miguel book that his father was George Flint of the Nacimiento ranch; George was his uncle, and is listed in the Pacific Coast Business Directory 1871-73 as R G Flint, sheep & cattle raiser, San Marcos, 36 miles north of San Luis Obispo. Robert G is mentioned several times in Thompson & West's *History of San Luis Obispo Co*, 1883; in the dry season of 1863-4 he was at San Juan Capistrano, in the valley of the San Juan river, a tributary to the Estrella river, in R16E T28S MDB&M, eastern San Luis Obispo co. His wife, Eliza, died @38 at San Juan Capistrano, SLO co, 25 July 1877, reported in the *Tribune*. Nephew Robert came to California at age 21, in the 1880's (census data is not consistent), to work for his uncle on the Nacimiento ranch, and became manager for

13 years. He was associated with Herbert Nelson in San Miguel as a wholesale butcher, and had a ranch in that vicinity, before moving to San Luis Obispo.

His father, Pirney Flint, came to California in 1849, later returning to Canada to marry and father 2 sons and 4 daughters. In 1933 two sisters were still in London, Ontario: Mrs A Baker and Miss E Flint; another sister, Mrs J K Granacher was in California, and Charlotte had died in 1929. His only brother, Peter, was still in San Miguel. Pall bearers were Carl Metzler, Charles Forbes, M L Stevens, L M King, T H Rougeot and W C Carpenter.

Note: The Rougeot family was in Estrella in 1904.

7. Charles N Davis   b. nr Bradley Monterey co 21 Feb 1864;
   bio Storke 570   m. of Gonzales (*Times*)
   1880 cen: w/parents   d. at home San Miguel 21 Oct 1932 @68;
   1892 GR: 23 (28) 5'9 lt blu lt   San Miguel cem; obit DT Sat Oct 22 p.6. wid, 2 dau 1
     small scar on r eyebrow   son 2 sis 1 bro 3 gch
     hotel keeper; CA
   San Miguel, same, same
   Constable San Miguel 16y
   1900 cen: San Miguel saloon keeper
   1902 GR: 38; San Miguel
   1910 cen: Mission st San Miguel retail dealer wines liquor etc
   1912 Dir: Chas saloon San Miguel
   1920-1 VR: 6'; CA; San Miguel
     m. San Luis Obispo 17 Dec 1892, by J.W. Van Cleve, VDM, D235
       wit: A S Chalmers, Santa Maria; R A Stubblefield, Paso Robles
   Ella Chalmers   b. Watsonville CA Oct 1866; m. of Santa Maria (*Times*)
     1900 cen: 2 births 2 living   d.
     1910 cen: 3 births 3 living   F: Alvin Smith Chalmers 1838-1916
     1920-1 VR: Mrs Ella 5'9½; CA   1910 cen: lodging house kpr, San Miguel
         m.2 c 1878 Ella 1850
  a. Zoe Davis   b. (San Miguel) 5 Mar 1894
    living in Vallejo 1932   d. Vallejo Feb 1983; SSDI
    m.
    Roy W Clinkscale   b. 6 Mar 1895
         d. Vallejo Oct 1973; SSDI
  b. Irma (Irmigard) Davis   b. (San Miguel) June 1898
    1916 SLO co Public Sch Dir: d.
     Irmagard Davis, tchr, San Miguel
    m.
    William E Higginbotham
     in Ventura 1932
  c. Irving Charles Davis   b. (San Miguel) 1903
         d.

"Saloons Flourished…1890 to the Dry Year of 1898…the Orpheum, run by Charlie Davis…perhaps the best appointed…gambling and pool tables, mechanical music box, and long bar with mirrors behind it and paintings of nude women above." "Young Charlie Davis, son of the proprietor of the Orpheum Saloon, became a brakeman and rode the passenger trains up and down the line for a number of years, leaving to enter the furniture business in Bakersfield."   –*San Miguel At the Turn…* op cit p.6, 69

Note: Charles N Davis vs Ella Davis Feb 16 1900 SLO co F125; if this was a divorce judgement, it didn't stick, for they were together on the 1900 and 1910 censuses, and she is listed as a survivor.

8.   Elecia Davis   b. CA Dec 1866
        1880 cen: w/parents   d. SLO co 28 May 1925 @58
        1900 cen: w/Joseph
        1910 cen: same
        in SLO 1913
          Single; lived with the brothers
        1920-1 VR: Miss Elecia 5'9; San Miguel

9.   George E Davis   b. CA 1869
        1880 cen: w/parents   d. before 1912
        1892 GR: 21 5'9½ fr blu fr stu; CA; San Miguel, same, same
        1902 SLO GR: not found

DAVIS
SANTA YNEZ VALLEY PIONEERS

William Lane Davis   b. IN 25 Dec 1850
  to CA 1887 by train; SYv 1888   d. at home of dau Mrs Carl Campbell, Los Olivos
  1890 GR: 39 IN f Ballard   8 Jan 1948 @97; Oak Hill cem Ballard
  1900 cen: Ballard pct lab   obit *SY Valley News* Fri Jan 9 p.1; 19gch 26ggch
  1910 cen: Orcutt   2gggch
  1920 cen: Ballard pct, trucking   F: Joab Davis
  1922-3 Dir: W L (Lydia) prop   M: Sarah Mull
    Davis Gar

Note: The Davis Garage was on the southwest corner of Alamo Pintado and Grand Avenues, diagonally across the flagpole intersection from the Los Olivos Garage, which is still standing; the Davis building is long gone, and the lot used as a small park.

  in Huntington Park 1936
  1948: 3 dau 2 sons
  "Will Davis promoted construction of the 'little white church in the lane.' " (1894)
                                                            -*Where The Light Turns Gold*, Rife, 1977 p.83
    Also D D Davis and Sofus Olson, store, Solvang…   -p.125
      m. Washington co IN 4 Dec 1873 (IGI)

Lydia Ann Garrison   b. IN 17 July 1852
  1900 cen: 7 births 6 living   d. 22 Mar 1930 @77; Oak Hill cem
  1930: 4 dau 2 sons   obit *SY Valley News* Mar 28 p.1, 19gch 3ggch
                                                and T Wed Mar 26 p.8; 42y Los Olivos

1.   Dallas Denver Davis   b. Chestnut Hill IN 29 Sep 1876
        to Los Olivos 1888   (Chestnut Hill p.o., Washington co IN, 107 m
        genl merch Los Olivos   s of Indianapolis. –*Fanning's Illus. Gazetteer of*
        1900-1925; SYv grange,   *the US 1850*)
        Hesperian Lodge #264, Al   d. Santa Maria 9 Aug 1966 @89
        Malikah Shrine, LA, SM Club   obit Fri Aug 12 p.2. 6gch 21ggch 1gggch
        1st Christian Ch.
      First theater in SYv. "The Flicks. A nickel got you a seat in Davis Hall the local movie palace…" A drawing shows the interior, with pianist, and screen surrounded by

advertising posters, including W H Down's Variety Store, and Davis Garage & Transfer Co, Auto Supplies, Work That's Right.
  –*Peerless Stoves and Other Poems*, Kroc, 1980, pp.44-6

1902: D D Davis…b. IN, to CA 15 yrs ago. Seven yrs ago began general merchandise business as member of firm of T J & W L Davis. Retired after 5 yrs; purchased E & J Heyman stock and business – oldest and largest store in Los Olivos; store + warehouse is 50x80…has everything in line of genl merchandise…no need of anyone here sending to San Francisco or elsewhere…sole agency of Deering Implement Co's implements and vehicles and Fred Kaufman's Chicago custom made clothing…present sole ownership… correct business methods employed…Knights of Pythias -*Times* May 31

1900 cen: mcht genl

1910 cen: Ballard pct

1914: City Happenings. D D Davis, proprietor of the Los Olivos general merchandise store, was a business caller in SM Thu. –Jan 17

1916: Locals. M/M D D Davis & children of Los Olivos visiting Mrs Davis' parents, M/M D V Dailey. –Nov 18

1917 phbk: D D Davis store Los Olivos

1920 cen: Ballard pct retail merch genl store

1922-3 Dir: D D (Maymie R) genl merch Los Olivos

1930 Dir: D D DAVIS "Your Neighborhood Grocer First" A Share of Your Patronage Solicited. Fountain Service 620 S Bwy Santa Maria

1940-1 Dir: D D Davis (Maymie R) gen mdse 620 S Bwy; res same

1947-8 Dir, 1955-6 Dir: same   1961 Dir: Dallas D (Mamie) h208 W Maple, Lompoc

Note: Member Laura Abeloe remembers patronizing the Davis fountain in her high school days, 1950's.

	m. 1902	
	Maymie R Dailey	b. (Abilene)? KS June 1884
	1910 cen: 4 births 3 living	d. Lompoc
		F: Davis V Dailey 1859-1940 d. at home 618 S Bwy SM
		M: Donna M 1864-1937 d. at home 618 S Bwy SM

a. Arlie Alberta Davis   b. 1903
    1920 cen: w/parents, S   d. Bremerton c1973
    in Oxnard 1937
    living in Bremerton WA 1966; moved there to be with Louise
        m. eloped to AZ 1920
        George Troup   b. (Goleta) CA 27 Sep 1894; SSDI
          1920 cen: bo w/Elsa Craig SY pct   d. Bremerton Feb 1964
          1922-3 Dir: George chauffeur F: James Troup 1867-
            S Ynez dist   1939 Goleta Valley Dir: James Troup f rte 1
          1926. Solvang & Vic: Mrs Geo   El Sueno Rd
            Troup & dau of Oxnard visiting M: Isabelle A Marr 1869-1927
            M/M D D Davis, Los Olivos   -*Times* Tue Feb 9
        = Louise Troup (Wm Kudera) came from Oxnard in 1941 to help out in D D
            Davis' store; Kudera U S Navy
        = Jack Troup deceased
        = George Troup retired from JPL, living Pacific Grove 1998
        = James Troup deceased
b. Oma Avenelle Davis   b. 20 Oct 1904
                                d. 2 Nov 1904; Oak Hill cem

    c.   Meredith W Davis   b. 12 Apr 1906; SSDI
        1920 cen: w/parents, S   d. Apr 1990; Oak Hill cem
        in Los Olivos 1937
        in Nojoqui Park 1966
            m. SLO co 3 July 1925; O 88
        Cash Wolford   b.
                                                           d. 1 Sep 1989; Oak Hill cem
      = Dorothy Wolford m. Steffensen; 3 dau
         1955-6 Dir: Steffensen Clinton W (Dorothy) plbr h1634 Elm Av Solvang
         1934. Women Study Diet. Mrs Wolford's Home Scene of Food Combination
             Demonstration. The Women's Home Club met for an all day session and potluck
             lunch at the home of Mrs Cash Wolford in Los Olivos. Mrs Fred Lang and Mrs
             Cash Wolford, project leaders, assisted Miss Nancy Folsom…showing good
             combinations essential to normal digestion…present…Miss Folsom, Mrs
             Wolford, Mrs Lang, Mrs J W Browning, Mrs Harry Neece, Mrs McCullough,
             Mrs Burd, Mrs Leon Cooper, Hester Stonebarger, Mrs Edgar Davison, Mrs John
             McGinnis, Mrs Fredericksen, Mrs B Davis, Mrs W Phelps and Mrs Otho
             Williams.   -*Santa Ynez Valley News* Fri Feb 16
         Social and Personal: M/M Lee Palmer spent Sunday at home of M/M Cash
             Wolford.   –ibid Feb 23
         1940 phbk: Cash Wolford rLos Olivos
         1947-8 Dir: Cash (Meredith) agt Seaside Oil Co Box 41 Buellton
         1957 phbk: Cash Wolford 1540 Elm Av Solvang
    d.   Beulah V Davis   b. 12 Feb 1908; SSDI
        "Plink"   d. Lompoc Apr 1983
        1920 cen: w/parents, S
        in Lompoc 1937, 1966
            m.
        Lee S Palmer   b. 30 May 1907; SSDI
                                                         d. Lompoc May 1978
        1940-1 Dir: Lee S (Beulah) clk D Davis h809 S Lincoln
        1947-8 Dir: Lee S (Beulah V) emp D D Davis h219 W Park
        1957 phbk: 204 W Maple, Lompoc; in Lompoc 1966
      = Pat L Palmer r 204 W Maple 1998
2.   Bernard Davis   b. IN Aug 1869; m. @28 of Orcutt
    1900 cen: tp 4 clerk gen merch   d. 22 July 1954; Oak Hill cem
    1906 Dir: Bernard eng PO&T; Mrs B Los Alamos, PO Careaga
    1910 cen: tp 6 Los Alamos-Orcutt Rd gauger oil well
    1917 phbk: B Davis garage Los Olivos; ad: Davis Garage & Transfer Co.
     B Davis, Prop. Oils, Gasoline and Greases, Vulcanizing, Repair Work of All Kinds,
     Tires, Tubes, and Rubber Supplies. Ford Parts. Auto Service and Truck Work. Telephone
     10-L Los Olivos, Cal.
    1920 cen: Ballard pct mech garage
    1922-3 Dir: Bernard (Martha) Davis Garage Los Olivos auto repairs
    1939 phbk: B Davis gar Los Olivos   1940 phbk: same
    1947-8 Dir: Bernard B mech PO B 24 Los Olivos
        m. San Luis Obispo 23 Nov 1907 by H E Smith, H91
            wit: Henry Cox, Los Olivos; Keturah Davis, Los Olivos
    Martha L Cox   b. on the Alamo (creek/ranch) SLO co
    to Los Olivos 1914   30 June 1889 (*Times*)

    2½ yrs Long Beach,   d. Santa Barbara 19 Nov 1946; Oak Hill cem
    defense work WWII   obit *SY Valley News* Fri Nov 22 p.1; 14gch
    7 ch surviving   F: James Marion Cox 1859-1932
    1910 cen: 1 birth 0 living   M: Elizabeth Frances Garrett 1862-1930
                                          see Garrett chart

    a. son   d. (13 July 1909 @1 day)
    b. William Lane Davis   b. 1911; (in Seal Beach 1946)
        m. 1933   d. 1968
        Helen D Cadwell   b. Vancouver CAN 18 Dec 1913; to U S 1932
        = Wm D Davis d. 1981   d. Orange co CA 14 Jan 1999; Oak Hill cem
        = Bernard L Davis (living 1999)   obit Sat 16 Jan; 9gch 6ggch
                                       F: Paul Cadwell   M: Jane
    c. Nina M Davis (Tom Cadwell)   b. 1913; (in Lomita 1946)
    d. N Boyd Davis   b. 1914
        in Lompoc 1946   d. living 1998
        1947-8 Dir: N Boyd (Katherine) frmr Central, Box 57 Lompoc RR
        m.
        Kathryn Beattie   b.
          1998 phbk: N Boyd & Edna K   d. living 1998
            2919 Blaisdl Av Redondo Beach F: Walter Ray Beattie 1886-1968
                                        M: Edna C Lind 1894-1987
    e. Elva M Davis   b. 1916
        in Lompoc 1946   d. living in Santa Ynez 1998
        m.
        James Edward Beattie   b. (Lompoc 1915)
          1947-8 Dir: J Edw (Elva)   d.
          frmr Artesia Av Box 62   F: Walter Ray Beattie 1886-1968
          Lompoc RR   M: Edna C Lind 1894-1987 See *Huyck Cousins*,
          1957 phbk: 322 North H   Manfrina, p. 149,152
        = James Beattie jr (Jeannie) ranch west hills, Miguelito Cnyn, Lompoc (Manfrina)
    f. Bernard G Davis   b. 1918
        in Morgan Hill 1946   d.
        1947-8 Dir: Bernie G (Pauline) blksm & mach wks welding POB 24 Los Olivos
    g. Dallas D Davis   b. 20 Feb 1920
        in Santa Ynez 1946   d. Westminster Apr 1976; SSDI
    h. Delbert James Davis   b. 20 Feb 1920
        in Santa Ynez 1946   d. (Downey) July 1979; SSDI
        1947-8 Dir: D J (Christine) Davis Gar POB 24; Christina (sic) hmkr same
          Davis Gar: D J Davis, R A Campbell Grand Av Los Olivos POB 24
          Campbell R A (Lavinia) Davis Garage Box 125
          m.
        Christine   b. 1 Dec 1922; SSDI
                                       d. Downey 12 June 1988

3. Keturah Davis   b. IN 16 Dec 1881; SSDI
    1910 cen: w/parents, S   d. SB co 1 June 1978
    1966 in Los Olivos
      m.
    Carl C Campbell   b. (Lompoc) 29 Sep 1889; SSDI
      in Huntington Park 1930, 1936   d. SB co 9 Nov 1963
      1936 LA phbk: C C Campbell   F: Elijah Reuben Campbell 1866-1929

   r6137 S Santa Fe Huntington M: Lily Dell Hoyt 1873-1930
  Park
 1947-8 Dir: rancher Box 156 Los Olivos; 1955-6 Dir: same
 No issue

4. Etalka Davis   b. IN 25 July 1885
  1900 cen: w/parents   d. 25 June 1971; Oak Hill cem "Mother"
  1920 cen: Ballard pct clerk PO
  1922-3 Dir: postmaster Los Olivos
   m. Santa Barbara 25 Sep 1907
 William Henry Downs   b. (Sacramento) 1 Aug 1871
  1900 cen: tp 4 Ballard pct   d. 25 Apr 1961; Oak Hill cem "Father"
   alone; also tp 5 w/Donald F: Wm Taylor Downs 1847-1943; to CA 1862
   Burton   M: Maggie Miller 1853-1905
  1910 cen: Ballard pct storekeeper
 1902. Los Alamos Notes. W H Downs has started a store and barber shop at Los Olivos – May 24. W H Downs…succeeded Mr W H Thrailkill about 2 months ago since which time by adding new lines of goods, and extensive and favorable acquaintance, he has rapidly increased the business. The building…is 30x55…stock of candies, fruits, lunch, and canned goods, nuts, soft drinks, ground barley, bicycles and bicycle sundries and ice cream on Sundays. Any bicycle, motor cycle or automobile…desired…obtained for the purchaser. No specialties…except to sell the best at the lowest prices and as several lines of goods are handled and a profit made on each, a bicycle will be sold at a reasonable profit and the purchaser need not pay a month's board for the dealer because he sells one wheel a month. Here the other lines pay expenses and a small profit on wheel is all that is wanted. Bicycles are repaired promptly. In the store is a barbershop under the same ownership. Outside…Mr Downs has teams…for heavy hauling…extensive acquaintance…has been in this country for 19 years.   -*Times* May 31

Note: Bicycles were very expensive in those days.

  1907. Orcutt. Downs & Drumm is the name of another new firm that believes in the future of our busy little city. The young men are opening a general merchandise store and already have their building completed.   -*Times* June 22
Santa Ynez. W H Downs of Los Olivos gave us a call Wed. In partnership with a Mr Drum (sic) he will conduct a general merchandise store at Orcutt in the near future. Santa Ynez ARGUS. (See Drumm chart)   -*Times* June 29
 1917 phbk: W H Downs Gents Furnishing, Sporting Goods, Harness, Saddlery and
  Supplies. Telephone 10-X Los Olivos, Cal. res. Los Olivos
 1920 cen: Ballard pct store genl merc
 1922-3 Dir: W H Downs Variety store Los Olivos; Los Olivos Variety Store,
  W H Downs, Prop.
 1940 phbk: Los Olivos
 1947-8 Dir: grocer Box 156 Los Olivos   1957 phbk: Los Olivos
For Downs, see *Where The Light Turns Gold*, op cit pp.100-102

  a. Rubirna R Downs   b. 1909; artist w/Walt Disney
  b. Wilma Downs   b. 1911
  c. Nielson Downs   b. 1913
    1957 phbk: Star Lane Ranch Santa Ynez
  d. Althea Downs   b. 1915

5. Indiana Davis b. 17 Sep 1887
 d. 4 Oct 1891; Oak Hill cem
6. Nora Davis b. CA 28 Feb 1891; SSDI
   1910 cen: w/parents, S d. (Eureka) 29 May 1973
   in Eureka 1930, 1936, 1948, 1966
   m.
   George C. Bartlett b.
     1922-3 Dir: Geo C (Nora) d. (11-5-61 Santa Clara co; SSDI
     contr trking Los Olivos spouse initial N)?
   a. Dorothy Bartlett
   b. George Bartlett jr
   c. twins Janice Bartlett
   d. Joyce Bartlett d. @18 leukemia
7. Della Davis b. CA Sep 1894
   1910 cen: w/parents, S d. Los Angeles co 22 Apr 1944
   1920 cen: w/parents, bkpr gar, S
   living in Compton 1930, 1936
   m.
   Charles J Emerson b.
     1936 Los Angeles phbk: Chas J Emerson r317 Culver, Compton
   = Marylyn Emerson (Colombo)
     1947-8 Dir: Marylyn Emerson Box 156 Los Olivos (lived w/Campbells after mother's
     death)

Thomas J Davis b. IN 1848
  1920 cen: retail mcht, S d. Santa Maria 6 Apr 1936; Oak Hill cem
   Ballard pct next to Bernard Davis obit T Tue Apr 7 p.4; also *SY Valley News* Apr 10 p.1
  1922-3 Dir: groc Los Olivos
  1936. Aged Los Olivos Merchant Passes…@88   Fifty years grocery store; died local hospital,
   uncle of D D Davis, Santa Maria merchant.   –*Times*
  Last Rites held on Thursday P M for 'Uncle Tom' Davis…pall bearers; Dallas Davis, Bernard
   Davis, William Downs, Charles Emerson, Carl Campbell, Edward Beattie, nephews,
   nephews-in-law, and grand nephews. Wife died many years ago. Brother William in
   Huntington Park.   –*SY Valley News*
  Mrs Thomas Davis d. SB 26 Oct 1900 @39/11/22. –T 3 Nov
  1900. Mrs Thomas Davis, eldest daughter of M/M Thos Saulsbury, postmistress at Guadalupe
   several years…funeral from Saulsburys'. Guad Cem.   –Nov 3
  In Memory of Mrs Ella A Davis…born Alameda co 4 Dec 1860; to Guadalupe @13. Married 2
   Feb 1879 Richard J Guthrie, 1 child. Widowed after 4 years. Married 16 May 1896 Thomas
   Davis. Daughter Dora Guthrie.   –Nov 10
Note: Unfortunately the 1896 volume of the *Santa Maria Times* is missing, so we can't check the marriage there.
  Card of Thanks. Thos Davis, Dora Guthrie, M/M Thos Saulsbury.   –Nov 10

GUTHRIE

Robert Julian Guthrie b. TX c1852; F: SCT; M: IRE; m. @27 of Guad
  1880 cen: Guadalupe d. 1882; Guadalupe cem
   m. Guadalupe 2 Feb 1879 by John Dunbar JP, B373
Ella A Saulsbury b. Alameda co 4 Dec 1860; m. @   of Guad
   d. Santa Barbara 26 Oct 1900

                            F: Thomas Saulsbury 1830-1911
                            M: Isabella Randall 1843-1920
1.   Dora P Guthrie   b. (Guadalupe) Nov 1879

Note: It is not certain which Thomas Davis Mrs Guthrie married. Could be this one.
   1900 cen: tp 4 Thomas Davis 1860 m. 5y b. MN; F: OH, M: WI; supt rr const
      (listed w/rr workers; wife not there)

DAVIS
SANTA MARIA BUSINESSMEN

Joseph Morse Davis   b. New Iberia LA 16 Dec 1883
  bio *Who's Who SM* 1930   d. Santa Maria 24 Mar 1967
    to SM 1913   F: Jacob Davis
    r611 S Bwy   M: Elise
  1922-3 Dir: J M – Auditor and Accountant, Notary Public, Rm4 Hart Bldg, r SM Club
  1925 Dir: Joseph M Acct fire & life ins agt r611 S Bwy; Mrs Phoebe J, same
  1928 Dir: Joseph M Auditor & Acct 122 N Bwy; 1930 Dir: acct 122 N Bwy r611 S Bwy
  1940-1 Dir: J M (Phoebe J) Genl Ins Auditing Acctg Income Tax Svc Notary
        Mgr SMVRR 122 N Bwy h611 S Bwy and so through the years
     m. Los Angeles 14 July 1926 – see 1925 Dir 1926 must be a misprint in *Who's Who*
Phoebe Jane Boyd Erkens   b. Los Gatos CA 4 Oct 1879
                                    d. Santa Maria 9 Dec 1964 @85/1/13; SM cem
                                       obit Thu Dec 10 p.2
                                    F: John Boyd 1854-1933 bio M/H 393
                                    M: Jane Griffith 1860-1935
No issue   son b. San Jose 14 Dec 1907 to M/M H Erkins (*Times*)
                                    Henry Erkins d. San Jose 4-26-1908 @32
    1901: Phoebe Erkens, Mizpah   –Apr
    1909 Dir: Erkens Mrs Phoebe School teacher 516 S Bwy
           Boyd John stock broker 516 S Bwy; Mrs J
    1916: Mrs Phoebe Erkens County Board of Ed.   –June 17
    1920: Mrs Pheobe Erkins on vacation to San Francisco.   –July
    1921. Local Briefs. M/M Geo Radke entertained Sunday. Guests: M/M E W Boyd, Mrs Erkens,
       Mrs Sadie Kelly, Miss Mildred Kelly, Miss May Kellogg and J M Davis. –Mon Jan 17
Note: Edw W Boyd (1882-1946) was Pheobe's brother; May Kellogg (1897-1984) was a niece of
       Leonora Sherrill (1885-1990), Ed's wife. Miss Kellogg taught at the high school for years.
    1922-3 Dir: Erkins Phoebe J principal Main st sch r528 S Bwy
           Boyd John (Jane) rancher r528 S Bwy
    1925. M/M Joe Davis spent a few days in the south.   –Nov 21

Note: Erkins/Erkens is closer than Erskine (ONT) and Atkins (M/H)

BOYD

Boyd brothers John (above) and Thomas (1850-1922) came from Ireland to California in the 1870's; they married Griffith sisters and, after coming to the Santa Maria valley, became land owners and influential in business circles. Biographies of both are found in Morrison & Haydon.
In 1895, the South Side Items reported that Thomas Boyd had two brothers, direct from Ireland arrive last week to live with him.   – May 18
One, Dave Boyd, married Carrie Winters, and is detailed in Earl chart.

Corrections and Additions [Page numbers refer to those in Quarterly]

Member Gail Benson of Lompoc has contributed corrections to the chart of William Lane Davis.
p.10.   Faye Marion Davis m.1 Earl Howerton, son of Harry Howerton (1888-1952) and Myrtle Upton (1892-1953). Their children were Sandra Howerton, whose first husband was Earl Green, and second ____ Sherer; Edward Earl Howerton was the second child. Faye's second husband was Nelson (Wimpy) Williams.

p.30.   Elva M Davis died at home in Santa Ynez 23 Jan 1999, aged 85. Survivors were son Daniel Beattie, Santa Ynez; daughter Maryanne Wilkins, Santa Ynez; 4 granddaughters, 4 grandsons; brothers Boyd Davis, Redondo Beach, and Bernard Davis, Ventura; sister Nina Cadwell, Torrance. She was preceded in death by husband, and sons Ray and Benjamin.
–*SM Times* Jan 25? Her husband was Ray Edward Beattie, not James Edward Beattie, and James, jr, is not her son. Gail credits her with 3 children: Ray Ed Beattie, Daniel Beattie, and Mary Ann Beattie.

Sylvester C Davis
p.19.   Mary C Davis, 80, widow, b. NY, 1060 Islay st, SLO, 1920 cen.
p.21.   Maggie F Davis, 35 divorced, ME, rooming house keeper, 1232 Morro, SLO, 1920 cen.
        Laura May/Mary L Davis, 27, CA, widow, living w/mother-in-law, Mary C Davis, SLO; son Freddie @4 7/12, 1920 cen.

George Davis
p.24.   1866 SLO GR: John Azbell 35 MO f Santa Rosa Ck; removed
                       Newton Azbill 23 MO f San Simeon cancelled removed
                       Wm Thomas Azbill 36 MO f Hot Springs removed
                       Jasper Azbill 27 MO f San Simeon removed

p.24.   1925. Tells of First Wedding at Fort Sutter, from *Sacramento Bee* Aug 12…July 17, 1843, Alecia Sumner @13, George Davis. Alecia born Feb 25, 1830 in MS…Mrs Mattie Hames, grandniece of pioneer has cape and bonnet worn for the wedding…Mrs Davis died in 1913…
                                                                    -*SLO Tribune* Fri Sep 18 p.3
Note: The cape and bonnet are on display at the Rios-Caledonia Adobe, San Miguel.

p.25.   Claude T Azbill. 1941. Succeeded as Police Chief Paso Robles by H P Knowles. –*PR Press* Mar 27. Azbell's car stolen first day he's off police job. –*PR Journal* Mar 20. Full-time employer of Grey Line Taxi Service. –*PR Press* Mar 27. Appointed superintendent of Paso Robles streets at $75 per month.   –*Paso Robles Journal* Apr 23
        1921. Santa Margarita. M/M J Azbill, son Eddie, nephew Lloyd Barnes visiting here. Azbills lived here until 9 yrs ago. M/M J Azbill motored to M/M Clark Hendricks and Araujos – all old friends.   –*SLO Daily Telegraph* Sep 6

p.26.   From *The Lands of Mission San Miguel*, Ohles, 1997, comes data on the Flint family. R G Flint's mother is thought to be Ann Elson. Ethel Flint married Everett John Hoy of Indian Valley; his 1920-1 voter registration says born CA 6'2, as printed in the SLOCGS *Bulletin*. Their daughter, Florence Hoy, married Donald E Butler.

p.27.   1921. San Miguel. M/M Roy Clinkscale and baby returned to Vallejo after visiting Charlie Davis. Miss Irma Davis returned to Fellows where she teaches.   –*SLO Daily Telegraph* Sep 6
        Zoe Davis was a teacher in Santa Margarita in 1916, married Clinkscale after the 1920 census, which found her with her parents.

Vol. XXXI, No. 3, Fall 1999, pp.5, 6

DAVISSON
SANTA MARIA VALLEY PIONEERS

Charles Obediah Davisson   b. MO Feb 1850 (cen)
   1880 cen: Yolo co Cottonwood tp   d. Woodland, Yolo co 28 Dec 1912 @63/10/13; SM cem
   1900 cen: Santa Maria drayman   obit Jan 4 1913; Card of Thanks
     4 births 4 living

   1900. Davisson & Bunce's big team were frightened by a big gate slamming to early Friday morning while the wagon was being unloaded at the rear of Fleisher's store, and they started out on a little run. Charlie Bunce stopped them before any damage occurred, further than tearing out a section of plank fence back of Fleisher's.   –April 14

   1901. ad. Davisson & Bunce Pioneer Truck and Transfer Line Furniture & Piano Moving Dealers in ICE   –Mar 30

     Davisson & Bunce will put on a truck and transfer line for freight between Guadalupe and Santa Maria in the near future. Watch for card of hauling days.   –Apr 6

     Note: Charles Alfred Bunce 1870-1941; see Bunce chart.

   1909 Dir: Davisson Mrs A rSo Lincoln st; James r same; Earl F stu r same
       Nicholson Harry, rancher; Mrs H

   1912. W E (sic) Davisson, formerly in the transfer business in this city, is seriously ill at a sanitarium in Woodland, owing to stroke of paralysis and not expected to live. His daughter, Mrs Harry Nicholson and husband are attending him leaving here Wednesday night.   –Dec 28

   1913. Death Claims C A (sic) Davisson, former Santa Maria Business Man…died Woodland Dec 18 @63; daughter Mrs Harry Nicholson; sons Earl and Louis in Los Angeles; son, James, deceased.   –Jan 4

      m. c1878

Almeda Marmora McHenry   b. Annally tp Sonoma co Dec 1860
                                      d. Oakland 24 Mar 1936 @75/2/23; SM cem
                                           obit Tue Apr 7 p.4; to Oakland 1920; 2 ch 2 gch
                                      F: James McHenry c1829-
                                      M: Sarah O   c1831-c1875
                                            See ONT for related McHenrys

   1898. Mrs Davisson went to the Tepesquet Thursday to visit with her sister Mrs P O Tietzen.   -June 18

     Note: Margaret McHenry m. 1883 Paul O Tietzen; see M/H; to Berkeley 1909

   1900. Mrs C O Davisson, Mrs P O Tietzen and James Davisson returned from Hueneme.   –Sep

   1919. Miss Letha Davisson of San Luis Obispo is visiting her aunt Mrs Alia Davisson, E Church.   –Dec 4

     Mrs Alia Davisson to go to Los Angeles after Christmas with son Lewis and wife. Dr Earl Davisson of Oakland, to arrive Dec 24 to spend Christmas holidays with his mother Mrs Alia Davisson and sister Mrs Harry Nicholson.   –Dec 20

1.   James Melville   b. Solano co 10 April 1879 (obit) 1878 (cen)
                                d. Santa Maria 9 July 1909 @30/2/29; SM cem
                                    obit July 17 p.1; SMVHS 1900; worked for San Francisco EXAMINER; to SM 1897; SMUHS

2.   Margie M   b. (Yolo co) 31 Aug 1881
                                d. Long Beach 16 Sep 1970 @89/1/15; SM cem
                                obit Thu Sep 17; 20y LB; 2gch 5ggch

     m. at home of bride's mother Mrs H Davidson (sic) 23 Jan 1904 by Rev Wm Clague -*Times*

   Harry Roland Nicholson   b. IA 1877
                                      d. Long Beach 1969

			F: Ellis Harry Nicholson 1856-1937
			M: Agnes Elizabeth Hall 1858-1912; see Nicholson chart

    a.   James R   1905-1972 m. 1924
        Ariel Roberta Glines   1905-1975
          No issue   F: Robert Cassius Glines 1877-1933
                                            M: Cora Victoria McCroskey 1878-1974
    b.   Dorothy   1908-1990 m. 1927
        Lemuel Elza Glines   1902-1962 brother of Ariel
        2 ch

3.   Louis P   b. CA June 1887
    1909 in El Centro   d. Los Angeles co 29 Oct 1928 @42; spouse P
    1912 in Los Angeles
    1914. Mrs Louise (sic) Davisson from Los Angeles is visiting her sister-in-law Mrs Harry
        Nicholson.   –Jan 17

4.   Earl Francis   b. CA 1 Jan 1890
    1912 in Los Angeles   d. Alameda co 5 Jan 1949 @58/11/26; SM cem
    1916 attending Dental College, San Francisco
    1919. Earl Davisson recent graduate of College of Physicians & Surgeons, San Francisco.
                                                                               -May 12

    1936 in Oakland (?)
        m.
    Esther Raughilda --   b. CA 12 Apr 1898
                                          d. Los Angeles co 2 June 1963 @65/2/2/; SM cem

THE DeNISE BROTHERS
PIONEERS OF THE CALIFORNIA CENTRAL COAST

William Henry DeNise   b. Montgomery co NY 28 May 1829; parents NY
   1875 Paulson Dir: W H Sr,   d. at home 1426 st between Pismo & Buchon, San Luis
     business SLO co; PO Cambria   Obispo 13 Mar 1906 @ 76/9/15; IOOF cem obits *SLO*
   1880 cen: San Simeon tp   *Tribune* Mar 14 (copied from bio T/W); *SLO Breeze*
   1890 GR: 57 NY f Cambria;   Mar 15; wid, son 2 dau; to CA 1854; Yolo,
     reg Sep 26 1887   Sacramento 4y; Gold Hill NV 6y teaming; Santa
   1892 GR: 63 NY 5'8 7/8 fair   Clara co 2y; San Jose 2y; to SLO co 1871, 456a
     complexion, grey eyes, grey hair   Santa Rosa Ck; retired to SLO
     both forefingers hand stiff f NY res SLO pct SLO #3 PO SLO; reg Aug 30
   1900 cen: San Simeon tp
   1904 GR: 74 SLO #4
       m. (San Jose) 30 Jan 1867
Carrie N Brown   b. NY June 1852; F:NY; M:NJ
    d. Watsonville 1 Feb 1932 @79; IOOF cem SLO
      obit *SLO Daily Telegraph* Wed Feb 3; son 2 dau 3gch;
      to Watsonville 7y ago to live w/gdau Mrs S H Elliott

1.   William Conover   b. (San Jose) 20 Jan 1868
    1890 GR: 22 CA clk SLO #2   d. Contra Costa co 29 Jan 1954
     reg Mar 25 1890
    1892 GR: 25 CA 5'8½" light complexion blue eyes brown hair cloud in left eye clk
     res SLO pct SLO #4   PO SLO; reg Oct 11
    1900 cen: w/parents
    1906. RE&Ins w/ W W Smithers
    1932 in Campbell CA
       m. nr Creston 15 July 1891, D34; wit: H M Knight, SLO; Rbt Steele, Creston
    Mattie Steele   b. KS 1862
    d. San Francisco 28 May 1898 @36; bur SLO
      notice *Breeze* Tue May 31; svc at res of G W McCabe
    F: James Barnes Steele 1837-1906
    M:
    a.   Neva   b. (SLO co) 28 May 1894
      1900 cen: w/gpar   d. Santa Cruz co 2 July 1976 surname Elliott
      1932 Mrs S H Elliott in Watsonville
2.   Carrie L   b. (SLO co) 1872
    1906 in San Jose   d.
    1932 in Oakland
       m. San Luis Obispo 15 Dec 1898, E357
    William John Dunstan   b. MI 15 Feb 1868
    1917 phbk: r359 Glendale av   d. Alameda co 4 Aug 1942 @74; M:Pearce
     Oakland
    a.   Charles   b.
      1932 in Oakland   d.
    b.   William   b.
      1932 in Oakland   d.
3.   Irene F   b. (Cambria) June 1874
    1900 cen: w/parents   d. Sonoma co 26 Mar 1963 @88 surname Harvard
    1906 in SLO
    1932 in Ontario surname Harvard

m. 1 Oct 1902   –*Santa Cruz Sentinel*
Warren William Smithers   b. (Cambria) Nov 1879
   1914 Dir: Wm W (Irene) ins   d. San Luis Obispo 31 Oct 1918 @38; IOOF cem
     & notary 848 Higuera,   F: Amos J Smithers 1852-1933
     h1132 Chorro   M: Ida Marcia Terrill 1856-1914
     W W Smithers General   For Leffingwell-Terrill-Smithers see Cambria Hist Soc
   Insurance Broker 848 Higuera SLO

Charles Sloan DeNise   b. NY 7 Oct 1843; parents NY; m. @30 of SLO
   1875 Paulson Dir: DeNice (sic)   d. Santa Maria 23 Nov 1912 @69; SM cem
     CE (sic) f SLO co; PO Cambria   obit Nov 30; 40y SM: wid dau; to Cambria to
   1880 cen: Santa Rosa st SLO   brother's ranch; drove stage for Flint Bixby who had
     stage driver   the through-route Gilroy-Los Angeles. Clk
   1887. Los Alamos. DeNise's   Cosmopolitan hotel SM for E B Morris, became
     lease on Union Hotel expired;   proprietor when Morris died; thence Snyder House
     back to J. Snyder. –May 14   Los Alamos; thence Santa Cruz, Watsonville,
         Hoffman House; leased Hart House SM; then SLO
         Cosmopolitan (not St James); retired to SM
   1888. Sloan DeNise is in San Francisco to get furniture for the Cosmopolitan Hotel, San Luis
      Obispo, which he recently rented.   –Sep
   1889. Sloan DeNise, proprietor of the Cosmopolitan Hotel, SLO, passed through yesterday
      morning on his return from Los Olivos and Los Alamos, having gone down the day of the
      excursion.   –May 4
      ad. Alamo Hotel Sloan Denise, Prop'r. Los Alamos, Santa Barbara Co, Cal.
        Excellent Accomodations For travelers and families. Table supplied with
        the best the market affords. No pains have been spared in making this a first-class
        house. Large Sample Rooms on ground floor. Coach at all trains.   –Oct 5
      Sloan DeNise of Los Alamos was in town Sunday. Mr DeNise says Los Alamos will
      surely be the county seat of Olive county. Railroad Putnam is on Mr DeNise's blacklist
      for having asserted that the gentleman's name was formerly Dennis and changed to DeNise
      by the dictates of frivolous fashion.   –*SLO Mirror* in *Los Alamos Progress* –Oct 19
      J W Tucker to take charge of the Cosmopolitan Hotel; he late of French Hotel.   –Oct 26
   1890. Alamos Hotel, Sloan DeNise, Prop
   1894. Hart House Changes Management… Hart to DeNise & Kunle.   –Jan 6
   1898. Sloan DeNise and wife are in Arroyo Grande straightening and cleaning up the old Ryan
      Hotel. When they open, Arroyo people will have cause to rejoice.   –Jan 29
      Mr Sloan DeNise of Arroyo Grande is in SLO today.   –*SLO Breeze* (June 1?)
      Note: for history of Ryan's hotel see Madge 235ff
   1902. Sloan DeNise is getting the Rice House in shape—open soon.   –May
   1903. Sloan DeNise to take charge of the Commercial Hotel Oct 1…has conducted hotels at
      different times in many towns in this part of the state…has lived in Santa Maria where for
      a time he conducted the Hart House.   –Sep 27
   1904 GR: Sloan DeNise 58 SLO #3
   1909 Dir: rancher W Main Santa Maria; Mrs C
   1910 cen: 210 W Main, Santa Maria, his second marriage, her first; 1 birth 1 living
   1912: pall bearers: John Boyd, R L Jones, Chas Black, A McNeil, Geo Trott, Thomas Preisker
        m. Cambria 10 Feb 1874 by O S Palmer, A180
           wit: Elias Conway, Cambria; Fannie Fine, Cambria

Caroline Fine b. Sonoma co 18 Jan 1850; m. @24 SLO
d. Berkeley 14 Feb 1938 @83; SM cem
obit Tue Feb 15 p.1; gdau, 3 gsons all Berkeley
dau d. 1934
F: Irby Hoyt Fine 1821-1879
M: Mary Elizabeth 1829-1920
m.2 1887 Morgan B Martin 1826-1898

1904. Mrs C S DeNise SLO wit to m. of John S Logan, Los Alamos, Leona C Holt, SM
1910. Twins 60th birthday: Mrs C S DeNise, SM, Mrs Fred Engles, SLO; born Sonoma co
first whites after the raising of the Bear Flag. –*SLO Telegram* in *SM Times* Jan 22
1914 Dir: Caroline wid Sloane h503 W Main SM
1925 Dir: hskpr r503 W Main

1. Edna DeNise b. (Cambria) 1874; m. @20 of SM
d. at home Oakland 30 Jan 1934 @59/7/22; SM cem
obit Wed Jan 31 p.4; 3 sons dau; mother w/them
m. Hart House 7am 25 Dec 1894 by C H Lawrence ME; wit: Alvin W Cox, father
They left on train for Oakland to attend m. of J G Black. -*Times*

Arthur Elmer Cox b. Santa Maria valley (or MO?) Aug 1873; m. @21
  1894. clk Hart House d. at home Oakland 6 May 1924 50/8/21; SM cem
  bio M/H 860: rancher, obit Wed May 7 p.1; 3 sons dau; bro Chester B Cox,
  PCRR, Asst PM SM
  1900 cen: SM f 1 birth F: Alvin Warren/Warner Cox 1843-1951
  1906 Dir: rancher 1m nw M: Mary A Powers 1852-1922
  1909 Dir: rancher nw cor city limits; Mrs
  1910 cen: W Stillwell st SM
  1914 Dir: Arthur f n end Elizabeth av SM
  1920 cen: N Bwy
  1922-3 Dir: Arthur E f rAlvin st
  1924. Mrs Arthur Cox of Oakland sons Sherwood and Roswell, visiting her mother Mrs
     Sloane (sic) DeNise. –Mon July 21
  1934. pall bearers: Walter E Smith, Rell Laughlin, Chas F Black, Jas W Herron, Dudley D
     Brady, Paul Fox

  a. Orville E b. nr SM 27 Jan 1900 (*Times*)
     1949 in San Leandro d. Alameda co 28 July 1977 @77
  b. Iola Frances b. SM 7 Aug 1902 (*Times*)
      d. SM 27 Nov 1902 @3m20d; SM cem (*Times*)
  c. Zetta b. SM 25 June 1904
     1924 single d.
     1938 Berkeley CA surname Dunsten (sic)
     1949 Jacksonville OR surname Dunsten (sic)
     (William Dunstan b. 29 Dec 1899; d. Medford OR Feb 1974; SSDI)
  d. Roswell W b. SM Dec 1908
      d. buried Jan 19 1949 @40/1/3 SM cem
      obit Jan 7 p.7; "returned war dead"; sis bro
  e. Sherwood Francis b. SM 5 Aug 1912
      d. Shasta co 9 Oct 1942 @30/2/4; bur Dec 19
      SM cem

DOANE
PIONEER BUSINESSMEN OF SANTA MARIA

The Doane Building Company was established in Santa Maria in 1880, and is in business yet in 1994. A photo of Doane's clapboard building, taken about 100 years ago, is on page 254 of *This Is Our Valley*. Unlike other early settlers, George Doane came directly from the east to the Santa Maria Valley, influenced, one may guess, by someone like Melford P Nicholson, possibly an uncle, who had come to Guadalupe in 1870, and was a prime mover in the valley until his untimely death in 1888 occasioned by a kick in the groin by his favorite horse.

Doane was the principal builder in Santa Maria for several decades; only by the time of the Great War does O C Marriott's name appear in the paper as a competitor. The biographies list some of the many private and public buildings for which Doane was responsible. The *Santa Maria Times*, in a special issue, Dec 17, 1904, printed a photo of J B Bonetti's large Victorian house as an example of Doane's work; a few months later it was noted that Doane had completed a two-story, eleven room house complete with pantry, bathroom and nine closets for H D Freeman; "it is hard finished throughout and is one of the best finished and most commodious buildings put up anywhere in the valley". – Mar 4, 1905. In 1914 Doane built a new garage for W H Crakes' machine shop and automotive business, a 50x100 frame structure with galvanized roof and sides, which rather primitive structure is still in use – unrecognizable under present modification. Contrast that with the 100' brick building, to be built in 90 days, contracted by Stephen Campodonico, Guadalupe merchant, in 1924; it, too, is still in use.

The most famous of Doane's buildings is the Santa Maria Inn. The original inn opened in 1917; Oscar Doane, who, with brother Clarence, was taken into partnership with their father in 1912, was the architect. Twenty-two rooms were added in 1922. It has undergone more than its share of modifications since.

In 1919 Doane turned the business over to his sons so as to devote his attention to the Santa Maria Planing Mill, in which he had been interested since its beginning in 1907. Its history is found in the 1909 Santa Maria Directory, with photo; the officers were G M Doane, pres.; A H Heller, v-pres.; T B Adam, sec; L P Scaroni, treas; and John Thomas, mg. Doane was active in this business until his death.

George Doane, Jr, was the one son to eschew the building trades; he went into grain and bean brokerage, investing, along with members of a San Francisco brokerage house, in a large ranch in Solano County in 1912; his death at age 50 in San Bernardino was not explained in the local newspaper.

Clarence moved to Santa Cruz about 1918 and opened his own contracting business, into which he took his son when he came of age, but the untimely death of the son in an accident cut short the life of both namesake and business. Mrs Doane died instantly upon hearing of her son's demise; Clarence lived only nine months thereafter.

A few scraps from the Santa Maria Times: In 1890 the Personals from June 11 noted that G.M Doane was badly injured on his right leg Wednesday and was compelled to use crutches…Contractor Doane has begun laying the foundation for the new building adjoining the Bank of Santa Maria. In 1914 "Accidental Shot Fired by Geo Doane Wounds Dover Rice…Doane had been carrying the pistol on account of tramps infesting his home place."   – Sep 5 1916

Build Now Never before such a chance to build in Santa Maria as right now. I will furnish the lot and build you a house on the installment plan. See me at the Hotel Bradley. Melford Doane
– Feb 5

George Mason Doane   b. nr Rockford IL 27 Sep 1849
   To SM 1880   d. Santa Maria 14 Jul 1923 @73/9/17; SM cem
   1888 Polk Gazetteer: architect SM   obit Sat July 15 p.1
   1896 GR: carp 47 5'9½   F: Matthew M Doane 1812-1896
      lt gry br IL SM   M: Tryphena Jane Albright
   1906 Dir: Contr & Bldr, offc Main st., r Broadway
   1920: 213 S Pine w/Mary G Mattocks
   1922 Dir: Prop SM Planing Mill, r 213 S Pine
      bios: *Santa Maria Times* Dec 17 1904; Guinn p.1447; M/H p.521
         m. Elgin (Fayette) IA 1869
Mary Marilla Hatfield   b. PA Mar 1848
   1860: Fayette co IA   d. Santa Maria 4 Mar 1919 @70/11/23; SM cem
                                           obit Sat Mar 8 p.2; from Tue Daily
                                        F: Joseph Griswold Hatfield 1810-1893
                                        M: Sarah C (Rhodes? Nicholson?) 1821-1890

1.   George Marion   b. IA Aug 1871 (cen); m. @21
                                        d. San Bernardino CA 15 Sep 1920 @50/1/15; SM cem
      1896 GR: 26 5'7 lt blu br IA farmer   obit Sep 19
      1904: Wineman Bldg, grain & beans
      1906 Dir: grain buyer, r 2½ mi NW; Mrs   1920: grain buyer
         m. at home of Wm McPhaul, Guadalupe, 3 Aug 1892 by Rev Jos W Smith   -(*Times*)
      Jennie Freelove McPhaul   b. Guadalupe Mar 1874; m. @18
      1922 Dir: 611 W Cypress   d. SM 13 Jan 1943 @68/9/11; SM cem
      1930 Dir: 623 S Pine   obit Thu Jan 14 p.1
      1938, 1943: 217 N Vine   F: Wm McPhaul 1828-1893
                                        M: Alice Lucina Battles 1849-1933

            4 births, 4 living 1910
   a.   Marion R   b. Guad 6 Apr 1894 (*Times*) (obit: 16 Apr 1889)
         1920: ranch hand Sisquoc   d. Taft CA 24 Nov 1970 @76; Westside cem
         1922 Dir: lab w/W Stillwell   obit *Taft Daily Midway Driller* Fri
1943: Santa Maria   Nov 27; r 433 California st Maricopa
         1947 Dir: dairyman, Los Olivos
               m.1
         Elsie I   d. Los Olivos 18 May 1946; Ballard cem
                                           notice Mon May 20 p.1
         = George Robert   d. 13 Jul 1929 @4; SM cem; obit Mon Jul 15 p.5
         = Mildred   b. 1927 (in Lompoc 1970)
         = Irene (in San Luis Obispo 1970)
         = James (in Olanche 1970)
         = Elmer L (Willa M) (in Santa Maria 1970)
               m.2
         Edna P
   b.   Mabel H   b. 5 Oct 1901; m. @18 of SM
         NDGW r 213 S Pine   d. SM 10 Oct 1974 @73; obit Mon Oct 14 p.2
            m. San Luis Obispo 19 Nov 1919 by Wm Mallagh, L113
               wit: John O'Connor, SLO; Jeff Johnson, SLO
         Albert L "Curly" Phillips   b. 25 May 1896
                                        d. SM Jan 1982

```
                1922 Dir: truck drvr r 611 W Cypress;   1940 Dir: Tel Co emp r 123 S Russell
         No issue                                       retired from Gen Tel Co
    c.  Leila M                                    b. 24 Dec 1904
                                                   d. Bakersfield 15 Oct 1978
                m.
         James Elmer Reynolds                      b. Dexter/N. Branch KS 9 June 1915
            to SM 1935                             d. Goleta 23 Jan 1983 @67/7/14*
         WWII Army Air Corps; 38y SM Police; 18y Asst Chief Police
         = Dennis (in Methuen MA 1983)                 *obit Mon Jan 24 p.2; Tue Jan 25
         = David (in Salinas CA 1983)
    d.  Cecile M (Hibbard)                         b. SM 20 Nov 1906 (Times)
         1947 Dir: emp Home Lndy                   d. SM 20 Nov 1976 @70/0/0; SM cem
         1951 Dir: emp Home Lndy; r 217 N Vine     obit Mon Nov 22 p.3; r 211 S Pine
         = Kenneth      1940 Dir: emp Univ Auto Parts, r 217 N Vine
                        1947 Dir: Slsmn Reak Auto Parts, r 217 N Vine
                        1950 Dir: Santa Maria Airbase
                        1976 in Placerville
         = Glen         1947 Dir: emp City of SM, r 217 N Vine
                        1950 Dir: r 217 N Vine
                        1962 Dir: foreman Gen Tel, r 217 N Vine
                        1976 in Camarillo
2.  Mary G                                         b. Elgin IA 13 May 1874; m. @25 of SM
                                                   d. Santa Maria 6 Aug 1946; SM cem
                                                   obit Tue Aug 6 p.8
            m.1 San Luis Obispo 21 Sep 1899 by Rev J C Eastman, Pres. F12
                wit: Mrs Mary P Eastman, SLO; Miss Mary I Hall, Oakland (Times)
    Walter A Mattocks                              b. IA 1874; parents PA (there were several Mattocks
      1906 Dir: carp Pine st                          families in Fayette co IA 1870)
      1909 Dir: carp 207 S Pine st                 d. Santa Maria 13 July 1914 @40/6; SM cem
                                                   eulogy in T; no data
      1910 cen: sexton, cemetery; r Pine st
      1902: Mrs G M Doane and Mrs W W Mattocks left Wed for Pelchuck WA where
            Mrs M's husband is employed.                                    -Times date lost
      1909: Roses for sale at Mrs Mattocks'.                                -Times date lost
      1909 AD: W A Mattocks. Agt for Monuments, Coping, All Kinds Cemetery Work
            Phone Home 1672                                                 - Times Aug 14
      1908: visited his family in Seattle                                   - Times date lost
    a.  Gertrude Georgina                          b. SM 24 Feb 1901
                                                   d. SM 7 June 1908 @7; SM cem; obit,
                                                   card of thanks

                m.2
         George C Sibley                           b. VT 1871
                                                   d. Alameda co CA 31 Dec 1920 @49
                                                   F: Albert Monroe Sibley 1840-1891
                                                   M: Mary Young 1844-(1918)
            1896 GR: lab 25 5'5 lt haz br VT SM
            1922, 1930, 1940 Dir: Mrs Geo/Mrs Mary r 215 S Pine
                No issue
3.  Clarence Murray                                b. Elgin IA 14 Jan 1879
                                                   d. Santa Cruz CA 6 Jan 1955 @76
      1906 Dir: carp Cypress st; Mrs               obit Fri Jan 7 p.8
```

1910: W Cypress; to Santa Cruz 1918; contractor/builder
  m.1 Yuma AZ 30 April 1900 (*Times*)
Gloria M Frago/Frates Mrs   b. CA 1879; parents Portuguese
 2 births, 0 living 1910
  m.2 (after 1910)
Isabelle E   b. Stockton CA 1883
 1920: 10 Roberts av Santa Cruz   d. Santa Cruz 30 Mar 1954 @70
      m.1 ____ Vandyke
 obit Apr 2 p.2; also *Santa Cruz Sentinel* Tue Mar 30 p.1; Wed Mar 31 p.14; Thu
  Apr 1 p.8; her dau: Hazel M Vandyke   b. 1905 m. ____ Ball
       = Bonnie Jean (Angell)
 a. Clarence Murray jr   b. Santa Maria c1916
  builder   d. Capitola CA 30 March 1954 @38
   m. (Santa Cruz) 1 Dec 1937   accident; obits as above
  Josephine R Scott   b. Santa Cruz 1919
  = Mary Karon   F: David Silas Scott 1875-1969
  = John Murray   M. Elizabeth Connor 1886-
  = Jeffrey Alan
  = James Nathan
4. Melford L   b. Santa Maria 19 Oct 1880; m. @19
 1900: farm lab SM   d. San Jose CA 16 July 1947
 1906 Dir: carp, Lincoln st; Mrs   obit Sat July 19 p.1
 1910: Santa Cruz, mgr lbr yd, r rooming hs w/Mrs Bloomer
 1918: to San Jose, Lumber contractor   1920: 23 Clay, Santa Cruz
 1900: 4th July Melford & Clarence in foot race and broad jump   -(*Times*)
 1927: Melford won fat man's race at Pioneer Picnic, SM   -*Times* Apr 30, 1930
  m.1 Santa Maria 24 Jan 1900 by S S Sampson ME ch
   wit: Geo M Doane Sr, Santa Maria; Clarence Doane, Santa Maria   (*Times*)
 Sarah I Bloomer   b. CA Aug 1880; m. @19 of Templeton
      F: William Bloomer 1852-1901
      M: Elizabeth   1861-
 1910: 364 Pacific av Santa Cruz; see above
 a. Cyril   b. Santa Maria 1 Jan 1901 (*Times*)
   m.2 (after 1920)
  Hortense
 b. Katherine (Alexander)   (in San Jose 1947)
 c. Buddy   "
 d. Norma   "
5. Perry P   b. Santa Maria Dec 1884
 1922 Dir: carp 215 S Pine st   d. At Mrs Sibley's 10 June 1934 @49/5/30 SM cem obit
  survived by 7 nieces and nephews
6. Oscar Mason   b. Santa Maria 28 Nov 1886 (*Who's Who SM*)
      d. Santa Maria 4 Jan 1960 @73/11/6; SM cem
 1920; w/Dick, 215 S Pine   obit Mon Jan 4 p.1
 1922 Dir: supt constr, Doane Bldg Co; r 609 E Church
 1938: Tepesquet 1960: 609 E Church
  m. San Luis Obispo 7 May 1905 (*Who's Who*; not found SLO)
 Genevieve Gertrude Bowers   b. Rome NY 6 Feb 1887
      d. Santa Maria 3 Oct 1974 @87/7/27; SM cem
       obit Fri Oct 4 p.2
      F: Francis Joseph Bowers 1866-1945

```
                              M: Katherine Hellen Baulig 1866-1943
  a.    Geraldine L            b. SM 10 Nov 1906
                               d. Guadalupe 11 May 1981 @74; Guad cem
                                  obit Tue May 12 p.7; Wed May 13 p.10
              m. (after 1926)
         Albert H Perona       b. Pinckneyville IL 16 June 1907
                               d. at res 331 Campodonico st Guad 7 Oct 1964
                               @58; Guad cem obit Wed Oct 7 p.16 Thu Oct 8
                               F: Peter P Perona 1876-1957
                               M: Emma          1890-1982
         1940 Dir: clk newsstand r 217A Guad st Guad
         1951 Dir: clk Perona newstnd r 962 Campodonico st Guad
            = Mace Doane (in Southwick MA 1964; in Santa Barbara 1981)
            = Peter Paul  b. 15 June 1930; d. 27 July 1975; Guad cem; USAF
  7. Richard V (Dick)          b. Santa Maria 18 Feb 1891 (Who's Who)
     1910: w/ parents          d. Santa Maria 9 Mar 1977 @86; SM cem
     1920, 1922, 1930: 215 S Pine   obit Fri Mar 11; photo
            m. Santa Maria 4 April 1921
     Anna Mae Breen            b. Rome NY 9 May 1887
                               d. Santa Maria 28 June 1975 @88/1/19; SM cem
                                  obit Mon June 30
     1922 Dir: Doane Bldrs Bldg Mats    F: Frank Eugene Breen 1858-1921
       Cypress & Pine; also 215 W Cypress  M: Mary Bowers 1859-1932; r 215 S Pine
     a.  Betty Jean            b. Santa Maria 7 Sep 1922
            m.
         Parnell Waldon Tilley  See Tilley chart
           1978 Dir: Doane Bldg Co, Parnell W Tilley Pres, Betty Tilley Sec-Treas,
             Contr; 212 N Russell
         =6 children
```

Vol. XXVI, No. 1, Spring 1994, pp.9, 10

Corrections and Additions   [Page numbers refer to those in Quarterly]

p.7.   Mary Hatfield's mother was Sarah Cynthia Howard, sister of Samantha Howard Nicholson. See Nicholson chart.

p.8.   Walter Andrew Mattocks was son of Lavina Abigail Howard, sister of above, and Jacob Cline Mattocks 1852-1909

Vol. XXX, No. 1, Spring 1998, p.9

DODGE
SANTA MARIA VALLEY PIONEERS

Rinaldo Dodge   b. MI May 1846 (cen); parents NY
- 1890 GR: 40 MI f Arroyo Grande; reg Sep 7 1888
- d. at home W Chapel 1 Mar 1922 @74/9/14; SM cem obit Mar 2; wid 3 sons 3 dau
- 1892 GR: 45 5'8 lt complexion grey eyes brown hair f MI Arroyo Grande; reg Aug 22
- 50 y CA, 22 y SM; grocery 16 y, ret 6y ago. CW GAR
- 1900 cen: Arroyo Grande tp; 6 births 6 living
- 1906 Dir: Dodge & CO Dealers in Groceries, Broadway
    Dodge R Grover rMain & Miller; Mrs
    Clara Miss stu; Celia Miss, stu; Walter, lab; John, rancher, Emmitt, rancher
- 1909 Dir: Dodge R Dealer in Produce 221 W Mill & Pine; Mrs Clara L
    E E, Teaming; Miss Clara, tel op; Miss Celia, tel op
- 1910 cen: 221 W Mill peddler (sic) groc; parents WI
- 1914 Dir: Dodge Rinaldo (Clara) h221 W Mill
- 1922 Survived by widow Clara; sons Ernest (sic) and John, Santa Maria; Walter, Chico; daus Mrs Jessie Rice, Santa Maria; Mrs Clara Ringo, Owensmouth; Mrs Celia Close, San Jose; sister Mrs Alsie Bartrum (sic), Santa Maria

m. Hanford 20 Apr 1876

Clara Lenora Cheadle
- b. IL Feb 1860
- d. Santa Maria 19 Sep 1931 @71/6/26 obit Sep 19 p.1; here 51y. To CA from IL @5 (sic) 3 sons 3 dau
- F: George Lafayette Cheadle 1844-1922 bio M/H 419: to CA 1863, to Hanford 1870
- M: Sarah Jane Ramage 1848-1923

- 1922-3 Dir: Dodge Celia L Widow (Rinalde) (sic) r221 W Mill
    Mrs Clara, hskpr; Emmet (sic) E, pumper; John J. oil wkr
    Cheadle Sarah, widow r221W Mill; Willis H, lab r221 W Mill
- 1925 Dir: Dodge Mrs Clara L hskpr r221 W Mill; Emmett E cement contractor same
- 1928 Dir: Dodge Clara L wid; Emmett mech; John J mech all 221 W Mill
- 1931 Survived by sons Emmett and John, Santa Maria; Walter, Chico; daus Mrs Jessie Rice, San Jose; Mrs Clarence (sic) Ringo, Reseda; Mrs Celia Close, Watsonville; sisters Mrs Ella Conner, Central City NE: Mrs Annie Ables, Torrence; Mrs Nettie Griffin, Tucson; bro Geo Cheadle, Santa Maria

1. Emmett Elmer Dodge   b. Hanford CA July 1877
   Single
   - d. 31 May 1934 @56/10/10, SM cem obit Fri June 1 p.1; Fall from Tower Fatal to Emmett Dodge Yesterday: working w/bro John to repair windmill on Bello ranch, Oso Flaco, fell 12'. Lived many yrs at Black Lake w/parents; to SM 1901.
   - K of P, 3 sis, 2 bro, uncle Geo Cheadle, Santa Maria, other relatives

2. John Jensen Dodge   b. (Hanford)? 9 Sep 1880
   Single
   - d. San Luis Obispo 26 Dec 1956 @76/3/17; SM cem obit Thu Dec 27 p.3; 3 sis. Lived SMv and Guadalupe, recently moved to Oceano. Eagles.

3. Jessie Mae Dodge
   - b. CA 15 Dec 1878
   - d. Santa Clara co 13 May 1968 @89

      m. San Luis Obispo 15 Oct 1905 by Rev James Blackledge, Pres ch   *-Times*
  George Siddons Rice   b. CA 14 Feb 1883; m. of Santa Maria
   1906 Dir: Geo S bkpr rMain; Mrs   d. Santa Clara co 6 Feb 1941 @57
   1909 Dir: Rice Geo Bkpr   F: William Thomas Rice 1845-1899
    r215 W Fesler; Mrs Geo   M: Louisa Russell 1841-1921
   1914 Dir: Rice Geo S (Jessie) bkpr Bryant & Trott h215 W Fesler
   1922-3 Dir: Rice Geo S (Jessie) Pulliam & Rice r215 W Fesler
     Pulliam & Rice (A W Pulliam & G S Rice) dry goods cor Main & Lincoln
     Pulliam and Rice SW cor Main & Lincoln
     Prices Are Right
   1925,1928 Dir: no. In San Jose 1931
   a. Velma M Rice   b. 7 Jan 1907   *-Times*
   b. Donald W Rice   b. SB co 7 June 1908
 4. Walter R Dodge   b. CA 25 Jan 1885
   1910 cen: w/parents   d. Butte co 21 Dec 1945 @60
   1914 Dir: W R Arroyo Grande
    m. San Luis Obispo ME parsonage 2 June 1906 by Rev James Blackledge;
     to reside in Arroyo Grande -T
  Alice V Mozier   b. MO 23 Aug 1885
             d. Butte co 1 Dec 1974
             F: Frank Mozier 1856-
             M: Mary Ann Brant 1867-1954
   a. Gwendolyn R Dodge   b. Arroyo Grande 25 July 1907   *-Times*
   b. Thelma M Dodge   b. SB co 11 Mar 1911
   c. Lenora E Dodge   b. SLO co 31 Jan 1914
   d. Walter Russell Dodge   b. Betteravia 24 Feb 1916
             d. Butte co 5 Dec 1997 @81
 5. Clara L Dodge (Ringo)   b. CA 28 Sep 1886
   1900 cen: w/parents   d. Los Angeles co 16 Sep 1961 @74
   m.
  W Ringo
   a. Earldeen Ringo   b. SB co 14 Sep 1910 (mother's name Dodge)
 6. Celia A Dodge (Close)   b. CA 11 Aug 1888
   1910 cen: w/parents   d. Santa Clara co 16 Jan 1973 @84
   1914 Dir: Celia Dodge h1410 Broad st SLO
   a. James Allen Close   b. Alameda co 7 Aug 1925 (mother's name
               Dodge)

This chart was composed by Barbara Cole from resources at hand plus California birth and death records on www.rootsweb.com.

Vol. XXXIII, No. 2, Summer 2001, pp.14, 15

Corrections and Additions   [Page numbers refer to those in Quarterly]

p.15   MARRIAGE: Clara Dodge m. SLO 22 Sep 1909 by H S Munger, ME, George D. Ringo
                     -Santa Maria Times Sept 25

Vol. XXXIV, No. 1, Spring 2002, p.19

DRUM - DRUMM
LOS ALAMOS VALLEY PIONEERS

The Drum brothers of Los Alamos were born in the same decade as the Drumm brothers of Orcutt. The spelling is interchangeable in the public record, often in the same article; however, their origins distinguish them, as the single-m Drums were natives of Pennsylvania, the double-mm Drumms coming from Kentucky by way of Missouri.

A compilation of surnames from the 1790 census, published by the government in 1909, shows 20 heads of families under Drum-Drom-Droom (no Drumm). Of these, one was in Massachusetts, eight in Pennsylvania, and eleven in New York. "Drum Family Notes," in the *New York Genealogical & Biographical Record*, Vol. 90, p. 181, says "Andreas Tron, the progenitor of the Drum (Tron) family, was a Palatine emigrant who came with his family to East Camp, Columbia Co, NY, in 1709, from the Duchy of Zweibrucken…recorded in registers of the Reform parish of Niederkirche in Ostertal." This might merit pursuit.

Adding to the confusion caused by indifference to specific spelling is Jacob Durm, a longtime resident of the Lompoc area, whose name was occasionally represented as Drum. The Great Register of Voters is rife with typographical errors as well as those apparently stemming from misread handwriting. Durm-Drum is one; another might be Morgan Drum's middle name – Gruer. It has not been found elsewhere for corroboration; could it be Greer? Green? Gruen?

The information herein presented has been gathered from public sources, with the exception of some data on the later Drums from Nona Hall, an erstwhile SMVGS&L member. There is obvious inconsistency in some of the birth and death calculations; birth dates on census are often erroneous and such given at time of death are not much more accurate. Dates in parentheses are from the California Grand Death List, not corroborated by obituaries or other sources.

DRUM

Morgan Gruer Drum   b. PA 1819
  1879 GR: 61 PA farmer Santa Rita   d. Santa Rita 30 May 1887 @67/10/28 Los Alamos cem
           Co H PA Inf
  1880: tp 4 (nr Lompoc)   F: NJ   M: PA
  1887: Brief Items. M G Drumm (sic), from his mountain home in the Santa Rita, was in town
       Monday and reports crops and feed good in his section. Mr Drumm expects to see that
       region yet covered in English walnuts and vines and all manner of fruit.
                                                               -Lompoc Record May 21
  1887: IN MEMORIAM . . . M G Drumm, who was a member of the 122d regiment of the
       Pennsylvania Volunteers, Infantry, and served nine months in the war of the Rebellion, in
       defense of his Country's flag, and also a member of Robert Anderson Post, GAR, and
       departed this life on the 30th day of May 1887…our sincere sympathy to the bereaved
       family and friends of our late comrade…
         W B Gray, Wm Jackson, A C Warwick, Committee   -Ibid June 11
  m. (Luzerne co PA)?
Sarah   b. PA 1825
               d. 11 Feb 1898 @73; Los Alamos cem; parents PA
  Known children:
1. Francis M   b. PA 1848
    1870: Sonoma co, Salt Point,   d. (Los Angeles co 10-18-1928 @81)
         PO Timber Cove; lumberman
    1900: (Siskiyou co PA Sep 1840 alone)?
    1920: Los Alamos @72 w/brother JR
2. Lyman   living in Flagstaff AZ 1921

3. George M   b. PA 1852
    1870: lumberman w/Francis; living in San Francisco 1921
4. John Rosbin   b. nr Wilkes-Barre PA July 1854; m.1 @29
                                              of Los Alamos
      1879 GR: 24 US f Guad   d. Los Alamos 19 Dec 1921 @67; Los Alamos cem
      1880: w/parents   obit Mon Dec 19 p.3
      1890 GR: 36 PA f Santa Rita
      1892 GR: 38 5'11 dk br br PA Santa Rita PO Los Alamos; reg Oct 5
      1896 GR: rancher 42 5'11 lt br br PA Santa Rita
      1900: tp 5 (nr Lompoc)   1906 Dir: Los Alamos 5m S; Mrs Q (?) stock raiser
      1920: Los Alamos
         m.1 San Luis Obispo 8 May 1884 by D S Gregory, A612; wit: Ernest Graves, Esq.
      Winnie J Hickman   b. IL 1866; m. @18 of Los Alamos
                                            d. 18 Apr 1897; Los Alamos cem; no obit
                                            F: IL
                                            M: Emma J 1848-
                                                m.2 Frederick Jack Welborn 1838-1909
                                                     1879 GR: Lompoc; 1890 GR: Santa Rita
         m.2 @45 of Santa Rita in Los Alamos 6 Jan 1900, F237
           wit: Mathilda Kahn, Los Alamos; J B Hankerson, Los Alamos
      Elizabeth M Morss (Mrs)   b. MO Mar 1854; m. @45* (!)
                                             (she was 21 in 1870 with 4 children)* of S Rita
                                             d.
                                             m.1 c1861 Geo W Morss 1841-1919
                                             1900: 10 births, 7 living; household incl. Clarence
                                                  J Morss b. 1882
         m.3   Is he "Drum C farmer Los Alamos 5m S" 1906 Dir?
      Delphine   b. IL (1920 @63)
      1920: Los Alamos   d. (not mentioned in JR's obit)
Children by first wife
4-1   Morgan Frank   b. 29 Mar 1885; m. @23 of Los Alamos
      Frank M   d. 1 Sep 1949; Los Alamos cem
        1906 Dir: Los Alamos 5m S
        1910: nr Los Alamos, blacksmith
        1920: Sisquoc w/Dott Webber
           m. San Luis Obispo 15 Nov 1907 by Harry Hillard, H88. Wit: Mr and Mrs* J T Cullen,
               Santa Margarita (*Grace Funk - for Cullen genealogy, see ONT p.223ff)
      Lilah Ophelia Funk   b. KS 30 July 1886; m. @21 of Los Alamos
      1920: Sisquoc w/fam   d. Sacramento 9 Jan 1961; Los Alamos cem
                                           F: John G Funk, blacksmith
                                           M: Ella D
          a. Eunice A (Ted Larson)   b. 1908; living King City 1973
          b. Lyman Grant   b. Los Alamos 26 Feb 1910
             1940 Dir: oil wkr Los Alamos   d. 315 Perkins St, Los Alamos May 1973 @63
             1947, 51 Dir: same   (spouse R E)
             m.1
             Marie Olive Saulsbury   b. Girard KS 30 May 1909
               355 Coiner st Los Alamos   d. Santa Maria 16 Feb 1965 obit Wed Feb 17 p.4
                                                   F: Roy Saulsbury (in Santa Susana 1965)
             = David   M: (Minnie Shoemaker)

= Lynnette	m.1 Murdock; son Myrten
c. Minnie D	b. 1913; living Santa Maria 1993
(Plinio Edward Gnesa 1905-1989)	
d. Jack R (Ruth Cullen)	b. 1914; living Nipomo 1973
e. Frank L (Gladys F Pico)	b. 1917; res Los Alamos
f. Clarence H (Catherine Pico)	b. 1918; res Los Alamos
g. Delena (Leo Gnesa)	living in Lompoc 1976
h. Helen (Manuel Perry)	living in Lompoc 1976
i. Hazel (Martin)	living in Santa Barbara 1973

4-2 Sarah/Sadie E — b. May 1887
    m.1 Santa Rita 23 Sep 1901 — d. before 1961
    William W Bullock — b. CA Dec 1880
        d. (San Francisco 1-5-1919 @50)?
    4 children — F: Robert J Bullock; 1900: tp 5
        M: Nancy Ann

    m.2 before 1921 -- Terry

4-3 Harry Saxon — b. Drum Canyon June 1888; m. @21 of Los Alamos
    1906 Dir: Los Alamos 5m S — d. Los Angeles co (Lakewood) 3-3-1961
    1940-1 Dir: oil wkr Los Alamos
    1947-8 Dir: pumper, Signal Oil & Gas, Los Alamos
        m. San Luis Obispo 15 Nov 1907 by Harry Hillard, H89
            wit: Mr and Mrs J T Cullen, Santa Margarita; consent of parents
Mary Edith Funk — b. CA 1891; m. @16 of Los Alamos
    1910: Santa Rita rd — d. Los Angeles co 5-28-1967
    1920: Careaga — F: John G Funk
    1940 Dir: Hmkr Los Alamos — M: Ella D (Shoemaker)?

a. John R (Gertrude Irwin)	b. 1909
= Mary	d. 1951
= John	
b. Lloyd James	b. 1910/11
1939-40 Dir: 1243 E Meta, Ventura (Ruth)	
m. 1	
Ruth E Page	
m.2 Dorothy	
No issue; adopted Susan	
c. Dell Earl	b. 1911/12
1947-8 Dir: oil wkr Los Alamos	
m.1	
Erma Irene Fickle	b. San Simeon 24 Aug 1907
	F: Alva W Fickle (in Bicknell 1914)
	M: Annie May – suicide 1909 @39
m.2	m.1 Eagon; dau Winona (David Hall)
Helen Ayres	Thanks for your help, Nona!
d. Grace Viola	b. 1913
m.1	
Edward Kaucher	1940 Dir: Los Alamos
= William Thomas	
m.2	
Carlos De la Guerra	1947 Dir: oil wkr Los Alamos (Grace)

    e. William T (Martha Pico)   b. 1915
        1940 Dir: mt ctr Los Alamos Mkt
        1947, 1951 Dir: oil wkr Los Alamos
        = Bernard

4-4 Ralph Owen   b. Jan 1891 (cen) or 11 July 1890 (SS)
    1906 Dir: Los Alamos 5m S   d. (Fresno co 11-1-1956)
    1920: 159 Lincoln Coalinga   1921: Los Angeles
      m.1
    Margaret Whitson   b. TN (1920: @19)
    a. Glen   b. CA 1918
    b. Ralph jr   b. CA 1919
      m.2
    Vera V   b. 12 July 1906
                                            d. Bakersfield 7 Feb 1981

4-5 Marian A/S   b. Los Alamos Sep 1892; m. @16 of Los Alamos
                                            d. living in Long Beach 1961
      m. San Luis Obispo 13 Apr 1908 by Harry Hillard, MG, H159
        wit: A W Marshall, Cayucos: H Hillard, SLO. Consent of father John A (sic) Drum
                                          – See *SLO Tribune, SM Times* "John R"

    James M/F Foster   b. CA 1886; m. @22 of Los Alamos
        1910: tool dresser, oil fields   d. (Chico Jan 1968)?
    a. Glen
    b. Bonnie

4-6 Earl Rosbin   b. 18 Apr 1894
    drafted Aug 18 1917 (*Times*)   d. 12 Dec 1961; Los Alamos cem obit Thu Dec 14 p.2
    1920: Santa Fe av, Orange   (mother's maiden name Milburn!)
    1921: Los Alamos
      m.
    Edna Hitchcock   b. CA 1900
                                              d. (before 1961)

    a. Cherrille (Felt)   b. 1920; in Florina CA 1961
    b. Ronald   in Long Beach 1961
    c. Thomas   in Pittsburgh 1961

5.   William Henry   b. PA 4 March 1857
      1879 GR: 22 PA f Los Alamos   d. nr Los Alamos 3 Jan 1924 (at home of nephew
      1880: w/parents   Morgan F Drum) @66; Los Alamos cem;
      1890 GR: 33 PA Santa Rita   spouse initial R obit Jan 3 p.5, Jan 4
      1896 GR: 39 5'9¾ lt br br cattle buyer PA Santa Rita
        m.1 (both of Los Alamos) aboard Steamer Santa Rosa Nov 1887
            by Capt John M Ingles (*Times*)
    Gracie Powell   b. CA 1870
                                              d.
                                              F: Wales
                                             M: Grace Maria   b. IA 1832
                                                   d. Santa Rita 5 May 1889 @56; Evergreen cem
                                                   Lompoc. m.2 James Nash
                                                    1879 GR: 50 Eng Santa Rita, trans from Butte co
    a. Nettie (Dillwood) living in Academy 1924
    b. Jessie (Sample) living in Berkeley 1924
        m.2 San Luis Obispo 4 May 1896, E35
    Ray/Rachel R Hilliard   b. NC 1873

    1920: Los Alamos   d. (not mentioned in his obit)
    1922 Dir: Wm H Drum shoemaker Los Alamos
6. Maria Gennett   b. PA
                                  d. (before 1900)?
    1887: Mixed Items from Los Alamos: Last Wednesday a large concourse of people
        attended the funeral of Morgan Drum, father of Mrs Dr Graham . . . he died at his
        residence in Santa Rita . . . buried Los Alamos Cemetery   -(*Times*) June 11
         m. San Francisco 1882 (Storke)
    James William Graham MD   b. Hancock co IL 1 Oct 1850
       grad Willamette U   d. Lompoc 9 June 1914 @63; Evergreen cem
       Portland OR 1883   bio Storke p.601; Guinn 1907 p.2230
       to Los Alamos 1884   obit *Lompoc Record* June 12 front page
                                     F: Benjamin Franklin Graham 1815-1903 to CA 1852
                                     M: "Safrano"
                                         m.2 Lompoc 14 Feb 1900 Lena F Rucker 1879-1931;
                                         dau Marian b. & d. 1901
                                               F: Geo F Rucker 1851-1928
    1890 GR: 39 IL phys Los Alamos   M: Susan F Barker 1858-1912
    1892 GR: 41 5'9 dk hz blk scar on finger 1h IL Los Alamos
    1896 GR: phys 45 5'9 dk dk dk scar on forefinger 1h IL Los Alamos
    1900, 1910: Lompoc

JOHN R. DRUMM OF LOS ALAMOS
Los Alamos – The Productive Valley Equal to Any in the State

Paragraphs on Los Olivos, Juan B Careaga, Wm Gewe, H P Morrey, G Muscio, J R Drumm, W.H. Downs, Peter Scolari, D D Davis, A Leslie, John McGillivray, H H Harris & Co, Los Alamos Market (Manuel Den and Fred Kreigel), and Hotel Bar (C W Short)

J R DRUMM*
    J R Drumm was born near Wilkes-Barre, PA, where he received a common school education. After his school days he worked for the J Dupont Powder Co. in Lucerne County. Thirty-five years ago he came direct to California. At Pt. Sal he went to work for Harmon & Clayton building warehouses on the wharf, and continued to work for them for a year and half. Then he engaged in buying and selling cattle and went to Kerney Junction, Nebraska by way of Arizona…, New Mexico and Colorado. He stayed at Concordia, Kansas for 11 months and at Kerney Jct., Neb. 6 weeks. Then he returned to the Salinas valley where he worked for a year for wages upon a thrashing machine. In 1878 he removed to what is now known as Drum* Canyon, four miles (from) Los Alamos where he has since resided. Here he bought a possessory right and afterward secured title. He now owns 700 acres of land, 200 acres of which is planted to wheat, barley, mustard, oats, (and) corn. The land is very rich the loam being at least 75 feet and has produced the same crop year after year. It usually averages 25 sacks of grain per acre.
    Mr Drum also raises stock, has been and proposes to again commence raising Percherion (sic) – Norman horses, because nothing pays so well; raises shorthorn cattle and dish-faced Berkshire and Poland China hogs. He has 300 acres surrounded by hog tight fences and aims to turn off 300 head of hogs per year.
    Chickens in this Canyon do well.

Vegetables grow without irrigation, but are not raised for market. Cabbage weighing 65 pounds to the head and radishes of tremendous size have been grown. Apricots, peaches, pears, apples, figs, prunes and walnuts do well but their success is interfered with by gophers.

Last year, a dry year, 640 (the number hard to read) sacks of grain of 140 pounds each were raised from 25 acres.

The land is especially adapted to raising mustard, Chevalier and common barley, oats and corn. Last year 14 sacks of mustard to the acre were raised and frequently 30 sacks of barley raised. As many beans cannot be raised to the acre as on sandy soil.

An improvement this year will be the erection of a new grain warehouse.

There are wells on the place showing water to be easily obtained. In one well, a bored one, the water ran out of the top but has not done so since 1895. The water in the well is now rising.

Fifteen years ago a well was dug and abandoned because so much oil collected that the (water) could not be used. The State Mineralogist reports the indications for oil here to be of the best.

The climate in Drumm Canyon is one of the best in the US. This year Mr Drumm also farms 500 acres of land in the Los Alamos valley.

Mr Drumm is a director on the Los Alamos Creamery and is a member of the local AOOW lodge. -*Santa Maria Times* May 31, 1902

*spelling copied as found

J R Drumm visited in town on Saturday. (to import the above, no doubt) -Ibid May 24

FARMERS ATTENTION
Squirrel poison
Prepared and Ready to Use
In quantities of 20 gals up at 40¢
Per gal. at the
Los Alamos Deport
Smaller quantities in proportion
Address J.R. DRUMM, Los Alamos, Cal

-Mar 18 1904

DRUMM

Benjamin Howard Drumm   b. Fayette co KY 14 Feb 1816
   1850: Jackson co MO, Sniabar tp   d. Santa Maria 23 Apr 1900 @84/2/9; SM cem
   1860: Sonoma co CA, Santa Rosa tp   obit April 28
   1870: Monterey co CA, Castroville   parents VA; to CA 1852
   1879 GR: 62 KY f Guadalupe
   1880: Santa Barbara co 8th tp (Guadalupe)
   1890 GR: 74 KY f Santa Rita
   1892 GR: 77 5'11 florid complexion blue eyes grey hair scar on nose; KY,
       res. Lompoc; reg Sep 12
    m. KY 1841
Jane N Smith   b. KY May 1820 (1900 cen)
   1900: w/Millard   d. Santa Maria 28 Oct 1902 @86/6/18 (*Times*)
       or @82 SM cem record
   9 births, 5 living   F: born at sea;   M: Scotland
1.
2.
3. Benjamin Franklin   b. (Jackson co) MO 1846
       d. (not with family 1870)

Vol. XXVI, No. 4, Winter 1994, pp.10, 11, 12

4. Calvin Rice 1848-1926; see chart
5. James Howard   b. Jackson co MO 19 July 1850; m.1 @28
   1879 GR: 29 MO f Grad   of La Graciosa
   1880: 8th tp (Guad)   d. Santa Maria 4 May 1916 @65; Pine Grove cem
   1890 GR: 40 MO f La G   obit May 6; Patron T/W: to CA 1852; to co. 1875;
   1896 GR: f 45 5'9 lt gry   res. Green Canon, PO Gradalupe; 400a
      lt MO La Graciosa
   1910: Orcutt, mcht, genl store
     m.1 5 Nov 1879 by M Thornburgh, B415. Wit: Thomas Brookshire, M G Foster
  Mary C Stubblefield   b. CA 17 Aug 1864; m. @15
                                               d. 21 Dec 1894 @30/4/4; Pine Grove cem obit Dec 22
  8 children; to be presented later   F: Robert Coleman Stubblefield 1834-1924
                                               M: Sarah Lewis 1826-1915
     m.2 1896/7
  Frances E   b. IN Apr 1848; parents OH
6.
7. Mildred A (Moore)   b. CA 1854
8. Henry Clay   b. CA 1856
   1880: w/parents   d. Ventura 14 May 1939 @83; Ivy Lawn cem; obit
                                               Oxnard Daily Courier Mon May 15 p.1
                                               "no relatives"
     m. San Luis Obispo 20 Oct 1891 by J H Barrett JP, D72
       wit: J L Wilson, SLO; Peter S Meyer, SLO
  Mary Bell Scott   b. CA 1870? m. of Santa Maria
                                        d. (11 Jan 1895)
                                        F: John Cowhick Scott 1839-1901
                                        M: Ella Elizabeth Cook 1848-1901
  a. Mabel J   b. 1892
    1909 Dir: stu 617 S Lincoln w/H W Scott
    1910: cousin w/B W Scott, Santa Maria
  b. Alphoretta J   b. Santa Maria 6 June 1893 (*Times*)
    1909 Dir: as above   d. (not mentioned in Willis' obit)
      m. San Luis Obispo 4 Aug 1911 by Wm Mallagh JP, I252
        wit: Regina Hopper, SM; F J Rodriguez, SLO
    Willis G McMillan   b. CA 1888
      electrician   d. Santa Maria 26 Oct 1943 @55/7/7; SM cem
                                          obit Wed Oct 27 p.3
                                          F: John McMillan 1850-1910
                                             bio Phillips II 199
                                          M: Ellen C Robertson 1864-1936
       = dau (Marshall Elberson) in Los Angeles 1943
9. Millard Fillmore   b. CA Feb 1857; m. @21
   1879 GR: 22 CA f Santa Barbara   d. Los Angeles 11 Nov 1919 @62
   1880: Santa Maria   obit Wed Nov 13/19 p.3
   1890 GR: 33 CA f Santa Rita
   1892 GR: 35 lt blu br CA SM #1; Reg Aug 8
   1896 GR: livery 39 5'10 lt blu br CA Santa Maria
   1900: tp 7 (Santa Maria)   1904 GR: 47 Arroyo Grande #2
   1910: foreman sugar factory (Betteravia) alone

	m. Santa Maria 13 Nov 1878 by M Thornburgh, B348
Hattie G Jared	b. IL Aug 1859; m. @19
1920: 4337 Hillsdale av	d. Los Angeles 17 Feb 1946
Los Angeles, alone	F: Lorenzo D Jared 1831-1909
	M: Margaret 1838-

7? births, 4 living 1919; no children 1880
- a. Margaret J   b. April 1881
    - m. Santa Barbara 20 Dec 1902
  - John H Cowan
- b. Agnes S/G   b. Oct 1883
    - SMUHS 1903; grad LA Business College, Berkeley. Steno, in Los Angeles 1913
    - (per Alum notes, SMUHS *Review*)
- c. Katie M   b. March 1886
- d. Charles M   b. 23 Mar 1888; SSDI
    - 1920: 4327 Hillsdale av Los Angeles   d. (Van Nuys) 2 Sep 1975
  - Edith   b. CA 1892
    -                         d. Los Angeles co 3-24-1935 @42
    - = Anita b. 1916
- e. Anne (Banner) twin   b. Santa Maria 11 May 1891 (*Times*)
- f. Benjamin J twin   b. Santa Maria 11 May 1891 (*Times*)
    -                         d. Alhambra 4 July 1973 spouse initial MC
- ? (Mary   b. 2 Sep 1894
    -                         d. Norco Oct 1972; SS records)?

DRUMM–NORRIS
SANTA MARIA VALLEY PIONEERS

Calvin Rice Drumm	b. Jackson co MO 30 Dec 1848
1879 GR: 29 MO f SM	d. Santa Maria 26 June 1926 @77/5/26; SM cem
1880: La Graciosa	obit Mon June 28 p.1
1887: trustee Suey sch (ONT)	bio M/H 494
1890 GR: 42 MO La Graociosa	
1892 GR: 43 5'10½ blu br lt 1st finger broken 1h, MO LaG PO SM	
1900: Santa Maria	
1906 Dir: f 9m SE; Mrs	
1910: 2 listings: 63 m/33 MO VA KY or 61 div MO3 farmhand	
1920: 71 div Sisquoc, lodger w/Fred Baker	

      m. Guadalupe 7 Dec 1876 by W J Leach, B244; div/sep by 1910

Mary Bell Norris	b. Mariposa CA 6 June 1858
	d. Santa Maria 28 Dec 1929 @71; SM cem
1910: 10 births, 10 living	obit Mon Dec 30 p.5; res 505 N Lincoln
	F: See Norris chart

- 1922: Local Briefs. Mrs Mary Drum (sic) is now established in her home in the Tunnel tract on North Lincoln   -Mar 14 p.5
- 1924: Local news. Mrs Mary Drum left Monday for Santa Barbara to reside. She was preceded last week by her son, Ben Drumm, who has been transferred to the Santa Barbara music store of W H Saladin.   -Feb 26
- 1929: 5 sons, 4 daughters living

1. Louis Seymour   b. Guadalupe 8 Nov 1877; m. @35 of Orcutt
   1906 Dir: f 9m SE   d. Santa Barbara 26 Apr 1954 @78 (*Times*) or

       1910: w/parents   76/5/18 SM cem record;   obit Tue Apr 27 p.8
       1920: Park av Orcutt   bio O'Neill 239; Orcutt Mercantile Co 1907-;
       1922 Dir: Mcht Orcutt   custodian Orcutt school 1926-
       1940 Dir: jan Orcutt sch
       1945: to Santa Barbara
           m.1 Orcutt 12 March 1914 by H J Harrington, min
  Ferne Marguerite Hatch   b. nr San Lake (Grand Rapids) MI 12 Jun 1893
    1922 Dir: hskpr Orcutt   d. Richmond CA 1 Mar 1982 @88/8/19; SM cem
                                                   obit Mar 4 p.9
                                                   F: Henry H Hatch (d. SF 4-7-31 @72)?
                                                   M: Myrtle
      a. Ruth Aileen   b. SM 19 Nov 1914
                                                    d. SM 16 Sep 1989; SM cem
           m.1 (before 1940)   obit: Ruth's Café S Bwy 1954-69
    William A Walker   b. Appleton City MO 23 June 1904
     to SM 1928   d. SM 5 Mar 1980 @75/8/12; SM cem
      1940 Dir: Lion Head Ser Sta   obit Sat Mar 8 p.4
      320 N Bwy; h 616 E Main (Ruth)
  = ...gdau JoAnn Cavaletti, SB 1989
        m.2
    Clarence Ernest Ontiveros 1899-1977; see ONT p.79
      b. Donna Evelyn   b. SM 19 Feb 1916
          m.1 Barling   d. Santa Barbara 15 Oct 1987 @71; SM cem
          m.2 Hauman   obit res. Summerland & SM
      c. Louis Lambert   b. Orcutt 7 Jan 1921
                                                  d. (living in Kodiak Alaska 1989)
      d. Clarence Curtis   b. & d. 1 July 1925 (*Times*) SM cem
1.   m.2
   Millie C   1949 Dir: 826 Bath st Santa Barbara
2. Susan/Susie Bell   b. Nov 1879
   1910: cook bdg hs   d. 505 N Lincoln SM 1 Jan 1929 @49/1/30 SM cem
                                             Wiley plot; obit Wed Jan 2 p.1
     m.1 nr Los Alamos at the home of bride's parents 7 Nov 1897 by Rev Jas Smith
         wit: Mrs Anna E Smith, J R Norris
  Wyatt Cecil Wiley   b. CA July 1877; m. @20
                                            d. Hollister CA 24 June 1937 @59/11/3
                                            F: Benjamin Taylor Wiley 1827-1902
                                            M: Abigail Trott 1840-1924; wid of FM Bryant
                                            m.2 1920 Jennie L Huston
                                            m.3 Dolores
    1906 Dir: 3 listings: W C Wiley tmstr 10 m SE, Mrs; W C Wylie f 10m SE, Mrs;
       Wiley Wyatt f Orcutt, Mrs
    1910: Kern co tp 9 tmstr next to Henry A Bryant
 3 births, 2 living 1910 (Elsie b/d1900)
   a. Mabel G (Ridgeway)   b. 1 Feb 1903 (*Times*)
                                           d. (living in Watsonville 1929)
   b. Benjamin L/Bennie   b. 31 Oct 1904 (*Times*)
     res Hollister 1929, '37   d. Fallon NV Dec 1972 (SSDI)
      (m.2 Wade Hawkins, living in Palmdale 1926 per father's obit)?

3. Grace Marie b. 1881
 d. Ventura 6 May 1962 @80; Ivy Lawn cem
 obit *Ventura Star-Free Press* Mon May 7 p.6
   m.1 nr Santa Maria Thu 22 Feb 1900 by Rev S S Sampson (*Times*)
Edmund M Wiley b. (Santa Maria valley) 1879
  1910: 8th st Pomona, tmstr d. (living in Paso Robles 1924)
 F: Benjamin Taylor Wiley as above
1 birth, 1 living 1910 M: Abigail Trott as above
  a.   Freda (Hammon) b. Pine Grove 1 Mar 1901 (*Times*)
 d. (before 1962)
      = Donald (in Bakersfield 1962)
      = Edwin Jr (in Cleveland 1962)
      = Alice (Knoles) (in Bakersfield 1962)
      = Grace (Resch) (in Bakersfield 1962)
  m.2 c1915
Lewis P Brown b. MO c1882
  1920: 122 N 7th, Santa Paula d. Ventura co 3-26-41; no obit available
4. Eva Lena b. March 1884; m. @23 of Orcutt
 d. Santa Barbara 26 Dec 1946 @62 of Orcutt; obit *SB*
 News-Press Fri Dec 27 Sec 2 p.1, called widow
  m. San Luis Obispo 28 March 1907 by Carl M Ross MG, G478
    wit: Mrs Martha C Hughes, SLO; Mrs Mary B Drumm, Orcutt
Walter Hughes b. MO Jan 1884; m. @23 of Orcutt
 d. (living Anaheim 1947 when his mother died)
 F: Wm B Hughes 1851-1898
 M: Martha C 1865-1947; m.2 John Ow
  1906 Dir: Church st; also foreman Union Pipe line, Orcutt
  1910: tp 10 teamster oil
  1920: Del Mar av, San Gabriel
  a.   Marvin Elden b. Orcutt 29 Mar 1908 (*Times*)
     in Suez 1946 d. SM 31 Mar 1977 @69/0/2; SM cem
       m. obit Sat Apr 2 p.7 no children mentioned
    Danita Anderson
  b.   Edith M b. 1909
 d. (before 1920)?
5. Albert Leonard/Jack b. Martin dist 29 Nov 1887 (*Times*)
  WWI; single d. SM 1 Apr 1958 @70/4/2; SM cem
  1910: w/parents obit Tue Apr 1 p.1; hit by car
  1922 Dir: oil wkr Orcutt 1940-1 Dir: f Sisquoc
6. Henry b. Santa Maria 26 Oct 1889; m. @25 of Orcutt
  1910: w/parents, groc adv d. Santa Barbara 27 May 1969 @79; SB cem
  1920: grocer, Orcutt Mercantile obit May 28; also *Santa Barbara News-Press*
  1949 Dir: slsmn M G Hart, r 1012 C Laguna, Santa Barbara
    m.1 San Luis Obispo 18 Aug 1914 by E P Unangst, Sup Ct Judge J223
      wit: Chas Shaw, Orcutt; Margaret Walker, Orcutt
Lula Ellen Brown b. NE 1896; m. @19 of Orcutt
  1920: no children d.
 F: b. IA; d. before 1910
 M: Rose b. IL c1868
    m.2 Arnold NE 1949   1910: Ice cream & candy store, Orcutt
Nettie Ida P Hayes (Mrs) b. Norfolk NE 19 Jan 1891

                         d. Santa Barbara 18 Dec 1974 @83
                             obit *Santa Barbara News-Press* Fri Dec 20 B-3
                             her ch: Vera (Blomquist) in Sacramento
                             Vernon Hayes, in SB 1969, 1974

7. Eugene C   b. 15 Oct 1893
    1910: w/parents in Taft   d. Lodi CA 1 Apr 1969; no obit *Stockton Record*
    1926: in Goleta   1929: in Lodi 1958-
    1962 Dir: prod dir 1119 S Central Lodi   1969: same, retired
     Edna C   still at 1119 S Central 1984

8. Ellen   b. 2 Apr 1895
                                 d. Ventura May 1974 (SSDI)
       m. San Luis Obispo 4 June 1917 by Wm Mallagh JP, K180
          wit: Mrs M B Drumm, Orcutt; Joseph Pruitt, Orcutt
    Albert W Pruitt   b. OR 4 Nov 1892
     1929: Long Beach   d. Ventura, at home, 16 Sep 1975 @82
     1944: Ventura   obit *Star-Free Press* Wed Sep 17 A-7
     Mgr McCullough Tool Co   F: Joseph Pruitt 1860-1944
                               M: Lucy   1870-1963
     a. Clifford (in Ventura 1975)
     b. Michael (in Thomasville GA 1975)   (b. 9 Jan 24
                                              d. Mar 1981 Savannah GA; SSDI)?
     c. John (in San Francisco 1975)
     d. Norma (Reiman) (in Ventura 1975)

9. Benjamin Franklin   b. Los Alamos 11 June 1897
    1910: w/parents   d. Westminster CA 18 Dec 1976
    1920: Orcutt, alone   no obit found *Santa Ana Register*
    1939: Union Sugar;   in Westminster 1958, 1962
    1930 Dir: 505 N Lincoln

10. Edith T   b. Orcutt 1901
                               d. Santa Maria 22 July 1993 @92; Ivy Lawn cem
                               Ventura; obit July 25, last of 10 children
     1926 Dir: Miss, clk, WU Tel co; r 817 N Milpas, Santa Barbara
       m. c1927
    Wilbur Sawyers DDS   b. (Santa Barbara) 22 Nov 1895
                               d. Ventura Sep 1984 (SSDI)
                               F: George Edwin Sawyers 1862-
                               M: Mary Lillard 1874-(1934)?
       No Issue

BIOGRAPHY 1917

Calvin R Drumm. – An employee of the county of Santa Barbara in the fifth supervisorial district, Calvin R Drumm, of Orcutt, is engaged in the care of Waste oil in the Orcutt field, in the Santa Maria valley. This oil is used for road purposes, and its salvage is a considerable factor in the furtherance of public economy…

       He has lived in the West from a child of two years of age, had undergone hardships and disappointments, and is today respected by all who know him. He has been engaged in farming and stock-raising for years, and is now employed by the board of supervisors in the Orcutt oil fields in pumping the waste oil into tanks; and this is used for road-making. Over thirteen thousand pounds were thus applied during the year 1915…ten children…Louis S is with the Orcutt Mercantile

Company; Susie B is the wife of Wyatt Wiley of Fillmore; Grace is now Mrs Brown of Santa Paula; Evalina is married to Walter Hughes of Fullerton; Albert is a teamster in Orcutt; Henry and Eugene are with the Orcutt Mercantile Company; and Ellen, Bennie and Edith reside with their mother.

-Morrison & Haydon p.494

THE ORCUTT MERCANTILE COMPANY

Bob Nelson's *Old Town Orcutt*, 1987, has two photographs of the Orcutt Mercantile Company in its heyday, and one of its death by fire in 1959, accompanied by a quotation from Willard Forbes on its history. Forbes' father, James F (died 1926 @68) is said to have been the first merchant in Orcutt; the 1906 Directory lists Forbes & Son, Gen'l Merchandise and Aubrey Forbes (d. 1963 @78) merchant, in Orcutt. When that business burned down in 1910 Forbes was unable to rebuild, so "Charlie Webb and Lou Drumm formed the Orcutt Mercantile Company." The replacement edifice bore the date 1911. However, Lou started in business before that:

Orcutt. C O Dyer has finished putting the rustic on his new store building across from Logan's hall. When finished it will be occupied by Downs and Drumm. Mr Downs has been running a store in Los Olivos for some time past with a good deal of success. Mr Drumm has been working in the oil fields for quite a while. The goal is success and they invite the people's patronage as they claim this is the only way to find the path of their goal and when once found they expect to follow it. -*Santa Maria Times* June 8 1907

Wm H Downs was a brother of the second husband of Mattie Norris; he apparently preferred his Los Olivos location, as he returned there. Cerfee Luis worked for Drumm for some years, and bought the business possibly in the late thirties, or by 1940.

SCRAPBOOK - C R DRUMM

1891   South Side Scribbles...The next day after Mrs Drumm and family went to Lompoc to visit Cal was seized with a desire to his parents too, so hitched up and drove next morning before breakfast. Cal wasn't lonesome. Oh no. -*Santa Maria Times*, Dec 26

1892   Mr F. M. Drumm and family are on a visit to his parents, Mr and Mrs B. H. Drumm.
–Brief Items, *Lompoc Record* June 25

1894   South Side Items. The parents of Jim and Cal Drumm have been visiting them recently. Each year they come to spend a few weeks with their children here and to enjoy our warm sunshine which to the Lompoc people is one of the luxuries of life to be enjoyed only at rare intervals.
-*Santa Maria Times* Dec. 29

1894   The South Side. Cal Drumm, of the Maynard orchard of South Side was a business caller in town the 1st of the wk. -Ibid Dec 29

The South Side. C. R. Drumm and family spent Sunday with Father Norris of Pine Grove.
-Ibid June 16

1895   Graciosa Items. County Surveyor Flournoy, W W Stillwell and C R Drumm, road viewers, were on duty in our neighborhood last week appraising land, etc. –Ibid March 2

1897   Father Drumm, of Lompoc, made the *Times* office a very pleasant call Tuesday. He brought his wife, who has been very ill since January last, over to Santa Maria last Saturday in hopes that a change of climate and scenery would have a beneficial effect upon her. They are the guests of the family of their son, M F Drumm. –Ibid Apr 24

1897   Cal Drumm rancher and farmer from the sand hill country dropped into our office this week on business. -*Santa Maria Times* June 5

1897   Miss Susie Drumm spent Monday with Santa Maria friends. –Ibid Nov 6

1897   Married: Wylie-Drumm. Near Los Alamos Sunday Nov. 7, 1897 by Rev J M Smith, Wyatt C Wiley to Miss Susie Drumm.

Wyatt C Wylie and Miss Susie Drumm, of Los Alamos, were quietly married last Sunday at 11 am at the residence of the bride's parents. None but the family of the contacting parties being present. The young couple have gone to housekeeping in the Martin district where the groom will raise grain next year. Here's the *SM Times'* best wishes for their future happiness and prosperity.
–Ibid Nov 13

1897   The young people of Pine Grove district gave a dance last night in honor of W C Wylie and bride. Of course there was a most enjoyable evening spent.   –Ibid Nov. 20

1897   11th annual Masquerade…Cavalier: Louis Drumm.   –Ibid Nov 27

1897   Dude* Drumm went to Lompoc Tuesday returning Wednesday with his parent for Thanksgiving dinner under his roof.   –Ibid Nov 27

*"Dude" is M F Drumm

1898   Grandpa Drumm came over from Lompoc Monday for a short visit.   – March 12

1900   Died. DRUM (sic) In Santa Maria Monday April 23, 1900, Benjamin Howard Drumm aged 84 years, 2 months 9 days.

Another of our pioneers has gone – another link that connected us with the early days of California is severed. Grandpa Drumm passed peaceably away on Monday morning. He had suffered intense pain for a number of weeks past but was unconscious for some hours before death and the end was peaceful.

For the past five years he has been a sufferer from the painful and lingering disease of Cancer. He underwent several operations and surgical skill added unto his day several years. He died at the ripe old age of 84 years and two months.

Benjamin Howard Drumm was born in Lafayette co, Ky, Feb 14, 1816. He was married in the same state in 1841 at the age of 25. He and his bride immediately started West and settled in Missouri, living there nine years. The gold fever was then in the land and Mr Drumm resolved to try his fortune in California. He crossed the plains in 1850 and after a year returned by way of Panama and brought his wife and family to this state. They settled in Sonoma County near Healdsburg and engaged in farming til 1860. In that year they moved to Texas and made it their home for four years. Returning to California and Sonoma county they lived there til 1867 when they moved to Monterey County and resided there eight years. In 1875 they came to Santa Maria Valley and a few years later moved to Lompoc, which was their home until about a year ago.

Declining health induced them to leave Lompoc where they were so well and favorably known and return to Santa Maria to be with their family. Of nine children born to them, five are living: C R Drumm, J H Drumm, Henry C Drumm, M F Drumm and Mildred A Moore.

Mrs Drumm has been for some years in delicate health. Much attention and care has been shown to Mr and Mrs Drumm by the many friends of the family during their long illness. Mr & Mrs Drumm were members of the Presbyterian church at Lompoc.

Card of Thanks . . . Jane M. Drumm and Family.   -April 28

1914   Local News Notes. Married Today - Henry Drumm and Lula Ellen Brown by Judge Unangst . . . both of Orcutt . . . he is engaged in merchandising business . . . Present: Mrs Rose Brown, Mrs Mary B Drumm, Mrs Susie Collins, Miss Margaret Walker, Chas. Shaw, Mrs Shay (sic), Thos. Ash, J A Hayes . . .   -*SLO Daily Telegram* Aug 18

1925   A little son was born this morning to Mr and Mrs Louis Drumm at their home in Orcutt. The infant passed away and will be laid to rest in the Santa Maria Cemetery.
-*SM Times*, July 1

1926   Calvin Drumm, Aged Pioneer, Called By Death

Calvin Drumm, 77, a native of Missouri and a resident of the Santa Maria Valley for the past 51 years, died here late Saturday following a brief illness. Mr Drumm was a retired rancher and was widely known through the entire community.

Mr Drumm moved to California with his parents 73 years ago and the family lived in Sonoma county for several years. Moving to the Santa Maria valley a little over a half century ago he made his home in this county since that time.

The widow, May Belle Drumm, and ten children survive. The children are Ben, of Santa Maria; Lewis of Orcutt; Henry of Santa Barbara; Albert of Whittier; Mrs Wade Hawkins of Palmdale; Mrs Lou Brown of Whittier, Mrs Walter Hughes of Long Beach; Mrs Albert Pruitt of Whittier, and Miss Edith of Santa Barbara, and Eugene of Taft.

Funeral services will be held Tuesday afternoon at the Albert A Dudley Funeral Home. Rev George B Cliff, pastor of the Methodist Church in Santa Maria, will be in charge of the service. Interment will be in the local cemetery.   -Ibid Mon June 28 p.1

1929   Obituary. Mary Belle Drumm

Mary Belle Drumm, 71, pioneer resident of Santa Maria Valley, died Saturday evening, December 28, at her home, 505 North Lincoln.

Deceased was a native of California, born in Mariposa county, and had been a resident of this city for the past 53 years.

She is survived by the following: five sons, Louis of Orcutt, Jack, Henry, and Ben of Santa Maria, and Eugene of Goleta; four daughters: Mrs Grace Brown of Hunting Park, Mrs Eva Hughes of Whittier, Mrs Ellen Pruitt of Long Beach, and Mrs Edith Sawyers of Santa Barbara. One brother, John N Norris of Santa Maria; and two sisters, Mrs Mattie Lewis (sic) of San Luis Obispo, and Mrs Nettie Earl of this city, also survive.

Services will be held in the chapel of the Dudley-Bradford Funeral Home tomorrow afternoon at 1 o'clock with the Rev John Gray officiating. Interment will be in the local cemetery.
-Ibid Mon Dec. 30, p.5

1930   Mrs H. H. Hart and Mrs L. S. Drumm of Orcutt were hurt when their auto crashed into a Pacific Coast railway train south of the city.   -Ibid Feb 13

Vol. XXVI, No. 4, Winter 1994, p. 20

Corrections and Additions   [Page numbers refer to those in Quarterly]

Morgan G DRUM family
p.5.   1882 GR: Morgan Groer (sic) Drum 64 PA Santa Rita; reg Oct 3
             George Morgan Drum 30 PA lab Los Alamos; reg Aug 16
         Francis M Drum died in Sawtelle 1928 –Oct 26

A famous incident of Lompoc's temperance history is the pulling down of a saloon by means of ropes with "drys" providing the power. One of Lompoc's murals represents this event. Four prominent Lompoc citizens were tried for the crime and they had their picture made with their counsel, W W Broughton and Sheriff Robert Broughton; Joseph Dimock, George Frick, James Saunders and George Anthony –See *Lompoc: The First 100 Years*, 1974 p.14. The *SM Times* reported it: A High Sounding Drum. The (SLO) *Mirror* says – "Drumm (sic), one of the fellows who recently opened a saloon in Lompoc, and had it demolished by the citizens of that burg was in San Luis the first of the week. He had been to San Francisco where he has engaged the League of Freedom lawyers to bring a suit against Santa Barbara county for damages. He threatens to have other citizens of Lompoc arrested for complicity in the riot and claims as a grand finale, that after all the suits pending are decided, he will again build and open his saloon in Lompoc. The people of the town however, do not intend to allow any one to run a saloon in their midst." We advise Drumm (sic) to desist from further persecution of Lompoc. If we mistake not the temper of the people there, the next time they have use for their historical rope it will not be to pull down his building. They may conclude to string something up to the kettle-drum pitch.   -June 23 1883 p.5

The next week the *Santa Maria Times* quoted the *Lompoc Record*: "George Drum, of Lompoc, has had J W Rogers of Lompoc arrested for shooting deer before the time fixed by law." – July 7. Seems Rogers had permission from some official with faulty information, and George must have been out to get him.

Vol. XXX, No. 1, Spring 1998, p.6

Four years later "George Drum of Los Alamos has been awarded a patent for a potatoe (sic) masher" –Oct 8 1887. His name is not on the 1890 Great Register; he must have moved away.

In La Reata No. 12, *History of Zaca Lake*, by Jim and Lynne Norris, p.168, is a brief biography of George Morgan Drum, aka Grover. He was born in Bell Bend, Lucerne co PA in 1852; blinded in an explosion at the Ocean View Rock Quarry 3 Nov 1895, he ended up in San Francisco, where he took a second wife, Lottie Sterling, in 1903. Together they wrote stories and poems, including *The Bottomless Lake and Mysteries of the Haunted Cavern; a Story of Zaca Lake*. The Norris book can be consulted at the Santa Maria Valley Historical Society.

1882 GR: John Rosebin (sic) Drum 27 PA carp Los Alamos; reg Aug 16

Los Alamos News. Judge Drum has had his residence & barn repainted which makes his property a credit to the town. We would like to see the Judge build a few cottages on his property which would be rapidly rented as there are not vacant houses here for rent fit to live in.
–Dec 25 1909

p.6. Marie Saulsbury's mother was Minnie Elizabeth Shoemaker, who died after a lingering illness in Los Alamos 4 Aug 1914 @23/8/17; SM Cem. She left two little girls, 5 and 14 months, and husband Roy D Saulsbury, aka David Roy Saulsbury, born KS Jan 1884. The Card of Thanks was signed by Roy Saulsbury and Mrs Nettie Shoemaker. –Aug 8 1914 p.1,4

Clarence H Drum d. 1990

Minnie Drum Gnesa b. Los Alamos 2 Apr 1912 d. SM 5 Dec 1997. Survivors: son Edward C Gnesa, SM; 1 gson 1 ggson. –Tue Dec 9 1997 A-7

p.7. Martha Pico Drum b. Los Alamos 5 June 1917 d. Long Beach 5 Dec 1997. Survivors: husband William Drum, 3 sisters, Anita Carroll, Solvang; Gladys Drum & Katherine Drum of Los Alamos, 2 bros: Mervin Pico, Ontario, Richard Pico, SM. 3 gch 3 ggch –Tue Dec 9 1997 A-7

p.8. 1882 GR: Wm Henry Drum 25 PA f Los Alamos; reg Oct 3

W H Drum, of Santa Rita, while riding a colt recently was thrown from the animal, the colt falling on him, severely spraining his ankle and injuring his leg. –Mar 14 1885

Los Alamos Locals. Will Drum and Miss Gracie Powell, of Santa Rita, were married out at sea last week; the bride's mother refusing her consent as the girl was only 16 years old.
–Nov 19 1887

Los Alamos News. Mrs Dr Graham is visiting friends in Colusa. –Nov 5 1887
(Dr Graham had gone there earlier to visit his father.)

Benjamin H Drumm family
p.13. Mary Bell Scott to be deleted; see Scott chart Corrections and Additions.

Calvin R Drumm family
p.16. MARRIAGE: Mrs Eva Walters formerly of Santa Maria m. in Paso Robles April 29 1930 Henry Drumm, to live in Santa Barbara. –May 12 1930. That makes Nettie his third, not second, wife.

p.17. MARRIAGE: Edith Drumm @18 and Maxton Albert Laughlin @19 m. ME ch Santa Barbara 16 Jan 1920 (Anc West op cit). Max was son of Rell Hayward Laughlin 1875-1948 and Rebecca M Faulkner 1878-1959 – see *Who's Who in Santa Maria*. The 1922-3 Directory has Max and Edith listed separately at the same address; in 1925 he is alone, and in 1926 she is shown under her maiden name in Santa Barbara. Max was still single in 1928, but soon married Beatrice Evangeline Missall 1909-1980; they moved in with her father, Wm C Missall, veterinarian, on West Chapel st. Max died in 1946 @45.

Santa Marians motoring to Santa Barbara to spend Sunday included Mr & Mrs Rell Laughlin, son Max, and Miss Beatrice Missall. (not married yet!) —Mon Mar 10 1930

Max Laughlin was survived by widow, Beatrice, children Albert & Margaret, parents, and brother, Wm T, San Diego. When Beatrice, born in Santa Maria 27 Oct 1909, died in Fresno, 26 March 1980, Albert was in Pleasanton, and Margaret (Mrs McLean) was in Fresno. 4 gch.
—obit Mar 28

Forbes & Son incorporate. Five directors: James H Drumm, F E Drumm, Frank Drumm, James F Forbes, Jessie Forbes. —Dec 28 1907

Vol. XXX, No. 1, Spring 1998, p.7

p.6.   Frank L Drum b. Devil's Den, CA 2 Nov 1916; died at home, Los Alamos 26 Mar 1999 @82; Los Alamos Cem. Survivors: wife Gladys, Los Alamos; daughters Anita Withers and Judy Trabucco, Los Alamos; Jacqueline Duncan, Santa Maria; son Frank jr, Los Alamos. Sisters Delena Gnesa and Helen Perry, Lompoc; Hazel Martin, Nipomo; 3 gch. Son Gary Lester Drum d. 1945.
—*Santa Maria Times* Mon Mar 29 1999

Minnie Della Gnesa b. Los Alamos 2 Apr 1912; died at home Santa Maria 5 Dec 1997. Husband Plinio Gnesa d. 13 June 1989. Survived by son, Edward C Gnesa, Santa Maria; 1 gson, 1 ggson.   —*Santa Maria Times* Tue Dec 9 1997 A-7

Hazel M Martin d. at home Nipomo 5 June 1999 @73; b. Los Alamos 7 May 1926. Husband Manuel M Martin d. 8 Nov 1985. Survivors: daughter and son-in-law, Lilah and Edward Chavez, Nipomo; 2 granddaughters; sisters Mrs Delena Gnesa, Mrs Helen Perry, Lompoc; 3 ggch.
-*Santa Maria Times*

p.7.   William T Drum b. Cat Canyon 13 July 1914; d. Long Beach 20 Dec 1998. Survivors: son Bernardo, 3 gdau, 3 ggch.   —*Santa Maria Times* Dec 22 1998

Martha Rose Drum b. Los Alamos 5 June 1917; d. Long Beach 5 Dec 1997. Survivors: husband, William; son, Bernardo; 3 sisters: Anita Carroll, Solvang; Gladys Drum, Katherine Drum, Los Alamos; brothers Mervin Pico, Ontario; Richard Pico, Santa Maria, 3 gch, 3 ggch.
—*Santa Maria Times* Dec 9 1997 A-7

p.15. Jeanette L Drumm b. Gadsden, AL 17 Feb 1924; d. Santa Maria 5 July 1999, buried Gadsden. Moved to Santa Maria from Kodiak AK 1990. Survivors: husband Louis L Drumm, Santa Maria; children: Gail Christensen, Glencoe, AL and Donald Jett, Gadsden AL; sister Venetta Gray, Gadsden; brother Soule Lynn, Birmingham AL; 2 gch, 2 ggch.   —*Santa Maria Times*

Vol. XXXI, No. 3, Fall 1999, p. 6

The DUNCAN EARL Family
SANTA MARIA VALLEY PIONEERS

"Grandfather Earl was a crotchety old Scotsman", according to Carrie Winters Boyd, whose reminiscences are included in *This Is Our Valley*, published by the Santa Maria Valley Historical Society in 1959. The verification of the Scottish origin we will leave to Daniel Earl of San Jose, a descendant. However, Earl is a surname found in colonial Massachusetts, and Duncan's father, said to have a Vermont birthplace, may well have been among those New Englanders who moved north into Vermont and northern New York in revolutionary days, and when the westward call became strong in the first two decades of the 19th century, trekked west through Canada, some recrossing later into Ohio or Michigan with Canadian-born children.

Mrs Earl was also a native of Canada, her father having emigrated from England, but settling afterwards in Lee county, IL, where, possibly, Duncan and Esther were married. Their first child was born in Canada, but they soon came back to Lee county, and from there to California in 1872, residing for several years in Gilroy before coming to the Santa Maria Valley.

They lived at first in the Pt. Sal area, the wharf there being an important shipping point for the valley, they acquired farmland about two and one half miles south of Santa Maria, in the vicinity of the present Santa Maria Country Club. Grandfather Earl "had great hope for this country. 'The ox road in front of this place will be famous someday', he said. Now there are oil wells there, too. The whole area is one of wealth". (*Valley* p.202) Indeed, to this day there remains a solitary "grasshopper" oil pump across that "ox road" near K-Mart.

The California Great Registers of Voters for the 1890's give physical description of the registrants; thus we learn that Duncan was 6 feet tall with light complexion, blue eyes, and at the age of 69, grey hair. Robert, too, was 6 feet tall, but with dark complexion, eyes and hair, inherited from his mother, "tiny, black-eyed 'Grandma' Earl". (*Valley*, op.cit)

A notable characteristic of this family was their interest in education. Mary Olive as a teenager was private tutor to the children of C H Clark, wharfinger at Pt. Sal, and in her widowhood devoted at least 30 years to the high school district as trustee. Her husband, J H Winters, was trustee in the Suey district (pronounced "sway") near Sisquoc, as was Robert Earl, who was, conceivably, influenced by his father-in-law, J R Norris, a trustee in La Graciosa district and the Santa Maria high school district. Fred Earl, in his turn, served as trustee in the Suey district; lists of these officials are found in *San Ramon Chapel Pioneers*, by SMVGS&L founding member Erlinda Ontiveros. Carrie Winters' husband, Dave Boyd was for years engineer and custodian of the contiguous high school-junior college campus; the playing field was named in his honor some years ago. Lizzie Earl Jessee's part was played for 17 years in the high school cafeteria.

Most of the valley residents were farmers, and this fruitful valley produced well – in rainy years. In 1888 a number of locals charged O W Maulsby with a wagonload of produce to take for exhibition at the Los Angeles Fair; among those listed were G W Battles: apples, pears, peaches, grapes; G M Doane: grapes; Mr Hobbs: squashes, beans, beets, and other vegetables; George Klink: general fruit display; J. R. Norris: grain and vegetables; Duncan Earl: fruit and vegetables; Mr Foster: fruit; John Winters: marine curios… (40 Years Ago, *Santa Maria Times*, Tue, Sep 18 1928) See Hobbs, Foster, Norris, Battles, and Doane charts

Following are a few items from the *Santa Maria Times* touching the social and agricultural activities of our subjects.

South Side Items   Robert Earl and family spent Christmas with his parents near Santa Maria. John Winters and family were among the number that gathered at the residence of Mr and Mrs Earl to partake of their hospitality Christmas.

We had two Devils in our peaceful community a few days ago. Fred Maulsby the Bam Print of the *Santa Maria Times*, spent Sunday with Frank Winters. Farming has begun in earnest, Trott & Boyd, Bob Earl, Nicholson Bros, Frank Clark, John Houk, Witzen & Smith, John Winters, Wm. Forrester, Ables Bros., Martin's (sic) and many others of our extensive farmers are all engaged in plowing and seeding.   -Dec 30 1893

John Winters and F A Baker were working the South Side roads the past week – between showers. All road grading should be done within the next month thus giving them a chance to settle before the heavy rains are over. We had abundant evidence of the non-observance of this the past year.   -Dec 30 1893

Washington District   Mr D. Earl intends enlarging his orchard this winter. He has some of the finest apples in the valley.   -Jan 6 1894

South Side Items   Ed. Times: The stockholders of the Alliance Milling Co. of Los Alamos met Tuesday April 3d for the election of a new board of directors.

The new board is, J H Stewart, Pres; A H Davis, Sec-Treas; C W Martin, Mg; C H Glines, D Spaulding, Wm Forrester, C O More, J H Winters, C R Drumm. The business was found to be in a prosperous condition and everything pointed to a continuation of the same. The profit to stock holders being about 26% on paid up stock.

This is not a bad showing for six months business. If farmers generally could make half that much on their capital invested in farms and machinery there would be no more complaints of hard times. Moral: Co-operation leads the way.   -Apr 6, 1894

The South Side   Our three schools, Martin, Suey and Highland have closed for vacation. C R Drumm, B T Wiley, and Wm Forrester are making hay. Bob Earl and John Houk are heading. The McCrakey Bros. expect to begin harvest soon. Grain and hay here will make about half a usual crop. (*Note*: dry year)   – June 16 1894

South Side Items   J H Winters is putting in his crop on the Twitchell place at present…
  – Dec 29 1894

Duncan Earl died in Santa Maria at the age of 85, an age exceeded by his son, Chauncy, but not so much as approached by Bob or Fred and his sons. "The latter years of his life spent in darkness and enfeebled to the point of utter helplessness…extreme old age undermined his former hardy constitution . . . was but a shadow of the days when he was known as one of the most active residents of this section.   (*Santa Maria Times* July 25 1908)

The pallbearers at his funeral in the Methodist Church were T C Nance, L W Blosser, M Thornburg, Chas. Bradley, J H Haydon and W T Norris. Haydon, a school teacher in La Graciosa in the 1890's, must have been well acquainted with the Earl and Norris families, which explains the inclusion, with some redundance, of the biographies of Robert Earl, sons Fred and John Robert, and the youngest Norris son, John M., in *History of San Luis Obispo County and Environs*, 1917, the "environs" including the Santa Maria Valley. The data is flawed but interesting and helpful on the pre-California days of the families.

Robert Earl and wife, Nettie Norris, farmed in the Sisquoc district for years before retirement brought them into town where they lived at 315 East Cypress, a site now under the

Town Center Mall. Bob died in Los Angeles at the age of 62, having gone there to seek medical attention. He was a member of the Masonic Lodge, the Elks, and Knights of Pythias, and had been road overseer since 1904. Mrs Earl died at the Cypress Street house fifteen years later; at the time she was possessed of real estate bringing in income of $500 per annum, which, in today's terms, sounds like nothing at all, but during the Depression, rents for ordinary little houses ran from $15 to $25 per month, so she must have owned several.

Their son, Fred, farmed with his father in the Suey district, near Sisquoc, then rented land on the Suey ranch, which straddles the Santa Maria River, as did his brother Bob and uncle Chauncy. A few years before his untimely death, he moved to King City. His wife died in 1934; he and two surviving sons came to Santa Maria for his mother's funeral in 1935, returning to King City only to have death claim Toots, the younger son, former Santa Maria High School athlete, by hemorrhage the next day, and Fred, himself, eight months later.

Mable's husband, Frank Gates, came to Santa Maria in 1902; he was city clerk and engaged in real estate until moving to Sisquoc about 1912, where he operated the general store until 1921, after which he went into the sand and gravel business. In 1912, he and Mable traveled to West Virginia and other eastern cities to visit relatives; at his death in 1952, his sisters Jessie Lyon and Kate Gates were still living in Charleston, WV.   (*Santa Maria Times* Dec 7 1912; Dec 17 1952)

Alice's second husband, Howard Frew, worked for Gates' Sand and Gravel after a stint with Union Sugar, then went into real estate. His surviving relatives, all in Pennsylvania, were a sister, Ella Fritges, three others unnamed and two brothers.   (*Santa Maria Times* May 9 1957 p.1)

John Robert (Bob) farmed successfully during the 'teens on the Suey Ranch, apparently spending some years thereafter in Sacramento and returning to Santa Maria about 1927, where he, too, worked for Gates' Sand & Gravel. In 1950, he and his wife moved to Los Alamos.

Lottie's first husband, Aten Johnston, was a barber at the Bradley Hotel. Like Gates, he had been in Santa Maria about a year when he married an Earl girl. He was a member of the Elks and the Santa Maria Rifle Club. His early demise was caused by a stroke during a hunting trip near the Beard Ranch, in the vicinity of Figueroa Mtn. His son-in-law, James Hoey, along with Charles and William Hoey and Wayne Engel went looking for him when he failed to meet his partner, Claude Aguirre, at the pre-arranged time. "A crew of men from the Gates Sand & Gravel Co. of Sisquoc, under the direction of Bob Earl, brother-in-law, 'went to bring the body out'; it took three hours to get it to the road and Dudley's hearse." (*Santa Maria Times* Aug 25 1941) Lottie's third husband was Guillermo/William Roman Ruiz of Sisquoc, whose family is well documented in *San Ramon Chapel Pioneers*.

Winters. The size of a community is not an accurate indicator of the size of mentality of energy of its inhabitants. Garey Items, a column in the *Santa Maria Times*, documents the efforts of the ladies of the area:

Ed. Times: The ladies of this section have now fully organized. The Society is to be known as the "Ladies Social Union" of Garey. The objectives are: Social, educational and financial. They propose giving a series of balls the net proceeds to be applied to the purchase of material for building a hall. The initial ball to be given the evening of the 4th of July proximo.

There is to be a basket picnic and literary entertainment during the day. The proceedings will open by a succinct statement of the objectives of the society by the president, Mrs L J Garey.

The orator of the day is Mrs Winters. Reader of the Declaration of Independence, Miss Nellie Hathaway. So it is apparent the celebration of the glorious 4th will be of a unique character at Garey. The ladies anticipate a nice representation from Santa Maria. The officers of the society are Pres, Mrs L J Garey; Vice, Mrs Hathway (sic); Sect'y, Miss Lizzie Brown; Treas, Mrs Carr. Executive Committee: Mrs Winters, Mrs Stuart, Mrs James Elliott, Mrs Carr.

(*Santa Maria Times* June 12 1893)

Mrs Winters was active in the Red Cross for many years, beginning in World War I; her niece, Mabel Gates, was chairman of the membership drive in 1928. Other activities were Eastern Star, Minerva Club, and the Santa Maria Valley Pioneer Association. Frank Winters spent his life in San Francisco; the city directories chronicle his rise in the police department from corporal in 1912 to sergeant in 1921 to lieutenant in 1924. He was a Mason and member of the Widows and Orphans Association of the SFPD. (*San Francisco Chronicle* Apr 7 1965, p.22)

Jessee. The Jessees were not so devoted to farming as other families: John was a surveyor, Frank and Henry ran a saloon; Cox & Jessee ran an express and transfer company, in which Mat engaged in the 1890's and a decade or two thereafter when he wasn't engaged in public service as the first night watchman in town, or constable, or helping Mrs Winters on her farm. His obituary, on the front page of the *Santa Maria Times* is valuable historically, and has an old photograph of him in his turn-of-the-century constable's uniform, complete with "bobbie"-type helmet. His brother, John, survived him by one month, and his life story is interesting, too. (*Santa Maria Times*, Mar 23, Apr 26 1937) These two Jessee brothers were members of the Santa Maria Star baseball team, in 1882 composed of them and another brother, Perry, two brothers-in-law, C B Dutcher and James Wilkinson, and Wilkinson's brother Dennis, and Tom Welch, Will Tunnell and Henry Morris. Their chief rival was the San Luis team, and the papers carried news of their conflicts.

In 1943, Bert Jessee died in Oakland at the age of 55 on a visit to his daughter from his home in Sacramento where he was a grain and bean broker; Clarence, who had been a blacksmith for Union Sugar before going north to help build Camp San Luis and then to the bay area for defense work, fell ill and came home to die less than three months after his brother. Ray, on the other hand, who moved to Hayfork in 1924, followed in his father's footsteps with a long life and career as constable. It is safe to assume that his 60 years in the tranquility of Trinity County gave him more contact with the cattle he raised than the criminal element of mankind he was charged with controlling. (*Trinity Journal*, Mar 20 1985)

J H Haydon not only helped write San Luis history, but also spurred development of the telephone company in Santa Maria, which may explain why Chauncy Earl found employment in that line. Otherwise little is known about Chauncy; his obituary contains no history at all.

Lulu, the youngest of Duncan's children, married Bert Ward, a law student; they lived for years in San Jose where he was secretary for the Building Trades Council and later Vice President of the Surety Building & Loan Association. Their sons were carpenters, but Ernest spent some time as superintendent of Alum Rock Park, and was first to leave San Jose, living in Boulder Creek, then Santa Cruz, where his brother joined him. Bert survived Lulu fifteen years, finally going to be with his sons in Santa Cruz, where he died in 1964. (*Santa Cruz Sentinel* Dec 27 1964, p.15)

Much more information from newspapers and city directories was collected than can be presented in this summary. Some of the articles are confusing and contradictory; however, Ye Ed. will be happy to send additional information to any inquirer.

Duncan Earl   b. Canada East 5 June 1823; imm 1840 (cen)
                                      d. Santa Maria 20 July 1908 @85; SM cem
                                      F: VT   M: C/E
    1880 cen: Santa Maria tp
    1890 GR: 67 CAN farmer SM #2 citizen by virtue of naturalization of father; Reg. Aug 25
    1892 GR: 69 6' light complexion blue eyes grey hair, fingers left hand disfigured; CAN;
            SM #1; nat. of f; reg. Sep 6
    1900 cen: Santa Maria
    1906 Dir: ret, res Church st Santa Maria
              m. (IL) 1857
Esther Reilly   b. Canada East 10 Apr 1835; imm. 1840 (cen)
                                      d. Santa Maria 7 Aug 1910 @75; SM cem
                                      F: Eng   M: Ire
    1909 Dir: Mrs D 305 E Church st Santa Maria
    1910 cen: Santa Maria w/Wm C
              6 births, 5 living 1900

1. Robert Wesley 1859-1920; m. 1882 Nettie Moore Norris 1863-1935
        See Norris chart
2. Mary Olive   b. Ashton IL 7 Nov 1861; m. @17
                                      d. Santa Maria 3 Aug 1946; SM cem
        1910 cen: Santa Maria, alone
        7 births, 5 living 1900; survived by 1 son 3 dau
              m. Central City 18 Sep 1878 by H R Stevens ME ch B339
   John Hugh Winters   b. IL 29 June 1853; m. @25
                                      d. Santa Maria 10 Feb 1908 @54/7/12; SM cem
    1880 cen: SM tp   F: NY (Nathaniel Ths Winters 67 NY SM 1890)?
    1890 GR: 37 IL f Sisquoc; Reg Sep 1 M: NY
    1900 cen: Santa Maria
    a. Frank E   b. Santa Maria June 1879 (cen)
          m. (after 1910?)   d. San Francisco 6 April 1965
        Beatrice O   d. San Francisco 5-29-1965
    b. Gracie Olive   b. nr Santa Maria 17 Sep 1884 (*Times*)
                                      d. 15 Oct 1884, stone SM cem
                                      (buried 1 July 1884 cem record)
    c. Elsie Lovilla   b. 7 Nov 1886
                                      d. 18 Oct 1887 @ 10 mos stone SM cem
                                      (d. Pt Sal 26 Mar 1887 croup @10 mos 15 days
                                      SM Times; buried 27 March 1887 cem record)
    d. Maude M   b. (Pt Sal) 12 May 1886 (*T*) or Sep 1886 (cen)
          m.   d. Los Angeles co 7 May 1960
        Edgar S. Maxson   d. c1950; rancher Whittier
         1917: City Briefs. Mrs Mary Winters visiting daughter in Los Angeles –*SM Times* Oct 13
    e. Carrie E   b. Pt Sal 13 Aug 1888 (*Times*)
          m.   d. Santa Maria 1979 @90 (undated obit
                                         in SM Hist Soc files)
        David Allen Boyd   b. Eniskillen IRE 14 Mar 1880
                                         naturalized 1896 PA
                                      d. Los Angeles 18 Dec 1963
        1920 cen: 1858 16th, Oakland CA, riveter
        1921 Dir: same

        1940 Dir: Bldg Engnr & Custdn H Sch & Jr Col r W Stowell Rd SM
        1951 Dir: ret r 501 E Chapel SM
  = Harold R (Clara)   b. 1914   d. 19 Mar 1977
        1951 Dir: ins 501 E Chapel SM
  = Dempster A (Virginia)
        1970 Dir: 257 Lake Louise Dr SW, Tacoma WA

  f.   Lillian Esther   b. Aug 1891 (cen); m. @19
                                          d. Orcutt 31 May 1938 @46
      m. San Luis Obispo 4 Dec 1910 by H Selah Munger MG, I103
        wit: Mrs Earl, Santa Maria; Ward Martin, SLO
  William Alexander Findley   b. CA 1877 (cen); m. @23
    1920 cen: Sisquoc   d.
  = Earl   b. 1914
  = Hazel   b. 1918

  g.   Ruth Esther   b. nr Santa Maria 9 Dec 1897 (*Times*)
                                          d. (before 1942)

3. Margaret Elizabeth (Lizzie)   b. Ashton IL 5 Oct 1864
                                        d. 29 Aug 1947 @82
    1920 cen: San Jose w/dau Edith, and Grace Morrison (dau of John H & Annie Swain
        m. 1883   Morrison of SM)
  Madison Jessee (Mat)   b. Napa Valley CA Dec 1859 (cen)
    1880 cen: w/ mother SM   d. Santa Maria 23 Mar 1937 @79
    1882: Star baseball team SM   F: Archer C Jessee 1821-1877
    1890 GR: 33 CA lab SM #1   M: Mary A Harbin 1822-1901
    1900 cen: Santa Maria tp farm lab   1896: Cox & Jessee, Express & Transfer Co –
    1906 Dir: r Cook st nightwatchman   ad in *SM Graphic*
    1909 Dir: 303 E Cook, works for transfer co
    1920 cen: living w/bro Frank SM;   1930 Dir: 826 S Pine SM

  a.   son   stillborn 13 Sep 1884 (*Times*)

  b.   Clarence Leonard   b. (SM) Mar 1886 (cen)
      Single   d. Santa Maria 21 Aug 1943 @57
      1906 Dir: lab r Cook st
      1909 Dir: blksmth 303 E Cook st
      1910 cen: w/parents

  c.   Bertram Earl   b. Santa Maria 16 Nov 1887 (*T*); m. @24 of SM
      1906 Dir: clk r Cook st   d. Oakland CA 29 May 1943 @55
      1909 Dir: Asst Cashier Bank of SM 303 E Cook st
        m. Santa Barbara 16 Dec 1911 (*Times*)
    Florence L Bonetti   b. (Green Canyon 23 June 1888 (*Times*))
      m. @24 of SM   F: John Baptista Bonetti 1855-1917
      bio M/H p. 916   M: Albina E. Vanina 1866-1936
    = Albert W
    = dau (James Warren)

  d.   Essie Belle   b. July 1890 (cen)
      1906 Dir: stu w/par   d. c1975
      1909 Dir: same
        m.1 Santa Maria 21 Nov 1910
    Robert Clayton McMichael   b. Tulsa OK
      policeman SM 2 mos   d. Santa Maria 25 Oct 1932 @46
      1918: in Taft   motorcycle accident
    = Edith   b. 1912; living Santa Maria 1993

      m. Alfred Wm (Bill) Gregory   b. SLO 1917
        (Bill & Nick's Liquor)   d. SM 1975 @57; SM cem
                                   GF: Francisco Jose Gregorio
          (1892 GR: Gregorio Francisco Jose 25 5'8 light complexion,
           black eyes black hair; scar under chin; lab Pt Harford
           nat. 1 July 1892 SLO Sup ct; Reg. Aug 23) (native of Azores)
  (d.)   m.2 after 1943
      Marion Francis Turnage   b. Snow Hill NC 22 Oct 1878
        bio *Who's Who in*   d. SM Apr 1959 @80/5/10; SM cem
        Santa Maria, 1931   F: Alfred A Turnage
                                 m: Mary Francis
      to SM 1924   Children by 1st marriage:
      1930 Dir: Mrs Georgia   Gertrude Saling, (Palos Verdes)
      210 S Vine SM   Katherine Grottkau, (Palo Verdes)
                                 m.2 Carson City NV 1911
                                 Georgia True Gifford d. 3 Apr 1930 @41
                                 Marion Florence (John Simko) b. 1912
                                 Frances True (Allison) b. 1913
                                 Clarence Lee b. 1914
      1940 Dir: M F Turnage Real Estate & Ins 112 W Church r MacIntyre
        Motor Hotel 1640 N Bwy;   1947 Dir: same
      1951 Dir: M F (Essie B) rl est & ins 112 W Church; r S Hwy
        Turnage Motel So 101
 e.   Ray E   b. Santa Maria 14 Oct 1893 (*Times*) or 12 Oct
                                       1895 (obit)
                                   d. (Weaverville) CA 12 Mar 1985; Hayfork cem
      1918: US Marines, guard duty Mendocino Co – *Santa Maria Times* Dec 28
      1922 Dir: Ray (Georgia) rancher Vine & Main SM
        m. (Humboldt) 1920
      Georgia G Cuddeback   b. Humboldt co 1901
                                 d. Redding CA 19 Jan 1973 @71; Hayfork cem
                                 F: Grant Cuddeback
      = Richard/Dick
      = Millicent (Sunday)
 f.   Edna R   b. Santa Maria 21 Aug 1898 (*Times*)
                                 d. (in SM 1985)
        m. after 1920
      Westbrook S Law   b. CA c1894 (cen)
                                 d.
      1920: Sisquoc, bunkhouse, single
      1965, 1972, 1976 Dir: 216 E Junipero, Santa Barbara
 g.   Edith Aileen   b. 1900
                               d. 22 Feb 1922 @ 21/2; SM cem
      1920 cen: w/mother in San Jose
4.   William Chauncy   b. IL 13 May 1871
    Single   d. Grover City CA 31 Mar 1963 @92; SM cem
    1906 Dir: farmer, r Church st w/mother
    1892 GR: 21 5'7 light complexion hazel eyes brown hair; left leg (off?) IL SM #2; reg Sep 1
    1909 Dir: wks for Home Telephone co, r E Church st w/mother
    1910 cen: Santa Maria w/mother   1920 cen: Sacramento w/J R Earl

1944 Earl Recovers. Chauncy Earl, well-known valley pioneer, is able to be about once more following a serious illness as the result of ptomaine poisoning.
-*Santa Maria Advertiser* Jun 15

5. Lulu Mable   b. CA June 1877 (cen)
     d. San Jose CA 6 June 1949

    m. (Santa Maria?) 1895 (cen)
Bertram Philip Ward   b. (Petaluma) CA June 1874 (cen)
    1900 cen: SM   d. Santa Cruz CA 26 Dec 1964 @88
    1910 cen: San Jose   F: Abraham Ward 1855-
    1920 cen: San Jose   bio Storke p 611; 1900 cen: Santa Maria
    M: Lucina Lusk 1856-

   a. Lawrence Abraham   b. Santa Maria 18 Mar 1896 (co.rec.)
     d. (Santa Cruz)

     1920 cen: 97 N 14th, San Jose
     1963 Dir; ret, Santa Cruz
   Elva P   b. WI 1899 (cen)
   = Esther (Hitchman)
   = Richard L
  b. Ernest R   b. 1902 (cen)
    Alice M   d. (Santa Cruz)
    = Raymond
     1963 Dir: ret, Santa Cruz

Robert Wesley Earl   b. Montreal CAN 19 Dec 1859; imm. 1861 (cen)
    m. @23
    d. Los Angeles 13 Aug 1920 @59; SM cem
    bio M/H p. 413

1892 GR: 33 6' dark complexion dark eyes dark hair, CAN, SM #2; nat of father. Reg Sep 1
1896 GR: 37 6' same as above
1897, 1900, 1902: trustee Suey school
1906 Dir: 2 entries: Santa Maria, farmer, 9 mi SE rfd, Mrs Garey, farmer, Mrs
   m. La Graciosa 15 Nov 1882 by W E King min, C10
     Wit: Nicholas Klink; Mary Winters
Nettie Moore Norris   b. Mariposa CA 4 Dec 1862; m. @19 of SM
    d. Santa Maria 19 Apr 1935 @72; SM cem
    F: John Richard Norris 1827-1909
    M: Mary Thomas Mattingly 1838-1910

    5 births, 5 living 1900
1. Frederick E   b. nr Garey 20 Nov 1883
   1906 Dir: Garey   d. Salinas CA 24 Dec 1935 @52 of King City; SM cem
   1914: trustee Suey sch
   1922 Dir: farmer Suey   bio M/H p.922
    m. Nipomo at res of bride's parents 21 Sep 1904 (*Times*) by W F S Nelson, ME ch, H23
     wit: R W Earl, Santa Maria; G C Orand, Nipomo
  Nellie Grand   b. (Cowley co) KS 18 July 1878; m. @25 of Nipomo
    d. Salinas CA 20 Feb 1934; of King City; SM cem
    F: Gideon Clark Orand 1843-1913
    M: Lydia Grimes 1856-1922
   a. Leo Lambert   b. Santa Maria 30 Mar 1906 (*Times*)
    1922 Dir: Musician Suey district   d. 1961
    Lillian Mercedes Beyer 1907-1988

```
            = Richard Leland         b. 1930 (Patricia Ann Harrison)
            = Dorothy Janice         b. 1932 (Marion Walter Jr)
            = Robert Frederick       b. 1941 (Phyllis Jean Webb)
      b.  Harold Gideon (twin)            b. SM 12 April 1913 "Tiny"
                                          d. SM 31 Mar 1916 @2 /11/19; SM cem
      c.  Herbert R (twin)                b. SM 12 April 1913
                                          d. King City CA 23 April 1935; SM cem
2. Mable E                                b. (nr SM) Dec 1884 (cen)
                                          d. Los Angeles co 2/25/1966, res Long Beach/
                                             Palos Verdes
      m. at home of parents 5 Nov 1903 (Times)
   Franklin Henry Gates                   b. Bristol NY 9 Nov 1880* or 1875 (obit)
                                          d. Santa Maria 16 Dec 1952 @77
      1909 Dir: city clk         F: John Gates    M: Matilda
      1920 cen: 405 S McClel'd Real Est. broker
      bio *Who's Who in Santa Maria, 1931; 1 birth 1 living 1910
      a.  Earl Francis, Dr                b. Santa Maria 9 Nov 1909
                                          d. (res Palos Verdes)
3. Alice M                                b. Suey district 3 March 1888 (Times)
      1910 cen: w/ parents                d. Santa Maria 17 June 1956; SM cem
      1909 Dir: telephone op, cor Lincoln/Cypress
      1902: 7th grade Suey school
            m.1
   William Grant
      1919: Local news. Mrs Wm Grant arrived from Gilroy to visit her parents
            Mr and Mrs R W Earl.                        - Santa Maria Times Nov 10
         m.2 after 1920
   Howard A Frew                          b. (PA) 2 Aug 1893
      1940 Dir: Union Sugar                d. Santa Maria 9 May 1957; SM cem
      1951 Dir: 516 E Orange; Real Estate 119A E Church, SM
            No issue
4. John Robert (Bob)                      b. Suey district 20 Aug 1889 (Times)
                                          d. Santa Maria 9 June 1962; SM cem
      1902: 5th gr Suey sch, res 535 Perkins Los Alamos
      1910: cen: w/parents
      1918: … arrived from ranch near Sacramento …        - Santa Maria Times Dec 28
      1920 cen: Sacramento; also Chancy Earl, uncle; Hazel Eames, 24, cousin
      1939 Dir: Tepusquet
      1947 Dir: 2 listings. Supt SPRock & Granit, 406 E Tunnell SM;
            w/FH Gates & Co, 621 E Central
         m. 29 Oct 1916
      Clara Belle French                  b. CA/IL 6 Sep 1883/4
                                          d. Santa Maria 6 Dec 1956; SM cem
                                          F: Charles French 1866-1920
                                          M: Ada Brookshire 1876-
                                          m.1 (Stevenson)
                                             = Fred Stevenson
                                             = Marion (called Earl) (Ray Hardy)
                                                + Robert Ray Hardy b. 1932
                                                   m. Mary Jane Bianchi 1932-1981
```

5. Lottie L   b. nr Garey 27 Aug 1893; m.1 @20 of SM
     1902: 2d gr Suey sch   d. Santa Maria 20 Jan 1986 @93
     1909 Dir: stu cor Lincoln/Cypress w/Alice
        m. Santa Maria 9 Aug 1914 by Wm F S Nelson
   Aten E Johnston   b. Burnett TX 14 Feb 1888, m. @26, of SM
     1930 Dir: 415 S Lincoln   d. east of SM 24 Aug 1941; hunting
     1940 Dir: same; he w/Bradley Brbr & Beauty Shop; she slsldy Ames & Harris
   a. inf dau   d. 7 Apr 1920; SM cem
   b. Alberta <u>Maxine</u>
     1940 Dir: stu w/parents
     James F Hoey   b. 1919
       1956: in Portland OR   F: Ray E Hoey b. 1891
                                       M: Emma L Pfeiffer
                                           bio *Who's Who in Santa Maria*, 1931
     1950 Dir: Lottie Johnston 314 N Miller SM
      m.2 Harrison/Hoefling (in Porterville 1956)
      m.3
     Guillermo/Wm Roman Ruiz   b. Garey 2 Aug 1896
       See Ontiveros, *San Ramon*   d. Santa Maria 4 July 1985
         Chapel Pioneers   F: Caesario Antonio Ruiz 1871-1916
                                           M: Maria Anita Felicidad Vidal 1866-1924
                                              m.1 Dora Sanchez 1901-1933
                                              m.2 Nellie Forrester

Vol. XXV, No. 3 & 4, 1993, p.18

Corrections and Additions   [Page numbers refer to those in Quarterly]

Duncan Earl family
2.   Mary Olive Earl
       John Hugh Winters   b. Amboy IL
          Bio Phillips pp. 362-4   F: Wyman W Winters of Philadelphia
                                           M. Mary Churchill, born England

Mary Winters' recollections were printed in Vol., XIII No. 2, as copied from the *Santa Maria Times* Pioneer Edition, 1938. The *Review* 1938, Santa Maria Union High School yearbook, was dedicated to Mrs Winters, and a full page photograph was included.

Vol. XXVI, No. 1, Spring 1994, p. 5

p.13.   Mrs Duncan Earl, who had been suffering from a lame shoulder for several months, planning to go to Newsom's Warm Springs for treatment when Dr Lucas discovered it was a dislocated shoulder.   –50 Years Ago Oct 1 1940
        Surprise Birthday Party for Esther Earl @75   –article Apr 17 1909
        John Hugh Winters; Mrs Johnny Winters met with a serious accident on Thursday last. While out riding on horseback the saddle turned which threw her off and resulted in breaking her right ankle.   –Sep 17 1887
        Former Santa Marian Is Considered "Brains" of Bay City Police Force. Police Lt Frank Winters, detective bureau … son of Mrs M O Winters of south Lincoln st …
        -article under San Francisco News Wed Jan 15 1930 p.2
        Frank E Winters, Lt SFPD, retired, died in San Francisco 1965. Late wife Beatrice; grandchildren Constance Halter, Rudolf G Luft and Frank F Luft; 11 ggch. Cypress Lawn Mem Park.   –*San Francisco Chronicle* Wed Apr 7 1965 p.22

Vol. XXX, No. 1, Spring 1998, pp.9, 10

Mr & Mrs E F Maxson and children visiting Mrs J H Winters, returned to Los Angeles; Mrs Maxson is principal of a school in Whittier. —Sep 1 1923

Mrs M Maxson of Los Angeles visiting Mr & Mrs Alex Findley. —Dec 2 1936

p.14. The children of Lillian Earl and William Alexander Findley are Earl, Hazel, Helen (Haines), and Ella J (Hoyt V Law). Hazel was born in Santa Maria 6 Aug 1917, and died here 19 Dec 1997; she married Conrad W Kurtz in 1939. Their children are Lillian R Aughe, George L Kurtz, of Orcutt, Joyce K Chrisman of Santa Maria, and Earl C Kurtz of Arroyo Grande; 11 gch, 17 ggch. Surviving are the husband, and sister, Ella Law, as well as the children. —Mon Dec 22 1997 A-5

Hoyt Vernard Law died in 1986 @72.

Scorched by Flames at Home of Chauncy Earl ... his sister, Mrs Matt Jessee, nearly burned to death ... poured a cup of gasoline into a pail of hot water ... caught fire. —Nov 16 1907

The 1940 SMUHS *Review* was dedicated to Dave Boyd; the football field was given his name in 1948. Son Dempster Boyd was born in Oakland 8 Nov 1918. *-SM Times*

Dave Boyd died in 1963; in Santa Maria 65 years. (leaving out the time in Oakland—Ed.) Spanish-American war. Son Harold in Ventura, son Dempster with US Army, Germany. 5 gch 2 ggch –Fri Dec 20 p.12. When Carrie died, Dempster was in Tacoma; she had 5 gch 11 ggch.
—1978 obit SMVHS scrapbook

Farewell Party for Mrs Elizabeth Jessee at Home of Mr & Mrs Henry Strong 610 S Lincoln ... going to San Jose. —July 30 1919

See also Morrison chart. *Note*: Edith Jessee and Grace Morrison grad SMUHS 1919, went to Heald's Business College, per 1920 *Review*. Mama must have gone as chaperone.

Mrs Lizabeth (sic) Jessee has sold her home on E Cook to Ben Chacon and bought lots on S McClelland st where she expects to build a modern bungalow. —Jan 1920

When Lizzie Jessee died in 1947, she was survived by her daughter, Mrs Turnage, with whom she made her home, Mrs Edna Law of Lafayette LA, and son Ray of Hayfork CA; 6 gch, 3 ggch. —Sat Aug 29 p.1

Nightwatchman Matt Jessee has purchased an elegant new uniform with a helmet. He looks like a real policeman. –June 11 1907. *Note*: This must be what he was wearing in the photo accompanying his obituary. He was survived by Mrs Essie McMichael of Santa Maria; C L Jessee, King City; Bert Jessee, Sacramento; Ray Jessee, Hayfork; Mrs Edna Law, Jennings LA; also sisters Mrs Parlee Wilkinson, Long Beach; Mrs Virginia Largo, Los Angeles; and his one surviving brother, John Victor, at death's door at the time, and J V's daughter, Mrs Elma Crakes.
—Tue Mar 23 1937 p.1

Marriage: Clarence L Jessee @26 of SM m. SLO 20 July 1912 by H H Hocker MG, I444; wit: Margaret Campbell, SLO; Mrs Hocker, SLO.   Bernice Doak b. WA m. @24 of SM

When Clarence died while visiting his daughter in Oakland 1943, Mrs Law was in Conroe TX.

(ad) Jessee & Brant Genl Blacksmiths Horseshoeing a Specialty Work promptly turned out and guaranteed. Broadway & Chapel sts Santa Maria Cal. —Sep 1912

C L Jessee bought out Brand's (sic) interest in the blacksmith and horseshoe business.
—Feb 1 1913

Bert Jessee has been entered as a clerk in the Bank of Santa Maria. —Mar 11 1905

Marriage: Hymen's Knot Tied for Popular Young Couple ... Bert Jessee eldest son (sic) of Matt Jessee, and Florence L Bonetti, daughter of J B Bonetti —Dec 23 1911

B E Jessee here from Stockton to attend the funeral of his uncle, Perry Jessee.
—Nov 12 1919

p.15   Personals. Miss Essie Jessee had the misfortune to fall and break her arm on Friday evening last at the skating rink. —Jan 16 1909

Marriage: Essie B Jessee m. @20 of SM, phone operator m. SLO 21 Nov 1910 by H Selah Munger, I99; wit: M R Winter, SM; Mrs D A Boyd, SM.   Robert C McMichael b. PA m. @25 of Los Angeles, machinist. Wedding in the parlors of the James Hotel at 2pm; to live in Los Angeles.
–*SLO Tribune* Tue Nov 22 1910

Much comment was published in the *Santa Maria Times* about the accident that killed Traffic Officer McMichael. He had but recently returned to Santa Maria as a police officer, and was chasing a speeder on west Main street when Mrs C L Preisker in a car with her sister, Miss Mary Adam, pulled a U-turn at the intersection of Main and Thornburg, not realizing that the motorcycle was fast approaching from the rear. The motorcycle struck the car, and McMichael died shortly thereafter of his injuries. Mrs Preisker was not held liable. Survivors were wife, Essie; daughter, Edith; brother Clyde McMichael, and sister, Winifred of Tulsa.
–Mon Oct 24 1932 p.1; Wed Oct 26 p.1,3; Thu Oct 27; Fri Oct 28 p.1

Edith McMichael was born in Los Angeles 11 Mar 1912, and was 7 when her parents moved to Santa Maria; later they moved to Tulsa, her father's former residence, where she was schooled, returning to Santa Maria in 1930. She died in Santa Maria 9 Feb 1996, survived by her daughters, Susan D Lowe of Santa Clara, and Berry A Eames of Santa Maria; 2 gch. –Feb 11 1996. Her husband, Bill Gregory, died in Santa Maria 14 Jan 1975, son of Frank F Gregory (1893-1957 IOOF Cem SLO) and Eva Virginia ____ (1889-1946 SM cem). Bill was survived by Edith, daughters Susan Andrade of Sunnyvale and Berry Eames of Santa Maria; brothers Irving Gregory of Hemet and Francis Gregory of Oxnard; 3 gch. (grandson Christopher Eames died in 1979.)

Miss Edna Jessee, in Oakland to visit cousin, Mrs Ruth Ruh, was forced to remain when the apartment building was quarantined ... visited by phone, also, another cousin Mrs David Boyd of Oakland.   –Paragraphs of the past 25 Years Ago Thu Oct 28 1943
Note: 1918 flu epidemic. Ruth Ruh must be the younger sister of Carrie Boyd. See p.14

Robert W Earl family
p.16.   Robert Earl gave a Christmas reception for 40 relatives. (lengthy article)   –Dec 29 1894

p.17.   Fred and Leo Earl went to the rodeo in Salinas.   –July 23 1923
Fred Earl is moving from his ranch on the Suey to the Jesus Maria ranch near Casmalia ... leased for farming ... one of the most prominent farmers on this section.   –Sat July 15 1924
F H Gates Sell Gravel Business to Southern Pacific Milling ... established 37 years ago ... (lengthy article) –Tue Jan 15 1946 *Note*: Many men whose names appear in these pages were employed by Gates and successor in Sisquoc.
Mrs Alice Grant home from Los Angeles and Santa Barbara where she visited friends.
–Mon Nov 14 1921

1922-3 Dir:	Grant Mrs Alice opr SB Tel Co r315 E Cypress	
	Frew Howard S (sic) steno P A Oil co, Casmalia	
1925 Dir:	Frew H A (Alice) bkpr Union Sugar Co r213 S Miller	

p.18.   Marriage: John Robert Earl @27 of nr SM m. nr SM 29 Sep 1916 by Wm S F Nelson, SLO co K15; wit: R W Earl, SM; Frank Gates, SM.   Belle French b. CA m. @23 of nr SM
An ad for KSMA (radio station) has a line drawing of Maxine Hoey.   –Apr 30 1955

EDMANDS
TWENTIETH CENTURY CALIFORNIA PIONEERS

    Thomas R Edmands   b. Wales; immigrated @14
      Civil War vet   d.
           m.
    Rhoda M Wilson   b. MI/WI
                             d.

1.   Fred M   b.
                             d. Santa Barbara co 4 Nov 1921 @50
2.   Chauncy T   b. IA/WI 1872
                             d. Santa Barbara 13 Aug 1922 @50; AG cem; rSanta
                                 Maria obit *SLO Daily Telegraph* Aug 15; widow, 3 ch
          1910 cen: AGpct/Huasna-Verde Cyn Rd; mason; 4 births, 4 living also bro/law Milo
             White 25
              m/3 NE IA2; Lela 25 IA3; Ray 11/12 OK
           m. 1898
      Mary H White   b. NE 4 Sep 1875; parents PA/IA
        to CA 1907   d. at home of dau Mrs T J Wright, Huasna district
                                 21 Aug 1939 @64; AG cem obit *SM Times* Wed
                                 Aug 23, p.6; 9 mos w/Wright; hus, 3 dau son 6 gch
                                 ggdau; 2 bro 2 sis in NE; n/n
          1920 cen: 121 W Morrison SM
          1922-3 Dir: Edmands Chester L drvr AM Exp r305 S Lincoln
                      Mrs Mary A (sic) hskpr r305 S Lincoln
                      Verna steno r305 S Lincoln
          1925 Dir: Mrs M H hskpr r 509 S Pine; Chester mech r same
          1928 Dir: Mrs Mary H hskpr 509 S Pine
          1930. Mrs Mary Edmands (sic), M/M Bob Wilson and little son, and Elva Thompson of
             Santa Maria visiting M/M Walter Edmands (sic).   –Nov 13
      Mary   m.2
      Harry Rollins   b. Clarion co OH* 4 Aug 1870
                                 (*no such; is it Clarion co PA?)
                                 d. at home of dau Mrs Harry Stringer, Taft, Tue 9 Sep
                                    1947 @77/1/5; SM cem; obit Thu Sep 11, p.4;
                                    12 days in Taft; 37 y CA Union Oil, ret 1935; Moose
          1922-3 Dir: Harry (Mary) pumper Orcutt; Stringer Morris H (Minnie) pipe fitter Orcutt
          1925 Dir: Harry (Mary) oil wkr Orcutt
      Mary Ann Rollins   b. Zane OH 1868 (Zanesville? Zanesfield?)
                                    d. nr Atascadero 30 June 1925 @56; SM cem
                                       obit July 1; many yrs Fox lease; son Emory, AZ
                                       dau Mrs Minnie Stringer, Taft
          1928 Dir: Harry f Orcutt
          1940-1 Dir: Harry (Mary) lab P O Box 1886 Orcutt
          1947-8 Dir: Harry ret 310 Union, Orcutt, Box 1886
          1955-6 Dir: Stringer, Minnie (wid of Henry) ret h 310 Union, Orcutt, Box 1886
          1972 Dir: same

Note: member Gerri Brown, a Santa Maria native, now of Fort Wayne IN, knew "Uncle Hal" Rollins; his family and Gerri's grandparents, Jonathan B (1884-1952) and Aley Hughes (1889-1978) came together from West Virginia to work in the Orcutt oil fields. They were close neighbors in

Orcutt, and Gerri used to play her violin for Uncle Hal; his favorite song (and hers) was "Carry Me Back to Old Virginny". However, nobody did, his bones lie in the Santa Maria cemetery, as do those of his wife, his daughter, Minnie Louise Stringer (1889-1974) and his son-in-law, Maurice Henry "Hank" Stringer (1887-1951), both born W VA. Gerri has two photos of Uncle Hal, should anyone be interested.

    a.   Gladys May   b. WY 24 Dec 1894; m. @18 of Santa Maria
                                              d. Santa Barbara co 19 Aug 1950 @55; AG cem
                                                no obit found
                m.1 (AG) 17 Dec 1913 by Edw Whitlock, ME, J82
                     wit: Geo W Hulett, AG; Lucy D Hulett, AG
            Clarence A Thompson   b. NE 1893; m. @20 of AG
             1925 Dir: C A Oil wkr   d. at res of Mrs M H Edmands 509 S Pine 4 Mar
              Orcutt   1930 @36; AG cem
             1928 Dir: C A (Gladys)   obit Thu Mar 6 p.5; widow, dau SM; mother
              pumper Union Oil Co   Mrs J M Emmert, Madera; sis Mrs Jennie
              Orcutt   Edmands, AG; bro John Thompson
                                                  (1882-1936), Berros
            = Elva   F: Jasper N Thompson 1852-1912 AG cem
                                                  M: Lydia Jane Harding 1859-1952 AG cem
              Gladys m.2   m.2 J M Emmert (see Walter's wife next page)
            T J Wright   b. CA 18 July 1892; M: Cripe
            (Thomas Jefferson)   d. SLO 5 Mar 1952; AG cem
                                                  obit Thu Mar 6 p.7; Huasna farmer 18 y
    b.   Myrna (twin)   b. Ritzville WA 27 Feb 1902
                                               d. Santa Barbara 8 Oct 1968 @68 (sic)
            1917. Promoted. 8th grade diplomas…Vyrina Edwards (sic), Myrina Edmonds (sic)
                                                                                            -June 16
            1920 cen: w/mother
            1923. M/M Arthur Torgeson (Myrna Edmands) and baby of Santa Barbara   –Dec 24
            1925 Dir: Torgeson Arthur (Myrna) mgr Wolf Auto Top Shop r509 S Pine
            1928 Dir: Torgenson (sic) A E (Myrna) Mgr Wolf's Top Shop rMayer Tract
            1928 Dir: Wolf's Auto Top Shop, A E Torgeson, mgr, 207 N Broadway
            1939 in Santa Barbara
            1948 phbk: Torg's Top Shop 423 State Street Barbara
                     Arthur E Torgeson 2435 Castillo St Santa Barbara
            1961 phbk: Torgeson Myrna 833 Kentia Av Santa Barbara
                     Torg's Automotive Paint Store 423 State St
                     Torg's Top shop 423 State St. est. 1941.
                     Torgeson Arthur jr 2435 Castillo St SB
               m. c1922
            Arthur E Torgeson   b. MN 9 June 1896; M: Peterson
                                              d. Ventura co 7 Feb 1959 @62
            = Arthur E jr   b. (SB) 2 Jan 1923
                            d. (SB) 2 Feb 1963 @40
    c.   Vyrna (twin)   b. Ritzville WA 17 Feb 1902 (sic)
            1920 cen: w/mother   d. (SM) 6 Feb 1959 @57; AG cem
            1922-3 Dir: w/mother   obit Mon Feb 9 p.8; r510 E Church; 43y SM
                                                gdau, 3 gsons
            1923. Verna (sic) Edmands and R C Wilson are visiting friends in Los Angeles and
                 Pomona.   –Sep 4

        1925. M/M R C Wilson (Verna Edmunds, sic) went to Pennsylvania to stay six
           months or a year.   –June 17
        1928 Dir: R C "Bob" (Vyrna) elec h510 E Church
        1940-1 Dir: same h501 (sic) E Church
        1947-8 Dir: Rbt C (Vyrna) elec Anderson Shop h510 E Church
           Mrs Verna (sic) record libr OLPH Hospital r510 E Church
           (Our Lady of Perpetual Help)
        1955-6 Dir: Robert C (Vyrna) cust Alvin Av Sch h501 (sic) E Church
           Vyrna ofc emp OLPH r501 E Church
      Vyrna   m. c1924
      Robert Charles Wilson   b. PA 21 Feb 1901
                            d. Santa Maria 31 Dec 1965 @63; AG cem
                                  obit Fri Jan 1 1965 p.8; SM 41y; electrician,
                                  IBEW, Eagles; dau son 4 gdau sister Mrs
                                  Jennie Ostendorf, WinterHaven FL
      = Beverly (Stone) in Santa Fe Springs CA 1959, 1965
      = Robert C jr in SM 1959, 1965
   d.   Chester L/T   b. KS 1905
        1930 Dir: C T 509 S Pine   d.
3.   Walter LeRoy   b. Cottage Grove IA 27 May 1874
      1908 to AG from Stamford NE   d. San Luis Obispo 29 Sep 1956 @82; AG cem; obit *SLO*
      1910 cen: Huasna pct, AG &   *Telegram-Tribune* Sep 29 p.2, Oct 2 p.2; *SM Times*
        SLO Rd 3 births 3 living;   Sep 29 p.1 r Huasna Rd AG; 48y AG valley; 6 gch 5
                                          5 ggch farmer
      1919. dug up Indian burials near his property on the old AG-Huasna Rd; 1951 found other
          bones.   –Ditmas p.212
      1920 cen: AG #2 teamster 4 ch at home
          m. Beaver City NE 18 Mar 1896; 50th anniversary *SB News-Press* Mar 17 1946
          son 3 dau 5 gch
      Jennie E Thompson   b. Hastings IA 23 Aug 1878
                                  d. Arroyo Grande 12 Aug 1971 @92; AG cem; obit *SLO*
                                    Telegram-Tribune 63y south county; *SM Times* Thu
                                    Aug 12 p.2; also Sat Aug 14 p.4; 4211 E Branch AG;
                                    63y SLO co; 2 dau 5 gch 10 ggch
                                  F: Jasper N Thompson 1852-1912; AG cem
                                  M: Lydia Jane Harding 1859-1952; AG cem
                                    obit Sat Jan 12 1952 p.8; b. Boskobell (=Boscobel)
                                    WI Sep 1859; to AG 1903; to Madera w/Emmert;
                                    returned c1942. F: Stephen D Harding 1832-1907;
                                    M: Nancy Virginia 1833-1906; brother Charles
                                        Harding, Canada. 10 gch 16 ggch 4 gggch
                                  m.2 Jonathan Masterson Emmert
                                          b. IL 28 Feb 1853; d. Madera 2 July 1942
                                                1902 GR: Jonathan M 49 pct Los Osos PO SLO
   a.   Edgar Y   b. Stamford NE 12 Mar 1897
                                  d. AG 18 Sep 1970 @73; AG cem; obit *SLO*
                                    Telegram-Tribune Sat Sep 19 p.4; 62y AG;
                                    r146 LePoint st; wid dau 3 sis 1 gch
        1915. Arroyo Grande: Walter Edmands exhibited a 4-point buck head in Commercial
            store window, killed by son Edgar on Porter Ranch.   –Nov 10

1930. M/M Edgar Edmonds (sic) and little daughter of SLO visited his parents
M/M Walter Edmonds and her parents M/M Ellis Coale. —Nov 13

Edgar m.
 Elizabeth Louella Coale   b. Long Beach CA 14 June 1907
     d. AG Nov 1988 @81; AG cem
      obit Fri Nov 25 p.10; rGrover City. 3 sis,
      gdau Sharon Brazell, ggson Joseph Darrell
      Brazell, SLO
     F: Ellis Pusy Coale
      b. Huntington IN 23 July 1868; M: Moore
      d. Santa Maria 1 Mar 1965 @96; AG cem
      obit Tue Mar 2 p.2; 5 dau son 10gson 5gdau
      17ggch 3gggch
     M: Grace Lowenza (sic) Rowley
      b. IL 27 Aug 1873; M: Swan
      d. Napa at home of dau Rowley
       4 Mar 1952 @70; AG cem
       obit Thu Mar 6 p.7; 5 dau son 15 gch
       14ggch
     1. Edna Mae Coale 1895-1986
      (Robert Oscar Schilling 1890-1970)
     2. Charlotte Irene Coale 1898-1990
      (Wm L J Barker 1897-1961)
     3. Dorothy Noel Coale 1902-1998
      (Gerald or Gerard S Dana 1896-1972)
     4. Herbert Ellis Coale 1897-1976
      (Jeanette DeVries 1897-1994)?
      1852 in Martin (Marin) City; 1965 in San
      Anselmo
     5. Elizabeth
     6. Lucille (C) Coale 1910-1993
      (James E Rowley Jr -1964) or is this a son?
     all in AG cem except Herbert
  = Barbara (Blumhorst) single 1946; in AG 1970, 1988
   1999 phbk: Blumhorst Harry Edward 707 Bennett Av AG
b. Velma Idelle   b. NE 26 Feb 1899; m. @20 of AG
     d. SLO 11 Jan 1971 @71; AG cem;
      surname Rodoni; obit Wed Jan 13 p.4; ret reg
      nurse r535 Traffic Way AG space 9; 54y
      SLO co; mother, 2 sis

  1946 Velma Cipresso in San Jose?
   (Francesco Cipresso 1899-1941? Battista Becoi Cipresso 1897-1947?)
  1956 Velma Rodoni in Petaluma
  1970 AG
   m.1 (Arroyo Grande) 21 Jan 1920 by Edwin Whitlock, AG ME ch, L179
    wit: A E Henderson, SLO; David W Harding, AG. (David Winslow Harding
    1866-1939 AG cem; Alva Edgar Henderson 1878-1959, Henderson is Stuart's
    brother-in-law)
   Stuart Elwood Hampton   b. (See Cyn) 19 Aug 1896; m. @23 of SLO
     d. SLO 18 Apr 1966; IOOF cem
     F: Valentine Austin Hampton 1844-1911

                                          M: Fanny Bolen 1857-1919
       Velma m.2
       Leo R Rodoni   b. CA 19 Apr 1906; M: Crrea
                                         d. SLO 7 July 1965 @59; AG cem

  c.   Bernice Chlorus (sic)   b. Stamford NE 9 Feb 1908
       1946 Holmes AG   d. 12 May 1987 @79; AG cem
       1956 Lapp AG   obit Wed May 13 p.10; to AG @9 mos
       1970 Holmes AG
       1971 Holmes AG
       m.
       Floyd Glenn Holmes   b. Youngstown KS 17 June 1901
                                         d. (AG) 12 Sep 1954; AG cem
                                         obit Mon Sep 13 p.8; 28y AG; supt Mechs,
                                         US Disciplinary Barracks, Lompoc. wf dau
                                         son AG, son Korea; 2 bro 6 sis 3 gch
     = Elta Lea (Murphy) in AG 1946, 1987
     = Floyd Leroy 10 May 1930 – 24 Mar 1961; AG cem
     = Kay Allen Cpl US Army Korea 1954
  d.   Lenora Irma   b. (AG) 3 Jan 1914
                                         d. San Jose 8 Oct 1985; surname Nelson
       1930. M/M Walford Maguire of SLO visiting her parents M/M Walter
           Edmonds (sic).   –Nov 13
       1946, 1956 in San Jose, surname Menzie
         (Henry A Menzie 1907-1965)?
       1970, 1971 in San Jose, surname Nelson
     = Henry Edmond Menzie living 1946
4.   Myron Wilson   b. Iowa Falls IA 13 Oct 1877
                                       d. San Luis Obispo 14 Aug 1952 @74; AG cem
                                       obit Fri Aug 15 p.11; 14y AG, formerly of Colorado,
                                       wf, 4 dau 2 sons, bros Walter & John, both AG
                                       11gch 6ggch
       m.
       Lucinda/Lula L Smith   b. NE 21 Jan 1885
                                       d. San Luis Obispo 19 Aug 1956 @71; AG cem
                                     obit Tue Aug 21 p.8; 14y AG from Colorado 4 dau
                                     2 sons bro Otis Smith, NE
  a.   Mrs Virgie Martin in AG 1952, 1956
  b.   Mrs Dorothy Lambeth in AG 1952, 1956
  c.   Mrs Lois Casady in AG 1952, Shell Beach 1956
  d.   Mrs Lena Shaffer in Denver 1952, Colorado 1956
  e.   Loren Oscar   b. NE 22 Oct 1905
       in AG 1952, 1956   d. Santa Cruz co 29 Apr 1980
  f.   Merl in Denver 1952, 1956
5.   John Delos   b. NE 1 Dec 1887
                                     d. Santa Cruz 10 Nov 1953 @65; AG cem
                                   obit Thu Nov 12 p.8; 44y AG valley wf Dora,
                                   Boulder Creek; bro Walter, AG
      1939. Arroyo Grande Feb 13: M/M John Edmands of Monterey are guests of M/M
          Walter Edmands.
        m. (after 1926)
      Dora Logan   b. (Orcutt) 14 Oct 1888

                d. Santa Maria 13 Sep 1979 @94; SM cem
                   obit Sat Sep 15 p.12; 2 sons 3 dau 17 gch 36 ggch
                   20 gggch; sis Amyee Dierlan (sic), Bakersfield
                F: John Hulet/Hugh Logan 1859-1933
                M: Emily J Garrett 1863-1897
     1933 Dora Edmands in Watsonville CA

Note: See the Hopper, Logan, and Garrett charts. Dora's death date on California records was given as Sep 23, so no obituary was found then; however, more careful search of the *Santa Maria Times* turned up the correct date, Sep 13, which opened up additional windows, so the following is presented in detail as both additions and corrections to the Logan chart.

Logan chart: Aymee Gene Logan Dierlam died in Bakersfield 3 Sep 1986 @96; last residence Tooele Utah; buried Bakersfield; brief notice *Bakersfield Californian* Sep 5.

    Dora m.1 Santa Maria 5 Apr 1903 (*Times*)
    Frederick E Strong   b. (Butte co) 8 June 1879
                                        d. San Mateo co 3 Nov 1957
      1880 cen: Butte co   F: John Henry Strong 1833-1927
       Kimshaw tp Paradise   M: Mary Emily Calkins 1845-1937
       Ridge   m.2 1894 Charles Haskell Clark 1838-1900
      1900 cen: w/mother Santa Maria
      1906 Dir: Fred & Mrs lab SM; also listed in Orcutt
      1909. Fred Strong back from Maricopa co (sic: it's Mariposa); bought a ranch, will move
          after settling affairs in Orcutt.   –Apr 17? 24?
        Note: Fred moved to Indian Peak, Mariposa co, where already had settled Hopper
        and Logan relatives; see Logan chart.
      1910 cen: Mariposa co Indian Peak tp 4 births 4 living
      1914 Dir: Fred (Dora) house mover r301 E Mill
           Logan Hugh (Nettie) house mover h301 E Mill
      1920 cen: SM
      1922-3 Dir: F E (Dorac-sic) wet wash 601 W Fesler
      1925 Dir: F E (Dora) engineer r601 W Fesler
      1926. Notice. I will not be responsible for any debts contracted by any one except
          myself. Dated Oct 20 1926. F E Strong   –Oct 20 and repeated
      1937. in SM one of 127 descendants of Mary Clark; children of Fred born in SM; Mrs
          Jennie Reims (sic). Emory and Freddie Strong, Mrs Mona Truesdale, Mrs Dorothy
          Crews, Edith Strong.   –(Mrs Clark' obituary Tue Apr 27 1937 p.1)
      1956 in Redwood City
   a.   Emily Jennie   b. SM 6 Nov 1904 (*Times*)
       (Genevieve)   d. Oberlin LA 17 Nov 2001; surname Rheams
        1979 Genevieve Rheams, Mittel LA
   b.   Emery H   b. SM 21 Aug 1906 (*Times*)
       1979 in Boulder Ck   d. Boulder Creek 26 Aug 1987; spouse MT
   c.   Mona G   b. SM (1908)
       1979 in SM   d. probably still living, in San Jose (?)
       m.
       Thomas Elmo Truesdale   b. Shandon 12 Oct 1902
                                          d. SM 19 Apr 1970 @67/6/7; SM cem
                                            obit Tue Apr 21 p.2; 34y SM; 42y Union Oil
                                            ret 1965. wid 3 dau 3 bro 2 sis parents
                                          F: Willis Truesdale 1872-1974; Shandon cem

        M: Zora Grainger 1874-1974; Shandon cem
        see M/H; also *The Lands of Mission San*
        Miguel, Ohles, 1997, pp.249, 250; photo
        Note: Truesdale twins, Willis and Hillis m. 1895
        Grainger twins, Zora and Nora.
        twins Lillie and Millie Truesdale, infants
        d. 1900; Shandon cem

   1970. Survivors: Orville Truesdale (1904-1987), Bakersfield; Clarence Truesdale,
      AG; George Truesdale (1909-1982), Buellton; Mrs Ruth (1912-1989)
      Jacobson, Cottonwood; Mrs Bernice (1900-1989) Anderson, Atascadero;
      parents Palo Robles; 9gch

      Pall bearers: Phillip C Reiner, W A Word, Chester A Davis, Donald E
      Thomas, Edward J Pryor, Louis Grabil. Honorary: K E Trefts, M J Stephan,
      M W Hite, DeWitt Meredith, Arnold L Nickson, Marian (sic) A Smith, J P
      Fraser, Vernon R Edwards, H B Hughes, Ray A Olson, W D Wisener,
      Dewitt (sic) G Deming, John D Wilkins, Hugh O Pope jr

  1938-9 Dir: Truesdale Thos E pumper U Oil co 213 A W Morrison
  1940-1 Dir: Thos E (Mona G) engnr U Oil co h524 E Central
  1945-6 Dir: same; 1947-8 Dir: same
  1955-6 Dir: Thos E h904 N Elm Belva emp Arrow Photo r904 N Elm
  1970 Dir: Thoms E (Mona G) ret h904 Elm ave
  1976 Dir: Mona G wid ret 904 Elm;   1979 in SM;   1982 Dir: 904 Elm
= Belva (Reik) SMUHS 1953, in Fairfax MO 1970
= Sharon (Boydstun) in San Jose 1970
    1955-6 Dir: Boydstun Able L (Lilly M) oil wkr Pac WO Corp h700 E Cypress
      Thos E stu r 700 E Cypress
    1970 in San Jose Thomas Boydstun tchr Cupertino
= Linda m. 1960 Manoah (Robbie) Robison police officer
    SMUHS 1959; in San Jose 1969, 1970; Boulder Creek 1984

    d.   Frederick E   b. SM 4 Mar 1910
                                        d. (Prunedale) 21 Aug 1993
      1928 Dir: Fred lab r609 W Cypress (father or son?)
      1934. Mrs Fred Strong's father died in Denver Friday.   –Mon Mar 26
      1938-9 Dir: Fred E (Edith A) emp S B Co h513 W Park; 1940-1 Dir: same
      1979 in Salinas
        Note: Edith Strong is listed as a survivor of Mrs Clark, 1937, but not mentioned
          in Dora Edmands's obituary

    e.   Dorothy/Dorothea E   b. SM (1913)
      1937 Dorothy Crews   d. (Dorothy E Hatch 7 July 1912-11 Mar 1999
                                                 Fresno)?
      1945-6 Dir: Hatch Wm E (Dorothy) major Air Corp Base h514 E Cook
      1979 Dorothy Hatch in Huntington Beach

ELVIDGE
SANTA MARIA VALLEY POINEERS

Joseph Elvidge   b. England 11 Apr 1859; imm 1889
- 1900 cen: tp 7 (SM)   d. Santa Maria 18 Mar 1922 @62; SM cem
- 1906 Dir: 5m SW   obit Sat Mar 18 p.1; FOE #7741
- 1910 cen: Orcutt pct   res lower Orcutt Rd
- 1922 Dir: Orcutt Rd farmer
- 1922: siblings John, Mrs Sarah Marshall, Mrs Anne Surgy, England; Charlie, South Africa
  m. England c1879

Stella Spencer   b. England 13 May 1860
- 1926 Dir: Mrs Joe hskpr   d. at home 15 Jan 1930 @69; SM cem
  lower Orcutt Rd   obit Thu Jan 16 p.4. 41 yrs in SM
- 1930: siblings Mrs S R Waite,   F: _____ Spencer
  SM; 1 bro, 2 sis in   M: Elizabeth 1815-1914
  England   m.2 Paul Bradley 1820-1890; bio Storke 419
                             3 dau: Mrs Seth Waite, Mrs Jos Elvidge, SM;
                              Mrs John Graham, Los Angeles

1900, 1910: 9 births, 9 living

1. Sarah Elizabeth   b. Nottinghamshire Eng 14 Feb 1881; imm @6
   bio M/H 943; trustee   d. Visalia CA 8 June 1966 @85/3/24; SM cem
   Washington Sch Dist   obit Thu June 9 p.10. 2 gch
   left SM 1953; in Oakdale 1961; in Visalia 1962
   m. Santa Maria 25 March 1908
   George W Chaffin 1881-1953   See Chaffin chart
   a. Lela Vivian (Hudson)
   b. George William

2. Joseph   b. England 30 March 1883; imm @6
   - 1900 cen: w/parents   d. in a So Cal hospital @69/11/16; bur
   - 1910 cen: w/parents   19 Mar 1953 SM cem. obit Tue Mar 17 p.8
   - 1922 Dir: Casmalia   ranch lower Orcutt Rd
   - 1930 Dir: SM
   (infant of Joseph Elvidge b. Aug 29 1920; bur Aug 30 SM cem)

3. William   b. England 8 July 1885
   - 1900, 1910, 1920 cen: d. at home 29 Apr 1961 @75/9/21; SM cem
     w/parents   obit Mon May 1 p.2. 70 yrs SM. 2gch 4ggch
   - 1940-1 Dir: lower Orcutt   res 115 S Vine SM. Pioneer Assn
     Rd, farmer
   m. (after 1924)
   Nell_____   b. Carrollton AR 18 March 1884
   to SM 1924   d. Santa Barbara 2 Jan 1969 @84/9/25; SM cem
   1945-6 Dir: Wm (Nell) emp   obit Fri Jan 3 p.2; res 1866 S Bwy
   Paramount Clnrs h 115 S Vine
   1969: survivors sisters Mrs Helen Potter, Fairplay MO; Mrs Dixie Stover, Long Beach CA;
   niece Sue Howell (?), Escondido; gch Edwin M Johnson, Hemet, Ida Mae Tinsley, SM
   4ggch
   a. (her dau) Ida Mae   b. Boone AR 18 May 1909; to SM @13
      Ida Mae's Gown Shop   d. SM 27 Nov 1978 @69/6/9; SM cem
      217 S Bwy 20 yrs   obit Tue Nov 28 p.10. 3 gch 1ggch
      m.

      Edwin William Johnson   b. Santa Barbara 6 Nov 1910
        1933 K of P; 201 E Cook   d. San Luis Obispo 10 July 1968 @57/8/2
        1940-1 Dir: Mgr Sanitary   SM cem. obit Thu July 11 p.2; 2 gch
          Lndy & Linen Sply   F: Edwin Siegfried Johnson 1882-1964
          r301 E Cook   bio Phillips 1 427
        1955-6 Dir: Sanitary Lndy   M: Elise Hagen 1891-1972
          & Clnr r801 S McClelland
     =Edwin M "Buzz" living in Hemet 1968, 1969; Atascadero 1978
    Note: Johnsons owned the house at 201 E Cook st, built by Rembusch (see Adam chart) until it was moved out for the construction of the Mall; Eddie's home on S McClelland was the "castle" built by E D Rubel.

4.   George   b. England 11 Jan 1888; to SM @1
     1910 cen: w/parents; also   d. Santa Maria 14 Aug 1953 @65/6/15; SM cem
       w/Geo Chaffin   obit Sat Aug 15 p.8; Mon Aug 17 p.8; res 221 E Cook
     1920 cen: Pct #5 Co Rd   retired to Cook st from farm
     1945-6 Dir: RR #2 Box 338;   1945 phbk: Newlove Dr
       m. c1919; divorced?
     Annie Agnes   b. San Francisco 15 Dec 1890
                                       d. 18 Nov 1954 @63/11/3; SM cem; obit Sat Nov 20 p.8
                                       5 gch, 35 yrs SM; sis Mrs R D Dickinson, San Fran
       a. (her dau) Helen Caughell (Madsen) b. CA c1912; F: OR
         SMUHS 1928; CSF Seal Bearer; living in Bell Gardens 1953, 1954
       b. (her son) Jewel A Caughell   b. CA 28 July 1915
     Note: 1910 census shows two Caughell   d. 15 Mar 1989; SSDI; living in Crescent City 1954
       families in Eureka/Humboldt Co   (or Garberville); Richardson Grove 1953
       1940-1 Dir: Jewel N ser sta opr Gen Del SM
       c. George jr   b. c1922
         SMUHS 1941   d. in action WWII, Navy

5.   Stella Myrtle   b. (Santa Maria) 6 Jan 1890; m. @22 of Orcutt
     1910 cen: w/parents   d. (Walnut Creek) CA 6 Apr 1984; SSDI; living in
                                       Richmond 1950, Walnut Creek 1953, 1961, 1962, 1966
        m. San Luis Obispo 12 June 1912 by Gustav Kirchner, Ev-Luth Ch, I429
          wit: Ruth Elvidge, Orcutt; Bertha Kirchner, SLO
     Charles C. Garing   b. PA 24 Aug 1882; m. @29 of Orcutt
     1920 cen: Kern Co, foreman   d. (Concord) CA 18 Oct 1975; SSDI
       machine shop, Std Oil Co Pipe   living in Bakersfield 1922, 1930
       Line Dept, Fuel Oil Depot
       a. Merrill/Merle Ward   b. 22 Aug 1913; SSDI
                                       d. (Walnut Creek) 12 May 1994

6.   Spencer John   b. Santa Maria 5 March 1892 (*Times*)
     1917: of Orcutt, drafted   d. Santa Maria 18 Aug 1962 @70/5/13; SM cem
       18 Aug (*Times*)   obit Mon Aug 20 p.2; res 868 Lakeview Rd
     1920 cen: w/parents   County Parks & Rec Dept – Waller Park
     1940-1 Dir: farmer Gen Del SM
     1955-6 Dir: 860 Lakeview Rd; single

7.   Ruth   b. (Santa Maria) 7 April 1895; SSDI
     1920 cen: w/parents   d. Riverside Co 22 Dec 1983; SS benefits to Orcutt
        m. San Luis Obispo 18 Aug 1920 –25 Yrs Ago, Sat Aug 18 1945
     Alfred Tomasini   b. (Guadalupe) 4 Nov 1893; SSDI
     1922, 24: Casmalia   d. Riverside Co 19 Sep 1982

	1930, 1950, 1953, 1961, 1962: Wilmington	F:	Abramo Tomasini 1860-1924
		M:	Teresa 1874-1955
8.	Catherine J	b.	at home lower Orcutt Rd 24 Apr 1897
	1920 cen: w/parents	d.	Santa Maria 23 Nov 1950 @53/6/29; SM cem
	1922: SM		obit Fri Nov 24 p. 3. res 317 E Cook St
	1930: Wilmington		Culinary Alliance
	single		
9.	Mariellen	b.	(Santa Maria) 2 Dec 1899; SSDI
	1920 cen: w/parents	d.	Dec 1983; SS benefits to Orcutt
	1922: SM single		

1930 Dir: r Orcutt Rd, single
1926 Dir: Miss Mary E tel op lower Orcutt Rd
   m. (after 1930)

Harvey <u>Deane</u> Walker		b.	Guadalupe 15 Oct 1899
		d.	Santa Maria 7 May 1996 @ 96
			obit Thu May 9. 3gch, 2ggch
		F:	Robert Oliver Walker 1866-1945
		M:	Mary Irene Laughlin 1869-1950

1930 Dir: Walker's Hiway Groceteria, Orcutt
1940-41 Dir: Vic & Deane Mkt 125 Clark av, Orcutt; r 137 Clark av
   (Deane Walker & Vic Osborn, props—brothers-in-law)
1955-6 Dir: merch; h 105 N Gray, Orcutt
   See *Old Town Orcutt*, Nelson, 1987

a. Jay D		living in Santa Maria 1996
1950: USAF Philippines		
b. Roberta (Allison)	b.	1936
SMUHS 1954	d.	at home May 1993; @57; SM cem
		obit Mon May 3 A5
		3 nephews, 1 cousin

Vol. XXVIII, No. 3, Fall 1996, p. 13

Corrections and Additions   [Page numbers refer to those in Quarterly]

p.11.   Marriage: William Elvidge married Nell Melfert of Whittier in SLO; wit: Mr & Mrs F L Tilley.   –Tue May 27 1924

p.12.   Marriage: George Elvidge m. SLO Wed Jan 16 1919 Mrs Annie A Caughell, widow of late Ensign Caughell, sister of Mrs R D Dickinson.   –Sat Jan 18 p.5

   Mr & Mrs George Elvidge and children of Casmalia visited Mr & Mrs R D Dickinson in Santa Maria – the wives are sisters.   –1925

   1925 Dir: Dickinson R D (Sarah) lumberman r708 S Lincoln; Miss Margaret, stu

Vol. XXIX, No. 4, Winter 1997, p.19

FINE
CALIFORNIA PIONEERS

Irby Hoyt Fine b. TN Feb 1821
  d. Paso Robles Rancho 23 Apr 1879 @58; Cambria cem
  notice *SLO Tribune*

  Bancroft's Pioneer Register and Index: Fine J H (sic) 1846 nat of KY; claimant for Suisun rancho; d. Paso de Robles 1879 @58

  Land Grants In Alta California, Perez, 1996: Suisun (Fine) Solano co; Grantee, Solano, Francisco 1/28/1842; Patentee, Fine J H (sic) 12/16/1882
    Commission 660, Expediente 266, 482. 19 acres. District Court 396 ND
    Appeal Dismissed by District Court

  To CA from MO w/Lilburn W Boggs' party, which also included the A C Jessee family who later settled in the Santa Maria valley. Fines settled first in Sonoma; 7 children

  1850 cen: Sonoma co: J H (sic) Fine 29 TN, Elizabeth 21 KY, William 2 CA
  1860 cen: Sonoma co Vallejo tp PO Petaluma: Holt (sic) Fine 38 f 7000 4000 TN wf 7 ch
  1875 Paulson Dir: I H Fine farmer Morro
    m. KY 1844

Mary Elizabeth b. KY 1829; m. @15
  d. at home of dau Sherwood Santa Barbara 16 Dec 1920
lived w/DeNise 1898-1909 @91/5/23; SM cem. obit *SM TIMES* Fri Dec 17 p.1;
1909 to Santa Barbara also *SM Vidette* Wed Dec 22 p.1. 3 dau
  m.2 @58 1887 Morgan B Martin 1826-1898;
  Cambria cem 1890 GR: Morgan B Martin 61 MO
  saloonkpr Cambria; reg July 19 1887

1. William b. (Sonoma) 1848
2. Caroline (twin) b. Sonoma co 18 Jan 1850
  d. Berkeley 14 Feb 1938 @83; SM cem
    m. Cambria 10 Feb 1874 by O S Palmer, A180
      wit: Elias Conway, Cambria; Fannie Fine, Cambria
  Charles Sloan DeNise 1843-1912; see DeNise chart
3. Elizabeth (twin) b. Sonoma co 18 Jan 1850
  d. San Francisco 28 Dec 1916 @66
    1910. Twins 60th Birthday: Mrs C S DeNise, Santa Maria, Mrs Fred Engles (sic), San Luis Obispo; born Sonoma co, first white children after the raising of the Bear Flag. –*SLO Telegram* in *SM Times* Jan 22
    m.
Frederick Phillip Engels b. NY 1847
  d. San Francisco 18 Sep 1923 @76
  1890 GR: Frederick P Engels 37 NY saloonkpr Beach; reg July 21 1887
  1892 GR: Frederick Phillip Engels 43 5'11¾ ruddy complexion grey eyes grey hair
    saloonkpr NY res Pismo pct Beach PO Arroyo Grande; reg Sep3
  1902 GR: Fred P 52 SLO #3
  a. Irby H(oyt) Engels b. CA Apr 1872
  d. San Francisco 25 Mar 1934 @61
    1900 cen: Avila, Asst light hs kpr; 1 birth 1 living
    1902 GR: Irby H 30 Beach pct PO Pt Harford
      m. Pismo 18 Sep 1892, D188
    Elizabeth Peppermon b. CA Aug 1875
      (Pepperman?) d. San Francisco 21 Aug 1934 @58
    = Angelica L Engels b. CA Aug 1892 (cen)

4. Frances — b. Petaluma 1852
   1920 in Santa Barbara — d. Santa Maria 4 Jan 1927 @74/4/23; SM cem obit Tue Jan 4 p.2; new home W Chapel; svl yrs SM; 2 sisters, nieces/nephews
   m.
   C E Sherwood (Charles E Sherwood d. San Benito co 17 May 1913 @73)?
5. Josephine Fine — b. (Petaluma) c1854
   1920 in Grangeville ID — d.
   1927 in Seattle
   m.
   George Washington Vaughan — b. MS c1838; parents TN
     1880 cen: San Simeon tp — d.
     1890 GR: 53 5'10 fair haz grey scar on wrist l h dairy MS Cayucos Cayucos Cayucos; reg Sep 2
   a. Alison — b. CA c1875
   b. Martin — b. CA c1877
   c. Ray — b. CA Mar 1880
6. Martin E — b. (Petaluma) c1856
   — d. (before 1920)
   1890 GR: 31 CA dairy Cambria; reg Oct 21 1887
7. Emma Fine — b. (Petaluma) c1858

FLECK
GUADALUPE PIONEERS

John Fleck   b. Johnstown PA (obit) Somerset co (cem) 1820
   1860 cen: SCz co SCz tp   d. Guadalupe 16 June 1891 @71/3/26; Guad cem
     millwright w/Rbt Woodcock   Dolcini plot. obit June 20
     (a miller) & family   rheumatic sufferer.   F&AM
   to Guadalupe 1872
   1879 GR: 58 millwright PA Guadalupe
   1880 cen: Guadalupe
   1890 GR: 73 PA millwright Guadalupe
     m. (Santa Cruz) after 1860
Mary Theresa Clark   b. NY (cen) or Co Cavan IR (cem/*Who's Who* SM)
   1860 cen: SCz dressmaker   17 Mar 1840
     w/David Post family   d. (Guadalupe) 20 Oct 1901; Guad cem
   1880: 5 ch; 1900: 6 births 6 living   F: IR; M: Julia (in SCz 1860)
1. Henrietta Mary   b. Santa Cruz June 1864; m. @17
    Confirmed Guadalupe   d. Guadalupe 3 May 1919 @54; Guad cem
    8 Jul 1877 @13; sponsor   obit Mon May 5 p.2
    Elizabeth Adams (sic)
      m. Guadalupe 6 Dec 1881 by M Lynch, B579
         wit: Joseph Dolcini,
         Theresa Fleck
Henry Dolcini   b. Switzerland 1853; m. @28
   1880: Guad milker @27   d. Guadalupe 23 Nov 1893 @40; Guad cem; Masonic
     also Joe Dolcini 35, Felipe Dolcini 25, milkers   funeral
   1900: Guad 6 births 6 living
    a. Leonora D   b. Oct 1882 (living in SF 1952)
      nurse   d. (before 1961)?
    b. Mabel D   b. 5 Feb 1884 (Co birth rec)
      nurse   d. (before 1961)? (living in SF 1952)
    c. (Alice) Corinne   b. nr Guad 9 Sep 1885 (*Times*)
      Confirmed St Pat's Ch AG   d. SM 19 Nov 1977 @92; Guad cem
      7 Oct 1901 @16; sponsor   obit Mon Nov 21 p.16, Nov 22 p.5
      Asunta Grisingher   bio O'Neill 98: Flecks PA Dutch
      Post Mistress Guadalupe 1915-1945
      Norte Dame College, San Jose
      Single
    d. Henry J   b. (Guad) 14 Oct 1886
      1906 Dir: stu Guad   d. 6 Sep 1961 @74
      1940-1 Dir: clk PO Guad   obit Thu Sep 7 p.2
      1947-8 Dir: Asst PO Guad   1919: 316 Engs, 91st Div, France
         home for mother's funeral
        m.
      Minette A Dana   b. (Nipomo) 6 July 1903
         d. Aug 1991; SSDI
         F: Joseph A G Dana 1875-1938 OM cem SLO
         M: Lucretia E Deleisseigues 1881-1965 "
         Confirmed St Pat's Ch AG 3 Je 1894 @12
     =Henry (living in Richmond 1961, in Yorba Linda 1977)
     =Bernardine Perales (living in Guadalupe 1961, in SM 1977)

    e. Clair C/G   b. (Guad) 4 Feb 1890
        1906 Dir: stu Guad   d. San Francisco Apr 1952; bur Apr 22 SM cem
                                              obit Mon Apr 21 p.1; to Tiburon 1950
       m. 1916
     1952 Pall bearers: Henry J. Nieggemann, Lester Van Pelt, SM; Albert J Dolcini,
        Sacramento; Rbt Franklin, Gilroy; Dr Wm Franklin, Watsonville;
        George Kennedy, Pasadena
         John Henry Franklin MD   b. Gilroy CA
                                              d. @54/0/22; bur 25 Apr 1934 SM cem
                                              bio M/H 590
                                              F: Warham Easley Franklin d. 1908 @65
                                              M: Marion Fife d. 1918 @69
         1913. Dr Franklin, who administers to the sick in Guadalupe, was in Santa Maria
            the first of the week. He states that Guadalupe is coming to the front gradually
            but surely, and before long the snug little town will have paved streets and
            several other necessary improvements.
            "...after World War I he gave up a medical practice...to become a plant
            breeder" for Waller-Franklin Seed Co. Principals: L D Waller, J H Franklin,
            and P Giacomini.   See *This is Our Valley* p.239
            The 200 block of E Morrison boasts two fine houses built by Waller and
            Franklin, on opposite corners. Waller's is a New England-style house, restored
            by Harrell Fletcher some years ago; Franklin's was built in the Mediterranean
            fashion, and has but recently been entirely refurbished to its original condition.
            = Mrs Wm D Thorp (living in Tiburon 1952)
            = Beatrice   "   "   "   "
            =John B   "   "   "   "
            = Warham H, Lt USAF d. 1944
                1940-1 Dir: Franklin Beatrice stu r223 E Morrison
                           Claire C hskpr h 223 E Morrison
                           Warham H stu r223 E Morrison
     f. Valente J   b. (Guad) Dec 1890
                                              d. (in Davis before 1952)?
Note: nephews and nieces of Corinne Dolcini 1977: Albert Dolcini, Red Bluff; Valente Dolcini,
    Davis; Henry Dolcini, Yorba Linda; Claire Guichard, Walnut Creek; Jean Bailey, Colusa;
    Mary Ellen Dolcini PhD, Davis; Carol Porter, Carmichael; Lenore Arneson, San Francisco;
    Beatrice Stejer, Palo Alto; Bernardine Perales, Santa Maria
2. Ferdinand   b. (Santa Cruz)
   (Thomas F)?
   1893 T F Fleck of Frisco, formerly of Guadalupe, brother-in-law of the late Henry Dolcini.....
       came in to pay Mr Dolcini's subscription to the, *Santa Maria Times* as he had stated on the
       day he was killed that he intended paying it that day.   -Dec 2
   1906 Dir: Thomas F Fleck foreman oil wks, Guadalupe
3. Francis   b. (Santa Cruz) 1867 (cen)
   Confirmed Guadalupe   d.
   1 Apr 1886 @17; sponsor
   Ambrose Fox
   1891 Frank Fleck is down from San Francisco...absent two years...
                                                                -*Guadalupe Telephonies*, June 27
4. Grace C   b. Guadalupe 28 Sep 1875
    teacher   d. San Francisco 8 Mar 1947; Guad cem
       Single   obit Mar 10 p.1

1893 High School Notes. Miss Grace Fleck was summoned to her home at Guadalupe
on Thursday by the death of her brother-in-law, H Dolcini. -Nov 25
1947 Pall Bearers: Fred & Raymond Abernathy, Chas Campodonico, Leo Acquistapace,
Fred Malizzia, Lavern Evans

5. Charles	b. Guadalupe 2 May 1879 (co birth rec)
	d. 11 May 1919; Guad cem
6. William Alexander	b. Guadalupe 1881
Confirmed St Pat's Ch AG	d. (San Jose) 28 May 1964; Guad cem
3 June 1894 @13; sponsor John Ormon	
m.	
Hilda Olsen-Wong	b. Oslo Norway; d. 1958; Guad cem
a. Marie Henrietta	b. San Jose (Guad cem; no dates)

Vol. XXVIII, No. 1, Spring 1996, p. 20

Corrections and Additions   [Page numbers refer to those in Quarterly]

p. 19   Mrs John Fleck, @60. 9 July 1890-6 Oct 1891, resident of Guadalupe.
– List of Aged Persons Supported by Santa Barbara County Outside of Hospital.
(-*Ancestors West*, Santa Barbara co Gen Soc)

Vol. XXVIII, No. 2, Summer 1996, p.14

p. 19   Guadalupe Items. Mrs John Flick (sic) three children with scarlet fever; two almost well, 3 yr-old Charlie seriously ill. -Sep 30 1882

p. 20   T F Fleck, well borer, died in Los Angeles 30 June 1938 @71.
-Knights of Pythias records, SM Lodge #90

FORRESTER

Pottawatomie Co KS   Santa Barbara Co CA

George Washington Forrester   b. PA, 4th of the name
    m.
Cassandra Pinick   b. OH c1817; d. Manzana 3 Feb 1895
    1888: L L Forrester's mother returned on Wednesday from Nevada.   -June 12
    1895: Manzana Notes. Mrs Forrester, mother of the Forrister (sic) boys has been quite
        sick during the past week. -Jan 12. …not expected to live. She is 78 years old.   –Jan 26
    Mrs C Forrester died at the ripe old age of 77 years on Sunday last.   -Feb 9
    5 sons, 3 daughters; 3 sons to CA, per bio of E E Forrester

1. Joann (James L Porter)   b. (W)V c1847
    a. George F b. WV 1867   1870: Pottawatomie co KS
    b. John T b. KS 1869
        others?

2. George Washington   b. Mason co (W)V 1848; d. Pottawatomie co KS 1926
    1870: w/Porters. bio *Pioneers of the Bluestem Prairie*, Riley co KS Gen Soc,
    1976 p. 194. To KS 1868
        m. Pottawatomie co 1871
    Nancy Ellen Anderson   b. IN 1854; d. Pottawatomie co KS 1913
        F: James Anderson; M: Martha J Plummer
    a. Edgar G 1872-1964 (Nora Ott 1873-1959)   Upper Sisquoc Items. Rev George Forrester and
    b. Sylvester W 1877-1946 (Anna Fox)   wife, of KS are at the ranch of his brother, Ed E.
    c. Martha C 1879-1967 (Frank Fox)   The guests are also excursionists from Kansas.
    d. Cora E 1881-1973 (David W Atkinson   -July 24 1897
        1874-1954)
    e. Laura M 1886/7-1973 (Robert F Kolterman) Upper…Mr and Mrs Geo Forrester
    f. George W 1889-1937 (Lydia Grutzmacher)   returned to Kansas this week.   -Aug 7 1897

3. Lucean Leonidas   b. (W)V 1849; d. Riverside CA 1923
    bio *History of Santa Barbara Co*, Storke 1891 p. 436; 5 children. 1900: 8 births, 2 living
        m.1 Pottawatomie co 1872
    Martha A Clark   b. MO 1856; d. (Bakersfield? after 1900)
    a. Nora C b. KS 1874; m. San Luis Obispo 1894 Edward Francis Montgomery 1871-1935
        (divorced); F: Josiah T Montgomery 1852-1919; M: Ellen
    b. Laura b. NV 1877; m. NV 1893 Wm M Miller b. IL 1860; d. Arroyo Grande 1900
    c. Lilly F 1882-before 1900   Manzana Items. Wm Miller
    d. Lucien 1885-before 1900   and family have returned from Inyo
    e. Clara M 1888-before 1900   co; they expect to make their future
    f. Edwin 1889-1889 SM cem   home here.   -Mar 2 1895
    g. Lorenzo 1890-1890 SM cem
    h. George H 1892-before 1900
        m.2 1905
    Sarah W Gilbert 1858-1935, widow of Wm L Gilbert?

4. --

5. Sarah Ellen   b. (W)V 1853/4; death date unknown
    1870: w/Porters
        m. 1870/1
    Frederick Montgomery Davis   b. IN 1839
    1870: Pottawatomie co KS   d. Manzana 1897; buried Manzana- "impracticable to
        remove the body to Santa Maria" -May 29
    1880: Elko co NV, Star Valley,   F: Frederick Montgomery Davis: M: Betsy Spencer

next to L W St Clair See *Pioneers of the Bluestem Prairie*, op.cit, p. 184
To KS 1869; to NV 1876; to CA 1886; to Manzana 1894
  a. Alonzo Edwin b. KS 1871; d. Santa Maria 1933; m. Pacific Valley, Monterey co 1905
    Lucy Elizabeth Plaskett 1886-1975. F: Byron G Plaskett; M: Corrine Martha
  b. Arthur Curtis b. KS 1874; d. Santa Maria 1937; single

6. William Merchant   b. (W)V 1856; d. San Luis Obispo co 1912
   1870: w/Porters   See bio of granddaughter Minnie Holland Martin,
     m. c1876   *History of Santa Barbara Co*, O'Neill, 1939 p. 429
  Catherine Elizabeth Wheat Wells   b. MI 1845; d. Los Angeles co 1918
                             F: Hiram P Wheat 1822?-1903; M: Elizabeth Catherine
                                m.1 1865 William Harvey Wells
  a. Eva/Evelyn b. Tulare CA c1877   d. San Bernardino co 1949; m. SLO 1895
    Henry Holland 1873-1957   F: Richard Watson Holland 1832-1900
                                M: Catherine C Bell 1837-1914
  b. Isabelle Elizabeth b. Tulare 1882/4; d. San Luis Obispo 1969; m. Santa Maria 1903
    William David Holland 1882-1971. Parents as above
  c. Charity Elizabeth b. Santa Maria (valley) 1885; d. San Luis Obispo 1977; m. SLO 1911
    George Walter Warren 1879-1982.   F: Joseph A Warren 1840-1913
                                  M: Calista A Stiltz 1859-1944
  d. Bertha b. Santa Maria 1887;   d. San Bernardino co 1974; m.1 Carpinteria 1908
    Albert Lee Treloar F: Samuel Treloar 1832-1914; M: Elizabeth Lee 1847-1916
      m.2 -Wright

7. Helen R   b. (W)V 1857?
   1880: Elko co NV Star Valley next to Fred Davis
  L W St Clair   b. VA c1846
  a. Annie M b. NV c1877; m. San Luis Obispo 1894
    Charles Wells 1865-1918   F: Wm Harvey Wells
                                M: Catherine Elizabeth Wheat 1845-1918
  b. Maude G b. NV c1878   Sisquoc Local News. Mrs St Clair of Nevada is
  c. Lottie E b NV 1880   visiting her brother, E E Forrester.   -Feb 9 1895
    others?

8. Edward Everett   b. (W)V 1860; d. Imperial Valley 1936
      m. Santa Maria 1884
  EmmaLinda M Wells   b. WI 1866; d. Yolo co CA 1947
                                F: Wm Harvey Wells
                                M: Catherine Elizabeth Wheat 1845-1918
a. Jerome L b. (Santa Barbara co) 1883; d. nr Brawley 1934; auto accident Emily J
b. George Washington b. Santa Barbara co 1885; d. Imperial Valley 1950
c. B Everett b. Santa Barbara co 1887
d. Emma May (Rosenbaum) b. Santa Barbara co 1889; d. Orange co 1988
e. Anna b. Santa Barbara co 1891; single in 1936
f. Elmer b. Santa Barbara co 1893; d. Imperial co 1976; m. (of El Centro) SLO 1923
   Edna Minnie Sherwood of Santa Ana
g. James Arthur b. Manzana 1895 (*Times*); d. El Centro 1989
h. William H b. (Santa Barbara co) 1897; d. Imperial co 1934, spouse initial M
i. Edward Everett Jr b. Santa Barbara co 1900; Loraine d. El Centro 1933 @24
j. Arthur b. Santa Barbara co 1902; d. (Ballard) 1992; m. Santa Barbara co 1935
   Bernice Mackey
k. Lena (Smalley) b. (Imperial Valley) 1912
    bio *American Biography & Genealogy, California Ed.* (1912) Burdette, Vol. II, p. 553

The First Thirty years...Imperial Valley, 1931, Tout, p. 66
   to Imperial Valley 1901; sent for family 1903
(All items taken from the *Santa Maria Times* unless otherwise noted)

1883   LL Forrester and Woon, blacksmiths, on Central City and Santa Ynez Road ½ mile from Juan Flores –Thompson and West. *History of Santa Barbara and Ventura Counties.* 1883. (Section 17 – The road runs diagonally across the corner.)

1885   The frame building lately vacated by James P (sic) Goodwin & Co. took a walk Thursday through the persuasive influence of Mr Forrester, and is now safely located on Main Street, adjoining Hart's blacksmith shop   –*Santa Maria Times* Feb 7 (should be James F Goodwin)
   Personal Mention. L L Forrester has gone to San Francisco to prove up on his land.
–Nov 28
   (Homestead #6536 N2NE4, N2NW4, S17 T9N R32W Notice from San Francisco –Oct 24) Wm Miller witness to the Notice of Intent of James W Goodchild.
   Land Notice. San Francisco Oct 16, 1885. Lucian L Forrester Homestead 6536 N2NE4 N2NW4 S17 T9N R32W –Wit: F Fugler, E E Forrester, Cassander Walker, J J Holloway, all Santa Maria PO.

1887   L L Forrester made a special trip to take in Los Angeles and other counties south of us quite recently. He said until he had made the trip that he was really very anxious to sell his place in Santa Maria Valley, but after making his tour and taking a good look at the country south of us, he came right back and withdrew his land from the market. He says the *Santa Maria Times* and the real estate men of Santa Maria are doing a big thing for the valley in advertising it, that he found out by its being talked of so much in Los Angeles and other places, and says just as soon as the railroad is completed a great rush will be made for Santa Maria   –Jul 16
   Land Notice San Francisco—Sep 6, 1887—Henry Irving Roberts Homestead App. #8328 lot 3 S32 T9N R29W NE4SW4 N2SE4 S25 T9N R30N. Wit: G A Woon, SB PO; H P Wheat, Ed Forrester, Wm Forrester SM PO.   –Sep 17
   We paid Mr L L Forrester's place of business a visit this week and found his machine shop entirely complete. Mr Forrester proposes to saw lumber and manufacture door and window frames to order and attend promptly to barley crushing. We also found Mr Forrester erecting a blacksmith, carriage and wagonmaking shop in connection with the above named establishment. We invite your attention to his new advertisement in this issue.   –Sep 17

L L Forrester
Blacksmith
And
Machinist
Blacksmithing, carriage and wagonmaking
in all the branches skillfully attended to.
Horses shod by experienced workmen a specialty.
Manufacturing of window and door frames
to order and other sawing done.
Also barley crushing.
Moving Houses Promptly Attended To.   –Sep 17

   E E Colby, who bought the blacksmith shop of Forrester Bros, about fifteen miles up the valley some two years ago gave us a pleasant call on Monday last. He expresses himself as being well pleased with his purchase and says that he is kept busy at his trade, have a good patronage.
–Oct 8

      L Forrester engaged during the week removing the machine shop bought from R Hart to corner of Broadway and Chapel on his lots . . . to add building 40 x 70 for planing mill and other manufacturing.   –Oct 15

      Fair Play Items. Forrester Bros sold their stock to R T Buell.   –Oct 22

      L Forrester moved J H Logan's dwelling from his ranch south of town and attached the same to his restaurant on the north side of Main Street.   –Oct 29

      L L Forrester has bought a lot on Church Street opposite Dr Bagby's residence to move the cottage building which stood on his lots in the north part of town on to the same, which he will occupy, with his family, for a permanent residence. L Forrester has moved Dr Lucas' barn from the West End to the north east part of town and located it on Dr's lots not far from his residence. –Nov 5

      The buildings of Forrester's machine and blacksmith shop show off quite nicely from the center of town. The front facing town being nicely painted.   –Nov 19

      G B Hopper with whom all our citizens are well acquainted desires to inform the public that he has leased the blacksmith shop of L L Forrester and is prepared to do first class blacksmithing and horseshoeing. For further reference see his permanent card in this issue.

  –Nov 26

      G B Hopper, blacksmithing, horseshoeing, having leased the blacksmith shop of L L Forrester I am now prepared to do all kinds of work in this line and guarantee satisfaction to all my patrons.   –Nov 26

      L L Forrester moved school . . .   –Dec 10

      L L Forrester has moved the old two-story school building on to Mr Crosby's lots on Chapel Street and the same will be fitted up and put in order for a lodging house.   –Dec 10

      Mr Davis of Kansas has erected a residence in the north part of town on Broadway Street. He is the woodworkman in Forrester Bros Carriage shop.   –Dec 10

      L L Forrester's blacksmith shop had received its second coat of paint by J R Weeks.

  –Dec 10

1888   Street Sprinkling by L L Forrester ...   -Jun 6, Jun 30
        L L Forrester's mother returned on Wednesday from Nevada.   –Jun 12
        L L Forrester proposes to sprinkle . . .   –40 Years Ago, Thur, Jun 14, 1928 p.8

1890   Blacksmith Ad: Marsh and Forrester, Broadway and Chapel . . .   –Apr 26

      L L Forrester met with rather a lightning and painful accident the other day. He had the end of his index finger of the left hand taken off by his buzz saw, at his shop at the corner of Broadway and Chapel streets. It is a piece of old advice—"Never monkey with a Buzz Saw."

  –Jun 7

      Blacksmith Ad: L L Forrester, Broadway and Chapel . . .   –Jul 26

      Robert Braun is again on deck—after two years rest—wagonmaker . . . L L Forrester turned out a finely constructed spring wagon. All our blacksmiths . . . have a round at this work—all understand their business, too.   –Jul 28

      Ad: L L Forrester wagons blacksmith horseshoer mechanic, Broadway and Chapel . . . –Oct 4 Mr G B Hopper, who sold his blacksmith business to Harry Marsh, and he to L L Forrester some time ago, has bought the same back and asks a renewal of acquaintance with his old patrons and solicits the patronage of others. Mr Hopper is a fine workman and his patrons of old will be pleased to learn of his purchase. He will be found at the same old stand on the corner of Broadway and Chapel, as formerly. L L Forrester will remove to his ranch. L L Forrester has bought Mr Hopper's place north of town.   –Nov 15

      Forrester Bros have removed the Cole building, belonging to Harry Marsh, from Main Street down Broadway and located it on Mr Marsh's lot for residential purposes.   –Dec 13

      Note: Ex-Cambrian Charles Cole, shopkeeper, left town.

1891   L L Forrester, a rancher of Santa Maria, was born in West Virginia in 1850. He lived at home until 18 years of age, and then worked in a saw mill and in oil works in Parkersburg, and there learned the science of well boring. He then went to Kansas, and for several years followed farming and stock-raising. In the spring of 1875 he came to California, and farmed one year in Butte County, then he went to Tulare, where he ran a saw mill and teamed until 1878, when he went to Oregon and helped build and run a saw mill, until he returned to California and settled in Santa Maria, in 1880. He then opened a blacksmith shop in the Santa Maria district, where he continued until 1885, when he returned to Santa Maria and built his present spacious shop, 46 x 70 ft, corner Broadway and Chapel streets. He also has a machine shop and barley crusher, all running by steam power, and he is prepared to do blacksmithing in all its branches, also carriage building and repairing, always keeping on hand two blacksmiths and one wood workman. He has 20 acres in fruit, mainly prunes and apricots, and also grows barley and beans. He breeds horses and cattle, keeping from forty to sixty head. In 1878 (sic) (1887?) he started the waterworks, pumping by steam from the well to an elevated tank, and is prepared to supply the town; this interest he sold to his brother in the fall of 1889. Mr Forrester is a professional house-mover, and has moved some of the largest houses in the surrounding country. He was married in Pottawatomi, Kansas, in 1872, to Miss Martha Clark, a native of Missouri, and they have five children. Mr Forrester's father was born in Philadelphia.   –Storke. *History of Santa Barbara . . . Cos.* 1891 p.436

Estray Notices. Estrayed from my place on the Sisquoc, a bay mare and colt. The mare was branded on the left hip with a L. A libral (sic) reward will be given to anyone returning the animals to me or giving any information as to their whereabouts. L L Forrester   –Sep 26

1892   On the Alamo . . . M Logan moved from the Alamo to the Forrester Ranch where he is to be a Majordomo.   –Apr 17
Note: The Alamo ranch is north of the Santa Maria river in San Luis Obispo County.
    (Dictionary: Majordomo is a steward of a royal household.)

1893   Five Horses Eaten Up. E E Forrester was in the early part of the week from Sisquoc country. He says the California lions have become so numerous and voracious as to threaten the destruction of his entire band of horses. Heretofore they have not attacked anything but young colts, but recently they killed and ate a three year old filly and they have devoured five of his young horses within the past few weeks. These animals seem partial to horse flesh and as Ed has a fine band on the range he is feeling rather sore over the proposition. He reports lot of feed and cattle looking well.
    –Apr 29
    Long Valley Items. Miss Nora Forrester who has been stopping at Mrs Triplett's for some time will leave for Nevada where her parents now reside.   –Aug 26
    Married: Wm Miller of Idaho and Laura Forrester, formerly of Santa Maria, 25 August 1893, Eliso (sic) (Elko), Nevada, Elko County.   –Sep 16
    We hear that L L Forrester is now very well pleased with Nevada climate . . . in all probability will return to Santa Maria next spring.   –Oct 14
    G C Cochran with L L Forrester in Death, Nevada . . . glad to be home.   –Oct 21
Note: Death and Elko are in Elko County, Nevada (Should this be Deeth?)
    Wm Forrester says his brother L L is now at Stockton and unless he finds something there to do he will return to Santa Maria in a short time. He has been hunting for a better place but has failed to find it.   –Dec 30

1894   Ed Forrester says there is more ice to be seen on the Sisquoc River, about 20 miles east of this place, than any winter since 1885. This of course indicates that it is the longest continued cold spell that we have had since the winter of '85.   –Jan 20
    Delinquent Tax List . . . Forrest L L   Forrest Wm

Garey. L Forrester in town Monday with a load of apricots. –Jul 28
Note: Garey is a town near Sisquoc.

1895 Manzana Items. A few interesting notes from up the river. L L Forrester is in your valley and has been for some time. We are lost without him. –Jan 16

Manzana Notes: Mrs Forrester, mother of the Forrister (sic) boys has been quite sick during the past week. –Jan 12 . . . not expected to live. She is 78 years old. –Jan 26
Note: This is Cassandra (Pinnick) Forrester.

Mrs C Forrester died at the ripe old age of 77 years on Sunday last. –Feb 9

Sisquoc Local News. Mrs St Clair of Nevada is visiting her brother, E E Forrester. –Feb 9

Manzana Notes. L L Forrester is absent on a business run. –date lost

Manzana Items. Wm Miller and family have returned from Inyo County. They expect to make their future home here. *Note*: Wm Miller is Laura Forrester's husband. –Mar 2

Long Valley Items. Wm Miller hauled a load of machinery for the new saw mill to the Manzana last week for Davis and Co. –May 11

Manzana Items. Wm Miller has taken up a place by the river and is making hay. –May 18

Manzana Notes. Mr Ed Montgomery and wife are the guests of Mrs M's parents this week.
Note: Mrs Montgomery is Nora Forrester. –Jan 12

Manzana Items. Mr Ed Montgomery and wife are stopping at her father's place until the river falls. –Jan 26

. . . High water . . . E E Forrester lost land . . . –Feb 9

1896 L L Forrester of the Sisquoc was in town Wednesday after fruit trees which he will set out on his farm. –Feb 22

1897 Mrs Spittler and Mrs L L Forrester of Sisquoc were visitors in town.
–50 years ago, April 12, 1947

Upper Sisquoc Items. Messrs John and Wm Miller were down to the valley on business the past week. Ed Forrester and your contemporary correspondent returned safely, which seems to surprise some of their neighbors. They had a large demijohn of wine aboard the wagon –May 15

Upper Sisquoc. J H Miller is assisting Ed Forrester on the ranch this week. –May 29

Upper Sisquoc Notes: Ed Montgomery was assisting Ed Forrester in haying this week, and will soon go to the valley to stay during the harvesting season. –May 29

L L Forrester, of Sisquoc, a brother of Wm Forrester, the contractor, is here on a business trip. He reports grain coming out but during the past two weeks so much better that everyone has gone to work with smiling countenances. –*Santa Barbara Press* in *Santa Maria Times*, -Jun 5

Upper Sisquoc Notes. M/M Ed Montgomery returned from the valley "loaded to the guards." –Jun 5

Upper Sisquoc Notes. Lucien Forrester spent a couple of days with his brother. We learn that he may return here to live on his ranch. –Jun 12

Upper Sisquoc . . . M/M Ed Montgomery were among the pilgrims lately. –Jul 3

Upper Sisquoc. The home of M/M Ed Montgomery was burned on the 4th during their absence at the schoolhouse. The loss falls very heavily as nothing was saved except the clothing they wore during the day. The origin of the fire is a mystery. –Jul 4

Fourth of July Fire. Ed Montgomery, who resides on the Upper Sisquoc, about forty miles east of Santa Maria, lost his dwelling and contents by fire Sunday. With his family he went to the picnic at Castro's Sunday and remained during the night. Upon their arrival the next morning, nothing remained of their home except an ash pile. The house was a new one and had just been furnished with new furniture. Three valuable guns were also destroyed. It is not known how the fire originated but it is thought that some coals were left in the ash can from which the fire started. The loss to Mr Montgomery is about $800. -Jul 10

G W Forrester and wife arrived Monday evening from Wamego, Kansas on a visit to his brothers, L L and Wm Forrester of Upper Sisquoc. –Jul 17

Upper Sisquoc. Ed Montgomery will rebuild his dwelling soon. His father began the erection of an adobe of large dimensions on the Potreros this week. It is a much colder climate in winter. –Jul 21

Upper Sisquoc. A number of ranchers are digging wells this summer—J J Twitchell, Calvin Davis and Miller Bros, as far as heard from. –Jul 24

Upper Sisquoc Items. Rev George Forrester and wife, of Kansas, are at the ranch of his brother, Ed E Forrester. The guests are also excursionists from Kansas. –Jul 24

Upper Sisquoc Items. Mr and Mrs George Forrester returned to Kansas this week –Aug 7

Upper Sisquoc. M/M Ed Montgomery are down to Santa Maria this week purchasing household goods. –Aug 14

Upper Sisquoc. John Miller passed down the creek on route to the ranch of E E Forrester where he will engage in cutting peaches for drying. –Aug 21

Upper Sisquoc. Mr Miller who has been busily drying apricots at Mr Forrester's for the past two weeks made a hurried trip to the valley the forepart of the week. –Sep 4

Upper Sisquoc. Joe Montgomery and son made a trip to the valley this week. –Sep 4

Upper Sisquoc. L L and E E Forrester visited the valley this week. Lucien and Ed Forrester made a trip into the pinery this week. –Oct 23

Garey Notes. L L Forrester is down from his place at Sisquoc. –Dec 25

Upper Sisquoc. Ed Montgomery and wife were down to the valley, preparing for Christmas. –Dec 25

1898 Upper Sisquoc. Mrs Ed Montgomery did not return with her husband, remaining in Santa Maria until after the holidays. A H Davis and family, Alonzo and Arthur Davis, Capron and D Spaulding celebrated Christmas at the ranch of Will Tunnell, W J Twitchell and family with M/M H Wells, Ed Montgomery with L L Forrester. The balance of the settlement were at their homes. All report a very enjoyable time. –Jan 1

South Side Notes. L L Forrester has had to suspend building operation on his new house which he is building on his brother's ranch here until the Manzana saw mill can turn out some lumber of extra length, that is needed for its completion. –Mar 12

Note: Many other Manzana items are in the Twitchell family article, see Twitchell charts. The Manzana saw mill was operated by Frederick M Davis and sons; Davis was a brother-in-law of the Forrester brothers, and detailed in the Davis chart. See also Hopper and Logan charts.

1900 News of Arroyo Grande. W H (sic) (s/b M) Miller of Oceano, died last week from what is thought was a cancer of the stomach. The interment took place Friday and the remains were followed to their last resting place in the IOOF cemetery by a large number of sympathizing friends of the bereaved widow and fatherless little ones. *–San Luis Obispo Breeze,* Fri Sep 7

1912 J C Naylor and Violet Naylor of San Luis Obispo witnesses to the marriage of Charles A Harp of Orcutt and Helena A Buffington of San Luis Obispo. –Oct 27

1921 Directory: Miller, Carl H inspr Burroughs Add Mach h214 Prospect Av

1923   Vital Statistics: Death Notices. Forrester—In Riverside, Cal, Feb 19, 1923, Mr Lucean L Forrester, aged 72, beloved husband of Mrs Sara Forrester, late residence 1290 Chestnut St. The funeral services will be announced later by Amstutz Glenn and Preston.
-Riverside Daily Press, Feb 19 p.5

Funeral Notices. The funeral services for Lucean L Forrester will be conducted from the chapel of Amstutz, Glenn and Preston, Saturday morning, Feb 24th at 10:30 a.m. (postponed from Wednesday morning.) Dr Ira W Barnett officiating, interment in Olivewood Cemetery.
–Ibid., Tue eve Feb 20 p.6

Card of Thanks Mrs L L Forrester and Family –Mon Feb 26, p.2. r1290 Chestnut Str. Olivewood Cemetery.

Directory: 1923 Forrester, Saul (Bessie) carp h1290 Chestnut, Riverside
Miller, Doris stu (student?) r1290 Chestnut
Miller, Carl H (Frankie) inspr Burroughs Add Mach h203 E 7th
Sherwood, Jas B watchmn r1177 Almond

1924   Riverside County: Forrester, Sara L from Elizabeth Jourdan April 12, 1924; rec. July 3, 1924; 607:503.

1926   Riverside Co. Deeds: Forrester, Saul and Bessie A from C F Collier 1926: 665-427.

1934   Directory: 1934 Forrester, Sarah L (wid L L) r4290 Chestnut, Riverside
Gilbert, W M (Lois V) mech Albrights & Brown h6767 Brockton Av
Miller, Carl G (Sarah) h2921 8th
Forrester, Saul and Bessie A chauf h4290 Chestnut
Miller, Doris F r4290 Chestnut
Sherwood, Wibur (sic) P (Anna) mech Roubidoux Motor Co h1161,
    El Dorado

1935   Death Notice. Forrester—In Riverside, Calif, Oct 2, 1935. Sarah L Forrester, aged 76 years, beloved mother of Sterling C Gilbert of Watsonville, Calif; Mrs Violet Naylor of San Luis Obispo, Calif; Mrs Bessie Forrester of 4290 Chestnut Street, Riverside and Mrs Ann Sherwood of Riverside; grandmother of Doris Miller of Riverside, Lyle Sherwood, Rose-Mary Sherwood, Don Sherwood, all of Riverside; Clyde Gilbert, Stella Dicks, both of Watsonville, Calif; Pearl Love of Taft, Calif, and Ruby Webber of Los Angeles. Services will be conducted Saturday afternoon at 3:30 o'clock in the M H Simons & Co Chapel, Dr W W Catherwood officiating. Interment in Olivewood cemetery.
–Ibid, Wed eve Oct 2 p.14

1938   Riverside Co Deeds: Estate of Bessie G Forrester to Saul Forrester and Doris F Miller, in Riverside. Court Order Bk 384 p459 22 Aug 1938; recorded Sep 1.

1969   Obituaries. Violet J Naylor . . . Rebeka (sic) Lodge @ 89 years. Born June 24, 1879 Visalia; 60 years in San Luis Obispo. Past resident Dept Assn Ladies Auxiliary Patriarch Militant. Survivors: two daughters, Mrs Pearl Robert, Taft; Mrs Ruby Webber, Huntington Park. Three grandchildren, 5ggch, 6gggch . . .   *–San Luis Obispo Tel-Trib,* Tue Feb 18

Submitted by: Ms. Jerry P. Webber, Tacoma, WA Information Gathered by: Barbara Cole

FORRESTER DESCENDANTS

1 Forrester (b. 1694-Ireland; d.____)
   Sp: Nancy Brown (b. 1698-Ireland; m.____; d.____)
  2 Ralph Forrester (b. abt 1726-Ireland (?) d. aft 1764-probably Chester, PA)
     Sp: Tamer Gregory (b. abt 1730-Goshen, Lancaster, PA; m. abt 1743;
     d. 1842-Chester, PA)
    3 Ezekiel Forrester (b. 30 Apr 1744-Westchester, Chester, PA.; d. 19 Nov 1770)
    3 Ralph Forrester (b. 28 Mar 1746-Westchester, PA.; d. bef Oct 1796-PA.)
       Sp: Ann Catherine (Kitty) Elliott (b. 1756-Chester, PA; m. 23 Oct 1777;
       d. 1842-Chester, PA)
      4 George Washington (1st) Forrester (b. abt 1785-PA or VA;
         d. aft 1860-Philadelphia, PA)
         Sp: Sarah Griffiths (b. 1788-Wales; d. aft 1861)
        5 George Washington (2nd) Forrester (b. abt 1815-Letart, VA.;
           d. abt 1868-__)
           Sp: Cassandra Pinick (b. abt Jun 1818-PA or OH; m. 21 Apr 1845;
           d. 3 Feb 1895-Horse Gulch, Santa Barbara, CA)
          6 Joanne Forrester (b. 23 Sep 1846-Wheeling, Mason County, W VA; d.____)
             Sp: James Lathan Porter (b. 16 Aug 1843-Meigs County, OH; m. 21 Apr 1864;
             d.____)
            7 George Taylor Porter (b. 30 Oct 1866-New Haven, W VA;
               d. 1959-San Pedro, CA)
               Sp: Ida Mae Cowling (b.____; m. 4 Nov 1895; d. 1 May 1962)
            7 George Edgar Porter (b. 1867; d.____)
               Sp: Sophia M. E. Mosing (b. 1868; m. 1893; d. 1952)
            7 John Thomas Porter (b. 5 Oct 1869-Wamego, KS; d. 1 May 1962-La Crescenta, CA)
            7 Maggie (Kitty) Casandra Porter (b. 5 Jan 1873-Wamego, KS;
               d. 1920-Pomona, CA)
               Sp: Bert Lewis (b.____; m. 2 Jan 1893; d.____)
            7 Nena Porter (b. 23 Dec 1873-Wamego, KS; d. 30 Oct 1956-Starr Valley, NV)
               Sp: Charles Henry Black (b.____; m. 4 Nov 1891; d.____)
            7 Emma Gertrude Porter (b. 6 Apr 1876-Deeth, NV; d. 15 Jan 1905)
               Sp: George Ferguson (b.____; m. 6 May 1895; d.____)
            7 William Merchant Porter (b. 23 Jan 1881-Deeth, NV; d.____)
            7 Lee Porter (b. 29 Sep 1882-Deeth, NV; d. 14 Apr 1903-Ogden, UT)
            7 (Addie) Belle Porter (b. 23 Mar 1886-Deeth, NV; d. 15 Mar 1919-Wilson, WY)
               Sp: Robert Lundy (b.____; m. 3 Nov 1904; d.____)
            7 Grace Irene Porter (b. 10 Apr 1890-Deeth, NV; d. 24 Jun 1958-Glendale, CA)
               Sp: Robert Steven Marshall (b.____; m. 2 May 1909; d.____)
               Sp: John Miller Riddell (b.____; m. 24 Feb 1914; d.____)
          6 Jerome Forrester (b. 1844-W VA; d.____)
          6 George Washington (3rd) Forrester (b. 3 Oct 1848-Mason County, W VA
             d. 1 Jun 1926-Wamego, Pottawatomie County, KS)
             Sp: Nancy Ellen Anderson (b. 26 Sep 1854-Green Castle, IN; m. 17 Dec 1871
             d. 1 Aug 1913-Wamego, KS)
            7 Edgar G. Forrester (b. 13 Oct 1872; d. 1964)
               Sp: Nora A. Ott (b. 15 Nov 1873-Arispe, KS.; m. 27 Nov 1895; d. 4 Jul 1959)
            7 Sylvester W. Forrester (b. May 1877; d. 1946-Peabody, ____)
               Sp: Anna Fox (b.____; m.____; d.____)

7   Martha C. Forrester (b. 31 May 1879; d. 18 Aug 1967)
      Sp: Frank Fox (b.____; m.____; d.____)
7   Cora E. Forrester (b. 22 Feb 1881; d. 1973)
      Sp: David W. Atkinson (b. 1874-Louisville, KS; d. 1954)
7   Laura M. Forrester (b. 28 Aug 1887; d. 18 July 1973)
      Sp: Robert F. Kolterman (b.____; m.____; d.____)
7   George W. Forrester (b. 22 Mar 1889-Indian Creek, Pottawatomie, KS
    d. 12 Jan 1937-Manhattan, KS)
      Sp: Lydia Grutzmacher (b.____; m. 15 Dec 1908; d.____)
  8   Leva Ermine Forrester (b.____; d. in infancy)
  8   Bernadine Twilla Forrester (b.____; d.____)
      Sp: ____ Taylor (b.____; d.____)
    9   Nonavee Aldene Taylor (b.____; d.____)
  8   Georgia Ellen Forrester (b.____; d.____)
      Sp: ____ Cottle (b.____; d.____)
  8   Wilma Aldine Forrester (b.____; d.____)
6   Lucian Leonidas Forrester (b. 1849/1850-Mason County, W VA;
   d. 1923-Riverside, CA
   Sp: Martha Ann Clark (b. 2 Apr 1856-Richland, Livingston, MO;
   m. 6 Apr 1872; d. bef 1905-Bakersfield, CA)
  7   Nora Catherine Forrester (b. 8 Aug 1874-Pottawatamie County, KS
     d. 29 May 1947-San Luis Obispo, CA)
     Sp: Edward Francis Montgomery (b. Dec 1871; m. 13 Dec 1894; div.
     d. 12 Mar 1935)
     Sp: Alfred Rupp (b. 17 Feb 1870-PA; d. 29 Jun 1955)
    8   Gerald Myers/Rupp {Living} (Adopted by Aunt Nora when his mother,
       Clara Maude, became ill with Tuberculosis, abt 1927)
       Sp: Ellen Baker {Living}
      9   Mary Alice Rupp {Living}
         Sp: Daniel Bennett {Living}
        10   Wardell Clark Bennett {Living}
        10   Lucia Ruth Ellen Bennett {Living}
        10   Rose O'Grady Bennett {Living}
      9   Johanna Laura Rupp {Living}
      9   Sophia Simone Rupp {Living}
      9   Gia Calista Rupp {Living}
    8   Sp: Nancy Davis {Living} div.
      9   Forrester Davis Rupp {Living}
      9   Alexander Alfred Rupp {Living}
  7   Laura Belle Forrester (b. Feb 1877-NV; d. abt 1902____? CA?)
     Sp: Henry J. Ehlers (b. abt 1882-San Diego, CA; m. 28 Aug 1902-
     San Diego, CA; d. abt. 1902____?-   CA ?)
     Sp: William Morris Miller (b. Mar 1860-IL; m. 25 Aug 1893; d. 30
     Aug 1900-Arroyo Grande or Oceano, San Luis Obispo, CA)
    8   Carl Laurel Miller (b. 28 Jul 1894-Carson City, NV; d. 6 Apr 1974-
       Bakersfield, CA)
       Sp: Sara Viola (Sally) Ralls (b. 22 Aug 1894-Kern County, CA
       m. 11 Sep 1917; d. 25 Sep 1998- Kern County, CA)
      9   Lyla June Miller (b. 12 Jul 1918-El Centro, CA; d. 15 Mar 1993-
         Bakersfield, CA)
         Sp: Henry C. Breilein (b. 25 Dec 1914-SD; m. 29 Oct 1939

             d. 22 Jan 1978-Bakersfield, CA)
       10   Bonnie Jean Breilein {Living}
             Sp: Jerry Lackey {Living} div.
          11   Lea Jean Lackey {Living}
                Sp: Douglas Grant {Living}
             12   Tiffany Jean Grant {Living}
             12   MacAuley Sarah June Grant {Living}
             12   Channing Hope Grant {Living}
       10   Sp: Gordon Lindbery {Living} div.
       10   Raymond Henry Breilein {Living}
             Sp: Barbara Knapp {Living} div.
          11   Lance E. Breilein {Living}
                Sp: Jennifer Wilson {Living}
          11   Stuart E. Breilein {Living}
       10   Sp: Susan L. Hale {Living} div.
     9   Betty Miller (b. 15 Nov 1922-Wasco or Bakersfield ?, CA;
         d. 15 Mar 1964-Moses Lake, WA)
         Sp: Noble Hyde {Living}
   8   Nina Miller/Torchiana (b. 23 Mar 1897-El Centro, CA;
       d. 23 Dec 1984-CA ?) (Adopted by Torchiana about 1908)
       Sp: Allyn Lorraine, Sr. (b.____; m.____; d.____)
     9   Eulalie S. Lorraine (b. 17 Oct 1917-Seattle, WA.; d. 16 Mar 1957)
         Sp: Theodore Franklin Twisselman (b. 17 Apr 1910; m.____;
         d. 13 Apr 1968)
       10   Theodore Franklin Twisselman {Living}
             Sp: Patricia Rowena Cooper {Living}
          11   Elena Patricia Twisselman {Living}
                Sp: Peter Clark {Living}
          11   Lonnie Franklin Twisselman {Living}
                Sp: Junis Smith {Living}
             12   Curtis Lee Twisselman {Living}
          11   Michael Lee Twisselman {Living}
          11   Cheryl Marie Twisselman {Living}
     9   Betty Lorraine (b.____; d.____)
   8   Sp: James W. Tausig (b.____; m.____; d.____)
   8   Eva Belle Miller (b. 8 Apr 1899-Bakersfield, CA; d. 31 Jul 1965-Seattle, WA)
       Sp: Charles Bonham (b.____; m. abt 1914 div. or annulled; d.____)
       Sp: Chester Elwood Maines (b. 23 Apr 1906-South Bend, WA;
       m. 1928; d. 3 Jan 1979-Raymond, WA)
       Sp: Richard Lee Ralls (b. 4 Feb 1885-Upper Santana, CA; m. 4 Aug 1919
       (div.); d. 26 Feb 1955-Kern County, CA)
     9   Nina Patricia Ralls (b. 20 May 1924-Lost Hills, CA; d. 20 Mar 1968-
         Raymond, WA)
         Sp: Chester Christian Haines (b. 11 Oct 1921-St Paul, MN;
         m. 3 Jun 1939 (div.); d. 6 July 1986-Raymond, WA)
       10   Jerry Patricia Haines {Living}
             Sp: James Webber {Living}
             Sp: Harry Alan Kohn {Living} (div.)
             Sp: Harwood Leigh Scouten {Living} (div.)
          11   Grant Leigh Scouten {Living}
                Sp: Christina Elaine Boat {Living}

- 12 Stephen Tyler Scouten {Living} – Birth Father Kellar
- 12 Dillon Leigh Scouten {Living} – Birth Mother Sharon Marie Hughes
- 12 Jared Allen Scouten {Living} – Birth Father Kellar
- 12 Samantha Christine Scouten {Living}
- 11 Sundee Marie Scouten {Living}
- 11 Rachel Starr Scouten {Living}
  - Sp: Jason Anthony Charles Hudgins {Living}
- 10 Neena Jean Haines {Living}
  - Sp: Donald Lee Church {Living}
  - Sp: Alvin Denton Davis (b. 18 Aug 1934-Chance, OK; m. 1961 (div.); d. 1977-Long Beach, WA)
- 11 Becky Ann Davis {Living}
  - Sp: Carl Edward Huddleston {Living}
- 12 Stacy Elise Huddleston {Living}
- 12 Elaina Denise Huddleston {Living}
- 10 Judy Christine Haines {Living}
  - Sp: Ribhi Allinie {Living} (div.)
  - Sp: Robert J. Connery {Living} (div.)
- 11 Annette Marie Connery {Living}
  - Sp: Scott Duane Bundy {Living} (div.)
- 12 Scott Duane Bundy {Living}
- 12 Natasha Christine Bundy {Living}
- 13 Isaiah Collin Bundy {Living} – Birth Father Carlos Jaime Mamejia
- 12 Kristiana Rashelle Bundy {Living}
- 11 Debra Lee Connery {Living}
  - Sp: Doyle Dean Sanford {Living}
- 12 Ryon Thomas Sanford {Living}
- 12 Chelsie Clara Sanford {Living}
- 12 Joshua Keith Sanford {Living}
- 10 Sp: Thomas Neal Trotter {Living} (div.)
- 11 Tonya Lynn Trotter {Living}
  - Sp: David Mickelson {Living} (div.)
- 12 Sarah Ann Mickelson {Living}
- 11 Thomas A. Trotter {Living}
  - Sp: Dorothy (Dodie) Leanne Craig {Living}
- 12 Thomas Colten Trotter {Living}
- 12 Nathanial Craig Trotter {Living}
- 12 Garrett Young Trotter {Living}
- 12 Morganne Brook Trotter {Living}
- 9 Sp: John Paul Wiley {Living}
- 10 Janelle Paulette Wiley {Living}
  - Sp: Melvin James Long {Living}
- 11 Daniel Alan Long {Living}
- 12 Danielle Ann Long {Living}– Birth mother, Kimberly Beatty {Living}
- 11 James Albert Long {Living}
  - Sp: Season Narvasa Ceton {Living}
- 12 Skylar-Lynn Lamberton {Living} – Birth father Lamberton {Living}
- 11 Brian Elwood Long {Living}
  - Sp: Hanna Elizabeth Sheldon {Living}
- 12 Wyatt James Long {Living}
- 10 Jackie Kaye Wiley (b. 14 May 1949-Seattle, King, WA;

                    d. 14 Feb 1950-Alderwood Manor, Snohomish, WA)
9   Sp: Carl Floyd Black (b. 25 Jul 1926-Dennison Jack, KS;
         d. 11 Aug 1991)
    10   Joylita Carla Black (b. 11 Jul 1954; Tacoma, WA;
              d. 17 Feb 1999-Ocean Park, WA)
          Sp: Denton Eugene Morgan (b. 30 Mar 1950-Ilwaco, WA; m. 1969 (div).;
              d. Feb 1983-Ilwaco, WA)
      11   Gregory Jerome Morgan {Living}
              Sp: Kara Santee {Living}
        12   Alissa Joylita Morgan {Living}
    10   Sp: Randall Cole {Living} Div.
9   Sp: Woodrow Maines {Living} Div.-Marriage to step-uncle, no children
9   James Alfred Ralls/Maines (b. 4 Jun 1926-San Luis Obispo, CA;
         d. 11 Aug 2001-AL) Changed name to Maines
     Sp: Rose Marie Veit {Living}
    10   Dennis Patrick Maines {Living}
9   Sp: Darlene Shirley Seals {Living} (div.)
    10   Chester Elwood Maines {Living}
          Sp: Vickie {Living}
          Sp: Linda {Living} (div.)
          Sp: Cheryl {Living} (div.)
      11   Chester Elwood Maines
    10   Della Shellene Maines {Living}
          Sp: Leonard Schutt {Living} (div.)
      11   Rebecca Schutt {Living}
      11   Jennifer Schutt {Living}
      11   Christina Schutt {Living}
    10   Sp:_____?
      11   Boy {Living}
      11   Boy {Living}
      11   Boy {Living}
9   Sp: Naoma Jean Minor (b. 20 Apr 1928-Quilicine, WA;
         m. Tacoma, WA (div.); d. 22 Jun 2001-Tacoma, WA)
    10   James Alfred Maines II {Living}
          Sp: Gretchan Gail _____ {Living} (div.)
      11   James Alfred Maines III {Living}
      11   Gayla Lorraine Maines {Living}
    10   Sp: Elizabeth Ann _____ {Living}
      11   Richard Maines {Living}
      11   Gerald Maines {Living}
    10   Jeannette Marie Maines {Living}
      11   Brett Michael Maines (b. 1978; d. 1978)
      11   Ross Joseph Maines (b. abt. 1980; d. 1980)
    10   Joanne Ann Maines {Living}
          Sp: Patrick Jack Ferante {Living} (div.)
      11   Peter James Ferante {Living}
      11   Kathleen Javette Ferante {Living}
              Sp: Trevor William Sauders {Living}
    10   Sp: John Wesley Polk {Living}
7   Lilly Frances Forrester (b. Apr 1882; d. bef. 1900-Manzana, CA or NV)
7   Francis Lucian (Saul) Forrester (b. 16 May 1885-CA;

    d. 30 Mar 1946-Imperial, CA)
   Sp: Bessie A. Gilbert (b. Nov 1887-CA; m. Mar 1921;
   d. 7 Apr 1937-Riverside, CA)
 7 Clara Maude Forrester (b. Apr 1888-Sisquoc, Santa Barbara, CA;
   d. abt 1927-Olive View, CA)
  Sp: Clifton D. Myers (b. 7 Feb 1886-Sierraville, CA
  d. 8 May 1944-Orange County, CA)
  8 Rex N. Myers (b.____; d.____)
  8 Laura Myers (b.____; d.____)
   Sp: ____ Short (b.____; d.____)
  8 Gerald Myers/Rupp {living} Birth Mother: Clara Maude Forrester
   Adopted by Nora Forrester/Rupp (aunt)
 7 Edwin Forrester (b. 1889-Santa Maria Valley, CA
  d. 12 Oct 1889-Santa Maria, CA)
 7 Lorenzo Forrester (b. 24 Nov 1890-Santa Maria Valley, CA;
  d. Dec 1890-Santa Maria, CA)
 7 George Henry Forrester (b. 6 Jun 1892-CA; d. 22 Aug 1982-Los Angeles, CA)
  Sp: Jewel _____ (b.____; m.____; d.____)
6 Sp: Sarah Wheeler or Wheeland married name Gilbert (b. Feb 1858
 m. 1905; d. 2 Oct 1935)
6 Baby Forrester (b. abt 1851; d. abt 1851)
6 Sarah Ellen Forrester (b. abt 1853-Mason County W VA; d.____)
 Sp: Frederick Montgomery Davis (b. 1839-IN; d. 1897-Manzana, CA)
 7 Alonzo Edwin Davis (b. 1871-KS; d. 1933-Santa Maria, CA)
  Sp: Lucy Elizabeth Plaskett (b. 1886; m. 1905; d. 1975)
 7 Arthur Curtis Davis (b. 1874-KS; d. 1937-Santa Maria, CA)
6 William Merchant Forrester (b. 1856-Mason County, W VA;
 d. 1912-San Luis Obispo, CA)
 Sp: Catherine Elizabeth Wheat (b. 1845-MI; m. 1876;
 d. 1918-Los Angeles County, CA)
 7 Evelyn Forrester (b. 1878-Tulare, CA; d. 1949-Highland, CA)
  Sp: Henry Holland (b. 1873; m. 1895; d. 1957)
 7 Isabelle Elizabeth Forrester (b. 23 May 1882-Tulare, CA;
  d. Oct 1969-San Luis Obispo, CA)
  Sp: William David Holland (b. 9 Sep 1882-Santa Maria, CA;
  m. 18 Feb 1903; d. 4 Jul 1971-San Luis Obispo, CA)
  8 Elizabeth Holland (b.____; d.____)
   Sp: _____ Wicksom (b.____; d.____)
 7 Charity Elizabeth Forrester (b. 1885-Santa Maria Valley, CA;
  d. 1977-San Luis Obispo, CA)
  Sp: George Walter Warren (b. 1879; m. 1911; d. 1982)
  8 Stuart George Warren (b.____; d.____)
  8 Forrester W. Warren (b. 1919; d. 1992)
   Sp: Mary Ellen Willard (b. 1911; d. 1981)
 7 Bertha Forrester (b. 1887-Santa Maria Valley, CA
  d. 1974-San Bernardino County, CA)
  Sp: Albert Lee Treloar (b.____; m. 1908; d.____)
  8 William Treloar (b.____; d.____)
6 Helen R. Forrester (b. 1857-Mason County, W VA; d. 1880-Elko City, NV)
 Sp: L. W. St Clair (b.1846-VA; d.____)

- 7 Annie M. St Clair (b.1877-NV; d.____)
  Sp: Charles Wells (b. 1865; m. 1894; d. 1918)
- 7 Maude G. St Clair (b. 1878-NV; d.____)
- 7 Lottie E. St Clair (b. 1880-NV; d.____)
- 6 Edward Everett Forrester (b. 1860-Mason County, W VA;
  d. 1936-Imperial Valley, CA)
  Sp: Emma Linda Wells (b. 1866-WI; m. 1884; d. 1947-Yolo County, CA)
  - 7 Jerome L. Forrester (b. 1883-Santa Barbara County, CA;
    d. 1934-Brawley, CA)
    Sp: Emily J. _____ (b.____; m.____; d.____)
  - 7 George Washington Forrester (b. 15 Feb 1885-Garey, Santa Barbara County, CA
    d. 1950-Imperial Valley, CA)
  - 7 Everett Forrester (b. 1887-Santa Barbara County, CA; d.____)
  - 7 Emma May Forrester (b. 1889-Santa Barbara County, CA;
    d. 1988-Orange County, CA)
    Sp: _____ Rosenbaum (b.____; m.____; d.____)
  - 7 Anna Forrester (b. 1891-Santa Barbara County, CA; d.____)
  - 7 Elmer Forrester (b. 1893-Santa Barbara County, CA;
    d. 1976-Imperial County, CA)
    Sp: Edna Minnie Sherwood (b.____; m. 1923; d.____)
  - 7 James Arthur Forrester (b. 1895-Manzana, CA; d. 1989-El Centro, CA)
  - 7 William H. Forrester (b. 1897-Santa Barbara County, CA;
    d. 1934-Imperial County, CA)
    Sp: M_____ _____; (b.____; m.____; d.____)
  - 7 Edward Everett Forrester Jr. (b. 1900-Santa Barbara County, CA; d.____)
    Sp: Loraine _____ (b.____; m.____; d.____)
  - 7 Arthur Forrester (b. 1902-Santa Barbara County, CA;
    d. 1992-Ballard, CA)
    Sp: Bernice Mackey (b.____; m. 1935; d.____)
  - 7 Lena Forrester (b. 1912-Imperial Valley, CA; d.____)
    Sp: _____ Smalley; (b.____; m.____; d.____)
- 5 Lucean Bonapart Forrester (b. 9 Dec 1831-Harrison, OH; d.____)
- 5 George Forrester (b. abt 1811-Philadelphia, PA; d.____)
- 5 Joseph Tarpley Forrester (b. abt 1820-Harrison, Ohio; d.____)
- 5 Mary Forrester (b. abt 1825-Harrison, OH; d.____)
- 5 Margaret Forrester (b. abt 1829-Harrison, OH; d.____)
- 5 Cassell Griffiths Forrester (b. 6 Jan 1818-Philadelphia, PA;
  d. 30 Dec 1892-Laramie, Larimer County, WY)
  Sp: Mary Clark (b. 2 Jun 1829-Lexington, Richland County, OH;
  m. 6 Nov 1843; d. 16 Jan 1883-Laramie, Larimer County (sic), WY)
  - 6 Sarah Forrester (b. 9 Jun 1846-MO; d. 1862)
  - 6 Tamerlane Forrester (b. 27 Jun 1846-MO; d. 8 Oct 1925)
  - 6 George Forrester (b. 8 Aug 1850-MO; d. 1861/1862)
  - 6 Mary E. Forrester (b. 28 Sep 1852-MO; d. 17 Jun 1917)
    Sp: John Falkenstein (b. abt 1848-MO; d.____)
  - 6 Margaret Forrester (b. 16 Jan 1855-MO; d. 16 May 1913)
    Sp: John Detro (b. abt 1851-MO; d.____)
  - 6 Abner Clark Forrester (b. 14 Feb 1857-Springhill, Lewiston County, MO
    d. 19 Aug 1917-Riverside, Okanagan County, WA)
    Sp: Stella Evangeline Fisk (b. 2 Apr 1868-Dover, NY; d.____)

      6   Ethleen Forrester (b. 6 Apr 1859-Springhill, Larimer, MO.; d. 7 Dec 1903)
           Sp: Arthur Peck (b. abt 1855-Springhill, Larimer, MO; d.____)
      6   William Lucean Forrester (b. 25 Oct 1861-KS; d. 25 Oct 1938)
           Sp: Gertrude _____ (b. abt 1865-KS; d.____)
      6   Cassell Chase Forrester (b. 9 Mar 1864-KS; d. 25 Dec 1936)
           Sp: Mary Kelly (b. abt 1868-KS; d.____)
      6   Clara Forrester (b. 12 Feb 1866-KS; d. Mar 1932)
           Sp: Zenas Zin (b. abt 1862-KS; d.____)
      6   Nevada Forrester (b. Jul 4 1868 or 1869-KS; d.____)
           Sp: Fred Delay (b. abt 1864-KS; d.____)
  4   Ralph E. Forrester (b. abt 1786-Baltimore, Baltimore, MD; d.____)
      Sp: Sara Gantz (b. abt 1790-Baltimore, MD; m.____; d.____)
    5   Elizabeth Forrester (b. abt 1810-Baltimore, MD; d.____)
    5   Jane Forrester (b. abt 1814-Baltimore, MD; d.____)
    5   George W. Forrester (b. abt 1816-Baltimore, MD; d.____)
    5   Ralph Forrester (b. abt 1818-Baltimore, MD; d.____)
    5   Sarah Forrester (b. abt 1820-Baltimore, MD; d.____)
    5   Mary Forrester (b. abt 1822-Baltimore, MD; d.____)
    5   Anne Forrester (b. abt 1824-Baltimore, MD; d.____)
    5   Margaret Forrester (b. abt 1826-Chester County, PA: d.____)
  4   Margaret Forrester (b. abt 1789-Chester County, PA; d.____)
      Sp: John Silver (b. abt 1785-Chester County, PA; m.____; d.____)
  4   Ann M. Forrester (b. abt 1789-Chester County, PA; d.____)
3   Margaret Forrester (b. 4 Apr 1749-West Chester, Chester, PA; d.____)
3   Mary Forrester (b. 10 Mar 1752-Probably Goshen, Lancaster County, PA;
    d. 5 Sep 1840-Goshen, Lancaster County, PA)
    Sp: Joseph Hoopes (b. 10 Mar 1748-Goshen, Lancaster, PA; d.____)
  4   Paschell Hoopes (b. 22 Feb 1779-Goshen, Lancaster, PA; d.____)
      Sp: Sarah Temple (b. Apr 1789-Goshen, Lancaster, PA; d.____)
    5   John Temple Hoopes (b. 17 Oct 1810-W. Goshen, Chester, PA.; d.____)
        Sp: Rebecca Hallowell Stemple (b. May 1795-E. Goshen, Chester, PA.; d.____)
      6 Azaria Williamson Hoopes (b. 10 Feb 1833-E. Whiteland, PA.; d.____)
      6 Sarah Jane Hoopes (b. 2 Jul 1836-E. Whiteland, Chester, PA.; d.____)
    5   Jane Temple Hoopes (b. 29 May 1813-W. Goshen, Chester, PA.; d.____)
        Sp: William Robbins (b. abt 1810-Chester County, PA; d.____)
      6 Sarah E. Robbins (b. abt 1833-prob. Chester County, PA.; d.____)
      6 Mary M. Robbins (b. abt 1835-prob. Chester County, PA.; d.____)
      6 Emma Robbins (b. abt 1837-prob. Chester County, PA.; d.____)
    5   George Hoopes (b. 20 Dec 1815-West Goshen, Chester, PA.; d.____)
    5   Melinda Hoopes (b. 22 Jul 1818-West Goshen, Chester, PA.; d.____)
    5   Elizabeth Temple Hoopes (b. 20 Aug 1819-W. Goshen, Chester, PA.; d____)
    5   Alban Hoopes (b. 25 Jul 1823-West Goshen, Chester, PA; d.____)
        Sp: Sarah Elizabeth Smith (b. abt 1825-Philadelphia, PA.; d.____)
    5   Paschell Joseph Hoopes (b. 25 Dec 1827-W. Goshen, Chester, PA.; d.____)
        Sp: Lydia E. Eves (b. 3 Sep 1831-prob. DE, PA; d.____)
      6 Elizabeth H. Hoopes (b. Feb 1855-Philadelphia, PA; d.____)
      6 Fannie Hoopes (b. 13 Mar 1857-Kingessing, Philadelphia; PA; d.____)
      6 Horace B. Hoopes (b. 23 Oct 1859-Kingessing, Philadelphia, PA.; d.____)
      6 Helen Crittenden Hoopes (b. 15 Jan 1863-West Philadelphia, PA.; d.____)
      6 Fannie Hoopes (b. abt 1865-Philadelphia, PA; d.____)
      6 William E. Hoopes (b. 21 May 1869-Kingessing, Philadelphia, PA.; d.__)

4   Joseph Jr. Hoopes (b. 1 May 1790-Bradford, Chester, PA; d.____)
    Sp: Jane Woodward (b. 14 Feb 1783-West Bradford, Chester, PA.; d.____)
  5   Forrester Hoopes (b. 6 Sep 1811-East Goshen, Lancaster, PA.; d.____)
  5   Charlotte Hoopes (b. 17 Nov 1813-West Bradford, Chester, PA.; d.____)
  5   Elizabeth Hoopes (b. 18 Nov 1815-West Bradford, Chester, PA.; d.____)
  5   Lydia Ann Hoopes (b. 9 May 1820-East Goshen, Lancaster, PA.; d.____)
4   George Hoopes (b. 17 Nov 1785-Goshen, Lancaster, PA; d.____)
    Sp: Albina Woodward (b. 14 Jan 1789-West Bradford, McKean, PA.; d.____)
  5   George Washington Hoopes (b. 5 Jul 1809-E. Goshen, Lancaster, PA.; d.____)
  5   Mary Ann Hoopes (b. 8 Jan 1811-East Goshen, Lancaster, PA.; d.____)
      Sp: David Dutton Yearsley (b. 3 Mar 1808-Thornbury, Chester, PA.; d.__)
    6   Elizabeth Yearsley (b. 25 May 1831-Phoenixville, Chester, PA.; d.__)
        Sp: Jacob Cloward (b. 24 May 1830-Phoenixville, Chester, PA.; d.____)
        Sp: Alonzo Hazeltine Raleigh (b. 7 Nov 1818-Francistown, Hillsborough, NH
        d.____)
    6   Lavenia Elizabeth Hoopes Yearsley (b. 1 Sep 1833-Phoenixville, Schuylkill, PA
        d.____)
        Sp: Rufus Chester Allen (b. 22 Oct 1827-Mansfield, Deposit, NY; d.____)
        Sp: James Cloward Berry (b. 1829-Westchester, Chester, PA.; d.____)
    6   Nathan Yearsley (b. 8 Nov 1835-Westchester, Chester, PA.; d.____)
        Sp: Ruthinda Emma Stewart (b. 17 May 1845-Dallas, Jackson, MO.; d.____)
        Sp: Julia Ann Gibbs (b. 1865-Ogden, Weber County, UT; d.____)
    6   Mary Jane Yearsley (b. 18 Feb 1838-prob. Phoenixville, PA.; d.____)
        Sp: Benjamin Frankland Cummings (b. Mar 1821-Farmington, Franklin, ME
        d.____)
    6   George Hoopes Yearsley (b. 16 Mar 1840-prob. Phoenixville, PA; d.____)
        Sp: Lorinda Bess (b. 19 Dec 1842-Greenwood, Stebuen, NY; d.____)
        Sp: Annette Adelaide Miles (b. abt 1844-Westchester, Chester, PA; d.____)
    6   Emma Smith Yearsley (b. 14 Nov 1842-prob. Phoenixville, PA.; d.____)
        Sp: William Brockerman Wright (b. 10 Feb 1836-Philadelphia, PA; d.____)
        Sp: Joseph Vance (b. 1838-Nauvoo, IL)
    6   David Dutton Yearsley (b. 2 Jun 1845-prob. Phoenixville, Chester, PA; d.____)
        Sp: Alice Eldridge (b. 26 Oct 1848-Salt Lake City, Salt Lake, UT; d.__)
    6   Heber Chase Yearsley (b. 27 Sep 1848-prob. Phoenixville, Chester, PA; d.____)
        Sp: Addaline Malinda Poole (b. 24 Feb 1852-Centerville, Davis, UT; d.____)
  5   Robert F. Hoopes (b. 9 Jun 1813-East Goshen, Lancaster, PA.; d.____)
      Sp: Eliza R. Lewis (b. Jan 1822-prob. West Whiteland, Chester, PA.; d.____)
    6   George R. Hoopes (b. 1 Nov 1848-West Whiteland, Chester, PA.; d.____)
    6   Thomas Lewis Hoopes (b. 28 May 1850-W. Whiteland, Chester, PA; d.____)
    6   Ella Emma Hoopes (b. 18 Nov 1853-West Whiteland, Chester, PA.; d.____)
    6   Anna Mary Hoopes (b.30 Jun 1859-West Whiteland, Chester, PA.; d.____)
    6   Carrie S. Hoopes (b.4 Jul 1863-West Whiteland, Chester, PA.; d.____)
  5   Lavina Miller Hoopes (b. 25 Dec 1815-East Goshen, Lancaster, PA.; d____)
  5   Elizabeth Garrett Hoopes (b. 8 Sep 1817-East Goshen, Lancaster, PA; d.____)
      Sp: David Brinton (b. 29 Dec 1814-Thornbury Township, Near Dilworthtown, DE,
      PA; d.____)
    6   Robert Brinton (b. 11 Nov 1845-Winter Quarters, Nebraska; d.____)
  5   Abigail S. Hoopes (b. 14 Jan 1820-East Goshen, Lancaster, PA.; d.____)
      Sp: Caleb T. Pennock (b. 1816-prob. Chester County, PA; d.____)
  5   Esther Painter Hoopes (b. 21 Jun 1823-Birmingham, Huntingdon, PA; d.____)

5　Caroline T. Hoopes (b. 28 Jun 1829-Birmingham, Huntingdon, PA.; d.____)
　　　　Sp: Lee Spackman (b.____; d.____)
　　　6　William Spackman (b. 28 Oct 1852-Chester County, PA.; d.____)
　　　6　Robert Spackman (b. 29 Jul 1856-Chester County, PA.; d.____)
　　　6　Mary Albina Spackman (b. 11 Jul 1859-Chester County, PA.; d.____)
　4　Lydia Hoopes (b. 9 Jan 1786-Goshen, Chester County, PA.; d.____)
　　　Sp: John Walton (b. 14 May 1776-Goshen, Chester, PA.; d.____)
　　5　Joseph Walton (b. abt 1803-Goshen, Chester, PA; d.____)
　　5　Tamar Walton (b. abt 1805-prob. Goshen, Chester, PA; d.____)
　　　　Sp: William Sylvester (b. abt 1805-prob. Goshen, Chester, PA.; d.____)
　　5　William Walton (b. abt 1806-Goshen, Chester, PA.; d.____)
3　Tamer Forrester (b. 18 Apr 1754-West Chester, Chester, PA.; d.____)
　　Sp: Brown (b. abt 1750-West Chester, Chester County, PA; d.____)
3　Lydia Forrester (b. 10 Feb 1757-West Chester, Chester, PA.; d.____)
　　Sp: Fitzgerald (b. abt 1753-West Chester, Chester County, PA.; d.____)
3　Aaron Forrester (b. 22 Feb 1759-West Chester, Chester, PA.; d.____)
　　Sp: Sarah Hemphill (b.____; d.____)
3　Ruth Forrester (b. 5 Aug 1762-West Chester, Chester County, PA.; d.____)
　　Sp: Israel Hoopes (b. 14 Apr 1763-Chester County, PA; d.____)
　4　Susan Hoopes (b. 1788-Goshen, Chester County, PA; d.____)
　4　Jane Hoopes (b. 17 Nov 1790-Goshen, Chester County, PA.; d.____)
　　　Sp: Robert M. Martin (b. abt 1790-prob. Chester County, PA.; d.____)
　4　George Hoopes (b. 1791-prob. Chester County, PA; d.____)
　4　Anne Hoopes (b. 1792-prob. Chester County, PA; d.____)
　4　Charity Hoopes (b. abt 1794-prob. Chester County, PA; d.____)
　4　Jane Hoopes (b. 17 Nov 1799-Chester County, PA; d.____)
3　John Forrester (b. 10 Oct 1764-West Chester, Chester County, PA;
　　d. 10 Oct 1764-West Chester, Chester County, PA)

Compiled by:　　　　　　　　　　　　　　　　Contributors: Barbara Cole, SMVGS
Ms. Jerry P. Webber　　　　　　　　　　　　　　Forrest Warren, Cambria, CA
　　　　　　　　　　　　　　　　　　　　　Gerald Rupp, Morro Bay, CA

The GEORGE FOSTER Family of La Graciosa
SANTA MARIA VALLEY PIONEERS

The town of La Graciosa was the earliest settlement in the Santa Maria Valley; a school was built there in 1869, followed the next year by one at Pine Grove, which eventually became the name of the district serving the area. The town of La Graciosa was short-lived because of land title disputes, but the name persisted, and the history is recounted in the county histories, from Thompson & West, 1883, to Morrison & Hayden, 1917, and in personal recollections, such as Marie Dunlap's in the SMVGS&L Quarterly XI, 3-4, 1979, and the recent *Old Town Orcutt*, by Bob Nelson. *This Is Our Valley* repeats the list of original settlers among whom are the Foster and Hobbs families.

The Foster family came to the central coast area about 1868, probably from Visalia, the origin of a number of Cambria families. They are found on the 1870 census of Santa Rosa township, San Luis Obispo County. George W Foster's name is on a lengthy list of payments made by the San Luis Obispo Board of Supervisors in January 1872, but by 1876 he was established in La Graciosa, being the proprietor of the store in which was held the election of the trustees of the La Graciosa school district, per the oft-quoted minutes of May 2, 1876. In April 1876 he had been a witness to the marriage of C W Martin and Winnie Evans, and "in 1877 Mr G W Foster lost his granary, 800 sacks of barley, and a number of fowls, by a fire, supposed to be incendiary." (Thompson & West, p. 324). The 1880 census-taker found Mrs Foster, 58, a sufferer from heart disease, in La Graciosa with her daughter Laura Crabtree and family; Mr Foster may have gone to the Bay area with others of the family. Mrs Foster is buried in Haywards (in those days Haywards, like Ballards, still carried the "s") where Belle Chisholm and family were living in 1900, with Mr Foster in the household; Mr Foster skipped across the bay before the census-taker got to Stewart's house, for he was enumerated with them, too.

George W Foster's death in San Francisco occasioned a fairly lengthy obituary in the *San Luis Obispo Morning Tribune*, Friday, February 16, 1906, in which are named his children, both living and dead, which is helpful, but his life story was told in general terms, so the peregrinations of the family must be reconstructed from the public record. The obituary carried the notice "Boston papers please copy"; his two oldest children were born in Massachusetts; one would hope to find him on the 1850 census in that vicinity. Having searched out the half-dozen or more George Fosters listed in the AIS Index, it is still not obvious which is he; the Irish-born ones may be eliminated, of course.

Although he is called a '49er in his obituary, the first hint of California residence is found in the birth date of the third child, age 15 in 1870, born June 1855, per 1900 census and June 1861 in 1910 (at which time she was married to a much younger man). The California birthplace is consistent, as it is for the next two girls. George, Jr, was born in Oregon in 1861, but the family soon came back to California where the last boy first saw light.

CRABTREE

The Crabtree family is listed on the 1860 census for Tulare county: John, 65, blacksmith, born Tennessee; Rebecca, 53, born Missouri, and Ephraim, 17, born Texas. R W (William) Crabtree died at Adelaida, San Luis Obispo county, August 21, 1894, aged 49, according to the Paso Robles INDEPENDENT, and his tombstone is in the Adelaida cemetery; otherwise, the name is not represented on the central coast, as Ephraim left La Graciosa after his wife's death in 1886. He registered to vote at San Simeon in 1892, but thereafter moved to Kern county, his children, apparently following him.

LEFFINGWELL

Emma Jane, the first of the girls to marry, was wife of a German surnamed Gisin; their son was born in Visalia in 1867, and widow and baby accompanied the Foster family to the central coast. Early in 1879 Emma Jane married Adam Leffingwell, youngest son of the pioneer Cambria family. They became parents to four daughters and a son, the latter living but a few weeks; a daughter died, likely of diphtheria, less than two months before Adam was killed at the family sawmill when a two inch plank, hurled from the saw, crushed his temple, in August 1882. Her oldest daughter died as a young wife with two small boys; the youngest died at 16; she was left with Clayton, her firstborn, who managed her ranch for her, the two of them remaining single, and the next youngest daughter, Lena, the only one to outlive her. A photograph of Emma Jane Leffingwell, three other Leffingwells, and 16 other early Cambria residents are in *Where The Highway Ends - Cambria, San Simeon and the Ranchos*, by Geneva Hamilton.

KAYS

Anna married during the La Graciosa years; her husband, William Kays, was the fifth son of John Charles Kays, an Irishman who settled in the Santa Ynez valley in the 1840's. Kays' wife was Maria Josefa Burke whose father, James Walter Burke, was also Irish, having come to California from Galway and settling in Santa Barbara county in 1828, the year he married Maria Josefa Bruna Boronda Cota, daughter of Jose Manuel Boronda and widow of Manuel Antonio Cota. (For the lineage of these families, see *Spanish-American Families of Early California: 1769-1850*, Vol. II, by Maria E Northrup, Southern California Genealogical Society, 1984.) By 1870 the Kays family had moved from the valley, ranching and raising cattle, to Santa Barbara, where J C Kays was a dealer in general merchandise. His son learned bookkeeping and clerking, and, in 1875, when he came of age, he registered to vote in La Graciosa, occupation clerk. It could be that he was working in George Foster's store, and that year he married the boss's daughter. In 1879 he registered in Guadalupe, probably because Foster closed the La Graciosa store. In 1882 he registered in Los Alamos, and some time later returned to Santa Barbara, where, in September, 1890, about 2 o'clock on a Saturday night, William Kays, during a "friendly scuffle" was shot dead outside a saloon, both participants being well "under the influence". "Everybody knew William Kays as a quiet, inoffensive young man. Somewhat inclined to drink, to be sure, but not known in any sense as a bad man. He has been bookkeeper in the upper part of the county and in truth quite an able young man. Himself was his worst enemy. His father is an octogenarian well known in this city. His brother, John, was formerly sheriff of Los Angeles county." That is the second paragraph of an 18 paragraph article on the shooting, which includes the inquest, in the *Santa Barbara Daily Independent*, Sep. 20, 1890.

Anna took her three boys to San Francisco, and, like many another widow, took in boarders; in 1900 she had in her household, her brother Elmer, and John Henry Charles Leffingwell. Son of Adam Leffingwell's oldest brother, he was born in the Cambria area in 1876 or 1878, so was about the age of Anna's oldest child. He saw fit to marry her, but despite his youth, she outlived him. Nothing has been found of him after the 1910 census, so whether the union was successful or not cannot be judged.

STEWART and CHISHOLM

Little is known about Addie and Belle beyond the census records. Both predeceased their husbands who are found on the 1910 census as boarders: Stewart with Leland Green in Berkeley where he died in 1914; Chisholm with Hester Kennedy in Santa Cruz where he died in 1919.

Although Chisholms were living in Haywards in 1900, his occupation blacksmith, his obituary in the Santa Cruz paper said he had been a "lumberman in this section of the state for 45 years."

GEORGE ALONZO FOSTER

Both George and his wife were objects of lengthy obituaries, hers being the more accurate. He was born in Oregon but the family left when he was but a few months old, thence to San Francisco, which remains to be ascertained; their arrival in San Luis Obispo county when George was 7 is correct. The Scott family was in Santa Maria in 1880, so why George and Mary Scott married in Santa Rosa is not known. George died in Oceano, which led the newspaper writer to the conclusion that he had lived there ever since his arrival, which is not the case. Her obit. said eight of their ten children were born in Santa Maria; the 1886 birth was noted in the *SM Times*. He filed Notice of Intention in 1887 for N2NE4 S1 T9N R34W, P.O. Santa Maria, witnesses Wm W McPherson, B McPherson, Lee J McPherson, and David Foster (of the Missouri Fosters). This land is about a mile east of Bradley Road on a line with Lakeview. His voter registration for 1888 was in Sisquoc but in 1892 in Cambria. G A Foster was delinquent for 3.23 in taxes in the Tepusquet district in 1897, but on the 1900 census he is listed in Santa Maria. The 1906 directory shows him on Main street, and the 1909 directory at 608 S Pine St. It was this property for which he failed to pay his taxes in 1909, according to the Delinquent Tax list printed in the Santa Barbara MORNING PRESS. Described as lot 12, block 4, Thornburgh's Addition to the City of Santa Maria, it is now 614 S. Pine St. He was also delinquent on property in the Martin district, south east of Orcutt: Lot 2 S19 R33W, 100 acres. He may have been slow on the taxes because of having moved to Mariposa county (1909) (George Foster is now residing in Mariposa. –*SM Times* Feb 12 1910) The census-taker found the family there in 1910, Indian Peak district. Mary's sister, Nettie Phillips and family, had moved to Mariposa about 1899. Phillipses stayed but Fosters came back to the coast, living in Santa Maria until 1915, per Mary's obit., but they are listed in the 1917 Santa Maria phone book. Moving to Arroyo Grande they operated the Ryan Hotel for several years, until they built a house in Oceano, where they ended their days.

ELMER ALEXANDER FOSTER

Elmer was born in Wilmington, California, according to his brief obituary in the *Santa Maria Times*. Wilmington was the port for Los Angeles, and grew rapidly during the Civil War as a base for government supplies. Patriots gathered there in hopes of being sent east to the fray; it may be that George Foster went there for business purposes.

Elmer was a single man and apparently lived with one or another relative. He registered to vote in Cambria, as did George, in 1892; in 1900 he was with his sister Anna in San Francisco; in 1910 he was enumerated twice on the census: in Santa Maria at 620 W. Church St, Laborer, and in Ballards with George W. Scott, a brother-in-law of George Foster. They were employed in a gravel pit. He made news in Santa Maria when he, "a teamster at the sugar factory, was thrown from his wagon last Tuesday afternoon and sustained a fracture of the right wrist. He was otherwise badly bruised and after the accident laid unconscious for nearly an hour before being picked up. He is now being cared for in town." (*Santa Maria Times* May 16,1908) Later this item appeared in Local News Notes, *San Luis Obispo Daily Telegram*, Wednesday, February 4, 1914: "Archie (sic) Foster and Elmer Foster, well known Santa Marians, are among the out-of-town guests registered at the Golden State Hotel today."

This is a condensation of material gathered for a book tentatively entitled, Related Pioneer Families of the Central Coast-families related in a round-about way, or, as Fosters, a circular way, to Laurentine S. Cole, 1828-1894 (from Wisconsin to Cambria in 1874), thus: Cole's step-daughter

Abigail Williams married Wm H Bright, whose brother George married Lizzie Woods, whose sister, May, was wife of Wm Leffingwell, whose brother and nephew married Foster sisters, whose brother, George, married Mary Scott, whose sister, Nettie, was wife of Newton Phillips, son of Georgiana Music, whose sister Blandina married Jack Bright, brother of William, son-in-law of Laura Culver Williams Cole, second wife of Laurentine S Cole. Several dozen families are being collected, most having settled earlier than Coles; there is much intermarriage, and scattering, to the north as far as Santa Cruz and south to Santa Maria.

FOSTER SCRAPBOOK

1885 La Graciosa Dew Drops...Mrs Crabtree has been very sick, but we are glad to learn, is improving... -*SM Times* July 4

Personal Mention. The little nine year old son of E J Crabtree, 7 miles south of this place, was thrown from a horse a few days ago and one of his arms dislocated at the elbow, besides being considerably bruised up otherwise. -Ibid Aug 29; also SLO paper

La Graciosa Frost. With the frost nipping at our nose this morning we hadn't the heart (or the cheek) to dub our scratching "Dew Drops" as usual...Mr E J Crabtree and Mr T J Brookshire have been seriously ill, but we are glad that they are both convalescing.
-Ibid (date lost)

1888 ...raise funds for La Graciosa....Judges: S Mudgett, F C Twitchell; Inspector: E J Crabtree...
-Ibid (date lost) (indicating Crabtree still here; not listed on 1890 SB co voter list)

1892 A quiet wedding took place at the Methodist (sic) parsonage on Sunday last; the contracting parties were Elmer Gale and Miss Carrie Crabtree, both well and favorably known in this section.
-Ibid Nov 26

1933 E E Gale, Dead; Field Engineer Elmer Ellsworth Gale, 55, field engineer with United States Engineers' office of Stockton, died Saturday night at his home, 1225 North Sierra Nevada street, after eight months of illness of hardening of the arteries.. Surviving are the widow, Carrie, a daughter, Verna LaVerne Gale, the latter a teacher in the public schools here; two sisters, Mrs James Wilson of Glendale and Mrs Clara Bowers of Seattle, and a brother, Charles Gale of Los Angeles.

Previously to affiliating with the government engineers' office here, Gale was for many years engineer with the Harris Manufacturing Company. His first work was with the Santa Fe as steam engineer.

Funeral services will be held at 3 o'clock tomorrow in the chapel of B C Wallace, North Sutter street. -*Stockton Record* Mon Jan 23 p.1
Ed. Note: Father probably S M Gale, d. Santa Maria June 1887 @44; mother E. Della Gale, who married John Ball of Lompoc in 1895.

George W Foster	b. Maine May/Jun 1823 (cen) or 1820 (obit)
	d. San Francisco 9 Feb 1906 @85/9/3
	buried Haywards, CA
m. (Boston?)	
Martha J	b. New Hampshire 1820/22
	d. before 1900; buried Haywards
	1880: in La Graciosa with Crabtrees
1. Laura E	b. MA 26 Mar 1848 (tombstone)
	d. La Graciosa 26 July 1886; Peritonitis
	(d. @43 per Reg. of Death;) Pinegrove cem
m. (Visalia) 1 Jan 1868; Tulare Co A163	

Ephraim Jasper Crabtree   b. TX 1853
   1892 Voter reg: 6'1¼, fair   d. Old River Dist., Kern Co, CA 9 May 1908 @66,
     complexion, blue eyes, brown   Cancer of the stomach
     hair, rancher, res. San Simeon   F. John Crabtree (1860; Tulare Co)
                                          M. Rebecca
   a. Cora Edna   b. (Cambria, CA) July 1869
                                          d. Kern Co 26 Dec 1948
               m. Pine Grove 7 Sep 1887 by S K Morton, JP, Santa Maria
   William Adrian Hobbs   b. Stockton CA 1858
                                        d. Kern Co 27 Mar 1943
                                        F. Samuel K Hobbs 1833-1901
                                        M. Mahala J Gann 1841-1925

     = 11 children by 1910; see Hobbs chart
   b. Carrie E   b. (La Graciosa) 1874; m. @18
                                         d. (Stockton 8 Nov 1947)
           m. Santa Maria 20 Nov 1892 by Geo T Weaver, ME ch
   Elmer Ellsworth Gale   b. CA; m. @21
                                         d. Stockton CA 21 Jan 1933 @55 (?)
     = Verna LaVerne   b. Pine Grove 2 Oct 1893 (*Santa Maria Times*)
   c. Clyde   b. (La Graciosa) 1876
   d. Cleoro (?)   b. (La Graciosa) 1878
     others?
             J H Freer, son-in-law, in Old River, Kern co 1908
2. Emma Jane   b. MA Sep 1849
                                        d. San Luis Obispo 8 Dec 1941 @92; Cambria cem

       m. 1
    _____ Gisin
   a. George Clayton   b. (Visalia) Nov 1867
     Single   d. San Luis Obispo 7 Jan 1932 @64
                                          Cambria cem
             m. 2 San Luis Obispo 20 Feb 1870 by G W Murphy, A111
   Adam Charles Leffingwell   b. Montrose IA 5 Aug 1845
                                        d. Cambria 15 Aug 1882; Cambria cem
                                        F. Wm Leffingwell 1805-1884
                                           (Joseph^7, Benjamin^6, Samuel^5, Samuel^4,
                                           Nathaniel^3, Thomas^2, Thomas^1)
                                        M. Eunice^5, Bigelow 1805-1889
                                           (John^4, John^3, John^2, John^1.)
   b. Laura Jane   b. Cambria 6 Jan 1872
                                        d. before 1900
                m. c1890
   William Henry Morss   b. CA Nov 1868
                                        d. San Jose 28 Feb 1907
                                        F: Wm. Morss 1846-1907
                                        M: Rosannah L. 1851-1922

     = Clayton Leonard 1891-1967
     = Ralph Gordon 1893-1911
   c. Leroy G   b. Cambria 27 Feb 1873
                                          d. 11 Apr 1873; Cambria cem

   d. Lucy M.   b. Cambria 19 Aug 1874
                                          d. 21 June 1882; Cambria cem

   e. Lena Ivy   b. Cambria 1877
                  d. Oakland CA 12 Aug 1953 @76;
                  Cambria cem
     m. Cambria 29 Nov 1899 by Rev J. H. Chase, F76
      wit: H K Cass, Cayucos; Ira Whittaker, Cambria
  Dick Sanders   b. Cayucos 15 May 1877
                  d. San Luis Obispo 28 Apr 1943
                  F: Davis G Sanders
                  M: Martha
   = Lorena Jeannette (Garrett) b. 3 Apr 1905
  f. Emma Lorena   b. Cambria Apr 1880
                  d. 2 Aug 1896; Cambria cem
3. Anna F   b. CA June 1855
                  d. San Francisco 18 Aug 1939 @84; Olivet cem
   m. 1 La Graciosa 16 Oct 1875 by Chas H South JP, B147
  William Charles Kays   b. (Santa Ynez) 1853
                  d. Santa Barbara 20 Sep 1890 @c33; shot
                  F: John Charles Kays 1813-1896
                  M: Maria Josefa Burke 1830-
  a. William F   b. (La Graciosa) Aug 1876
                  d. (San Francisco 25 Sep 1935 @59,
                    spouse initial M.)
  b. Ernest   b. (Guadalupe) 14 Jan 1879
                  d. (Sacramento 1 Sep 1946)
  c. Alfred August   b. (Los Alamos) July 1882
                  d. (San Francisco 18 Dec 1944,
                    spouse initial L.K.)
     m. 1908 (1910: letter carrier, San Francisco)
  Veronica H   b. CA 1889
3.   m. 2 (San Francisco) 1901
  John Henry Charles Leffingwell   b. CA 29 Aug 1876/8
   1910: Carpenter, San Francisco   F: Joseph Lyman Leffingwell 1833-1884
                   brother of Adam C. Leffingwell
                  M: Margaret Ashworth 1835-1917
4. Mary A(ddie)   b. CA Feb 1856/7
                  d. (San Francisco) before 1906
   m. 1882
  Andrew Galloway Stewart   b. Scotland May 1848; imm. 1870
                  d. Berkeley 8 Feb 1914 @67
   No issue. Was survived by nephew William Case
5. Isabel (Belle) V   b. CA July 1859/60
                  d. (Haywards?) before 1910
   m. 1885
  Daniel Chisholm   b. Antigonish NS Sep 1852/5; imm 1877
                  d. Santa Cruz 20 Apr 1919 @67¼
                   See Heritage Quest #31 Nov-Dec 1990
                   p.21 for Chisholm, Antigonish NS
    a. Zelda G   b. Aug 1886
    b. Trello A   b. Feb 1890
    c. Verna B   b. Mar 1892

6. George Alonzo					b. Roseburg OR June 1861
						d. Oceano CA 27 Oct 1932 @71;
						    Arroyo Grande cem
	1892: @32 5'11, light complexion, blue eyes, brown hair, scar under rt eye, teamster,
	    res: Cambria. Reg. Aug 27
	1922: 5'10, res. Arroyo Grande
		m. Santa Rosa 15 Apr 1883 by G O Burnett, Min Christian Ch, H80
   Mary Ellen Scott				b. Healdsburg CA Dec 1863/4
						d. Oceano CA 23 Apr 1942 @79 or @78
						    Arroyo Grande cem
						F: Benjamin Welcome Scott 1830-1909
						M: Eliza Jane Freshour 1838-1909
		1922: 5'4, res. Arroyo Grande
		10 births, 8 living in 1910; 8 born Santa Maria, per obit
	a. Fay					b. Sep 1884; m. @21 of Santa Maria
						d. before 1932
			m. San Luis Obispo 11 Sep 1905 by Geo Willett, Congl min, G191
				wit: Mary Cathryn Egan, SLO; Rbt D Fuller, SLO
	   Benjamin W. Scott			b. CA 1881; m. @24 of Santa Maria
	      (bride's uncle)			d. before 1933 (Kern Co 30 Jan 1912 @30)?
						F: Benjamin Welcome Scott 1830-1909
						M: Eliza Jane Freshour 1838-1909
	   =Bernice P				b. Santa Maria 25 Nov 1905
	b. Raymond				b. Santa Maria 14 Aug 1886 (*SM Times*)
		1922: 5'7½ , res. Arroyo Grande
	c. Lottie					b. (Sisquoc) Dec 1888
						d. before 1932
			m. 1907
	   Marion/Martin J Braiden Scott	b. CA Nov 1885
	      (1st cousin once removed)
						F: John C. Scott 1839-1901
						    brother of Benj W Scott
						M: Ella Cook 1848-1901
	d. Gladys					b. Feb 1892
						d. before 1932
	e. Ernest					b. Apr 1898
	f. Ruby					b. Feb 1900
						d. before 1932
	g. Frances (Annis)			d. 16 Nov 1938 @38; AG cem
	h. George Alfred				b. Santa Maria 28 Dec 1903
						d. San Luis Obispo 24 Feb 1973; AG cem
			m.
	   Florence _____
	i. Lucile (Sugden)
	j. --
7. Elmer Alexander				b. Wilmington CA 27 May 1865
	   Single					d. Santa Maria 6 Aug 1944
		1892: @27, 5'10, light complexion, blue eyes, brown hair,
		    laborer, res. Cambria. Reg. Aug 27

Corrections and Additions   [Page numbers refer to those in Quarterly]

pg. 6.   Mary Ellen and George A Foster
10 births, 8 living, 1910; 8 born in Santa Maria (obit)
    a. Myrtle <u>Fay</u>   b. SM Sep 1884; m. @21 of SM
                                                                 d. Arroyo Grande 30 Oct 1918 @34;
                                                                 AG cem   obit Nov 2
                                                                 m.2 Monroe NELL
         m.1 San Luis Obispo 11 Sep 1905 by Geo Willett, min, G191
             wit: Mary Cathryn Egan, SLO; Rbt D Fuller, SLO
      Benjamin Wirt Scott   b. Siskiyou co May 1882; m. @24 of SM
        1906 Dir: Scott Wirt   d. nr McKittrick CA 30 Jan 1912 @30; obit
          lab r Chapel st SM   *Bakersfield Californian* Wed Jan 31 p. 2
        1910: Santa Maria   F: John Cowhick Scott
                                                M: Ella Elizabeth Cook
      =Bernice P b. SM 25 Nov 1905 (*Times*)
         1920: @18 (!) w/Jack & Lottie Scott, Kern co
    b. Raymond Elmer   b. SM 14 Aug 1886 (*Times*)
       1910, 1920: w/parents   d. (Oceano) 1 Sep 1947; no obit found
       1931-2 Dir, 1938 Dir: Oceano; 1942: living w/mother
    c. Lottie Hazel   b. Sisquoc 3 Dec 1888
                                                d. Taft CA 14 Sep 1928 @39; obit
                                                Bakersfield Californian Mon Sep 17 p. 10
             m. 1906   Union cem, Bakersfield
     Marion <u>Jack</u>son Braiden Scott 1885-1961; see J C Scott chart
    d. Gladys Ellen   b. (Cambria) 20 Feb 1891
       1910: w/parents   d. Arroyo Grande 24 Oct 1918 @26;
          m.   AG cem; obit Nov 2
       Fred D Hobbs   b. SM valley 4 Dec 1888
        1914 Dir: Fred S & Gladys, lab,   d. (Oceano) 14 Apr 1959* @70; AG cem
          W end Grover, SM   F: Joseph Lane Hobbs 1863-1936
          (now Boone st)   M: Nancy Elnora Stubblefield 1867-1909
               m.2 Larena   *obit *SLO Telegram-Tribune* Thu Apr 16 p. 2
        1920: Careaga   See Hobbs chart
      =Elizabeth (Bessie) Ellen (Roads)   b. 5 Feb 1910
                                                d. Napa 27 Oct 1988
      =Virginia Geraldine (Jane)   b. c1915
         m. Albert LaBorde   b. (Huasna, SLO co) 1908
                                                F: Pierre/Peter LaBorde 1862-1935
                                                M: Martha Olive Mahurin 1880-1958
    e. Ernest E   b. (SM) 4 Apr 1898
       FBI   d. Huntington Park CA 13 Aug 1981
             m.1 Pauline Miller; 2 children
             m.2 Gertie Wideman
    f. Frances Ruby   b. SM Feb 1900
                                               d. Los Angeles 16 Nov 1938 @38
           m.   AG cem; obit Fri Nov 18 p. 3
      Edward B Annis   (b. ME; d. SCz co 6-3-1921 @44)?
        1934 Dir: Frances E Annis (wid EB) r 3809 Brunswick av Los Angeles
        1938 Dir: same

      g. George Alfred   b. SM 28 Dec 1903
                                                                        d. SLO 25 Feb 1983; AG cem; obit *SLO*
                m.   *Telegram-Tribune* Mon Feb 26 p. 2
      Florence Carr   living San Luis Obispo 1994
        No Issue
   h. Lucile N   b. (Santa Maria) 1907/8
     1920: w/parents   d. Cedarville CA 1961
         m.
  Walter R Sugden, whose mother died in WA 1935   -*San Luis Obispo Daily Telegram* Jan 18
   ?(Walter F Sugden b. 23 May 1902; d. Placer co 11-18-1986 SSDI, benefits to Roseville)?

Vol. XXVII, No. 2, Summer 1995, p.14

Corrections and Additions   [Page numbers refer to those in Quarterly]

p.13.   Marriage: Lottie Foster Married Jack Scott last Friday.   -Sep 29 1906
          Frances Foster born Pine Grove 14 Feb 1900. (*Times*)

Vol. XXX, No. 1, Spring 1998, p.4

p.24   G W Foster's wife was Martha Jane Sawyer; she died in San Francisco 9 May 1896. Cuyama & Bakersfield (news). Bakersfield, Dec 12, 1892. Ed. Times: … Since I began this, Marcellus Brown and Wm Hobbs of upper Cuyama have made their appearance, accompanied by Eph Crabtree, son and daughter from everywhere but here; Eph is an old La Graciosa inhabitant…J.M.   -Dec 17 1892

Vol. XXX, No. 3, Fall 1998, pg 19

FOX
GUADALUPE PIONEERS

Michael Fox   b. IRE Aug 1830; imm. 1847/1850
    1860 cen: Nevada co CA   d. Santa Barbara 11 Oct 1928 @98
    Eureka tp PO Morris? Flat
    1875: to Guadalupe   -*This is Our Valley* 36
    1879 GR: 49 IRE f Guad; naturalized July 1867 SF Dist Ct
    1880 cen: Guadalupe
    1892 GR: 62 5'4½ fair complexion brown eyes grey hair scar on l h;
        farmer; IR; res Nipomo; precinct Oso Flaco; PO Nipomo. nat 11 July 1867 SF Cir Ct
    1900 cen: Nipomo; 1900 GR: Oso Flaco/Nipomo
    1902 GR: 71 Oso Flaco PO Nipomo
    1920 cen: 1910 Laguna St Santa Barbara, widower
       m. c1857
Jane Connelly   b. IRE Nov 1838; imm. 1851
                  d. (SB 13 Aug 1916 @76)

9 births, 7 living 1900
1. Ambrose   b. c1858; m. @28 of SLO co
               d.
     1886: Ambrose Fox sponsor for Francis Fleck, confirmation, Guad
     1888: ad The Hart House Livery Stable, A A Fox, Prop. Main St
       next to Hart House.—Ag Fair program
     1895: Military Band, A A Fox…   -*Times* Sept 21
        m. San Luis Obispo 19 Oct 1886 by G W Barnes JP, B163.
          wit: H H Doyle, SLO; F P Collins, SLO
    Teresa Toquini, widow   b. CA   m. @30 of SB co
                          d.   parents b. Germany
2. Basil   b. CA June 1860
    Confirmed St Isidore's   d. (Los Angeles co 25 Oct 1938 @78 CS)
      Ch Guad 8 July 1877 @17; sponsor Peter Meade
    1880 cen: w/parents
    1892 GR: 32 5' 9½ fr gry dk f CA Oso Flaco PO Nipomo
    1900 cen: Nipomo, single;   1902 GR: 40 Oso Flaco PO Nipomo
    1902 GR: 42 Oso Flaco PO Nipomo
    1910, 1920 cen: 431 E Pedregosa St SB; mother-in-law in household
    1936 Los Angeles Extended Area phbk: 1330 N Louise, Glendale
       m. 1910
    Clarinda Stafford   b. CA 1881-2
                       d. (Los Angeles co 1-5-1958)
                       F: IRE (Owen A Stafford 1882-____)?
                       M: Clarinda M 1838-1921
     a. Katherine J   b. c1912
     b. Elizabeth C   b. c1915
     c. Mary E   b. c1919
3. Thomas Francis   b. CA Dec 1863
    Confirmed St Isidore's Ch   d. (Los Angeles co 5-15-1935 @73 N)
      Guad 8 July 1877 @13; sponsor Peter Meade
    1880 cen: w/parents
    1892 GR: 29 5'10 lt gry blk scar on l wrist stu CA Nipomo
    1900 cen: Lompoc, Lawyer; 2 births, 2 living

1936 Los Angeles Extended Area phbk: 1803 Crenshaw Blvd
m. Lompoc 9 Nov 1897 by Rev Lack (*Times*)

Mary Ann Sanor	b.	(Santa Clara co) CA 18 Jan 1871
(Mamie)	d.	(Lompoc) 21 Nov 1905; Evergreen cem
	F:	Martin Van Buren Sanor 1840-1921
	M:	Annie Mullen 1852-1908
		to Lompoc 1874; see O'Neill 165

    a. Angela C   b. Lompoc 16 Aug 1898 (*Times*) also SSDI
       1920 cen: w/Michael Fox   d. SB 1-6-1982; SSDI
       1948, 1960, 1973 phbk: 1910 Laguna St SB
    b. Leo   b. Lompoc 27 Jan 1900; SSDI
       1920 cen: w/Michael Fox   d. (San Francisco 9-30-1971)
       1936 Los Angeles Extended Area phbk: Leo S Fox 8039 Selma Av (?)
       1973 Santa Barbara phbk: L J Fox 1910 Laguna St (?)
    c. Lucile   b. (Lompoc) 1903
       1920 cen: w/Michael Fox
       (Lucile E Fox b. 14 Oct 1903 SSDI)   d. SDiego Co 11-11-1979)
    d. Evelyn   b. (Lompoc) 1905
       1920 cen: w/Michael Fox

4. Mary E   b. CA July 1866
    Confirmed St Isidore's Ch   d.
       Guad 8 July 1877 @11; sponsor Jane Donovan
    1900: w/parents, single;   1920: w/father, single;   1932 phbk: M Fox 1910 Laguna SB

5. Catherine   b. CA Feb 1871/2
    Confirmed St Isidore's Ch   d. (Kate C Fox d. SB 3-13-1968)
       Guad 1 Apr 1886 @15; sponsor Artemisa Arellanes
    1900: w/parents, single
    1948, 1960 SB phbk: Kate C Fox 1910 Laguna St

6. Angela   b. CA c1874
                                 d. (Angela F Mitchell Marin co 9-2-1955)
          m. Santa Barbara 11 Sep 1907
    Harold L Mitchell   d. (Santa Barbara co 7-29-1942 AM)

7. Paul   b. Fox ranch nr Guad 13 Dec 1876
    Confirmed St Isidore's Ch   d. Santa Barbara 22 Feb 1971 @94/2/9; SM cem
       Guad 1 Apr 1886 @10   obit Feb 24 p.2. 11 neph/nc
       sponsor Daniel Donovan   Stanford U; LLB Georgetown U 1902
    1902 GR: 25 Oso Flaco   bio *Who's Who SM* 24
       PO Nipomo   in Bakersfield 1910-1918
    1930 Dir: h 1201 S Broadway   City Clerk Lompoc 6 y   -*This is Our Valley* 40
    1940-1 Dir: same
          m. Los Angeles 15 April 1906
    Lizetta Edna Tolladay   b. (Lompoc) 1876
                                 d. (1) Feb 1950 @73/9/11; SM cem
    No issue   obit Feb 2 p.1. r 1201 S Bwy
                                 F: Lemuel Tolladay 1837-1891; Evergreen cem
                                 M: Martha   1853-1901; Evergreen cem
      1950: pall bearers: Tony Souza, Geo Scott, L T Thompson Sr., Ray Saunders,
          Howard Frew, Allan Crews.

1880 Honor Roll Guadalupe School: Katie, Angela, Paul Fox…   -*This is Our Valley* 40
Early teachers at the Nipomo School: Lottie Wise, Kate Fox, Mollie O'Connor who married Pat Moore, and Mollie O'Connor who married John Brown…   -*California Pioneers*, Alonzo Dana,1966

Who Are These: 1904 SLO Dir: Mrs T Fox 1132 Chorro
                       Died in county hospital 13 Jan 1881 John Fox.   -*SLO Tribune*
                       J W Fox Insolvent debtor.   -Ibid 12 Mar 1881

Vol. XXVIII, No. 2, Summer 1996, p.16

Corrections and Additions   [Page numbers refer to those in Quarterly]

p.15.   A Fox is now proprietor of Santa Maria Stables… new rigs, well kept stables…purchased new fine carry-all…runs for American House guests.   –Oct 8 1887

      1900 cen: SLO. Theresa Fox Apr 1856 m.13 5 births 5 living CA GER GER; Lena Jan 1876 CA SWTZ CA; Mary Oct 1879 CA SWTZ CA; Ernest May 1882 CA SWTZ CA; Ambrose Nov 1895 CA CA CA. First 3 children apparently from first marriage, surname not given.

GANOUNG
PIONEERS OF THE CALIFORNIA CENTRAL COAST

Edwin E Ganoung   b. MI 22 June 1837; m.1 @22. Parents NY
   to CA 1860   d. at home Corbett Canyon, Arroyo Grande
   1870 cen: AG tp   15 July 1911 @74
   1874. IOOF #3 installation…E Ganoung… -Jan
   1875 Paulson Dir: Ganoung Ed, contr Nipomo st SLO
   1880 cen: Buchon st SLO lab
   1892 GR: 55 5'4 dark complexion brown eyes brown hair farmer MI res AG pct AG #1PO AG
   1900 cen: AG farmer
   1902 GR: 65 AG #1
   1910 cen: AG
   1912 Dir: Arroyo Grande: Ganoung Albert J farmer; Edwin Ganoung farmer
   1911: Visits Bedside of Father in Arroyo. Mrs C J Whisman, wife of Chas Whisman, cashier of the First National Bank of Salinas, was a visitor in SLO yesterday, en route home after a visit to the bedside of her father, Edward (sic) Ganoug, who is ill at his home in Arroyo Grande. Mr Ganoung is a pioneer resident of the Arroyo Grande valley, and at present resides in Corbit (sic) canyon, near that town. His many friends will regret to hear of his indisposition. Mrs Whisman returned to Salinas last night. The lady is a former resident of San Miguel and well known to many in this section.   –*SLO Daily Telegraph* Thu May 11 p.1
   1911: Local Paragraphs. Edwin E Ganoung, one of the best known pioneers of SLO Co passed away at his home near Arroyo Grande @74…wife, 1 dau, 2 sons.   –*SM Times* July 22
     m.1 San Luis Obispo 2 April 1860 by Lewis H Bouton at house of Augustin Garcia, A27; wit: John Haskins, F A Simpson

Elizabeth Ellen Kester   b. IA c1842; m. @17
    d. San Luis Obispo 11 March 1868 @25/4/21
                     -*SLO Pioneer* Mar 14

1. Harvey A Ganoung   b. CA 1862
    d.

2. Clara Alice Ganoung   b. Sep 1863
   tchr San Miguel 1887   d.
   m. 1889
   Charles J Whisman   b. CA Jan 1861; parents MO
    d. Alameda Co 4 Dec 1918 @58
     1887. Came from Chualar, replaced J J Bullock as Wells Fargo agent, San Miguel.   -*The Lands of Mission San Miguel*, Ohles, 1997
     1892 GR: 32 5'8½ fr blu dk expr agt CA res, pct, PO San Miguel
     1899. Wells Fargo agt, San Miguel. –Ohles
     1900 cen: San Miguel agt WF&Co 2 births 2 living
     a. Henry S Whisman   b. Jan 1890
        d.
     b. Clara J Whisman   b. Aug 1898
        d.

3. Edwin Ganoung   b. SLO 10 Feb 1868   –*SLO Pioneer*
   E Ganving (sic) Constable   d. (after 1939)
   San Miguel tp (after 1888)   –*The Story of Adelaida*, MacGillivray, 1992
   1900 cen: Monterey Co San Antonio tp grocer 4 births 4 living
   1910 cen: Lockwood-Jolon rd 4 births 3 living; postmaster Jolon
   1926 in St Helena
   1934 in Oakland

        m. 1892
   Susan A   b. WI Aug 1868; parents IRE
                                       d. Butte Co 31 Aug 1932 @64
     1916-17 VR: Lynch pct: Edwin 5'6 CA, Miss Nellie 5'2½ CA; Mrs Susan A 5'6½ WI
     1920: San Miguel. Mrs E Ganoung of Napa returned home after visiting Mrs Geo
        Sonnenberg.   -date lost
    a.   Nellie M Ganoung   b. June 1893
                                        d.
    b.   Clarence C Ganoung   b. Apr 1895
                                        d. before 1910
    c.   Nettie A Ganoung   b. Jan 1898
                                        d.
    d.   Raymond A Ganoung   b. Mar 1900; (20 Mar 1900; SSDI)
                                        d. (Yuba Co July 1985)
(3.)   m.2 at house of Thomas Whiteley Esq San Luis Obispo Tue Feb 14 1871
         by Rev J W Allen, A124. "Taunton Mass papers please copy."   –*SLO Tribune*
Priscilla Whiteley Smith   b. Manchester ENG 19 Jan 1847; imm 1855; m. of SLO
  to San Francisco @13   d. at home of son 404 W Cook, Santa Maria
  in CA 66y   23 Nov 1926 @79; AG cem
  1900 cen: 3 births 3 living   obit *SM Times* Tue Nov 23 p.1. 10 gch 2 ggch
  bio M/H 443: 6 births 3 lvg   F: Thomas Whiteley 1819-1899. Bio M/H 443
                                         na 1872 Bristol MA
                                        M: Margaret Ann Longshire 1827-1902
4.   Ida/Cora Maud Ganoung   b. SLO Fri 16 Feb 1872, 10#.   –*SLO Tribune*
     bap 4 Aug 1872 St. Stephen's   d. SLO 6 Nov 1873 @1/10   –*SLO Tribune*
     Epis Ch SLO
5.   Albert Jason Ganoung   b. SLO 27 Oct 1874 (St. Stephen's Ch records)
     1900 cen: San Miguel   d. Contra Costa Co 22 Feb 1933 @59
     1 birth 1 living   spouse initial D
     1902 GR: 28 AG #1
     1912 Dir: AG farmer
     1926: in Martinez
       m. 1898
     Emma B   b. CA Feb 1882; parents AR
                                          d.
    a.   Albert H Ganoung   b. Feb 1899
                                      d.
     1895: Albert Ganoung of Arroyo Grande arrived in town yesterday, on his way overland
       from Paso Robles. He reports the roads as in a very demoralized condition and most of
       the bridges missing. The Salinas river is higher than it was two years ago and the current
       is very strong.   –*SLO Tribune* Sun Jan 20
     1900: Albert Ganoung, a former resident of this city who now conducts a general
       merchandise store in San Miguel, is a visitor in the city. He is on his way to Arroyo
       Grande to visit his parents.–"14 Years Ago in SLO" *Daily Telegraph* Tue Aug 18 1914 p.2
     1902 GR: 28 AG #1
     Note: 1875 Paulson Business Dir: A Ganoung mcht Cambria – who is this?
6.   Mary/May Isabel Ganoung   b. 17 Sep 1878 (St. Stephen's Ch records)
                                         d. SLO 28 July 1880 @1/11   –*SLO Tribune* (?)
7.   Charleston Thomas Ganoung b. 28 May 1882 (St. Stephen's Ch records)
                                         d.

8. Oliver (E) Vanda Ganoung   b. Sep 1883
   bap 16 Feb 1896 St   d. San Luis Obispo (20) Dec 1934 @51/3/14;
    Stephen's Epis Ch SLO   bur Dec 22 SM cem; inf: W H Gannug (sic)
   1926: in Pismo   obit *SM Times* Fri Dec 21 p.2
    m. ?
   a. Catherine Ganoung in Berkeley 1934
   b. Oliver Ganoung in Berkeley 1934 (10 Oct 1909; SSDI d. Berkeley Feb 1992)

9. William Henry Ganoung   b. San Luis Obispo 29 Nov 1887; m. @26 of AG
   bap 16 Feb 1896 St   d. Santa Maria 15 Oct 1964 @76/10/16; SM cem
    Stephen's Epis Ch SLO   obit Fri Oct 16 p.10. 50y SM 4 gch
   1917 phbk: 420 S Lincoln SM   res 219 E Tunnell
    m. SLO 22 Sep 1914 by H H Hocker ME Ch. J240
     wit: Mrs B Mae Hocker, SLO; Mrs D Beth Williams, SLO

Mary Jane Zerfing   b. rural Arroyo Grande 6 June 1895; m. @19 of
  res SMv, Lompoc, Paso   nr Orcutt SLO co; SSDI
    Robles;   d. SM 5 Feb 1988 @92; SM cem
  to SM 1940's   obit *SM Times* Sun Feb 7 p.5
       F: Nathan C Zerfing 1863-
1920 cen: SM   M: Nancy C/J 1866-
1922-3 Dir: Wm (Mary) foreman SM Gas Co r406 W Cook SM; Mrs Priscilla hskpr same
1925 Dir: W H (Mary) shop foreman SM Gas Co r same; Mrs Priscilla same
1928 Dir: Wm (Mary) gas fitter r628 E Cypress SM
(1940-1 Dir: not in SM, possibly Paso Robles)
1947-8 Dir: Wm H (Mary) oil wkr Hancock h510 N Lincoln SM
1955-6 Dir: same
1972 Dir: Mary J (wid Wm H) 219 E Tunnell SM; 1982: same

   a. Muriel Ganoung   b. 1 July 1915; SSDI
     1964: in Lompoc   d. Lompoc 21 April 1986
     m.
    John Hennessy. In Lompoc 1988. Lompoc High Sch football team 1931
     1947-8 Dir: Hennessy John M chf cost acct JMP Corp h335 So D Lompoc
     1988 phbk: Hennessy John M 1020 E Walnut Av Lompoc
   b. Wilma P Ganoung   b. 6 Feb 1917; SSDI
       d. 1 Nov 1975 (mother's obit)
         or Feb 1976 (SSDI)
     m.
    John Hannah. In Guadalupe 1988. Lompoc High Sch football team 1931
     1963. John Hannah, Seaside Sta, Laurel & O, Lompoc
     1988 phbk: John J Hannah 4831 Sanchez Dr Guadalupe
     1988. Grandchildren: Robert Hannah, Lancaster
                       Judy Smith, Moorehead City NC
                       Val Morgan, Fukuaka, Japan
                       Patti Hennessy, Lompoc

GARRETT
VALLEY PIONEERS

(Joseph) Martin Garrett   b. SC 1825
   1860: Tulare Co next to Mahurins   d. before 1880? to TN, to TX, to CA
     m. c1857
Martha Mahurin   b. TX 26 Aug 1841
     d. Santa Maria 28 May 1909, SM cem
   1850: Milam Co TX   F: Thomas Mahurin
   1880: Lynns Valley tp Kern Co   M: Nancy
   1897: La Graciosa. Mrs Garrett, mother-in-law of Hugh Logan, has moved from her home
       on the Alamo and is keeping house for Mr Logan.   –Sep 11
   1909: Personals. Mrs Garrett, mother of Mrs L J Morris, is very ill at her daughter's
       home, Mrs Joel Hopper   -June 5 (no obit)

1. Stonewall Jackson (Jack)   b. Visalia 5 March 1858
   IOOF: LOOM: KKK   d. Santa Maria 7 June 1928 @70/3/2, SM cem
   1892 GR: 34 5ft 10 lt blu ltbr   obit June 7 p.5; 45 years SM valley; ranch
     rancher CA Huasna PO SM   3m E of Orcutt. Will 15 June 1928 (Probate
     reg. Sep 16   #3-24); wit: A W Fickle, Orcutt;
   1906 Dir: 6m SE   H T Bailey, Santa Maria
       m. 1 on the Alamo 28 Feb 1892 by Rev Amon (*Times*); (divorced)
   Georgia A Logan 1872-   See Logan chart
     m. 2 1910
   Ida May Kemp Smith   b. (Watsonville) Jan 1862
     1880: Guadalupe, svt w/Zederian   d. (int.12) Jan 1946 @84/0/7; SM cem
     1900: Guadalupe w/parents   (no obit) 'Police seeking Warren Kemp
       of Guadalupe...his aunt died...'   -Jan 10
     1938-9 Dir: Ida May Garrett,   F: Wm Parker Kemp 1830-1912
       quilting h401 W Cook SM   M: Clara Jane 1835-1907
         m.1 Geo L Smith 1862-1908

2. Anna Eliza   b. (Visalia) Feb 1860
     m. 1888   d. Hughson 11 Nov 1925 @66
   Joel Leigh Hopper 1864-1939   See Hopper chart

3. Elizabeth Frances   b. Tulare Co 1862 (cen)
     d. at home Los Alamos 25 July 1930 @69 or 70
       Oak Hill cem Ballard; obit Jul 25 p.4
     m.
   James Marion Cox   b. Ukiah or Modoc Co May 1860
     d. Los Alamos 28 Oct 1932 @73, Oak Hill cem
       obit Sat Oct 29 p. 1
     F: Henry Cox 1825-1898
     M: Mary Yarnell 1818-1902

4. Emily/Emma J   b. (Visalia) May 1863; m. @20
     d. Washington district 5m S 22 Aug 1897
       @34/3/2; SM cem; obit Aug 28
     m. Santa Maria 25 Nov 1883 by Wm Shaw, ME ch, C89
   John Hulet Logan 1859-1933   See Logan chart

5. Sarah Josephine   b. Tulare 3 Jan 1863;
     d. Santa Maria 5 Sep 1942 @79/8/2; SM cem
   m.1 c1878   obit Sat Sep 5 p. 1

Henry Twiman Cox	b. MO 1850
	d. Sep 1885 @32 (*T*) or @34/9/1 (cem) SM cem
	F: Henry Cox 1825-1898
	M: Mary Yarnell 1818-1902
m. 2 San Luis Obispo 31 Jul 1889	
Louis Joseph Morris	b. Victoria BC 23 June 1859; imm.1870
Justice of the Peace 44 years	d. Santa Maria 28 July 1948 @88/1/5
r420 W Mill	SM cem. obit Thu July 29 p.1; bio *Who's Who SM;* bio *Times* Pioneer Ed May 3 1940 4-B photo *SM Times* May 19, 1924
	F: John Morris; M: Maria/Martha Josephine
6. Cinthia L	b. Tulare Co 1864/5
	d. at res of brother-in-law Hugh Logan 5 Dec 1885 @18 *(Times)* or @20/10 (cem); SM cem; Enteritis
7. Joseph Martin	b. Tulare Co Nov 1872
	d. Santa Maria 14 June 1942 @70/6/17; SM cem obit June 15 p. 1; rodent exterminator w/County Horticultural Dept 12 years
m. Pine Grove 26 Aug 1900 (*Times*)	
Clara Catherine Norris 1882-1962	See Norris chart

Vol. XXVII, No. 1, Spring 1995, p. 12

Corrections and Additions   [Page numbers refer to those in Quarterly]

p.12.   Marriage. Stonewall Jackson Garrett and Georgia A Logan recorded SLO Co D140; wit: J L Hopper, SM; E T Norris, SM.

GATES
LOS ALAMOS PIONEERS

Lorison Gates	b. Malone, Franklin co NY 3 Mar 1813 (IGI)
1850 cen: Lake co OH	d.
Kirtland dist farmer	F: Ira Gates
1860 cen: Porter co IN	M: Clarissa Heath
Porter tp PO Valparaiso	
m.	
Salome Parker Felt	b. Cavendish, Windsor co VT 11 Oct 1815 (IGI)
	d.
1. Stillman Gates	b. Ellington, Chautauqua co NY 6 Oct 1835 (IGI)
1860 cen: next to parents	d.
m.	
Mary Elizabeth McNeal	b. NY 1839 (cen)
	d.
a. James L Gates	b. Porter co IN 21 Feb 1858 (IGI)
b. Herbert Phidelio Gates	b. Porter co IN 26 Sep 1859 (IGI)
(others?)	
c. Salome Hope	b. Jasper co IN 28 Dec 1868 (IGI)
2. Lorison Lucius Gates	b. Norwalk, Huron co OH 1 Sep 1837 (IGI)
1879 GR: 41 OH f Los Alamos	d. (Los Alamos) 13 Oct 1887 @50/1/13
1880 cen: 42 OH f Los Alamos	Los Alamos cem, no obit found
next to E A Waite	
1884-5 Dir: Gates Lorison L f 98a (Abeloe file)	
m.1	
Eliza Ann (cen)	b. OH 1849
Nancy Maria McNeil (IGI)	d. (Los Alamos) 16 Sep 1882 @33/8
	Los Alamos cem
	F: NY; M: VT (same as his?)
a. Lucius Darwin Gates	b. Porter, Porter co IN 18 Jan 1864
1890 GR: 26 IN mach SB #5	d. Santa Barbara 7 May 1906 @42 (IGI)
1900 cen: 720 Bath St Santa Barbara	
bio Storke 531: to Chico 1875; to Los Alamos 1877; to SB, foundry, back to	
Los Alamos, father ill, 1884-6; then SB	
m. 1890	
Emma Jane Brooks	b. Bath, Steuben co NY 18 May 1871 (IGI)
1910 cen: SB widow	m. @19
	d. Santa Barbara 23 Feb 1930 @58
	F: Ralph Mills Brooks
	1879 GR: 52 VT milkman SB
	1890 GR: 63 VT printer SB #5
	M: Sarah Ann Murphy (IGI)
=Carrie May	b. SB 30 May 1891 (cen, IGI)
=Lucius Brooks	b. SB 21 July 1892 (IGI) 1893 (cen)
=Olive C/E	b. 19 Dec 1893 (IGI) 1894 (cen)
=Earl Ingram	b. SB 21 July 1895 (IGI) 1896 (cen)
=Ralph Lorison	b. 4 Apr 1897; d. SB Apr 1972; SSDI
=Barbara Emma	b. (SB) 1 Apr 1900 (IGI) (cen)
b. Charles Homer Gates	b. Porter IN 18 Jan 1866
1890 GR: 24 IN clk SB #3	d. (SB?) 28 Dec 1895; Los Alamos cem

        m. (see below)   no obit found
    c. Ida B Gates   b. IN 1878 (cen) (1868?)
2.   m.2 @47 of Los Alamos in Los Alamos 21 Sep 1884 by Rev Mitchell, Pres, C148
         wit: H H Wait, M M Sturgeon. 2nd marriage for both
  Harriet Maria Prouty Waite 1842-1921: see E A Waite chart
    1884: Los Alamos Letter. Mr Hixon and family are going to Montecito to live and
      L L Gates and wife will move to his res.   -Nov 15
      1893: Interesting Facts About the Late Fire…By great efforts Mr C H Pearson saved
        his store and very materially helped to save the back buildings to the hotel. If they
        had burned, Mrs Gates dwelling house would certainly have burned.   -Feb 25
3.   Salome Electa Gates   b.   OH 31 May 1840 (IGI)
    1860 cen: sch tchr w/parents
4.   Ira Rufus Gates   b.   Norwalk OH 12 May 1842 (IGI)
5.   Lucy Jane Gates   b.   Munson, Medina co OH 23 Dec 1844 (IGI)
    (Lucy J Clark bo 65 OH wd 7 births 6 living, with Harriet Gates, 1910 census, Los Alamos)
6.   Hosea Felt Gates   b.   Kirtland, Lake co OH 1 Sep 1847 (IGI)
7.   Goodwin Gates   b.   Kirtland OH 3 Aug 1850 (IGI)

1882: Presbyterian Church of Los Alamos organized March. Rev S B King, presiding;
   S R I Sturgeon, Sec. Trustees: D Coiner, A Leslie, A Wilson, George E Klink, G C Hixon,
   L L Gates, W W Curtis, Esq.   -100 Years of Love (Pres Ch of Los Alamos, 1982)
1887?: (1 mi east of H Hilton) Just beyond is the farm of Mr L L Gates, who has another
   tract of thirty acres. His land is about one mile from town, and is well laid out for future
   development. Three acres are planted with fruit of various descriptions, including apples,
   pears, quinces, etc. The trees are very thrifty, and are from one to three years of age, giving
   a fine promise for the future. The owner very sensibly says he is not for sale, as he intends
   to keep the property for home use and home comfort.

THE SPANISH QUADRILLE

This famous performance of dancing horses, trained by Robert Wickenden and called by Jerry Muir, was a Fourth of July feature in Los Alamos in the 1890's. Performers on pairs of matched bays:

James D Wickenden	Miss Sarah Wickenden
Ernest Wickenden	Miss Ida Wickenden
Robert Wickenden	Miss Olivia Arata
Caesar Arata	Miss Adela Arata
Rudolph Arata	Miss De la Cuesta
Hannibal Arata	Mrs Jennie Hathaway
Frank Hathaway	Mrs Charles Gates
Charles Gates	Miss Ida Gates

Thanks to Laura Abeloe for these historical items.

GRAGG
FROM KENTUCKY TO LOMPOC

James Arminius Gragg   b. KY Nov 1839; parents KY
   1890 GR: 50 KY f Lompoc   d. (Lompoc) 24 March 1911 @71; Evergreen cem
   1900 cen: tp #5 Lompoc   Lompoc
   9 births 9 living; IGI:6 ch
      m. Barren co KY 1865 (IGI)
Mary Elizabeth H Payne   b. KY Jan 1848; parents KY
   1920 cen: Hollister, w/Jas   d. Santa Barbara co 18 May 1929 @81; Evergreen cem
1. Lura J   b. KY 1866 (IGI)
2. Lizzie H   b. KY 1868 (IGI)
3. Clarence P   b. KY 1870 (IGI)
    1910 cen: tp #4 Ballard pct   d. (Ventura co 5-24-1959)
     3 births 2 living
    1922-3 Dir: C Gragg welder Bicknell
    in Ventura 1944
       m. (Santa Barbara) c1892 (cen & IGI)
   Addie P   b. CA c1871; parents CA
    a. Elsie F (?)   b. c1896
    b. Henri G (?)   b. c1899
4. Mary E (Sinclair)   b. KY 22 Mar 1873
    "Mamie"; in Los Angeles 1944   d. Los Angeles co 28 July 1949 @76; Evergreen cem
5. Irvin James   b. Barren co KY May 1875
   (James Irvin)   d. San Francisco 30 Sep 1927 @52
    1900 cen: w/parents
    1910 cen: H st Lompoc 3 births 3 living
    1920 cen: 542 4th, Hollister
      m.1 Santa Barbara co 2 Feb 1903
Barbara Sheen (Shean?)   b. CA c1887 (cen); (10 Nov 1886; SSDI;
                           d. Laguna Beach 18 Jul 1970)?
                           F: KY; M: CA
    a. Arlene C   b. c1905
    b. Barbara   b. c1906
    c. Robert I   b. (18 Sep 1908; SSDI)
                           d. (Vets Hosp., San Diego co 21 Nov 1974
                           @66)
      m.2 Santa Barbara 17 Feb 1912 (*Times*)
Mila B More see More chart
    1912. Irwin Gregg (sic) of Lompoc married Miss Mila More, dau of M/M C O More,
      formerly of this place in Santa Barbara Saturday. He is a veteran of the Spanish-
      American war and well known to the writer as a fellow soldier.   -*Times* Feb 24
    d. Beverly M (Davis)   b. Los Alamos Nov 1914
      living in Orcutt 2000; see More chart
    e. Charles Robley   d. @12d; bur SM cem 6 Nov 1915
                           removed from Los Alamos cem
    f. James   b. (after 1920)
      called son of Maurice; in SLO 1944
6. Carrie P   b. CO May 1879
    1900 cen: w/parents
      m.1 Santa Barbara 3 Oct 1901

George W Pratt
m. (2) Brown; living in Hayward 1944

7. Lovell A — b. CO 8 July 1881; SSDI
   1900 cen: w/parents — d. SLO co 20 Aug 1958; Evergreen cem
   1910 cen: F st Lompoc bkpr 3 births 3 living(?)
   1925 Dir: L A (Eleanor) oil wkr Orcutt
   1928 Dir: L A (Eleanor) carp divide A O Co, Orcutt; Lloyd stu
  in Los Gatos 1944
      m. 1905
  (Leslie) Eleanor Kellogg — b. 23 Jan 1884; SSDI; F: MI; M: CA
       d. Montrose CA 6 Feb 1982 @98; Evergreen cem
       F: Charles M Kellogg 1856-1889
       M: Fannie E Wear

  a. Lois — b. c1908
  b. Merritt Kellogg — b. 4 Dec 1909; bur 17 Nov 1910
       Evergreen Cem
  c. Earle Maurice — b. 14 June 1915
       d. bur 28 Jul 1922 @7; Evergreen cem
  d. Lloyd Lovell — b. 8 Oct 1913; SSDI
       d. Sacramento 15 Oct 1979 @66

8. Maurice R — b. Sterling CO Sep 1887; m. @23 of Lompoc
   1900 cen: w/parents — d. at home chicken ranch, Willow Ck Rd W of
   1920 cen: Hollister w/Jas — Templeton, suicide 15 Mar 1944 @56/6/6;
      Templeton cem "CA 1Sgt US Army" WWI; obit *SLO*
   1920-1 VR: 6' CO Templeton — *Telegram-Tribune* Wed Mar 15 p.7; wife, son, 2 sis 2
  to Templeton 1920 — bro, 54y CA
      m. Santa Barbara 13 Mar 1911
  Goldie Catherine Ambler — b. (Belmont co)? OH 30 Nov 1891; SSDI;
   1920-1 VR: Mrs Goldie 5'6 OH — m. @19 of Lompoc
   Templeton — d. Templeton 11 Dec 1971; Templeton cem
      F: (John Ambler 1850-1909)?
      M: (Nancy Wilcox 1855-1938)?
  a. James, San Luis Obispo, called son in obit 1944.

9. Claude V — b. CA 13 Mar 1890; SSDI
   1922-3 Dir: Claude V — d. Ventura co 22 Oct 1940
  (Gladys M) foreman r407 So G, Lompoc
      m.
  Gladys M — b. 6 Jan 1895; SSDI
       d. Oak View, Ventura co 9 Feb 1986

Santa Barbara Co Deaths: Alice P Gragg 11-13-1915 @2 mos
                      unnamed Gragg 10-19-1920 @ 30 min

Vol. XXXII, No. 1, Spring 2000, pp.14, 15

Corrections and Additions   [Page numbers refer to those in Quarterly]

p.15   Eleanor Kellogg's mother, Fannie/Frances E Wear (1860-1932) married in 1890 Amos C Whittemore (1864-1937). Both are buried in the Evergreen Cemetery, Lompoc.

Vol. XXXII, No. 2, Summer 2000, p. 12

GRAY
IRISH PIONEERS OF THE CALIFORNIA CENTRAL COAST

Samuel (W) Gray   b. Ballyrobert Dough, Antrim, Ire Jan 1860; m. @22
  bio M/H 278; 7ch   imm. 1881; na 1892
  see also bio of O C   d. at home Santa Maria (2) Mar 1941 @81; SM cem
  Marriott, Phillips II 111   obit Mon Mar 3 p.1; 50 y SMv; wid 3 dau 3 sons,
         8gch; bro/law
         F: James Gray d. @64 GF: Robert Gray
         M: Mary Ann Boyd

1897. La Graciosa Items: Sam Gray is moving onto his Graciosa farm from Oso Flaco this week. –Oct 30. *Note*: Sam Gray owned NE4 S15 T9, the west line of which abutted the east line of the tiny town of Orcutt. As Orcutt grew with the oil industry, it expanded east into Gray's property. "Gray's division" and "Gray's addition" to the town of Orcutt comprise a strip two blocks north-south, Clark-Union-Pinal, and 6½ blocks east from the west side of Pacific past Gray and Dyer to Twitchell. Pacific, Union, and Pinal are oil company names; E W Clark was general manager of the Pacific Coast Railway; and Fremont Twitchell was a local pioneer, Twitchell dam, later being named for a son. Dyer has not been identified. See Twitchell chart.

1900 cen: tp 7 (Santa Maria valley) m/19y; 10 births 7 living
1902 moved to property on the Guadalupe road west of Santa Maria
1906 Dir: Samuel f 2m NW; Mrs
1910 cen: tp 7 county rd; m/28
1920 cen: Santa Maria
1922-3 Dir: Samual Gray rancher r W Main nr Guadalupe Rd
1923. Shandon June 22. Samuel Gray of Santa Maria arrived at Shandon Tuesday evening to help his son Robert with haying for a few weeks.   – *San Luis Obispo Daily Telegram*
    Note: he owned 2960 acres in the Shandon area, son Robert overseeing for 30-35 years.
1925 Dir: Saml (Jennie) f W Main
1928 Dir: Sam (Jennie) f W Main
1930 phbk: Gray Samuel r W Main
1940-1 Dir: Gray Saml f PO Box 432
    RR #2: Grey (sic) Sam Guad Rd Box 339
    Gray Samuel (Jennie) frmr Box 339
1941. Pallbearers: Israel M Burola, H E Filipponi, L H Adam, P J Mahoney, Henry Yelkin, Elmer Rice

         m. Ireland 1881; to US as newlyweds, first to Allegheny PA, soon to Oso Flaco to her brother Devid McKeen, who had come in 1878 to aunt and uncle Patrick (1832-1905) and Sarah McKeen Moore (1839-1900) See Madge

Janet/Jennie McKeen   b. Antrim Apr 1860
         d. at home Dec 30 1947 @89/8; SM cem
         obit Tue Dec 30 p.1; 3 dau 3 sons 8gch 4 ggch
         F: Robert McKeen
         M: Gordon? (David McKeen's mother was Gordon)

1914. Mrs Wells of San Francisco is visiting her sister Mrs Sam Gray. (date lost)
1919. Lt and Mrs W W Hedges, of New York, are on a month's leave from his ship the USS Plattsburg, and visiting her sister Mrs Sam Gray…had been guests of M/M Robert Gray, Shandon…left for San Francisco…   -Nov 14
1922-3 Dir: David McKeen ret rancher Oso Flaco r Gray Bros mail SMPO
1924. Local News…from San Pedro to visit M/M Sam Gray and M/M Robt H Brown are Lt and Mrs W W Hedges. Mrs Hedges is a niece of Mrs Brown…Mrs Robert Gray here

from Shandon to see her brother, Dr W H Reid of Chicago, who has been visiting his mother, Mrs R H Brown. –Feb 11

1942. Pioneer David McKeen died at the home of his sister, Mrs Gray, half-brother of Mrs Walker Kedges (sic), Long Beach; 2 half-sisters in Chicago and Liverpool, England, uncle of the Gray siblings. –Feb 3

Note: Jean McKeen Hedges b. 16 July 1865 d. San Bernardino co 29 Jan 1958 @92

1947-8 Dir: Jennie Box 339

1. Robert James Gray b. Oso Flaco 2 Nov 1882
   1900 cen: w/parents d. Santa Maria 2 Aug 1977 @94; SLO cem
   1906 Dir: R J lab 2mNE obit Tue Aug 2 p.3; wid Annie, bro John, n/n
   1907. Pacific Realty & Stock Co, Santa Maria, Wilbur T Smith, Robert J Gray, Jones Bldg, Santa Maria. –ad June 22
   1917: rancher in Santa Barbara co (M/H)
   1918. M/M Robert Gray sold Rancho del Rio in Cuyama, will move to Shandon to operate the 3000 acre ranch of Gray's father. –Oct 26
   1920-1 VR: Rbt J 5'8 CA Shandon
   1972 Dir: Rbt J (Anne) ret h720 E Cypress SM

   m. by 1915

   Marian Reid b. Ireland 18 Dec 1880
   1920-1 VR: Marian 5'6½ d. Oroville 11 May 1953 @72; funeral Paso Robles;
   IRE Shandon SLO cem; obit Wed May 13 p.6; hus, bro in Chicago
   F: Reid
   Shandon correspondent M: Joanna Hutchison Elliott 1866-1935
   to SLO OTel 1920's, '30's m.2 1909 Rbt Henry Brown 1867-1930
   The two Thomas Brown families were Irish also; see chart.

   No issue

2. Son b. Oso Flaco 27 Aug 1884 (*Times*)
   d. 18 July 1885; Guadalupe cem

3. Annie Gray b. Oso Flaco 24 June 1885
   1900 cen: w/Moores, w/whom d. Arroyo Grande 20 May 1977 @92; AG cem
   she lived most of her obit Mon May 23 p.3; 88y AG; 2 sons 2 bro 3 gch
   childhood, as they were 2 nc 3 neph
   childless. –see Madge
   1908 grad UC
   1917 in Oakland (MH)

   m. Berkeley 29 April 1908 (*Times*); lived in East Bay area until c1918

   John W Shannon b. Reno NV 3 Nov 1882 "Jack"
   to AG @11, back 1918 d. Arroyo Grande 28 Nov 1976 @94; AG cem; obit Tue Nov 30 p.2; wid 2 sons AG; neph Lester Liever, Saratoga; 3 gch. F: John E Shannon; GF: Wm Shannon GM: Betsy Everets; M: Catherine Brennan (1849-1930)? Pat Moore gave Shannons the Hillcrest farm on "Shannon Hill" south of AG. –See Yesterday

   a. John Patrick Shannon b. San Leandro 1910
      single d.
      sold ranch 1979, moved to Creston
   b. George Gray Shannon b. Dwight Way, Berkeley 1 Feb 1912
      1934 grad UC d. AG 9 May 2000; AG cem
      m. (AG after 1941)?

      Barbara Ernestine Hall   b. Madera 3 Sep 1917
         Santa Barbara HS 1935   d. at home 17 Nov 1993; AG cem
                                                obit Fri Nov 19 A5: to AG 1941; hus 3 sons
                                                bro Rbt Hall, Modesto sis Pat Dilbeck,
                                                Sacramento 4 gch
                                                F: Bruce Hall
                                                M: Eileen Cayce
     = John Michael Shannon (Nancy) in AG 1993
     = Gerald George Shannon single "Jerry" in AG 1993
     = Thomas Cayce Shannon (Debbie) Cayce in Templeton 1993

Note: Barbara Cole contributed the Shannon history to Yesterday, including photographs,
    pp.43-47, and the program for the World's Speed Trials, pp.171-80

1931. Organizers of World's Speed Trials August 30th 1931, Pismo Beach Oceanside
    Speedway & Racing Corporation, Ltd, Pismo Beach, California. John W Shannon,
    President W T Masengill, Vice President W Vaughan Scott, Vice President D A Terradell,
    Secretary R C Itjen, Treasurer…

4.   Annie's twin, stillborn
5.   Sadie Gray   b. Oso Flaco 21 June 1887(*Times*)
     1906 Dir: Miss Stu 2m NW   d. Santa Maria 3 June 1956 @66/11/12; SM cem
     1908 grad SMUHS   obit Mon June 4 p.5; dau sis 3 bro
     1910 cen: w/parents   r Oakland, returned to SM after husband's death
     1922 in Oakland
     1955-6 Dir: Sadie Fee (wid or A H) hmkr h712 E Orange
     m.
     Alexander H Fee   b. (IRE?) 11 Aug 1883 d. Alameda co 19 June 1948
                                           M: Hutchison; aunt Joanna Hutchison Reid Brown
     a.   Iva Jean Fee   b. Oakland CA 6 May 1913
         1956 in SM   d. Santa Maria 3 July 1974 @61/1/27
         1972 Dir: Ivajean (sic)   obit July 4 p.2; 2 uncles aunt, cousins;
                                            to SM 1951 ret h712 E Orange

        1974 pall bearers: Donald Gray, Jack Shannon, Geo Shannon, Bill Marriott, David
           Marriott, Jake Burchardi

6.   David Gray   b. (Oso Flaco) Oct 1889
     1910 cen: w/parents   d. San Francisco hospital 10 Aug 1922 @32/9/28; SM
     1922-3 Dir: David (Gladys)   cem; obit Thu Aug 10 p.2; WW vet; Camp Fremont,
       rancher r E Chapel   thence Siberia; farmed w/bros. wid,, parents 3 bro
                                                3 sis

     1922. Nipomo People Attend Funeral of David Gray   -*SLO Daily Telegram* Aug 14
     m. 2 Aug 1917 (*Times*)
     Gladys Lambert   b. Paso Robles 10 May 1899; m. of Santa Barbara
     1900 cen: Pine st Paso Robles   d. San Francisco 10 Apr 1981; surname Shuart
     1910 cen: N Pine st   F: Louis Adnirum Lambert 1866-1927
       Santa Maria   GF: James Lambert 1830-1899;
     1914. Misses Bessie and   GM: Frances E Wilson 18__-1921
       Gladys Lambert returned   M: Martha Ellen Matney 1875-1912
       from 2 wks visit at   GF: Carroll Sumner Matney 1850-1912
       Paso Robles. –Aug 1   GM: Terah Ellen Patterson 1858-1915
                                                see bio J R Matney (1877-1955) M/H
                                                Mrs Frances E Lewis M/H
                                                also see chart
                                                sisters Mabel Olivera 1896-19__, Bessie Irene Toy
                                                1897-1984

Gladys m.2 (Jack Shuart b. 16 Oct 1898; d. San Francisco Dec 1968)?

7. Jeanne (Jennie) Gray   b. (Oso Flaco) Oct 1890
    1906 Dir: Jennie Miss   d. Santa Maria 26 Nov 1953 @63/1/27; SM cem
       stu 2 m NW   obit Fri Nov 27 p.6; son dau 3 bro 2 sis 3 gch
    1910 cen: w/parents   owned/operated SM Storage & Transfer Co; r115 W
                                                Liberty

    1947-8 Dir: Jeanne SM Trans & St h115 W Liberty; same 1951

    1947. Mrs Marriott Buys $22,500 Property. Purchase of the block bounded by Jones, McClelland, and Oak streets here by Mrs Jeanne Marriott has been recorded with County Recorder Yris Covarrubias. Mrs Marriott purchased the property from the Southern Pacific Milling Company, which on the same day recorded the purchase of the same property from Mr and Mrs J H Kirk of San Luis Obispo. The milling company thus sent deeds for purchase and sale of the property through escrow at the same time. Purchase price by Mrs Marriott was reportedly $22,500.   –Apr 18 p.8

       m. at the home of Rev Nelson, Santa Barbara Sat Apr 29 1916; Mrs Gray, Miss Phyllis Adams (sic) and Frank Marshall attended. (*Times*)

Olin Clark Marriott   b. Cincinnati OH 14 Oct 1887; to CA 1907 from
    bio Phillips II 111   Indianapolis.
                             d. Santa Maria 10 Apr 1944 @56; SM cem
                               obit Tue Apr 11 p.1; brief illness; contracting
                               business; wid, son, dau, bro Earle E SM; 2 cousins:
                               Dr C H Marriott, SM; Leo Marriott, Santa Cruz
    F: William E Marriott 1857-1942
      GF: Elijah Marriott; GM: Louise
    M: Addie Frances Heiser 1859-1912

1909 Dir: Marriott W E Transfer, r408 W Church; Mrs Addie, bkpr same; O C same

1912. Mrs Wm Marriott Dies Very Suddenly…sons Olin C and Earl of Los Angeles…
                                                                                                            -Nov 30

Olin C Marriott returned to Los Angeles Wednesday to resume position with Pacific Sash
    & Door Factory.   –Dec 7

1922-3 Dir: O C (Jeanie) O C Marriott & Co cont & bldrs r 510 W Chapel O C Marriott & Co bldg mats 210 W Church

1925 Dir: Marriott O C (Jeanie) prop O C Marriott Co contractors r510 W Chapel

1928 Dir: Marriott O C & Co O C Marriott prop 120 (sic) W Church Marriott O C (Jeanie) bldg contr r501 W Chapel

1928. New Marriott Company Home Completed Soon. With their new office, shops and warehouses located on a private railroad spur, O C Marriott, contractor, will be able to offer a complete building and millwork service in the near future. The company, now on West Church street, will move into its new $5000 home at Jones and McClelland streets about December 1, Marriott said this morning. A Spanish stucco office building on the corner of the lot which takes in the entire block from McClelland to the S P Milling company warehouse, is expected to be completed by November 14. Besides the main building, there will be a shop, for sash, door and mill work, and warehouses for finished lumber and hardware. No rough lumber will be stored. However, there will be a complete line of tile, hardware and cabinet work for the home. The building, aside from the office, will be of corrugated iron.   –Oct 25

Note: this complex is still in use; son-in-law of compiler, a building contractor, rents space there.

1930 Dir: O C Marriott & Co 700 S McClelland; r 115 W Liberty; also 1931 phbk

1940-1 Dir: O C Marriott O C (Jeanie) Marriott Const Co, SM Trans & Stg Co h219 E Mill

    a. Lorraine Frances Marriott   b. SM 26 Feb 1917
        in Solvang 1941, 1953, 1963   d. Santa Ynez 19 Nov 1978; Oak Hill cem
                                               Ballard; obit Mon Nov 20 p.9; r160 Willow Dr
       m.   Solvang; 40y SM valley; hus dau bro 3 gch
    Johannes C Burchardi jr   b. 1 June 1909
      "Jake"   d. Oxnard 12 May 2000
       1947-8 Dir: Solvang, Burchardi J C Jr (Lorraine) engnr Hughes Sales Co L A
        in Solvang 1978   F: J C Burchardi
       1922-3 Dir: J C rancher Solvang
   = Susan Burchardi (Bott) in Goleta 1978.
        1967 phbk: Bott Ray C 344A Rosario Dr Santa Barbara
                  Bott Otto F 7064 Del Norte Dr Goleta
        1973 phbk: Bott Alice 7640 Cathedral Oaks Rd Goleta
                  Ray C 5700 Via Real Carpinteria
                  Robt 5720 Alondra Dr Goleta
    b. William C Marriott   b. (SM) 4 Apr 1922
                                           d. SM 9 Dec 2001
                                             obit Dec 11(?); 2 sons dau 6 gch
       1944. Sgt Wm C Marriott on duty in Southwest Pacific
       1955-6 Dir: Marriott WM C (Louise) mgr SM Transfer & Storage h115 W
        Liberty SM; Transfer & Storage Co 700 S McClelland
       1972 Dir: Marriott Wm C (Louise) ofc mgr Bee's Van & Stg h1116 S Miller
       1976 Dir: Wm C (Louise) ofc mgr Bee's…h1116 S Miller, Hollis J stu
        m. 1948
     Louise Lindsay   b. Atlanta; m. of Atlanta d. SM 15 Oct 1998
                                            obit Fri Oct 23 A7; hus 2 sons dau 5 gch
       = Hollis J Marriott in Laramie WY 1998, 2001
       = David Marriott 1982 Dir: Dave pntr h724 E Mariposa Way
           2003 phbk: David 1015 E Doane
       = Wm C Marriott jr in Woodacre CA 1998, 2001
8. Thomas Gray   b. (Oso Flaco) 19 July 1892
                                          d. Arroyo Grande hspl 20 Feb 1963 @70/7/1; SM cem
                                          obit Thu Feb 21 p.14; Gray ranch Guadalupe rd
    1910 cen: w/parents   wife dau 2 bro sis 2 gch
    1914. Messrs Tom Gray, Cornelius Donovan and Leonard Adam spent the weekend at
     Pismo.   –Aug 1
    1920 cen: w/parents, married
    1922-3 Dir: Grey (sic) Thos (Vallera L) rancher rGuad rd
    1925 Dir: same
    1928 Dir: Thomas (Vallera) f SM
    1940-1 Dir: Thomas & Valera f Guad rd; Valera slsldy Ida Mae Box 663
     Ida Mae Dress Shop Ida Mae Johnson 217 S Bwy
     Note: for Ida Mae see Elvidge chart
    1955: ranch SM
    1955-6 Dir: 1550 W Main (alone)
     Note: Jesse Razo, born in Betteravia in 1928 to Toribio and Nieves Ybarra Razo, died in
     Lakewood Oct 5 2003; before he joined the U S Army in 1954, he "worked for Mr Gray
     (a Santa Maria Valley rancher) supervising daily operations of the ranch."   –obit Oct 9
       m. by 1920
   Valera M Locey   b. Colusa CA 19 Jan 1898; F: IL; M: CA
     SMUHS 1918   d. Santa Maria 22 Oct 1996 @98; SM cem; surname

        Babigan; capt of basketball team 1915-1918
        obit Oct 24 A4; 85y SM; golf champion. She and Tom
        helped build golf course at SM Country Club.
       M: (Shelley)?
  1914. Mrs L L Locey of Guadalupe visited Santa Maria.   -July 15, Aug 1
   Note: This could be a sister-in-law. Lester L Locey 1889-1960, M: Shelly;
    Lucy L Locey 1892-1971, M: Stuart.
    Estelle M Locey, spouse LL, d. Merced co 5-29-1927 @43
  1930. Leslie Sharren (sic) former Santa Marian died at home in the north. Survived by
   widow Edith and niece Mrs Thomas Gray. M/M Gray and daughter went north during
   the weekend, Mrs Gray and baby will remain indefinitely.   –Tue July 22 p.3
  1914 Dir: Shearin Mark L (Edith) supt Santa Maria Valley RR Co h620 S Lincoln
   Note: Did Valera live with her uncle when going to high school?
   No Loceys are listed in directories.
     Valera m.2 c1964
  Robert R Babigan   b. Chicago 4 July 1914
   1976 Dir: Babigan Robt &   d. at home Santa Maria 26 Dec 1998
    Valera; electn h1016   obit Wed Dec 30 A6: journeyman electrician
    S Russell av Apt L   grad UCLA, merchant marines WWII; to SM 1958
           son Robert R Lakewood WA; 1 gson
  a. Edith <u>Colleen</u> Gray   b. (SM) 6 Dec 1926
    in Capistrano 1963   d. Capistrano Beach 2 Aug 1987; surname Hill
   = David Hill
   = Donald Hill
9. John Madison Gray   b. (Oso Flaco) Feb 1895
   1910 cen: w/parents   d. 20 Jan 1978 @82/10/22; SM cem
   1920: w/parents S   no obit found
   1922-3 Dir: John M (Frances L) rancher r505 W Main
    Mrs Francis (sic) L Asst Sec S M V Chamber of Commerce r505 W Main
   1925 Dir: John M f rW Main
    Mrs Francis L clk Pac & SoW Bank 419 E Church
   1928 Dir: John M f rW Main
   1940-1 Dir: John (Eva) r225 W Morrison; Mrs Eva J hswf PO Box 432
   1947-8 Dir: John & Eva J rancher h610 E Orange
   1953: rancher SM; 1955-6 Dir: John M (Eva J) frmr h610 E Orange
     m.1 Frances L
     m.2
  Eva June Wolverton   b. Duncan OK 19 June 1905; to CA as a child
   1925 Dir: Wolverton   d. at home 31 Dec 1987 @82
    Frank (Emma) carp   obit Sun Jan 3 1988; p.10; son dau 2 sis bro 4 gch
    r516 W Main   M: Wrinn (?) or Riggs
   1928 Dir: Frank (Emma)   sis: Jewell Krieger, Santa Barbara; Frances
    emp r203 E Church   Bickett, hwy Santa Cruz (Leona Frances Bicket
    Don hwy emp same   b. OK 12/24/1991 d. Santa Cruz 8/9/1992,
           F: Wolverton; M: Riggs);
           bro: Frank Wolverton, Canoga Park
  a. Donald M Gray
    in Foster City 1988
    (Donald M Gray b. 12 Sep 1935; d. SM 5 Jan 1998; no obit found)?
  b. Dorothy Mae Gray (Graham) in SM 1988
10. child   d. 9 May 1898; Guadalupe cem

H A A S
OF PHILADELPHIA

Matthias Haas   b. PA 1800
    1850 cen: Philadelphia co #432, Roll 825 p.282
        m.
Melinda   b. PA 1802
1.   Franklin   b. PA 1823
        1850 cen: trader
2.   Louis   b. PA 1825
        1850 cen: no occ
3.   Edwin (twin)   b. PA 1827
        1850 cen: clerk
4.   Edgar (twin)   b. PA 1827
        1850 cen: teacher
5.   Elizabeth   b. PA 1829
        1850 cen: no occ
6.   Holgate   b. PA 1832
        1850 cen: w/parents   d. NV 1894
7.   Nelson W   b. PA 1839 (1900 cen: Nov 1849)
        1850 cen: w/parents
        1880 cen: 910 12th, Sacramento; 1900 cen: 1434 Naud, Los Angeles
        m.
        Elizabeth/Lizzie   b. PA 1856 (1900 cen: GER May 1855)
          a.   Mary/May A   b. CA Jan 1878
          b.   Henry H   b. CA Feb 1882
          c.   Alfred J   b. CA Dec 1887
          d.   Nelson W   b. CA Apr 1891
          e.   Grace F   b. CA Feb 1897
8.   Jerome   b. PA Jan 1841
        1850 cen: w/parents; 1900 cen: 421 N Stanislaus, Stockton
        m.
        Louisa   b. CA Sep 1862
          a.   Clara   b. CA July 1882
             photo: Clara Pearl Haas @16 1898
          b.   Harriet Frances   b. CA June 1893
             photo: Harriet Frances Haas @5; both photos by McCullagh, Stockton
9.   Clara   b. PA 1845
        1850 cen: w/parents   d. 9 Jan 1930. This date from Cousin Clara per
                                           Whitney-Sanders letter

The Day Book and Ledger of Holgate Haas Coal Dealer Chestnut Hill Aug 30 1869
      A ton of stove coal sold for $8.00 in Philadelphia 1870. Last PA entry May 1871 (last 3 pages) Oct 1 1873. Louis Haas hired Holgate Haas to tend his sheep in Nevada for sixty dollars per month. John Desmond was hired Oct 1st 1873 for 35 dollars per month. I Holgate Haas have three hundred and six dollars and fifty cents due to Louis Haas for the sale of one house and some lumber.
      On Account with Jerome Haas: Mar 31st 1874 gave him to buy Stock &c 300.00; July 22 1874 Paid store bill & Lumber bill 104.92; Aug 8 two sacks of flour 4.00
      George Kennison came to work for me on the 3rd of April 1876 for thirty dollars per month. Stopped work on the second of June. Sore hands. Commenced work on 26 of June. June 26th gave him five dollars $5.00.

HOLGATE HAAS
NEVADA PIONEER

MARK WHITNEY
SANTA MARIA PIONEER

Holgate Haas   b. Germantown PA 1832 (IGI)
                                                 d. on his ranch, Clover Valley NV 5 Jan 1894 @62/0/4; bur Battle Mountain NV

1870 cen: dist 73, 22d ward, Philadelphia (M593 roll 1408 p.229); 1880 cen: not found

1894: Death of A Good Citizen. Holgate Hawes (sic), whose death is recorded in another place of to-day's *Gazette* died of heart failure at Clover Valley, Humboldt county, Nev. Mr Hawes was a native of Philadelphia, but had lived on the west coast since 1871. He was a good man, a good citizen, and a kind-hearted husband and father, and now that he is gone, it may truthfully be said of him that no person, living or dead, is or was the worse for having known him. He leaves a widow and three daughters and a circle of friends co-extensive with his circle of acquaintances. The funeral took place at Battle Mountain to-day.   –*Reno Evening Gazette* Jan 8

m.

Ellen Lee   b. Ireland 15 Aug 1834; imm. 1850/1
  1900 cen: North's ranch pct,   d. at home of dau Mrs Whitney Santa Maria
    Humboldt co NV; ranch & stock   3 Jan 1911 @76/4/19; bur Battle Mtn NV
  4 births 4 living

  1910 cen: same; 5 births 3 living

   lived at Jake's Creek ranch north of Golconda; sold in 1910, moved to Winnemucca

1911: Ellan Haas Gone to Her Reward...resided at North's ranch 37 years, one of the first settlers...came to Santa Maria 3 months ago...a daughter, son, and Mrs Whitney survive. "She died at ten minutes past seven just with the awakening of a new day and a new year and went to sleep like a tired child. Just as the rosy orb of dawn gave way to the glistening rays of the morning sun filling the eastern sky with a sheen of glory. Surely a most fitting time for a pure spirit to take its flight heavenward..." etc
                                                                          -*Santa Maria Times* Sat Jan 7 p.1

her son

John T Desmond   b. PA May 1854
  1870 cen: w/Haas   d. (San Jose) 20 Nov 1934 @80
  1900 cen: w/mother Single   F: PA or Ire

  1910 cen: same;   1911: Estate of Ellen Haas, JT Desmond, Ex;

    Jan 20. Mrs M E Whitney. Advance on funeral 130.35; Share of Estate of Ellen Haas to each heir.   Aug 17. John T Desmond $4860.48 1/3
                        Mrs M E Whitney   4860.48 1/3
                        Mrs Minnie Sanders   4860.48 1/3

  1920 cen: 102 Los Gatos Rd, San Jose

    m. 1917. (License sent from Recorder, Sacramento, to Mr John T Desmond, Hotel Bronx,
      640 E Main St, Stockton, post mark Jan 8 1917)

Elizabeth E   b. IL 1872
                                       d. (San Jose) 26 Aug 1926 @55
  her children: Elizabeth   b. CA 1902
              Catherine   b. CA 1904

1.   Melinda Haas   b. 15 1862
                                       d. 29 July 1865

2.   Mary Elizabeth Haas   b. Chestnut Hill PA 2 Feb, 1865
     to NV @7   d. at home 219 W Cypress SM 9 Nov 1940 @75/8/19;
     1910 cen: SM   SM cem. obit Tue Nov 12 p.6 41y SM
     1925 Dir: hskpr rN of SM**   sis: Minnie Sanders, Winnemucca

1928 Dir: wid r219 W Cypress;   1940-1 Dir: ret h219 W Cypress
1940-1 Dir: **Whitney Rd E of N Bwy at city limits: 1947-8 Dir: same (now E Donovan)
1940 pall bearers: Harry Nelson, Bert Young, Joseph Martin, George Dudley, Frank
  Clark, Joe S Brown

m. Winnemucca NV 28 Aug 1884

Mark Wilkins Whitney	b. Litchfield MI 29 May 1855
to SM 1899	d. Thu 7 Sep 1905 @50/3/9; epileptic fit
1900 cen: SM 1 birth 1 living	obit Sep 9 p.12(?)
1906 Dir: f 1¾ m NE; Mrs	F: Mark G Whitney 1821-1885
	M: Isabel Nelson 1822-1866

a.   Mark Holgate Whitney   b. Biggs (nr Gridley) CA 29 May 1886
    bio M/H 919   d. Santa Maria 15 Mar 1949
    to SM 1900 (sic)   obit Wed Mar 16 p.1. Masonic Funeral
  1910 cen: w/mother, single, rE of Whitney Rd
  1916: Surprise Party Given. M H Whitney given surprise birthday party on
     Wednesday evening at his home by a number of friends. Refreshments of ice
     cream and cake served, an enjoyable evening spent.   –June 10
  1925 Dir: Mark H (Edna) f N of SM
  1928 Dir: Supt SM cem h300 E El Camino. 1940-1 Dir: same
  1934: March House of Month Award by Garden Section of Minerva Club; 300 E
     El Camino, Mr & Mrs Mark Whitney.   –Mon Apr 1 p.1
  1934: Mark H Whitney admin of estate of J T Desmond 5 Dec 1934
  1944: Father Complains…Mark Whitney, 300 E El Camino reported to police that a
     1st Lieut driving along N Miller indecently exposed himself to Whitney's
     daughter, Edna Mae, while she was returning from school yesterday afternoon.
                                                                         -Wed Sep 30 p.3

    m. SM 10/11 Nov 1922

Edna Louise Young	b. Creston IL 7 Nov 1901
1951-2 Dir: Edna L (wid Mark H)	d. Santa Rosa 1 Jan 1990 @88; SM cem
hmkr 300 E El Camino	obit Fri Jan 5 p.12; 10gch 4 ggch
	m. last Ralph (Dale) Smith
	in Carmichael 1959, Sonora 1972, 1975
	F: Floyd Clarendon Young 1872-1959
	M: Mary Bell Anderson 1876-1947

= Mary Ellen Whitney 1923-1995; m. Las Vegas 1942
  Arthur Kenneth Schultz; 3 ch
= Edna May Whitney 1927-   m. SM 1946
  Harry L Powell, in Sacramento 1990 3 ch
    1947-8 Dir: Harry L (Edna-May) asst caretkr SM cem h304 E El Camino
= Shirley Ann Whitney 1932- m. SM 1950
  Alvin Dean Van Stone, in Santa Rosa 1973, 1990 4 ch
    1947-8 Dir: Alvin D emp Free Advertiser r409 E Orange
       H S (Alva) mach Cal Tool & Mach wks h409 E Orange (Elva Purkey)
         Harry Stephen Van Stone d. 21 Aug 1973 @73/7/26; SM cem, obit Fri Aug 24

3.   Melinda Holgate Haas   b. Philadelphia PA 16 May 1866
    "Minnie"   d. San Francisco 28 March 1941 @74; bur Winnemucca
                               r Winnemucca. obit *Humboldt Star* Mon Mar 31

    m. Battle Mountain NV July 1900

Philander Vernon Sanders	b. Lancaster co OH 31 May 1864
to TX @18; to Battle Mtn	d. Orovada NV at home of dau Mrs Christensen
c1900, cattle ranch Clover	16 June 1948, obit *Star* Fri June 18 p.1;
Valley	bur Winnemucca

To Winnemucca, stationary   F. VA; M: IRE
   engineer w/Western Pacific RR. Retired 1916. Later Orovada Mercantile Co.
1910 cen: Humboldt co, Gold Run tp, Golconda pct
1920 cen: he in Golconda on the ranch; she in Winnemucca, Bridge St, w/ch

   a. Bessie Ellen Sanders   b. Santa Maria 14 May 1902 (*Times*) (visiting
      bio Winni Mini Mart 1 Nov 1977:   Whitneys)
      Winnemucca HS 1922; tchr   d. Santa Maria 28 Oct 1992 @90 bur NV
      McDermitt, Pleasant Valley,   obit Oct 30 A-8
      Schurz and Winnemucca. To Reno, real estate. Postmaster Orovada 22y.
    To Winnemucca 1967; to Santa Maria 1982.
        m. Reno NV 14 July 1928
      Peter Christensen   b. Copenhagen DK 2 June 1901
        to US @22   d. Santa Maria 31 Jan 1991
        to San Francisco c1939   obit Feb 3 A-6. Sis:Vera Petterson,
        in Orovada 1946-1968 – Orovada   Copenhagen; Hetty Jakobsen, Jylland DK;
        Mercantile   neph: Erland B Christensen, Edmond OK
        No issue

   b. Bird M Sanders   b. Golconda NV 1 Apr 1908; m. @19 of
                                                  Winnemucca
                                                  d. Santa Maria 18 June 1991 @83
                                                  obit Sun June 23 A-10. 9y SM
                                                  artist, painter
        m. Reno NV (license) 13 June 1927
      James Donald Edwards   b. 17 Jan 1901: m. @26 of Reno
      "Don"   d. Los Angeles co 17 Apr 1974
     1930: Don got work in Paso Robles
     1938: Magic Cleaners, 26 California av, Reno
     1938-40: McGillivray Const co Sacramento;
     1948: Lynwood
     1961: Norwalk Asphaltic Concrete Inc, Jas D Edwards, plant supt Santa Fe Springs
     1966: Magic Dog Grooming Studio 3819-C E Century Blvd, Lynwood
     No issue

   c. Robert Vernon Sanders   b. (Golconda) NV 9 May 1912
      fireman SPRR   d. March 1947; bur Winnemucca
      Single

4. Ellen Lee Haas   b. (Chestnut Hill) PA 14 Sep 1870
    to NV as a child   d. Santa Maria 22 Jan 1901 @30; pneumonia
    to SM 1898   SM cem. obit Jan 16 (sic) Card of Thanks: Walter E
      m. 7 Dec 1892   Jones, Mrs Hass (sic), Mrs Whitney
    Walter E Jones   b. CA Nov 1863
    1900 cen: SM, farm lab   d.
    1899: Card of Thanks for father   F: Samuel Taylor Jones 1829-1899; obit Mar 18
    and brother: M/M W E Jones,   M: Minnie Long
    M/M T A Jones
    No issue

Our thanks to Julia Garcia who cared for Bird, Pete, and Bessie in their last years, thus becoming heir; she shared with Ye Ed. the family's historical collection, which has since been transferred to Shirley Whitney Van Stone. She, in turn, introduced us to Martha Nelson, a cousin in the Young family; both have been helpful.

HARRIMAN
SAN LUIS OBISPO COUNTY   SANTA BARBARA COUNTY   and   ELSEWHERE

John Fellows Harriman left his hometown of Searsmont, Maine, some time in the 1860's, possibly as a Civil War soldier; somehow he got to Wisconsin where he married Josephine Williams, a step-daughter of L S Cole, about 1866. They farmed in Trempealeau until 1873 when they sold their farm in Hale township to Cole by deed dated February 24. The family, enlarged by Ada, 6, and Forrest, 2 made the trek to California; their presence confirmed by J F's voter registration in Cambria August 18, 1873, they became property owners in November when $300 in gold was put into the hand of Samuel B Whitsett for a 1¾ acre lot in the town of Cambria.

The next year they were joined by a group of Wisconsin émigrés, among whom were the Cole family, the Bresette family (Josephine's sister Wilda), and possibly the large family of John Bright whose oldest son, William, was the husband of Josephine's youngest sister Abigail; this young couple had lived next-door to Harrimans on the farm.

On July 25, 1876, Harriman bought another ½ acre of land contiguous to the first 'off the public road to the beach'. A farmer in that period of his life, he was taxed for a Spanish horse, 3 American cows, 5 calves, furniture, and machinery. Where he was when the 1880 census was taken is not known; his wife and children were enumerated in the household of his brother, Atwood O Harriman, in Cambria. He was a member of the San Simeon Lodge No. 196, F&AM, and is included as Master Mason on a list for 1881, according to Angel's 1883 San Luis Obispo county history. However, he was a resident of Los Angeles when he sold his Cambria property to George Bright in October 1883.

John and Josephine came to the parting of the ways either in Los Angeles or Phoenix. The first directory published for Phoenix is for 1892, by which year Josephine had already married Edward Farley. That year John, now a carpenter, and Forrest were living together on Buchanan, corner Maricopa. The 1895 directory has Ed Farley operating a hotel and lodging house at 27 South Fourth. In 1900 the census shows the Farleys, now with a daughter, Ruth, (born in 1894 when Josephine was in her 45th year), at 127 Jackson W, and Harriman boarding at 207 E Buchanan.

Forrest came from Phoenix to marry Addie Clark in Los Angeles in 1902; he must have become acquainted with her on visits to his mother's half-sister, Aunt Laurie (Cole) Nixon, later Mrs Charles W Paine, who lived in San Fernando as did Addie. Aunt Laurie was an official witness to the marriage, with the bride's father, F M Clark. Lucia, the only child of Forrest and Addie, was born in 1905 in Nevada, but by 1910 the family was living in Burbank, near Farleys, Grandma Cole and the Bresettes. At that time Forrest was a carpenter, doing mill-work, but by 1920 was proprietor of Pollock and Harriman Garage, 4449 Sunset Blvd., Los Angeles, with Earl A Pollock, husband of his half-sister, Ruth. In 1922 Josephine died at Forrest's house, 2303 Childs Avenue, Los Angeles and about 1924 Forrest and Addie moved to Santa Barbara. They lived way out on Modoc Road, and directories list his occupation as carpenter and oil worker. After Addie's death in 1940 he remarried and moved out to Montecito. A staunch Seventh-Day Adventist, he died in the White Memorial Hospital in Los Angeles, and is buried in the Santa Barbara cemetery.

There is little information at hand about Ida. The 1908 Phoenix directory lists Mrs Ida M Harriman as proprietor of the DeMoss Rooming House, 401 South Fourth, and her father one of the roomers. The 1909 directory, under Furnished Rooms, lists the Moss Rooming House, 401

West Washington, Mrs Ida M Collyer, Prop. In residence are John F Harriman, saw filer, and James M Collyer, painter.

This advertisement appeared in the *Santa Barbara Morning Press*, October 26, 1912.

J. M. Collyer
Painter and Decorator
Uses Alabastine. All Work Guaranteed
If you want the best possible in this line call me up
Estimates   Reference   and   Bonds Furnished
Shop 735 Chapala St. Phones Home 1210 Pacific 919
Res. 322 E. Victoria St.

The 1912-13 Santa Barbara directory lists him at 32<u>4</u> E Victoria St, and John F Harriman, carpenter, RD No 1. By 1914 Collyer was working for Wm R Hayward, painting contractor. It was during this sojourn in Santa Barbara that "Grandpa Jim" painted some wood-graining, a popular artiface at the time, at the Mission, an accomplishment he was pleased to be able to point out to his grandson, Bob Brune, some decades later when they visited from the San Joaquin valley. Their stay on the coast ended in 1914 when Collyers moved to Reedley and Harriman to San Fernando, where he died in 1917, and was buried in the Morningside cemetery, where Grandma Cole lay. Ida died in Reedley in the '20's; Grandpa Jim remarried and lived a full nine decades, dying in Fresno in 1962.

Atwood Oscar Harriman was the older brother of J F, and something less of a traveler. He and John were living in their parent's domicile in 1850 and 1860; in 1870 A O was a married man with a baby daughter living in Montville, a few miles northwest of Searsmont. They may have come directly from Maine to California; if so, it was likely by ship, as Downeasters are sea-faring people.

His presence in California is shown in his voter registration on April 10, 1879, in Cambria. The 1880 census-taker found him there, with wife, three children, sister-in-law and her two children, Charley Bright (from Wisconsin), Eva Burns, cousin of the Brights, and another Maine man, Joseph E Miservey (?) in the house. He registered to vote again in Cambria in the spring of 1882, but later that year moved to Santa Barbara county, buying a "suburban" lot in Los Alamos valley from Charles D Patterson December 8, 1882. The acreage was not quite 6½ acres, so he surely wasn't trying to farm: in fact, the 1884-5 Coast Counties Directory lists him as a carpenter. He sold that property, half to Elena M Botiller, half to Louise M Botiller de Foxen, on April 12, 1887, and the next day bought lots 14-17, block 9, in Los Alamos, which is the northwest corner of Main and Centennial. Soon after he re-registered to vote in Cambria, but came back to Los Alamos. In June 1888 he and Dr J Will Graham bought lots 1-4, block 21, Los Alamos, which is the southwest corner of Shaw and Centennial. Not long after that he decided to take out a pre-emption on public land over the hills to the south near Santa Rita, and was living there in 1890. He received the patent in 1892 and sold it to Dr Graham.

This Business Card ran in the *Los Alamos Central* in 1892.

A. O. Herriman
Carpenter And Contractor
Estimates given on all kinds of building
plans, and especial attention given to job-work
Address orders to A. O. Harriman, Contractor
Los Alamos, Cal.

The following item from the *Santa Maria Times* for November 24, 1894 illustrates the working conditions as well as the reporting style of the era.

Los Alamos Explodes
Throws Some People Up–Some Down–
and Shakes The Town

On last Wednesday morning the denizens of our quiet little city were thrown into a fever of fear and excitement, that equaled or surpassed that of the big fire of a year or so ago. The cause of this great commotion was the explosion of a steam engine. Our townsman Mr B P Whitney had an old style Garr and Scott engine, that he used with his barley crusher, and on Wednesday morning he steamed it up for work. After running for an hour or so, the drive belt gave way and they were compelled to stop and mend it, while engaged in doing this the explosion took place. Mr Whitney, Owen and Evert Holloway and Eugene Herold were working in front of the engine, Messrs. A O Harriman and Mariano Ruiz, were doing some carpenter work on a bench which sat only a few feet from its side; and strange as it may appear, not one of them were seriously injured, although they were thrown head over heels in every direction by the violent concussion. The fearful report, which could have been heard for miles, brought excited men, women and children to the scene of disaster, expecting to find only the mangled remains of their neighbors and friends, who they knew were working near the ill fated engine. Their happy surprise, however, is better imagined than described when they found them unhurt and seemingly unconcerned. How all of those who were working only a few feet from the explosion, escaped with their lives, is a problem to hard for those who have seen the situation the men were placed in, to solve.

Notes Of The Wreck–
    Window glasses were broken in homes a quarter of a mile away.
    Owen and Evert Holloway were perfectly serene during the whole time of the excitement.
    A piece of the engine weighing fully 500 pounds was thrown over two houses into the middle of the street.
    Mr Ruiz, as he climbed down off the ridge where he had been placed by the terrible force of steam, remarked: "For God's sake, Harriman, what hit us?"
    Mr J J Holloway was standing near the Alliance Mills and was struck by a flying piece of iron, but fortunately it had spent its fury and did no damage.
    Mr Whitney when he had crawled out from under the debris by which he had been buried, called out: "Say, boys, did any of you see which direction my spectacles took?"
    A section of the large balance wheel was blown into the air fully 100 feet and in descending went crashing through the roof of Mrs Gates dining room, fortunately doing no damage to those inside.
    Mr Harriman, who had been deposited in the fence corner some 50 or 60 feet from the scene of destruction, arose and said: "To hades with the 'injine', you can buy another one, but can't put life in a dead man."

Harriman sold two of the lots in block 9 that he had bought in 1887 from L L Gates and Dr Graham to B F Whitney in 1889, and, the same day in February, turned over the lots in block 21 to Dr Graham. In 1894 half of lot 16 in block 9 was sold to J D and W F Wickenden, the rest in 1896 to Dr Graham. On June 27, 1896, A O and his son, Lot, registered to vote. A O was 5'7", down from 5'8¾" in 1894, sandy complexion, blue eyes (grey in '94), brown hair, AOH tattooed on left arm, occupation carpenter. Lot was 5'6½", light complexion, blue eyes, light hair, occupation printer. Both were residents of Los Alamos. Four days later Lot died of acute alcoholism.

Where the rest of the family was is anybody's guess. After Lot's death, A O moved out to the Jesus Maria ranch, where he continued to work as a carpenter. His death certificate was signed by his old friend, Dr Graham, coroner, now in Lompoc. No obituary has been found, so a number of questions remain.

Death Claims Mrs Harriman

Mrs Forrest J Harriman of 2442 Modoc Road died Saturday night in a local hospital following a lingering illness. She had resided in Santa Barbara for the past 16 years.

Born in Los Angeles in 1882, she was the daughter of the late Mr and Mrs Francis M Clark both of whom died in Santa Barbara in recent years. (Francis M Clark 6-17-32)

Besides her husband, she is survived by a daughter, Mrs Lloyd D Near of La Crescenta, a sister, Mrs Cora Hunter of Santa Barbara, brother L F (?) Clark of Manitoba Beach, Mich., two grandchildren, three nephews and one niece.

Mrs Harriman has been a member of the Seventh-Day Adventist Church of Santa Barbara for many years, and Rev Arthur D Armstrong pastor of that church will officiate at the services in the Charles T Holland chapel this afternoon at 2 o'clock. Committal services will follow in the Santa Barbara cemetery. Pallbearers, all members of the church will be . . . (illegible)

-*Santa Barbara News-Press* Monday Morning May 20 1940

Montecitan Died In Los Angeles

Forrest Harriman, 73, two decades a resident (!) of Montecito, died Wednesday morning at a Los Angeles hospital, where he had been under treatment.

A native of Wisconsin, Mr Harriman was an active member of the Seventh Day Adventist Church until his recent illness. He leaves his widow Mrs Rose Harriman of the home here; a daughter, Mrs L B Near of La Crescenta, and two grandchildren.

Rev C R Webster will conduct funeral services from the Welch and Ryce Chapel on Saturday afternoon at 2:30 o'clock. Committal will be in Santa Barbara cemetery.

William Solomon Harriman was also a native of Maine, and the following information was collected on the off-chance that he was related to the foregoing; apparently he isn't.

In San Luis Obispo W S Harriman, 36, seaman, registered to vote October 2, 1868. He, 38, clerk in lumber yard, and Mary A, 24, born Indiana, were on the 1870 census in San Luis Obispo township. On 10 February 1872 he bought some property in San Luis Obispo which he, a resident of Santa Cruz, sold to A M Loomis 18 February 1878.

April 5 1873, a girl born to W S and Mary A Harriman, San Luis.

1875   Handbook and Directory of Southern California: W S Harriman lumber dealer, Main Street, Guadalupe.

June 1 1880 Amador county census, township 3 Volcano

William Harriman, 50 laborer, born ME, father FR, mother ENG
Mary   33 wife   IN   PA   IRE

Died: Harriman. At Santa Cruz Oct. 18 1887 Mary, widow of the late W S Harriman, and daughter of the late Benjamin Grable.   –*Santa Maria Times* Oct 29 1887

July 31 1896. Benjamin F Grable, 44, blacksmith, born PA registered to vote in Los Alamos, Santa Barbara Co., California

History of the City of Belfast in the State of Maine, Vol. II, 1875-1900, Joseph Williamson, 1913: necrology
Marriages Waldo County Maine, compiled and typed by Dr Benjamin Lake Noyes, Stonington, ME. (Film, LDS Family History Center, LA)

Jesse H Harriman/Herriman   b. Montville, Waldo Co, ME c1808
    farmer   d.
         F: possibly Dudley Harriman
       m. before 1830 census; both 20-30, no children
Mary   b. Appleton Maine c1816
         d.
Children:
1.   Alonzo J   b. Montville ME 1831
         d. Montville ME Oct 27 1897 @66
       m. Belfast ME May 15 1856
     Mary J Morrison   d. Waterville ME Jan 30 1900 @68
         F: Jonathan of Boothbay

2.   Atwood Oscar   b. Searsmont ME Jun 1835
         d. Jesus Maria ranch, near Lompoc, CA
           October 28 1910
       m. 1868
     Ellen M (Nell)   b. Maine 1840
      a.   Lettie   b. Montville Sep 1869
      b.   Lot Atwood   b. Montville? 1871
         d. Los Alamos CA Jul 1 1896 @25
           bur. Los Alamos cemetery

      c.   Olin R   b. Maine c1874

3.   John Fellows   b. Searsmont ME Oct 17 1837
         d. San Fernando CA Nov 10 1917
         bur. Morningside cemetery, San Fernando
       m. Iowa? Wisconsin? c1866. Div.
     Josephine Williams   b. Lorain? Co. OH Nov 22 1849
         d. Los Angeles Jun 15 1922
         F: Riley Williams   M: Laura Anne^7 Culver
           (Oliver^6 Francis^5 Asher^4 Daniel^3 Edward^2 Edward^1)
         m. 2. c1891 Edward Farley
      a.   Ida M   b. Wisconsin c1867
         d. Reedley CA
       m. James M Collyer 1872-1962
      b.   Forrest Jesse   b. Trempealeau Co WI Aug 10 1871
         d. Los Angeles Nov 29 1944
         bur. Santa Barbara cemetery
       m. Los Angeles Feb 20 1902
     Addie Frances Clark   b. Los Angeles 1882
         d. Santa Barbara May 18 1940
         F: Frances M
     =Lucia Ellen   b. Nevada Apr 11 1905
         d. Carmichael CA Apr 27 1970

4.   Mary A   b. Searsmont ME c1842
5.   James W   b. Searsmont ME c1847

ED HECOX
LOMPOC'S KID STAGE DRIVER

Until 1900, public transportation to Lompoc was by stagecoach. Ed Hecox was the driver on the Lompoc-Gaviota-Arroyo Honda run in the 1890's, and is pictured in *Lompoc. The First 100 Years,* page 10, photo dated 1901. A story in the *Lompoc Record*, July 1926, says Hecox lost his job "27" years ago, although an accident to a stage Hecox was driving was reported in February 1900; later that year the census-taker found him and family in San Francisco. His name appears in Walker Tompkins' *Stage Coach Days in Santa Barbara County* on page 118.

Myra Manfrina of the Lompoc Historical Society has provided us with an account of some of Hecox's adventures written by Ronald Adam, longtime editor and publisher of the *Lompoc Record*, (and nephew of Wm L Adam of Santa Maria; see Adam chart), who started his career, like Ed, as a youth. He worked with Ed's father, Oscar Hecox, at the paper before Oscar's death in 1903, and continued until his own death fifty years later. He says Ed started running the stage at age 14, a four-horse rig between Lompoc and Los Alamos; he graduated to the main line horse stage while still in his teens. The stage company was owned by N W Wines of Santa Barbara whose policy "was to run on schedule, horse flesh didn't count; 'you make the schedule and I will buy the horses' was his edict." The coach, horses, and driver, too, "had to be slicked up before they left every morning, stage washed every night, every horse had its own harness and it had to be washed and polished every night."

Unpaved roads, rain, and no bridges made for a muddy mess to be cleaned before the next run; sometimes the stage didn't return to Lompoc until late at night, but it was to be clean and ready to go at six a.m. Storms occasionally prevented the completion of the trip. One night, pitchblack and stormy, Ed couldn't get the stage through the raging Salsipuedes Creek, so "upholding the old rule that the mail must go through . . . he unhooked one of his leaders, shouldered the mail sacks, mounted the animal and attempted to ford" but "the horse floundered and threw Hecox into the flood, but he grasped a tug and hung onto the mail bag and his staunch leader finally got them across. Later that stormy night while a few anxious folks waited up for the stage, a wet and weary lad rode into town with mail bags on his shoulder."

Ed married Belle Phillips in 1893. The Phillips family lived near Stuart, a post office on the road from Lompoc to Los Alamos. Belle died the next year, and the same issue of the *Lomppoc Record* that announced her death said that "James Meyers, formerly stage driver on the San Luis Obispo-Santa Margarita run is in Lompoc . . . now in employ of N W Wines of Santa Barbara." Thus Ed became acquainted with that family, and subsequently married Meyer's daughter May.

The romantic ideas associated with stagecoach travel don't take into consideration the vagaries and dangers of that method of transportation as some contemporary reporting will show.

SCRAPBOOK

1891. A six horse stage driven by Jim Myers (sic) overturned with five passengers on the Cuesta grade between San Luis and Santa Margarita on Wednesday evening. No one was seriously injured. The night was dark, the road muddy, the horses became frightened and ran away throwing the stage and occupants into the bank. Any other termination of the frightful accident could but have proven fatal to at least some of those on board the stage. –*SM Times* Jan 2

1892. Mr Wines, general manager of the Santa Barbara and Los Olivos Stage Co, appreciating the superior scenic attractions along his route, has added two new coaches, constructed with special reference to the requirements of tourists who demand "outside seats."
–*SM Times* Oct 22

(And what happens to the occupants of those outside seats?)
1875. Stage Accident. Thursday evening as Hecox was returning from the landing to San Luis with his coach and three passengers on board, his horses took fright as he finished watering them at the water station and run (sic) away, upsetting the coach. In his efforts to catch and stop the horses he was thrown under them, and the wheels passed over both thighs, fortunately without breaking them. A gentleman by the name of J W Mumford who was riding outside was thrown off as the coach went over and was considerably bruised but not seriously injured. The inside passengers escaped unhurt.
–*SLO Tribune* Nov 13

Note: This must be Adna H Hecox (1845-1922) cousin of Ed's father, Oscar, who operated a livery stable in San Luis Obispo in the late 1870s to about 1881, when he returned to the Santa Cruz area, where the Hecox family had settled in the 1840s.

Hecox Didn't Jump He Was Thrown From the Coach   The Driver's Account of the Recent Accident on the Santa Barbara Stage Line.

The *SLO Breeze* last Monday, Feb 12th, gave the particulars of an accident on the Santa Barbara Stage line which occurred near Gaviota on Sunday, 11th inst. The account published in the *Breeze* was furnished by a passenger, named J J Hutt, who was aboard the stage when the accident occurred. Mr Hutt blamed the driver, Hecox, accusing him of throwing the lines down and jumping. The *Lompoc Record* has interviewed Hecox and published his statement of the affair which places the matter in a different light, and vindicates him of the charge of carelessness or cowardice. From Hecox's statement, and he was in a better position to know what occurred than those inside the coach, the accident was, so far as the driver was concerned, unavoidable. He did all that a man under the circumstance could be expected to do, and used good judgement. Following is the driver's explanation of the accident:

The stage from Santa Barbara being half an hour late in reaching the dinner station made it necessary to make up that time on a short run between Ortegas and Las Cruces, hence the extra speed over parts of the road where possible. On reaching the Gaviota Hill, and just as the descent was reached, a singletree of one of the swing horses broke loose, coming forcibly against the horse's heels, causing the horse to jump on the swing pole which broke, letting the leadbars come against the leaders' heels. At this juncture Hecox told the lady to jump out which could have been effected with no injury had not some one present held her back until the infuriated horses were flying down the hill, when to jump was almost certain death, when the lady did jump and was injured as stated. Hecox says further that he was thrown from his seat and in attempting to recover it, dropped three of the reins which lost him control of the team. He was next thrown from the coach, and just how he escaped being crushed he does not know, all was so quickly done. No one who knows Ed will believe the report that he threw down the lines and jumped to save himself; and accepting his version of the cause of the accident, we cannot see how the casualties could have been averted. The injured parties are all doing well.
–*SLO Breeze* Feb 16

Former Stage Driver Greets Friends Here
1926. Mr and Mrs Ed Heacock (sic) of Reno, formerly of Lompoc, accompanied C M Tucker on his return from Santa Cruz Wednesday. Mr Tucker and Mr and Mrs Heacock were in Santa Cruz

to attend the funeral of W W Oney, Mr Heacock's step-father, and after the services they motored to Lompoc.

Mr Heacock was one of the stage drivers in Lompoc in the early days before the railroad was extended to this part of California. He is now a railroad engineer out of Reno, Nev. Mr Heacock is greeting the old timers who can recall the time when every one who arrived in Lompoc came in the stage driven by Mr Heacock. –The *Lompoc Record* Fri July 9

Hecox's Visit Recalls Stage Days Of Old
1926. Twenty-seven years ago Ed Heacock lost his job. It was one of the best paying jobs in Lompoc in those days, $60 per month, and he worked 365 days in the year. And Ed liked this particular job—but there came a day when the "iron horse" took the place of the stage coach and broncos and he was out of a job.

Ed Heacock was one of the old-time stage drivers. Not "old" like Jim Meyers, Tom Coe and some of the other veterans—any of them were old enough to be his father. Rather he was just a kid among those characters, but just the same he was a real stage driver, and a good one too.

When Ed lost his job as stage driver he took up railroading. First he became a fireman, and afterwards graduated into the ranks of locomotive engineer. Now he is piloting the Overland Limited east of Sparks, Nevada, and has the fastest run in the world. He is on a mail and express train and covers over 250 miles in a little over five hours, whereas in the old days of the stage coach he drove twelve hours to make 60 miles.

Mr Heacock was here yesterday in company with his wife, and meeting him recalled old times to the writer. We remember when Ed "held the ribbons" on the six-horse stage coach. If one was an early riser you would see the stage pull out at 6 o'clock every morning, rain or shine. The horses would be somewhat stiff and lame as they pounded along on Ocean avenue, and the vehicle would seem to be in "second gear" until they warmed up.

The San Julian was the stage road and it was one of the most delightful and picturesque drives in the state. However, it was not so well improved as it is now. Heacock drove as far as Arroyo Honda, which was the "noon station." Twenty minutes was taken off for lunch and for changing teams, and then he would head back for Lompoc, arriving here at 6 p.m. if the roads were good and none of the animals had failed.

Heacock said yesterday that he liked stage driving and that in the old days he hated to lay off a single trip for fear that he would miss the pleasure of a ride with some old and interesting friend. Ed was a great conversationalist and his stories never failed to interest the passengers. Prominent men, such as Bishop Johnson of Los Angeles, have told us of the interesting trips which they made thirty years ago with Heacock.

Getting back to jobs, sixty dollars per month was considered a good salary thirty years ago. Heacock said yesterday that during a five-year period he did not miss a single day—worked Sundays and every other day and over twelve hours a day. He drove stage for twelve years out of Lompoc. In the winter time the San Julian road was in bad condition and the stage was often late from one to six hours. In rainy weather the adobe on the San Julian would roll up on the brakes until it would lock the wheels of the stage and Heacock would have to dig it off. Sometimes one of the horses would become exhausted and have to be left by the roadside. But Ed carried on day in and day out and brought through the mail, passengers and express. If he did not get in at night until 11 o'clock, it made no difference with the next day's schedule, for he would leave promptly at 6 o'clock next morning.

This strenuous life seemed to agree with Heacock, and his appearance yesterday denoted that he is in fine physical condition.

The job that he now holds as engineer is a "snap." He says he only works eight hours per day and about five days per week, and gets five times as much pay as when he was laboring 12 to 18 hours per day as stage driver. He frankly confesses that he is glad that the "good old days" are gone. The old song that "people lived better in those days because things were cheaper" is all bunk, in Heacock's opinion, for he is quite sure that he is enjoying more of the luxuries of life on a salary of $300 per month than he used to a $60 per month.

Mr Heacock's father, Oscar Heacock, was the printer on the *Lompoc Record* thirty years ago. The paper was then edited by W W Broughton, and Mr Heacock set the type by hand and performed all the other duties in the "back office." Both Mr Heacock and Mr Broughton have been dead for many years. –The *Lompoc Record* Fri July 9 1926

Note: The confusion on the spelling probably originates with the fact that there was another family, unrelated, in Lompoc, who spelled their surname Heacock.

1933. Visit Enjoyed by Former Resident. Mr and Mrs Ed Hecock (sic) and daughter, Mrs Helen McAvoy of Sparks, Nev, were Sunday visitors in San Luis Obispo, enroute north from Lompoc ... former San Luis Obispo residents, Mr Hecock have been employed by Southern Pacific Company here for many years. Mrs Hecock will be remembered as May Meyers...daughter of Jim Meyers, pioneer stage driver here in former years...

–*SLO Daily Telegram* Mon Aug 21 p.5

1935. Daughter of Pioneer Stage Driver Visits Here. Mr and Mrs Ed Hecox of Sparks, Nev, were visitors at the home of Miss Rose Lee, ... enroute to San Diego ... California Pacific International Exposition. Mrs Hecox will be remembered as Miss May Meyers, who spent her girlhood and school days in San Luis Obispo ... daughter of Jim Meyers, who was one of the pioneer stage drivers of this city, having driven for many years the stage coach over Cuesta grade to San Francisco (sic) ... –*SLO Daily Telegram* Tue May 28

When the stage business became obsolete, Hecox became a railroad man. Even that line of transportation has its difficulties. He was the engineer on the City of San Francisco streamliner when it was sabotaged near Elko, Nevada, in August 1939. Jumping out and running down the track to the nearest section house, about a mile away, stumbling in the dark, was another sort of adventure. There was much about the incident in the Reno papers, as well there might be, as twenty were killed and 114 injured. Another wreck, an unfortunately similar sabotage, occurred to an Amtrak train near Hyder, Arizona, in October 1995. The newspaper account concludes with a mention of the 1939 wreck, implying that a recent story about it in a "train buff" magazine might have inspired the "anti-government" saboteur.

Ed Hecox was in the 8th generation from Samuel Hickocks/Hicox of colonial Farmington, CT. Much information has been gathered on 6th generation James and Adna Hecox, brothers who came to California in the early days. Interested persons may request it.

HOBBS
SANTA MARIA VALLEY PIONEERS

Farlon Hobbs b. OH 7 Sep 1838 (obit) or Aug 1837 (1910 census)
 d. Santa Maria 15 Nov 1919 @82/2/8; SM cem
   m. 1861
Mary Catherine Garrett b. VA Aug 1842
 d. Santa Maria 28 Jun 1922 @81/10/6; SM cem

1. Duskin Ernest b. Jefferson OH 28 Sep 1861; m. @25
 (only child) d. Santa Monica CA 2 Dec 1952 @90/2/3; SM cem
    m.2 Sophia
    m. Santa Maria 26 Jan 1887 by F A Thomas, C378
     wit: Garrett Blosser, Henry Stowell
 Susan Arminta Stowell b. Cayucos/Old Creek CA May 1869; m. @17
 6 births, 6 living, 1910; d. Santa Maria 13 Mar 1926 @57; SM cem
 8 living 1919 F: George Stowell 1830-1910
  M: Lydia Smith 1835-1903

  a. Leonard Arthur b. 16 Jul 1887
 electrical engineer d. 24 Aug 1976 Orange co CA
   m.1 San Juan Capistrano, CA 9 Sep 1911
 Olga Conwell b. 1890 Chicago, IL
  d.
  F: Cornelius L Conwell
  M: Alice Bunker
   m.2 23 Jun 1928
 May Monica Jones See Marquis' *Who's Who in the West* 1963-4
   a Leonard

  b. George Stowell b. Santa Maria 22 Sep 1889
 carpenter d. Santa Maria 12 Sep 1967 @77/11/20;
  SM cem
   m.
 Myrtle Launders b. 1896
  living in family home 319 W Park 1992
 =Alice G (Griffith) teacher Cook St sch 1938; Miller sch 1940
 =Hizzoner George Stowell jr Mayor of Santa Maria
 =Dorothy Sue (Baker)
 =William
 =Joan (Johnson)
 =Jean (Farrell)
 =Leslie

  c. Edwin Ira b. Santa Maria 21 Oct 1899
  d. Corning, CA 4 Jan 1984
   m. 1926: rancher, 201 E Morrison w/2parents
 Grace B

  d. Angus Guy b. 15 Sep 1901
 dentist d. 31 Oct 1981 Laguna Beach, CA
 1922 Grad. SM High School Activities: entered from Hughson High (2) Football (3,4) Class Pres (3) Senior Bazaar (4), "Last Will & Testament": Personal Property. "I, Angus Hobbs, leave my jar of 'Stacomb' to Mr Breneiser." Senior Prophecy: ... Harold Rosenblum playing piano in Angus Hobbs' café in Tia Juana.

    e.   Dorothy K Fannie   b. 10 May 1904 Santa Maria
        m.
        Alfred G Harker   b. 15 Dec 1902
                                                            d. 13 Aug 1985 Riverside co CA
                                                              (res. Cathedral city, CA)

    f.   Clifford Byron   b. 27 Nov 1908
                                                            d. 24 July 1970 Ojai, CA
        m. & div.   (spouse initial P P)
        Lorabeth Daniels   b. Santa Maria Valley
        nurse 1940   F: William Daniels
                                                         M: Esther Trott

    g.   Donald Elmer   b. 8 Jan 1912
        m. & div.
        Thelma Maxine Lyon   b. 1 Dec 1910 Arroyo Grande, CA
                                                         d. Santa Barbara @36/4/13; bur 16 Apr 1947;
                                                             SM cem
                                                             F: Roy L Lyon
                                                             M: Martha Josphine Morris 1891-1959**
                                                                  m.2 George Robinson

        = Darlene Gaye
            m. 8 Oct 1949 @16 yrs; Los Angeles co
        Richard Wells m. @21 yrs
    h.   Ottalie Helen   b. 1914
        m.1
        Ernest Migele
            m.2 @44 Ventura co (Ojai)? 5-13-1958
        Floyd Parslow m. @66

**These markers in one plot in Santa Maria cemetery:
    Louis J Morris 1860-1948; Sarah J Morris 1863-1942; Josephine M Robinson
    1891-1959; Thelma M Hobbs 1910-1947. (See *Who's Who in Santa Maria* 1931, for
    Judge L J Morris)

Ed. Note: This chart was formulated from public records, not intended to be complete, but to differentiate this Hobbs family from the La Graciosa Hobbs.

HOBBS SCRAPBOOK

1908   Attention is called to Leonard Hobbs' Adv. which tells about motors for making washing easy.   –*SM Times* April 25

1919   Farlon Hobbs Dies Of Injuries
        Farlon Hobbs died at his home south of town this morning at 4 o'clock as a result of the burns and shock which he received at the New Penn. service station fire Wednesday evening. He was a native of Ohio born September 7, 1838. He is survived by his wife, Mary C Hobbs, and an only son, Duskin Hobbs and eight grandchildren.
        Mr Hobbs was a resident of this valley for 35 years. He came here from Oregon. For a year before he moved to this valley he lived at Gridley, Calif. He farmed the 80 acre tract south of town, known as The Hobbs Tract.
        The funeral will take place from the A A Dudley chapel Monday afternoon at 2 o'clock. The interment will be in the local cemetery.

Mr Hobbs will be greatly missed by the community where he has many friends. Nearly every day of his residence here he would walk to town for a visit with his friends in the afternoon. On the day of the fatal accident, Mr Hobbs had stopped in at the service station to talk with Mr Lewis. He was standing at the door of the oil room when the explosion came. His burns at first were not regarded as serious but together with shock, they proved more than his advanced age could stand.

His family have the sympathy of the community in the departure of husband and father.

Gasoline Explodes Station Total Loss Three Are Injured
From Thursday's Daily: A fire caused from an explosion of a high gravity drum of gasoline completely destroyed the New Pennsylvania Oil service station a mile south of town last evening at five-thirty, and severely injured three men. The loss is estimated at over $5,000.

D A Lewis is in charge of the station at that hour. He went to the oil room to fill a gallon can with the high gravity gasoline for Mr Hopkins of the Perkins Cement company near Orcutt. When he took the plug from the top of the barrel the explosion occurred hurling gasoline and fumes all over the place for a large radius. Mr Lewis put the plug back in. It was only a minute he said from then that the whole place was in flames caught when the fumes reached a gas heater in the office eleven feet away and separated by a wall. The barrel which exploded contained forty-five gallons of gasoline.

L A* Hobbs, a neighbor who had been visiting Mr Lewis and Mr Hopkins were standing in the door watching when the fire broke out. All three were badly burned. Mr Lewis ran out into the street and rolled in the sand to extinguish the flames. His outer clothing was completely burned off. His face and hands were badly burned.

Mr Hobbs started for his home a little distance west of the station while his clothing was afire.

Mr Hopkins had driven up in a Packard. When the explosion occurred his wife and children jumped from the machine and ran to a place of safety, escaping injury.

The automobile was a complete wreck. The fire is still burning.

It was one of the most spectacular fires in town. The flames and smoke shot up into the air sometimes five hundred feet when the drums of gasoline would explode.

The injured men are getting along as well as can be expected, according to reports received early this morning. –*SM Times* Sat Nov 15 p.4

Ed. Note: error; L.A. Hobbs was the oldest grandson.

Card Of Thanks …Mrs Mary C Hobbs   D E Hobbs and family   –Ibid Sat Nov 15 pg 5

Ed Note: the 1906 Santa Maria Valley Directory shows F Hobbs, 1½ M,. sw; The La Graciosa Hobbses, Samuel's widow and son William, were 5 m. S and 6 m S, respectively.

1924   Local News. It is reported that John Morrison has sold to D E Hobbs 37 acres near the high school subdivision for a consideration of $38,000.   –Ibid Feb 28

1926   Mrs Susan Hobbs, Valley Pioneer, Called By Death
Mrs Susan Hobbs, wife of Duskin E Hobbs, and a resident of this city for the past 43 years, passed away at the family residence, 201 E Morrison St., early Saturday night as a result of illness of several months' duration. She had been a patient sufferer, but for some time she gradually failed until the end came.

Mrs Hobbs was a devout Christian woman and a member of the Methodist Episcopal church of this city, the Ladies' Aid Society and of the Woman's Relief Corps in which organization she had been active.

She was born in Cayucos, San Luis Obispo county, and was aged 57 years.

The following bereaved ones are left to mourn her death: the husband, Duskin E Hobbs; six sons, Leonard A Hobbs, of San Francisco, George S, Edwin I, Angus G, Clifford B, and Donald E, and two daughters, Dorothy and Helen Ottalie Hobbs, all of Santa Maria. There are also three grandchildren, Alice G, George S jr, and Dorothy Sue Hobbs; a sister, Mrs Fannie Stowell Tunnell of this city and a half-brother, Al Smith, living at Kerman, Calif.

The funeral was held this afternoon at 2 o'clock, services being conducted at the Methodist church by the pastor, Rev George B Cliff. Interment was in the Santa Maria Cemetery, under the direction of Albert A Dudley, funeral director. The pallbearers were W C Oakley, George May, W H Tunnell, E T Ketcham, M P Baker and Isaac Miller Jr. –*SM Daily Times* Mon Mar 15 p.1

1952   Duskin Ernest Hobbs Dies, Former Resident

Duskin Ernest Hobbs, well known former resident of Santa Maria, died yesterday in Santa Monica. He was 91 years old.

Mr Hobbs was born Sept 28, 1861, in Jefferson City, Mo.* A retired farmer, he had lived in Santa Monica for the past 22 years. He was a charter member of the Santa Maria Elks Club.

He was the husband of Mrs Sophia Hobbs of Santa Monica; father of George S Hobbs of Santa Maria, Leonard H Hobbs of Los Angeles, Edwin J Hobbs of Orland, Dr Angus G Hobbs of Long Beach, Mrs A G Harker of Long Beach, Clifford B Hobbs of Ojai, Donald B Hobbs of Santa Monica, Mrs Ernest Migele of Fresno. He is also survived by 16 grandchildren and five great grandchildren.

Funeral services will be conducted tomorrow at 3 PM in the Chapel of the Dudley Mortuary. Mrs P H Eakin will give the Christian Science reading. Burial will follow in the Santa Maria Cemetery.   –*SM Times* Wed Dec 3, p.8

Ed. Note: Jefferson, Ohio.

1967   George Hobbs, Sr., Local Pioneer Dies Suddenly   A funeral service for George Hobbs, Sr, 77, a pioneer Santa Maria resident, will be held at 11 AM Thursday in the chapel of the Magner Funeral Home with the Rev Stanley Smith, First Methodist church, officiating.

Burial will follow in the Santa Maria Cemetery. Friends may visit at the mortuary from 7 to 9 tonight.

Mr Hobbs died suddenly Tuesday afternoon in his home at 319 West Park St. He was born Sept 22, 1889, in Santa Maria and was a lifelong resident here. His mother was a member of the pioneer Stowell family.

He worked as a carpenter his entire life and was a member of the Carpenters Union No 2477 of Santa Maria. He was also past leader of the Eagles Lodge and belonged to the Native Sons of the Golden West.

Survivors include his wife, Mrs Myrtle Hobbs of the home address; three sons, George Hobbs, Jr, mayor of Santa Maria, William Hobbs of Lompoc, and Leslie Hobbs of San Fernando Rey Ranch; four daughters, Mrs Alice Griffin of Tracy, Mrs Dorothy Baker of Fresno, Mrs Joan Johnson of Hacienda Heights and Mrs Jean Farrell of Santa Maria; five brothers, Edwin Hobbs of Corning, Angus Hobbs of Long Beach, Clifford Hobbs of Ojai, Donald Hobbs of Joshua Tree and Leonard Hobbs of Laguna Heights; two sisters, Mrs Dorothy Harker of Long Beach and Mrs Ottelie Parslow of Ojai; 23 grandchildren and 22 great grandchildren.   –Ibid Wed Sep 13 p.1

1992   Wilding finds a new home for her old house… Tracing back the history of her home, Kathy Wilding explained that Duskin Hobbs (Santa Maria Mayor George Hobb's (sic) grandfather) purchased the 70 ft by 105 ft lot for $10. The R-3 lot is now for sale for just under $100,000.

By 1904 the home and lot sold again for $1,200. The Wildings believe, and George Hobbs confirms, that the home was constructed in 1896…**   –Ibid Sun May 31 A-7 with photos

***Ed. Note*; it stood on the southwest corner of Jones and Pine streets.

1992   Stained glass reflects a rich local history… The first United Methodist Church's large stained glass windows were put in when the current church was built in 1922.
. . . One window was dedicated to George and Lydia Stowell, who joined the church in the later 1880's and the following year became trustees. Stowell Road was named for this family and a descendant is Mayor George Stowell Hobbs   –Ibid Sun Nov 15 C-8

Vol. XXIV, No. 1-4, 1992, p.7

SAMUEL HOBBS
SANTA MARIA VALLEY PIONEERS
La Graciosa, Orcutt, Lompoc & Kern Co

The Samuel Hobbs family is not related to Santa Maria's mayor, whose ancestors originated in Ohio and settled in the town of Santa Maria. After the demolition of La Graciosa in 1877, the Samuel Hobbs family remained south of Santa Maria; the 1906 Santa Maria Valley Directory lists Mrs Mahala Hobbs and James Hobbs 5 miles south of town, and William, farmer, and Mrs Hobbs 6 miles south, in which vicinity the family is memorialized in Hobbs Lane. Jake and Stella, the last surviving members of the family in this valley, lived on Union St in Orcutt.

The following information had been gathered, for the most part, from locally available sources: census, obituary notices, the Pine Grove Cemetery file at the Santa Maria Valley Historical Society, the Evergreen Cemetery book in the Lompoc city library, and the newspaper extracts and county records published in the Quarterly SMVGS&L, wherein, also may be found earlier generations of the Hobbs family in the ahnentafel chart of Gail H Benson of Lompoc in Vol. XX, 1-2, pp. 16-17. There is a fine collection of photographs of the Hobbs-Howerton-Martin clan in the scrapbook file at the Lompoc Historical Society.

The following does not pretend to be complete. Dates in ( ) not corroborated by obituaries.

Samuel Kelsey Hobbs   b. IN 22 Nov 1833
  1892: @58, 6' light complexion   d. 28 Apr 1901 @ 87/5/6; PG
    blue eyes, brown hair, scar on   F. Abner Hobbs 1797-1881
    left hand (Voters registration)   M. Annie Kelsey 1800-1884
    m: O'Neal (Madera co) CA., 8 Sep 1857
Mahala Jane Gann   b. (Pike co) MO 18 May 1841
                                       d. Orcutt 9 Apr 1925; PG
                                       F. Nicholas Broyles Gann 1807-1887
                                       M. Ruth Melvina Freshour 1824-1890
  13 births, 10 living in 1900; 8 living 1910; 7 living 1925
1. William Adrian   b. Stockton, CA Nov 1858 m. @28 (obit)
                                       d. Kern Co, CA 27 Mar 1943
  1896: @ 37 yrs: 5'-11½", dk complexion, drk eyes, drk hair. (Voter's reg.)

Vol. XXIII, 1-4, 1991, p. 28

m: Pine Grove 7 Sep 1887 S. K. Morton, JP Santa Maria, C431
         wit: Joseph L Hobbs, David Foster.
Cora Edna Crabtree   b. (Cambria) Jul 1869 m. @18
                              d. (Kern Co) 26 Dec 1948
                              F. Ephraim Jasper Crabtree 1843-1908
                              M. Laura E Foster 1848-1886
  11 births, 11 living, (Kern co) Twp 12, 1910; 7 sons, 2 daughters living 1943
  a. Jasper   b. La Graciosa 13 Jun 1888
                              d. Alameda Co 18 May 1966
  b. Clara P   b. La Graciosa 29 Apr 1890
  c. Jesse E (twin)   b. La Graciosa Nov 1891
                              d. (Bakersfield 11 Sep 1974)
  d. Joseph Clay (twin)   b. La Graciosa Nov 1891
                              d. Arroyo Grande 13 Oct 1917 (age 25)
                                 or 14 Oct 1917 (age 26) AG cem.
  e. Lillie B (Townsend)   b. La Graciosa Apr 1894
  f. Ira L/V   b. La Graciosa May 1896
                              d. bef 1943
  g. William Brian   b. Bakersfield (26) Apr 1899
     (Ruth)   d. Arroyo Grande 25 Oct 1971
  h. Lena E   b. Palm Dist, Kern co 13 Dec 1902 (*SM Times*)
                              d. (Arroyo Grande 22 Apr 1928 @ 26 AG cem)
  i. John P/C   b. (25 Feb) 1905
                              d. (Dec 1986 Roseville CA)
  j. Frank J   b. (7 Nov) 1907
                              d. (South San Francisco May 1981)
  k. Clyde R/L   b. Old River, Kern co 30 Jun 1909
                              d. (Grover City Mar 1986)
  l. Jay Dee   b. 1913
                              d. (Kern co 6 Nov 1953)

Note: Jasper 31, Wm B 20, both single, together 1920 census SLO co

2. John Henry   b. CA Mar 1860; d. bef 1920
     1896: age 36 5'11½ dk complexion, dark eyes, dark hair
       m. 1883
   Emma   b. OR 1864
     6 births, 6 living 8th twp Santa Barbara co 1900
  a. William Edgar   b. Baker, OR 26 Jun 1884
                              d. Santa Maria 13 Apr 1958; EV

        m.
     Lillian Viola   b. 29 Dec 1880
                              d. 28 Dec 1978; EV
  b. Henry S /L   b. OR Aug 1887
     (Pearl)   d. (Kern co 15 Jul 1946)?
  c. Clarence (Alice)   b. OR May 1890
  d. Earl*   b. CA Jun 1891
  e. Earnest (Clara)   b. CA Aug 1894
  f. Hazel (Mathis)   b. CA 1898
  g. Maud (Harrison)   b. after 1900
     George E*   d. (Bakersfield 26 Mar 1965) ?
     Others?   (b. 4 Sep 1892 Social Sec recs)

Note: 1920 census soundex, Kern Co: Ernest 24, Clara 20 wife, Emma 56 mother, George* bro 27 Henry L 32 b. OR, Pearl 22 wife, Rola D 3, Cecil 2/12 Clarence 31, Alice 36 wife, Mable 14, Thelma 14, Roy 3 4/12?

3. Joseph Lane   b. CA Aug 1863
       d. Bakersfield 19 Aug 1936 @73; PG cem
   1896: age 34 5'9, dk complexion, br eyes, dk hair.
     m Santa Maria 30 Jul 1887 by Samuel K Morton, JP, C423.
       wit: Thomas Martin, Berdina Hobbs
   Nancy Elnora Stubblefield   b. Sonoma co CA Jul 1867
       d. Santa Maria 18 Jun1909 @42/l0/23; PG cem
       F. Absolom Stubblefield 1841-1934
       M. Nancy Harris 1845-1930
   5 births, 5 living Santa Maria 1900; he in Kern co 1910
     a. Fredrick D   b. Santa Maria Valley 4 Dec 1888
       d. Oceano 14 Apr 1959 (wife Larena)
     b. Lewis Guy   b. Aug 1891
       Hired man w/Chas French   d. SM 13 Oct 1969; AG cem
       Santa Maria 1910
     c. Robert Nelson   b. 15 May 1893
       d. AG 3 Feb 1975
     d. Emmett Jesse   b. May 1895
       d. (SLO Co 5 Mar 1962)
       m. @25 (of Orcutt) in San Luis Obispo 12 May 1921, by Wm Mallagh, JP L575
         wit: Barbara Lopez, Santa Maria, Manuel Costa, Orcutt
         Written verified consent of father, Frank E Costa, first had & filed
       Gloria E Costa   b. CA; m. @17, of Los Alamos
     e. William L   b. 8 Dec 1896
       d. aft 1975
     f. boy   b. 18 Jun 1909; stillborn; PG cem

4. Melvina Jane   b. CA 17 Feb 1865; m. @18
     m. Pine Grove 15 Sep 1883 by Wright, C70
       wit: WB Scott, Coleman Stubblefield.
   Thomas Henry Martin   b. MO 1863; m. @20
       d. Lompoc 1 Apr 1926 @ 63/2/10; EV cem
       F. Thomas J Martin 1821-bef 1891
       M. Sarah A Goatley 1824-1891
   10 births, 10 living Lompoc 1910; 9 living 1926.
     a. Myrtle Lee   b. 1884; d. 1963
       m. 1903
      Irving J Daniels   b. 1882; d. 1962
     b. Annie Laurie   b. 1888; d. 1986
       m. 1908
      Elmer E Elliott
     c. Rufus Henry   b. 29 Apr 1890; d. 2 Feb 1943; EV cem
       m. 1917
      Trina Kolding   b. 1896; d. 1967
     d. William Thomas   b. 23 Dec 1892; d. 10 Aug 1979; EV cem
       m. 1916
      Emily Deitzman   b. 2 Aug 1895; d. 27 Dec 1954; EV cem
     e. Charles Roland   b. 19 Aug 1895; d. Lompoc 12 Aug 1925
       m. 1919

Marian Smith	b. 1895; d. 1924
f. Ruth Jane	b. 1897; d. 1978 (killed acc. Anaheim)
m.1 1921	
Luther Sidney Douglass	b. 23 Oct 1877; d. 1 Jan 1961; EV cem
m.2	
Paul Metraud	b. 1896; d. 1978 (killed acc. Anaheim)
g. Delbert Leonard	b 4 Oct 1900; d. 2 Aug 1961; EV cem
m. c1918	
Kathleen Day	
= Thomas Henry d. 29 Oct 1920 @6 mo. Spinal Meningitis; EV cem	
h. Sarah E	b. 1903; d. 1982
m.1922	
Richard Huseman	b. 1899; d. 1952
i. James Nelson	b. 11 Jun 1906; d. 11 Nov 1969; EV cem
m.1 1927	
Blanche Gilkeson	b. 1906; d. 1936
m.2 1940	
Blanche Winans	b. 1911/19; d. 1945
m.3 1948	
Lulu Aldeane Williams	b. 12 Dec 1909; d.10 May 1977; EV cem
j. Perry Dean	b. 1909
m. 1931	
Lucile Sanor	b. 1909
5. Berdina	b. CA 1867; m. @20; d. 1896

m. 7/9 Nov 1887 Santa Maria/SK Morton, JP c443
    wit: Joseph L Hobbs & Mrs Cora Hobbs

Mattison Warren Howerton	b. IL 19 Mar 1863
	d. Santa Barbara 27 Feb 1941 @78
	F. Wm Patton Howerton 1829-1905
	M. Nancy Candace Groves 1830-1871
a. Harry R	b. 19 Nov 1888; d. 27 Jan 1952; EV cem
m. 1910	
Myrtle Upton	b. 1892; d. 1953
b. Alice Elsie	b. May 1891; d. 1973; m. @19 of Lompoc
m. Lompoc Oct 1910	
Andrew L Huyck	b. Jul 1884; d. 1968; m. @26 of Lompoc

Note: (Howerton m. 2) Garey, CA 22 Apr 1899 @36 Elder John Houk, LDS
    wit: Candace Houk, Angeline Houk, of Garey

Clara L Moore	b. ME Mar 1855. m. @44;
	d. Casmalia 24 Apr 1904 @49/0/25.
m.3 1906	
Elizabeth Bradley	b. 12 Aug 1873; Santa Maria
	d. 30 May 1957 Santa Barbara, CA
	F. Charles Bradley 1839-1913
	M. Elizabeth Boothe 1840-1893

m.1 Samuel J Singleton b. MO 1861; d. Lompoc 15 Nov 1905; SM cem
    Singleton issue:

a. James Fred	1891-1957
b. Walter	1894-1916; EV
c. Evelyn	1899-1907; EV
d. John D	1902-1979

6. Rosette L   b. CA 25 Dec 1869 (cem) or Sep 1869 (Census)
                                     d. 29 Apr 1887 @17/5/4; PG cem
7. James A   b. La Graciosa 21 Nov 1872
   (single)   d. Santa Maria 18 Sep 1954; EV cem
8. Bertha Mae   b. La Graciosa 13 Dec1874; m. @15
                                     d. Lompoc 30 Aug 1964 @89; EV cem
       m. Santa Maria 26 Feb 1889; A.R. McCullough, Christian Ch
           wit: Eliza McCorkle, Victoria Thornburgh
   Thomas Frank Howerton   b. Johnson co KS 3 Feb 1868
   10 births, 10 living, Ocean Av   d. Lompoc 24 May 1953 @85; EV cem
     between Lompoc & Surf   F. Wm Patton Howerton 1829-1905
     1910 12 living 1965   M. Nancy Candace Groves 1830-1871
   a. Lucy   b. nr Pine Grove 18 Jan 1890; d. 1983
            m. 1911
       Meinard Kalin   b. 1886; d. 1947
   b. Wm F (Bud)   b. 1892; d. 1982
            m.1 1918
       Rachel Lewis   b. 1898; d. 1988
            m.2
       Margarita Tico   b. 1905; d. 1900; m.1 Eugene E Hess
   c. Nellie   b. 1894
            m.1
       J Fred Singleton   b. 1891; d. 1957
            m.2 Cox
   d. Samuel T   b. 1896; d. 1972
            m. 1919
        Ella (Mae) Baber   b. 1900; d. 1969
   e. Sarah (Sadie)   b. 1899; d. 1969
            m.
       Harry Kehew
   f. Edith   b. 1901; d. 1967
            m. 1924
       Harry Sorensen   b. 1901; d. 1975
   g. Bessie   b.1903
            m. 1924
       Wilbur O Hooker
   h. Roland (Rod)   b. 1905
            m.
       Connie Lewellyn
   i. Albert   b. 1907
            m.
       Ruth Wolford
   j. Hazel I   b. 1910
            m. 1947
       Bert Jory
   k. Lawrence (Smitty)   b. 1912; d. 1978
            m. 1936
       Ruby Perry
   l. Mildred May   b. 28 Aug 1916
            m. 1936
       Donald Eugene Headrick   b. 1915; d. 1969; EV cem

9. Ruth Ann*	b. 1876; d. bef 1925
10. Minnie E*	b. 1879; d. bef 1925
11. Nicholas Nathaniel (Jake) single	b. Orcutt 18 Jan 1882 (obit); 11 Jan (cem) d. Orcutt 7 Sep 1962 @80; PG
12. Edith Estella (Stella) single	b. Orcutt 5 Oct 1884 d. Santa Maria 9 Feb 1963 @78; PG
13. Infant girl "S H"	Pine Grove Cemetery- no dates.

* Mrs Burnham of Watsonville arrived Wednesday night on a visit to her parents, Mr and Mrs Samuel Hobbs. -*SM Times* Apr 6, 1901

Additional References
Howerton Family, Valley Pioneers, by Myra Manfrina, The *Lompoc Record* Fri Sep 3 1965.
W.F. (Bud) Howerton of Los Alamos, in the Galaxy section. - *Santa Maria Times* Sep 18, 1971.
From Boomtown to Bedroom Community; A History of Orcutt, (1904-1982), Sally L Simon, Sect 4, "Pioneer Days: La Graciosa 1868-1877" pp 11-14.
Huyck Cousins, by Manfrina, 1987
San Ramon Chapel Pioneers, by Ontiveros, 1990.

SAMUEL HOBBS
Scrapbook
(Items from The *Santa Maria Times* unless otherwise noted)

1894 Residents of Pine Grove District voted to send J R Norris, C Martin, S. Hobbs, C Glines and Wm Brooks as delegates to the County Division Convention.
-Paragraphs of the Past. Fifty years Ago. Sat. July 29 1944 p.4

1895 Sam Hobbs of Pine Grove was in last Monday and tells of roads out his way that would be called good in the old country. -Jan 5

La Graciosa Items. Mrs S Hobbs' sister from Santa Cruz is visiting. -Nov. 23

1897 La Graciosa Items. Samuel Hobbs returned from San Francisco Friday of last week...medical attention.. -(date lost)

1901 Mrs Burnham of Watsonville arrived Wednesday night on a visit to her parents, Mr and Mrs Samuel Hobbs. -Apr 6
Sam Hobbs, an old resident of this valley died a week ago last Sunday at Pine Grove. He was well advanced in age and suffered with a cancer for many years. Thus death was a welcome relief to him. -May 11

1902 Social dance at the Martin school house May 1st. Good Music. Tickets 50 cents. Everybody invited. Nicholas Hobbs. -Apr 26

1925 Orcutt Notes: Mrs Howe of Lompoc spent the week with her grandmother, Mrs Hobbs, who is very ill at her home in Orcutt.
Mr and Mrs Martin of Lompoc are visiting at the Hobbs home in Orcutt. Mrs Hobbs is the mother of Mrs Martin.
"Grandma" Hobbs is still very ill at her home in Orcutt. -Tue Apr 7 p.5
Orcutt Notes:-Bill Hobbs of Los Alamos was a caller at the home of his grandmother in Orcutt.

"Grandma" Hobbs who has been very ill at her home for the past two weeks, passed away early this morning. -Fri Apr 10 p.5

Ed. Note: Compare the following.

Death Calls Pioneer Resident Of S M. Valley

Mrs Mahala Jane Hobbs, aged 83 years, a native of Pike County, Missouri, passed away at the family home in Orcutt yesterday. Mrs Hobbs was an old-time resident of this state, having come here in 1847, in the Hopper train. Mrs Hobbs first settled in Stockton. In 1868 she came to this valley. Mrs Hobbs is of a very well known family. Her husband, Samuel K Hobbs, passed away 24 years ago. The children surviving are W A Hobbs of Bakersfield, J L Hobbs of Los Alamos, Mrs T H Martin, Mrs Frank Howerton, James A Hobbs, all of Lompoc, and Nicholas N Hobbs and Stella Hobbs of Orcutt. There are also fifty grandchildren and forty-five great-grandchildren surviving. Funeral services will take place at the Orcutt church at 2 o'clock, Friday afternoon. Rev W F S Nelson will conduct the services. Interment will be in Pine Grove cemetery. Funeral arrangements are in charge of the Albert A Dudley Funeral Home. -Thu Apr 9 front page

1925 Last Survivor of Hopper Train Crosses Divide   Mahala J Hobbs passed away at home in Orcutt on Wednesday, April 8, at the age of eighty-four, after an eventful and useful life.

She was born in Pike County, Missouri, May 18, 1841; crossed the plains with an ox team and settled in Germantown near Stockton. She and Mrs Dutton are the last survivors of the Hopper train-those hardy pioneers who endured such hardships to come to the land of gold.

Mrs Hobbs was the oldest child of Mr and Mrs Nick Gann. She was married to Samuel Hobbs in 1857 and to them was born 13 children, seven of whom are still living, four sons and three daughters who were with her during her last illness. She also leaves 50 grandchildren and 45 great grandchildren and seven nieces and nephews.

The surviving children are: W A Hobbs, of Bakersfield; Mrs Henry Martin, Mrs Bertha Howerton and James Hobbs of Lompoc; J L Hobbs, Los Alamos, and Nicholas Hobbs and Stella Hobbs of Orcutt. -The *Lompoc Record* Apr 10 front page

1925 Hopper Train Survivor Dies   Pioneer Sta. Maria Woman Was One of First Residents. Mrs Mahala Jane Hobbs, one of the last survivors of the Hopper train which left Pike County, Missouri, for California in 1847, died at her home in Santa Maria yesterday at the age of 84.

Mrs Hobbs was born in Pike County in 1841 and was six years of age when the eventful journey to California started. Arriving in Sacramento her family resided there until 1853*, when they moved to Santa Barbara County,* settling in Santa Maria valley.

There* she married S K Hobbs, who died 24 years ago. Only two other members of the Hopper train are still alive, one of them being Mrs James Dutton, who also resides in Santa Maria.

She is survived by four sons, three daughters, 50 grandchildren and 45 great grandchildren.

Her sons are W A Hobbs of Bakersfield, J L of Los Alamos, James A of Lompoc and Nicholas of Orcutt; while the following are daughters: Malvina J. Martin and Bertha Howerton of Lompoc, and Miss Stella Hobbs of Orcutt.

Funeral services will be held from the Orcutt church at a time to be set today, and interment will be made in Pine Grove cemetery, Rev W F S Nelson officiating.
* Incorrect -*Santa Barbara Press* Apr 10 front page

1926 Well Known Resident Is Suddenly Stricken   T H Martin, for twenty years a resident of the valley and head of one of the community's best families suffered a heart attack and died at 6:30

o'clock last evening… Yesterday he was at his place of business here in town greeting his friends in his usual jovial manner. In the afternoon he became ill...

Thomas Henry Martin had spent most of his life time in northern Santa Barbara County. His parents settled in the Santa Maria valley in the early days and he received part of his schooling at Guadalupe public school. Later they moved to what is now known as Martin district, which is east of the town of Orcutt.

Mr Martin was born in Missouri, the son of Mr and Mrs Thomas J Martin. The family came to California when he was three years of age and first located in Lake county. In 1875 they moved to the Santa Maria valley and lived at Guadalupe, later locating on the farm east of Orcutt. Mr Martin was married to Miss Melvina Hobbs, of Santa Maria in 1883, and ten children were born to this union. Mrs Martin and nine children survive him. The latter are Mrs Irwin Daniels, of Santa Barbara, Mrs Elmer Elliott, of Sisquoc, Rufus and William Martin, Mrs Luther S Douglass, Delbert Martin, Mrs Richard Huseman, James and Dean Martin, all of Lompoc. Charles Martin, also a son, died here last August.

Mr Martin was aged 63 years, 1 month and 10 days at the time of his death. He had lived in Lompoc valley for 20 years, having moved here with his family in 1906 from Santa Maria. In 1911 he purchased from the late C K Hardenbrook the ranch in Cebada canyon which has since been his home. Following the death of his son Charles last August, Mr Martin has looked after the auto electric business of which the son had been proprietor, and this work brought him to town almost daily...   -The *Lompoc Record* Apr 2

1936   Orcutt Notes: Mr and Mrs B Hobbs motored to Bakersfield to attend the funeral of the late Joe Hobbs, a brother of Jake and Stella Hobbs of this locality.   -Thur Aug 27

1941 "Matt" Howerton Passes at 78 La Graciosa Pioneer Dies in Countyseat (sic)
Mathew* W Howerton, age 78, husband of one of the members of the pioneer Bradley family of Santa Maria, died in his Santa Barbara home early this morning.

Deceased came to California from his native Illinois in November, 1881, when 18 years of age, having been born in 1863. He located with his parents in what was then Graciosa, an early settlement south of Orcutt, where the family lived for many years.

Deceased worked as a young man for Paul Bradley, first of the Bradleys to arrive in the valley and uncle of Chas Bradley, whose name the Bradley hotel bears and who was the father of Mrs Howerton. She was Elizabeth Bradley, sister of Mrs Agnes Forbes, Mrs Rachel Niverth and Mrs Sadie Kelley of Santa Maria, and Mrs Ellen Elliott of Los Angeles. Another sister, Mrs Mary Tunnell, died in Santa Maria on Feb. 12.

Deceased leaves two children, Harry Howerton, born in 1888, and Mrs Alice Huyck, born in 1891. Both live in Lompoc.

A sister of deceased was married to Pioneer John Houk, who built the Houk building on the corner of Chapel and North Broadway.

Moving from this locality to Lompoc, the Howertons resided there until about 20 years ago when they moved to Santa Barbara, where they lived at 823 Jennings avenue. They have extensive farming interests in the Lompoc vicinity.

Funeral arrangements had not been announced today.   -Feb 27
*Mattison

1885 La Graciosa Dew Drops. Ed. *Times*:-...It is customary to say something about the weather we in common with other residents of the valley are enjoying the daily west winds and gusts of sand …We see Mr Wm Hobbs at work with his header, doing good work for the farmers...Chas Hecox and family, Wm and Has Hobbs and B F Hyder spent several days of last week on the beach below Point Sal fishing. They report food success and a jolly time...Resp. SATISFIED   -*SM Times* July 4

La Graciosa Dew Drops...Another fishing excursion to the coast, consisting of Mr Bellew and family, Mr Brookshire and family, Misses Birdie and Rosa Hobbs, Messrs Wm Hobbs and James Miller...We are sorry to learn of the severe illness of Miss Rosa Hobbs of Pine Grove. While enjoying a fishing excursion she was suddenly taken sick, and grave fears were entertained as to her recovery. But under the skillful treatment of Hon Dr Lucas we hope for and expect a speedy recovery... -Ibid July 11

Vol. XXIII, No. 1-4, 1991, p.37

Synopses of obituaries

1959 Fred D Hobbs d. @70...Arroyo Grande cemetery...resident of Oceano 20 years...owned Hobbs Wood yard...wife Larena; daughters Jane LaBorde, Oregon, Bessie Roads, Napa. Brothers: Emmett and Lewis, Oceano; Robert, Orcutt; William, Avenal. 12 grandchildren, 18 great-grandchildren. -*SLO Telegram-Tribune* Thu Apr 16 p.2

1960 Lewis Guy Hobbs b. Santa Barbara co, d. @78. World War I. Resident of Oceano, d. Santa Maria hospital. Brothers: Robert N, Oceano; William L, Fresno.
-*Santa Maria Times*

1971 William Brian (Bryan) Hobbs d. Arroyo Grande...Wife Ruth; brothers: John, San Luis Obispo; Clyde, Grover City; Jesse, Bakersfield; Frank, Sonora. Sisters: Lillie Townsend, Taft; Olive Leonare, Bakersfield. -Ibid

1975 Robert Neson Hobbs of Oceano d. @81 in Arroyo Grande. Brother: W L Hobbs, Oceano.
-*SLO Telegram-Tribune* Feb 5

Vol. XXIII, No. 1-4, 1991, p.27

Corrections and Additions [Page numbers refer to those in Quarterly]

Farlon Hobbs family

p.3. Hizzoner George Stowell Hobbs jr lost the election of Nov 1994 to Roger Bunch. Hobbs had been involved in the city government of Santa Maria for nearly 35 years, 22 of those as mayor. He became nationally famous in 1990 when his remarks about the "Mexican problem" allegedly caused by illegal immigrants made the news.

p.4. Marriage: Clifford B Hobbs @22 of Santa Maria m. San Luis Obispo 22 March 1930 by A H Brazil, police judge, R14; wit: Aditha Hibbard, Santa Maria; Vera Jones, San Luis Obispo. Ethel May Hibbard b. OR m. @19 of SM. F: John Bert Hibbard 1868-1941; in 1941 she was Ethel Bolls, in Santa Maria. M: Aditha Beulah Chamberlain 1877-1953; in 1953 she was Ethel Brown, in Exeter.

A subsequent wife of Clifford's was Lorabeth Daniels, daughter of William Henry Daniels, who died in Santa Maria in 1934 @56; at that time Lorabeth was surnamed Daniels. Her mother was Esther Elizabeth Trott 1881-1956; by 1956 Lorabeth Hobbs was living in Ojai with daughters Susan and Diana.

Marriage: Donald E Hobbs, Nipomo 17 Sep 1932, S245, and Thelma Maxine Lyon. Thelma's father, Roy L Lyon, died in 1966 @80; at that time his granddaughter, Darlene Wells, was living in Northridge.

p.5. L A Hobbs, working for Western Electric Co in Los Angeles visited aunt Mrs H C Tunnell.
-*Santa Maria* Vidette June 12 1917

Vol. XXX, No. 1, Spring 1998, p.13

Samuel Kelsey Hobbs family

p. 29   John P(erry) Hobbs, 89, died in Santa Maria 17 April 1994, Arroyo Grande Cem. Born in Bakersfield 21 Aug 1904, longtime resident of San Luis Obispo co, Santa Maria past five years. Retired heavy equipment operator. Survivors: sons John P Hobbs, jr, Carlsbad NM; Joseph L Hobbs, Santa Maria; Paul T Hobbs, El Monte; 10 gch, 21 ggch, 2 gggch.   -Tue Apr 19 1994 A-5
   Marriage: Wm B Hobbs 57 Santa Barbara co 28 Aug 1956. Ruth Crowder/Crocker 49.
   Henry Hobbs and family moving to Bakersfield county.   -June 4 1898
   Southside Squibs. Henry and Joe Hobbs with their families have left us for the Sunset Oil Co district where they expect to get profitable employment.   -Sep 1 1900

p. 30.   Marriage: Lewis Guy Hobbs b. CA @38 of Los Alamos, divorced, mechanic m. Arroyo Grande 2 Nov 1931 by W H Dowell JP, S25; Wit: Mary E Foster, Oceano. Maria Costa Rosa Brown b. CA @20 of Los Alamos, waitress. Her F: Joseph V Brown, b. MA, M: Effie Harris b. MO.
   Los Alamos: J V Brown of Long Beach, father of Marcia Hobbs visiting; also Mrs Fred Hobbs of Santa Ynez, and Mrs Leroy Eiland and Elmer G Eiland. Mary Saulsbury of Zaca ranch recuperating at home of nephew Fred Hobbs, Santa Ynez.   -1932 (date lost)
   Frederick D Hobbs' first wife was Gladys Ellen Foster 1891-1918, daughter of George A Foster and Mary Ellen Scott. See Scott chart for additions and corrections to Foster family.
   Emmett G (sic) Hobbs, wounded, arrived (Tue) evening from France; two fingers shot off right hand; son of J Hobbs of Orcutt. He is also on the casualty list, of Orcutt, nearest relative Joseph C Hobbs.   -Dec 28 1918

p. 32.   Marriage: James Fred Singleton @22 of Lompoc license Lompoc 27 Sep 1913 Nellie May Howerton @18, of Lompoc
   Marriage: Meinard Kalin b. MT @25 of Lompoc in Lompoc 2 Nov 1911 Lucy Annie Howerton m. @21 of Lompoc
   Bess Howerton Hooker, 90, died in Lompoc 1 Oct 1993. Survivors: daughter Glenna Brown, Goleta; sons Richard and Kenneth Hooker, Fresno; Ronald Hooker, Lompoc; sister, Hazel Jory, Lompoc; brother Bert Howerton, Lompoc; 9 gch; numerous nieces and nephews. Husband Wilbur C Hooker died 1976.   -Mon Oct 4 1993

p. 34.   Sam Hobbs returned from San Francisco; was there 6 weeks for cancer treatment. He considers himself well.   -June 4 1898

HOPPER
CALIFORNIA PIONEERS

Charles Hopper came to California with the Bidwell-Bartleson party, the first overland trek to California, in 1841. (Illegal immigrants?) In 1842 he led some of the company east; in 1847 he returned to stay, the captain and guide of a train including his own family and other relatives. There is some confusion among the descendants about a connection with the Donner party. Let it be noted that the Donners were snowed in in the late fall of 1846, at which time Hopper was, presumably, still safe in Missouri.

Bancroft, in his *History of California*, makes mention of Hopper's *Narrative*, which, he explained, was the result of an interview with Charles Hopper by R T Montgomery in 1871. This *Narrative* is cited several times as authority for Bancroft's statements.

In the Hopper train were two nephews, Ari and John. Both spent decades in the Mendocino county, leaving in the 1880's. Ari came south to Ventura county, where his name is memorialized in Hopper Canyon, east of Fillmore, and Hopper Peak, elevation 4524 ft. There is material on the Ventura county Hoppers in the files of the Ventura County Historical Society, and a biography may be read in Guinn's *History of California and its Southern Coast Counties*, 1915. His accidental death was reported in the *Santa Maria Times* Feb 12 1898.

John, the progenitor of the Santa Maria Hoppers, was brought here in his old age in 1888 by his son Greenberry, and is buried in the Santa Maria cemetery, although his place of residence was Ballard, near his youngest daughter, Emma Tunnell. He is mentioned by Bancroft as having been on the first jury in San Jose; his son, George, is said to be the first white child born there. They spent but a year or so in San Jose, moving north to Sonoma county, thence to Mendocino, and by 1862 in Potter Valley. A history of Potter Valley, 1855-1985, entitled *From Acorns to Oaks*, by Delight Corbett Shelton, is a compilation of stories of the valley pioneers, largely anecdotal, with rather casual family charting. What is here presented is more detailed, chart-wise, especially for local people, but limited as to history because of space. Much has been gathered from local newspapers, and C G Hopper has provided copies of some of the literary effort of bygone generations, which will be supplied upon request to the reader.

C G Hopper's grandfather, Kenneth Hopper, joined his brother-in-law Wm Keeney to publish the *Guadalupe Moon*, commencing in May 1900 and lasting into the next year when they accepted the same sort of employment in Hawaii. Gertrude Keeney Hopper wrote memoirs of her pioneer adventures, some having been published, such as The Gentleman Stage Robber, and the Keeney family's trek to Oregon and back from San Luis Obispo county. Her description of life on the ranch in Mariposa county in the early twentieth century was published by her daughter, Thelma. Greenberry Hopper composed a fine historical encomium upon his mother's death, and Ken Hopper did the same for his Uncle Luther, the cowboy, although it has little family information. Another Luther, son of George, wrote up the legend of Carpella, an Indian story from Mendocino county, to fulfill his literary assignment as a member of the junior class of the Santa Maria high school for the 1905 yearbook.

Besides literary ability, another characteristic seems to have been a serious mein. Thelma Hopper described her little brother Bud as being more serious than she; he would "look at you solemnly with those big blue eyes and seldom laughed". George's son, Luther, often confused with his Uncle Luther, as in Mrs Ontiveros' book, with the Santa Maria valley's barbecue king in the '20's; he "ate pea gravel after a big meal and all the kids would watch....never saw a Hopper smile; they took life seriously".   -ONT p.160; see also *This Is Our Valley*

It was noteworthy to the local press that the last two survivors of the Hopper train died in Santa Maria in April 1925. First was Mahala Gann Hobbs, who had come to La Graciosa in the early years with her husband, Sam Hobbs. Their story is in Samuel Hobbs' chart. The second, who died a few days later, was Sarah Hopper Dutton, eldest daughter of John Hopper. Pauline Lownes Novo was a small girl when Mrs Dutton died, but remembers her long hair, and the comfort she gave when Pauline accidentally swallowed a piece of ice, a temporarily terrifying experience.

The Tunnell family came from Mendocino county to the Santa Maria valley in 1869, the year that a number of well known pioneer families arrived from Sonoma county as well as Mendocino. The Tunnell family is well represented in Mrs Ontiveros' book, *San Ramon Chapel Pioneers*. It was, no doubt, following them that brought the Hoppers here. Their prime interest was not farming, however, as Greenberry and John were blacksmiths, and George was a carpenter, working sometimes with William Dutton, who became his brother-in-law. Luther was a blacksmith early in life, but in later years gained fame as a horsebreaker and rider, winning prizes well into the ninth decade of his life. He was a short man—some say 5 ft 3", the voter registration says 5 ft 6", likely with boots on—but on a horse he could do anything. The Hopper family group photograph, furnished by C G Hopper, shows him definitely the shortest.

Greenberry arrived in Santa Maria in 1885; there was no shortage of blacksmiths, neither a shortage of work for them all. Besides the usual horseshoeing, there was wagon-making, building and repairing farm machinery such as bean planters and mowing machines, plus the ubiquitous "barley-crushing on Saturdays." (or sometimes "on demand" to beat the competition, no doubt.) In 1888 Hopper's "stand" at Broadway and Chapel was ornamented with a sign built by L T Jeter, painter, "18 ft long with a semi-circle rounding upwards in the center of about 5 ft wide, at the highest point. This sign shows off well from the center of town and is put there to tell what is done in this building, wagon and carriage making first-class blacksmithing." -Apr 14 1888. In 1890 G B Hopper had "a fine two seated spring wagon for sale—of his own manufacture. It was brought up from Hart & Son's shop at Guadalupe, the other day where it had received the required number of coats of paint and varnish." –Nov 15

In 1888 Ed. E Colby, whose wife, Emma Logan, was a niece of Greenberry's, moved his pregnant wife, child and blacksmith business into Santa Maria from his location out near Sisquoc, with the intention of going into partnership with Greenberry. They bought L L Forrester's machinery and supplies, and Forrester, doubling as housemover, brought in a house to the rear of the shop to be used for a Chinese laundry. –Feb. 11. It had been a little over two years before that Colby had bought the Sisquoc blacksmith business from the Forrester brothers; Forresters had their hands in many a pie. Unfortunately, a few days after the announcement was made, Colby died, "taken sick with congestion of the brain," so Greenberry continued alone, later taking his son Joel into the business, and, for a time in 1891, his brother John, who had been plying the trade in Ballard. Like many in the valley, Joel went into the oil industry as it developed. In 1906 he was burned lighting the boiler at the Logan Oil Co. near Arroyo Grande; "Joel Hopper Scorched", proclaimed the headline. -July 28 p.1

Some of the pioneers moved away after the turn of the century to pursue oil in Kern county or to farm elsewhere. One of Greenberry's daughters married a Stowell, and they, as well as others of the Stowell clan, went to farm near Hughson, in Stanislaus county. (See Stowell chart.) George Hopper was the only one to remain in Santa Maria, well known as a carpenter and a member of the Pioneer Association. His wife was a daughter of Henry W Baker, who had been a justice of the peace in Mendocino county before coming to Santa Maria in the '80's, and continued his public service in this area. His large family intermarried with other pioneer families; we hope to profile them in these pages some time.

Only sketchy information on Luther Hopper's family has come to hand, so the listing of his children on the chart has not been verified. Emma, on the other hand, having married a Tunnell, is documented in Mrs Ontiveros' book. Since they were life-long residents of the Santa Ynez valley, no doubt the local historical society has data about the family that is not available in Santa Maria. Some of the sons-in-law were railroad men, working for the Pacific Coast Railway, the narrow-gauge which connected Los Olivos and San Luis Obispo. One of them, Lemuel W Thompson, graduated to the Southern Pacific and moved to San Luis Obispo, where he was killed in a freak accident. "Two Killed As Auto Plows Into Crowd...L W Thompson, 1845 Broad St., Southern Pacific conductor, was instantly killed and Ray Alford, 940 Chorro St., carpenter, died from injuries received when Sullivan's car plunged into a group of people that had gathered about a minor automobile accident on Broad St near Upham at about three o'clock in the morning..." Seems they were having a party, and a couple of inebriated drivers collided nearby, upon which the partygoers went outside to inspect, and were hit by a third drunk driver.–*SLO Daily Telegram* Mon Apr 22 1935. Poor Lem! He married into a pioneer family of long-lived individuals, but outlasted his parents-in-law only two months, dispatched by that modern day wonder, the automobile.

A FOILED ROBBERY

Mrs Hopper's story about the Gentleman Stage Robber is too long to print here; instead we offer a local story submitted by SMVGS member Elaine Miller, concerning relative, William A Hartnell, who, like Elaine, was a descendant of William EP Hartnell, an Englishman who came to California and integrated into Mexican society by marrying Maria Teresa De la Guerra y Noriega of Santa Barbara. He was the founder of a large family, many of whom lived in the Salinas valley as well as in Santa Barbara county. A son, Jose G Hartnell and his wife, Maria Ignacia Watson, daughter of another Englishman, lived in the La Graciosa area in the late 19th century, and it was in that vicinity that son William experienced the following:

My father, William A Hartnell told me this story and he said that it was true.
Just before the turn of the century in the late 1800's my father was a bartender in
Santa Maria. When he closed the bar about midnight he would have to take the
money for the day home with him. He would ride horseback along Graciosa
Road to his sister Teresa's house where he stayed. It was about 15 miles.
There was a Spanish bandit about during that time who would rob the Gringos
and sometimes kill them.

One night on his way home from work my dad was waylaid by the bandit; he spoke
to dad in Spanish and asked where he was going. My dad spoke fluent Spanish and
he answered the bandit and told him that he was a Spaniard. The bandit talked to
him for a while then shook his hand and let him go on his way.
Dad always thought that it was Solomon Pico the notorious bandit of that day.
-Rosalie Hartnell McDonald

When Jose G Hartnell died in 1911 at the age of 77, he was survived by his daughters, Teresa Hernandez, Matilda Antognazzi and Mrs James Dominguez; and sons, James, Albert, and William Hartnell -Nov 25. The 1906 Directory shows J G and W A Hartnell living two miles southeast of Santa Maria—no Solomon Pico there! On June 1st, 1910, William Hartnell, 32, married Miss Alice Munoz, 22, in San Luis Obispo (H619). See also *SM Times* June 4. There is a photograph of the three Hartnell sisters on display in the Santa Maria Valley Historical Museum.

John Hopper   b. Lafayette Co MO 8 Aug 1821
  to CA 1847   d. Ballard 16 Mar 1889 @69; SM cem
  to Ukiah 1856   F: William Hopper
  to Potter Valley 1862   M: Nancy Armstrong
  1860: Ukiah
  1870: MEN Co Calpella tp
  1884-5 McKenney Coast Counties Dir: 400a PotterValley, sheepraiser, f
      m. Lafayette Co MO 9 Nov 1837, B108
Jan Leigh   b. TN 17 Feb 1814
                                                    d. Santa Maria 20 Sep 1898 @84/7/3; SM cem
                                                        obit Oct 4
                                                        F: GA;   M: TN
1. Sarah J   b. Lafayette Co MO 2 Dec 1840
    1884-5 McK: Mrs Sarah J   d. Bicknell at home of dau Marcia Lownes
      Logan, farming 510a,   3 May 1925 @84; SM cem, obit May 4 p.1
      Potter Valley
        m.1 Healdsburg 4 Feb 1858 by J T Barnes, A116, divorced
    Samuel Hays Hulet Logan 1839-1914; see Logan chart
        m.2
    William F Dutton   b. c1828
      1888: Polk Gazetteer: SM,   d. 5 Jan 1896 @68; SM cem
      carpenter
2. Greenberry Barton   b. Lafayette Co MO 12 Jan 1843
    1860: w/parents   d. Turlock CA 27 Aug 1918 @75; obit *Modesto*
    1870: Calpella tp   *Morning Herald* Wed Aug 28 p.8
    1880: Calpella tp blacksmith
    1884-5 McK: blksm & wgnmkr 65a Potter Valley
    1888 Polk: SM blksm
    1890 GR: 47 MO blksm SM
    1896 GR: blksm 53 6ft lt gry br MO SM #2
    1900: SM 6 births, 3 living
    1910: Stanislaus Co
        m. Ukiah 27 March 1862
    Sarah E Vann   b. MO Dec 1847
                                        d. nr Hughson 12 May 1935 @87
                                        obit (attribution lost)
                                        F: Pitt Woodward Vann 1819-1910
                                        M: Spicy E Davidson 1823-1913
  a. (Paul)
  b. Joel Leigh   b. (Calpella tp) Mar 1864
    1890 GR: 26 CA lab   d. Santa Cruz Co 5-16-1939 @75 spouse I U
      LaPatera   no obit *Santa Cruz Sentinel*
    1892 GR: 29 5ft 10½ lt blu br CA SM #2; reg Sep 19
    1896 GR: f 33 6ft ½ lt gry lt CA SM #2
    1900: SM 5 births, 5 living
    1906 Dir: oil man r Bwy; Mrs
    1910-11 Dir: oil well driller 703 S Bwy SM
        m. 1 1888
    Anna Eliza Garrett   b. (Visalia) Feb 1860
                                          d. Hughson 11 Nov 1925 @66; obit
                                          Modesto News-Herald Nov 14 p.4
                                          F: Martin Garrett

                                                M: Martha Mahurin 1841-1909
   =Mabel C b. OR May 1889; 1906 Dir: Miss stu r Bwy
   =Garrett R b. SM 31 Jan 1893 (*Times*); d. (Santa Cruz Co 3-20-43 spouse BH)
   =Paul L b. SM 27 Mar 1895 (*Times*); d. Campbell CA 25 Dec 1969 SSDI
   =Percy Amilton b. nr SM 14/5 May 1897 (*Times*); (d. STAN Co 1-9-47 M C)
        1920: 1023 Sutter, Stockton, w/Geo C Turner
   =Chester H b. Nov 1898
        1920: 7th St., Hughson
     Leone b. NH c1900 (cen) or (9 Nov 1899-18 Dec 1987 LA Co)?
  c. Mary Jane   b. MEN Co Oct 1866/7
     1910: w/parents   d. San Anselmo 24 Apr 1957 @90
     1920: 88 Bently Dr Los Gatos   IOOF cem Modesto
        m.1 c1890
     Frank Leon Stowell   1865-1904; see Stowell chart
   =Floyd C   b. Gilroy Dec 1890;   d. Stockton 15 Feb 1949 @58/2/13
       1910: lodger w/Patrick Tobin, Stockton
        m. after 1910
      Mabel Jeanette Siegel b. Clements CA 9 Nov 1895; d. Stockton 27 Mar 1978
      + Jeanne b. 1914 (Robert Dixon)
   =Mildred E b. 1896; d. (Los Gatos) 14 Mar 1928 @32; TB; single
        m.2
      John Metzler
  d. Hattie   b. MEN Co 1868
                                        d. (before 1900)
   =(Edwin b. CA July 1890; parents CA; gson w/Greenberry 1900)
  e. Lora Mae   b. Potter Valley Jan 1872
     1900: w/parents   d. Turlock 15 Mar 1968 @96
                                            obit Modesto BEE? date lost

        m. before 1910
     Joseph T/F Fritts   b. NJ Oct 1862
       1900: Fremont tp   d. Turlock 13 July 1947 @84
         Santa Clara Co   obit *Modesto Bee* Mon July 14 p.4
       1910: Santa Clara Co   m.1 Laura C Burton 1868-1905
       1920: Stanislaus Co   His ch: Joseph B 1895-
                                            James Wm 1897- (before 1968)
                                            Mary Grace 1899-1968 (E P Squire)
                                            Harriett Martha 1903- (Sinclair)
  f. (Chester)   (Holshauser)
3. Jonathan Ari   b. MO 21 Apr 1845
                                        d. Sonoma Co 7 Sep 1856
4. George Leigh   b. San Jose 2 March 1848
     1870: Calpella tp   d. Santa Maria 28 Jan 1931 @82/10/26; SM cem
     1880: Calpella tp; no ch   obit Jan 29 p.1
     1890 GR: 42 CA lab Ballard
     1892 GR: 43 5ft 6 dk gry dk CA Ballard; reg Sep 8
     1896 GR: lab 47 5ft 5 lt blu br CA SM #2
     1906 Dir: sexton r Pine St; Mrs
     1910-11 Dir: res 709 S Lincoln (where he died)
        m. Potter Valley 30 March 1869
     Lucinda Emelina Baker   b. St Joseph MO 23 Dec 1852/3
       1900: SM 4 births 2 living   d. Santa Maria 5 May 1939 @85/4/12 at the

  1910: SM   home of G L Hopper 517 E Cypress: SM cem
  1920: 709 S Lincoln   obit Sat May 6 p.1
               F: Henry Womack Baker 1818-1909
               M: Elizabeth Wilkins/Wilkerson 1823-1899
  a. George T   b. March 1881
    1906 Dir: clk, r Pine St   d. (SON 1-30-54 spouse L H)? SSDI
    1910: Oakland
    1920: 5237 James, Oakland
    1931: Boise ID; 1939: Vallejo
      m. Oakland Thanksgiving Day 1905 (*Times*)
   Lulu Hamilton   b. CA 1885; m. of "northern CA"
               d. (12-23-67; SSDI)
   =Victor b. 1910
  b. (Gertie Bell)   buried 19 July 1883; SM cem
  c. Martin Luther/Lute   b. SM 30 Aug 1885; bio *Who's Who SM*
    1906 Dir: clk r Pine St   bio Phillips I 371
    1920: w/parents   d. (SON Co 4-4-62; SSDI)?
      m. Portland OR 29 Aug 1912
   Inez Clovinger   b. St Helens OR (1896)?
    1940 Dir: Broadway   d.
     Bootery SM   F: John Clovinger
               M: Mary McNulty

  d. -
5. John Thomas   b. Santa Rosa 30 April 1850
  1870: w/parents   d. at home of dau Mrs Mark Beck, S Lincoln
  1880: Calpella tp   SM 7 Dec 1918 @68/7/7; SM cem; obit (date lost)
  1884-5 McK: blksm w/GB
  1890 GR: 40 CA blksm Ballard; reg Sep 1
  1892 GR: 42 5ft 10½ lt blu br SM #1; reg Sep 24
  1900: Guadalupe w/Kenneth; divorced
   m.1 26 June 1872; divorced
  Eliza Jane Tunnell   b. SON Co 30 Dec 1854
               d. SM at S Lincoln St res 29 May 1931
                 @76/4/29; SM cem, obit Fri May 29 p.3
               F: Martin Luther Tunnell 1824-1903
               M: Salina Haskins 1829-1903
                m.2 Lompoc 28 Nov 1877
                Wm Kinison Hobson 1849-1917
                for Tunnells see ONT pp. 159-164
     m.2 Mendocino Co 16 Dec 1877
  Helen S Griffitts   b. Hopland CA 1 Dec 1858/9
               d. San Luis Obispo 24 Nov 1916
                obit *SLO Daily Telegram* Sat Nov 25,
                also *Atascadero News*, buried Vallejo
               F: Isaac Yokum Griffitts 1832-1911
               M: Mary Jane Snively 1835-1903
                m.2 C G "Albert" Wheeler 1867-
                1900: 418 Golden Gate Av San Francisco
  a. Kenneth Carl   b. Potter Valley 22 Apr 1880
    1900: 2 listings   d. Castro Valley 13 May 1961
     Guadalupe, pub newspaper; also w/mother, SF

    1910: Honolulu
        m. Guadalupe 2 July 1900 by E H Wise JP (*AG Herald* July 14)
  Gertrude Keeney   b. OR Oct 1876
    1900: Guadalupe, printer/   d. Mariposa Co 28 June 1974
      compositor,   F: Wm Thomas Keeney 1839-
      newspaper   M: Julianna Hoque 1839-1895
  =Thelma Beatrice b. Honolulu 3 Jan 1902 d. Puyallup WA 21 Mar 1987
    William Hadley
  =Kenneth Leverett b. Honolulu 29 Nov 1905; d. Menlo Park Mar 1962
  =Charles Glen b. Mariposa CA 1 Aug 1909; living 1995
 b. Leonardini Laura/Lennie   b. Potter Valley 15 Jan 1882/3
    1900: w/mother   deaf-mute   d. at home SM 17 July 1924
        m.   obit Sat July 19
  Marcus W Beck   b. CA c1890
    1920: 412½ S Lincoln   d. (27 May 1962)?
  No issue
6. William Brown   b. Petaluma 12 Aug 1853
    1870: w/parents   d. Potter Valley 23 Apr 1927 @73
    1880: Calpella tp
    1884-5 McK: 160a Potter Valley, sheep raiser
   1900: Potter Valley
      m. Potter Valley 26 March 1873
  Elizabeth Lownes   b. CA 23 Apr 1854
                                            d. Ukiah 1955
                                            F: Caleb Pancoast Lownes 1803-1891
                                            M: Sophronia Applegate 1828-1883
  a. Lulu/Luella (Clyde Rippey) 1874-1962
  b. Annie Lorena 1876-1962: m. 1897 Marcellus Bevans 1856-1922
  c. Lydia Pearl 1880-1970: m. John D Brower III 1878-1970
  d. Elmer Martin 1884-(1965)?: m. c1910 Etta-- 1888-
    =Harry M: =Hazel
  e. Harry Lownes 1888-1972: m. c1913 Nellie R McKee 1890-1980
    =Evangeline M
7. Luther Washington   b. Sonoma Co 14/5 July 1855
    1870: w/parents   d. at home of dau Mrs Osborne Oakland
    1880: Centerville/Calpella tp   11 Mar 1940 @85: obit Mariposa paper
      blacksmith
    1884-5 McK: 75a Potter Valley farmer
    1890 GR: 35 CA f Ballard: reg Sep 10
    1892 GR: 37 5ft 6 dk gry br cut on little finger rh CA Ballard PO Los Olivos;
      reg Aug 17
    1900: Vanderbilt tp San Bernardino Co: wd: miner: 8 ch born 2 w/him
    1910-11 Dir: lab 703 S Bwy SM
    1920: (Bakersfield) w/Wm Murray
      m. Potter Valley 14 Apr 1874
  Julia Alice Armstrong   b. CA 1856
    1906 Dir: L W Hopper,   d. (before 1900)
      horsebreaker, no Mrs
  a. Lena Belle   b. CA 25 Sep 1875/6; m. of SM
    1905: Mrs Lena…   d. Redding CA 5 Apr 1963
      leased Crosby House.—Sep 9

     1910: Livermore, 2 ch, no husband
     1920: 1124 Sutter, Stockton
          m. Los Olivos 22 May 1893 by Rev S Gascoigne (*Times*)
             Portrait by N H Reed, Santa Barbara
     Henry Warren Osborn(e)   b. CA Mar 1863 (cen) or 1858 (GR)
        1890 GR: 32 saloon kpr   d. (SF 2-23-1927 @74; obit *SF Chronicle*
          Ballard: reg Aug 18   Thu Feb 24 p. 10: "native of Boston")?
        1920: 302 ½ Orange, Redlands, w/Etta M Barber
     =Edna A (Williams) b. Nov 1894
     =Elmer L b. Oct 1897; d. (Shasta Co 2-4-61); 1920: w/mother
  b. William L   b. CA Mar 1876/78
        1900: w/father, miner   d. (Kern Co 1-14-1956; SSDI)?
        1910: Wm L 35 CA Kern Co alone   1920: Riverside
            m.
     Fannie   b. IA c1878 (1920 cen; @42)
  c. Jessica
     (Jessie Hopper m. Goleta 9 June 1900 John A Warren)?
  d. John Albert   b. CA 21 Nov 1882 (obit)1883 (cen); m.@25 SM
        1900: w/father   d. San Luis Obispo 1 Feb 1962 @79 AG cem res
                                              res Avila Beach obit *SLO Telegram-Tribune* Fri
          m. San Luis Obispo 26 Oct 1909 by _ E Smith JP, h495   Feb 2 p. 2
             wit: A B Green, SLO. Also *SLO Tribune* Oct 29
     Regina Marie Donaldson   b. CA; m. @18 of SM (divorced?***)
  e. Kate May/Kittie (Paulus) living in San Francisco 1962
  f. Della Maggie
  g. Donald Ware
  h. Pearl Hazel (Del Monte) living in Los Angeles 1962
8. Emma Angeline   b. MEN Co 12 Jan 1857
     of Los Olivos   d. Santa Barbara 15 Feb 1935; Oak Hill cem
                                              obit Feb 16 p.1
               m. Potter Valley 19 Oct 1875
     Francis Marion Tunnell   b. nr Ukiah 18 Apr 1854
        1880: Calpella tp   d. Los Olivos 7 Feb 1935; Oak Hill cem
        1884-5 McK: Potter Valley f   double funeral
        1890 GR: 36 CA Ballard   F: Martin Luther Tunnell 1824-1903
        1900: tp 4 Ballard   M: Salina Haskins 1829-1903
        1910: tp 4 Ballard Rd   for Tunnells see M/H 426: *This Is Our Valley* p. 88
        10 births 10 living
  a. Fred Francis   b. (Potter Valley) 14 Oct 1876
        1896 GR: rr emp 21 5'5 ½, lt blu br d. 528 E Cypress St SM 1 Jan 1945
          Ballard PO Los Olivos   Oak Hill cem; obit Tue Jan 2
        1900: SLO lodger w/Geo N Zumwalt
        1910: tp 5 Santa Rita Rd eng pumping plant
        1940-1 Dir: Bwy Batt & Elec, h 528 E Cypress
          m. 1900
     Cora Vivian Hartley   b. KS 7 Sep 1880
                                           d. 16 Jan 1972; Oak Hill cem
     =LaVerne (Mike) b. 1901: single   F: (John Wiley Hartley 1846-1923)?
     =Muriel b. 1908   m.1 Frank A Hebard d. 1942; Bwy Batt & Elec
                        m.2 Cecil C Calvert 1894-1952
     =James F b. 27 Dec 1908; d. SM 21 Feb 1982: spouse A R

   b. Elbert J   b. (Potter Valley) 10 Oct 1878
      Single. Figueroa ranch   d. Los Olivos 23 Mar 1934; Oak Hill cem
   c. Elsie J   b. Aug 1881
                                         d. 1973 (ONT) or 1963 (IOOF cem SLO)
       m. 1
   Lemuel Wm Thompson   b. Springfield IL 1879
                                         d. SLO 21 Apr 1935 @55; accident
                               conductor Southern Pacific RR; obit *SLO*
    =Eugene C (living in Stockton 1935)   *Daily Telegram* Mon Apr 22; IOOF cem SLO
    =Helen (Sanders) (living in Salinas 1935)
    =Kathryn (Melchoir) (living in Paso Robles 1935)
    =Lemuel William Jr (living in Watsonville 1935)
        m.2
   Jay B Bryan (living in Salinas 1945) d. (Salinas) 5-31-1949
     1941 Dir: h524 E Market, Salinas
   d. Myrtle H   b. Sep 1883; living in San Jose 1935
                                         d. (Myrtle H Santa Clara Co 3-15-63)?
       m. 1905? 1907?
   George A Thorpe   b. TX 1881
     1910: w/Tunnells, eng oil co   d.
                                         F: SCT: M: TN
    =Claire E b. 1908 (Bob Bennett)
   e. Mabel C   b. Dec 1885
       m.
   Bert Hardison   d. (Santa Barbara) 6-5-48 spouse M C
    =Allen
   f. Raymond W   b. Oct 1889
      Single   d. Las Vegas NV 28 Jan 1962; Oak Hill cem
   g. Gertrude F   b. 16 Sep 1891
       m.1
   James R Torrence   b. Sep 1889
                                         F: John Torrence 1855-
                                         M: Mary A   1858-
    =Richard Vernon
    =Gwendolyn (Sydess)
       m.2
   Chris Sorenson   living in Santa Barbara 1935
                                         His dau: Fern
   h. Sadie Mildred   b. Los Olivos 18 Aug 1893; m. @22
                                          of Los Olivos
                                         d. Santa Barbara 16 Oct 1973; Oak Hill cem
     m.1 San Luis Obispo 20 Oct 1915 by Chas B Allen, MEch, J446
        wit: Frances B Allen, Chas B Allen, SLO
   Frank M Buell   b. Oct 1893; m. @22 of Solvang
                                         d. Fresno Co 30 July 1947
                                         F: Linus Buell 1868-1931
                                         M: Annie M Smith 1875-1944
    =Ada (Robert Silverton)   See Phillips I 325 for Buell
    =Eddie
    =Barbara H b. 1920 (Mel Phillips)
    =Frank Jr b. 1928

```
                m.2  c1950
        B F Gates of Dos Pueblos ranch
    i. Russell Dewey                        b. 18 Mar 1895
            m.                              d. 15 Apr 1974; Oak Hill cem
        Elsie Knight                        b. 23 Sep 1897
                                            d. 3 Jan 1975; Oak Hill cem
                                                m.1 Barnes; 4 ch
    j. Sybil A                              b. 23 May 1900
            m.                              d. (living in Wilmington 1935, Lomita 1945)
        Henry Chambers                      b. 13 Jul 1890
                                            d. Lomita 5 Feb 1971; SSDI
***7. a. San Luis Obispo Court Index, suit #5607 Regina M Hopper vs John Allen Hopper
        judgment #5044  23 Mar 1916  K126
```

JOHN BOLDEN HOPPER
PIONEERS OF THE CALIFORNIA CENTRAL COAST

```
John Bolden Hopper                      b. Lafayette Co MO 3 July 1834
    (Bowlin)?                           d. SLO Co 15 Aug 1913 @79; Shandon cem
    bio M/H 876                         F: Charles Hopper 1809-1901
1870: Monterey Co   San Antonio tp      M: Nancy E McClure 1814-1874
1874-5 SLO Co Asst Bk: S6 T27 R11 Salinas tp
1880: Salinas tp
1892 GR: 58 5'9½ fair blu gry, f MO Cholame PO Shandon; reg Sep 1
1900: Cholame: 13 births, 12 living
1904 GR: Paso Robles #1 @69
            m. Cloverdale 13 May 1861 by Eli Lester. A224
Mary Frances Grove*                     b. Trenton OH Feb 1842
    to Windsor CA 1853                  d. Shandon 31 May 1929 @86/3; Shandon cem; obit SLO
                                            Daily Telegram June 7 Sec 2 p. 1
                                        F: David Grove
                                        M: Catherine Richter
1. Elwood                               d. @4 (not on 1870 census)
2. Sarah Ellen                          1864-   : m. Las Tablas SLO Co 1885: B48
                                            Yancy McFadden 1862-1927
3. Nancy Isabel                         1867-1937: m. Moro tp SLO Co 1886: B156
                                            John Jefferson Brians 1861-1915
                                            F: Adam Thornton Brians 1830-1917
                                            M: Lucy Finley 1840-1894
4. Mary Eveline/Adeline                 1868-1916  m. Young
5. John Theodore                        1870-1947: m. after 1900: Ora Casteel 1877-1928
    bio M/H 873                                 F: Jesse Casteel 1833-1904
                                                M: Mary M Hingley 1840-1906
6. Lucretia                             1872-       m. SLO 1895 D631 Walter J Thompson
                                            (1862-1932)?
                                        F: John Thompson 1842- ; M:    Craiton d. 1880
7. George Larkin                            1873-1944 m. 1898 (cen) Theresa Antoinette Waite
                                            1876-1946; F: David Waite 1844-1925
                                        M: Elizabeth Hill 1846-1927
8. Emma J                               1875-       m. Estrella 1893 D318 Arthur W Waite
                                            1876-(1935)?; F: David Waite 1844-1925
                                                M: Elizabeth Hill 1846-1927
```

9. David LeRoy	1876-1958 m. Lemoore c1915? Laura McMillan
bio M/H 876	1897- ; F: Alexander McMillan 1861-1935
	M: Mary Frances Harte 1870-1943
10. Henrietta	1878- m. 1898(cen) Herbert E Waite 1874-1939
	F: David Waite 1844-1925
	M: Elizabeth Hill 1846-1927
11. Oliver William	1880-1971 m. after 1920? (Mrs Ollie Hopper, daus
bio M/H 374	Anna, Hazel, at Grange picnic, Shandon May 28 1941
	-*Paso Robles Journal*)
12. Everett Ambrose	1881-1964 m. Arroyo Grande 1920: L300: Susie
bio M/H 374	Clemons 1891- ; F: George B Clemons 1842-1917
	M: Arminda Nunn 1853-1925
13. Addie Mildred	1883-1960 m. Paso Robles 1905 G75 Charles Herbert
	Stanley 1881-1963; F: Hartwell Bernard Stanley
	MD 1851-191; M: Mary

**Sonoma County Marriages 1847-1902*, published by the Sonoma Co Gen Soc, Inc 1990, gives Johnson as the surname of J B Hopper's bride.

Hand-book and Directory of San Luis Obispo, Santa Barbara, Ventura...Counties, Paulson 1875
Santa Maria; John Hopper, farmer; John T Hopper, farmer; Martin Luther Tunnell, farmer
Paso Robles Hot Springs; J B Hopper, farmer, near Hot Springs San Miguel; W Hopper, farmer, near San Miguel

Las Tablas--Messrs Barnett, Gates, Shimmin and Hopper with their families leave Las Tablas, most of them going to Cholame. "A farewell party was given to Messrs Hopper, Shimmin, Barnett, Gates, Coffey and Burnett at the residence of H P Burnett, Corral De Mulos, last week. About 60 persons present..." -*SLO Standard* a Prohibition paper, Oct 6 1886

A Happy Hopper Hunter

Pirkey Colvin, a Hopper-Stowell descendant, whose mother, Jeanne Dixon (not THAT Jeanne Dixon), is listed on page 301, recently returned from a two-day visit to the land of her Hopper forebears, elated over the large amount of material she was able to accrue in that short time, which included a copy of *From Acorns to Oaks* from the author, who has sold a thousand copies! Pirkey highly recommends the Heald-Poage Memorial Home and Historical Research Library in Ukiah, operated by the Mendocino County Historical Society. Their collection is extensive and the staff is most helpful. It was Pirkey's finding that John B Hopper of Shandon, long in the files of Ye Ed. because of the connection to the Clemons family of San Miguel, Arroyo Grande, and Santa Maria, was related to the Santa Maria Hoppers, and for that reason we include an abbreviated chart. John B's biography in Morrison & Haydon gives later dates for the California arrival than indicated by earlier sources; let some family member resolve the discrepancy.

Vol. XXVII, No. 1, Spring 1995, p. 13

WILLIAM STEVENS HOPPER

William Stevens Hopper	b. Adair co KY c1803 (census, IGI)
1850: Sacramento, lab.	d. after 1874
1870: w/Jasper Twitchell, (no wife)	F: Joseph Hopper (IGI)
	M: Nancy Ann

1874: voter reg: @60 KY farmer San Juan, reg. May 28. (Probably transferred from Monterey Co when San Benito was formed in 1874 without updating)

Vol. XXV, No. 1 & 2, 1993, p.30

        m. Adair co KY 16 Feb 1826 (IGI)

Hannah Moore	b. Adair co KY c1802 (Adair formed 1802)
	d. (before 1870)?
1. Irene C (S L Twitchell)	1827-1905
2. Jno	b. KY 1828; 1850: Sacramento; eating house
3. Emeline E	1832-1912 (J H Twitchell)
4. Jacob	b. IL 1835
5. William W	b. IL 1842 (census) McDonough co (IGI)
6. Christopher C	b. IL 1844 (census) McDonough co (IGI)

Vol. XXV, No. 1 & 2, 1993, p.30

Corrections and Additions   [Page numbers refer to those in Quarterly]

p.9.   Mrs Lou Hopper, Luther Hopper & M P Baker returned from Ukiah from the funeral of Mrs Emma Young, sister of Baker & Mrs Hopper. Mrs Young, a resident of Willitts, visited Santa Maria often.   –Mon Sep 2 1936

    Luther Hopper departed yesterday to make his last trip for Nettelton Shoe Co of Syracuse NY will complete his route and return to Santa Maria to open new shoe establishment the latter part of May   –Apr 20 1921

    City Briefs. Mr & Mrs George Hopper and son of Portland, Oregon and Mrs Dora Griffith of San Francisco are the house guests of Mr & Mrs Luther Hopper this week.   –Wed Aug 21 1929 p.5

    Locals. Mrs E A Griffith of San Francisco and Mr & Mrs George T Hopper of Portland have returned to their homes in the north following a visit of four days with relatives and friends here.   –Mon Aug 26 1929 p.5

    Mr & Mrs Frank Buell, Mr & Mrs Frank Tunnell, Mrs L Buell in town yesterday from Los Olivos to attend funeral of John Hopper.   –Sat Dec 4 1918 Epitome of the Week

    Helen S Griffitts m.2 Charles Garry Wheeler who was on the USS Bennington when it exploded in San Diego, 1905

p.10.   Henry Warren Osborne died in Fresno 2 Sep 1925, not San Francisco 1927. He died at the home of L T Wallenback, 1021 Archie St, was former proprietor of Osborn Paint Store, N and Fresno Sts, and had operated paint stores in Long Beach, Redlands, Riverside, Fresno, and Centralia, WA. He was 77 years old; no survivors mentioned.   –The obits from Glen Hopper, St George, UT.

    Luther Hopper to work for Hammond Bros (car dealers). See Hammond chart   –Feb 7 1919

    Lute Hopper in Santa Maria for Christmas – been gone 18 years.   –Dec 26 1923

p.11.   Marriage: Muriel V Tunnell m.1 Frank Atwood Hebard 1908-1942; living in Los Gatos 1934, formerly of Santa Maria (*Times*). Muriel died 25 Nov 1985, survived by daughter Lois E DeSolminihac, Grants Pass; sons Frank Hebard, Millwood VA and Chuck Hebard, Santa Maria; Oak Hill cem Ballard.

    Marriages (both from *Ancestors West*, SB Co Gen Soc): Elsie J Tunnell m.1 LaPatera 17 Mar 1902 L W Thompson; Myrtle Tunnell @21 m. ME ch, Santa Barbara 19 Sep 1904, George C Thorpe @25.

    James R Torrence's mother was Mary Agnes Hails. –See Gidney's *History of Santa Barbara, San Luis Obispo and Ventura Cos*, 2 vol, 1917

    Marriage: Sadie Tunnell married Frank Buell 1915; story in *Santa Maria Times* Oct 23. Wedding trip to San Francisco.

Vol. XXX, No. 1, Spring 1998, p.5

G. W. Battles
Courtesy Lompoc Historical Society

G. M Doane, Sr
Courtesy Lompoc Historical Society

Gragg Family left to right: Carrie, Judge James A., Mamie, Mrs. Mary Elizabeth Payne Gragg, Irwin,
Front: Lovell
Courtesy Lompoc Historical Society

Adam Family

left to right:
Ronald McDonald Adam
Esther Bradley Adam
Alexander Adam
William Adam

Courtesy Lompoc Historical Society

Nora Davis & Verda Davis 1894
Courtesy Lompoc Historical Society

Top left to right
Edna Clare Blosser
Alida Christina Blosser

Bottom left to right
Mary Anna Blosser
Nellie Blosser

Courtesy Santa Maria
Historical Society

George Mason Doane
Courtesy Santa Maria Historical Society

Mrs. Duncan Earl
Courtesy Santa Maria Historical Society

George Elvidge & Sarah Elvidge (Mrs George Chaffin)
Courtesy Santa Maria Historical Society

Miss Margaret More 21 July 1901
Courtesy Santa Maria Historical Society

Earl Gates   Curtis Tunnell Sr.   ?
Courtesy Santa Maria Historical Society

Anna Albrecht Miller wife of Isaac Miller, Sr.
Courtesy Santa Maria Historical Society

Isaac Miller uncle of Joel Miller
Courtesy Santa Maria Historical Society

Joel Miller Nephew of Isaac Miller
Courtesy Santa Maria Historical Society

Edith Hamann Miller wife of Isaac Junior
Courtesy Santa Maria Historical Society

Nellie Bradley
Courtesy Santa Maria Historical Society

Paul Bradley
Courtesy Santa Maria Historical Society

Louisa Bradley
Courtesy Santa Maria Historical Society

Charles Bradley
Courtesy Santa Maria Historical Society

Blanche Morrison
Courtesy Santa Maria Historical Society

Nellie and Seth Waite
Courtesy Santa Maria Historical Society

www.ingramcontent.com/pod-product-compliance
Lightning Source LLC
Chambersburg PA
CBHW080729300426
44114CB00019B/2523